1920 • The Retirement Act creates the first federal civil service pension system.
• The Nineteenth Amendment gives women the right to vote.
1921 • The Budget and Accounting Act establishes (1) the Bureau of the Budget in the Department of the Treasury and (2) the General Accounting Office as an agency of the Congress.
1922 • Max Weber's structural definition of bureaucracy is published posthumously.
1923 • The Classification Act brings position classification to Washington-based federal employees and establishes the principle of equal pay for equal work.
1924 • Hawthorne studies begin at the Hawthorne Works of the Western Electric Company in Chicago; they will last until 1932 and lead to new thinking about the relationship of work environment to productivity.
1926 • Leonard D. White's *Introduction to the Study of Public Administration* is the first text in public administration.
• Mary Parker Follett, in calling for "power with" as opposed to "power over," anticipates the movement toward more participatory management styles.
1929 • The University of Southern California establishes the first independent professional school of public administration.
• Stock market crashes; Great Depression begins.
1930 • Durham County, South Carolina is first to install county-manager form of county government.
1933 • President Franklin D. Roosevelt's New Deal begins.
• Francis Perkins, the first woman in a president's cabinet, is appointed Secretary of Labor.
• The Tennessee Valley Authority (TVA) is established by Congress as an independent public corporation.
1935 • The National Labor Relations (Wagner) Act establishes the right of private sector employees to organize and bargain collectively.
• Social Security program created.
1936 • J. Donald Kingsley and William E. Mosher's *Public Personnel Administration* becomes the first text in this field.
• John Maynard Keynes publishes his *General Theory of Employment, Interest, and Money*, which calls for using a government's fiscal and monetary policies to positively influence a capitalistic economy.
• E. Pendleton Herring in *Public Adminstration and the Public Interest* asserts that bureaucrats, by default, must often be the arbiters of the public interest.
1937 • The Brownlow Committee's report says that the "President needs help" and calls for the reorganization of the executive branch.
• Luther Gulick calls attention to the various functional elements of the work of an executive with his mnemonic device POSDCORB.
1938 • The Fair Labor Standards Act provides for minimum wages, overtime pay, and limits on child labor.
• Chester I. Barnard's *The Functions of the Executive* foreshadows the postwar revolution in thinking about organizational behavior.
1939 • American Society for Public Administration is founded.

• The Reorganization Act enables the creation of the Executive Office of the President and the transfer of the Bureau of the Budget from the Treasury to the White House.
• The Hatch Act is passed to inhibit political activities by federal employees.
• The federal government first requires the states to have merit systems for employees in programs aided by federal funds.
1940 • *Public Administration Review* first published.
1941 • James Burnham's *The Managerial Revolution* asserts that as the control of large organizations passes from the hands of the owners into the hands of professional administrators, the society's new governing class will be the possessors not of wealth, but of technical expertise.
• Japanese attack on Pearl Harbor brings the United States into World War II.
1943 • Abraham Maslow's "needs hierarchy" first appears in *Psychological Review*.
• Withholding for federal income tax begins as a temporary wartime measure.
1944 • J. Donald Kingsley's *Representative Bureaucracy* develops the concept that all social groups have a right to participate in their governing institutions in proportion to their numbers in the population.
1945 • With the dropping of the atomic bomb and the end of World War II, the suddenly public Manhattan Project marks the federal government's first major involvement with science in a policy-making role.
• Paul Appleby leads the postwar attack on the politics/administration dichotomy by insisting in *Big Democracy* that apolitical governmental processes went against the grain of the American experience.
1946 • The Employment Act creates the Council of Economic Advisors and asserts that it is the policy of the federal government to maintain full employment.
• The Administrative Procedure Act standarized many federal government administrative practices across agencies.
• Herbert A. Simon's "The Proverbs of Administration" attacks the principles approach to management for being inconsistent and often inapplicable.
1947 • President Harry S. Truman announces his namesake doctrine.
1949 • The First Hoover Commission recommends increased managerial capacity in the Executive Office of the President.
• The National Security Act creates the Department of Defense.
1951 • David Truman's *The Governmental Process* calls for viewing interest groups as the real determinant of, and focal point of study on, public policy.
• Kurt Lewin proposes a general model of organizational change consisting of three phases, "unfreezing, change, refreezing" in his *Field Theory in Social Science.*
1954 • Peter Drucker's book, *The Practice of Management*, popularizes the concept of management by objectives.
• The Supreme Court, in *Brown v. Board of Education*, holds that racially separate educational facilities are inherently unequal and therefore violate the equal protection clause of the Fourteenth Amendment.

Introducing Public Administration

FIFTH EDITION

Jay M. Shafritz
Graduate School of Public and International Affairs
University of Pittsburgh

E. W. Russell
Centre for the Governance and Management
of Urban Transport
University of Melbourne

Christopher P. Borick
Department of Political Science
Muhlenberg College

PEARSON
Longman

New York San Francisco Boston
London Toronto Sydney Tokyo Singapore Madrid
Mexico City Munich Paris Cape Town Hong Kong Montreal

Editor-In-Chief: Eric Stano
Media and Supplements Editor: Kristi Olson
Senior Marketing Manager: Elizabeth Fogarty
Production Manager: Eric Jorgensen
Project Coordination, Text Design, and Electronic Page Makeup:
   Pre-Press Company, Inc.
Cover Design Manager: John Callahan
Cover Designer: Maria Ilardi
Cover Image: Courtesy of CORBIS, Inc.
Photo Researcher: Christine Pullo
Senior Manufacturing Buyer: Dennis J. Para
Printer and Binder: RR Donnelley & Sons Company
Cover Printer: Phoenix Color Corporation

For permission to use copyrighted material, grateful acknowledgment is made to the copyright holders which are hereby made part of this copyright page.

Cataloging-in-Publication Data on file at the Library of Congress

Page 4 left: Masatomo Kuriya/CORBIS; page 4 right: Paul Richards/CORBIS; page 43: Bettmann/CORBIS; page 105: Bettmann/CORBIS; page 111: Win McNamee/Hulton Archive/Reuters; page 124: Bettmann/CORBIS; page 135: Margaret Bourke White/Time Life Pictures/Getty Images; page 177: Palazzo Vecchio, Florence, Italy/Alinari/Art Resource, NY; page 187: Bettmann/CORBIS; page 189 left: Martin Luther King Memorial Library, Washington, D.C.; page 189 right: AP/Wide World Photos; page 218: The Kobal Collection/Paramount; page 235: Bettmann/CORBIS; page 264 left: WARNER BROS./THE KOBAL COLLECTION/ JAMES, DAVID; page 264 right: The Everett Collection; page 279: Jocelyn Augustino/ epa/CORBIS; page 280: Library of Congress; page 288: Culver Pictures, Inc.; page 296: Bettmann/CORBIS; page 308: Francis G. Mayer/CORBIS; page 341: Bettmann/CORBIS; page 376 left: Chateaux de Malmaison et Bois-Preau, Rueil-Malmaison, France/Enrich Lessing/ Art Resource, NY; page 376 right: EAGLES ROAR, INC./CORBIS SYGMA; page 388: Library of Congress; page 420: Minnesota Historical Society/CORBIS; page 452: Library of Congress; page 488: Library of Congress; page 505: Bettmann/CORBIS; page 524: Bettmann/CORBIS.

Please visit us at http://www.ablongman.com

ISBN 0-321-43943-0

12345678910—DOH—09 08 07 06

Contents

Chapter 7   **Organizational Behavior   259**

Chapter 10

Leadership   369

Chapter 11   **Personnel Management and Labor Relations   396**

Chapter 12

Social Equity   442

Chapter 13   **Public Financial Management   480**

KEYNOTE: Take Me Out to the Ball Game and *You* Buy the Ticket: Public Stadium Financing   481

The Importance of Public Financial Management   483

Six Principles   484
Balanced Budgets   485
The Fiscal Year   486

Budgeting Theory and Practice   486

The Taft Commission   487
The Influence of Keynes   489
The Objectives of Budgeting   490
The Two Types of Budgets   491

Waves of Innovation in Budget Making   491

The Executive Budget   492
Line-Item Budgeting   493
Performance Budgeting   493
Program Budgeting Versus Incrementalism   494
Zero-Based Budgeting   497

Contemporary Budget Reform   498

Integrated Budgets   498
Multiyear Budgets   499

Financing Public Expenditure   500

Taxation   502
The Ability-to-Pay Principle   503
The Flat Tax   505
User Charges   506
Grants   507

The Problem of Debt   507

Abuse of Public Debt   508
Municipal Bonds   508
The Rating Agencies   509
Bonds, Debt, and Emergency Recovery   510

Preface

In the original preface to this text we explained that we sought to create a text that would bridge two worlds: one that would be informal enough to be accessible to undergraduates yet comprehensive enough for beginning graduate students. We are pleased to now be able to report that we have succeeded—at least to the extent that the publisher, after scrupulously studying the adoption statistics, has asked us to prepare this fifth edition.

As we have said since the first edition of this text, public administration is an exciting and fascinating field of study, full of the stuff of fiction, only true. We try to capture this sense of drama and excitement by beginning each chapter with a good story—what we call a keynote—that highlights a major aspect of the subject. These accounts deal with a rich variety of topics including the attack on the World Trade Center in New York, the financing of sports stadiums, the famous mutiny on the *Bounty,* and the organization development techniques of Hollywood films. All of these keynotes have significant public policy and public management implications that are developed further in the chapter. We trust they will lead to many stimulating class discussions.

The material in each chapter is then presented in an order that should not surprise anyone familiar with public administration. We have made every effort to keep the tone lively so that students, as well as their professors, might take some pleasure in reviewing the material. When a word appears in **boldface** in the text, it is defined at the bottom of its page. The key concepts at the end of each chapter supplement rather than duplicate these boldfaced definitions.

Readers will also find a list of recommended books and a separate list of related Web sites at the end of each chapter. These have been included as guides to further information on chapter topics for any interested reader—student or instructor.

Every effort has been made to keep the material as current as possible. Thus there is extensive coverage of the reinventing government movement, privatization, and contracting out. Because American public administration is being increasingly influenced by practices in other countries, such as managerialism in Britain, a comparative perspective has been added wherever appropriate.

NEW TO THIS EDITION
- All statistical information and tables, bibliographies, and Web sites have been updated as appropriate.
- New initiatives of the second George W. Bush administration—especially those concerned with the war on terror—have been incorporated where appropriate.

- Numerous chapters examine the effects of Hurricane Katrina on areas of public administration such as financial management, leadership, and social equity.

- Five case studies and/or keynotes have been added or significantly expanded:

  Chapter 4: How Intergovernmental Management Became Intergovernmental Chaos: The Cases of United Flight 93 and Hurricane Katrina
  Chapter 6: Sherlock Holmes Makes the Case for Scientific Management
  Chapter 7: The Dangers of Groupthink from Pearl Harbor to the War in Iraq
  Chapter 10: The Hedgehog, the Fox or Henry V
  Chapter 13: Take Me Out to the Ball Game and *You* Buy the Ticket: Public Stadium Financing

- New sections have been added on the following topics:

  Chapter 3: Privatization in the Military
  Chapter 4: Councils of Government and Intergovernmental Agreements
  The Transformation of Governance
  Chapter 5: Was "Deep Throat's" Behavior Honorable?
  Chapter 6: The Staff Concept
  Complex Adaptive Systems
  Chapter 9: Game Theory
  Chapter 11: Privatizing Public Personnel
  Patronage Gone Bad
  Chapter 12: The Ongoing Role of Race in Public Administration
  Chapter 13: Bonds, Debt, and Emergency Recovery

- The fifth edition is also accompanied by a revised Instructor's Manual/Test Bank, written by Breena Coates of San Diego State University and Jeffrey Guiler of Robert Morris University.

There are no traditional footnotes in this book. Generally, if a work or author is referred to in a chapter, the corresponding full citation will be found in that chapter's bibliography. The major exceptions are works or statements so famous and existing in so many formats—such as the Bible and Shakespeare's plays—that further bibliographic information was deemed unnecessary. Most long quotations are kept in boxes, separate from the main body and rhythm of the text. This informal format was used very successfully through five editions of the Shafritz et al. text *Personnel Management in Government* (New York: Marcel Dekker, 1978–2001). Sometimes it was too awkward to incorporate a reference to a citation in the body of the text. These "fugitive" quotations have their sources identified in an appendix.

No book is born without debts. We wish to express our thanks to the reviewers of the fourth edition—Jane Hansberry of University of Colorado, Denver; Jared J. Llorens of University of Georgia; Theo Edwin Maloy of West Texas A&M University; Dale Nesbary of Oakland University—who helped to prepare this Fifth edition. We are also happy to acknowledge the helpful suggestions of David H. Rosenbloom of the American University; Albert C. Hyde of the Brookings Institution; Elizabeth Hecker of Boise State University; Carol Edlund of California State University–Hayward; Geert Bouckaert of the Catholic University of Leuven in Belgium; Larry Terry and

Jennifer Alexander of Cleveland State University; Richard Wandling of Eastern Illinois University; Barbara Yarnold of Florida International University; John Sacco of George Mason University; Gashaw W. Lake of Kentucky State University; Jerry McCaffery of the Naval Postgraduate School; Michael L. Vasu of North Carolina State University; Christopher A. Simon of University of Nevada-Las Vegas; Beverly Cigler of Penn State/Harrisburg; Jeffrey K. Guiler of Robert Morris University; Peter Foot of Kings College London, United Kingdom; Marc Holzer of Rutgers/Newark; Katherine Naff of San Francisco State University; Curtis R. Berry of Shippensburg University; Kenneth Warren of St. Louis University; Norma Riccucci and Frank J. Thompson of the State University of New York at Albany; Harry A. Bailey of Temple University; Ari Halachmi of Tennessee State University; William H. Stewart of the University of Alabama; Daniel Martin of the University of Baltimore; Kathy Boyd of the University of Colorado at Denver; Kenneth L. Nichols of the University of Maine; Gary S. Marshall of the University of Nebraska at Omaha; Gordon P. Whittaker of the University of North Carolina; Donald Goldstein, Kevin Kearns, Jerome McKinney, Lou Picard, and Harvey L. White of the University of Pittsburgh; Jean Wahl Harris of the University of Scranton; Sharon Ridgeway of the University of Southwest Louisiana; David H. Davis of the University of Toledo; J. Steven Ott and Sandra J. Parkes of the University of Utah; Frank Bryan of the University of Vermont; Richard Crockett of Western Illinois University; Robert E. Colvin of Christopher Newport University; William N. Thompson of the University of Nevada, Las Vegas; Arthur Sementelli of Stephen F. Austin State University; Dwight S. Cropp of George Washington University; Craig Curtis of Bradley University; Christine J. Brehan of Bentley College; John Carhart of Texas A & M University at Galveston; R. Steven Daniels of California State University at Bakersfield; Jeremy L. Eccles of Marygrove College; Anne M. Gurnack of University of Wisconsin, Parkside; Jeffrey Kraus of Wagner College; Michael E. Meagher of University of Missouri; Fred A. Meyer, Jr. of Ball State University; Norman H. Runge of Wilmington College; Samuel T. Shelton of Troy State University; Robert Stock of San Diego State University; Pamela Stricker of California State University, San Marcos; and R. Lawson Veasey of Jacksonville State University.

We also acknowledge the permission of Marc Holzer, editor-in-chief of *Public Voices,* to reprint in a slightly altered form (as the keynote to Chapter 7) the article "Organization Development in Hollywood War Movies," originally written by Jay M. Shafritz and Peter Foot.

Some colleagues have been especially helpful. We are particularly grateful for the many helpful suggestions of Breena Coates of San Diego State University; Jeffery K. Guiler and Michele Cole of Robert Morris University; Paul A. Danczyk, David Young Miller, and Sarah Pennock of the University of Pittsburgh; and Gerald Caiden of the University of Southern California, who had an entire class of graduate students write very useful critiques of the text that he then sent on to us. We would also like to thank Sarah Niebler and Jill Batdorf of Lehigh University for their tremendous assistance in gathering research for the book.

This book started many years ago as a collaboration by two friends at opposite ends of the world: Melbourne, Australia, and Pittsburgh, Pennsylvania. The collaboration has now grown by one with the addition of a younger colleague from

Allentown, Pennsylvania. While separated by generations and many miles, we are kindred academic spirits. Despite the fact that we were bred in differing administrative cultures, we were totally in accord on what we wanted to say. And we are very grateful that what we have had to say has found a wide audience. This is both a major responsibility and a great honor. We will continuously strive to live up to the former and thank you, the reader, for the latter.

JAY M. SHAFRITZ
E. W. RUSSELL
CHRISTOPHER P. BORICK

CHAPTER 1

Defining Public Administration

•KEYNOTE: GO TELL THE SPARTANS

At 8:48 on the morning of September 11, 2001, Adam Mayblum, 35, an investment firm employee, was in his office on the 87th floor of the north tower of the World Trade Center in New York. Suddenly, it seemed like a huge bomb exploded on the floors above—the building shook as if in an earthquake, lighting fixtures fell down, the ceiling collapsed in several areas, and paper flew everywhere. The halls quickly filled with smoke, but the phones were still working. Mayblum immediately called home and left a message for his wife that a bomb had gone off and he was on his way out. Next he took off his undershirt, tore it into three pieces, and gave two of the pieces to coworkers. They soaked the fabric in water and tied the torn T-shirt pieces around their faces as improvised air filters. Then the trio started down a smoke-filled staircase.

As Mayblum walked down the crowded and smoky stairs, he called his parents on his cell phone. Soon after, his sister-in-law called him. Everybody with a cell phone was making calls to or taking calls from friends and relatives. On the 53rd floor they found a "heavyset man" just sitting on the stairwell. Mayblum and his friends offered to carry him, but he preferred to wait for professional help. As they approached the 44th floor, they first started seeing firefighters and police officers on their way up. Mayblum stopped several of them and told them about the man on the 53rd floor and also about a friend who was missing on the 87th.

The next day, in a 2,000-word e-mail that was written for friends but ultimately distributed to thousands, Mayblum told of his narrow escape. He wrote that he "felt terrible" about telling the rescuers to go further up the stairs. "They headed up to find those people and met death instead. . . . I realize that they were going up anyway. But it hurts to know that I may have made them move quicker to find my friend."

Mayblum is only one of thousands who fled down the stairs to safety from the inferno of the World Trade Center towers as firefighters and other rescue workers raced up the stairs into deadly danger. The essence of the firefighters' bravery can be summed up by an old observation: Firefighters don't run from burning buildings; they run into them. Peggy Noonan, a speechwriter for Presidents Reagan and Bush (the elder), wrote, "You think to yourself: Do we pay them enough? You realize: We couldn't possibly pay them enough. And in any case, a career like that is not about money." But if it is "not about money," what *is* it about? The answer is that it is about duty.

For almost 2,500 years "Go tell the Spartans" has been the most famous classical reference to a duty done unto death. When it became shockingly evident that over 300 firefighters died that day, those who knew ancient history might well have thought of another group of 300 heroes who died in the line of duty. In 480 B.C.E. soldiers from the Greek city of Sparta fought a delaying action against invaders from Persia (now Iran). Taking up a defensive position in the mountain pass of Thermopylae, they fought off massive waves of assaulting Persians for three days. The Spartans knowingly sacrificed themselves—fought until they were all killed—so that their fellow Greeks would have the time to organize and eventually defeat the enemy.

The similarities between the New York City firefighters and the Spartans of ancient Greece go far beyond the number 300. And that number is not accurate in either case. The 343 firefighters who died were in the company of 136 other rescue workers (New York City police, Port Authority police, private security guards, etc.) who also died. The Spartans had auxiliaries (somebody had to cook) and small combat units from other cities, including about 1,000 Thespians (not actors, but soldiers from Thespiae). Nevertheless, the number 300 resonates because it was the Spartans who fought to the death while others retreated. And it was the firefighters who personified the rescue effort.

Societies have always expected their soldiers to die in large numbers if necessary. But not firefighters. They are pacifistic warriors seeking only to fight fires and save lives. In the past firefighters only occasionally died in the line of duty. Until 2001 about 100 died in the United States each year. Previously, in the worst fire disaster in New York City, 12 firefighters died. To have 343 die in a single day was, until September 11, unthinkable.

Both the firefighters and the Spartans sacrificed themselves according to the ethics of their crafts. And though their actions were separated by two and a half millennia in

TABLE 1.1   Annual Police and Firefighter Deaths in the Line of Duty

Year	Police	Firefighters
1992	157	75
1993	153	77
1994	170	104
1995	172	96
1996	133	95
1997	163	94
1998	156	91
1999	134	112
2000	151	102
2001	230	446
2002	147	102
2003	146	111
2004	153	110

SOURCE: Federal Emergency Management Agency/National Fire Data Center/National Law Enforcement Officers Memorial Fund.

time, they were both fighting the same enemy: a despotism from the East that then sought to suppress the budding democracy of ancient Greece and now seeks to wipe out the flourishing democracies of the Western World.

After the Greeks won their war, Simonides (556–468 B.C.E.), a famous poet of the time, was commissioned to write an appropriate inscription for a memorial plaque to be placed at Thermopylae to honor the Spartan heroes. Some Greeks were shocked when he turned in only two lines. But these two lines have become the most meaningful and best-known epitaph in the history of Western civilization:

Go tell the Spartans, thou who passest by,
That here obedient to their laws we lie.

There will eventually be a fitting memorial to all those who died on that infamous 11th of September. But the firefighters, police officers, and other doomed rescuers already have one memorial. They all share the epitaph of the Spartans because they died bravely in the line of duty, "obedient to their laws."

Although the approximately 3,000 dead from the attack were in New York, it was the whole nation that cried with their families. This was not just another office building complex. Towering over Wall Street, these office buildings represented the capitalistic might of the United States. The barbarous attack wounded the entire country because it was an act of war against all of us. In the days following the blast the news media put forth much banal talk about America's "loss of innocence" along with the increasing statistics, the body count, on the loss of the innocents.

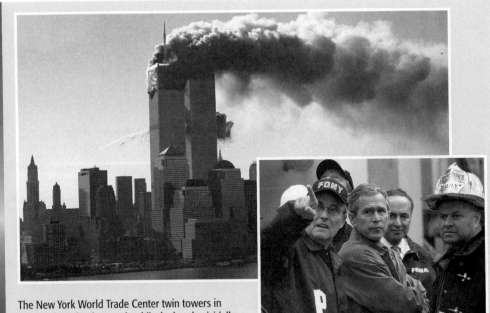

The New York World Trade Center twin towers in flames after Islamic terrorists hijacked and suicidally crashed commercial airliners into them on September 11, 2001. Two other airliners were also hijacked at the same time. One crashed into the Pentagon, and another, seemingly destined for the U.S. Capitol building in Washington, D.C., crashed into a rural area of Pennsylvania after passengers (who by cell phone learned of the other crashes) fought with the hijackers. In loss of life and property this was the worst sneak attack in American history—worse than the Japanese attack on Pearl Harbor on December 7, 1941, that brought the United States into World War II. The war on terrorism that has ensued has and will continue to have vast implications for public administration.

A grim-faced President George W. Bush with then-mayor of New York Rudolph Giuliani (left side) survey the wreckage of the World Trade Center on September 14, 2001. Bush told Bob Woodward of the *Washington Post* that as soon as he heard of the second plane hitting the World Trade Center, he thought, "They had declared war on us, and I made up my mind at that moment that we were going to war." But with whom? In a speech to the nation at 8:30 that evening he stated what would be called the Bush doctrine: "We will make no distinction between the terrorists who committed these acts and those who harbor them."

That no one would be found alive in the rubble after the first day was impossible to know at the time. Soon out-of-state rescue teams arrived to help. These teams, deployed by the Federal Emergency Management Agency, included search dogs. They are trained to bark if they detect a live person and whine when they locate a body. The dogs spent most of their time whining. While less dramatic, it is often just as dangerous to recover a body at a disaster site as it is to rescue a survivor.

The heroic efforts of the rescuers received massive publicity. The stories many of the survivors told of the bravery and daring of the rescue teams were heartrending.

But one point was largely missed in all the news reports. All these highly trained search and rescue professionals were public employees. They, and the administrative apparatus that sustains their organizations, are part of the government. They are representative of the bureaucrats whom so many people—even some who were then lauding them as heroes—had often described as overpaid and inefficient.

These everyday heroes got so much attention after September 11 because they were doing wholesale what they did retail on a daily basis. It is a common, if not everyday, occurrence in America for firefighters to rescue people from burning buildings. But this was the first time that they rescued thousands and died themselves in the hundreds.

Citizens the world over complain about their governments. But once disaster strikes—whether caused by nature or terrorists—they expect instant service. When there is an earthquake in California, when the Mississippi River floods, or when an Atlantic hurricane wreaks havoc in Florida, volunteers come running. But usually only those with special training can save someone from the raging torrent that was once a gentle stream or the cage of twisted metal that was once a car. And the lasting help that disaster victims need—from social services to low-interest loans for rebuilding—is generally available only from government. Suddenly these "bureaucrats" are angels of mercy. When danger lurks, they become our modern versions of medieval knights in shining armor. Call 911 in most U.S. cities and within minutes you'll have a career public servant at your door ready to risk his or her life for you and yours.

Yet, when our modern heroes do not live up to the high expectations that we place on them, the public disappointment is obvious. When many New Orleans police officers in a 2005 hurricane failed to uphold their solemn oath to defend and protect the citizens of their city, there was outrage throughout the nation. How could so many men and women who pledged to serve the public interest fail in the time of greatest need? For the many New Orleans police officers who stayed on the job, the disappointment in their colleagues must have been overwhelming. To be sure, the men and women of the NOPD who deserted their posts were no Spartans.

There were certainly heroes in New York and in New Orleans. And there are heroes in your city, too, but most of them are invisible to you. The modern public service allows vast scope for heroism. Throughout history, classic heroes used their special skills for the public good, usually by performing feats of military prowess and physical bravery. And some societies recognized other kinds of heroes, too. For example, Michelangelo, who became one of the greatest heroes of Renaissance Italy, was known only for his prowess with a chisel and a paintbrush.

Today's police officer and firefighter heroes are joined by great numbers of quiet unsung heroes: public works department engineers who provide safe drinking water, highway department drivers who work all night clearing snow in a blizzard, and public health officials who keep diseases from becoming epidemics. These virtually invisible heroes often hold our lives in their hands no less than their uniformed coworkers. More than that, they make modern life—civilization as we know it—possible.

Then there are those public employees who do not deal with life and death issues. Their concerns are instead with quality of life. They are, for example, the teachers who inspire students to excel, the social workers who find a loving home for a suddenly orphaned child, the economic development officers who bring hundreds of new jobs into a community, and the public managers who reinvent programs so that costs can be cut and taxes lowered. While not called upon to be physically brave, their efforts are often heroic. The public service has a wide variety of heroes. Some are just more visible than others.

For Discussion: *Are the first responders (police, firefighters, etc.) where you live more prepared now for a terrorist attack than they were before September 11, 2001? Has the response to Hurricane Katrina changed your attitude toward public servants and public service careers?*

The Definitions of Public Administration

It is easy to define public administration if you are content with being simplistic: it is government in action—the management of public affairs or the implementation of public policies. Such a facile definition, while accurate, is not adequate for such an important task. Consider the scene in Edmond Rostand's play *Cyrano de Bergerac* in which somebody insults the hero's big nose to provoke him into fighting a duel. But the challenger's insult of "rather large" is so commonplace that Cyrano then lectures him on "the great many things" he might have said if he'd had "some tinge of letters, or of wit." Defining public administration poses a similar challenge—even without the ensuing swordplay.

The authors of this book believe that nothing is more important to an introduction to public administration than the most expansive definition possible. How else can we explore its richness and subtlety and savor its historical significance, universal application, and present development? How else can we gain an appreciation for the later technical chapters? Nevertheless, the discussion that follows is inherently incomplete. Public administration is so vast that there is no way to encompass it all with only one definition. So we have written 18 of them and clustered them into 4 categories: political, legal, managerial, and occupational. This quartet of definitions essentially expands upon the trio—managerial, political, and legal—established by **David H. Rosenbloom**. But even with such an

---

David H. Rosenbloom (1943–) The leading authority on the constitutional aspects of public employment. His paradigm of public administration as the intersection of management, politics, and law has become a standard way to analyze and teach the subject.

array of definitions, the authors are in the uncomfortable position of Cyrano's challenger. We would have said more if we'd only had the wit!

Political Definitions of Public Administration

Public administration cannot exist outside of its political context. It is this context that makes it public—that makes it different from private or business administration. Consequently, our first definitions of public administration focus on its political nature.

Public Administration Is What Government Does   It is a White House chef preparing the menu of a state dinner for a visiting **chief of state,** a Department of Agriculture inspector examining beef at a slaughterhouse, and a Food and Drug Administration scientist determining the number of rodent hairs that food processors can safely and legally leave in chocolate, popcorn, and peanut butter. It is a firefighter rescuing a child from a disintegrating building, a meter reader attaching a ticket to your automobile for overlong parking, and a state prison official injecting deadly fluids into the veins of a condemned criminal. It is an astronomer exploring the furthest reaches of outer space, a CIA agent decoding captured messages from suspected terrorists, and a sewer crawler seeking to discover what has clogged up a municipal drainpipe. It is giving **food stamps** to the poor, mortgage interest deductions to homeowners, and hot meals to evacuees of a Gulf Coast hurricane.

Throughout the world, government employees do things that affect the daily lives of their fellow citizens. These things range from the heroic (as we saw in New York City) to the mundane. Usually these efforts are beneficial, but sometimes they are not. Most of the time in most countries public administrators tend to the public's business; for example, they build bridges and highways, collect garbage, put out fires, plow snow, spray for mosquitoes, and provide essential social services for the less fortunate. But in other lands public employees may torture the innocent and murder children. When **Amnesty International** publishes its annual report on the states that brutalize and violate the civil rights of its citizens, who do you think does all this brutalizing and violating? It is none other than the local public administrators! Of course, such nefarious activities are usually organized within some innocuous-sounding program having to do with "population control" or "internal security." Thus modern public relations try to put a friendly face on ancient atrocities.

---

chief of state The ceremonial head of a government, such as a king, queen, or president. This is in contrast to the chief executive of a government, such as a prime minister, chancellor, or president. The American presidency combines in one office—one person—the roles of chief of state and chief executive.

food stamps A welfare program designed to improve the nutrition of the poor. Administered by the Department of Agriculture and state and local welfare organizations, the program provides coupons (stamps) that can be used to pay for food at many grocery stores.

Amnesty International A worldwide organization that seeks to gain the release of political and religious prisoners by publicizing their plights and by lobbying governments. It has been especially effective in exposing cases of government-sanctioned torture. In 1972 the organization was awarded the Nobel Peace Prize.

> ## BOX 1.1   How the Inherent Criminality of Some Public Administrators Is Hidden by Political Language
>
> In our time, political speech and writing are largely the defense of the indefensible. Thus political language has to consist largely of euphemism, question-begging, and sheer cloudy vagueness. Defenseless villages are bombarded from the air, the inhabitants driven out into the countryside, the cattle machine-gunned, the huts set on fire with incendiary bullets; this is called pacification. Millions of peasants are robbed of their farms and sent trudging along the roads with no more than they can carry; this is called transfer of population or rectification of frontiers. People are imprisoned for years without trial, or shot in the back of the neck, or sent to die of scurvy in Arctic lumber camps; this is called elimination of unreliable elements. Such phraseology is needed if one wants to name things without calling up mental pictures of them. . . .
>
> Political language . . . is designed to make lies sound truthful and murder respectable, and to give an appearance of solidity to pure wind.
>
> SOURCE: George Orwell, "Politics and the English Language," in *Shooting an Elephant and Other Essays* (New York: Harcourt Brace, 1946). Orwell's rhetorical influence remains alive and well. A week after the September 11, 2001, attack, President Bush told a joint session of the Congress, "Whether we bring our enemies to justice or bring justice to our enemies, justice will be done." In the classic Orwellian tradition he was using a relatively innocuous word to mean something far harsher. Only those not familiar with the innate subtleties of the English language did not understand that his "justice" meant death to the terrorists. After all, only three days earlier he had told reporters that he wanted bin Laden "dead or alive." Only the most obtuse minds thought he did not have a preference.

As a profession, public administration has developed values and ethical standards. But as an activity, it has no values. It merely reflects the cultural norms, beliefs, and power realities of its society. It is simply government doing whatever government does—in whatever political and cultural context it happens to exist. In 1955 **Dwight Waldo** was the first to insist that analysts "see administration in terms of its environment" because "it enables us to understand differences in administration between different societies which would be inexplicable if we were limited to viewing administration analytically in terms of the universals of administration itself." So essentially similar administrative acts can be performed differently in different cultures. Thus a routine customs inspection in one state parallels the solicitation of a bribe by a corrupt customs official in another. The same act that is performed honestly in one state (because of a culture that supports honesty) may be performed corruptly in another (where the culture supports corruption by government officials).

Dwight Waldo (1913–2000) The preeminent historian of the academic field of public administration.

Public administration is the totality of the working day activities of all the world's bureaucrats—whether those activities are performed legally or illegally, competently or incompetently, decently or despicably! British scientist J. B. S. Haldane wrote that "the universe is not only queerer than we suppose, but queerer than we *can* suppose." Things are much the same with public administration. It is not only far vaster in scope than most people suppose, but it is so extensive and pervasive in modern life that not even the most imaginative of us can imagine it all.

Public Administration Is Both Direct and Indirect   It is direct when government employees provide services to the public as varied as mortgage insurance, mail delivery, and electricity. It is indirect when government pays private contractors to provide goods or services to citizens. For example, **NASA** operates the space shuttle, but the shuttle itself was built by private corporations. Similarly, security officers protecting American construction workers in Iraq's oil fields are not part of the U.S. armed forces but employees of private firms contracted by the defense department. Does the fact that these workers are employed by private companies put them outside the realm of public administration? Not at all. Remember that a government agency must hire, evaluate, and hold all employees and contractors accountable for the quality of their performance—whether they are building rockets or guarding oil rigs.

Governments have used private contractors since ancient times. For example, the executioner who once operated and maintained the guillotine in France was an independent contractor who earned a fee per head chopped off (literally severance pay). The current trend toward greater **privatization** of government functions, which began most notably in the 1980s during the Reagan administration in the United States and the Thatcher administration in the United Kingdom, is now worldwide. This trend has been reinforced by the growth of the nonprofit sector, which receives much of its funding from government contracts—especially for social services and research. By 1995, 40 percent of the budget of private nonprofit organizations providing human services was derived from government. According to former New York Governor Mario Cuomo, government funds account for two out of every three dollars spent by Catholic Charities USA, a national network of some 1,400 social service organizations. By comparison, Lutheran Social Ministries obtains 54 percent of its funding from government sources, and the Salvation Army obtains 15 percent from such sources. Thus we may conclude that privatization has not necessarily reduced the total amount of public administration in the world; it has simply forced it to take different forms.

NASA (National Aeronautics and Space Administration) The federal agency created by the National Aeronautics and Space Act of 1958 to conduct research on problems of flight and to explore outer space.

privatization The process of returning to the private sector property (such as public lands) or functions (such as trash collection, fire protection) previously owned or performed by government.

The increasingly expansive nature of public administration, its branching out into the private and nonprofit sectors, has given new meaning to the word _governance_. What was once a synonym for the process of government has evolved to refer to interorganizational efforts to cope with cross-boundary problems by using networks of people and organizations. Thus public administration has gone from being merely indirect to being extremely convoluted as well.

Public Administration Is a Phase in the Public Policymaking Cycle   Public policymaking never ends. Government perpetually suffers from a problem similar to that faced by Shakespeare's _Hamlet_, the indecisive prince of Denmark, who struggled with whether "to be or not to be." Governments are in a constant flurry over whether to do or not to do. And whatever they do or do not do is public policy. All such decisions (including decisions not to make a decision) are made by those who control political power and implemented by the administrative officers of the bureaucracy. Thus public policy and public administration are two sides of the same coin. One decides, the other does. They cannot be separate because one side cannot exist without the other. But because policymaking is a continuous process, it cannot end with **implementation**. Whenever government does something, critics will suggest ways to do it better. This feedback can be informal—from citizen complaints to journalistic investigations—or it can take the form of an agency or legislative program evaluation. In any case, new decisions must be made even if the decision is to avoid making a decision.

Public Administration Is Implementing the Public Interest   The public interest is the universal label in which political actors wrap the policies and programs that they advocate. Would any **lobby**, public manager, legislator, or chief executive ever propose a program that was not "in the public interest"? Hardly! Because the public interest is generally taken to mean a commonly accepted good, the phrase is used both to further policies that are indeed for the common good and to obscure policies that may not be so commonly accepted as good. A considerable body of literature has developed about this phrase, because it represents an important philosophic point that, if successfully defined, could provide considerable guidance for politicians and public administrators alike. **Walter Lippmann** wrote that "the public interest may be presumed to be what men would choose if they saw clearly,

---

implementation Putting a government program into effect; the total process of translating a legal mandate into appropriate program directives and structures that provide services or create goods.

lobby Any individual, group, or organization that seeks to influence legislation or administrative action. Lobbies can be trade associations, individual corporations, good-government public interest groups, or other levels of government. The term arose from the use of lobbies, or corridors, in legislative halls as places to meet with and persuade legislators to vote a certain way. Many lobbies provide legislators with reliable firsthand information of considerable value. However, some lobbies have given the practice an undesirable connotation because they often contribute money to political campaigns and offer special favors to officials in the expectation of favorable treatment on some issue in the future.

Walter Lippmann (1889–1974) A journalist who went beyond being the preeminent political pundit of his time to being a political philosopher who wrote pioneering analyses of public opinion and foreign policy.

thought rationally, acted disinterestedly and benevolently." Clear eyes and rational minds are common enough. Finding leaders who are disinterested and benevolent is the hard part.

In the early twentieth century, **E. Pendleton Herring** examined the problems posed by the dramatic increase in the scope of the administrative discretion of government. He accepted that laws passed by legislatures are necessarily the products of legislative compromise; thus they are often so vague that they need further definition. The bureaucrat, by default, then has the task of giving defining detail to the general principles embodied in a statute by issuing supplemental rules and regulations. "Upon the shoulders of the bureaucrat has been placed in large part the burden of reconciling group differences and making effective and workable the economic and social compromises arrived at through the legislative process." In effect, it becomes the job of the anonymous administrator to define the public interest.

Herring's discussion of the public interest and the critical roles played by bureaucrats and interest groups in public policy formulation correctly anticipated many of the critical issues still being grappled with in schools of public policy and administration today. Herring is a significant voice in what political science calls group theory, a school of thought that views government as representing various group interests and negotiating policy outcomes among them. According to Herring, the most basic task of a bureaucrat has been to establish working relationships with the various special interests so that their concerns can be more efficiently brokered.

The role that Herring would have public administrators play is that of **Edmund Burke's** trustee, a representative who exercises personal judgment and doesn't just follow the exact orders of a legislature or the perceived opinion of a constituency. In his classic 1774 "Speech to the Electors of Bristol" Burke told the voters, "Your representative owes you, not his industry only, but his judgment; and he betrays, instead of serving you, if he sacrifices it to your opinion." Few would argue with the desirability of using good judgment in the furtherance of the public interest. However, some would argue that the interest-group broker role that Herring espouses for high-level public administrators is inherently undemocratic.

Public Administration Is Doing Collectively That Which Cannot Be So Well Done Individually This is Abraham Lincoln's understanding of the "legitimate object of government, . . . to do for a community of people, whatever they need to have done, but cannot do, at all, or cannot, so well do, for themselves—in their separate, and individual capacities." Thus public administration is the mature manifestation of

---

E. Pendleton Herring (1903–2004) One of the most influential of the pre–World War II scholars of public administration. His *Group Representation Before Congress* (1929) was one of the pioneering works in the study of pressure groups. His *Public Administration and the Public Interest* (1936) remains a major analysis of the relations between government agencies and their formal and informal constituencies.

Edmund Burke (1729–1797) The British political philosopher and member of parliament who is often referred to as the father of modern conservative thought.

the community spirit. What started as voluntary service (such as fire protection or care for the poor) became institutionalized as people indicated a preference (via elections) to pay taxes so that once-voluntary activities could become government functions. Similarly, collective action is the remedy for the "**tragedy of the commons**," where individuals acting in their self-interest destroy public resources such as land and water. In this context public administration is central to the process of regulating individual behavior in the interest of the common good.

Twentieth-century communications have brought about a "revolution of rising expectations" whereby the people of traditionally poor countries realize just how poor they are relative to industrialized states. Similarly, the citizens of these rich states benefit from programs that they increasingly resent paying for. Senator Ernest Hollings of South Carolina often tells the story of the veteran who returned from Korea and went to college on the **GI Bill**, bought a house with a Federal Housing Administration loan, started a business with a Small Business Administration loan, got electricity from Tennessee Valley Authority, and, later, got clean water from an Environmental Protection Agency project. His parents, who were receiving Social Security, retired to a farm, got their electricity from the Rural Electrification Administration, and had their soil tested by the U.S. Department of Agriculture. When his father became ill, the family was saved from financial ruin by Medicare, and his father's life was saved with a drug developed through the National Institutes of Health. His kids participated in the school lunch program, learned physics from teachers trained in a National Science Foundation program, and went on to college with guaranteed student loans. He drove to work on the interstate and moored his boat in a channel dredged by the Army Corps of Engineers. When his home was flooded, he took **Amtrak** to Washington, DC, to apply for disaster relief, and while there, he spent some time in the Smithsonian Institution museums. One day he got mad, so he sent his congressman an angry letter. "Get the government off my back!" he wrote. "I'm tired of paying taxes for all those programs created for ungrateful people!"

But we all want—indeed expect—government employees to literally pull our backs out of the rubble when disaster strikes, as it did in New York City. Volunteers could do the easy tasks, such as driving the walking wounded to local hospitals, but only the highly trained public service professionals could do the real rescue work. Their organizations—the police and fire departments—were created, in Lincoln's words, to be available to do what the citizens "cannot do, at all, or cannot, so well do, for themselves."

---

tragedy of the commons A story illustrative of the principle that maximization of private gain will not result in the maximization of social benefit. When herdsmen sought to maximize individual gain by adding more cattle to the common pasture, it caused overgrazing, with the result that the common could no longer be used for grazing at all. The concepts involved with the tragedy of the commons apply to societal problems such as pollution and overpopulation.

GI Bill The American Servicemen's Readjustment Act of 1944. It provided low-interest, no-down-payment home mortgages and education benefits that allowed a whole generation of working-class veterans to go to college and advance into the middle class.

Amtrak The National Railroad Passenger Corp., the federally subsidized corporation created in 1970 to operate intercity rail passenger service.

Legal Definitions of Public Administration

Because public administration is what a state does, it is both created and bound by an instrument of the law. Indeed, in many communities, such as those of continental Europe, it is an academic subject that has never escaped from the faculties of law. While public administration in the United States is not a "legal" subject, its foundations are always legal.

Public Administration Is Law in Action Public administration is inherently the execution of a **public law**. Every application of a general law is necessarily an act of administration. Administration cannot exist without this legal foundation. In the United States, the Constitution of 1787 as amended is the law of the land. All legislation must conform to it—or at the very least not violate it in a manner obvious to the U.S. Supreme Court. The law that creates an agency or program is known as its enabling legislation—the law that legally "enables" a program to exist. In theory, no government administrator can do anything if it is not provided for in the legislation or in the rules and regulations that the legislation allows the agency to promulgate. And how much government money can the president of the United States spend on his own without the approval of the Congress? Not a penny! Everything the president does, if it involves spending public money, must have a basis in legislation. This is often difficult for people in less democratic regimes to understand. Tip O'Neill, the former **Speaker** of the U.S. House of Representatives, wrote in a memoir, "I must have met Deng Xiaoping of China a half-dozen times, and every time he would ask, 'The president has to go to you for his money?'" O'Neill always answered this question the same way: "Yes, and the president had better not forget it." And the same is true of governors and mayors who must go to their respective legislative bodies for appropriations.

While many books have been written about the implementation of this or that government program, there is ultimately only one thing that government is in essence capable of implementing: the law. Of course, the law is often in turmoil. The legislative basis of programs, or specific agency rules and regulations, is constantly being challenged in court by those who oppose as well as those who support the program involved. The opposition wants the enabling legislation declared unconstitutional and the program destroyed, while supporters often want the program administered even more generously. Ever since the **New Deal**, a pattern has emerged with controversial legislation. After its passage, opponents challenge its legality in court, hoping that the judicial branch will overturn it. In effect, there is a new final phase to the legislative process: a **judicial review** that confirms that the new law is constitutional.

---

public law A legislative act that deals with the citizenry as a whole; a statute that applies to all. This is in contrast to a private law that affects only one person or group.

Speaker The presiding officer of a legislature such as a House of Representatives or a House of Commons, elected by its members. Thomas P. "Tip" O'Neill was Speaker from 1977 to 1987.

New Deal The domestic programs and policies of the administration of Franklin D. Roosevelt, who was president from 1933 to 1945.

judicial review Any court's power to review executive actions, legislative acts, or decisions of lower courts (or quasi-judicial entities, such as arbitration panels) to either confirm or overturn them.

While public administration is the law in action, the law of how, when, and where these actions can be taken is called administrative law. In the American context administrative law does not deal with the substantive content of agency policies and practices. Instead, it focuses on the procedures that agencies use in exercising their authority. For example, Congress requires federal agencies such as the Environmental Protection Agency (EPA) to notify the public when the agency is creating a new rule that affects citizens. If the agency doesn't follow the specific guidelines on how and when to notify the public, its new rules can be declared illegitimate by the courts. In effect, administrative law is the totality of constitutional provisions, legislative statutes, court decisions, and executive directives that regulate the activities of government agencies.

Public Administration Is Regulation   It is government telling citizens and businesses what they may and may not do. Regulation is one of the oldest functions of government. The Code of Hammurabi in ancient Babylonia provided that "the mason who builds a house which falls down and kills the inmate shall be put to death." While not exactly a modern building code, this nevertheless proved an effective means of regulating the soundness of housing.

Modern-day regulation is so pervasive and so commonplace that we see it every day and accept it without thinking. Consider the simple act of going to McDonald's to buy a hamburger or a salad. You leave your house or apartment, which has been built according to local building codes—regulation. You get into your car, which has many safety features required by the federal government—regulation. You drive to an intersection and stop at a red light—regulation. Once at McDonald's, you notice a sticker on the door from the local public health agency indicating that the establishment has been inspected and found free of insect and rodent infestation—regulation. On the wall is a framed certificate from the local municipality indicating that the property is licensed to operate as a business—regulation. Then you give your order to a person whose minimum wages and maximum working hours are set by legislation—regulation—and whose supervisor is required by guidelines issued by the Equal Employment Opportunity Commission to maintain a workplace free of sexual harassment—regulation—and whose wages are reduced by mandatory deductions for income tax and Social Security—regulation. If after your meal you feel the need to visit one of the restrooms, you will find one oversized toilet stall designed for the physically handicapped—regulation.

Our lives are constantly governed, or interfered with, by regulation. We are not officially born until we have a birth certificate—regulation. We must attend school up to a certain age—regulation. We cannot engage in many occupations without a license from the state—regulation. Finally, we cannot be declared legally dead without a death certificate—regulation. And it doesn't even end there. We can be buried only in government-approved cemeteries, and our estate taxes must be paid—regulation.

As a general rule of thumb, the more crowded and economically developed a place is, the more regulations it has. Society needs rules so that people don't inadvertently bump into each other's cars, live in houses that fall down because they are structurally unsound, or get food poisoning from contaminated meat. Such catastrophes were

---

BOX 1.2   Why Regulation Came to the Meatpacking Industry

There was never the least attention paid to what was cut up for sausage. . . . There would be meat that had tumbled out on the floor, in the dirt and sawdust, where the workers had tramped and spit uncounted billions of consumption germs. There would be meat stored in great piles in rooms; and the water from leaky roofs would drip over it, and thousands of rats would race about on it. It was too dark in these storage places to see well, but a man could run his hand over these piles of meat and sweep off handfuls of the dried dung of rats. These rats were nuisances, and the packers would put poisoned bread out for them, they would die, and then rats, bread, and meat would go into the hoppers together. This is no fairy story and no joke; the meat would be shoveled into carts and the man who did the shoveling would not trouble to lift out a rat even when he saw one—there were things that went into the sausage in comparison with which a poisoned rat was a tidbit. There was no place for the men to wash their hands before they ate their dinner, and so they made a practice of washing them in the water that was to be ladled into the sausage. There were the butt-ends of smoked meat, and the scraps of corned beef, and all the odds and ends of the waste of the plants, that would be dumped into old barrels in the cellar and left there. Under the system of rigid economy which the packers enforced, there were some jobs that it only paid to do once in a long time, and among these was the cleaning out of the waste barrels. Every spring they did it; and in the barrels would be dirt and rust and old nails and stale water—and cart load after cart load of it would be taken up and dumped into the hoppers with fresh meat, and sent out to the public's breakfast.

SOURCE: Upton Sinclair, *The Jungle* (1906). This novel caused such a sensation that President Theodore Roosevelt authorized an investigation of the meatpackers. This led to the Pure Food and Drug Act of 1906, which provided for federal inspection.

---

common before government regulations—at least in the developed world—made them relatively rare.

Consider that in December 2003 both central California and southern Iran had earthquakes of similar magnitude. Yet, while just two people died in California, tens of thousands died in Iran. Erik Kirschbaum quotes Iranian officials as reporting that "poor design, primitive materials, and widely ignored building codes were prime causes of the high death rate." Government regulations in California requiring architectural approval, strict adherence to building codes, and building inspections saved lives.

Regulation has its origin in legislation. But since legislation can never be totally comprehensive on any subject, rules are typically needed to address the details that have not been specified in the written law. Thus rulemaking authority is necessarily exercised by administrative agencies; it is a power that has the full force of law. Agencies begin with some form of legislative mandate and translate their interpretation of that mandate into policy decisions, specifications of regulations, and statements of penalties and enforcement provisions. The exact process to be followed in formulating regulations is only briefly described in the federal Administrative Procedure Act (APA). The APA does distinguish between rulemaking that requires a hearing and rulemaking that requires only notice and the opportunity for public comment. Whether the formal or informal procedure is to be used is determined by the enabling statute: the Supreme Court's decision in *United States v. Florida East Coast Railway* (1973) held that formal rulemaking need only be followed when the enabling statute expressly requires an agency hearing prior to rule formulation. The APA also requires that rules be published 30 days before their effective date and that agencies afford any interested party the right to petition for issuance, amendment, or repeal of a rule. In effect, while the APA establishes a process of notice and time for comment, it accords administrative rulemakers the same prerogatives as legislatures in enacting statutes. There is, of course, the additional requirement that the rule enacted be consistent with the enabling statute directing the rulemaking.

All new federal rules must be pubished in the *Federal Register,* the daily publication (begun in 1935) that is the medium for making available to the public the forthcoming rules and regulations of federal agencies—as well as other legal documents of the executive branch, such as presidential proclamations and executive orders. Of course, any controversial proposed rules will quickly find their way into the mainstream press as well. All the states have similar rulemaking procedures involving the publication of proposed rules, mechanisms for receiving comments, and final action.

Public Administration Is the King's Largesse   The king's largesse is whatever goods, services, or honors the ruling authority decides to bestow. This was the earliest meaning of public administration. Since everything was owned by the crown, whatever was granted to the nobles and peasants was a gift. In the modern world this version of public administration can be seen in traditional monarchies and dictatorships, where hospitals, schools, parks, and such are touted as something given by the autocrat to a grateful people. The last vestige of this kingly largesse in **representative government** can be seen on the plaques often attached to public buildings and bridges indicating that the edifice was built during the tenure of Mayor Smith or Governor Jones. Of course, whenever representative governments grow corrupt, largesse as an operating mode of public administration reasserts itself. Then citizens may only get public services such as police protection and welfare benefits if they are deserving in the eyes of the rulers.

---

representative government A governing system in which a legislature freely chosen by the people exercises substantial power on their behalf.

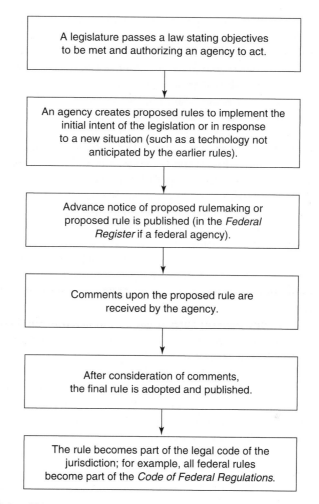

Figure 1.1 The Rulemaking Process

The traditional big-city **political machine** lasted only as long as there was largesse to distribute. For example, in Cambridge, Massachusetts, during the Great Depression, Democratic party **ward heelers** were authorized to distribute up to 50 "snow buttons" each time there was a major snowstorm. Each button entitled the holder to a day's work shoveling snow for the city. This was a highly prized benefit

political machine Historically, an informal organization that controlled the formal processes of a government through corruption, patronage, intimidation, and service to its constituents. A political machine usually centered on a single politician—a boss—who commanded loyalty through largesse, fear, or affection. The phrase is usually pejorative, because the machine works to achieve political control through those who run the machine, rather than through the popular will.

ward heeler A local political functionary; someone who is involved with, but insignificant in, party affairs. A heeler is not worthy of much respect. The term comes from the way a dog is brought to heel by its master; ward heelers are known by their obedience to their masters.

sought by unemployed men in each **ward**. While certainly at the low end of the **patronage** food chain, this largesse bought the ward heeler loyalty that translated into votes for the party. Snow buttons are a relic of the past. So are political machines, because welfare benefits as a matter of right, as an entitlement, have made them superfluous. Thus the comprehensive public services of the **welfare state** have driven out the informal welfare system of the machines. Without largesse, the political machines cannot hold the loyalty of their audience.

Public Administration Is Theft   There are those who believe that a government should do little more than provide police and military protection; other than that, it should not interfere—either for good or ill—in the lives of its citizens. A major intellectual force advocating such **libertarianism** was Ayn Rand, the **objectivist** philosopher who attacked welfare state notions of selflessness and sacrifice for a common good in novels such as *The Fountainhead* (1943) and *Atlas Shrugged* (1957). In *Capitalism: The Unknown Ideal* (1966), she wrote, "The only proper function of the government of a free country is to act as an agency which protects the individual's rights, i.e., which protects the individual from physical violence." Such **reactionary** attitudes are an extreme form of **conservatism**.

Conservatives are continuously fearful of public policies involving redistribution, such as social welfare policies and programs whose goal is to shift wealth or benefits from one segment of the population to another. The welfare state is founded on this notion of redistribution. The basic mechanism for redistribution is taxation. However, the laws themselves can sometimes redistribute benefits. For example, **tax loopholes** benefit one group of taxpayers at the expense of others; and civil rights legislation, through equal employment opportunity mandates, gives economic benefits to one segment of the population at the theoretical expense of another. Redistribution is one leg of political scientist Theodore J. Lowi's three-part classification of all domestic public policies into distribution, regulation, or redistribution. Obviously,

---

ward A subdivision of a city, often used as a legislative district for city council elections, as an administrative division for public services, or as a unit for the organization of political parties. A ward is often further divided into precincts.

patronage The power of elected and appointed officials to make partisan appointments to office or to confer contracts, honors, or other benefits on their political supporters.

welfare state A governing system in which it is a public policy that government will strive to provide a universal minimum floor of economic and social benefits for all of its citizens.

libertarianism A political doctrine holding that a government should do little more than provide police and military protection; other than that, it should not interfere—for either good or ill—in the lives of its citizens.

objectivist One who believes that reason and logic are the only means to knowledge, that self-interest determines ethics, and that capitalism should prevail in society.

reactionary A person who supports outmoded ideas of the past. The term is a derogatory reference to political malcontents who yearn for a previous status quo.

conservatism Adherence to a political disposition that prefers the status quo and accepts change only in moderation.

tax loophole An inconsistency in the tax laws, intentional or unintentional, that allows the avoidance of some taxes.

redistribution is more popular with some classes of society than with others. As **Alexis de Tocqueville** wrote in 1835, "Countries . . . , when lawmaking falls exclusively to the lot of the poor, cannot hope for much economy in public expenditure; expenses will always be considerable, either because taxes cannot touch those who vote for them or because they are assessed in a way to prevent that." Playwright George Bernard Shaw put it more succinctly: "A government which robs Peter to pay Paul can always depend on the support of Paul."

And just who is the government's chief robber in this Robin Hood game? None other than your local public administrator! This is why so many citizens with their assets at risk consider thieving the underlying occupation of the public administrator. It is a long-standing legal maxim that government regulation that goes too far amounts to a taking. This conservative attitude is strikingly similar to the famous invective issued in 1851 by anarchist **Pierre-Joseph Proudhon** against all governments: "To be governed is to be watched over, inspected, spied on, directed, legislated at, regulated, docketed, indoctrinated, preached at, controlled, assessed, weighed, censored, ordered about, by men who have neither the right nor the knowledge nor the virtue."

Proudhon was wrong about at least one thing. Public administrators *do* have the right under law to do what they do. A controversial example of the power of public administrators to "take" from the public was provided in a 2005 U.S. Supreme court ruling. The decision in *Kelo v. New London* allows government authorities to take private property from individuals for private sector economic projects in the same way that government can take one's land to build a new road. Thus, a local redevelopment agency seeking to bring in a new Wal-Mart can make you sell your property even if you wish to maintain ownership.

While many government actons could be construed as theft by portions of the populace, there is a line separating metaphorical and actual thievery. Just as the fictional British secret agent James Bond had a "license to kill," government employees in some countries consider their jobs a license to steal—usually by soliciting bribes. This is extremely common in developing countries where bureaucrats are not paid reasonable wages and have almost no choice but to engage in petty corruption. Often an informal system of fees evolves that tells the citizen, for example, how much is expected to "fix" a parking ticket or to speed up a building permit.

Managerial Definitions of Public Administration

Public administration is so much a branch of management that many graduate schools of management (or business or administration) are divided into public and private—and now increasingly nonprofit—programs. Its legal basis allows

---

Alexis de Tocqueville (1805–1859) The French historian who visited the United States in the early 1830s and went home to write *Democracy in America* (1835), a landmark description of American governance and a classic analysis of American political culture.

Pierre-Joseph Proudhon (1809–1865) The French journalist who is considered the intellectual father of anarchism.

public administration to exist, but without its management aspect, not much of the public's business would get done.

Public Administration Is the Executive Function in Government   In democratic states, whether they are republics or constitutional monarchies, it is government agencies putting into practice legislative acts that represent the will of the people. According to **Alexander Hamilton**, writing in *The Federalist,* No. 72, "The administration of government . . . in its most usual, and perhaps most precise signification . . . is limited to executive details, and falls peculiarly within the province of the executive department." In dictatorial regimes similar agencies do the bidding of the people who hold power. But the process is far more interactive and dynamic than any separation of powers diagram would suggest. While the executive, legislative, and judicial branches are separate and distinct in the United States, all sides struggle to influence the others. A president, governor, or mayor is constantly recommending new programs to the Congress, state legislature, or city council. Modern government executives at all levels do not meekly sit back and merely "execute" the will of the legislature. They actively compete to influence that will and to fight for the enactment of programs they are anxious to implement. Because this can lead to dramatic and highly publicized confrontations, the impression is often given that this is what executives do: fight for new legislation, fight for the annual budget, and fight for or against various interest groups. The reality is far less dramatic and more mundane. Most of what an executive does is to manage existing programs, to run the bureaucracy. This work is virtually invisible to the public except when something goes wrong and the media circus begins.

Public Administration Is a Management Specialty   Management refers both to the people responsible for running an organization and to the running process itself—the use of numerous resources (such as employees and machines) to accomplish an organizational goal. Top managers make the big decisions and are responsible for the overall success of the organization. In government the top managers are always the political leaders of society whether they gain power by election, appointment, or assassination. When a new president comes into office in the United States, he or she may appoint persons into approximately 3,000 jobs as the top managers who will be responsible for implementing policy. These appointees, while functioning as top managers with significant management responsibilities, are seldom professional managers and seldom think of themselves as management experts. They tend to be simply old friends, political-party loyalists, campaign contributors, and representatives of interest groups.

Consequently, the public administrators of a jurisdiction (the actual management specialists) are to be found in the vast area of middle management—the group responsible for the execution and interpretation of top-management policies and for

---

Alexander Hamilton (1755–1804) George Washington's aide and secretary during the Revolutionary
    War. A supporter of a strong national government, he signed the U.S. Constitution and coauthored
    the Federalist Papers to help get the Constitution ratified in his native New York. When Washington
    became president, he made Hamilton secretary of the treasury.

the day-to-day operation of the various organizational units. These individuals often have advanced degrees in general fields such as public administration or business administration or technical fields such as public health or social work. These are the people who have made the management of government programs their life's work. They typically have supervisory or first-level managers—those responsible for the final implementation of policies by rank-and-file employees—reporting to them. These middle managers, despite their disparity in functions and technical backgrounds, largely constitute the management specialty of public administration. They spend their working lives fighting as officers in the administrative wars started by their political leaders.

Public Administration Is Mickey Mouse   This otherwise innocent cartoon rodent has lent his name as a pejorative term for many aspects of governmental administration. When Walt Disney's famous mouse made it big in the 1930s, he appeared in a variety of cartoon shorts that had him building something (such as a house or a boat) that would later fall apart, or generally going to a great deal of trouble for little result. So Mickey gradually gave his name to anything requiring considerable effort for slight results, including many of the Mickey Mouse requirements of bureaucracy. The term is also applied to policies or regulations felt to be needless, inane, silly, or mildly offensive. For example, President Ronald Reagan used the term to good effect when he complained in 1982 that "the United States government's program for arriving at a budget is about the most irresponsible Mickey Mouse arrangement that any government body has ever practiced."

BOX 1.3   Saint Augustine Distinguishes Between Public Administration and Organized Crime—Is It Just a Matter of Size?

What are kingdoms but gangs of criminals on a large scale? What are criminal gangs but petty kingdoms? A gang is a group of men under the command of a leader, bound by a compact of association, in which the plunder is divided according to an agreed convention.

If this villainy wins so many recruits from the ranks of the demoralized that it acquires territory, establishes a base, captures cities and subdues peoples, it then openly arrogates to itself the title of kingdom. . . . It was a witty and a truthful rejoinder, which was given by a captured pirate to Alexander the Great. The king asked the fellow, "What is your idea, in infesting the sea?" And the pirate answered, with uninhibited insolence, "The same as yours, in infesting the earth! But because I do it with a tiny craft, I'm called a pirate; because you have a mighty navy, you're called an emperor."

SOURCE: Saint Augustine, *Concerning the City of God Against the Pagans* (London: Penguin Books, 1972). Charlie Chaplin summed all this up in one of his last films, *Monsieur Verdoux* (1947). Convicted of murdering a woman for her money, his character complains, "One murder makes a villain. Millions a hero. Numbers sanctify."

Mickey Mouse is often used to mean *red tape,* the symbol of excessive formality and attention to routine. This has its origins in the red ribbon with which clerks bound official documents in the nineteenth century. The ribbon has disappeared, but the practices it represents linger on. Herbert Kaufman of the Brookings Institution found that the term "is applied to a bewildering variety of organizational practices and features." Organizations create and retain such seemingly rigid "practices and features" because they promote efficiency and equity on the whole—even though this may not be true in many individual cases. After all, "one person's 'red tape' may be another's treasured procedural safeguard." Kaufman concluded that "red tape turns out to be at the core of our institutions rather than an excrescence on them."

Public Administration Is Art, Not Science—or Vice Versa   Some people have a gift for administration. We have all met such natural administrators. They are not only perpetually organized but have a knack for getting people to work together harmoniously. The administrative art is judgment, panache, and common sense. But the artist is useless without tools—without the technical skills (the science) that allow for the digestion and transference of information. Nothing is more pointless than to argue whether the practice of public administration is more art or science. It is inherently both. Of course, the more science you have, the better artist you'll be. But "book learnin' " won't make you an artist if you don't possess an element of the gift in the first place.

At the beginning of the American Civil War, Henry Wager Halleck was perhaps the most knowledgeable northerner on the art and science of war. His textbook *Elements of Military Art and Science* (1846) and translations of foreign military texts were used at West Point, where he taught. He was nicknamed "Old Brains," and much was expected when he was given a field command. But while he knew all the science, he just didn't have the art to be a leader in actual battle. Although he ended up as the **chief of staff** of the U.S. Army, he is on nobody's list of great generals. By contrast, Ulysses S. Grant, the winning general of the Civil War, dismissed books on tactics as "nothing more than common sense." He wrote in his *Memoirs* (1885) that he didn't believe his officers "ever discovered that I had never studied the tactics that I used."

So are you more likely to be an "Old Brains" Halleck—all science and no art, good at **staff** work but incapable of command—or a Grant—all art and no science, the archetypal line officer? Just because you have a master's or even a doctorate in public administration or a related field doesn't mean that you can function as a high-level administrator. Being highly educated does not always equate with being professionally able. If your goal is to make it as a city manager or agency administrator, you may wish to avoid staff jobs. Get out there and run something! Gradually prove with progressively more responsible jobs that you are an artist, that you can cope with and thrive among the usual administrative chaos.

---

chief of staff An army's highest-ranking officer.

staff Specialists who assist line managers in carrying out their duties. Generally, staff units do not have the power of decision, command, or control of operations. Rather, they make recommendations (which may or may not be adopted) to executives and line managers.

It is the same in all professions. You prepare yourself by doing smaller versions of the big thing you really want to do. Organizational theorist Antony Jay wrote of the advice traditionally given to aspiring actors: If you want to be a leading actor, you must only play leading parts—"much better to play Hamlet in Denver than **Laertes** on Broadway." You thus learn "to lead a big organization by leading smaller ones." But lead you must! When selection committees are seeking a manager for a major agency, those with only staff experience are not as likely to make the short list of finalists. Appointing authorities may not have heard of the historical Halleck, but they have all seen a Halleck—and don't want to see one in the administrative structure of their group.

Occupational Definitions of Public Administration

One of the joys of public service occupations is the frequent opportunity to participate in analyses and evaluations of public programs. However, not all public sector workers seek to engage in the public debate over policies, laws, and management practices. But all of them are interested in their jobs. So let's look at public administration—as an occupation.

Public Administration Is an Occupational Category   It is whatever the public employees of the world do. It ranges from brain surgery to street sweeping. Most of the people in this broad occupational category do not even think of themselves as public administrators. They identify with their specific professions (physician, engineer, or teacher) and trades (carpenter, electrician, or plumber). While it is true that they may not be administrators in the sense of being managers, they are nevertheless, whether they realize it or not, ministering (in the sense of providing services) to the public. In 2000 the United States had more than 20 million civilians working for its local, state, and federal governments. And only the smallest portion of them would define their work as public administration. They simply see themselves as police officers, social workers, or forest rangers, but they are also, unavoidably, public administrators.

In 1995 Richard Klausner became the director of the federal government's National Cancer Institute. He then defiantly told the *New York Times*, "I am not an administrator." He asserted that he was "a scientist and a physician." But the *Times* was not fooled by Dr. Klausner. Its lengthy profile of him was headlined "New Administrator Is 'Not an Administrator.'" Administrators, even if they, like Dr. Klausner, are in denial, are still administrators.

Public Administration Is an Essay Contest   People in bureaucratic careers tend to rise or fall on how well they can write. In a game of shuffling paper, the person whose memorandum ends up on top wins. It is a legendary truism in the U.S. State Department that nobody who's good writes his or her own memos. If you are considered talented enough, you will be asked to write your boss's memos. Then because you're too busy

---

Laertes A supporting role in Shakespeare's *Hamlet*; Laertes and Hamlet have the big sword fight in the final act.

writing the boss's memos, you find a younger talent to write yours. When your boss gets that big promotion, you go along for the ride with your own promotion. And, of course, you bring along the person who's been writing for you. Remember that Thomas Jefferson was offered the job of writing the Declaration of Independence because of his reputation as a fine stylist. And his eventual elevation to president came because he made the most of this writing opportunity. When General Douglas MacArthur was head of the U.S. Army in the 1930s, a young captain (later a major) wrote the general's reports and speeches. Coworkers knew that Dwight D. Eisenhower was an officer who was going places because he could write.

Oral presentation skills are also essential, but because more people can speak than write effectively, writing is more decisive in determining whose ideas get advanced. All organizations place great value on the person who can write succinctly in times of stress. That is the person who will be turned to when an important opportunity comes up. This is why public administration is an essay contest: because your writing reputation creates your administrative persona of winner or loser. According to a U.S. Department of State report, the Foreign Service "has prized drafting ability above almost all other skills. We emphasize this skill in recruitment and reward it generously in our promotion system. The prize jobs in the service are the reporting jobs." Donald P. Warwick, in his analysis of the State Department's bureaucracy, found that "following the classic model of the gentleman generalist, the Foreign Service exalts graceful prose and the well-turned phrase." Other agencies with fewer "gentlemen" are equally anxious to reward "graceful prose."

If you examine the personal histories of the best-known and most influential members of the George W. Bush administration—Vice President Richard Cheney, Secretary of State Condoleezza Rice, and Secretary of Defense Donald Rumsfeld—you will find that when they were lowly bureaucrats they each jump-started their careers because of their ability to write. Of course, their boss, President Bush, is widely known not to be one to whom "graceful prose" comes naturally. But he overcame that handicap through the combination of leadership skills and by being born into a political dynasty of great wealth and influence. Unless you are similarly wellborn, you have no choice but to enter the essay contest to advance in a public administration career.

Public Administration Is Idealism in Action   Many people enter public service careers because they are idealists; they believe in and seek to advance noble principles. "Noble" is the key word here because traditionally the nobility had public service obligations. They were the warrior class, so it was their obligation to heroically protect the weak and less fortunate, to accept the notion of **noblesse oblige**. Gradually, their duties expanded from military affairs to the whole realm of public affairs. High-level government service, which was once the prerogative of the wellborn, the financially well off, and the well connected, is now also open to those who were born with talent but without money or connections.

Idealism draws people into public administration because it provides them with worthwhile—and exciting—things to do with their lives. Nowhere else can someone

---

noblesse oblige A French term meaning "nobility obliges"; the notion that the nobles (or those of the upper class) have a special obligation to serve society.

without private wealth achieve such vast power so quickly. Even the children of the very wealthy—such as the Kennedys and Rockefellers—tend to enter public service for the same reasons other people do: because it's fun, it offers ego gratification, and, most importantly, because it satisfies their dual desires to do good works and exercise power. When someone asked the multimillionaire presidential candidate John F. Kennedy why he wanted to be president, he candidly replied, "Because that is where the power is."

The idealism associated with public administration goes far beyond the individual. The goal is the mystical one of building "a city upon a hill," an ideal political community thoroughly fit for others to observe as an example. This phrase comes from John Winthrop, governor of the Massachusetts Bay Colony. In 1630 he wrote, "For we must consider that we shall be as a city upon a hill. The eyes of all people are upon us." This is a famous statement in Massachusetts history, and both Presidents Kennedy and Reagan favored using it in speeches. It also illustrates how the nondenominational religious elements of public administration allow participants to gain satisfaction by becoming involved with a cause greater than themselves.

According to an old story, a supervisor asks three bricklayers what they are doing. The first replies, "I'm just putting one brick upon another." The second says, "I'm building this here wall." The third says, "I'm creating a cathedral." They are all doing the identical job, but the third worker is emotionally caught up in a great and noble enterprise. We cannot necessarily presume that the third bricklayer will do a better job, but he'll feel better about it. And because he feels better about it, it is more likely that he'll do a better job. His idealism is no different from the emotional high available to individuals engaged in any number of projects to improve their communities. A neighborhood free from crime or a city with safe drinking water for all are goals every bit as worthy as building a cathedral.

It is strange how these idealists in government who only want to do good for their fellow citizens are considered not much better than thieves and social parasites by others—usually not by those who need government help but by those **rugged individualists** who don't. Many who seek careers in public service believe that government is a legitimate vehicle for solving social problems—and they want to be driving that vehicle when the problem gets solved. What's the good of doing good if you can't have fun doing it? This attitude is similar to that of the sixteenth-century Spanish conquistador Bernal Díaz del Castillo, whom Samuel Eliot Morison quotes as saying, "We came here [to the Americas] to serve God and also to get rich." Today's public administration idealists know that getting rich in terms of money is unlikely; the riches they seek are those of the joys of experience, the sense of personal satisfaction, and the building of "a city upon a hill."

Public Administration Is an Academic Field   It is the study of the art and science of management applied to the public sector. But it traditionally goes far beyond the

---

rugged individualists Those who staunchly believe that citizens should take care of their own economic needs and not be dependent on government for the necessities of life. Rugged individualists also tend to oppose paternalistic government welfare programs out of concern that the poor will have their character undermined. This philosophy was most associated with Presidents Hoover and Reagan.

concerns of management and incorporates as its subject matter all of the political, social, cultural, and legal environments that affect the running of public institutions. As a field of study, it is inherently cross-disciplinary because it encompasses so much of political science, sociology, business administration, psychology, law, anthropology, medicine, forestry, and so on. Indeed, it can be argued that because public administration borrows so much from other fields, what is left as its core is hardly worthy of being considered a legitimate academic field at all. Yet, there is a center about which the parts of public administration have coalesced (see Figure 1.2).

While **Woodrow Wilson** and many others of the **progressive movement** called for a "science of administration," new intellectual fields evolve amorphously. It is difficult to trace the exact moment of their conception. What is certain is that the first real American public administration text is *Introduction to the Study of Public Administration* by **Leonard White**, published in 1926.

While Woodrow Wilson provided the rationale for public administration to be an academic discipline and professional management specialty, it remained for White to most clearly articulate its preliminary objectives. In his pioneering text, he noted four critical assumptions that formed the basis for the study of public administration:

1. Administration is a unitary process that can be studied uniformly, at the federal, state, and local levels.
2. The basis for study is management, not law.
3. Administration is still art, but the ideal of transformation to science is both feasible and worthwhile.
4. Administration "has become, and will continue to be the heart of the problem of modern government."

White's text was remarkable both for its influence over four decades (the fourth and last edition was published in 1955) and for its restraint in not taking a prescriptive cookbook approach to public administration. He recognized that public administration was above all a field of study that had to stay close to reality—the reality of its largely untrained practitioner base that still professed great belief in the art of administration. Even more interesting, his work avoided the potential pitfall of the politics–administration dichotomy. Defining

---

Woodrow Wilson (1856–1924) Before Wilson became president of the United States (1913–1921), he was a professor of history and political science who rose to be president of Princeton University (1902–1910) and governor of New Jersey (1911–1913).

progressive movement While the term has its origins in religious concepts that argued for the infinite improvability of the human condition, by the end of the nineteenth century it had come to refer to a political and cultural movement that focused on reforming industrialized societies to provide for greater democratic participation by the individual in government, and the application of science and specialized knowledge and skills to the improvement of life.

Leonard White (1891–1958) The University of Chicago professor who wrote the first public administration text in 1926. He is the author of the standard administrative histories of the U.S. government in the nineteenth century. Overall White is one of the most significant voices in the development of public administration as an academic discipline.

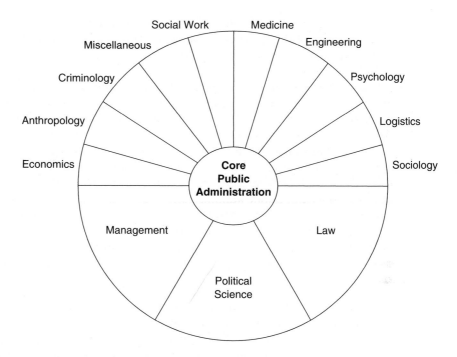

Figure 1.2   The Interdisciplinary Nature of Public Administration

public administration as emphasizing the managerial phase, he left unanswered "the question to what extent the administration itself participates in formulating the purposes of the state."

As an independent academic field, public administration has always been controversial. First, it was the stepchild of political science. And in many colleges, the field is still represented by a few courses within the political science curriculum. Later, schools of business or management began to offer it as one of a variety of administrative specialties. In recent decades, independent departments and graduate schools of public administration have been created. But as the field of public administration matured, its constituent elements began to intellectually fly away. The public policy analyst increasingly identified with the mathematical rigor of political science methodologists. Public finance has been claimed by the economists. The core management elements have drifted toward the field of public management. Increasingly, the field seems to be less a discipline than a holding company for disparate intellectual components. This is hardly new. In 1975 Dwight Waldo was decrying that "public administration is suffering from an identity crisis, having enormously expanded its periphery without retaining or creating a unifying center." A quarter-century later, this crisis shows no signs of abating.

In answer to the question "Is public administration a legitimate academic field?" honest people of differing views will argue both pro and con. We obviously side with Waldo and assert that, whatever its problems with unity, public administration is most decidedly a legitimate field. We also contend that the growth and frisky independence of its elements is both healthy and intellectually invigorating. An academic field without controversy must necessarily be in decline. Thus public administration is very healthy indeed.

Public Administration Is a Profession   It is the application of its unique arts and sciences to the problems of society. But is it a profession, such as law, medicine, engineering, or architecture? The case for public administration's status as a profession can be made by applying to it the test of professionalism. Does it possess the three core features common to traditional professions?

1. A body of academic and practical knowledge that is applied to the service of society
2. A standard of success theoretically measured by serving the needs of society rather than seeking purely personal gain
3. A system of control over the professional practice that regulates the education of new members and maintains both a code of ethics and appropriate sanctions

Public administration amply meets all three of these criteria even though, unlike law or medicine, it cannot control entry to practice through licenses and examinations. However, public administration acts like these long-established professions by drawing upon different fields of specialization to solve problems and prepare new practitioners. While public administration is not a pure social science, as some would have it, it is fully equal to these more traditional fields of study. Perhaps it supersedes many in one respect. Society's original professionals were clergy because they professed the word of God. Such people were said to have a "calling." Why? Because God was said to have called them. Public administration with its idealistic notions of building "a city upon a hill" is closer to this original religious conception of professionalism than many other professions today.

The Evolution of Public Administration

There was nothing preordained about the preceding discussion of definitions. It is a product of the life experiences of the authors. It could have been written in a radically different framework and accomplished essentially the same task. Similarly, public administration itself did not have to evolve the way it did. As with any evolutionary process, there were a seemingly infinite number of possible outcomes. Biologist Stephen Jay Gould in his book about the Burgess Shale, a fossil-rich limestone quarry in the Canadian Rockies, shows how animal evolution had any number of starts and stops. According to Gould, no "handicapper, given Burgess evidence as known today, would have granted very favorable odds" that the vertebrate creatures from which humans evolved would have survived. The most disturbing thing about this kind of natural selection, according to Gould, is the random nature of it—that so much of evolutionary history takes on the character of a lottery.

So it has been with public administration. The administrative institutions that we presently have could so easily have been radically different. How humans learned to approach the practice and definition of public administration could so easily have taken a surprising turn. For example, if the Greeks had insisted that administration was household management on a grand scale, they might have developed it as a female occupation. And it might have been copied that way by the Romans, who adopted so much else of Greek science and culture. If the classical world developed the notion that men were fit only for war and physical toil, women might have evolved a beneficent administrative matriarchy. And there is a third possibility: rule by eunuchs. (No joke!)

For over two thousand years and into the twentieth century, eunuchs—males with their external sex organs amputated—were the public administrators of choice. Why? Because their missing parts meant that they could be trusted—first with the rulers' wives and concubines, and then with other administrative chores. Eunuchs proved to be particularly effective and loyal administrators. As slaves usually long removed from any family, they knew that the only way to thrive was to do well by the only people who could enrich and protect them. The eunuchs formed a kind of civil service system. Entrance was typically limited to captured slave boys from the edge of the empire who were castrated by the thousands. While a large percentage died from the crude surgery, the survivors were put into service as court eunuchs. There they could work their way up to the highest level of administrative responsibility. Eunuchs grew to be the servant class most trusted by the rulers of ancient Syria, Persia, China, and Rome. In an era rife with nepotism (hiring of relatives), they were immune from such influences. While Christian Byzantium made extensive use of eunuchs in government posts, Western Christendom did not.

The last of the traditional bureaucrat-eunuchs were still to be seen in imperial China and the Ottoman Empire only a century ago. Thus for most of recorded history administration by eunuchs was a "normal" means by which states managed their affairs. The advantages they offered—absolute loyalty and apathy—are not to be sneered at. Fortunately today there are ways to instill high standards of ethics in government officials without sending castration technicians to visit the bureaucrats of Washington, **Whitehall**, and the **Kremlin**.

The Core Content

But even if public administration had evolved along radically different lines, it would have had to come out about where it is concerning its core content. While there is no agreement on all the details, there is broad general agreement about the subject matter. Thus all public administration introductory texts have chapters similar to those that follow, except for the method of presentation. But there is almost universal agreement that organization theory, bureaucratic behavior, personnel management, public finance and budgeting, policy analysis, program evaluation,

---

Whitehall That area of London between Trafalgar and Parliament Squares in which government buildings have historically (since the time of Henry VIII) been concentrated. Thus it has come to refer to the most senior members of the British civil service.

Kremlin The Moscow citadel where the main offices of the Russian government are located.

and administrative ethics, among other topics, are essential to a basic understanding of the field. This essential information is all here.

It is an underlying premise of this book that public administration cannot be properly understood without an appreciation of its political dynamics. All of the actors in the public administration world must accept their political fate—they cannot pretend either to themselves or to the public that they operate as a public sector counterpart to industrial management. And the political nature of public administration must be faced maturely. Just as the first step in arresting alcoholism is to have the alcoholic admit that he or she is an alcoholic and will always be an alcoholic even after he or she stops drinking, the first step toward putting public administration operations on a more realistic footing is for public managers to admit that public sector administration is an inherently political process.

Public administration is increasingly a cross-governmental field. Yet too many of the comprehensive texts available for introductory courses in the United States are decidedly parochial in that they focus on the national government. This is an incongruous situation when you consider that a relatively small percentage of American public administrators work for the federal government. While the United States has one federal government, it has more than 80,000 units of state, county, metropolitan, and local governments led by administrators as esteemed as governors and as unnoticed as the executive director of a mosquito abatement district. In all, state and local governments employed over 16.6 million Americans in 2004, compared to only 2.7 million individuals working for the federal government in civilian positions (see Table 1.2). Most public administration students in the United States will go into state and local government or are foreign nationals who expect to return home with readily applicable skills. Still others will work in nonprofit organizations. The end of the Cold War has only encouraged an ever-increasing worldwide market for Western-oriented public administration. Thus to a large extent this text takes a unified approach—appropriate for U.S. students at all levels (federal, state, and local) but generic enough to be truly useful to students of other countries and cultures.

Most of the content of introductory public administration texts can be universally applicable. There exists a unified whole (public administration in general) that is greater than the sum of its parts (public administration in each jurisdiction). The core concept of the unified approach to introducing public administration is to

TABLE 1.2 Government Employment in 2004

Level of Government	Number of Employees	Total Monthly Payroll*
Federal Government	2,733,869	$12.8 billion
State Government	5,041,143	$15.5 billion
Local Government	11,601,136	$40.4 billion

SOURCE: U.S Bureau of the Census Annual Survey of Government Employment, 2004.
http://www.census.gov/govs/www/apes.html

*Monthly payroll figures calculated from payrolls in March 2004.

write the material in such a manner that it can be readily applied to the differing political systems within the American federal system and throughout the rest of the world. Indeed, no public administration textbook can be comprehensive today if it is not cross-governmental in the most expansive sense. National administration figures from the president on down hardly ever make a major speech without some reference to government policies and practices in Asia, Europe, and elsewhere. This is just the latest evidence of how imperative it is that American students of public administration develop a greater international perspective.

This will not be a "how-to" book written for people who want to be public administration experts in ten easy lessons. It will be a "what is it?" book written for people who seek or are engaged in managerial careers in the public sector and are in need of a basic introduction to, or a review of, public sector administrative practices. The "nuts and bolts" of administrative processes vary considerably from jurisdiction to jurisdiction. Because of differing laws and customs, it would be futile to present the "one right way" for any given procedure. Instead, the procedural chapters (on personnel, budgeting, strategic management, etc.) concentrate on the historical evolution, essential theory, and future trends of their subjects. With this information, diligent readers will have the kind of conceptual foundation that will allow them to rapidly digest and master the procedural nuts and bolts that differ with every jurisdiction.

It's an Adventure!

The U.S. Navy once used this recruiting slogan: "It's not just a job, it's an adventure." So is it with public administration. A public service career is often the most exciting thing individuals can do with their lives. Walter Lippmann often observed that "the joys of private life" are much overrated. "For the truth is that public life, once a man [or woman] has been infected with its excitement and importance, is something that few ever get over." Whether one comes to a capital to expand government or to contract it, it is a worthy personal quest, a great personal adventure—and equally worthy and adventurous if you serve in a national capital, a state capital, a city hall, or a neighborhood association. Public service, like adventure, comes in all sizes.

Many of you would not be holding this book if you were not engaged in or contemplating a public service career. Consider what follows not so much as a guidebook—the field is too vast to be encompassed in one or even one hundred books—but as a reconnaissance. Herein is the lay of the land that you will encounter in a public administration adventure. Learn how to tinker with the machinery of government, discover the ancient secrets of modern strategic management, review the arcane rules of public personnel administration, buy into the politics of the budgetary process, and finally examine how ethical it all is. Public administration not only has a cast of millions, but it is a show that has been playing for more than 5,000 years. The goal of the authors has been to make your journey in the sometimes wild and woolly public sector more successful by giving necessary historical perspectives on this strange world and by alerting you to the dangers and opportunities that lie ahead. You, as the adventurer, must make the most of them. Enjoy the trip!

✦ A CASE STUDY: HOW A PRESIDENT UNDESERVEDLY RECEIVED CREDIT FOR FOUNDING A DISCIPLINE

In 1885 Woodrow Wilson, having not yet completed his doctoral program at Johns Hopkins University, began his teaching career at the newly founded Bryn Mawr College for Women. While reportedly a lecturer of genius, he resented having to teach women. As he told an associate, such an activity "relaxes one's mental muscle." In 1887 he summed up his life by saying, "Thirty-one years old and nothing done!" In retrospect Wilson seems to have been like many other ambitious academics seemingly stuck in a post that did not do justice to talent. And he chose as the way out the now traditional road to high academic fame, fortune, and position: He wrote and published and was saved!

American public administration as a field of study traditionally traces its origin to an 1887 *Political Science Quarterly* article by this frustrated young academic. In "The Study of Administration" Wilson attempted nothing less than to refocus the newly emerging field of political science. Rather than be concerned with the "lasting maxims of political wisdom," he argued that political science should concentrate on the more generally neglected details of how governments are administered. This was necessary because "it is getting harder to *run* a constitution than to frame one."

Wilson wanted the study of public administration to focus not only on the problems of personnel management, as many other reformers of the time had advocated, but also on organization and management in general. The reform movement of the time had an agenda that did not go beyond the abolition of the spoils system and the installation of a merit system. Wilson regarded civil service reform "as but a prelude to a fuller administrative reform." He sought to push the concerns of public administration into investigations of the "organization and methods of our government offices" with a view toward determining "first, what government can properly and successfully do, and secondly, how it can do these proper things with the utmost possible efficiency and at the least possible cost either of money or energy." He was concerned with overall organizational efficiency and economy—that is, productivity in its most simplistic formulation. What could be more current—then or now?

In his essay, Wilson also proclaimed the existence of a major distinction between politics and administration. This was a common and necessary political tactic of the reform movement because arguments that public appointments should be based on fitness and merit, rather than partisanship, necessarily had to assert that "politics" was out of place in public service. As Wilson said, "Although politics sets the tasks for administration, it should not be suffered to manipulate its offices." In reinforcing what became known as the "politics–administration dichotomy," Wilson was really referring to "partisan" politics. While this subtlety was lost on many, Wilson's main themes—that public administration should be premised on a science of management and separate from traditional politics—fell on fertile intellectual ground. The ideas of this then obscure professor eventually became the dogma of academic public administration.

And what happened to the young Bryn Mawr professor who plaintively wrote in 1888, "I have for a long time been hungry for a class of *men*"? Shortly thereafter he took up an appointment at Wesleyan University in Connecticut. From there he went to Princeton, made good, and became president of that university. In later life he found a job in Washington.

But if Wilson had not found that job in Washington, had not become president, his now seminal article would have continued to enjoy the obscurity its verbosity warrants. The article's significant influence came only after World War II—more than half a century after it was published. Administrative historian Paul van Riper found that none of the early public administration scholars, Wilson's contemporaries, cited the article in their otherwise heavily referenced works. "In reality, any connection between Wilson's essay and the later development of the discipline is pure fantasy! An examination of major political and social science works of the period between 1890 and World War I shows no citation whatever of the essay." So how did it get rediscovered and become required reading for generations of students? According to a historical analysis by Daniel W. Martin, "The simple answer . . . is the glowing reprint of Wilson's article in the December 1941 *Political Science Quarterly.* It was a masterwork of public relations, complete with a photostatic copy of Wilson's tentative letter of submission." Thereafter, Wilson's essay, cited only modestly in the interwar period, grew to its current influence.

For Discussion: *Do you think that public administration can ever be, or should be, totally separate from politics? Can the current Bush administration be considered "Wilsonian" in that it is similarly concerned with efficiency and economy?*

Summary

Public administration can be defined from political, legal, managerial, and occupational perspectives. However defined, its vast scope encompasses whatever governments do. Public administration cannot exist outside of its political context. It is this context that makes it public—that makes it different from private or business administration. Public administration is what a state does. It is created by and bound by the law and is an instrument of the law. It is inherently the execution of public laws. Every application of a general law is necessarily an act of administration. Its legal basis allows public administration to exist, but without its management aspect, not much of the public's business would get done.

Public administration as an academic field is the study of the art and science of management applied to the public sector. But it traditionally goes far beyond the concerns of management and incorporates as its subject matter all of the political, social, cultural, and legal environments that affect the running of public institutions. It is inherently cross-disciplinary, encompassing so much of other fields—from political science and sociology to business administration and law. American public administration as a field of study is traditionally traced to Woodrow Wilson's 1887 article "The Study of Administration." The discipline of public administration, after developing as part of political science, emerged as an independent field in the second half of the twentieth century.

As a profession, public administration offers significant opportunities for idealism in the pursuit of public service—and even heroism, as we saw on September 11. Concerns for an increasingly effective or more expansive public service ebb and flow with the changing political philosophies of differing administrations. But the provision of public services—whether by career public servants or by contracted private sector employees—remains the very essence of public administration.

Review Questions

1. How would you define public administration in one phrase, one paragraph, or an essay?

2. Is public administration among the oldest or newest areas of study or both?

3. Is public administration an amalgam of various areas of study or a field unto itself?

4. Is public administration a profession or just an occupation?

5. How does a public administration career offer the potential of a great adventure?

Key Concepts

administration The management and direction of the affairs of governments and institutions; a collective term for all policymaking officials of a government; the execution and implementation of public policy.

executive branch The part of a government responsible for applying or administering the law. Thus a president, governor, or mayor and the supporting bureaucracies are the executive branches of their respective jurisdictions.

management A word that refers to both the people responsible for running an organization and the running process itself; the use of numerous resources (such as employees and machines) to accomplish an organizational goal.

professional A member of an occupation requiring specialized knowledge that can be gained only after intensive preparation. Professional occupations tend to possess three features: a body of academic and practical knowledge that is applied to the service of society, a standard of success theoretically measured by serving the needs of society rather than seeking purely personal gain,

and a system of control over the professional practice.

public administration Whatever governments do for good or ill. It is public administration's political context that makes it public—that distinguishes it from private or business administration.

public interest The universal label in which political actors wrap the policies and programs that they advocate.

public policy Decision making by government. Governments are constantly concerned about what they should or should not do. And whatever they do or do not do is public policy.

red tape The ribbon that was once used to bind government documents; the term now stands as the symbol of excessive official formality and overattention to prescribed routines.

regulation The totality of government controls on the social and economic activities of its citizens; the rulemaking process of those administrative agencies charged with the official interpretation of laws.

Bibliography

Cuomo, Mario. (1995). *Reason to Believe.* New York: Simon and Schuster.

Edelman, Murray. (1964). *The Symbolic Uses of Politics.* Urbana: University of Illinois Press.

Friedman, Thomas L. (1998). "Desperado Democracies," *New York Times* (July 14).

Galbraith, John Kenneth. (1956). *American Capitalism.* Boston: Houghton Mifflin.

Gould, Stephen Jay. (1989). *Wonderful Life: The Burgess Shale and the Nature of History.* New York: Norton.

Haldane, J. B. S. (1928). *Possible Worlds and Other Essays.* New York: Harper.

Halleck, Henry W. (1863). *Elements of Military Art and Science,* 3rd ed. New York: Appleton.

Herring, E. Pendleton. (1936). *Public Administration and the Public Interest.* New York: McGraw-Hill.

Irving, Clive, ed. (1995). *In Their Name: Dedicated to the Brave and the Innocent—Oklahoma City, April 1995.* New York: Random House.

Jay, Antony. (1967). *Management and Machiavelli.* New York: Holt, Rinehart and Winston.

Kaufman, Herbert. (1977). *Red Tape: Its Origins, Uses, and Abuses.* Washington: Brookings Institution.

Kirschbaum, Erik. (2003). "Iran Asks Why Are Earthquakes So Deadly?" Reuters (December 30).

Kugler, Sara. (2001). "One WTC Survivor's E-Mail Touches Hundreds Worldwide," Associated Press (December 25).

Lippmann, Walter. (1955). *The Public Philosophy.* Boston: Little, Brown.

Lowi, Theodore J. (1969). *The End of Liberalism.* New York: Norton.

Martin, Daniel W. (1988). "The Fading Legacy of Woodrow Wilson," *Public Administration Review* 48 (March–April).

Morison, Samuel Eliot. (1974). *The European Discovery of America: The Southern Voyages.* New York: Oxford University Press.

Noonan, Peggy. (2001). "Courage Under Fire," *The Wall Street Journal* (October 5).

O'Neill, Tip. (1994). *All Politics Is Local and Other Rules of the Game.* New York: Times Books.

Rosenbloom, David H. (1990). *Public Administration,* 2nd ed. New York: Random House.

Rossiter, Clinton, and James Lare, eds. (1963). *The Essential Lippmann: A Political Philosophy for Liberal Democracy.* New York: Random House.

Shaw, George Bernard. (1944). *Everybody's Political What's What?* New York: Dodd, Mead.

Tocqueville, Alexis de. (1835; translation 1899). *Democracy in America.* New York: Appleton.

U.S. Department of State. (1970). *Diplomacy for the 70s.* Washington: U.S. Department of State.

Van Riper, Paul. (1983). "The American Administrative State: Wilson and the Founders—An Unorthodox View." *Public Administration Review* 43 (November–December).

Waldo, Dwight. (1955). *The Study of Administration.* New York: Random House.

———. (1975). "Education for Public Administration in the Seventies." In *American Public Administration: Past, Present, Future,* ed. Frederick C. Mosher. Tuscaloosa: University of Alabama Press.

Warwick, Donald P. (1975). *A Theory of Public Bureaucracy: Politics, Personality, and Organization in the State Department.* Cambridge, MA: Harvard University Press.

Wilson, Woodrow. (1887). "The Study of Administration," *Political Science Quarterly* 2 (June); reprinted 50 (December 1941).

Winthrop, Robert C. (1971). *Life and Letters of John Winthrop.* New York: Da Capo Press.

Woodward, Bob. (2002). *Bush at War.* New York: Simon and Schuster.

Recommended Books

Kettl, Donald F. (2002). *The Transformation of Governance: Public Administration for Twenty-First Century America.* Baltimore: Johns Hopkins University Press. An explanation of how governance—the set of processes and institutions, formal and informal, through which social action occurs—is transforming the nature of public administration.

Rosenbloom, David H., and Rosemary O'Leary. (1987). *Public Administration and Law,* 2nd ed. New York: Marcel Dekker. An extensive explanation of how the legal system—the courts—influences administrative values, decision making, organizational structures, policy implementation, and program evaluation.

Shafritz, Jay M., editor in chief. (1998). *International Encyclopedia of Public Policy and Administration.* Boulder, CO: Westview Press. Nine hundred articles defining and analyzing every aspect of public administration; the first place to go to look up a concept, practice, theory, or issue in the field.

Shafritz, Jay M., (2004). *The Dictionary of Public Policy and Administration.* Boulder, CO: Westview Press. A detailed collection of terms and definitions within the areas of public administration and policy.

Waldo, Dwight. (1984). *The Administrative State: A Study of the Political Theory of Amercian Public Administration,* 2nd ed. New York: Holmes and Meier. The classic work on the philosophy of public administration (originally published in 1948) wherein the prevailing "gospel of efficiency" is rejected and administrative value neutrality is denied.

Related Web Sites

American Political Science Association
www.apsanet.org/

Amercian Society for Public Administration
www.aspanet.org/

Amnesty International
www.amnesty.org/

Association for Public Policy Analysis and Management
www.appam.org

Council on Licensure, Enforcement, and Regulation
www.csg.org

Federal government laws and regulations
www.thecre.com/fedlaw/default.htm

Federal government statistics
www.fedstats.gov

National Association of Schools of Public Affairs and Administration
www.naspaa.org

Woodrow Wilson
www.whitehouse.gov/history/presidents/ww28.html

CHAPTER 2

The Political and Cultural Environment of Public Policy and Its Administration

• KEYNOTE: WHO DECIDES IF THE UNITED STATES SHOULD WAGE WAR?

A decision to go to war is arguably the most important public policy decision made by a state. The U.S. Constitution (Article I, Section 8) unambiguously gives Congress the authority "to declare war." However, the president, as commander in chief, has implied powers to commit the military forces to action. Article III, Section 2, of the Constitution says that "the president shall be commander in chief of the army and the navy of the United States and of the militia of the several states when called into the actual service of the United States." The last president to exercise his authority as commander in chief to literally command troops in the field was James Madison during the War of 1812. At Bladensburg, Maryland, the American forces, under the direct command of their president, met the British and were soundly defeated. The British then marched on Washington, DC, to burn the White House, the Capitol, and most other public buildings. No subsequent president while in office has sought to personally lead men in battle.

But many subsequent presidents have sent U.S. forces to fight in foreign lands without waiting for or even asking Congress to exercise its constitutional responsibility "to declare war." Formal declarations of war seem to be rapidly becoming quaint relics of diplomatic history. Declarations of war first came about when states felt it necessary to separate their military actions from the activities of bandits, pirates, and privateers (a pirate ship authorized by a government to prey on its foes). Therefore, before the beginning of hostilities, a formal statement of intention—a declaration—to make war on another state was promulgated. In 1907 this practice was formalized by the Hague Convention Relative to the Opening of Hostilities. This established an international obligation on the part of the signatories to announce that a legal state of hostilities existed with another state by making a formal declaration to this effect. And formal meant *formal*. For example, here is the declaration that started World War I.

> The Royal Serbian Government not having answered in a satisfactory manner the note of July 23, 1914, presented by the Austro-Hungarian Minister at Belgrade, the Imperial and Royal Government are themselves compelled to see to the safeguarding of their right and interests, and, with this object, to have recourse to force of arms. Austria-Hungary consequently considers herself henceforward in state of war with Serbia.

These are the courtly words that initiated the greatest mass slaughter the world had seen to date. When British Prime Minister Winston Churchill had to justify why the declaration of war against Japan on December 8, 1941, was made in similar diplomatic language, he responded, "When you have to kill a man, it costs nothing to be polite."

World War II was the last time formal declarations of war were widely used. Things started to get constitutionally messy with the Korean War—the war between communist North Korea and noncommunist South Korea—which began on June 25, 1950, when the North invaded the South. The American intervention was a symbolic signal to the Soviets that the United States was determined to halt the spread of communism. With the encouragement of the United States, the United Nations Security Council (with the Soviet Union temporarily absent) asked member nations to aid the South in resisting the invasion. Thus the war, called a "police action," was fought under the flag of the United Nations by U.S. forces with small contingents from more than a dozen other nations.

The Vietnam War of 1956 to 1975 was between the noncommunist Republic of Vietnam (South Vietnam) and the communist Democratic Republic of Vietnam (North Vietnam), which resulted in the victory of the North over the South and the unification of the two countries into the communist Socialist Republic of Vietnam on July 2, 1976. The United States first offered financial support to South Vietnam during the Eisenhower administration. Military assistance began with the John F. Kennedy administration in 1961. By 1963, the United States had 16,000 military "advisors" in South Vietnam. In 1964, the Gulf of Tonkin Resolution allowed the administration of Lyndon B. Johnson to expand U.S. involvement in spite of the fact that Johnson had promised, notably in a campaign speech in Akron, Ohio, on October 21, 1964: "We are not about to send American boys nine or ten thousand miles away from home to do what Asian boys ought to be doing for themselves."

With the Gulf of Tonkin Resolution the U.S. Congress sanctioned the Johnson administration's use of great numbers of American forces in an expansion of the Vietnam War. It was premised upon a presumed attack on U.S. ships in the Gulf of Tonkin by North Vietnamese naval units. The Johnson administration would treat this as the moral and legal equivalent of a declaration of war. Later, those who opposed the war would denounce it as a fraud because there was no solid evidence that there ever was an attack on American ships in the Tonkin Gulf. Indeed, Barbara W. Tuchman in *The March of Folly* (1984) would write, "With evidence accumulating of confusion by radar and sonar technicians in the second clash, [President] Johnson said privately, 'Well, those dumb, stupid sailors were just shooting at flying fish.' So much for *casus belli*." But there was little initial opposition. The House of Representatives passed it unanimously. In the Senate there were only two dissenting votes. Senator Jacob K. Javits, who voted for the resolution, would later write in *Who Makes War* (1973), "In voting unlimited presidential power most members of Congress thought they were providing for retaliation for an attack on our forces and preventing a large-scale war in Asia, rather than authorizing its inception."

By 1968, the United States had more than one-half million men engaged in the most unpopular foreign war in American history. As a direct result, the Democrats lost

TABLE 2.1 Wars: Declared and Undeclared

Declared Wars	Undeclared Wars
War of 1812	Korean War 1950–1953
Mexican War, 1846	Vietnam War 1962–1974
Spanish-American War, 1898	Grenada Invasion 1983
World War I, 1917	Panama Intervention 1989
World War II, 1941	Persian Gulf War 1990–1991
	War on Terrorism 2001–
	Iraq War 2003–

control of the White House to Republican Richard M. Nixon. The Nixon administration's policy of Vietnamization called for the South Vietnamese to gradually take over all the fighting from the Americans. The Americans continued to pull out, and the South held off the North for a while. As the American forces dwindled, the North got more aggressive and successful. Finally, the North's January 1975 offensive led to the South's unconditional surrender by April. More than 58,000 Americans died in the Vietnam War; another 150,000 were wounded.

Because of the unhappy experience of the Vietnam War, Congress passed the War Powers Resolution of 1973, the law that seeks to clarify the respective roles of the president and Congress in cases involving the use of military forces without a declaration of war. The president "in every possible instance" shall consult with Congress before introducing troops and shall report to Congress within 48 hours. The use of the armed forces is to be terminated within 60 days (with a possible 30-day extension by the president) unless Congress acts during that time to declare war, enacts a specific authorization for use of armed forces, extends the 60- to 90-day period, or is physically unable to meet as a result of an attack on the United States. At any time before the 60 days expire, Congress may direct by concurrent resolution that American military forces be removed by the president.

In one sense the War Powers Resolution has been a failure: It has not been able to remedy the problems of presidents ignoring Congress. President George H. W. Bush, for example, sent troops into action during the Panama Intervention and the Persian Gulf War without formally asking congressional consent. While Congress, at the last minute (on January 12, 1991) gave him legal authority to commit U.S. forces to combat (which he did on January 15, 1991), he asserted that he didn't really need it—that his authority under the Constitution as commander in chief was sufficient.

On the other hand, the desire to avoid putting their war powers to the test has led presidents to be somewhat more responsive to Congress than they might otherwise have been. The Reagan administration, for example, withdrew U.S. forces from Lebanon when it became clear that there was little congressional or public support for keeping them there. The Clinton administration conducted a major bombing campaign against Serbia to force the Serbian troops out of Kosovo in 1999. But it initially maintained that a ground assault was not an option because it knew that there was slight congressional support for the bombing.

If the president can, as Bush did, send 500,000 troops half a world away to fight for a country with which we had no treaty of obligation to defend, then what, if anything, is left of Congress's constitutional authority to declare war? The answer is that it has never amounted to much. The fallacy of Congress's authority "to declare war" was first exposed by James K. Polk, the president of the United States from 1845 to 1849. When in 1846 Mexico refused a U.S. offer to purchase New Mexico and California, Polk sent the army to provoke a war. The Mexicans obliged with incidents, were conquered, and forfeited (with payment by the United States of $15 million) land comprising the present states of California, Nevada, Utah, and most of New Mexico and Arizona. Former President John Quincy Adams then summed up the implications of this for Congress: "It is now established as an irreversible precedent that the president of the United States has but to declare that war exists, with any nation upon Earth, by the act of that nation's government, and the war is essentially declared."

So it was nothing new when in the wake of September 11, 2001, attacks that President Bush decided that the United States would be "at war" but that it would not be necessary for Congress to actually declare it. Besides, the traditional declaration of war was designed to be an honorable notice of intent from one sovereign state to another. It hardly made sense to apply it to a criminal gang with branch offices in dozens of states.

Instead of a declaration, the president on September 18, 2001, signed a joint resolution by Congress entitled "Authorization for Use of Military Force." While he was pleased to have the backing of the members of Congress and promised to "continue to consult closely with them," he also asserted—as did his father before him during the Persian Gulf War—that he didn't need their approval. "In signing this resolution, I maintain the long-standing position of the executive branch regarding the president's constitutional authority to use force."

In effect, the president has always had dictatorial powers concerning military operations. This is only tempered by his political concerns and the ultimate ability of Congress to stop him by cutting off funds. So the answer to the question of who decides if the United States should wage war is very simple: It is the president—alone. And because it is the president alone who makes this decision, it is the president that must accept the political fallout from failed military endeavors that eventually disenchant the public because they fail, cost too much, have too many dead and wounded, or simply take too long. Of course, with success, however defined, he gets the political credit for foresight and wisdom.

For Discussion: *Why is it that the War Powers Resolution of 1973, Congress's effort to curb the war-making powers of the president, is generally considered a failure? If the American president has, in effect, dictatorial powers in wartime, what has prevented the United States from succumbing to dictatorial government when this has been the fate of so many other nations?*

What Is Public Policy?

In the beginning there was chaos. Then came policy. "Let there be light" (Genesis 1:3) was a policy decision. Policy creates orderly structures and a sense of direction. Public administration cannot exist in a policy vacuum. It must have administrative structures that are directed by leaders who wish to do something—if only to maintain the **status quo**. Thus all of public administration is inherently an instrument of policy—whether that instrument plays well, poorly, or not at all.

---

status quo The existing state of affairs. This term is often used to describe policies designed to maintain the existing distribution of power.

Any policy is a decision. A public policy is whatever a government decides to do or not to do. It is what a government does in response to a political issue. A public program consists of all those activities designed to implement the public policy: Often this calls for the creation of organizations, public agencies, and bureaus, which in turn need to create more policies that give guidance to the organization's employees on how to put into practice the overall public policy.

Policy is hierarchical. The broadest, most overarching policy is made at the top. Then increasingly more focused policies must be made at every level on down. For example, the president of the United States sits at the top of the foreign policymaking pyramid. Dozens of layers below him sit thousands of clerks in the **visa** sections of hundreds of embassies and consulates making policy—that is, making decisions—on who may legally enter the United States. To be sure, policy at the bottom is heavily impacted by laws and regulations. But to the extent that these low-level officials—what Michael Lipsky calls **street-level bureaucrats**—have any discretion at all, they are making policy. And if you are on the receiving end of that policy, whether as a visa applicant or a motorist receiving a traffic citation from a police officer, the policy is as real to you as if it were coming from higher levels in the policymaking hierarchy.

Public Policymaking in a Republic

It is the sovereign who makes legitimate policy in a political community. In a traditional society, the sovereign (meaning the monarch) is the sovereign (meaning the boss). In the United States, the people are sovereign and government is considered their agent. In a 1916 speech, President Woodrow Wilson rhetorically asked, "Just what is it that America stands for? If she stands for one thing more than another, it is for the sovereignty of self-governing people." This kind of sovereignty is generally referred to as a democracy.

But democracy is not a simple or constant concept. Instead, it is an evolving notion regarding the relationship between the people and government. It started, like so many things having to do with government, with the Greeks. Their democracy consisted of rule by an elite group of male citizens, whose well-being was maintained by politically suppressed women and a large slave population (which was not a desirable situation if you were a woman and worse if you were a slave). The development of popular or universal democracy in the eighteenth century led to revolutionary conceptions of democracy that called for the placing of all power in the hands of the people—at first just white males. The problem remained of constructing a state that could exercise that power not just in the name of, but for all, the people. This is what President Abraham Lincoln, a man with strong

---

visa A document, usually in the form of a stamp in a passport, which allows a citizen of one nation to visit another.

street-level bureaucrats Those public officials who are literally closest to the people by being in almost constant contact with them. Examples are police officers, welfare caseworkers, and teachers.

As aides note the time, President Franklin D. Roosevelt signs the Declaration of War against Japan on December 9, 1941. World War II was the last war the U.S. Congress actually declared. The Congress was called into emergency joint session by President Franklin D. Roosevelt the day after the Japanese attack on Pearl Harbor (December 8, 1941). The president said:

> Yesterday, December 7, 1941—a date which will live in infamy—the United States of America was suddenly and deliberately attacked by naval and air forces of the empire of Japan. . . .
>
> I ask that the Congress declare that since the unprovoked and dastardly attack by Japan on Sunday, December 7, 1941, a state of war has existed between the United States and the Japanese Empire.

Pearl Harbor, the American Pacific fleet headquarters in Hawaii, had about 5,000 casualties, half of them deaths. The attack incensed the American public not just because it was a surprise, which is to be expected in war, but because it was a sneak attack when there was no state of war. Indeed, Japanese emissaries were in Washington at the same time purportedly negotiating in good faith to resolve United States–Japan differences. The Japanese had intended to notify the Americans that a state of war existed one-half hour before the attack. But because of decoding difficulties, the war message was not delivered until after the attack was well underway. This time difference is the difference between an honorable surprise attack and a dishonorable sneak attack. So how did Pearl Harbor cause the United States to fight Nazi Germany as well? Because Germany's 1937 treaty of alliance with Japan was a defensive one, its pact did not require Germany to declare war on the United States after the Japanese attack on Pearl Harbor. (It would have been required if the United States had attacked Japan.) Because Japan was clearly the aggressor, Hitler's declaration of war against the United States was both gratuitous and, as it turned out, stupid.

antislavery credentials, was concerned about in his 1863 Gettysburg Address: ". . . that this government of the people, by the people, for the people, shall not perish from the earth."

The modern problem with "the people" is that so many nasty individuals have done too many despicable things in their name. Because the term *democracy* often has been used by totalitarian regimes and their "people's democracies," one person's democratic regime is too often another's totalitarian despotism. So modern democracy, like the modern contact lens, is in the eye of the beholder. By being used to describe such a large range of institutional possibilities, the term *democracy* has lost its meaning—but not its vitality—in political debate.

The **founders** of the United States were rightly suspicious of the so-called "pure" democracy of the free male citizens of ancient Athens. As **Aristotle** had warned, time and again throughout history these pure democracies had been captured by **demagogues** and had degenerated into dictatorial tyrannies. John Adams wrote in an 1814 letter, "Remember, democracy never lasts long. It soon wastes, exhausts, and murders itself. There never was a democracy yet that did not commit suicide." This well-justified fear of "the mob" led the founders to create a **republic,** a form of government one step removed from democracy, that presumably protects the people from their own passions.

The frustration of coming to grips with the concept and the reality of democracy is illustrated by Winston Churchill's 1947 remark in the House of Commons: "No one pretends that democracy is perfect or all wise. Indeed, it has been said that democracy is the worst form of government except all those other forms that have been tried from time to time."

While the founders specifically wanted a governing structure that was insulated from a pure democracy, they also wanted a governing arrangement that, unlike the city-states of ancient Greece, could function over a large area. As James Madison wrote in *The Federalist,* No. 14, "In a democracy the people meet and exercise the government in person; in a republic, they assemble and administer it by their representatives and agents. A democracy, consequently, will be confined to a small spot. A republic may be extended over a large region." Yet the founders all knew that many republics in history, such as the Roman republic, had been replaced by despots. Consequently, when Benjamin Franklin was asked what sort of government had been hatched at the **Constitutional Convention of 1787,** he replied, "A republic, if you can keep it." He knew that "keeping it" was far from certain.

---

founders An imprecise phrase for all of those individuals who played major roles in declaring U.S. independence from Britain, fighting the Revolutionary War, and writing and adopting the U.S. Constitution.

Aristotle (384–322 B.C.E.) The Greek philosopher who originated much of the study of logic, science, and politics. For several years, Aristotle, who was a student of Plato, served as the tutor of the boy who would become Alexander the Great.

demagogue A political leader accused of seeking or gaining power through the use of arguments designed to appeal to a mass public's sentiments, even though critics may consider those arguments exaggerated or spurious. The term is loaded and is never considered a compliment except as an indirect way of referring to a politician's rhetorical powers. The term, derived from the Greek *demagogos,* meaning "a leader of the people," is one of the most time-honored epithets thrown at successful opposition politicians.

republic A Latin word meaning "the public thing"; the state and its institutions; that form of government in which sovereignty resides in the people who elect agents to represent them in political decision making. The United States is a republic.

Constitutional Convention of 1787 The meeting in Philadelphia, held from May 25 to September 18, at which 55 delegates from the various states designed the U.S. Constitution. The convention was called to revise the Articles of Confederation. Instead, the convention, presided over by George Washington, discarded the articles and designed an entirely new framework for American governance.

In a republic the legislature, whether parliament or **Congress,** is supreme. After all, it has the greatest number of enumerated powers and the executive and judicial branches must enforce its laws. As Madison wrote in *The Federalist,* No. 51, "In republican government, the legislative authority necessarily predominates." President Franklin D. Roosevelt in a press conference on July 23, 1937, put it another way: "It is the duty of the president to propose and it is the privilege of the Congress to dispose." Yet this system was perverted from World War II until very recently. Because of the necessities of both hot and cold wars, the president has been unusually strong vis-à-vis the Congress. With the end of the Cold War and without the need to rally behind a wartime leader, the power relationship seemed to be returning to its "normal" condition. At the least, until September 11, 2001, and the war on terrorism.

Executive Powers

Many political executives, whether mayors, governors, or presidents, have tried—often for sound cause relating to the public good—to take more policy-making power unto themselves than may be constitutionally warranted. Just how far can an executive deviate from the legislative will or the letter of the constitution in a republican government? This is usually a function of the political strength of the executive as evidenced by a large electoral mandate, control by the executive's party in the legislature, or public opinion poll ratings. Strong executives are able to put into place more of the policies they espouse. But just how much strength should an executive ideally have or be allowed to have? Fortunately, we can answer this question with the help of three famous statements on executive power, all made by past presidents of the United States—and all equally applicable to any political executive, whether president, governor, or mayor, in any constitutional system: the restricted view, the prerogative theory, and the stewardship theory.

The Restricted View   This is the limited (or literalist) view of presidential power espoused by President **William Howard Taft.** He, as an archconservative, held that "the president can exercise no power which cannot be fairly and reasonably traced to some specific grant of power or justly implied and included within such express grant as proper and necessary to its exercise." Furthermore (and directly contrary to President Theodore Roosevelt's stewardship view that follows), "there is no undefined residuum of power which he can exercise because it seems to be in the public interest." Taft viewed the president as the agent of the Congress—in no way a free agent. In a

---

Congress The legislative branch of the U.S. government. Congress was created by Article I, Section 1, of the Constitution, which provides that "all legislative powers herein granted shall be vested in a Congress of the United States, which shall consist of a Senate and House of Representatives."

William Howard Taft (1857–1930) The only person to be both president of the United States (1909–1913) and chief justice of the Supreme Court (1921–1930). Taft, at 321 pounds, also holds the record as the largest of all presidents.

constitutional sense, Taft was a **strict constructionist.** He was disdainful of those who asserted the presence of a "residuum of power" when he clearly saw none. As an administrator, he felt his political hands were tied by the constraints of his office. And he was happy in his bondage. Today he remains a role model for all those public managers who would instantly solve public problems with new public policy if only they had the power. Not having it, they sit back, survey the poor conditions in their administrative realm, and feel quite strongly that they too are a victim of "the system."

The Prerogative Theory   This theory of executive power was espoused by President Abraham Lincoln and supported by **John Locke** in his *Second Treatise of Government* (1690). Under certain conditions, they believed that the chief executive possessed extraordinary power to preserve the nation: "Many things there are which the law can by no means provide for; and those must necessarily be left to the discretion of him that has the executive power in his hands." This power, as Lincoln saw it, might not only exceed constitutional bounds but act against the Constitution. A president, according to this view, could at least for a short while even assume dictatorial powers. Lincoln explained this theory in an 1864 letter:

> [T]hat my oath to preserve the Constitution to the best of my ability imposed upon me the duty of preserving, by every indispensable means, that government—that nation, of which that Constitution was the organic law. Was it possible to lose the nation and yet preserve the Constitution? By general law, life and limb must be protected, yet often a limb must be amputated to save a life; but a life is never wisely given to save a limb. I felt that measures otherwise unconstitutional might become lawful by becoming indispensable to the preservation of the Constitution through the preservation of the nation.

Lincoln's attitude was commendable enough in the middle of a civil war. However, when recent presidents have sought extraordinary powers, even with claims of national security and **executive privilege,** they have been "checked" by the Supreme Court. For example, when President Franklin D. Roosevelt sought to expand the federal government's scope and size during the Great Depression, many of his efforts were rejected by a Supreme Court that viewed his initiatives as exceeding the bounds of executive power established by the Constitution. Similarly, during the Korean War President Harry S. Truman's attempts to exert executive power over labor and industry were blocked by a skeptical judicial branch. As the war in Korea

---

strict constructionist One who believes the U.S. Constitution should be interpreted narrowly and literally. A loose constructionist, in contrast, believes that the Constitution should be interpreted liberally in order to reflect changing times.

John Locke (1632–1704) The English physician and philosopher whose writings on the nature of governance were a profound influence on the founding fathers. It is often argued that the first part of the Declaration of Independence, which establishes the essential philosophic rationale for the break with England, is Thomas Jefferson's restatement of John Locke's most basic themes.

executive privilege The presidential claim that the executive branch may withhold information from the Congress or its committees and the courts to preserve confidential communications within the executive branch or to secure the national interest. Although the Constitution does not explicitly grant the executive a privilege to withhold information from Congress, presidents have from the beginning of the republic claimed it.

waged on during the 1950s, Truman issued an executive order directing the secretary of commerce to take possession of and operate the nation's steel mills because of a labor dispute that threatened to disrupt war production. In response, the Supreme Court held in *Youngstown Sheet and Tube Co. v. Sawyer* (1952) that the president exceeded his constitutional powers. Two decades later the Court in *United States v. Nixon* (1974) rejected President Richard M. Nixon's claim that the Constitution provided the president with an absolute and unreviewable executive privilege—specifically, the right not to respond to a **subpoena** in connection with a judicial trial. The Court held that "neither the doctrine of separation of powers nor the need for confidentiality of high-level communications, without more, can sustain an absolute, unqualified, presidential immunity from judicial process under all circumstances." The Court allowed there was a limited executive privilege that might pertain in the areas of military, diplomatic, or security affairs, and where confidentiality was related to the president's ability to carry out his constitutional mandates. This was the decision that forced Nixon to give the Watergate **special prosecutor** tape recordings of criminal activities in **Oval Office** meetings and, in effect, that forced Nixon to resign as president in 1974.

The prerogative approach is not a theory for all seasons. Since it is applicable only in times of extraordinary national emergency, presidents have been able to "get away with it" only during wartime when Congress has been compliant (as it was during the Civil War) or kept ignorant (as it was during the Vietnam War). The important thing to remember is that this theory of executive power is quietly reserved to support the efforts of a leader who sees the nation through in a time of crisis, or, alternately, it lurks in the hands of an unprincipled opportunist or demagogue to stifle republican institutions.

The Stewardship Theory   This is President Theodore Roosevelt's view that the president, because he represents and holds in trust the interests of all the people, should be free to take any actions in the public interest that are not specifically forbidden by the Constitution or statutory law. Although he only articulated this doctrine in his autobiography, published in 1913 after he left office, Roosevelt certainly lived it. For example, he sent the U.S. Navy's battleships on an around-the-world training cruise without congressional permission. He then told Congress that if they wanted the ships back, they would have to appropriate funds to buy fuel for the return journey. Roosevelt believed strongly that "every executive officer . . . was a steward of

---

subpoena A written order issued by a judicial officer requiring a specified person to appear in a designated court at a specified time, either to serve as a witness in a case under the jurisdiction of that court or to bring material to that court.

special prosecutor A prosecutor appointed to consider the evidence in a case and, if necessary, to undertake the prosecution of a case that presents a possible conflict of interest for the jurisdiction's regular prosecutor.

Oval Office The oval-shaped White House office of the president of the United States. Although the office itself was built in the 1930s as part of an expansion of the West Wing of the White House, the term did not come into general usage until the Nixon administration. Until then, the president's office was just called the president's office.

the people bound actively and affirmatively to do all he could for the people." Roosevelt felt, in sum, that he was free to do as he pleased in that twilight zone lying between the prohibitions of the law and the duties required by specific constitutional or statutory enactments.

These three models of executive leadership are all still very much with us. Of course, the prerogative approach of Lincoln and Locke is not much in evidence except in despotic regimes. But the war on terrorism may force a future American president to temporarily suspend some constitutional privileges in the wake of a subsequent disastrous attack. While Lincoln's example remains as a last resort, the more common situation at all political and organizational levels is illustrated by the two ends of a continuum with a literalist (a Taft) at one end and a steward (a Teddy Roosevelt) at the other. The choice for leaders, then, is to be inactive in terms of policy initiation—basically to just maintain what is—or to be **proactive** in terms of policy and to be at the forefront of continuous change and reform. Or to be where most political and administrative executives are—somewhere in between. That is, they are proactive only on a limited number of issues.

The Policymaking Process

A new policy proposal is frequently presented to the public as a policy paper—a written argument in favor of (or opposing) a particular public policy. Political candidates typically generate a variety of policy papers on issues of importance to their constituents. Political campaigns often become a "battle" of opposing policy papers. And the modern battleground for these opposing policies is frequently in cyberspace, on political candidates' Web sites. Such Web sites are promoting not only the candidate but the policies of that candidate, as well. Consequently they usually contain **white papers** about where the candidate stands on various issues and why. In theory, the voters can read these thoughtful papers on a wide range of policy issues. They may even believe the illusion that the papers were actually written by the candidate. In reality the papers are read by few because most voters are content with the minimally informative **sound bites** that the candidates spit out on TV.

But no matter how astute and detailed the arguments are for or against a particular policy, the media tend to distill them into a few words. Thus an extremely thoughtful review of the utility of capital punishment often comes down to the fact that the candidate is "for" or "against" the death penalty. Voters prefer to think that their favored candidates have given great thought to all the subtle aspects of their policy positions. Consequently, it is more important that such policy papers exist than be

---

proactive An administrative style that encourages taking risks on behalf of one's clients or one's moral values; the opposite of a reactive style.

white paper Any formal statement of an official (or would-be) government policy, with its associated background documentation.

sound bite A political campaign slogan or short statement that summarizes a candidate's beliefs. Such simplistic policies can backfire if they promise more than can be delivered. In 1988 George H. W. Bush became president by shouting, "Read my lips! No new taxes!" But less than two years into his presidency he was forced to eat his sound bite and agree to raise taxes.

BOX 2.1   How War Studies Became Case Studies

The study of the policymaking process is often undertaken by means of a case study, an in-depth analysis of a single subject. It is a history that offers an understanding of dynamic, constantly moving and changing processes over time. Most traditional news stories use the case study approach. Note that aspiring journalists are taught that a story should contain all the essential elements of a case study: "who, what, why, when, where, and how."

Wars make excellent case studies because they each have a beginning, middle, and end. Indeed, the first case studies examined battles and wars. Thucydides' *History of the Peloponnesian War* (404 B.C.E.) is the progenitor of these military case studies. Military colleges—and general staffs—have long used the case study method to review battles and study generalship. This same technique is now widely used in a civilian context to examine how policy proposals become law, how programs are implemented, and how special interests affect policy development.

College courses in business and public administration often use a case study approach. An entire course may consist of case studies (frequently combined into a casebook) of management situations to be reviewed. The goal is to inculcate experience artificially. Any manager rich with years of service will have had the opportunity to live through a lifetime of "cases." By having students study many cases, each of which may have extended over many years, the case study course compresses both time and experience. In this way, a relatively young student can gain much of the insight and wisdom of a manager who has had hundreds of years of experience. In theory, this makes them so wise beyond their years that employers will eagerly seek them out.

---

read. However, policy papers put out by advocacy groups and academics—and not related to political campaigns—tend to be both more sophisticated and better received.

Policy papers, while currently written, have an ancient unwritten tradition. When in the Bible, Moses said to Pharoah (Exodus 5:1), "Let my people go!" and when Ulysses, in Homer's *The Iliad,* told the Greeks besieging Troy to build the Trojan horse, they were presenting policies even before there was paper. There is still a strong oral policy paper tradition. However, the modern version of a would-be Moses or Ulysses is most likely to be found giving a speech on the campaign trail—either running for office or as the representative of a public interest group. The place where you will find this oral tradition flourishing every hour of every day is on TV and radio talk shows. There the most pressing public policy issues of any given day will be dissected, criticized, and/or supported ad nauseum. Academic policy papers are published in professional journals and read by few. Talk show hosts publish little and may be relatively ignorant—but they can be immensely influential.

Because public policymaking involves so many aspects, so many players, and so many issues, it is difficult to grasp it as one single thing. Of course, it is not a tangible

Political Environment

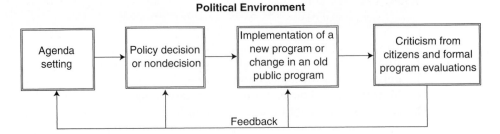

Figure 2.1   The Public Policymaking Cycle

thing; it is a never-ending intangible process. This process can be illustrated by the public policymaking cycle (see Figure 2.1), a conceptual model that views the public policy process as moving through a succession of stages: (1) agenda setting (or the identification of a policy issue), (2) policy decision or nondecision, (3) implementation, (4) program evaluation or impact analysis, and, finally, (5) feedback, which leads to revision or termination. Thus the process comes full circle—which is why it is called a "cycle." A review of this process will show that public administration is both at the heart of the process and a feature of every aspect of it.

Agenda Setting

Agenda setting is the process by which ideas or issues bubble up through the various political channels to wind up for consideration by a political institution such as a legislature or court. We have already mentioned the two greatest sources of agenda items—the executive and the legislators. Their constituents expect that they will seek the enactment into law of the policies that they advocated in their campaigns for elective office. Additionally, the administrative agencies of a government often generate legislative proposals. Sometimes, these are incorporated into the executive's legislative recommendations.

The agenda-setting process often makes extensive use of the mass media to take a relatively unknown or unsupported issue and, through publicity, expand the numbers of people who care about the issue so that an institution, whether it be city hall or the Congress, is forced to take some action. One example can be traced back to 1955, when Rosa Parks, an African-American woman, was arrested for refusing to take a seat in the back of a bus in Montgomery, Alabama. This confrontation sparked the modern civil rights movement. Dr. Martin Luther King Jr. would later use the tactics of nonviolent confrontation with southern segregational policies to arouse sufficient sympathy and support in the rest of the nation, which would lead to the passage of landmark civil rights legislation in Congress. When these nonviolent demonstrators turned violent, it was all the better—because it made better TV and thus ensured a bigger audience for the message of the cause. Starting in the 1980s, pro-life (meaning antiabortion) groups used demonstrators in front of medical offices providing abortion services to arouse the national consciousness about this issue. These, too, often became spontaneously violent and thus made for better TV. The lesson is clear. "Nonviolent" demonstrators that turn violent or at least contentious once the TV news cameras arrive are more likely to get on the six o'clock news. These approaches to placing issues on the public policy agenda are called pseudo-events by historian Daniel Boorstin because they are "nonspontaneous, planted, or manufactured 'news,' whose main purpose is to gain publicity for the person or cause which arranged the 'event.'"

The importance of TV in propelling an issue onto government's agenda is particularly notable when the policy issue maintains a highly visual element. For example, the stark visual aspects of air and water pollution helped drive environmental protection issues fully onto the federal government's radar in the late 1960s and early 1970s. From oil-covered marine mammals on California's once pristine coast to burning rivers in the petroleum-choked surface water of Cleveland, Ohio, the striking images of environmental destruction directly boosted environmental protection issues into the public consciousness and eventually into the halls of Congress.

Agendas are often set by public policy entrepreneurs, political actors who take a political issue and run with it. Thus certain senators might make particular issues their own by sheer force of expertise that, if respected, "forces" colleagues to take cues on the matter from them. Or a staffer might become such an expert on an issue that he or she can heavily influence legislation dealing with it. Thus a public policy entrepreneur can be anyone in the political environment whose expertise and actions can affect an issue.

Agenda setting, which is usually confined to professional politicians, is a game that anybody can play. A federal judge could rule that a state prison is unconstitutionally overcrowded and thus force the state's legislature to deal with the issue by appropriating funds for new prisons. A citizens' group could be so concerned about an issue that they gather enough signatures of registered voters to put the issue as a proposition on the next election's ballot. A public interest law firm could challenge the legality of an agency's action and force the courts to ascertain its constitutionality. Or an interest group could get thousands of its members to write (or e-mail) letters to their legislative representatives demanding action on a controversy. While there

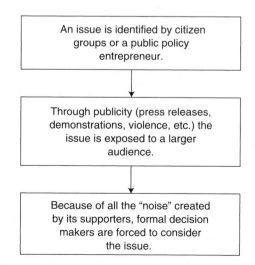

Figure 2.2   The Agenda-Setting Process

are only a few places—such as a legislature, court, or regulatory commission—where agendas can be formally enacted, there are infinite numbers of sources from which agenda items spring. And like hope, they spring eternally.

The issue-attention cycle is a model developed by **Anthony Downs** that attempts to explain the way in which many policy problems evolve on the political agenda. The cycle is premised on the notion that the public's attention rarely remains focused on any one issue, regardless of the objective nature of the problem. The cycle consists of five steps:

1. The preproblem stage (an undesirable social condition exists but has not captured public attention)
2. Alarmed discovery and euphoric enthusiasm (a dramatic event catalyzes the public attention, accompanied by an enthusiasm to solve the problem)
3. Recognition of the cost of change (the public gradually realizes the difficulty of implementing meaningful change)
4. Decline of public interest (people become discouraged or bored or a new issue claims attention)
5. The postproblem stage (although the issue has not been solved, it has been dropped from the nation's agenda)

According to policy analyst John Kingdon, "If Anthony Downs is right, problems often fade from public view because a short period of awareness and optimism gives way to a realization of the financial and social costs of action. As people become impressed with the sacrifices, dislocations, and costs to be borne, they lose their enthusiasm for addressing the problem." For example, early in the first Clinton administration there was great enthusiasm and support for a major reform in the nation's system of medical insurance. But as increasing attention was brought to the financial costs and difficulties of implementation, the issue faded from view while both political leaders and the public lost enthusiasm for dealing with what remains a major problem—at least for the nearly 44 million Americans without medical insurance.

Decision Making

Public policymaking is the totality of the processes by which a government decides to deal or not to deal with a particular problem or concern. It is a never-ending process. Nineteenth-century British statesman Lord Salisbury is usually credited with first remarking, "There is no such thing as a fixed policy, because policy, like all organic entities, is always in the making."

There are two distinct and opposite theories seeking to explain the mechanisms that produce policy decisions or nondecisions. The first might be called the rational

---

Anthony Downs (1930–) The economist and policy analyst who is generally credited with establishing the intellectual framework for public choice economics in his book *An Economic Theory of Democracy* (1957). His classic book on bureaucracy, *Inside Bureaucracy* (1967), sought to justify bureaucratic government on economic grounds and to develop laws and propositions that would aid in predicting the behavior of bureaus and bureaucrats.

decision-making approach, and it generally has been attributed to **Harold D. Lasswell.** In his book *The Future of Political Science,* he posited seven significant phases for every decision:

1. The intelligence phase, involving an influx of information
2. The promoting or recommending phase, involving activities designed to influence the outcome
3. The prescribing phase, involving the articulation of norms
4. The invoking phase, involving establishing correspondence between prescriptions and concrete circumstances
5. The application phase, in which the prescription is executed
6. The appraisal phase, assessing intent in relation to effect
7. The terminating phase, treating expectations (rights) established while the prescription was in force

Of course, there is an immediate problem with this and every other such list. It is impossible to complete. No matter how rational we would hope to be, there is no way anyone could gather *all* the facts and take into account *every* consideration. Therefore, decision makers exercise what Herbert Simon, the 1978 Nobel laureate in economics, calls "bounded rationality." The "bounds" are what people put on their decisions. Simon asserts that "it is impossible for the behavior of a single, isolated individual to reach any high degree of rationality. The number of alternatives he must explore is so great, the information he needs to evaluate them so vast, that even an approximation to objective rationality is hard to conceive." Consequently, humans make decisions on satisfactory, as opposed to optimal, information. Inventing a new word, Simon said that decision makers "satisfice" when they accept a satisfactory and sufficient amount of information on which to base a decision. Thus in the real world we are forced to reject the "rational comprehensive" approach and "satisfice" rather than "maximize."

A rejection of this rational approach was urged by **Charles E. Lindblom,** the leading proponent of the second theory of policy decision making—the incremental approach. In his most famous article, "The Science of Muddling Through," Lindblom took a hard look at the rational models of the decisional processes of government. He rejected the notion that most decisions are made by rational (total information) processes. Instead, he saw such decisions—indeed, the whole policymaking process— as dependent on small incremental decisions that tend to be made in response to short-term political conditions. Lindblom's thesis essentially held that decision making

---

Harold D. Lasswell (1902–1978) One of the most influential and prolific of social scientists. While he made major contributions to the fields of communications, psychology (he pioneered the application of Freudian theory to politics), political science, sociology, and law, his most lasting legacy is probably his pioneering work in developing the concept and methodology of the policy sciences.

Charles E. Lindblom (1917–) The Yale University political scientist who since the 1950s has been asserting that incrementalism is the most viable approach to understanding how public policies are made.

was controlled infinitely more by events and circumstances than by the will of those in policymaking positions. Disjointed incrementalism as a policy course was in reality the only truly feasible route, since incrementalism "concentrated the policymaker's analysis on familiar, better-known experiences, sharply reduced the number of different alternative policies to be explored, and sharply reduced the number and complexity of factors to be analyzed." Moreover, Lindblom argued that incrementalism was more consistent with the pluralistic nature of American democracy, where individuals are free to combine to pursue common interests, whose contention "often can assure a more comprehensive regard for the values of the whole society than any attempt at intellectual comprehensiveness."

The rational and incremental models, often viewed as two ends of a continuum, are useful intellectual tools for conceptualizing the decision-making process. There is even a "split the difference" compromise model that combines the two. Mixed scanning is the decision-making model put forth by **Amitai Etzioni**, which calls for seeking short-term solutions to problems by using both incrementalism and rational-comprehensive approaches to problem solving. For example, a foreign policy analyst responsible for reviewing political developments in Europe might superficially scan all recent developments (the comprehensive approach) but focus only on those political problems that have changed since the last scanning (the incremental approach). In this way the analyst saves time by dealing in detail only with those situations that truly demand attention.

A Single Calculating Decision Maker—Not!

A famous example of a conceptual model of public policymaking is provided by Graham T. Allison's classic study of government decision making, *Essence of Decision: Explaining the Cuban Missile Crisis* (1971). It showed the inadequacies of the view that policies are made by a "single calculating decision maker," such as a president who has complete control over the organizational units and individual officials within his or her government. Instead, Allison—using John F. Kennedy's **Cuban Missile Crisis** of 1962—demonstrated that differing bureaucratic viewpoints (such as the State Department, Defense Department, and National Security Council) fight over policy. Although Allison's ideas were not new, he helped crystallize thinking about foreign policymaking by dealing with the different approaches in terms of three models. He argued that the traditionally dominant model, that of the

---

Amitai Etzioni (1929–) The sociologist whose early work on organization theory steered him toward analyses of international political integration and communitarianism.

Cuban Missile Crisis The 1962 confrontation between the United States and the Soviet Union over the Soviet placement of nuclear missiles in Cuba. President John F. Kennedy demanded the removal of the missiles, imposed a naval blockade on Cuba, and waited for the Soviet response. In the end, the Soviets removed their missiles in exchange for a U.S. promise not to invade Cuba and an understanding that the United States would also remove its nuclear missiles from Turkey. Secretary of State Dean Rusk offered his now famous summary of the crisis: "We were eyeball-to-eyeball, and the other fellow just blinked." (*Saturday Evening Post,* December 8, 1962) "single calculating decision maker," obscured more than it illuminated. Allison called this the Rational Actor Model or Model One and believed that this model must be supplemented by two other models. Allison's Model Two, the Organizational Processes Model, basically argued that government action could be understood as the output of large organizations that operated according to standard operating procedures. Allison described Model Three as a Governmental Politics Model, the essence of which was that decisions were the outcome of a bargaining process between different groups and individuals with different bureaucratic perspectives and different political interests. Consequently, foreign policy decisions are not the product of a rational calculation about what is good for the state but a compromise—and often a compromised product of the internal bargaining process.

But in reality all these models are not much more than mind games for **policy wonks**. The real world of political executives and harried legislators is not so much an intellectual arena as it is a bare-knuckles political arena. Decisions in the political arena are influenced far more by the perception of a situation than by any rational concept of objective reality. It is far more than the differences between a pessimist seeing a glass half empty and an optimist seeing the glass half full. One actor in the decisional drama may view a program as absolutely essential for the national interest, while another actor is equally certain that it is nothing more than an example of petty bureaucrats wasting the taxpayers' money.

Policymakers bring two kinds of intelligence to bear on their thinking. First is their mental ability to cope with complicated problems. Second is the information they have about and the experience they have with the issue at hand. Both kinds of intelligence are then filtered through their ideological predispositions and personal biases before an attitude toward any given problem is set. Thus political decisions are seldom made on the objective merits of a case because a case only has merit in the eyes of a political decision maker if he or she is intelligent enough to see it and, equally important, is ideologically and politically predisposed to support it.

At the end of the day, the policy processes of government are not only about equity or justice but, fundamentally, about power. But once power is exerted, once a law is enacted, once a program is created, these power brokers—whether democrats or autocrats—turn to their public administrators to make their wishes, to make their power, a reality. Without the administrators of the state to do their bidding, the power brokers are quite literally broke.

Implementation

Implementation is the process of putting a government program into effect; it is the total process of translating a legal mandate, whether an executive order or an enacted **statute,** into appropriate program directives and structures that provide services or

---

policy wonk A compulsive analyst of public policy processes. "Wonk" is slang for a student who is a grind or a nerd.
statute A law passed by a legislature; legislative-made as opposed to judge-made law.

TABLE 2.2   The Polis Model

Policy analysts have long been critical of the "either/or" nature of the rational versus the incremental approaches to decision making. A model advocated by Deborah Stone holds that the political community, the polis, is better able to deal with the ambiguity of less-than-perfect information—information often "spun" by "spin doctors"—than with the "look at hard facts" approach of the rational model. While rational analysis does not lend itself to the inconsistencies of real life, the polis model assumes them. Stone's comparison of the two models follows. Note how the polis model is so much more congenial and digestible to the public.

Rational-Analytic Model	Polis Model
State goals/objectives explicitly and precisely.	State goals ambiguously and possibly keep some goals secret or hidden.
Adhere to the same goal throughout the analysis and decision-making process.	Be prepared to shift goals and redefine goals as the political situation dictates.
Try to imagine and consider as many alternatives as possible.	Keep undesirable alternatives off the agenda by not mentioning them. Make your preferred alternative appear to be the only feasible or possible one.
	Focus on one part of the causal chain and ignore others that would require politically difficult or costly policy actions.
Define each alternative clearly as a distinct course of action.	Use rhetorical devices to blend alternatives; don't appear to make a clear decision that could trigger strong opposition.
Evaluate the costs and benefits of each course of action as accurately and completely as possible.	Select from the infinite range of consequences only those whose costs and benefits will make your preferred course of action look "best."
Choose the course of action that will maximize total welfare as defined by your objective.	Choose the course of action that hurts powerful constituents the least but portrays your decision as creating maximum social good for a broad public.

SOURCE: Table adapted from Deborah Stone, *Policy Paradox: The Art of Political Decision Making* (New York: W. W. Norton & Co., 1997).

create goods. Implementation, the doing part of public administration, is an inherently political process. Architects often say that "God is in the details." So is it with implementation. A law is passed, but the process of putting it into effect requires countless small decisions that necessarily alter it. According to President Carter's National Security Adviser Zbigniew Brzezinski, "Policymakers are overwhelmed by events and information. . . . A great deal of decision making is done through implementation by the bureaucracy, which often distorts it."

"Distort" is a harsh word that implies intentional change. Most administrative implementors, however, act in good faith, with little intentional distortion. But there is substantial friction. This concept has been well expressed by Prussian General Karl von Clausewitz, who held that no matter how well planned a large operation is, the reality of delays, misunderstandings, and so forth will make its inevitable execution

BOX 2.2   Seven Reasons for Incrementalism

Why is emphasis on alternatives closely related to existing reality an aid to rational calculation? **First,** the consequences of alternatives that bear a remote relation to existing reality are generally more difficult to predict.

Second, . . . people cannot accurately foresee their own wants. . . . To be sure, they can exclude many unwanted alternatives without actually testing them. . . . But it is much more difficult to know which of the remaining alternatives is preferable. . . .

Third, because an individual has many goals, some of which conflict with one another, . . . a marginal adjustment will bring about a gain in goal attainment. This is incrementalism in individual action, and the logic applies equally to social action.

Fourth, incrementalism is an aid to verifying the results of one's choices. This is in keeping with the principle of isolating a single variable. Results after one has acted can be compared with conditions before the change, and the relation of the particular choice to the particular changes is more easily determined.

Fifth, incrementalism helps to ensure control. Incremental change gives prescribed superiors an opportunity to issue rather detailed instructions or to check in detail the actions of their subordinates. As a general matter, the larger the increments of change, the more difficult it is for prescribed superiors to check on their subordinates or even to give instructions that are any more than a blank check.

Sixth, incrementalism is reversible. When mistakes are made, they can more easily be repaired.

Seventh, incrementalism permits both the survival and the continual alteration of the operating organization. The attempt to secure abrupt change by prescription usually fails because the operating organization, with its own codes and norms, resists sudden, large-scale change.

SOURCE: Robert A. Dahl and Charles E. Lindblom, *Politics, Economics, and Welfare* (Chicago: University of Chicago Press, 1953).

less than ideal. While military in origin, friction has become a generally recognized phenomenon in all aspects of the administration of public and **international affairs.**

While implementation is obviously at the heart of public administration, it has only recently been self-consciously studied. The first major analysis of implementation as a new focus for public administration was Jeffrey Pressman and Aaron Wildavsky's 1973 study of federal programs in the city of Oakland, California. The unabridged title of their work tells part of the story: *Implementation: How Great Expectations in*

---

international affairs A term that is loosely used as a synonym for international politics. It can include almost anything that is not exclusively domestic in nature.

Washington Are Dashed in Oakland; Or, Why It's Amazing that Federal Programs Work At All; This Being a Saga of the Economic Development Administration as Told by Two Sympathetic Observers Who Seek to Build Morals on a Foundation of Ruined Hopes. What Pressman and Wildavsky related in their landmark book seems almost simplistic—that policy planning and analysis were not taking into account the difficulties of execution or "implementation." The goal of their book was to consider how a closer nexus between policy and implementation could be achieved. A direct result of this book was a spate of works explaining how policy analysis can accomplish this objective—an objective, it is fair to say, that has yet to be comprehensively implemented.

Pressman and Wildavsky define implementation as "a process of interaction between the setting of goals and actions geared to achieving them" as well as "an ability to forge subsequent links in the causal chain so as to obtain the desired results." This definition usefully calls attention to the interaction between setting goals and carrying them out. This helps clarify that implementation is political in a very fundamental sense in that the activities that go on under its banner shape **who gets what,** when, and how from government. Like lawmakers, administrators and those with whom they interact during the implementation process exert power over program objectives and influence program inputs and outcomes. Implementation involves administrators, interest groups, and other actors with diverse values mobilizing power resources, forming coalitions, consciously plotting strategies, and generally engaging in strategic behavior designed to ensure that their point of view prevails. The terrain may be different from that found in Congress or other legislatures, but the basic staples of the political process are very much present.

Never forget that the goal of program implementation is necessarily the creation of the myriad details of everyday administrative life. Policy analyst Charles O. Jones maintains that implementation consists of "those activities directed toward putting a program into effect." This involves the "translation of program language into acceptable and feasible directives," as well as creating appropriate organizational structures and routines. A major virtue of Jones's definition is that it explicitly points to the role of routine and other aspects of organizational structure in implementation. In order to conserve time and energy, as well as to promote the equal treatment of clients, organizations develop **standard operating procedures.** These procedures plus other informal **decision rules** greatly simplify choices for administrators. Decisions can be made almost without thinking. Any effort to comprehend how implementation processes affect program outcomes cannot, then, ignore the collective impact of countless procedures and simple decision rules. Implementation is always a mix of the consciously strategic with the daily routine.

---

who gets what This is the very definition of politics provided by the title of Harold Lasswell's classic 1936 book *Politics: Who Gets What, When, How.*

standard operating procedures The established routines by which organizations accomplish their objectives.

decision rule Any directive established to make decisions in the face of uncertainty. For example, a payroll office might be given a decision rule to deduct one hour's pay from an employee's wages for tardiness that exceeds ten minutes but is less than one hour.

Evaluation

Any evaluation is an assessment. A program evaluation is the systematic examination of activities undertaken by government to make a determination about their effects, both for the short term and the long range. Program evaluation is distinguished from management evaluation (also called organization evaluation) because the latter is limited to a program's internal administrative procedures. While program evaluations use management and organizational data, the main thrust is necessarily on overall program objectives and impact. Thus a program is less concerned with the management of a police department than with that department's overall effect on crime and less concerned with a welfare agency's internal administration than with its effectiveness in dealing with clients.

The concepts of **efficiency** and **effectiveness** are the standard criteria against which programs are pitted by evaluation. In addition, these concepts helped to forge a workable distinction between **audits** and evaluations. Audits, primarily financial accounting audits, were traditionally geared to control—to ensure that every dime of public funds is accounted for and that every regulation is complied with. This law-enforcement style of management is being increasingly displaced by program evaluation—a far more comprehensive management tool. We still expect programs to be administered efficiently, just as we expect complete fiscal accountability for funds and receipts. But efficiency is not enough. A work unit could be terribly efficient while working toward the wrong goals. Because of this, evaluations, if they are themselves to be effective, must also deal with the questions of effectiveness and relevance. It is not unreasonable to demand that programs have an effect on problems—and the right problems at that. Simply put, the most basic objective of a program evaluation is to assay the impact of a program on its target problem.

Program evaluations, while usually undertaken by the executive and legislative branches of government, are sometimes even done by the courts in response to petitions by client groups. While the three regular branches of government are heavily involved in evaluation, so too is the so-called "fourth branch of government": the press. It conducts evaluations with every exposé of a mismanaged agency. However, journalistic evaluations often tend to be too superficial to serve as instruments of reform, although they do serve to provide impetus for full-scale evaluation efforts by others.

Feedback   The public policy cycle comes full circle when evaluative information creates new agenda items for subsequent decisions. This is called feedback because

---

efficiency Competence as well as speed in performance. Americans have historically been suspicious of a too-efficient government, feeling that a truly efficient administration of public affairs could eventually eat into political liberties.

effectiveness The extent to which an organization accomplishes some predetermined goal or objective; more recently, the overall performance of an organization from the viewpoint of some strategic constituency.

audit The final phase of the government budgetary process, which reviews the operations of an agency, especially its financial transactions, to determine whether the agency has spent its money in accordance with the law, in the most efficient manner, and with desired results.

the new information feeds back into its original source. In its purest form feedback can either drive new items onto the policy agenda or reshape issues that are already being considered. But remember, everything about this cycle is impacted by politics. This is because the whole process takes place in a political environment, as shown in Figure 2.1 on page 50.

Feedback is effective to the extent that it is noisy. The people who set the goals and make the decisions must hear it. Sometimes feedback is heard as a complaint about slow service or poor-quality products. Sometimes it is the silent noise of the citizens voting to **throw the rascals out.**

Power—The External Perspective

Power is the ability or the right to exercise authority over others. Traditionally, according to the founder of the People's Republic of China, Mao Zedong, "Political power grows out of the barrel of a gun." More recently power has been residing in the checkbooks of large corporations and powerful lobbyists. Those with traditional power or the power to make large campaign contributions get to make or heavily influence public policy. Whether they do it with a gun or a check is dependent on local conditions. The world is organized into an immense **hierarchy** of power: Political leaders have power over their followers, managers over their workers, and parents over their children. We are all subject to the powers that be that force us to work or school and constrain us from straying too far from what is expected.

One of the best ways to visualize and understand an administrator's power environment is to do a force field analysis of the pressures that bear upon any agency. Field theory originated in physics. It was borrowed by psychology to explain how an individual's behavior at any given time is the result of his or her personality interacting with the psychological forces in the environment. Organizational analysts refocused field theory from the individual to the group, the group that made up an organization. By systematically examining all of the forces—all of the powers—in the organization's field (meaning environment)—thus a force field analysis—they were better able to understand why the organization acted the way it did. Those wishing to understand why a government or an agency does seemingly irrational or contradictory things use a force field analysis to arrive at an explanation. For example, the federal government has a variety of laws and programs designed to prevent people from smoking tobacco. It forbids cigarette advertising on television and demands health warnings on tobacco products. But at the same time it encourages the growing of tobacco by American farmers and the sale of tobacco overseas by American companies. Thus the federal government is at the same time both for and against the use of tobacco.

---

throw the rascals out An oft-heard campaign slogan of the party not in power. Sometimes all it really means is that it is time for a change of rascals.

hierarchy Any ordering of persons, things, or ideas by rank or level. The administrative structures are typically hierarchical in that each level has authority over levels below and must take orders from levels above.

This contradictory policy seems silly on the surface. But the forces of good health work their will on the system to curtail tobacco use at the same time that the forces of commerce work their will on the system to encourage profit from tobacco—and the latter were here first. The obnoxious weed was introduced to Europe by none other than Christopher Columbus. For hundreds of years tobacco has been a major part of the economic foundation of colonial and later republican America. Only in the 1960s did the government "discover" the health hazards related to it. But by then it was just so profitable in terms of **excise tax** yields to both federal and state governments that forbidding the sale on health grounds would mean higher taxes elsewhere. Besides, an illegal market for tobacco would immediately arise in its place as it did with alcohol during the era of prohibition, thus yielding "tax" revenues only to the smugglers.

This all goes to show how governments as well as people get addicted to addictive substances. We as citizens are all addicted in the sense that we depend on smokers to disproportionately pay taxes for their vice and then graciously die prematurely without collecting their fair share of Social Security retirement benefits. What self-sacrificing patriots they are! The same can be said of alcoholics. Here we have **public choice economics** in action. The citizen smoker (or drinker) as the sovereign consumer makes intelligent (or stupid) choices in the marketplace of products and ideas. If you feel this is irrational, you are right, but it is political, too. To understand why administration is so often irrational, we have to look at some of the underlying premises of American government.

Pluralism

The "problem" begins with the fact that American government is inherently pluralistic—composed of multiple elements. First, its constitutional arrangement requires a separation of powers, the allocation of powers among the three branches of government so that they are a check upon each other. This separation, in theory, makes a tyrannical concentration of power impossible. The U.S. Constitution contains provisions in separate articles for three branches of government—legislative, executive, and judicial. There is a significant difference in the grants of power to these branches: The first article, dealing with legislative power, vests in Congress "all legislative powers herein granted"; the second article vests "the executive power" in the president; and the third article states that "the judicial power of the United States shall be vested in one Supreme Court, and in such inferior courts as the Congress may from time to time ordain and establish." Justice Louis D. Brandeis offered the opinion of the U.S. Supreme Court in the 1926 case of

---

excise tax A tax on the manufacture, sale, or consumption of a product such as gasoline or tobacco.
public choice economics An approach to public administration and politics based on microeconomic
 theory that views the citizen as a consumer of government goods and services. It would attempt to
 maximize administrative responsiveness to citizen demand by creating a market system for government activities in which public agencies would compete to provide citizens with goods and services.
 This might replace a portion of the current system, under which most administrative agencies in
 effect act as monopolies under the influence of organized pressure groups, which, the public choice
 economists argue, are institutionally incapable of representing the demands of individual citizens.

> **BOX 2.3   James Madison on Angels and the Separation of Powers**
>
> Ambition must be made to counteract ambition. The interest of the man must be connected with the constitutional rights of the place. It may be a reflection on human nature that such devices should be necessary to control the abuses of government. But what is government itself but the greatest of all reflections on human nature? If men were angels, no government would be necessary. If angels were to govern men, neither external nor internal controls on government would be necessary. In framing a government which is to be administered by men over men, the great difficulty lies in this: you must first enable the government to control the governed; and in the next place oblige it to control itself. A dependence on the people is, no doubt, the primary control on the government; but experience has taught mankind the necessity of auxiliary precautions.
>
> SOURCE: James Madison, *The Federalist*, No. 51 (1788).

Myers v. United States: "The doctrine of the separation of powers was adopted by the Convention of 1787, not to promote efficiency but to preclude the exercise of arbitrary power. The purpose was not to avoid friction, but, by means of the inevitable friction incident to the distribution of the governmental powers among three departments, to save the people from autocracy." The "friction" that Brandeis refers to is not the friction inherent in implementation that Clausewitz analyzed but the friction of conflict caused by independent power.

Second, American political processes, being inherently pluralistic, emphasize the role of competitive groups in society. Pluralism assumes that power will shift from group to group as elements in the mass public transfer their allegiance in response to their perceptions of their individual interests. In his book *Who Governs?*, Robert Dahl established key tenets of the pluralist perspective. According to Dahl, pluralism involves varying degrees of political engagement among citizens, with the ability of individuals to impact political decisions in selected areas of public policy. However, according to **power-elite theory**, if democracy is defined as popular participation in public affairs, then pluralist theory is inadequate as an explanation of modern U.S. government. Pluralism, according to this view, offers little direct participation, since the elite structure is closed, pyramidal, consensual, and unresponsive. Society is thus divided into two classes: the few who govern and the many who are governed. So pluralism is covert elitism instead of a practical solution to preserve democracy in a mass society.

---

power-elite theory The belief that the United States is basically ruled by a political, military, and business elite whose decisional powers essentially preempt the democratic process. C. Wright Mills (1916–1962) wrote in *The Power Elite* that "the leading men in each of the three domains of power—the warlords, the corporation chieftains, the political directorate—tend to come together to form the power elite of America." Most contemporary analyses of elitism in American governance have their intellectual foundations in Mills's work, even if Mills himself is not acknowledged.

Those who subscribe to elite theory often have a paranoid political orientation, the belief that there is a nationwide conspiracy against them. Examples include homosexuals who believe that AIDS was "invented" by the government to destroy them, African-Americans who believe that the drug epidemic is encouraged by the government to hurt them, right-wing militia members who believe that the federal government is conspiring to confiscate all firearms in the hands of the citizens, and politicians who—especially during the Cold War—believed that a Communist conspiracy was on the verge of taking over the country.

In the wake of Hurricane Katrina there has been considerable discussion that the failure of the levees and the slow government response were part of an intentional plot to eradicate the large African-American population in New Orleans. This concept was first identified in 1965 by historian Richard Hofstadter in *The Paranoid Style in American Politics*:

> There is a vital difference between the paranoid spokesman in politics and the clinical paranoiac: although they both tend to be overheated, oversuspicious, overaggressive, grandiose, and apocalyptic in expression, the clinical paranoid sees the hostile and conspiratorial world in which he feels himself to be living as directed specifically against him, whereas the spokesman of the paranoid style finds it directed against a nation, a culture, a way of life whose fate affects not himself alone but millions of others.

Finally, pluralism has a cultural dimension. Those who espouse this believe that a nation's overall welfare is best served by preserving ethnic cultures rather than by encouraging the integration and blending of cultures. This is in contrast to the assimilationist belief that all immigrants should take their turn in a national **melting pot** and come out homogenized. But studies have consistently shown this not to be the case. Historian Carl N. Degler wrote, "The metaphor of the melting pot is unfortunate and misleading. A more accurate analogy would be a salad bowl, for, though the salad is an entity, the lettuce can still be distinguished from the chicory, the tomatoes from the cabbage." In recent years the term has become less fashionable and has been replaced in political rhetoric by the image of a mosaic. Without using the term, then Speaker of the House Newt Gingrich resurrected the melting pot concept in 1995 when he asserted that America is a distinct civilization—and that the way for immigrants to become "civilized" is to accept the mainstream "melting pot" values.

Group Theory

The importance of pluralism and the significance of groups in the democratic political process has been recognized for over two thousand years: Aristotle noted that political associations were both significant and commonplace because of the

---

melting pot A sociological term that implies that (1) each succeeding wave of immigrants to the United States blends into the general society and (2) this melting is ideally what should happen. The term originated in Israel Zangwill's (1864–1926) play *The Melting Pot* (1908), in which he wrote, "America is God's Crucible, the great Melting-Pot where all races of Europe are melting and reforming!" The phrase became the symbol of assimilation for several generations of American immigrants.

"general advantages" that members obtained. One of the first specific references to groups in the American political process was James Madison's famous discussion of factions in *The Federalist,* No. 10 (1787). In Madison's view, the group was inherent in the nature of people, and its causes were unremovable. Therefore, the only choice was to control the effects of group pressure and power. A more elaborate discussion of group theory can be traced to John C. Calhoun's 1853 treatise *A Disquisition on Government.* While essentially an argument for the protection of minority interests, the treatise suggested that ideal governance must deal with all interest groups, since they represent the legitimate interests of the citizens. If all groups participated on some level of parity within the policymaking process, then all individual interests would be recognized by the policymakers.

Modern group theory has taken greater impetus from the work of **Arthur F. Bentley, David B. Truman,** and **Earl Latham**. Latham viewed the legislature as the referee of the group struggle, responsible for "ratifying the victories of the successful coalitions and recording the terms of the surrenders, compromises, and conquests in the form of statutes." The function of bureaucrats is quite different, however. They are like "armies of occupation left in the field to police the rule won by the victorious coalition." Although Latham's description was aimed primarily at regulatory agencies, he saw the bureaucrat being deluged by the losing coalitions of groups for more favorable actions despite the general rules established. The result is that "agencies are constantly besought and importuned to interpret their authorities in favor of the very groups for the regulation of which they were originally granted."

Latham distinguished three types of groups, based on phases of development: incipient, conscious, and organized. An incipient group is one "where the interest exists but is not recognized" by the potential members; a conscious group is one "in which the community sense exists but which has not become organized"; and finally

---

Arthur F. Bentley (1870–1957) The political scientist who was one of the pioneering voices in the behavioral analysis of politics and the intellectual creator of modern interest group theory. In *The Process of Government* (1908), Bentley argued that political analysis has had to shift its focus from forms of government to actions of individuals in the context of groups, because groups are the critical action mechanisms that enable numbers of individuals to achieve their political, economic, and social desires. Bentley's work was effectively "lost" until it was rediscovered and publicized by David B. Truman.

David B. Truman (1913–2003) A political scientist and one of the most influential interest group theorists. Truman's principal work, *The Governmental Process* (1951), views group interaction as the real determinant of public policy and as the proper focal point of study. Truman defines the interest group as "a shared attitude group that makes certain claims upon other groups in the society. If and when it makes its claims through or upon any of the institutions of government, it becomes a public interest group." Group pressure is assured through the establishment of lines of access and influence. Truman notes that the administrative process provides a multitude of points of access comparable to the legislature. What Truman provides for group theory is a complete description and analysis of how groups interact in, function in, and influence the overall political system.

Earl Latham (1907–1977) The group theorist whose *The Group Basis of Politics* (1952) was particularly significant because of his conceptualization that government itself is a group just like the various private groups attempting to access the policy process. Latham ascribed to government the same characteristics and concern for power associated with all other organized groups. Thus the state becomes more than a referee between groups in conflict because it is also developing its own goals.

an organized group is "a conscious group which has established an objective and formal apparatus to promote the common interest." Latham's incipient and conscious groups are essentially the same as Truman's potential groups, which always exist but do not come together until there is a felt need for action on an issue.

The concept of potential groups keeps the bureaucratic policymaking process honest (or perhaps balanced), given the possibility that new groups might surface or some issues may influence decision making. The potential groups concept also serves as a counterargument to the claim that group theory is undemocratic. Once the concept of potential group is married to the active role of organized groups, the claim can be made, in Truman's words, that "all interests of society by definition are taken into account in one form or another by the institutions of government" (see Figure 2.3).

So much for the theory. The problem is, according to political scientist Theodore J. Lowi, too much public authority is parceled out to private interest groups and results in a weak, decentralized government incapable of long-range planning. Powerful interest groups operate to promote private goals but do not compete to promote the public interest. Government becomes not an institution that makes hard choices among conflicting values but a holding company for interests. These interests are promoted by alliances of interest groups, relevant government agencies, and the appropriate legislative **committees** in each issue area. This is furthered by cozy triangles, the mutually supportive relations among government agencies, interest groups, and the legislative committee or subcommittee with jurisdiction over their areas of

Figure 2.3 Typical Outside Forces on a Public Agency Manager

---

committee A subdivision of a legislature that prepares legislation for action by the respective house or that makes investigations as directed by the respective house. Most standing (full) committees are divided into subcommittees, which study legislation, hold hearings, and report their recommendations to the full committee. Only the full committee can report legislation for action by the entire legislature.

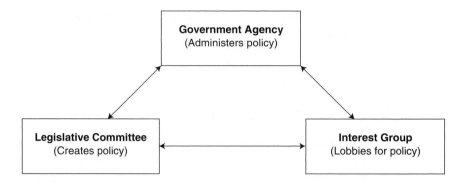

Figure 2.4 The Cozy or Iron Triangle

common concern. Such coalitions constantly exchange information, services, and money (in the form of campaign contributions from the interest groups to the members of the legislative committee and budget approval from the committee to the agency). As a whole, they tend to dominate policymaking in their areas of concern. These triangles are considered to be so strong that others elected or appointed to control administrative policy as representatives of the public's interest are effectively prohibited from interfering on behalf of the public (see Figure 2.4).

All government agencies rise and fall, are created or dissolved, in response to an ever-changing external environment made up both of broad historical trends and everyday political maneuvering. NASA is a perfect example of this. It rose in 1958 as the American response to the space race of the Cold War— certainly a broad historical trend. Political maneuvering by cold warriors in the Truman administration allowed Nazi war criminals such as Wernher von Braun, the German rocket scientist, to give American rocketry a decided boost during the early days of the space program. Morality and ethics aside, von Braun and

---

BOX 2.4 Power and Administration

There is no more forlorn spectacle in the administrative world than an agency and a program possessed of statutory life, armed with executive orders, sustained in the courts, yet stricken with paralysis and deprived of power. An object of contempt to its enemies and of despair to its friends.

The lifeblood of administration is power. Its attainment, maintenance, increase, dissipation, and loss are subjects the practitioner and student can ill afford to neglect. . . . Power is only one of the considerations that must be weighed in administration, but of all it is the most overlooked in theory and the most dangerous to overlook in practice.

SOURCE: Norton E. Long, "Power and Administration," *Public Administration Review,* Autumn 1949.

his team of refugees truly were the best rocket scientists available to the United States at the time. Sometimes administrative necessity is as strong a force as **military necessity.** Now that this necessity has lessened in the wake of the Cold War, it is not surprising to find NASA significantly declining in budget and numbers of employees.

Power—The Internal Perspective

George Orwell, one of the most astute political observers of the twentieth century, was, however, very wrong about one thing. In his book *1984* he wrote that "power is not a means, it is an end" and that "the object of power is power." This highly influential attitude was taken by a man whose only large organizational experience was as a policeman in colonial Burma for a few years in the 1920s and as the most minor of bureaucrats for little more than a year in the World War II British Broadcasting Corporation (BBC). He loathed the inherent and subtle politics of large bureaucracies—mostly because he saw such wicked ones in the fascist Europe of the World War II era. Indeed, his creation of **Big Brother** in *1984* is the ultimate expression of that loathing. Orwell is a wonderful model for a political writer because he was such a great stylist, but his analysis and disdain of power are hardly useful for would-be and practicing public administrators—because public administration in essence is the exercise of power.

One sure thing about power is that we all understand it. We learn about power in organizations as soon as we go to school. Most of us have a pretty good intuitive grasp of the basic concepts of organizational power by the time we reach the third grade. So the newest thing about power in organizations is not our understanding of it but rather our intellectualizing about it.

Discussions of power and politics go back to Aristotle and other writers from antiquity. All of political theory is concerned with the exercise of power. The ancient field of political theory is now frequently applied to the comparatively young concepts of organization theory. Those who would limit themselves to the wisdom of modern writers are putting on intellectual blinders. Remember, it is frequently said of those who rise to rule the nation's largest organizations that they are "natural politicians." Niccolo Machiavelli is the most famous management and political analyst of the Italian Renaissance. His 1513 book of advice to would-be leaders, *The Prince,* is the progenitor of all "how to succeed" books that advocate practical rather than moral actions. In 1967, British Broadcasting Corporation executive Antony Jay reintroduced Machiavelli's concepts to a modern audience with his best-selling book *Management and Machiavelli,* which applied Machiavelli's insights for managing a state to the problem of power and politics in organizations. Jay concluded that Machiavelli's principles are as valid now as they were 450 years ago because they are

---

military necessity A justification for actions that violate the laws of war.
Big Brother George Orwell's (1903–1950) symbolization, from his novel *1984* (1949), of government so big and intrusive that it literally oversaw and regulated every aspect of life. The term has evolved to mean any potentially menacing power constantly looking over one's shoulder in judgment.

"rooted in human nature." According to Jay, "The new science of management is in fact only a continuation of the old art of government, and when you study management theory side by side with political theory, and management case histories side by side with political history, you realize that you are only studying two very similar branches of the same subject."

Ordinary people—as well as scholars—have hesitated to talk about power. For many, power is not a subject for polite conversation. Many of us—including Orwell—have often equated power with force, brutality, unethical behavior, manipulation, connivance, and subjugation. Harvard sociologist Rosabeth Moss Kanter contends that "power is America's last dirty word. It is easier to talk about money—and much easier to talk about sex—than it is to talk about power." Yet we must.

Organizational Goals

The traditional thinking is that organizations are institutions whose primary purpose is to accomplish established goals. Those goals are set by people in positions of formal authority such as elected officials or appointed agency directors. Thus the primary question for organization managers is how best to design and manage organizations to achieve their declared purposes effectively and efficiently. The personal preferences of organizational members are restrained by systems of formal rules and authority and by norms of rational behavior. But these assumptions about organizations may be naive and unrealistic when organizations are viewed as being complex systems of individuals and **coalitions,** each having its own interests, beliefs, values, preferences, perspectives, and goals. These coalitions—just like the larger group theory of politics—compete with each other continuously for scarce organizational resources. While the battles between groups such as automobile manufacturers and environmentalists over new clean air regulations often play out in the public spotlight, organizational competition is less obvious but every bit as real. The public may not be aware of a deep competition between agencies within the Department of Homeland Security for control over a newly hired group of agents, although such small-scale battles are quite common. Under the reality of scarce resources and individual aspiration, conflict is inevitable. Influence—and the power and political activities through which influence is acquired and maintained—is the primary "weapon" for use in competition and conflicts. Within an organization this weapon of influence can be based on factors ranging from an employee's knowledge and abilities within a given field to a staff member's skill in "sucking up" to the right people. Therefore, to fully understand an organization, we must get beyond its formally established goals and recognize that power, politics, and influence are critically important and permanent facts of organizational life.

Only rarely are organizational goals established by those in positions of formal authority. Goals result from ongoing maneuvering and bargaining among individuals

---

coalition A temporary joining of political actors to advance legislation or to elect candidates. It is often the case that the actors in a coalition are poles apart on many issues but are able to put their continuing differences aside in the interest of joining to advance (or defeat) the issue at hand.

and transitory coalitions. Just as it is with outside politics in general, coalitions tend to shift with issues. Thus, organizational goals change with shifts in the balance of power among coalitions. Organizational goals are important in the same way organizational power and politics are because they provide the "official" rationale and the legitimacy for resource allocation decisions: who gets which money.

Internal Power Relationships

Power relationships are permanent features of organizations primarily because specialization results in the creation of many interdependent units with varying sizes and degrees of importance that compete with each other for scarce resources. Organization theorist Jeffrey Pfeffer emphasizes this point in his book *Power in Organizations*: "Those persons and those units that have the responsibility for performing the more critical tasks in the organization have a natural advantage in developing and exercising power in the organization. . . . Power is first and foremost a structural phenomenon, and should be understood as such."

Power is related to dependence. Lower-level organizational members have an arsenal of weapons—such as expertise and personal attractiveness—with which to make others dependent on them. Servants who use their cleverness to take advantage of social betters are a stock-in-trade of classic drama. This is an intellectualization of something we all know instinctively: that some people are treated like prima donnas or "get away with murder" in organizations because they possess some special skill that gives them power in a specific context. The most ready examples are the characters Hawkeye and Trapper from the $M*A*S*H*$ movie and television series. If they had not been surgeons badly needed at the battlefront, they would have been court-martialed for their college boy antics.

Traditional organization theory places high importance on "legitimate authority" (authority that flows down through the formal organizational hierarchy) and formal rules (promulgated and enforced by those in authority) to ensure that organizational behavior is directed toward the attainment of established organizational goals. Such "structuralists" tend to define power synonymously with authority. In contrast, others argue that in today's organizational world, the gap is increasing between the power one needs to get the job done and the power that comes with the job (authority). For example, Rosabeth Moss Kanter, in her article "Power Failure in Management Circuits," identifies three groups of positions within organizations that are particularly susceptible to powerlessness: first-line supervisors, staff professionals, and top executives. However, she carefully distinguishes between "power" and "dominance, control, and oppression." She identifies her primary concern: At higher organizational levels, the power to "punish, to prevent, to sell off, to reduce, to fire, all without appropriate concern for consequences" grows, but the power needed for positive accomplishments does not. Managers who perceive themselves as being powerless and who think their subordinates are discounting them tend to use more dominating or punishing forms of influence. Thus in large organizations powerlessness (or perceived powerlessness) can be a more substantive problem than possession of power. Authority is only one of many available sources of organizational power. Power, no respecter of position, exists in *all* directions—not just down through the hierarchy.

Other forms of power and influence often prevail over authority-based power—for example, control over scarce resources (office space, discretionary funds, current and accurate information, and time and skill to work on projects), easy access to others who are perceived as having power (important customers or clients, members of the board of directors, someone else with formal authority or who controls scarce resources), a central place in a potent coalition, ability to "work the organizational rules" (knowing how to get things done or to prevent others from getting things done), and credibility (believing that one's word can be trusted). Historian Richard E. Neustadt's landmark analysis of the presidency, *Presidential Power,* asserted that a president's real powers are informal, that presidential power is essentially the power to persuade. Neustadt quotes President Harry S. Truman contemplating General of the Army Dwight D. Eisenhower becoming president: "He'll sit here, and he'll say, 'Do this! Do that!' *And nothing will happen.* Poor Ike—it won't be a bit like the Army. He'll find it very frustrating."

Jeffrey Pfeffer defines power as "the ability to get things done the way one wants them done; it is the latent ability to influence people." This definition offers several advantages for understanding organizations. First, it emphasizes the relativity of power. As Pfeffer points out, "Power is context or relationship specific. A person is not 'powerful' or 'powerless' in general, but only with respect to other social actors in a specific social relationship." Pfeffer's phrase "the way one wants them done" is a potent reminder that conflict and the use of power often are over the choice of methods, means, approaches, and/or "turf." They are not limited to battles about outcomes. This point is important because power is often a structural phenomenon—a consequence of organizational specialization. For example, competing organizational coalitions often form around professions: hospital nurses versus paramedics, sociologists versus mathematicians in a university, or business school-educated staff specialists versus generalists from the "school of hard knocks." Organizational conflicts among people representing different professions, educational backgrounds, sexes, and ages frequently do not involve goals: They center on questions about the "right" of a profession, academic discipline, sex, or age group to exercise its perception of its "professional rights," to control the way things will be done, or to protect its "turf" and status. This point is important because it reemphasizes that organizational behavior and decisions frequently are not "rational"—not necessarily directed toward accomplishing the formally stated goals of the organization (see Figure 2.5).

All would-be administrators should be aware of the personal danger in possessing significant power. Say the word "power," and half the people hearing it will immediately think of **Lord Acton**'s 1887 statement that "power tends to corrupt and absolute power corrupts absolutely." Certainly men like Hitler, Napoleon, Stalin, and Mao all grew more grossly corrupt the longer they held power. But petty tyrants grow proportionately corrupt. Perhaps the best advice on handling power came from Harry Truman in *Plain Speaking:* "If a man can accept a situation in a

---

Lord Acton (1834–1904) English historian; original name was John Dahlberg.

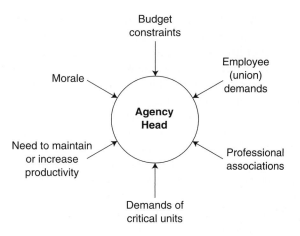

Figure 2.5   Typical Inside Forces on a Public Agency Manager

place of power with the thought that it's only temporary, he comes out all right. But when he thinks that he is the cause of the power, that can be his ruination."

The Cultures of Public Organizations

Administrative institutions are part of the greater culture of their society at the same time that they develop and nurture their own organizational cultures. We learn how to cope in these differing worlds almost instinctively from childhood. How we act in school or at home (each a relatively closed organization) is different from how we act on the street—in the outside world. This is a recognition that each culture demands different behaviors. Thus we talk differently to our friends on the street than we do to our parents or teachers. This literally acculturates us to the fact that each time we join another organization—whether for work, worship, or weight lifting—we expect to—and are usually eager to—learn the new jargon and accepted ways of the new group's culture. To talk of the "two cultures" of public organizations is a gross oversimplification. There are an almost infinite variety of public organization cultures. However, they all have this in common: They interact with the outside environment of the overall culture. In this sense alone it can be said that all public organizations must deal with two cultures: their unique internal culture and the common outside culture.

The Outside Cultural Environment

Public management is constantly being judged in the wrong context. It is erroneously viewed as a public sector counterpart to industrial management systems. The private sector analogy holds true only for a portion of the total public management function, and the size of that portion depends on the degree to which the administrative operations of the jurisdiction are politicized. Thus public sector operations cannot be properly understood or evaluated outside the political context—the political culture—of the host jurisdiction.

The determinant of any community's attitudes toward the quality and vigor of its governing institutions is the political culture of the geographic area concerned. Political culture is that part of the overall societal culture that determines a community's attitudes toward the quality, style, and vigor of its political processes and government operations. The only way to explain the extreme variations in public bureaucracies is by examining the cultural context of the host jurisdictions. The quality of bureaucratic operations measured by levels of citizen satisfaction, efficiency, or corruption varies for a variety of reasons—not the least of which is the substantial disagreement on just what constitutes a quality operation. But the quality or style of operations is determined only in the lesser part by critics and public officials; the crucial determinant is the political will of the community. It determines the values and resources to be applied to any given public problem, it helps establish the obligations of **citizenship,** and it establishes the parameters of activities in which an official may participate.

Even when corruption is rife, it is the political culture that sets the limits and direction of such dishonesty. For example, James Q. Wilson, in *Varieties of Police Behavior,* demonstrated that the style of **police** operations in eight communities reflected not some abstract standard of quality or professionalism but the expressed and/or implied desires of the community. Thus the police were either exceedingly lenient or exceedingly strict with minor legal violations, depending on the perceived degree of community concern one way or the other. Wilson considers a police department to have a "watchman" style of performance if it is one in which order maintenance is perceived to be the prime function of the department. Such a police operation will tend to ignore law infringements that do not involve "serious" crimes, such as minor traffic violations, bookmaking, and illegal church bingo. Of course, all these activities or nonactivities are subject to occasional crackdowns. The police periodically shut down illegal gambling operations in response to the political needs of the police chief or mayor. The thrust of the "watchman" style is to maintain order, to ensure a smooth, nondisruptive running of the community or bureaucracy. Legal considerations and official operating mandates are paramount only when the "heat" is on. Of course, the standard operating procedures of police will tend to be more legalistic in communities that are so disposed.

Cultural Values and Administration   While a community's political culture is seldom articulated, it nevertheless serves as a source of definition. By determining the values

---

citizenship The dynamic relation between a citizen and his or her nation. The concept of citizenship involves rules of what a citizen might do (such as vote), must do (pay taxes), and can refuse to do (pledge allegiance). Increasingly, the concept involves benefits or entitlements that a citizen has a right to demand from government. In some jurisdictions, citizenship is a requirement for public employment. Citizenship also requires loyalty to and primary residency in one's state.

police Paramilitary state and local government organizations whose most basic responsibilities include maintaining public order and safety (through the use of force if necessary), investigating and arresting persons accused of crimes, and securing the cooperation of the citizenry. The term *police,* while referring to all law enforcement officers in general, is usually a reference to municipal law enforcement officers. County officers are sheriffs; state officers are usually called the state police, state troopers, or highway patrol.

to be applied to any given problem, the political culture ensures that the decisional process is filtered through its value system before administrative action is taken. How values influence administrative actions is illustrated by George Orwell's 1936 essay "Shooting an Elephant." In 1920s Burma, where Orwell was a police officer representing the British colonial administration, trained elephants were used for moving heavy logs. When an elephant suddenly disdained his domesticated labors in the timber industry and went on a rampage, it was the job of the local cop on the beat, in this case Orwell, to shoot him. The problem was that by the time Orwell and the local onlookers caught up with the elephant chronicled in the essay, it was peacefully eating grass and no danger to anyone. But an ever-increasing crowd expected this lone officer, this symbol of imperial presence, to act decisively. "A sahib [a master] has got to act like a sahib; he has got to appear resolute, to know his own mind and do definite things." Orwell was expected by the prevailing culture to shoot the elephant. Orwell says he felt like "an absurd puppet" who was being "pushed to and fro by the will of those" villagers. Despite the fact that there was no public safety reason to do so, he shoots and kills the elephant "solely to avoid looking a fool." The culture made him do it. Of course, today's attitudes are radically different, and it is almost unthinkable that a police officer anywhere in the world would feel pressured to kill any endangered species—let alone a nonthreatening elephant.

The United States is so vast and geographically diverse that while there is an overall American political culture, it is often less influential than the local political subcultures of the individual states and regions. Differing sources of political culture, such as race, ethnicity, and religion, combine with historical patterns of political behavior to yield the distinct political cultures of, for example, the Rocky Mountain West or the Deep South. All political cultures change—some more quickly than others. Germany and Japan have vastly different political cultures today than they did when they were the exemplars of **fascism** prior to and during World War II. In the wake of the Cold War the once Communist states of Eastern Europe almost overnight found themselves with new political cultures. The American political culture, with the notable exception of the Civil War of 1861 to 1865, has, in historical terms, been very stable.

The Inside Cultural Environment

An organizational culture—the culture which exists within an organization—is a parallel but smaller version of a societal culture. It is made up of intangible things such as values, beliefs, assumptions, and perceptions. It is the pattern of these beliefs and attitudes that determines members' behaviors in and around the organization, persists over extended periods of time, and pervades all elements of the organization (albeit to different extents and with varying intensity).

An organizational culture is transmitted to new members through socialization (or enculturation) processes; it is maintained and transmitted through a network of

---

fascism A political philosophy that advocates governance by a dictator, assisted by a hierarchically organized, strongly ideological party, in maintaining a totalitarian and regimented society through violence, intimidation, and the arbitrary use of power.

rituals and interaction patterns; it is enforced and reinforced by group **norms** and the organization's system of rewards and controls. It is the unseen and unobservable force that is always behind those organizational activities that can be observed. According to Kilmann and others, "Culture is to the organization what personality is to the individual—a hidden, yet unifying theme that provides meaning, direction, and mobilization."

Organizational culture is created by the attitudes and behaviors of the dominant or early organizational "shapers" and "heroes"; by the nature of the organization's work; and by the attitudes, values, and "willingness to act" of new members. It is transmitted by often-told stories and legends and by the formal and informal processes of socialization. An organization's culture provides a framework for shared understanding of events, defines behavioral expectations, and serves as a source of and focus for members' commitment and as an organizational "control system" (i.e., through group norms). But while a strong organizational culture can control organizational behavior, it can also block an organization from making those changes needed to adapt to a changing environment.

Organizational culture is particularly useful as an intellectual construct because it helps us to understand or predict how an organization will behave under different circumstances. A cultural pattern is similar to a genetic inheritance: Once you know the patterns of basic assumptions, you can anticipate how the organization will act in differing circumstances. Most importantly if it can be deduced that an organizational culture led to poor performance by an agency, it becomes necessary to find ways to break down the problematic elements of that culture. Such a scenario took place during the examination of intelligence breakdowns that allowed the terrorist attacks of September 11, 2001, to succeed. During joint Senate and House hearings in 2002 heavy criticism was targeted at the FBI for creating and fostering an organizational culture where cooperation between varied divisions within the bureau was not valued. More specifically, the hearings called attention to a culture at FBI, and a similar culture at the CIA, that did not promote interaction between intelligent officers and law enforcement officials.

Such concerns about the damaging effects of organizational culture at the Federal Emergency Management Agency (FEMA) have mounted in the aftermath of Hurricane Katrina. In particular, many questions have been raised about the culture at FEMA under the leadership of then agency director Michael Brown. Brown had very limited experience in emergency management before being appointed by President George W. Bush in January 2003. This lack of experience appears to have alienated many FEMA employees, who saw him as unqualified to lead the agency and unwilling to fight against budget cuts that were diminishing the organization's capabilities to respond to catastrophes.

Like snowflakes, every organizational culture is different. What has worked repeatedly for one organization may not work for another—so the basic assumptions differ. And all organizational cultures are shaped by myriad factors—from

---

norms The socially enforced requirements and expectations about basic responsibilities, behavior, and thought patterns of members in their organizational roles.

the societal culture in which it resides to its technologies and competing organizations. Some organizations have strong, unified, pervasive cultures, whereas others have weaker cultures; often "subcultures" evolve in different functional or geographical areas. The most common example of this last phenomenon is the more formal culture of a headquarters office versus the informality of a field office.

Although phrases like "organizational culture" and "culture of a factory" can be found in a few books on management written as early as the 1950s (for example, *The Changing Culture of a Factory* by Elliott Jaques and William H. Whyte Jr.'s book about corporate conformity, *The Organization Man*), few students of management or organizations paid much attention to the nature and content of organizational culture until the late 1970s. Nevertheless, today organizational culture is one of the hottest issues in the field of public administration—so much so that whenever there is an organizational breakdown, people start to shout (figuratively if not literally), "It's the culture!"

Professional Socialization

During the 1960s and early 1970s, several books on organizational and professional socialization processes received wide attention. As useful as these earlier works were, they assumed the presence of organizational or professional cultures and proceeded to examine issues involving the match between individuals and cultures. Two of the more widely read of these were *Boys in White* by Howard Saul Becker, et al., which chronicled the processes used to socialize medical students into the medical profession, and Herbert Kaufman's *The Forest Ranger*, a study of how the United States Forest Service developed the "will and capacity to conform" among its remotely stationed rangers. Once again, however, these earlier writings did not address important questions such as how cultures are formed or changed, how cultures affect leadership, or the relationship between culture and strategic planning (establishing organizational directions); rather, they focused on the process of socializing employees into existing organizational cultures and the impacts of existing cultures on organizational members. Without attention paid to the effect of culture on outcomes, important issues can be overlooked. For example, while it's important to understand how an FBI agent is socialized into the bureau, it's probably more important to understand how the organization's culture stressed the examination of crimes after the fact rather than stopping terrorism from occurring in the first place.

An entirely different orientation to organizational culture that focused on symbols started to appear in the late 1970s. Symbols are things like flags and logos, which carry a wider (or different) meaning than their intrinsic content. For example, the Stars and Stripes is a symbol because it embodies values, traditions, and emotions. Symbols also can be things such as words (IBM's famous sign "Think"), phrases (*Semper fidelis*, the motto meaning "Always faithful" of the U.S. Marine Corps), and organizational structures. Because the top or seventh floor is the location of the highest officials of the U.S. Department of State, policy is frequently said to come from the "seventh floor"—not any particular official. Similarly, the White House is a building that can, as a symbol, speak. Reporters and political commentators frequently state that the "White House said" this or that. The building speaks because it is the architectural embodiment of the bureaucratic institution that is the modern presidency. Thus the building speaks through press releases, news conferences, deep as well as shallow background briefings, and **leaks**. While the president is the main and most desired speaker, there are a few hundred other people who work there and also give it voice.

Romanticized stories about organizational heroes and ritualistic ceremonies can also be symbols—if they carry meanings that go beyond their intrinsic content. Military medals and other types of organizational awards for unusual achievement are a major example. When a member of Napoléon's government described military decorations as "baubles," Napoléon replied, "You are pleased to call them 'baubles.' Well, it is with 'baubles' that mankind is governed." Wise managers will create multiple opportunities to use symbols to motivate, inspire, and thank their employees.

Symbolic Management

The manipulation of symbols and the **dramaturgy** of symbolic acts are essential elements of managing people in organizations. While such manipulations may be conscious or unconscious on the part of management, they are invariably there. Frequently, symbolic acts are easily identifiable because of their obvious **beau geste** quality. They form an integral part of everyday manners and courtesies. When an organization's chief executive accidentally meets a lower-echelon employee in a crowded elevator and says, "How's your job coming along?" the executive is not expecting an answer to this question; the words are used simply to communicate sociability—a symbolic ritual. It would be quite out of place and both annoying and surprising to the executive if the employee really answered the question instead of replying with a simple "Fine, thank you." In cases like these, language ceases being an instrument of communication and becomes a symbol— a thing that carries a different meaning than its intrinsic content.

Symbolic management attracted only limited attention during the 1970s. The turning point for the organizational culture (and symbolism) perspective did not arrive until the early 1980s. Then, almost overnight, organizational culture became a very hot topic in books, journals, and periodicals aimed at both management practitioners and academicians. Because of the youthfulness of organizational culture as a perspective, minimal consensus exists about much of anything concerned with it. There are only a few organizational culture issues on which there is widespread agreement, including the following:

1. Organizational cultures exist.
2. Each organizational culture is relatively unique.

---

leaks The deliberate disclosure of confidential or classified information by someone in government who wants to advance the public interest, embarrass a bureaucratic rival, or help a reporter disclose incompetence or skulduggery to the public.

dramaturgy The manner in which a person acts out or theatrically stages his or her organizational or political role. Political candidates who make an effort to look or sound senatorial or presidential are engaging in dramaturgy. Of course, if they have to make an effort to look it or sound it, they may not have it. One is reminded of the traditional advice to actors: "Always be sincere. If you can fake that, you've got it made."

beau geste A noble and/or gracious gesture.

3. Organizational culture is a socially constructed concept.

4. Organizational culture provides its members with a way of understanding and making sense of events and symbols.

5. Organizational culture, because of its ability to informally approve or disapprove of behavior, can be a powerful tool for guiding organizations.

Each organization has its own unique culture that determines how it will respond to the same stimuli. At the Pentagon, the story is often told about how the same words can have vastly different meanings in different organizations. A good example is the use of the word *secure* in the U.S. Department of Defense. If the Army is told to secure a particular building, it will post guards at all the entrances and exits. The Marine Corps, given the same instructions, will assault the building until everyone inside surrenders. And the Air Force will achieve its mission to secure the building by negotiating a three-year lease with the owners.

Because the same words used in different organizational cultures can mean radically different outcomes, all would-be managers must be aware that organizational culture is not just something we live in. J. Steven Ott, a professor at the University of Utah, elaborates on this idea in *The Organizational Culture Perspective*. Managers must use organizational culture "as a frame of reference for the way one looks at, attempts to understand, and works with organizations." Thus, even though the vocabulary may be the same, the meaning of words in their organizational context may require a manager to effectively learn a new language. Any manager who doesn't learn to "walk the walk" and "talk the talk" is walking and talking alone—not managing.

✦ A CASE STUDY: WERE THE SPACE SHUTTLE ASTRONAUTS KILLED BY FOG?

In 1961 President John F. Kennedy told a joint session of Congress, "This nation should commit itself to achieving the goal, before this decade is out, of landing a man on the moon and returning him safely to the Earth." As with much grand policymaking, this was easy enough to say. Few believed that the National Aeronautics and Space Administration (NASA), the federal agency created in 1958 to beat the Soviet Union in the Cold War space race, could achieve this "man on the moon" goal in the allotted time.

NASA not only won the space race, but it became the national exemplar of managerial excellence—at least until a clear day in January 1986 when the space shuttle *Challenger* blasted off into the Florida skies to become a now classic example of managerial incompetence. The shuttle, with six astronauts and New Hampshire schoolteacher Christa McAuliffe aboard, blew up 73 seconds after liftoff because an O-ring seal on one of the booster rockets failed. Yet this was not a complete surprise to anyone who followed the shuttle program in the news media. It was widely reported that such seals nearly failed on earlier shuttle flights. They were most likely to fail when the outside air temperature was close to freezing, as it was on the day of the *Challenger* launch. The problem seems so obvious now. NASA managers had more information than they could adequately process. So while the skies were sunny when the *Challenger* last "slipped the surly bonds of Earth," it can be said that the crew truly died from fog—caused by a blinding array of information that led to a faulty decision by public administrators.

The "fog of war" is the wonderfully descriptive phrase for the confusion and uncertainty that is inherent in combat. Prussian General Karl von Clausewitz originated this meteorological metaphor in his 1832 classic on military strategy *On War.* It is as if a literal fog descends on the battlefield and blinds the combatants to what the enemy and even other elements of their own forces are doing. In the days of black powder, the fog was almost as literal as it was proverbial.

Today, wherever far-flung or large-scale operations have to be coordinated, whether military or managerial, fog or uncertainty is a possibility. The field of management information systems has grown up in recent decades to reduce the inevitable fog to manageable proportions. But the reduction mechanisms themselves—computer data and memorandums in a seemingly endless stream—often create more problems than the fog they were designed to dispel.

And sometimes the fog is made all the more blinding by political considerations. It was not just that NASA had developed an organizational culture that inhibited bad news from getting to the top in a timely manner. Those who decided to launch that day were under the most exquisitely subtle political pressures as well. If the shuttle had kept its schedule on that ill-fated day, it would have returned in time for Ms. McAuliffe—who had been selected in a highly publicized national search—to sit in the balcony of the chamber of the House of Representatives during the State of the Union speech while President Ronald Reagan pointed her out as an inspiration to the nation and all those desirous of winning lotteries.

Of course, as soon as the accident occurred, all those responsible went into deep denial. Top NASA managers denied having heard of O-ring problems. The White House denied it put any pressure on NASA that would compromise safety. To sort out the denials and gather the facts, the Presidential Commission on the Space Shuttle *Challenger* Accident was promptly appointed. Six months later the commission reported that the failure of the O-ring seals was the physical cause of the *Challenger* explosion. But it also declared that the "decision to launch the *Challenger* was flawed." It further concluded that "if the decision makers had known all the facts, it is highly unlikely that they would have decided to launch." In essence, the commission found that the NASA managers responsible for the launch decision were ignorant—because they were blinded by the fog of competing information.

The commission's report also absolved managers of succumbing to political pressures to prove that shuttle flights were routine and routinely on schedule. It simply denied that there were any political pressures. This was only polite. It certainly would have been unusual for a presidential commission to criticize the president who appointed it. But denial fooled no one and only made them look foolish. According to Barbara Romzek and Melvin Dubnick, writing in *Public Administration Review,* political "pressures existed and came from a variety of sources outside of NASA, including the White House." Charles Peters of *The Washington Monthly* reported that "top NASA officials didn't want to hear the bad news [about the O-rings] because they were determined to launch the next day so that President Reagan could point to this accomplishment in his State of the Union message. They had even written a suggested insert for the speech."

Good managers with the facts before them can make good decisions. However, good managers with an overwhelming volume of data to digest often become unable to make timely or wise decisions; they are reduced to incompetence by the efforts to make them more competent. We live in a contradictory world when the fog does not come in, as poet Carl Sandburg suggests, "on little cat feet," but rides on the crest of an endless wave of computer printouts. The *Challenger* disaster leads an infinite list of things gone wrong despite the best efforts of highly talented and otherwise able individuals—people who have banded together to create an organization that as a whole is less talented than the sum of its very talented human parts.

And just how did NASA respond to this problem of perceived incompetence? A few weeks after the *Challenger* disaster, NASA awarded bonuses to dozens of its top managers for the excellent work they had done. The media made a big joke of this by pointing out the incongruity of giving $10,000 bonuses to members of a team that couldn't "shuttle straight." NASA managers promptly complained that they shouldn't all be punished for the screwups of a few. True, the O-ring failed, but the other 30,000 parts of the shuttle worked just fine!

Even the best-run organization, of which NASA is still an example, can be befuddled by fog. As with real weather, this kind of fog is a sometimes thing. It can be disrupted by more effective management information systems, by supportive organizational cultures, and by determined top managers. The best managers will use a bout of fog as a learning experience—as an opportunity to change their information system, organization culture, and decisional processes so this particular bad weather can never happen again. That is exactly what NASA has proceeded to do. But then NASA failed again, and for the same reason—fog.

Seventeen years passed and shuttle flights once again seemed to be routine. Then on February 1, 2003, the *Columbia* disintegrated while returning from an otherwise successful mission, killing its seven-member crew. The *Columbia* Accident Investigation Board's August 2003 report stated that while the physical cause of the accident was insulating foam from an external fuel tank that damaged a wing during launch, "the organizational causes of this accident are rooted in the Space Shuttle Program's history and culture." It turned out that, as with the O-ring problem, many people also knew of the insulating foam problem, but the fog created by the culture—once again—prevented that information from getting to the appropriate decision makers. In response to the Accident Investigation Board's findings, NASA set out to change its safety culture in order to avoid the fatal errors associated with the *Challenger* and *Columbia* missions. The results of this overhaul could be seen during the 2005 flight of the shuttle *Discovery*. During the first flight since the *Columbia* failure, *Discovery*'s crew was prepaired to make in-flight repairs to the shuttle on damage sustained during the launch.

For Discussion: *Why are all large organizations so susceptible to Clausewitz's fog? Are political pressures for performance a common or an uncommon part of public administration?*

Summary

Public administration is an instrument of policy. But public policymaking in republican government is constrained by the very nature of republican institutions. Executive leadership is inherently limited, both by the leader's philosophic views on how to exercise power and the legal constraints of constitutional checks and balances.

Public policymaking is cyclical. As policy decisions are made and implemented, criticism in the form of feedback puts new decisions on the policy agenda. This starts the policymaking cycle all over again. While decisions can be radical departures for the current situation, they are most likely to be incremental.

Public processes, whether public policymaking or public administration, take place within a polity, an overarching political jurisdiction. All public managers have two polities with which to contend—internal (their agency) and external (the outside political world).

Just as public policy and administration exists in two polities, it has a similar double life as a culture. It is part of the greater culture of its society at the same time that it develops and nurtures its own organizational cultures.

Review Questions

1. What are the major checks on the American president's power to wage war?
2. What are the differences among the three major views of executive power: restricted, prerogative, and stewardship?
3. What are the major elements in the public policymaking cycle and how do they interact?
4. How does the pluralistic notion of the American political process influence public agency managers?
5. What is the difference between the internal and external cultures of public organizations?

Key Concepts

agenda setting The process by which ideas or issues bubble up through the various political channels to wind up for consideration by a political institution such as a legislature or court.

implementation Putting a government program into effect; the total process of translating a legal mandate, whether an executive order or an enacted statute, into appropriate program directives and structures that provide services or create goods.

incremental decision-making model A view of the public policymaking process that assumes that small decisions made at the margins of problems are the usual reality of change.

organizational culture The culture that exists within an organization; a parallel but smaller version of a societal culture.

pluralism A theory of government that attempts to reaffirm the democratic character of society by asserting that open, multiple, competing, and responsive groups preserve traditional democratic values in a mass industrial state. Pluralism assumes that power will shift from group to group as elements in the mass public transfer their allegiance in response to their perceptions of their individual interests.

political culture That part of the overall societal culture that determines a community's attitudes toward the quality, style, and vigor of its political processes and government operations.

program evaluation The systematic examination of any activity undertaken by government to make a determination about its effects, both short-term and long-range.

public program All those activities designed to implement a public policy; often this calls for the creation of organizations, public agencies, and bureaus.

rational decision-making model A view of the public policymaking process that assumes complete information and a systematic, logical, and comprehensive approach to change.

republic A form of government in which sovereignty resides in the people who elect agents to represent them in political decision making.

separation of powers The allocation of powers among the three branches of government so that they are a check upon each other. This separation, in theory, makes a tyrannical concentration of power impossible.

Bibliography

The 9/11 Commission. (2004). *The 9/11 Commission Report: Final Report of the National Commission on Terrorist Attacks Upon the United States.* United States Government Printing Office: Washington, DC.

Becker, H. S., et al. (1961). *Boys in White: Student Culture in Medical School.* Chicago: University of Chicago Press.

Bell, Daniel. (1960). *End of Ideology: On the Exhaustion of Political Ideas in the Fifties.* Glencoe, IL: Free Press.

Bemis, Samuel Flagg. (1956). *John Quincy Adams and the Union.* New York: Knopf.

Boorstin, Daniel J. (1961). *The Image: A Guide to Pseudo-Events in America.* New York: Atheneum.

Congressional Research Service. (1993). The Intelligence Community and 9/11: Congressional Hearings and the Status of the Investigation. www.fas.org/irp/crs/RL31650.pdf.

Dahl, Robert A., and Charles E. Lindblom. (1953). *Politics, Economics, and Welfare.* Chicago: University of Chicago Press.

Degler, Carl. (1970). *Out of Our Past.* New York: Harper and Row.

Downs, Anthony. (1972). "Up and Down with Ecology—The Issue-Attention Cycle." *Public Interest* 28 (summer).

Easton, David. (1963). *A Systems Analysis of Political Life.* New York: Atheneum.

Etzioni, Amitai. (1967). "Mixed Scanning: A 'Third' Approach to Decision Making," *Public Administration Review* (December).

Galbraith, John Kenneth. (1956). *American Capitalism.* Boston: Houghton Mifflin.

Gingrich, Newt. (1995). *To Renew America.* New York: HarperCollins.

Hofstadter, Richard. (1965). *The Paranoid Style in American Politics.* New York: Knopf.

Jaques, Elliott. (1951). *The Changing Culture of a Factory.* London: Tavistock Institute.

Jones, Charles O. (1977). *An Introduction to the Study of Public Policy,* 2nd ed. North Scituate, MA: Duxbury Press.

Joseph, Peter. (1974). *Good Times: An Oral History of America in the Nineteen Sixties.* New York: William Morrow.

Kanter, Rosabeth Moss. (1979). "Power Failure in Management Circuits." *Harvard Business Review* (July–August).

Kaufman, Herbert. (1960). *The Forest Ranger.* Baltimore: Johns Hopkins University Press.

Kilmann, R. H., et al., eds. (1985). *Gaining Control of the Corporate Culture.* San Francisco: Jossey-Bass.

Kingdon, John W. (1995). *Agendas, Alternatives, and Public Policies,* 2nd ed. New York: Longman.

Lasswell, Harold D. (1963). *The Future of Political Science.* New York: Atheneum.

———. (1936). *Politics: Who Gets What, When, How.* New York: Smith.

Latham, Earl. (1952). *The Group Basis of Politics.* Ithaca, NY: Cornell University Press.

Lindblom, Charles E. (1959). "The Science of Muddling Through." *Public Administration Review* (spring).

Lipsky, Michael. (1980). *Street-Level Bureaucracy.* New York: Russell Sage Foundation.

Lowi, Theodore, J. (1979). *The End of Liberalism,* 2nd ed. New York: Norton.

Markham, Felix. (1964). *Napoleon.* New York: New American Library.

Miller, Merle. (1974). *Plain Speaking: An Oral Biography of Harry S. Truman.* New York: Berkley.

Mills, C. Wright. (1956). *The Power Elite.* New York: Oxford University Press.

Orwell, George. (1946). *Shooting an Elephant and Other Essays.* New York: Harcourt, Brace.

Ott, J. Steven. (1989). *Organizational Cultural Perspective.* Pacific Grove, CA: Brooks/Cole.

Peters, Charles. (1993). "Tilting at Windmills." *The Washington Monthly* 25 (November).

Pfeffer, Jeffrey. (1981). *Power in Organizations.* Marshfield, MA: Pitman.

Pressman, Jeffrey, and Aaron Wildavsky. (1973). *Implementation.* Berkeley: University of California Press.

Romzek, Barbara S., and Melvin J. Dubnick. (1987). "Accountability in the Public Sector: Lessons from the *Challenger* Tragedy," *Public Administration Review* 47 (May–June).

Sheldon, Michael. (1991). *Orwell.* New York: HarperCollins.

Taft, William Howard. (1916). *Our Chief Magistrate and His Powers.* New York: Columbia University Press.

Whyte, William H., Jr. (1956). *The Organization Man.* New York: Simon and Schuster.

Wilson, James Q. (1968). *Varieties of Police Behavior.* Cambridge, MA: Harvard University Press.

Woodward, Bob, and Carl Bernstein. (1974). *All the President's Men.* New York: Simon and Schuster.

Recommended Books

Barzelay, Michael. (2001). *The New Public Management: Improving Research and Policy Dialogue.* New York: Columbia University Press. How policymakers should treat the denizens of the bureaucracy.

Bratton, William, with Peter Knobler. (1998). *Turnaround: How America's Top Cop Reversed the Crime Epidemic.* New York: Random House. A biographical account of how the author used modern management techniques to change the organizational culture of four major local police agencies (including the police departments of the cities of Boston and New York); this resulted in greater morale, increased productivity, and less crime.

Heady, Ferrel. (1996). *Public Administration: A Comparative Perspective,* 5th ed. New York: Marcel Dekker. The standard survey of worldwide public administration, providing both historic and contemporary contexts.

Neustadt, Richard E. (1991). *Presidential Power and Modern Presidents.* New York: Free Press. An analysis of how the essence of the power of the president—indeed, of any executive—is not to order but to persuade.

Pipes, Daniel. (1997). *Conspiracy: How the Paranoid Style Flourishes and Where It Comes From.* New York: Free Press. An updating of Richard Hofstadter's 1965 *The Paranoid Style in American Politics.* This volume deals with the latest batch of wacky theories as well as the golden oldies.

Simon, Herbert A. (1997). *Administrative Behavior: A Study of Decision-Making Processes in Administrative Organizations,* 4th ed. New York: Macmillan. The fifth anniversary edition of the groundbreaking analysis of how organizations make decisions within the context of their social values.

Related Web Sites

Abraham Lincoln online
www.netins.net/showcase/creative/lincoln.html

Association for Public Policy Analysis and Management
www.appam.org

Center on Budget and Policy Priorities
www.cbpp.org/

Civics and Politics
www.civicsandpolitics.com/index.htm

Government-related servers
www.eff.org/

John Locke
www.utm.edu/research/iep/1/locke.htm

National Aeronautics and Space Administration
www.nasa.gov

National Center for Policy Analysis
www.public-policy.org

National Center for Public Policy Research
www.nationalcenter.org/

National Civic League
www.nlc.org

Niccolo Machiavelli
www.www.philosophypages.com/ph/macv.htm

Public Agenda Online
www.publicagenda.org/

Public Policy Forum
www.ppforum.com/english/index.html

Theodore Roosevelt
www.pbs.org/wgbh/pages/amex/tr/index.html

CHAPTER 3

The Continuous Reinventing of the Machinery of Government

•KEYNOTE: THE NEW FEUDALISM

In 1958, economist John Kenneth Galbraith published *The Affluent Society*. This book described American society as one in which scarcity of resources was not a major problem but where "private affluence and public squalor" existed continuously side by side.

Today, this trend is becoming even more pronounced. Journalists such as Michael Lind are observing a "<u>new feudalism</u>" that "reverses the trend of the past thousand years toward the government's provision of basic public goods like policing, public roads and transport networks, and public schools." Lind concludes that "in the United States—to a degree unmatched in any other industrialized democracy—these <u>public goods are once again becoming private luxuries.</u>"

When public services deteriorate—especially in urban areas—those with enough money, increasingly, buy their way out of the problem. They send their children to private schools and hire private police. And in the best feudal tradition, they retire each night behind walled towns where guards at a gate check the identity of all who seek to enter. And we are not just talking about an apartment building with a door-keeper. We are talking about millions of citizens living in suburban "gated communities" with their own private police, private streets, and private parks.

While most popular in California, Texas, Arizona, Florida, and Virginia, such private residential communities are springing up throughout the United States, patterned after the comprehensive minicities that have long been popular with retirees in the sunbelt. What is new is that middle- and upper-income families of all ages are opting to pay hefty private taxes (community fees) and submit to stringent environmental regulations to lead the good life away from urban ills. It is estimated that over 5 million Americans already live in such closed-off communities, and that number is expected to double over the next decade. Ironically, according to political analyst Timothy Egan, "The very things that Republicans in Congress are trying to do away with for the nation as a whole—environmental protection, gun control, heavy regulation—are most pronounced in these predominantly Republican private enclaves."

These new-fashioned feudalists, who are decidedly libertarian concerning the out-side world, are surprisingly socialistic concerning the private inside world of their gated minicities. They willingly accept a wide variety of community regulations that they would challenge as unconstitutional in other contexts—from gun control to restrictions on exterior paint colors, lawn maintenance standards, and prohibitions on basketball hoops over garages. Homeowners must abide by common mandates, including the carrying of special identification, getting permission for more than a set number of visitors, and paying user fees for a wide variety of services such as trash collection, cable TV connections, and time on tennis courts.

The new feudalism also extends beyond the guarded gates. During the Middle Ages, many of the castles on the Rhine River in Western Europe were built to enforce the collection of tolls on that portion of the river controlled by a local warlord. Today electronic "castles" are enforcing the collection of tolls on a similarly private means of transport. For example, the California Private Transportation Corporation, with state approval, has built a ten-mile, $128 million, four-lane road in the median strip of an existing but highly congested southern California freeway. This new road is certainly a way to avoid the almost daily commuter gridlock, but it is not free. Users must have a transponder installed on their vehicle's windshield that can be read by an electronic monitor—the "castle"—as they enter the road. Periodically a computer bills the driver's credit card or mails an old-fashioned paper invoice. Anyone seeking to avoid these silent sentries will have their license plates photographed and face state-sanctioned fines of up to $300.

Gerald S. Pfeffer, the managing director of the corporation that owns the new road, explains his company's philosophy: "We're another example of private enterprise filling a gap in government services—the Federal Express of roads." But critics complain that the highway is elitist in that people who can afford the $2.50 rush-hour toll speed along in their luxury cars, while those who can't afford an extra $5.00 a day—more than $1,000 a year—for the round trip must creep along with the poor on the old public freeway. Pfeffer sees nothing wrong with that: "You get what you pay for—the great American way." Besides, toll roads and bridges have long been common in the United States. What is new here is someone collecting tolls for profits and not for governments.

Millions of citizens obviously feel that having the private police, roads, and parks are well worth the cost in money and possible personal restrictions. The problem is that the larger sense of community is often lost. Citizens living in their affluent private enclaves are less likely to vote for spending on public services that they do not use, such as traditional public schools, public parks, and public roads. Indeed, the California legislature specifically authorized the private road because it perceived that there was not sufficient public support to pay additional taxes for new public roads.

The result of this trend toward private services is that the needs of citizens who do not have a "going private" option may be ignored. And since these enclaved communities tend to be overwhelmingly white, this leads to a further balkanization of the body politic. The essential question here is, if certain citizens can afford to buy their way out of common public problems, what kind of public services does that leave for the rest of us? It used to be that the "leading" (meaning richer) citizens would make an effort to solve the problems of their communities because, for better or worse, they were part of it. Now they can just hide behind their walls.

Even people living in the heart of a big city can buy better public services for themselves by creating a "business improvement district"—a quasi-government paid for by taxes on property owners within the district. Almost a thousand of these districts nationwide provide extra sanitation, policing, and other services for their residents. Thus many of the richer neighborhoods in New York City are cleaner and safer because their residents can afford to pay for private sanitation services and private police.

The balkanizing of communities in the Unites States was all too evident in the evacuation of New Orleans before the arrival of Hurricane Katrina. The scenes of the city's poor lining up outside of the Superdome and convention center raised questions about the provision of even the most basic government services. But unlike the moats that kept the masses out of the feudal castles, the masses in the Superdome were trapped by a moat of floodwaters that kept them in.

This new feudalism is just one side of the increasing privatization of the public sector: here, citizens, as is their right, buy the amount of "public" services they can afford. The other side of privatization has government itself contracting for the private provision of public functions. Thus increasingly trash is collected, public buildings are cleaned, and streets are repaired not by public employees but by private sector employees of companies with government contracts. This is often less expensive because such workers are typically paid less than public employees—especially when fringe benefits are considered.

The traditional machinery of government—the administrative structures by which public purposes are achieved—is increasingly being called into question by an angry citizenry that does not always see the contradiction between wanting ever greater government services at ever decreasing costs. Thus privatization, even with its feudal aspects, is seen by some as one means of lowering the overall costs of government, by others as a means of reducing services to the poor, and by still others as a means of eliminating large elements of government altogether. But however it is viewed, and despite the continuing danger of social balkanization, it remains one of the most important tools in reinventing the machinery of government for the twenty-first century.

For Discussion: *Why is it that citizens living in gated communities are less likely to be involved in civic affairs? What does the trend toward gated communities imply for overall public support for increasing taxes and improving public services?*

What Is the Machinery of Government?

The machinery of government consists of all of the structural arrangements adopted by national, state, or local governments to deliver their legally mandated programs and services. This of necessity includes the central management arrangements of government. In all jurisdictions, the organization and eventual reorganization of executive branch agencies is the everlasting machinery of government issue.

Fine-Tuning the Machinery

In 1733 English poet Alexander Pope wrote the following:

For forms of government let fools contest—
That which is best administered is best.

These two lines from his *An Essay on Man* became so well known that Alexander Hamilton, in *The Federalist*, No. 68 (1788), took the trouble to quote them, denounce the sentiment as "political heresy," and then go on to acknowledge, "Yet we may safely pronounce that the true test of a good government is its aptitude and tendency to produce a good administration." Ever since, one test of governing efficacy has been Hamilton's ideal of "good administration." The machinery that a government creates to work its will must be judged by the quality of public administration that it yields. But many political analysts of Hamilton's generation as well as today would argue that no matter how good the quality, it is the quantity that is the crucial thing. Senator Barry Goldwater's often stated warning during his unsuccessful 1964 presidential campaign still resonates: "A government big enough to give you everything you want is a government big enough to take from you everything you have."

Hamilton's contemporary, Thomas Paine, the pamphleteering propagandist of the American Revolution, wrote in *Common Sense* that "society in every state is a blessing, but government, even in its best state, is but a necessary evil; in its worst state an intolerable one." This certainly reflects the sentiments of the modern Republican Party in the United States. Indeed, this party took control of the U.S. Congress during the 1994 midterm election, running on a platform that differs only in detail with Paine's contention. This can all be summed up in the proposition that "government is best which governs least." New England writer Henry David Thoreau began his famous 1849 essay "Civil Disobedience" with this motto, which has also been attributed to Thomas Jefferson, Thomas Paine, and many another doubting Thomases about government.

But if so many good and wise people believed so strongly that government should be "least," how and why did it grow so large? Has the machine grown too big for its most elemental task of producing Hamilton's "good administration"? The task of this chapter is to examine the machinery of government and its effects on administrations good and bad. Always remember, however, that most of the debate over reinventing government and the best public management practices are not about fundamentally changing the nature of governing institutions but about fine-tuning the machinery. To use a mobile metaphor: It's not about reinventing the automobile; it's about getting more miles per gallon of fuel using fewer and less-expensive parts.

The Rise and Fall of Governmental Machinery

Whenever government seeks to address a major issue, it leaves new machinery in its wake. Thus the civil rights movement that began in the 1950s left the Commission on Civil Rights (created in 1957) and the Equal Employment Opportunity Commission (created in 1964). The environmental movement that began in the 1960s left the Environmental Protection Agency (created in 1970). And the war on terrorism that started at the World Trade Center in 2001 has created the Department of Homeland Security. Governmental entities, once established, tend to last a long time and not change easily. They develop constituencies that support their cause. Often they take on new causes that also enhance their support. For example, the Equal Employment Opportunity Commission initially dealt only with cases of workplace discrimination. Today, as federal courts reinterpret the nature of discrimination, it is the nation's prime enforcer of workplace sexual harassment prohibitions as well (see Chapter 12 for more on this).

There is gravity at work in the machinery of government. What goes up can also fall down. For example, the Civil Aeronautics Board, created by the federal government to regulate the airline industry in 1938, was abolished in 1985 as economic deregulation became fashionable. The Office of Technology Assessment, created in 1972 as a support agency of Congress to be an objective source of information on policy alternatives for technology-related issues, was abolished in 1995 as a newly elected Republican-controlled Congress sought to cut costs. In 1996 the Bureau of Mines within the Department of the Interior gave 1,200 of its employees the shaft. This 85-year-old agency was abolished by a Congress less interested in the concerns of

big labor than in big-budget savings. But even when a piece of the government machine is sliced off, it is seldom completely thrown away. For example, Bureau of Mines' workers engaged in coal mine safety were transferred to the Fossil Energy Division of the Department of Energy. And even the most fervent advocates of abolishing the Department of Commerce believe it would be wise to retain the National Weather Service and the Bureau of the Census, albeit in scaled-down forms.

In the United States, the national machinery of government is far more inherently conservative and, in consequence, far more hesitant to change than many other comparable—albeit smaller—democracies, such as Britain, Australia, and New Zealand. However difficult to change, the elements of the machinery of government are not immutable. They can and should be changed as societal needs alter. There is one commonly asked machinery of government question. It was posed by Representative Newt Gingrich in a December 1994 speech accepting his party's nomination to be Speaker of the House: "When you see a large government bureaucracy, is it an inevitable relic of the past that can't be changed, or is it an opportunity for an extraordinary transformation to provide better services and better opportunities at lower cost?" This is one of those questions for which there is only one possible answer: Everybody wants "better services" and "lower costs." But are you willing to tinker with your government machine to get them?

The Administrative Architecture of the U.S. Government

A constitution provides the basic political and legal structure, the architecture, which prescribes the rules by which a government operates. James Madison wrote in *The Federalist*, No. 57 (1788), that "the aim of every political constitution is, or ought to be, first to obtain for rulers men who possess most wisdom to discern, and most virtue to pursue, the common good of the society; and in the next place, to take the most effectual precautions for keeping them virtuous whilst they continue to hold their public trust." While Madison asserted that the first aim was to find appropriate "men," he would certainly reconsider that word if he were writing today. To be sure, he would use a sexually neutral term such as *people, individuals,* or *persons.* But this does not go far enough—because the primary task of rulers in all modern constitutional systems is administration. So "administrators" should replace "men" in Madison's political philosophy because administrators are those who run a constitution. The echo of Woodrow Wilson's famous statement that "it is getting harder to run a constitution than to frame one" is loud and clear. Madison is generally considered the primary framer of the Constitution. But if he had lived to see what his handiwork had wrought, he would be much more concerned about running it.

The Constitution, with its famous opening words "We the people," asserts that the source of its authority is the people as opposed to the states. It then assigns powers to the various branches of government and in doing so structures the government. It

---

big labor The major American labor unions and their federations.

limits the powers that any branch may have through a system of **checks and balances.** Most significantly, it denies certain powers to the national government by reserving them for the states and the people.

American politics has grown up around the Constitution and has been, thereby, "constitutionalized." Many domestic political issues are eventually treated in constitutional terms—for example, civil rights, crime, pornography, abortion, and impeachment, to name but some of the more obvious cases. Only the realm of foreign affairs has substantially escaped this tendency, although the war on terror has increasingly brought back questions of the rights of prisoners to the American courts. In addressing matters of government and politics, Americans are likely to pose as the first question "Is it constitutional?" Only afterward are the desirabilities of policies and government arrangements considered on their own merits. In the 1819 case of *McCulloch v. Maryland,* the Supreme Court explained how to tell if something is constitutional: "Let the end be legitimate, let it be within the scope of the Constitution, and all means which are appropriate, which are plainly adapted to that end, which are not prohibited, but consist with the letter and spirit of the Constitution, are constitutional."

Unlike the British parliamentary machinery of government that evolved over hundreds of years, the American machinery was created at one moment in time for its specific purpose. The Constitutional Convention of 1787 was truly the world's first reinventing government movement. And the government it invented was designed to be inefficient. Because of their experiences under British rule, Americans have historically been suspicious of a too-efficient government, feeling that an overly efficient administration of public affairs could eventually eat into political liberties. Chief Justice Warren Burger, writing for the Court in *Immigration and Naturalization Service v. Chadha* (1983), offered this opinion:

> It is crystal clear from the records of the [Constitutional] Convention, contemporaneous writings and debates, that the Framers ranked other values higher than efficiency. . . . The choices we discern as having been made in the Constitutional Convention impose burdens on governmental processes that often seem clumsy, inefficient, and even unworkable, but those hard choices were consciously made by men who had lived under a form of government that permitted arbitrary governmental acts to go unchecked.

The modern U.S. Supreme Court then reaffirmed the value of inefficiency when it asserted in the *Chadha* case that "there is no support in the Constitution or decisions of this Court for the proposition that the cumbersomeness and delays often encountered in complying with explicit Constitutional standards may be avoided, either by the Congress or by the president." The Court unanimously declared its support for red tape, the treasured procedural safeguards that protect us even when

---

checks and balances The notion that constitutional devices can prevent any power within a nation from becoming absolute by being balanced against, or checked by, another source of power within that same nation. The U.S. Constitution is often described as a system of checks and balances. For example, it allows the president to check Congress by vetoing a bill and Congress to check the president by overriding a veto or refusing to ratify treaties or confirm nominees to federal office. The Supreme Court can check either by declaring laws passed by Congress or actions taken by the president to be unconstitutional.

we do not wish to be protected, and the law's delay. And they have done this as they stated in the *Chadha* case because "with all the obvious flaws of delay, untidiness, and potential for abuse, we have not yet found a better way to preserve freedom than by making the exercise of power subject to the carefully crafted restraints spelled out in the Constitution."

Executive Branch Machinery

One glance at an organization chart of the U.S. government and we can see immediately that the most complex part of the machinery of government lies in the executive branch; the other two branches seem small by comparison, with comparatively few subdivisions (see Figure 3.1). While the inefficiency of the separation of powers is to be highly valued for its protection of basic liberties, this is no excuse for individual agencies to be inefficient as organizations. Indeed, the whole thrust of American public administration reform over the past century has been to create efficient subunits within an overall inefficient system.

Although the executive branch has the most complex structure, the other two branches are also of interest from a machinery-of-government point of view. For example, the U.S. Supreme Court has ultimate administrative responsibility for the entire federal court system. And while most citizens know that the legislative branch contains the Senate and the House of Representatives, not so many realize that other important agencies are located in this branch, ranging from the Architect of the Capitol and the U.S. Botanic Garden to the Library of Congress and the Government Accountability Office (GAO). This last agency is of critical importance, allowing Congress to exercise financial oversight of the executive branch. The GAO would be severely diminished if its functions were located within the executive branch, as it frequently is within democracies based on the British **parliamentary system.** (The GAO's work is discussed in more detail in Chapter 14.)

The executive branch, headed by the president, contains the machinery that serves to implement national policies established by both constitutional and legislative means. There are three main categories of organizations in the structure of the executive branch: (1) executive office agencies, (2) executive departments, and (3) independent public bodies.

---

parliamentary system A means of governance whose power is concentrated in a legislature, which selects from among its members a prime minister and his or her cabinet officers. The government—that is, the prime minister and the cabinet—stays in power as long as it commands a majority of the Parliament. When the government loses its majority (loses a vote of confidence), elections must be held within a prescribed time period (or at least every five years in British practice). The main differences between a parliamentary system (which most of the democratic countries of the world use) and the American system are (1) the ease with which a parliamentary government can be changed if it falls out of favor with a majority in the legislature and (2) the lack of checks and balances in a parliamentary system. The legislative and the executive branches are one in a parliamentary system. The prime minister represents the legislature and, through them, the voters. The major check on his or her power is the constant possibility that his or her party will lose its working majority.

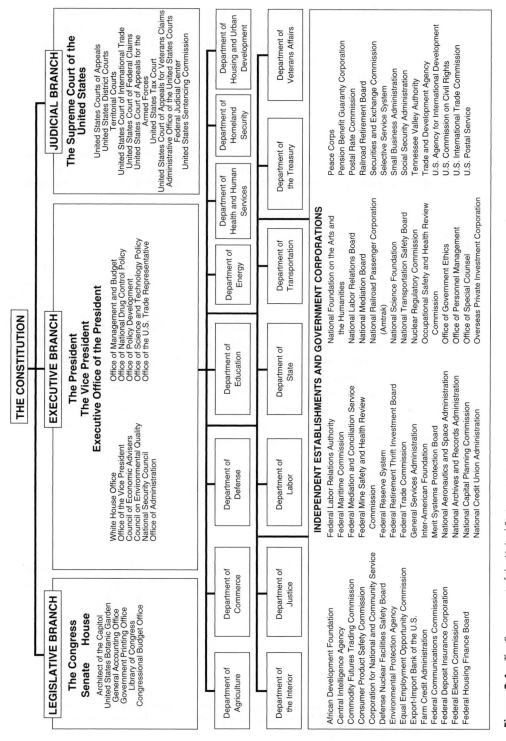

Figure 3.1 The Government of the United States   SOURCE: *U.S. Government Manual 2003/2004.*

Executive Office Agencies   The Executive Office of the President (EOP) is an umbrella office consisting of the top presidential staff agencies that provide the president help and advice in carrying out major responsibilities. These include, as you might expect, some agencies that are concerned with "head office" functions of policy, planning, and resource allocation, such as the Office of Management and Budget, the Council of Economic Advisers, and the National Security Council. But some exist to signify important national priorities, such as the Office of National Drug Control Policy and the Council on Environmental Quality.

Executive Departments   There are 15 executive **departments.** As a group they constitute the president's cabinet. This is an institution whose existence rests on custom rather than constitutional provision, even though its chief members, the secretaries of the federal executive departments, must be approved by the Senate. It came into being as a single body because President George Washington found it useful to meet with the chiefs of the several executive departments. While all subsequent presidents have considered it necessary to meet with the cabinet, their attitudes toward the institution and its members have varied greatly. Some presidents have convened their cabinet only for the most formal and routine matters, while others have relied on it for advice and support. The president's cabinet differs from the cabinet in the British parliamentary system in that in the United States the executive power is not shared by the cabinet as a whole but is constitutionally vested solely in the president. This is famously illustrated by a story about Abraham Lincoln. During the Civil War he called his cabinet together to discuss a pressing matter of war policy. Wanting to get a sense of their feelings, he called for a vote. They all voted "nay." Lincoln alone voted "aye." Yet, as president, he declared, "The ayes have it."

At the present time, cabinet membership consists of the secretaries of 15 executive departments, the newest member being the secretary of Homeland Security. But a substantial part of the executive branch is not represented in the cabinet. From the earliest days, presidents have accorded to others the privilege of attending and participating in cabinet meetings. In recent years, the United States ambassador to the United Nations and the director of the Office of Management and Budget, among others, have been accorded cabinet rank to symbolize the importance of the functions they represent. However, not all cabinet members are equal. The "inner" cabinet refers to the federal departments of State, Defense, Treasury, and Justice—because they (and their secretaries) tend to be more prominent and influential in every administration than the rest of the cabinet. While all cabinet secretaries are equal in rank and salary, the missions of those in the inner cabinet tend to give them an advantage in prestige, access, and visibility denied to those who head the rest of, or the "outer," cabinet.

But for better or worse, according to political scientists Edward Weisband and Thomas M. Frank: "Cabinet meetings in the United States, despite occasional

---

department A confusing word. While it can refer to a cabinet-level agency of the U.S. government, it can also refer to one of the three branches of government: executive, legislative, or judicial. But it is also used as a general term for any administrative subdivision. Thus the Department of the Navy is within the Department of Defense.

efforts to make them into significant decision-making occasions, have, at least in this century, been characterized as vapid nonevents in which there has been a deliberate nonexchange of information as part of a process of mutual nonconsultation." The president's cabinet has never functioned as a unified team. The American machinery of government, which requires cabinet secretaries to be responsible both to the president and the Congress (with its competing interests) makes that virtually impossible.

The structure of U.S. government departments is a reasonably deft selection of topics likely to need a national focus by government. But these topics are not the only ones that could be represented at this level. They represent choices among competing priorities. There is no federal Department of the Environment, for example, which means that environmental issues must be voiced through other departments. While the Clinton administration called for such a new department, its **loyal opposition** in the Congress not only opposed it but made efforts to repeal much of the environmental protection legislation such a department would administer.

Independent Public Bodies   The third main area of the U.S. national machinery of government is formed by independent establishments and government corporations. They range in purpose from public business **corporations** (such as the U.S. Postal Service, the Export-Import Bank of the United States, and Amtrak—the National Railroad Passenger Corporation) to important regulators and watchdogs (such as the Environmental Protection Agency and the Commission on Civil Rights) to foundations committed to worthy purposes, such as the National Science Foundation and the African Development Foundation.

A regulatory **commission** is an independent agency established by Congress to regulate some aspect of U.S. economic life. Among these are the Securities and Exchange Commission (SEC) and the Federal Communications Commission (FCC). Such agencies are, of course, not independent of the U.S. government. They are subject to the laws under which they operate as these laws are enacted and amended by Congress. Independent agencies and regulatory commissions can be divided into two categories: (1) those units under the direct supervision and guidance of the president, and therefore responsible to him, and (2) those not under such supervision and guidance, and therefore not responsible to him.

---

loyal opposition In a two-party system, the party out of power but loyal to the interest of the nation as a whole.

corporation An organization formed under state or federal law that exists, for legal purposes, as a separate being or an artificial person. It may be public (set up by the government) or private (set up by individuals), and it may be created to carry on a business or to perform almost any function. It may be owned by the government or by a few persons, or it may be a "publicly owned corporation"—owned by members of the general public who buy its shares on an open stock market such as the New York Stock Exchange.

commission A group charged with directing a government function, whether on an ad hoc or a permanent basis. Commissions tend to be used (1) when it is desirable to have bipartisan leadership, (2) when their functions are of a quasi-judicial nature, or (3) when it is deemed important to have wide representation of ethnic groups, regions of the country, differing skills, and so on.

Independent executive agencies, with rare exceptions, are headed by single administrators appointed by the president and confirmed by the Senate. These administrators serve at the pleasure of the president and can be removed by the president at any time. In addition, they must submit their budget requests to the Office of Management and Budget (OMB), which is located within the Executive Office of the president, for review and clearance. Examples of independent executive agencies include the Central Intelligence Agency, the Environmental Protection Agency, the General Services Administration, and the Small Business Administration.

Independent regulatory commissions (such as the FCC and SEC) and government-sponsored enterprises (such as the Tennessee Valley Authority) are bodies headed by several commissioners, directors, or governors, who are also appointed by the president and confirmed by the Senate. But unlike administrators of independent executive agencies, they serve for fixed terms and cannot be removed at the pleasure of the president. When Franklin Roosevelt sought to dismiss commissioners of the Federal Trade Commission (FTC) for disagreements over policy, the Supreme Court ruled in *Humphrey's Executor v. United States* (1935) that the FTC "occupies no place in the executive department." Thus all such commissioners can serve to the end of their fixed terms unless impeached by Congress. This independence from direct executive control can be a source of considerable strength to individuals who serve on regulatory boards and commissions. Nowhere is this power more evident than with the Federal Reserve Board and its panel of governors. The "Fed," as it's commonly known, has the authority to set monetary policy in the United States and therefore can directly impact the performance of the nation's economy. Not surprisingly, then, the chair of the Fed's Board of Governors is one of the nation's most powerful government officials.

Note that many regulatory functions are also performed by traditional cabinet departments. For example, the Food and Drug Administration is located within the Department of Health and Human Services. And the Office of Federal Contract Compliance, which monitors behavior of corporations that do business with the government, is located within the Department of Labor.

Government corporation is the term used for a government-owned corporation or an agency of government that administers a self-supporting enterprise in the following situations:

1. When an agency's business is essentially commercial

2. When an agency can generate its own revenue

3. When the agency's mission requires greater flexibility than government agencies normally have

Examples of federal government corporations include the Saint Lawrence Seaway Development Corporation, the Federal Deposit Insurance Corporation, Amtrak, and the Tennessee Valley Authority. At the state and municipal levels, corporations (often bearing different names, such as authorities) operate enterprises such as turnpikes, airports, and harbors. As we discuss later in this chapter, there has been an increased push, especially under Republican administrations, for many government corporations to be dissolved or sold to private entities.

State and Local Government Machinery

American subnational governments are individually smaller than the national government but collectively far larger (see Table 3.1). The number of public employees is a good indicator of this disparity. The federal government, excluding the armed forces, has just about 2.7 million civilian employees. But state and local employment exceeds 17 million. The machinery of government at the state and local levels parallels the national model with legislative, executive, and judicial branches. The Tenth Amendment, the last part of the Bill of Rights, holds that the "powers not delegated to the United States by the Constitution, nor prohibited by it to the states, are reserved to the states respectively, or to the people." This means that whatever the federal government cannot constitutionally do for the people, the states and their subunits must or may do. Significantly, the national Constitution does not mention cities, counties, or any other type of local government. They are all creatures of their states; their powers are derived from state law; and what a state gives a state may later take away.

The primacy of state over local law is the essence of Dillon's rule—a rule famously formulated by Judge John F. Dillon in his 1911 *Commentaries on the Law of Municipal Corporations*. The rule outlines criteria developed by state courts to determine the nature and extent of powers granted to local governments. It holds that municipal corporations have only those powers (1) expressly granted in the city charter, (2) necessarily or fairly implied by or incidental to formally expressed powers, and (3) essential to the declared purposes of the corporation. "Any fair, reasonable, substantial doubt" about a power is to result in denying that power to the corporation. In some states, the rule has been relaxed, especially in dealing with **home rule** cities. The essence of Dillon's rule was upheld by the Supreme Court in *City of Trenton v. State of New Jersey* (1913).

TABLE 3.1   Governments in the United States

Type	Number
National	1
State	50
County	3,034
Municipal	19,429
Townships/Towns	16,504
School Districts	13,506
Special Districts	35,052
Total	87,576

SOURCE: *Statistical Abstract of the United States* (2004).

---

home rule The ability, the power, of a municipal corporation to develop and implement its own charter. It resulted from the urban reform movement of the early twentieth century, which hoped to remove urban politics from the harmful influence of state politics. Home rule can be either a statutory or a constitutional system and varies in its details from state to state.

State Government

The elected chief executive of a state government is the governor. The responsibilities of a governor usually parallel those of a U.S. president, on a smaller scale, but each governor has only the powers granted to the office by the state constitution. Some states severely limit executive powers, while others give their governors powers, such as the **item veto,** that are greater than those possessed by the president of the United States. The term of office for a governor is four years in all states except Arkansas, New Hampshire, Rhode Island, and Vermont, where it is two. Currently 38 states have limits on the number of terms that their governors can serve, with most allowing two or three four-year terms. In one sense, it is a misnomer to call a governor the chief executive of a state. The reality is that most state constitutions provide for what amounts to a plural executive, because governors, in marked contrast to the U.S. president, typically must share powers with a variety of other independently elected executive branch officers, such as a secretary of state, an attorney general, a treasurer, and an auditor (or controller). Consequently, a governor's informal powers as a lobbyist for his or her initiatives and as head of his or her party may often be far more useful than the formal authority that comes with the office. Nevertheless, the management job of a governor compares favorably in terms of responsibility to those of the highest-paid corporate executives. For example, in terms of revenues, more than half the states would rank among the top 100 corporations in America. Most would be among the top 200 of the **Fortune 500.**

The lieutenant governor is the elected state official who would replace the governor should he or she be unable to complete a term of office. The office parallels that of the vice president in the national government but differs in that in many states the lieutenant governor is separately elected and thus may be of a different party from the governor. This can sometimes cause considerable friction when the two officeholders are political rivals—and especially when, as in California, the lieutenant governor assumes some of the governor's powers to act whenever the governor is out of the state. Arizona, Maine, New Hampshire, New Jersey, Oregon, West Virginia, and Wyoming have no lieutenant governors. In four of these states, the president of the state senate would succeed to the governorship; in the other three, the secretary of state succeeds.

The story is often told of Calvin Coolidge, then the lieutenant governor of Massachusetts, who met a woman at a dinner party. She asked him, "What do you do?"

He replied, "I'm the lieutenant governor."

"How interesting, you must tell me all about it," she said.

Coolidge then replied, "I just did." While Coolidge was notoriously tight-lipped, his summation of the limited responsibilities of the office of lieutenant governor was drawn from reality.

---

item veto The executive power to veto separate items in a bill. This is also known as the line-item veto.
Fortune 500 A size-ordered (based on gross revenues) directory of the 500 largest U.S. corporations published each year since 1955 by *Fortune* magazine.

BOX 3.1   The Meaning of Gubernatorial

Gubernatorial is the strange word that refers to things pertaining to the office of governor. It comes from the Greek *kybernan,* meaning "to direct a ship." The Romans borrowed the word from the Greeks as *guberno.* Then the French took it and sent it across the English Channel as *"governor."* When the word is used as an adjective, it goes back to its Latin roots: *"gubernatorial."*

County Government

The county is the basic unit for administrative decentralization of state government. Although it is typically governed by an elected board or commission, there is a movement at present toward a county administrator or executive (sometimes elected). In Louisiana, the comparable unit is called a parish; in Alaska, it is a borough. In 2002, the United States had 3,043 county governments. Each state determines for itself how many counties it will have. The elected officials of county government have a bewildering array of titles. According to Dade County, Florida, Commissioner Harvey Ruvin, speaking in 1989, county officials "are supervisors in California, judges in Texas, jurors in Louisiana, freeholders in New Jersey, county legislators in New York, commissioners in Dade. If I tell somebody from New York I'm a commissioner, they think I'm the dog catcher. No wonder the public and the media focus on governors and mayors."

The county seat is the capital of a county, where the courts and administrative offices are located. In much of the United States, the county seat was located in the geographical center of the county so that it would not be more than one day's ride on horseback from the farthest part of the county. This is why there are so many counties. Since few citizens ride horses to government offices today, it would seem to make a lot of sense to combine many counties and thus realize substantial savings from having fewer county clerks, county sheriffs, county courts, and so on. But which clerk, sheriff, or judge is going to quietly resign? The conundrum of reforming the machinery of government can often be summarized by the phrase "You can't get there from here!" Of course, the multiplicity of governing entities allows for greater democratic control in that government is kept closer to the people. Nevertheless, reformers constantly ask if the benefits derived are worth the extra costs of fragmented government, with a number of consolidations between county and municipal governments occurring in recent decades. A prominent example is the recent consolidation of Jefferson County Kentucky with the city of Louisville into a unified metropolitan (metro) government. We will examine the concept of metro government later in this chapter.

Tanis Janes Salant has classified the forms of county government as follows:

1. **Commission Form.** An elected county commission or board of supervisors, which is the most common form of county government, has legislative authority

(e.g., to enact ordinances, levy certain taxes, and adopt budgets), as well as executive and administrative authority (e.g., to administer local, state, and federal policies, appoint county employees, and supervise road work). Typically, however, administrative responsibilities are also vested in independently elected constitutional officers, such as a county sheriff, treasurer, coroner, clerk, auditor, assessor, and prosecutor.

2. **Commission-Administrator.** There are three basic types of this form, some of which also have additional, independently elected constitutional officers. About 786 counties have one type of this form.

   A. **Council Manager.** The county council or board, which is the legislative body, appoints a county manager who performs executive functions, such as appointing department heads, hiring county staff, administering county programs, drafting budgets, and proposing ordinances.

   B. **Chief Administrative Officer.** The county board or commission, as the legislative and quasi-executive body, appoints a chief administrative officer to supervise and coordinate county departments, but not appoint department heads, and to prepare budgets, draft ordinances, and oversee program implementation.

   C. **County Administrative Assistant.** The county board or commission, as the legislative and executive body, appoints an administrative assistant to help carry out the commission's responsibilities.

3. **Council-Executive.** A county executive is independently elected by the people to perform specific executive functions. The county board or commission remains the legislative body, but the county executive may veto ordinances enacted by the commission, with the commission having override power by an extraordinary majority vote. The county executive's authority and responsibilities are much like those of a mayor in a strong mayor-council municipality. About 383 counties have this form.

Municipal Government

Municipal refers to something of local government concern—such as municipal bonds or municipal parks. It implies that the thing it modifies is of internal concern to a state—as opposed to international concern. It comes from the Latin word *municipium,* which was a self-governing body within the ancient Roman Empire. A city is a municipal corporation chartered by its state. A political subdivision must meet various state requirements before it can qualify for a **city charter;** for example, it must usually have a population above a state-established minimum level.

---

city charter A document that spells out the purposes and powers of a municipal corporation. To operate, a municipal corporation must have a charter like any other corporation. The municipality can perform only those functions and exercise only those powers that are in the charter. If the particular state permits home rule, a city can develop and implement its own charter. Otherwise, it is limited to statutory charters spelled out by the state legislature.

A city council is the legislative branch, typically **unicameral,** of a municipal government. The duties of city council members vary greatly, but in almost all cases the most significant functions include passing ordinances (local laws) and controlling expenditures.

A mayor is the elected chief executive officer of a municipal corporation, the chief ceremonial officer of a city. In most modest-sized and small cities, the office of mayor is a part-time job. He or she may be directly elected. The smaller the city, the more likely that the election will be nonpartisan or that the city council will select a mayor from among its members; then the mayor simply presides as the first among equals on the council. While many big-city mayors have become national figures, no mayor has ever been able to make the leap directly from city hall to the White House—or has even been able to get a major party's nomination for president.

There has long been a bias in American government and American political thought against cities. For example, Thomas Jefferson expressed a common opinion when he wrote in a December 20, 1787, letter to James Madison, "I think our governments will remain virtuous for many centuries; as long as they are chiefly agricultural; and this will be as long as there shall be vacant lands in any part of America. When they get piled upon one another in large cities, as in Europe, they will become corrupt as in Europe." But a more tangible harm to cities was found in state and federal policies that denied their residents their fair share of representatives in the Congress and in state legislatures. This bias existed until the Supreme Court, beginning in 1962 with *Baker v. Carr,* issued a series of decisions that finally ended **apportionment** in favor of rural areas. The cities were finally made political equals.

Towns and Special Districts

A town is an urban population center—larger than a village but smaller than a city. Typically, its state statutory powers are less than those possessed by cities. The New England town combines the role of both city and county. It usually contains one or more urban areas plus surrounding rural areas. The town meeting is a method of self-government, suitable for only the smallest jurisdictions, where the entire citizenry is eligible to meet to decide local public policy. The town meeting is still the governing body for 88 percent of all New England municipalities. According to journalist Robert Preer, town meetings today are most likely to be controlled by special interests and the town's bureaucracy. Attendance is slight. Even though quorums

---

unicameral A legislature with only one chamber, as opposed to a bicameral one with two—typically a house and a senate. Nebraska is the only state with a unicameral legislature.

apportionment A determination of how many legislators should be sent to a legislative body from a given jurisdiction. The U.S. Constitution provides that each state is entitled to two senators and at least one representative. Beyond the minimum, representatives are apportioned among the states according to population. This apportionment is adjusted after every ten-year census. Under the Apportionment Act of 1929, Congress fixed the size of the House of Representatives at 435 seats, and after each census Congress assigns the appropriate number of seats to each state. The states themselves carry on from there. The actual redistributing process is a matter of state law, with one major exception: In 1967 Congress prohibited at-large elections in all states entitled to more than one seat in the House.

are set at only 1 or 2 percent of registered voters, meetings are often canceled because of the lack of a quorum. "Raises and promotions pass with ease because meetings are so often packed with employees and their families and friends." Preer concludes that the modern town meeting "is a microcosm of national politics. In both cases, power has shifted from an apathetic and unorganized public to special interests, the mass media, and a bureaucratic-technocratic elite."

A special district is a unit of local government typically performing a single function and overlapping traditional political boundaries. Examples include transportation districts, fire protection districts, library districts, water districts, sewer districts, and so on. Because special districts are such useful devices, they have been multiplying rapidly. In 1942 there were only 8,299 of them in the entire United States. Today there are more than 35,000—not including school districts. They constitute more than one-third of all American government entities.

A school district is a special district for the provision of local public education for all children in its service area. An elected board, the typical governing body, usually hires a professional superintendent to administer the system. School districts often have their own taxing authority. Many are administratively, financially, and politically independent of other local government units. The total number of school districts has been constantly shrinking because of the increasingly common phenomenon of merging two or more districts. There were more than 108,000 school districts in 1942; today there are fewer than 14,000.

Local Management Machinery

Local government leadership in the majority of jurisdictions overwhelmingly consists of part-time elected volunteers. Tens of thousands of citizens of middle- and small-sized local governments serve as elected or appointed unpaid (or symbolically paid) council, commission, and board members. Often these amateurs appoint a full-time professional manager. The council-manager plan is a form of municipal government in which an elected city council appoints a professional city manager to administer the city government. A county-manager system offers the same essential structure at the county level.

A city manager is the chief executive of the council-manager system of local government. In contrast to the heads of other types of government, the city manager is an appointed chief executive serving at the pleasure of the council. The concept originated early in the twentieth century by progressive reformers who wanted to replace political **bossism** with municipal experts. To do this effectively, they created the concept of an administrative chief executive armed with critical administrative powers, such as appointment and removal of administrative officials, but denied any political

---

bossism An informal system of local government in which public power is concentrated in the hands of a central figure, called a political boss, who may not have a formal government position. The power is concentrated through the use of a political machine, whereby a hierarchy is created and maintained through the use of patronage and government largesse to ensure compliance with the wishes of the boss. It was a dominant system in American city government after the Civil War and was the main target of the American urban reform effort. Few authentic bosses exist today.

powers, such as the veto. The city manager concept was sold to the cities as being just like a corporation with its board of directors. The dichotomy between administration and politics (remember Woodrow Wilson) upon which the system was premised was implemented by putting all of the policymaking and political functions into the city council, essentially abolishing any separation of powers in the traditional sense at the local level. The decision making ability of the council was ensured by (1) creating a small council, typically from five to nine members, elected through at-large, nonpartisan elections, and (2) permitting the council to hire and fire the city manager, their expert in the implementation of community policies.

Present council-manager systems often deviate from this traditional model. Many, particularly in bigger cities, have large councils, partisan elections, and separately elected mayors, and some if not all of the council members are elected from a **ward** or district. In fact, some recent federal court decisions have required ward elections in some cities because **at-large** elections make it more difficult for minority candidates to be elected. In some larger cities, a variant of the system has evolved, utilizing a chief administrative officer often appointed by the mayor.

The council-manager system has been criticized by some political scientists as being unresponsive to some elements of the community and supported by public administration experts for its effective management in the public interest. Yet even when a city manager delivers effective public management, it is important to remember that he or she is working in an expressly political environment. The best managers are those who are able to neatly balance political pressures with service delivery, thus addressing the real needs of the public.

The mayor-council system is a form of urban government that has a separately elected executive (the mayor) and an urban legislature (the council) usually elected in partisan ward elections. It is called a strong mayor system if the office of mayor is filled by separate citywide elections and has such powers as veto, appointment, and removal. Where the office of mayor lacks such powers, it is called a weak mayor system. This designation does not take into account any informal powers possessed by the incumbent mayor—only the formal powers of the office. Hence, someone can be a strong mayor in terms of actual power in a weak mayor system.

Metropolitan Government

Most larger American cities today cover wide geographical areas. They may have an old urban center with sprawling suburbs extending for many miles, connected to the center by freeways and other forms of urban transportation. The governance of such large conurbations or metropolises presents several options and philosophical choices. There could be a single local government covering the whole area and

---

ward A subdivision of a city, often used as a legislative district for city council elections, as an administrative division for public services or as a unit for the organization of political parties. A ward is often further divided into precincts.

at-large An election in which one or more candidates for a legislature are chosen by all of the voters of a jurisdiction. This is in contrast to an election by legislative district, in which voters are limited to selecting one candidate to represent their district.

providing for all. There could be, at the other end of the spectrum, total fragmentation, with many suburban local governments, and even fragmentation within the old center. Or there could be a variety of compromises in between—such as the two-tier government in Miami-Dade County, Florida, where functions are split between an overall metropolitan government and particular localities. The Lakewood Plan, in force in California for many years, offers another option: Local governments remain within the county, but they contract for many of their services from the county.

The adoption of the appropriate machinery of government for a metropolis depends on values. Often, richer and predominantly white residents prefer to withdraw to the suburbs and live under a fragmented local government system, which can avoid the costs of aging urban infrastructure and the social costs of policing and welfare in poorer areas. But fragmented local government lacks the muscle to put investment into social capital that benefits everybody—such as extensive transit systems, museums, parks and land preserves.

It is also difficult to address regional issues such as transportation and economic development when government authority is highly dispersed among many small governments. A 2004 study by the Brookings Institution attributed many of the state of Pennsylvania's economic and environmental problems on one of the nation's most fragmented systems of local government (see Box 3.2).

Conversely, it's no coincidence that one of the finest transit systems in North America is in Toronto, Canada, where Metro Toronto provides a strong metropolitan government approach. Of course, many wealthier Americans would rather not have any local government at all, but rely instead on private corporations to service their (often gated) communities, distant from urban problems and exempt from both urban costs and urban politics. It's an option some like, but such a degree of civic disengagement is not for everybody. A major method for coordinating the efforts of metropolitan governments is through a council of governments (COG). These institutional forums for voluntary cooperation offer many advantages, especially in comprehensive planning and jointly seeking federal funding for regional programs. COGs are discussed further in Chapter 4.

Continuous State and Local Reform

The progressive reform movement left in its wake some reform institutions that continue to encourage improvements in state and local government machinery. At the beginning of the twentieth century, municipal research bureaus—private nonprofit good government organizations—were established in most major cities. This "bureau movement" emphasized fact finding and the application of the scientific method to urban reform; this was in marked contrast to the simplistic "throw the rascals out" tactics of earlier reform efforts. The New York Bureau of Municipal Research, founded in 1906, pioneered with investigations of wasteful municipal spending (double billing, work paid for but not performed, etc.) that, when it was published, so shocked the community that real administrative reforms followed. The investigatory approach of the New York Bureau (now called the Institute of Public Administration) was then imitated in Philadelphia, Cincinnati, Chicago, Milwaukee, Kansas City, San Francisco, and elsewhere.

> **BOX 3.2   Government Fragmentation: The Pennsylvania Story**
>
> Pennsylvania is known for many things. From its historical treasures of Indepen-
> dence Hall, Gettysburg, and Valley Forge, to its culinary masterpieces of
> cheesesteaks and soft pretzels, the Keystone State has many distinguishing
> qualities. For those interested in the study of local government, Pennsylvania
> may be most known for its incredibly fragmented system of local governance.
> According to the Census Bureau, Pennsylvania has 2,630 local governments,
> amounting to one unit of general government for every 4,760 residents of the
> state. While the abundance of local governments may provide for an intimate
> relationship between the government and the governed, the fragmented
> nature of the system has also come under increased criticism for its inability to
> deal with many of the problems facing the state. A recent study by the Brook-
> ings Institution in Washington, DC, found that the highly decentralized struc-
> ture of Pennsylvania's governments works against strategic planning for
> economic development, transportation, and environmental preservation—thus
> placing the state at a competitive disadvantage with other states. In particular,
> the thousands of small governments and authorities stymie planning for busi-
> ness development, open-space conservation, and growth supported by public
> infrastructure. The effects of fragmentation are most pronounced in the area
> of land management, where state law delegates land-use authority to 2,566
> municipalities, placing these important decisions at a level of government with
> very limited capacity to manage them. While many analysts both in and outside
> the state have brought the problems of fragmentation to the public's atten-
> tion, there have only been nine municipal mergers since 1956 and very limited
> changes to the state's planning code. Even with evidence accumulating on the
> disadvantages of fragmentation, Pennsylvanians are very hesitant to make any
> moves that transfer power from the level of government that is closest to them.
>
> SOURCE: Adapted from Brookings Institution, Back to Prosperity: A Competitive Agenda For Renewing Penn-
> sylvania, December 2003. http://www.brookings.edu/es/urban/publications/pa.htm.

The bureau movement was the primary vehicle for developing, and then advocating the implementation of, many administrative innovations that we take for
granted today—for example, executive budgeting, uniform accounting standards,
merit system selection and staffing procedures, retirement systems, uniform crime
statistics, and in-service training. This movement was the source of much of the
early scholarly research in public administration. Indeed, it is not an exaggeration
to say that academic public administration was almost wholly created in its initial
stages by scholars associated with the various bureaus. Today the movement continues with local good government organizations such as the Pennsylvania Economy League that focus on efficient and responsive implementation of government
policies.

Reforming the National Machinery of Government

It all started with the conquest of England in 1066. William the Conqueror appointed commissioners to make an inventory of the assets of his new kingdom. This report, known as the Doomsday Book (because its findings were as beyond appeal as a Doomsday judgment), is the predecessor of today's royal or presidential commissions and committees. Ever since, prime ministers and presidents have used these devices to investigate a matter of public concern and to issue recommendations for improvement. There is great public satisfaction to be had in bringing together a group of responsible, respected, supposedly objective but knowledgeable citizens to examine and report on a national problem or major disaster.

BOX 3.3   How Machinery Begins: Benjamin Franklin Invents the Fire Department in Colonial Philadelphia

I wrote a paper on the different accidents and carelessnesses by which houses were set on fire, with cautions against them, and means proposed of avoiding them. This was much spoken of as a useful piece, and gave rise to a project, which soon followed it, of forming a company for the more ready extinguishing of fires, and mutual assistance in removing and securing of goods when in danger. Associates in this scheme were presently found, amounting to thirty. Our articles of agreement oblig'd every member to keep always in good order, and fit for use, a certain number of leather buckets, with strong bags and baskets (for packing and transporting of goods), which were to be brought to every fire; and we agreed to meet once a month and spend a social evening together, in discoursing and communicating such ideas as occurred to us upon the subject of fires, as might be useful in our conduct on such occasions.

The utility of this institution soon appeared, and many more desiring to be admitted than we thought convenient for one company, they were advised to form another, which was accordingly done; and this went on, one new company being formed after another, till they became so numerous as to include most of the inhabitants who were men of property; and now, at the time of my writing this, tho' upward of fifty years since its establishment, that which I first formed, called the Union Fire Company, still subsists and flourishes, tho' the first members are all deceas'd but myself and one, who is older by a year than I am. The small fines that have been paid by members for absence at the monthly meetings have been apply'd to the purchase of fire-engines, ladders, fire-hooks, and other useful implements for each company, so that I question whether there is a city in the world better provided with the means of putting a stop to beginning conflagrations; and, in fact, since these institutions, the city has never lost by fire more than one or two houses at a time, and the flames have often been extinguished before the house in which they began has been half consumed.

SOURCE: *The Autobiography of Benjamin Franklin* (New York: Washington Square Press, 1955).

Such commissions have proven to be handy devices for a modern president who, when faced with an intractable problem, such as crime, pornography, or urban riots, can, at slight expense, appoint a commission as a gesture to indicate his awareness of constituent distress. Whether that gesture has meaning or sincerity beyond itself is inconsequential for its immediate effect. By the time a commission makes its report, six months to a year later, attention will have been diverted to other issues, and the recommendations can be safely pigeonholed or curtailed.

Often such commissions (or committees) have been used to tinker with the machinery of government. Evolution inexorably marches on. Just as birds are now thought to be all that is left of the dinosaurs, the modern performance review can trace its lineage to the Doomsday Book. Both are efforts by the prevailing regime to assess a present situation so that it can be better repositioned. William the Conqueror used his assessment to restructure England's tax system. A later William—President William Jefferson Clinton—used his to try to reinvent government.

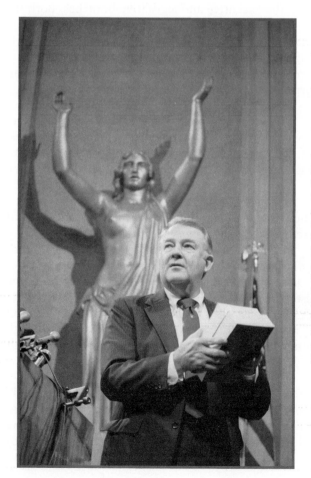

Then Attorney General Edwin Meese on July 9, 1986, holds up the final report of the Attorney General's Commission on Pornography, which called for sweeping changes in federal and state laws concerning the availability of pornographic materials. Here is an example of a commission appointed to assuage a traditional—in this case a moral values—constituency. Nothing came of it except for this famous picture of the attorney general of the United States incongruously denouncing pornography in front of a statue of a half-bare-breasted woman. This statue, known as *The Spirit of Justice,* had been in the Justice Department auditorium for decades. In 2002 Attorney General John Ashcroft had dark curtains placed in front of the statue—presumably because he did not wish to be associated with *The Spirit of Justice.* Nevertheless, when Attorney General Alberto Gonzalez became the leader at the Justice Department, the curtains came down and the Spirit of Justice was revealed in her original form.

(SOURCE: *Washington Post,* Saturday, June 25, 2005.)

ironies of gov't + governing

The Brownlow Committee

The advent of the 1990s reinventing government movement once again made reorganization a fashionable theme in the practice and literature of American public administration. However, the classic example of government reorganization, the one that to this day is still the most significant, is the structuring of the executive branch recommended by the President's Committee on Administrative Management in 1936–1937. This committee was popularly known as the Brownlow Committee, named after its chairman, Louis Brownlow, a major figure in the development of city management as a profession. The two other members of the committee were Charles Merriam of the University of Chicago and Luther Gulick of Columbia University and the Institute of Public Administration in New York City.

Government grew rapidly during the New Deal period, and there was little time or inclination for planning. It was largely believed that there existed many poorly conceived and poorly implemented organizational designs that were neither economical nor effective. These poor designs were often a reflection of the considerable political conflict between the executive and legislative branches. Both the president's office and the Congress had deliberately contributed to this problem by establishing programs in new organizations or agencies only with regard to political objectives—without taking managerial considerations into account. This persistent struggle over organizational control would be addressed by the Brownlow Committee—which provided the first formal assessment of government organization from a managerial perspective.

The Brownlow Committee submitted its report to President Roosevelt in January 1937. The core proposals of the committee were simple enough. Essentially the report indicated that "the president needs help" and professional staff members who possess a "passion for anonymity." This particular passion seems to have faded in recent years along with the public's belief that a modern president writes his own speeches.

Overall the committee recommended a major reorganization of the executive branch. The president agreed and appropriate legislation was submitted to Congress in 1938. But Congress, in the wake of the president's efforts to "pack"—to enlarge and thus control—the Supreme Court, and fearful of too much power in the presidency, killed the bill. The president resubmitted a considerably modified reorganization bill the following year, and Congress passed the Reorganization Act of 1939. This law created the Executive Office of the President, brought into it the Bureau of the Budget (later to be the Office of Management and Budget) from the Department of the Treasury, and authorized the president to prepare future reorganization plans subject to an after-the-fact congressional veto.

The Brownlow report, the Executive Office of the President, and many of the other recommendations of the Brownlow Committee that would eventually become law have been sanctified by time. Yet the Brownlow Committee's major proposals initially aroused considerable controversy. Modern scholars now recognize that there were different schools of thought regarding the development of public administration. The executive administration school, espoused by **Frank J. Goodnow,** viewed the roles and functions of government almost exclusively as opportunities for executive actions. In contrast, the legislative administrative school, as espoused by Brookings Institution head William F. Willoughby, viewed the relationship and especially the accountability of administration to the legislative branch as a central focus. This latter school believed that there was a considerable distinction between

---

BOX 3.4   The Brownlow Committee's Call for a Passion for Anonymity

The president needs help. His immediate staff assistance is entirely inadequate. He should be given a small number of executive assistants who would be his direct aides in dealing with the managerial agencies and administrative departments of the government. These assistants, probably not exceeding six in number, would be in addition to his present secretaries, who deal with the public, with the Congress, and with the press and radio. These aides would have no power to make decisions or issue instructions in their own right. They would not be interposed between the president and the heads of his departments. They would not be assistant presidents in any sense. Their function would be, when any matter was presented to the president for action affecting any part of the administrative work of the government, to assist him in obtaining quickly and without delay all pertinent information possessed by any of the executive departments so as to guide him in making his responsible decisions; and when the decisions have been made, to assist him in seeing to it that every administrative department and agency affected is promptly informed. Their effectiveness in assisting the president, will, we think, be directly proportional to their ability to discharge their functions with restraint. They would remain in the background, issue no orders, make no decisions, emit no public statements. Men for these positions should be carefully chosen by the president from within and without the government. They should be men in whom the president has personal confidence and whose character and attitude is such that they would not attempt to exercise power on their own account. They should be possessed of high competence, great physical vigor, and a passion for anonymity.

SOURCE: President's Committee on Administrative Management, *Administrative Management in the Government of the United States,* January 8, 1937 (Washington: U.S. Government Printing Office, 1937).

Frank J. Goodnow (1859–1939) A leader of the progressive reform movement and one of the founders and first president (in 1903) of the American Political Science Association. Goodnow is now best known as one of the principal exponents, along with Woodrow Wilson, of public administration's politics–administration dichotomy.

what was meant by "executive" and "administrative" and that the Constitution gave administrative power mainly to the Congress. The argument over who has more power over the machinery of government, the executive or the legislature, resonated in the mid-1990s with the budgetary struggles between the president and Congress over the size and scope of the governmental machine.

While Congress was considering the Brownlow Committee's various proposals, the forces opposed to an increase in the "administrative" powers of the president at the expense of Congress marshaled their arguments. One of the most eloquent was Lewis Meriam's 1939 *Reorganization of the National Government*. As the Brownlow Committee was arguing for increased presidential power, Meriam was cautioning against it. After "noting Hitler's rise to power within constitutional forms," he warned his readers that "proposals to vest great powers in the executive" might not work "to preserve democracy as we have known it but seriously to endanger it."

Forty years later the only surviving member of the Brownlow Committee would concede a point to Meriam. In considering Richard M. Nixon's abuses of the enhanced powers of the presidency, which the Brownlow Committee helped to create, Luther Gulick is quoted by Stephen Blumberg as saying, "We all assumed in the 1930s that all management, especially public management, flowed in a broad, strong stream of value-filled ethical performance. Were we blind or only naive until Nixon came along?" Nixon's 1970s subversion of constitutional government in the United States during the 1972–1974 Watergate scandal that forced his resignation differed only in degree from the subversion of republican governments that has been the hallmark of twentieth-century dictators.

Ironically, Nixon sought to enhance the power of the presidency with the creation of the Office of Management and Budget, yet he accomplished just the opposite. Congress, upset by Nixon's budgetary double-dealing, created a parallel Congressional Budget Office so that the legislature had its own number crunchers—who presumably would crunch numbers that could be believed. So in the game of constitutional checks and balances, new machinery of government is often created to check a would-be king.

The Hoover Commissions

The first Hoover Commission (1947–1949), formally the Commission on Organization of the Executive Branch of the Government, chaired by former President Herbert Hoover, was specifically charged to reduce the number of government agencies created during World War II; it did not, however, do so. Instead, it found that "disorder in the administrative machinery makes the executive branch of the Government work at cross purposes within itself" and focused on strengthening the executive branch by providing for a reorganization of agencies so that there would be a coherent purpose for each department. Instead of calling for a reduction of government agencies, the commission made a vigorous call for increased managerial capacity in the Executive Office of the President (EOP) through (1) unlimited discretion over presidential organization and staff, (2) a strengthened Bureau of the Budget, (3) an office of personnel located in the EOP, and (4) the creation of a staff secretary (what we now call a chief of staff) to provide a liaison between the president and his subordinates. The commission was considered a big success because

72 percent of its recommendations (196 out of 273) were adopted, including passage of the Reorganization Act of 1949 and the establishment of the Department of Health, Education, and Welfare in 1953.

A second Hoover Commission (1953–1955), also chaired by Hoover, is the unique example in the history of American public administration of an important commission being virtually reconvened after four years had passed to continue its work. This second commission recommended the elimination of nonessential government services and activities competitive with private enterprise, based on the assumptions that the federal government had grown beyond appropriate limits and that such growth should be reversed. In contrast to the first commission, the second commission's recommendations accomplished little. In a mere 18 volumes, the former president and his 11 fellow commissioners rigorously argued that a whole host of government activities should be turned over to the private sector. But the U.S. Congress was not so inclined, and this commission's recommendations got essentially nowhere. There was no political will to undertake massive privatization in the mid-1950s. This was a banner in the dust that would not be picked up and held high again until the Reagan administration of the 1980s and, more dramatically, with the Republican capture of Congress in 1994.

The Ash Council

President Richard M. Nixon's Advisory Council on Executive Organization, chaired by Roy Ash of Litton Industries, led to the transformation of the Bureau of the Budget into the Office of Management and Budget. The Ash Council's 1971 recommendations were extraordinarily ambitious in calling for a major restructuring of the cabinet agencies. President Nixon intended to implement this restructuring in his second term, beginning in 1973. But the Watergate scandal (see Chapter 14), which would force his resignation the following year, so dominated his aborted second term that no major domestic policy initiatives were possible.

The President's Private Sector Survey on Cost Control

If the second Hoover Commission is to be measured by 18 volumes of output leading nowhere, the 1982 President's Private Sector Survey on Cost Control can be measured by 47 reports from 36 major task forces with approximately similar results. The executive survey alone was 650 pages in two volumes. Like the second Hoover Commission, President Reagan's survey was appointed from an ideological position in which it was assumed that a little private sector know-how was all that it would take to put things right in Washington—an age-old belief that has been applied time and time again with great ardor but to somewhat limited effect. The PPSSCC was chaired by businessman J. Peter Grace, and its various subcommittees were composed of business figures from many large corporations.

It now seems that the PPSSCC, which came to be called the Grace Commission, was ill-fated from the start. The first problem was Grace himself. His true feelings notwithstanding, he came across in countless media interviews as an irascible old corporate patriarch who was condescending enough to disturb his well-earned repose by deigning to advise a misguided government on the multitudinous errors of *must leverage all assets*

its ways. The second problem was the commission's ignorance of one of the central precepts of modern management—employee participation. While Grace orchestrated this immense management audit by 2,000 private sector volunteers, the committee's task force largely ignored the expertise that was freely available from within the bureaucracy and the Congress.

poor leadership

Bureaucratic reform historian Donald Savoie reports that both the General Accounting Office and the Congressional Budget Office systematically reviewed the commission's conclusions and "undermine[d] the Commission's credibility" when they demonstrated that too many of the proposed savings were nonexistent and too many of the commission's facts were not factual after all. This however "did not stop the Reagan administration from applauding the findings of the commission and from reporting that it would press ahead with their implementation." But this was largely a public relations exercise of putting a good face on a poor effort. Perhaps the most highly touted recommendation of the commission that was actually implemented was the proposal that federal employees be issued corporate-type credit cards for official travel. While this offered legitimate savings on time previously spent on completing expense reimbursement vouchers, it was hardly worth the estimated $75 million cost (all private sector donated) for the report.

Reinventing Government

The most recent reinventing government movement was started in 1992 by the David Osborne and Ted Gaebler book with that title. It represents the confluence

TABLE 3.2 Major Commissions to Reform Federal Bureaucracy

Name	Chair	Year(s)	President	Result
Brownlow Commission	Louis Brownlow	1936	Roosevelt	Enhanced presidential control of bureaucracy
First Hoover Commission	Herbert Hoover	1947–1949	Truman	Strengthened the Executive Office of the President and enhanced agency management
Second Hoover Commission	Herbert Hoover	1953–1955	Eisenhower	Nothing significant
Ash Council	Roy Ash	1971	Nixon	The Bureau of the Budget became the Office of Management and Budget
Grace Commission	J. Peter Grace	1982	Reagan	A handful of minor bureaucratic adjustments
National Performance Review	Al Gore Jr.	1993	Clinton	A somewhat more stream-lined and customer-friendly bureaucracy

of two long-standing influences in American public life: the progressive reform movement and management faddism. Reinventing is logically the continuation of the progressive movement's philosophy of continuous improvement. This year's or this generation's most popular management fad is the comprehensive performance audit as a logically prior step in developing a new strategic vision for a business organization or a government operation. Next year, or next generation, there will be a new management fad, but it will still be within the progressive tradition.

Just as every new generation writes its own history, each new managerial generation has its own way of seeing the "one best way"—even if that one way means multiple ways. What has been genuinely new here is that governments at all levels are actually being forced by events to change the fundamental ways in which they operate. They must literally rethink—meaning reinvent—how they operate because they can no longer afford to simply do what they have been doing—with a reorganization here and a new public relations effort there—to assuage their critics. The simple overriding impetus to reinventing is a lack of money caused by the dual effects of the tax revolt and the Reagan revolution. *The truth be said!* √√

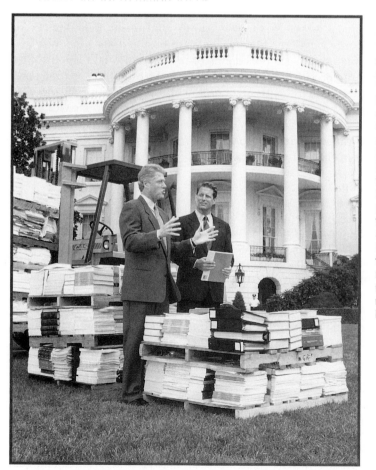

President Bill Clinton and Vice President Al Gore announce their reinventing government initiative on the White House lawn in 1993 surrounded by papers representing bureaucratic regulations they promise to discard. This was a truly great photo opportunity. Before most of the cabinet, many members of Congress, and the assembled press corps, Gore then told the president (for the benefit of the press): "Mr. President, if you want to know why government doesn't work, look behind you. The answer is at least partly on those forklifts. Those forklifts hold copies of budget rules, procurement rules, and the personnel code. The personnel code alone weighs in at over 1,000 pounds. That code and those regulations stacked up there no longer help government work, they hurt it; they hurt it badly. And we recommend getting rid of it." The lesson here is that there is not much political mileage in reinventing government in a closet. Better to do it on the White House lawn and let the whole world watch. •

(SMILE)

By 1980, the tax revolt movement forced 38 states to reduce or at least stabilize tax rates. Then the Reagan revolution came along and made state and local finances even more precarious. The Reagan administration, with its radical changes in the nation's fiscal and tax policies, redefined domestic priorities and curtailed federal programs—especially grants to state and local government—designed to solve social problems. As Reagan often said, "Government is not the solution to our problems. Government is the problem." In other words, the national welfare would be better served with general economic prosperity, brought about by tax cuts rather than with expanded welfare programs.

Necessity being the mother of invention, the latest reinventing government movement began in the early 1980s to cope with the declining revenues caused by the tax revolt and the Reagan revolution. In 1992, Osborne and Gaebler wrote *Reinventing Government*, a book that essentially categorized many of the things that thousands of state and local governments had been doing throughout the 1980s to cope with this crisis. Bill Clinton, as governor of Arkansas, endorsed the book. As president, he authorized the National Performance Review to seek these same kinds of innovations for the federal government—and for the same reason: money. The federal government was running record deficits. This had to be reduced by reducing (read reinventing) government.

If the federal government was off to the reinventing government races, Vice President Al Gore was the jockey riding the horse. This was unusual in itself because historically in the United States the vice president's only constitutional responsibility (aside from waiting for the president to die or be removed from office) is to preside over the U.S. Senate (except when it is trying a president for impeachment) and vote in the case of a tie. Recent presidents, however, have tended to give their vice presidents significant domestic and foreign policy assignments. Of course, having the vice president play with a president's **trial balloon** has always been an effective means of insulating a president from critics if the balloon pops.

The Gore Report

When President Bill Clinton launched the vice presidentially chaired National Performance Review in 1993—a six-month study aimed at making the federal government more efficient—the language he used was familiar: "Our goal is to make the federal government both less expensive and more efficient, and to change the culture of our national bureaucracy away from complacency and entitlement toward initiative and empowerment. We intend to redesign, to reinvent, to reinvigorate the entire national government." In pointed and emphasized contrast to the federal government's last major management reform effort (the Grace Commission), the Gore report would be researched and written largely by the in-house talent of the federal bureaucracy.

---

trial balloon A deliberate leak of a potential policy to see what public response will be. The term comes from the meteorological practice of sending up a balloon to test weather conditions. If public response is hostile, the new policy proposal can be quietly dropped (or deflated).

The National Performance Review made 258 agency-specific recommendations, affecting every national executive department, as well as the executive agencies in the Office of the President. As well, the review promised that it would spawn further reviews on more focused topics, such as the "antiquated" federal field office structure, the abandonment of obsolete programs, the elimination of unproductive subsidies, the redesign of failed programs, the redefinition of relationships between the federal government and state and local governments, and the reinvigoration of relationships between the executive and legislative branches. Whatever optimism or pessimism one might hold for the achievement of this program of change, the targets seemed right, and the prospect of the U.S. national government at last being freed up and "reinvented" seemed encouraging.

Whereas the Grace Report under the Reagan administration—which based its philosophy on the proposition that only private business executives could fix government—was an abject failure, the implementation of reinvention was quite different. The National Partnership for Reinventing Government relied on borrowed federal career officials to do its work. By 1998 it reported savings of $137 billion, a reduction of 351,000 positions in government, and the creation of 340 reinvention laboratories in government agencies. Instead of conflict, partnership was a key theme: between labor and management (occupational health and safety has been a key focus); between regulatory agencies and regulated businesses; and between government agencies. All this was for the common goals of best value for the taxpayer dollar, better service for customers, and better workplaces for employees.

The End of Reinvention

It must also be said, however, that the Gore report was not unlike its predecessors in that it focused on many specific programs and details, as would a conventional management consultant's report. It lacked the root and branch depth of change achieved in those bureaucracies where new fundamental principles have been adopted, rather than endeavoring to fine-tune, but not fundamentally change, the existing system. Some of the recommendations of the National Performance Review—for example, that the Railroad Retirement Board be reinvented—had a familiar ring, while others, like the recommendation that the management of the Department of Health and Human Services be reviewed, seemed to be like a Russian Matryoshka doll—a review that contained a recommendation for another review.

In marked contrast are the machinery of government changes that have taken place in the last decade in Britain, Australia, and New Zealand. These have involved fundamental principles and have been more radical than those of the National Performance Review. In fact, the specific machinery of government recommendations of the National Performance Review were relatively few—considering that an organization left in place after a review lives to fight another day and to disregard review recommendations it dislikes once the dust has settled.

The defeat of Vice President Al Gore in the 2000 presidential race ended reinvention. But by that time, after eight years of the Clinton administration's reform impetus, it badly needed reinventing itself. Its proposals were attacked both by those who felt that its principles didn't fit the traditional values of public administration and by those who felt that its proposals weren't radical enough. During Clinton's second term with a Republican-controlled Congress, reinventing efforts became more rhetoric than reality. The Republican's idea of reinventing meant two things: devolution and privatization. Thus the Republican Congress (with Clinton's support) devolved the national welfare program (discussed in Chapter 4), and privatization has become the watchword of the subsequent Bush administration. Reinvention has become a Clinton-Gore tainted word. While it is inevitable that many reforms will be achieved by the Bush administration, it seems fairly certain that nothing will be "reinvented."

The Micromanagers

Woodrow Wilson wrote in his famous 1887 essay "The Study of Administration" that "the field of administration is a field of business . . . a part of political life only as the methods of the counting-house are a part of the life of the society," and "administrative questions are not political questions." This was institutionalized by the Brownlow Committee recommendations for greater managerial capability on the part of the executive. But as David H. Rosenbloom has observed, Congress responded to this stronger, more managerially capable, presidency "in 1946 by establishing the legal and institutional bases for its contemporary role in federal administration." Thus, when Truman, a Democrat, was president while the Republicans controlled Congress, a **divided government** brought forth this quartet of laws that sowed the seeds of **micromanagement:**

1. Administrative Procedure Act (APA) of 1946: The basic law governing the way federal agencies operate to safeguard agency clients and the general public. The APA specifies the conditions under which administrative agencies (a) publicize information about their operations, (b) make rules, (c) engage in adjudication, and (d) are subject to judicial review. Thus agencies begin with some form of legislative mandate and translate their interpretation of that mandate into policy decisions, specifications of regulations, and statements of penalties and enforcement provisions. The APA requires that rules be published 30 days before their effective date and that agencies afford any interested party the right to petition for issuance, amendment, or repeal of a rule. In effect, while the APA establishes a process of notice and time for comment, it accords administrative rulemakers the same prerogatives that legislatures have in enacting statutes, as long as the rule enacted is consistent with the enabling statute.

2. Legislative Reorganization Act of 1946: A law that dramatically reduced the number of standing committees in the Senate and House, provided for a major expansion of the Legislative Reference Service (now known as the

---

divided government A government in which different political parties control the legislative and executive branches.

micromanagement A pejorative term for too-close supervision by policymakers in the implementation of programs. Congress has been accused of micromanagement when it writes detailed rules governing programs into legislation—thus denying line managers any real administrative discretion. But any manager is a micromanager if he or she refuses to allow subordinates to have any real authority or responsibility.

Congressional Research Service), and promoted the creation of a professional, nonpartisan staff for committees, as well as increased staff for individual members. This was the first attempt by Congress to establish an effective staff system to decrease its dependence on executive agencies for information.

3. Tort Claims Act of 1946: The law that made federal agencies responsible for their torts—legal harms done to another person that can be the cause of a civil court suit.

4. Employment Act of 1946: The law that created the Council of Economic Advisers in the Executive Office of the President and asserted that it was the federal government's responsibility to maintain economic stability and promote full employment.

The combined effect of these laws was to unleash a mob of micromanagers. Members of Congress, once largely limited to policy oversight, now had the opportunity to delve into the minutiae of administration on behalf of their constituents. The APA created a rulemaking process that offered unlimited possibilities for influencing rules for pork barrel motivations. The Legislative Reorganization Act gave Congress the staff it needed to constantly interfere for their specific political purposes. The Tort Claims Act meant that Congress could effectively lobby agencies to redress wrongs to constituents. And the Employment Act meant virtually unlimited justification to pump federal money into selected congressional districts. This process can be seen every time the Department of Defense has been forced into buying more of a weapon than it needs simply because the factory that makes it is in an influential member's congressional district. As Rosenbloom sarcastically noted, "Turning pork barrel politics into a virtuous national economic policy was no small achievement." But while pork by its nature is not kosher, for many Americans the very definition of a member of Congress is one who brings home the bacon. This, however, may be changing.

The import of all this is that Congress has never drawn—as the Brownlow Committee would have liked—a dichotomy between politics and administration. After all, the two are not separate anyway. So what made anybody think that the reinventing government movement—the latest effort to take politics out of administration by turning grumpy citizens into happy customers—was going to change the situation?

Now there is much tinkering that the executive branch can do on its own. It can get the Social Security Administration to answer its phones within a reasonable period. It can force Internal Revenue Service auditors to be polite. But this is minor compared to the power of Congress to determine the amount of Social Security payments and the level of taxes. Members of Congress are hardly likely to give up their ability to micromanage—with all the pork for constituents and reelection prospects that implies—for vague notions of greater efficiency. Members thrive on bureaucratic red tape and the opportunities it creates for constituent service. This is why the **ombudsman/ombudswoman** movement has never gone very far in the United

---

ombudsman/ombudswoman An official whose job it is to investigate the complaints of the citizenry concerning public services and to ensure that these complaints will reach the attention of those officials at levels above the original providers of service. The word is Swedish, meaning a representative of the king. Ombudsmen and ombudswomen are now found in many countries at a variety of jurisdictional levels. Many of the functions of ombudsmen in American local, state, and national governments are performed by members of their respective legislatures as casework.

States. This function is happily, even joyously, performed by the elected representatives. It is quite literally what they have their staffs spend most of their time on—because it is the key to reelection.

The conclusion of all this is in essence quite simple and obvious: To reinvent government, you must also reinvent Congress. And to reinvent state government, you must reinvent the state legislature. Few things are more obvious in the study of public administration than that there exists a strong relationship between the organization of a legislature and that of its executive branch. According to administrative analyst Harold Seidman, "One could as well ignore the laws of aerodynamics in designing an aircraft as ignore the laws of congressional dynamics in designing executive branch structure." Thus "what may appear to be structural eccentricities and anomalies within the executive branch are often nothing but mirror images of jurisdictional conflicts within the Congress. Congressional organization and executive branch organization are interrelated and constitute two halves of a single system." The British and other parliamentary systems have been able to go much further down the reinventing road precisely because they do not have this problem. There the executive and legislature, for policy purposes, are effectively one.

The Pressure for Privatization

Just as the Clinton administration wanted to reinvent government, the George W. Bush administration wants to privatize much of it—and has announced a major commitment to push into the private sector as many as 425,000 federal jobs. According to Ellen Nakashima, "The move will swell the contract corps, a shadow-government workforce whose numbers are estimated to be more than three times as large as the 1.8 million-strong civilian federal workforce." The rationale for this, as explained by Bush OMB Director Mitchell E. Daniels Jr., "is not to move jobs from the public sector to the private sector. The objective is to get the taxpayer the best deal." Notice that the underlying philosophy of this movement toward privatization comes directly from the Second Hoover Commission Report of 1955.

Nothing is more challenging, indeed threatening, to public administration than the now constant specter of privatization. Indeed, to many on the political right, reinventing is virtually synonymous with privatization. There are essentially two kinds of privatization. First, as discussed in the Keynote, there is the private provision of services with a "public" character, such as private police and private parks. These services are public only in the sense that they are available to any who can pay for them. Second, privatization is the process of returning to the private sector property or functions previously owned or performed by government. Conservative Republicans in particular tend to be in favor of privatizing those government functions that can be performed (in their opinion) less expensively or more efficiently by the private sector. Some extreme advocates of a wholesale privatization of government functions would even return Social Security, education, and public health to the private sector.

It may be somewhat of a misnomer to even label privatization as "a movement," but clearly public administration theorists and public sector practitioners are acutely aware of the increasing frequency of, and of the changes involved with, "contracting out," public-private partnerships, or whatever vehicle is being used to shift or separate the production of public sector goods and services from their provision. Privatization is a broad long-term trend, often fueled with strong and emotional conservative ideology, to reduce government expenditures, to turn (or return) government assets and operations to private enterprise and, thereby, to increase the effectiveness and efficiency of government.

Privatization is almost always predicated on assumptions about public sector versus private sector efficiency and productivity rates. The burden of proof is often on public sector managers to explain why they are not inferior to private enterprise managers and why they should retain their functions in the face of private sector alternatives. Perhaps no responsibility is greater for public managers today than developing the evaluation and management assessment tools needed to assure critics that public sector programs and enterprises are being managed efficiently and effectively.

Generally there are three basic forms or types of government privatization:

1. The sale of government assets (such as a railroad to a corporation or public housing units to their tenants)

2. The private financing of public facilities (such as toll highways in California or Virginia)

3. The private provision of services (such as trash collection or retirement benefits)

Strategies for Privatization

Privatization is the management ideology for those fearful, suspicious, or skeptical of expanding government. It is equally ideal as a tool for those who wish to reduce the size of government. Done properly, it dovetails with the first principle of the reinventing government movement: that government should be catalytic and steer (set direction) rather than row (do the work). A review of President George W. Bush's arguments for partial privatization of Social Security during the 2005 State of the Union address demonstrates the goal of steering rather than rowing. (See the case study in Chapter 13 for excerpts from Bush's address.)

However, privatization sometimes means that government will neither steer nor row. It will simply get out of an activity altogether. For example, some people strongly believe that government should have absolutely no role in birth control, sex education, broadcasting, or the arts. These activities, if undertaken at all, should be undertaken by private citizens at their own initiative. One counterargument was made by playwright **Arthur Miller.** He tells the story of the time he was speaking in defense of government support for theater. A man in the audience asked him, "I manufacture shoes. If the public won't buy enough of them, why shouldn't I demand government support?" Miller couldn't think of a logical and reasoned answer to this perfectly valid question. So he responded with a question: "Can you name me one classical

---

Arthur Miller (1915–2005) Pulitzer Prize–winning author of *Death of a Salesman* (1949).

Greek shoemaker?" Of course, Miller was emphatically not in favor of government control of the arts, but he felt, as many do, that government has an obligation to further its notions of civilization—and that this is often done by subsidizing the arts.

Political analyst E. S. Savas identified four strategies of privatization that together will "halt and reverse the growth of government."

1. Load shedding: A term that refers to government withdrawing from the provision of goods and services and allowing them "to be supplied by the marketplace or by voluntary arrangements."

2. Alternative delivery systems: Arrangements "in which government plays a relatively limited role," including services provided through voluntary or self-service arrangements, competitive markets, franchises, vouchers, grants, and contracts.

3. Imposing user charges for goods and services: Savas argues that government should do this whenever possible in order to expose the true costs of services and, thereby, to increase the chances that alternative delivery systems will evolve.

4. Restoring competition and minimizing government monopolies: Savas maintains that this "requires a conscious strategy of creating alternatives and fostering a receptive climate and mental attitude in favor of giving options to the citizen-consumers of public services."

Privatization of services usually is implemented in order to take advantage of one or more hoped-for benefits: reduced costs, improved services, short-term access to expensive specialized services, avoidance of service start-up costs, greater flexibility in service policy (through reduced inflexibility of labor and equipment), increased responsiveness to consumer demand, and improved control. In addition, privatization sometimes is pursued on the ideological grounds that government should not provide goods and services that firms in the private for-profit or nonprofit sector are able and willing to provide. Government should limit itself to activities that firms in the private sector cannot or will not provide.

Privatization also has limitations and problems that may lead to misuses or abuses. Policy analyst John Donahue has found that privatization brings both good news and bad news. The good news is that while privatization is not a "universal corrective," it does present some "real opportunities to make public undertakings more efficient and accountable by enlisting the private sector." The bad news is that political pressures could just as easily "tend to retain for the public sector functions where privatization would make sense, and to privatize tasks that would be better left to government."

Privatization in the Military

The military is the most fundamental unit of government often predating the government it serves. Remember that it was the Continental Army under George Washington that literally enabled the creation of the United States. But the traditional military is fading rapidly. Until recently, the military performed many of its own support functions. From cleaning sheets to digging latrines, basic aspects of military life were handled by members of the armed services. But increasingly, these basic support services are being handled by private, nonmilitary sources. While this "contracting out" of services is often seen as cost effective, there has been considerable criticism of the practice in recent years.

Privatization has been subjected to especially heavy criticism in its application in the war in Iraq. As noted in Chapter 1, the United States has hired private contractors to provide security services for construction workers who are rebuilding Iraq's worn-out infrastructure and oil industry. As the insurgency has continued to mount since 2004, there has been consistent criticism of the role that private security forces have played in the war theater. According to a 2005 PBS *Frontline* report, members of the U.S. military have reported numerous problems with the over 20,000 individuals who are serving as private security personnel. Among the complaints put forth by U.S. troops are claims that private contractors lack accountability and a clear relationship to the chain of command. There also exists a more emotional disconnect between active military personnel and private contractors that stems from vast differences in pay rates for similar levels of risk and position. Brookings Institution research fellow Peter Singer noted, "There's a bubbling resentment . . . and you're starting to sense a backlash from the military." Yet, with the military facing declining recruitment rates and the need for personnel remaining high, it appears privatization of military functions is likely to remain.

Although the potential problems differ somewhat among the various types of privatization, there is evidence that privatization leads to corruption because of its susceptibility to political influence, difficulties in monitoring contract performance and outcomes, reduced control over services, and limited numbers of competitors who are willing or able to provide services. The Halliburton Corporation has been a lightning rod for many of these concerns. This Texas-based construction company has been awarded a number of contracts from the federal government for reconstruction projects in Iraq. In particular, Halliburton was given a contract worth over $7 billion to help restore Iraqi oil production. The awarding of the contract was controversial not only because Vice President Dick Cheney was once the company's CEO, but because the contract was awarded without inviting bids from other firms. The *Washington Post* reported that Bunnatine H. Greenhouse, the top civilian contracting official at the U.S. Army Corps of Engineers, testified that Halliburton's subsidiary Kellogg Brown & Root (KBR) was given an unusual amount of control over the terms of its no-bid contract to rebuild Iraq's oil infrastructure. Greenhouse stated, "I can unequivocally state that the abuse related to contracts awarded to KBR represents the most blatant and improper abuse I have witnessed during the course of my professional career." To add fuel to the fire, the Defense Contract Audit Agency issued a 2005 report that questioned over $800 million in expenses that Halliburton charged to the Defense Department.

Indeed, it was exactly these kinds of problems that led to "publicization" of many privately provided services in the first place. The progressive reformers of the municipal research bureaus early in the twentieth century forcefully advocated that the government itself provide services such as street paving and trolley lines as a way of maintaining public accountability.

One of the most vocal opponents of privatization, the American Federation of State, County, and Municipal Employees (AFSCME), has published numerous examples to demonstrate that privatization results in poor performance, fraud, bribery, and graft. AFSCME and other government employee unions are fighting to keep the jobs of their members. In New York, Philadelphia, Indianapolis, and other major jurisdictions, the unions are being forced to prove that they can compete in price and quality with the private sector. The very fact that this is a matter of discussion has had a chilling effect on public employee union militancy and has inhibited demands for wage increases and lessened the likelihood of strikes.

The Nonprofit Gambit

In chess a gambit is a play, such as the sacrifice of a pawn, by which one seeks to gain a later advantage. Governments at all levels are increasingly using nonprofit organizations for just such strategic purposes. Services previously performed by government are being turned over to them—privatized since they are private organizations—so that government can both save money and get rid of perennially troublesome social programs that seek to improve the lot of the poor and unfortunate.

The nonprofit sector is a uniquely democratic phenomenon. In some respects it is the most capitalistic of our economic responses, reacting to **marketplace failure** by filling economic voids with **volunteers** and charitable contributions. In contrast, more socialistic economies tend to meet similar types of community needs through tax-supported government programs and services. Nonprofits provide a flexible alternative to tax-supported government action.

A nonprofit organization is in many respects a concept rather than a specific entity—and it can be defined in many different ways. The primary essence of a nonprofit organization, however, is that it is organized and operated for public or societal purposes (such as alleviation of poverty) rather than private benefit purposes (such as return on shareholders' investments). A second essential element of a nonprofit organization is its reliance on voluntary action for most of its financial and human resources. Despite common misconceptions to the contrary—and within well-defined limitations—nonprofit organizations can realize profits from their activities and programs, and they can engage in commercial-type enterprises. However, such profits must be returned to the operations of the agency.

Nonprofit organizations range in size and structure from large international religious denominations and seminational hospital chains to small, local, nonincorporated associations of people with common interests, goals, or concerns. From a relatively narrow, legalistic point of view, we can argue that a nonprofit organization is, in effect, an organization prescribed by the laws, rules, and codes of tax

---

marketplace failure The inability of a society's free markets to provide a needed service.

volunteer A person who provides a service without compulsion or requirement and typically without compensation. However, with the growth of the voluntary sector, the definition of a volunteer appears to be changing. For example, many volunteer ambulance services and fire departments now pay volunteers for their standby time and/or for making runs. These paid persons are still called volunteers or paid volunteers as long as their work with the ambulance service is not their primary source of income.

exemption. From a tax-exemption viewpoint, there are two basic types of nonprofit organizations:

1. Publicly supported charitable organizations that engage directly in religious, education, and social welfare programs
2. Private foundations, which tend to support other tax-exempt organizations' programs

The Reagan administration refocused the nation on the power of voluntary, nongovernmental responses to community problems. The Reagan agenda was predicated on the assumption that issue identification and action responsibility should be returned to local communities, thus increasing community reliance on nonprofits at a time when the government was simultaneously decreasing the size of, and the sector's access to, its traditional funding sources. Never in the history of the United States had the **third sector** been called upon to do so much more with so much less.

The first Bush administration did not signal the arrival of less complex times for the nonprofit sector. In fact, Bush's 1988 presidential campaign may be most remembered for its "thousand points of light," a reference to volunteerism and Bush's belief that a new, more altruistic age had begun throughout the land. Bush first used this metaphor for volunteerism and charity in American life in his acceptance speech at the 1988 Republican National Convention. In his inaugural address he further defined the "points" as "all the community organizations that are spread like stars throughout the nation doing good." Peggy Noonan, who wrote Bush's acceptance speech, said in her memoirs *What I Saw at the Revolution* (1990) that the "thousand points of light . . . became Bush's shorthand way of referring to the network of helping organizations throughout the country, and it became in some circles the object of derision, or at least of good-natured spoofing." The public as well as the press were initially confused about the exact meaning of the "thousand points." The metaphor had to be explained so often that it became a symbol of the fractured syntax of Bush's speech patterns.

As became his political trademark, President Bill Clinton carved out an interesting middle ground between private philanthropic organizations and the federal government. In 1993, Clinton signed the National and Community Service Trust Act, which established the Corporation for National and Community Service. This act brought a wide range of domestic community service programs under the umbrella of one central governmental organization known as AmeriCorps. Members of AmeriCorps serve with more than 3,000 nonprofits, public agencies, and faith-based and community organizations throughout the country. For example, an individual who volunteers with AmeriCorps may be placed with a group such as the Christian Appalachian Project, which builds homes in the impoverished areas of eastern Kentucky.

---

third sector All those organizations that fit neither in the public sector (government) nor the private sector (business); a generic phrase for the collectivity of nonprofit organizations or organizations that institutionalize activism to deal with issues and problems that are being ignored by the public and private sectors.

Despite programs such as AmeriCorps, the national inhibition toward more direct government funding for social programs has continued. The bottom line is that because of their charitable objectives and highly motivated, often volunteer, workforces, nonprofit organizations are a cheap way to fund a legislative mandate. In these instances, the subcontracting relationship to public funders renders the nonprofit organization at least indirectly accountable to the general public. In many cases, nonprofit board decision making is quite similar to that of a public utility: the nonprofit board is free to make decisions within legislative parameters.

The George W. Bush administration has been even more enthusiastic about using nonprofit agencies—especially religious organizations—to provide social services. Bush has even created an Office of Faith-Based and Community Initiatives to further this agenda. And five departments—Health and Human Services, Housing and Urban Development, Justice, Education, and Labor—have created centers to further faith-based efforts. The most controversial element of Bush's initiative has been a policy that allows religious organizations to compete for grants to provide federally funded social services such as drug rehabilitation and health clinics for the poor. This element of Bush's program has been criticized for blurring the separation between church and state by providing direct government payment to religious organizations, but most aspects of the faith-based initiative remain intact as of 2005. In fact, the Hurricane Katrina disaster once again called attention to the relationship between faith-based organizations and the federal government. As FEMA struggled to get aid to victims of the hurricane, many religious organizations quickly filled the gap with shelters and services. In response to these efforts, there has been renewed debate about whether these religious organizations should be eligible to receive federal funds.

Voluntarism and Philanthropy

Nonprofit management, third sector organizations, and independent sector programs are only new articulations of the old concepts of charity, philanthropy, and social action. The notions of charity and philanthropy are old, but how they are influencing today's society is new. In a country where the profit motive is supreme, it is both curious and inevitable that there also exists a pervasive nonprofit sector. In most other societies voluntarism does not play as significant a role in the lives of people as it does in the United States.

This Western tradition of voluntarism has roots in two diverse ideological streams:

1. The Greco-Roman heritage of emphasis on community, citizenry, and social responsibility. The Greco-Roman ideology rests on a foundation of social reform to relieve community social problems in order to improve the quality of life for all in the community.

2. The Judeo-Christian belief that relationships with a higher power affect our choices, our decision making. Thus our purpose is not to change people's lots but rather to alleviate the (preordained) suffering of others, particularly the poor. Under Judeo-Christian tradition, one does not help others solely from concern for oneself or one's neighbors but because a deity has given instructions to do so. We have been told to love our neighbor as we love ourself: One loves one's neighbor because one loves God first and thus seeks to obey.

These two distinct, historical, ideological themes remain clearly evident today. For example, we can distinguish between *cause advocacy,* or leadership for social reform, and *case advocacy,* or individual service to a person or a limited group of persons in need. The influence of the two ideologies has been replayed countless times and in countless ways in the history of the American nonprofit sector. Notice how it is reflected in the following definitions of two types of voluntarism.

- *Philanthropy* is the giving of money or self to solve social problems; it is developmental, an investment in the future, an effort to prevent future occurrences or recurrences.

- *Charity* is relieving or alleviating specific instances of suffering; it is acts of mercy or compassion.

We tend to view these two forms of voluntary action as complementary elements in a nonprofit system. We need philanthropy as well as charity. However, this is not always the case. For example, Andrew Carnegie, an ardent philanthropist, abhorred charity. "It were better for mankind that the millions of the rich were thrown into the sea than so spent as to encourage the slothful, the drunken, the unworthy. . . . So spent, indeed, as to produce the very evils which it hopes to mitigate or cure." Yet from the Judeo-Christian charitable tradition, almshouses, charitable hospitals, orphan homes, and charitable organizations such as the Little Sisters of the Poor, the Salvation Army, the International Red Cross, and countless others, have helped relieve untold instances of human suffering.

As this nation was founded on the democratic ideals of both individualism and pluralism, our fundamental notion of how domestic problems (such as poverty, health, childrearing, housing, mental illness, homelessness, and inequitable access to employment opportunities) should be addressed is returning to its historical stable state: community-level problem solving. Our basic approach to dealing with domestic problems has progressed from individual and family-level resolution, to community problem solving (as the country urbanized), to massive state intervention, and back toward community problem solving. In part this return to the past has been a negative reaction to the perceived failure of many New Deal and Great Society social programs. Thus as we enter a new century the nexus of responsibility for charity and social action once again shows signs of shifting from a national orientation back to one of local control.

From the provision of social services to the support of metropolitan symphonies, local structures now provide for the continued survival or decide the final fate of many nonprofit organizations. The role and responsibilities of the public sector have indeed contracted, in perception if not in fact. The pioneer barn-raising spirit of neighbors helping each other in good times and bad has become the foundation for domestic public policy reform. Returning responsibility to the people, allowing and requiring communities to decide which local problems should be addressed, has become vogue.

Until recently, philanthropy was largely limited to a leisure-time activity of the rich. In the last century, the great industrialists/robber barons and their families, after making their fortunes, might have donated funds for this or that public improvement. Andrew Carnegie was the most systematic example of this variety of traditional philanthropists. He gave away over $350 million while he lived. This is equivalent

A contemporary cartoon of Andrew Carnegie. The popular image of Carnegie is that of an enormously wealthy robber baron giving almost all of his money away before he died. But he is an important philosopher of the movement toward non-profit organization in twentieth-century America. He sought to create institutions whereby the working classes could better themselves. But they had to be worthy of his largesse. Thus he paid for the construction of 3,000 public libraries—but the local communities had to buy the books and maintain the buildings. He donated organs to 4,000 churches—but only to those that were financially sound and well managed. He created innumerable trusts and foundations as well as museums, institutions for art and music (Carnegie Hall but not the Carnegie Delicatessen across the street), and one of the world's great universities: Carnegie-Mellon. This man who said, "He who dies rich dies disgraced" did not die disgraced. And when he did die, he gave the world the secret to his success by having this engraved on his tombstone:

Here lies a man
Who knew how to enlist
In his service
Better men than himself •

to $6 billion today. But this century's differing attitudes toward social responsibilities and tax laws have transformed philanthropy from the altruistic concern of a single individual or family to a huge enterprise that affects and sustains a major portion of our economy and our society.

To be sure, wealthy people as well as people of all economic means contribute money, time, energy, and property for socially desirable purposes. But the largest share of the available philanthropic dollar goes to endow foundations. There are tax advantages to the donor in doing this. Therefore, using a foundation helps to multiply the total amount of philanthropic funds available for good works.

Now that philanthropy has to a large extent been institutionalized, its role has changed from random charitable or community developmental efforts to systematic efforts to find causes for focused efforts, to alleviate poverty in certain regions, control world population growth, or preserve rare artifacts, to state only three examples. The large-scale nature of philanthropy has caused it to become bureaucratized. No longer will an emotional charitable appeal suffice. A systematic proposal must be written and maneuvered through the various levels of approval of the requesting organization to the granting organization's often equally elaborate bureaucracy. Thus the alternative to government becomes, by trying to do what government has so far failed to do, more like the government than it finds comfortable to admit.

✦ A CASE STUDY: THE REVOLUTION IN THE BRITISH MACHINERY OF GOVERNMENT (1979–2005)

The British machinery of government differs in important respects from that of the United States. It is a system of cabinet, rather than presidential, government. In the British system the cabinet, the collectivity of ministers, is the ultimate seat of authority, although its existence and role are not provided for in a written constitution. Each minister is an elected member of Parliament, a politician of the ruling party of the day, and is assigned his or her post by the prime minister. The clear division of powers between the executive, legislative, and judicial branches is blurred in the British system, since the executive and the legislature are more closely tied.

Just as the U.S. system puts the three dominant classes of government agencies within the Executive Office of the President, the national executive departments, and independent public bodies, we find in the British system the parallels of Crown agencies, portfolio (cabinet) departments, and public bodies. As in the United States, some of the oldest departments, like the Treasury and the Foreign Office, have long and independent traditions, and the bureaucracy of "Whitehall" has had a reputation for intransigence and self-serving behavior no less negative than that of the U.S. bureaucracy.

By 1979 the British central machinery of government had evolved into the ideal candidate for substantial reform. It had become large, unwieldy, costly, and secretive. The numbers of public bodies had grown to a point where it was difficult for any one person to understand what they did or to whom they were accountable, much less to assess whether their activities served the public interest or some narrower sectional interest. The legacy of the **nationalization** of a number of heavy industries that had not been well managed in the 1960s and 1970s represented a serious problem for the country, and their poor performance seemed to play a big part in the overall decline in British economic performance. With this in view, significant reform was necessary. The British system of unitary government in which there are few of the checks and balances that exist in the U.S. Constitution and in U.S. policymaking behavior provided circumstances in which far-reaching reform could be undertaken.

The most famous of these reforms, privatization, was not part of **Margaret Thatcher**'s explicit platform when she was elected in 1979, although it was certainly part of the Conservative Party's program. Privatization was particularly focused on the nationalized industries and utilities. In Britain these included the petroleum,

---

nationalization The taking over by government of a significant segment of a country's private sector industry, land, transportation, and so on, usually with compensation to the former owners. Socialist governments tend to favor extensive nationalization. Indeed, the level of nationalization is an accurate measure of the degree of a nation's socialism. Ironically, even conservative and nonsocialist governments have resorted to nationalization but in an effort to save a collapsing firm or service, rather than in ideological fervor.

Margaret Thatcher (1925–) The conservative prime minister of Great Britain from 1979 to 1990. Elected as the first female prime minister in British history, she then held that office longer than any other twentieth-century British politician. Her championing of free-market economic policies, coupled with an assertive role in world affairs, created an ideological style of leadership that came to be known as "Thatcherism."

aerospace, and automotive industries, as well as gas, electricity, and water. Since the 1980s, these were successively sold to the private sector.

The massive reform of the national government departments, the "Next Steps" program, was launched in 1988. By 1992 more than half the British civil service—290,000 people—was included in the 76 new Executive Agencies. In a U.S. context, this would be comparable to a million federal government employees being reassigned to several hundred new agencies whose executives could be immediately removed if they did not achieve their performance targets. Some former departments, like Inland Revenue (equivalent to the U.S. Internal Revenue Service), were split into as many as 34 Executive Agencies, and each of these was pursuing stated quantitative performance targets. While these reforms are relatively recent, they do represent a disciplined and systematic program of reforming one of the most difficult parts of the public sector to reach and to manage—that is, the work conducted normally within civil service departments, albeit the "operational" rather than the "policy" aspects of that work. In effect, half of the traditional civil service has been placed in corporate-like structures where they will be treated more like corporate employees than public servants. This is the essence of corporatization—more flexibility for managers and less job security for all.

The results to date are encouraging, although the "arm's length relationship"— meaning no political interference—central to the Executive Agency concept can sometimes break down under sufficient political pressure. Within a decade, the British public sector was changed beyond recognition, with machinery of government changes of the most profound significance taking place. Overall, according to British professor Chistopher Pollitt, "in the decade from 1979 to 1990, 800,000 employees were transferred into the private sector, and the share of the gross domestic product accounted for by state-owned industries fell from 11 percent in 1979 to 5.5 percent in 1990." In effect, the Thatcher revolution cut the British public sector in half.

This revolution in the machinery of government continued even after the revolutionary party was voted out of office. In 1997 when the Labour party led by Prime Minister Tony Blair took over the British government, he declared, to the chagrin of many of the traditionally socialists members of his party, that the reforms would stay. He espoused a "third way" that went beyond the old left's preoccupation with state control but not so far as the far right's "belief that free markets are the answer to every problem." He has sought to have his "New Labour" party "rebrand Britain." And a major part of this "rebranding" was Labour's acceptance of the Conservative party's radical reforms of the machinery of government.

A key concept in the British reforms is market testing—a process that requires agencies to buy goods and services from the private sector if savings are to be had. This has led to private contractors building and managing prisons, the Passport Agency hiring outside companies to print passports, and the Inland Revenue contracting out the management of its computer databases. According to reinventing guru David Osborne, "The U.K. has gone further in reinventing government than any other country [other] than New Zealand." True, New Zealand has jumped into the deep end of the reinventing pool, but it is so small in population (less than 3.5 million) that its reinventing efforts are more comparable to those of big municipal rather than national governments.

In Britain, the late 1990s saw the headlong dive into privatization slowing a little. The incoming Labour government of Tony Blair in its July 1998 white paper on local government scrapped the compulsory local government outsourcing the Conservatives had insisted on, replacing it with a broader concept of "Best Value." In April 1999, a true watershed was reached when Conservative opposition leader William Hague, in a major public lecture, conceded that privatization should not displace predominant public funding in health, education, and welfare. This does not mean that the pendulum of privatization will swing back to the division between public and private functions which once existed, but it does indicate that, in Britain at least, a practical rather than an ideological stance on these issues is emerging on both sides of the political fence.

In the United States, the reinventing government movement renewed interest in bureaucratic innovation in general, and in aspects of commercialization in particular, but it would be fair to say that the United States has not been a leader in changes in this area. Indeed, if you read the formally stated "Principles of the National Performance Review," espoused by former Vice President Al Gore, you will see that they could easily and honestly be labeled "made in Great Britain."

But the proof of all this is in the implementation. Great Britain is way ahead in this game. Of course, it started a decade earlier. Nevertheless, the U.S. machinery of government is radically different, and there is no guarantee that the United States could ever catch up. Different political cultures and different machinery require different administrative solutions.

For Discussion: *How have the British reforms influenced public administration in the United States? Has the "third way" espoused by British Prime Minister Tony Blair and embraced by former President Bill Clinton been continued by President George W. Bush?*

Summary

The machinery of government consists of all of the structural arrangements provided by a constitutional provision or a statute requiring the delivery of government services. These arrangements are not immutable. The functions of public agencies can and should be altered from time to time to reflect emerging needs and changing values.

Executive branch machinery has three main categories of organizations: executive office agencies, executive departments, and independent public bodies. State and local arrangements parallel those of the federal level.

The advent of the 1990s reinventing government movement made reorganization once again fashionable. But this followed a long tradition of appointed bodies given the task of recommending improvements in governing structures. The Brownlow Committee of the 1930s and the Hoover Commissions of the 1940s and 1950s was followed by the National Performance Review of the 1990s. But because of the micromanagers in the Congress, executive agency reforms can never get too far ahead of the legislative will.

Privatization has two faces: (1) the private provision of services for those who can afford to pay for them and (2) the returning to the private sector functions previously performed by government. The various aspects of privatization are pivotal to reinventing government efforts throughout the world. The United States has a uniquely large nonprofit sector that it has been able to use as a vehicle for privatization.

Review Questions

1. What is the role of the U.S. Constitution in framing the national machinery of government?

2. How do state and local administrative arrangements mirror those of the federal government?

3. Why have the major efforts to reform the administrative machinery of the federal government—from the Brownlow Committee to the National Performance Review—been incomplete successes at best?

4. Why is the privatization of government services usually a more attractive option for Republicans than Democrats?

5. How does the nonprofit sector supplement the government's role in providing social services?

Key Concepts

Brownlow Committee A committee appointed by President Franklin D. Roosevelt in 1936 for the purpose of diagnosing the staffing needs of the president and making appropriate recommendations for the reorganization of the executive branch.

bureau movement The efforts of progressive reformers early in the twentieth century to apply scientific methods to municipal problems. Their efforts led to the creation of research bureaus, which in turn created the academic field of public administration.

cabinet The heads of the executive departments of a jurisdiction who report to and advise its chief executive; examples would include the president's cabinet, the governor's cabinet, and the mayor's cabinet.

cabinet government The British system, whereby the cabinet as a whole, rather than only the prime minister who heads it, is considered the executive, and the cabinet is collectively responsible to the Parliament for its performance. In addition,

the cabinet ministers are typically drawn from among the majority party's members in Parliament, whereas in the United States the cabinet secretaries are only from the executive branch.

constitutional architecture The administrative arrangements created by a government's constitution—from the separation of powers to the requirement that specific departments be created or services performed.

Dillon's rule The criteria developed by state courts to determine the nature and extent of powers granted to local governments.

Executive Office of the President (EOP) The umbrella office consisting of the top presidential staff agencies that provide the president help and advice in carrying out his major responsibilities. The EOP was created by President Franklin D. Roosevelt under the authority of the Reorganization Act of 1939. Since then, presidents have used executive orders, reorganization plans, and legislative initiatives to reorganize, expand, or contract the EOP.

Grace Commission An attempt made by the Reagan administration to have business leaders study and reform the federal government; much was studied, little was reformed.

Hoover Commissions The post–World War II efforts to reorganize the federal government.

nonprofit organization An organization created and operated for public or societal purposes (such as alleviation of poverty) rather than private benefit purposes (such as return on shareholders' investments).

privatization The process of returning to the private sector property or functions previously owned or performed by government.

regulatory commission An independent agency created by a government to regulate some aspect of economic life.

reinventing government The latest manifestation of the progressive tradition of continuously improving government—this time with an emphasis on privatization.

Bibliography

American Federation of State, County, and Municipal Employees. (1984). *Passing the Bucks: The Contracting Out of Public Services.* Washington: AFSCME.

Blair, Tony. (1998). "Third Way, Better Way," *Washington Post National Weekly* (October 5).

Blumberg, Stephen. (1981). "Seven Decades of Public Administration: A Tribute to Luther Gulick." *Public Administration Review* 41 (March–April).

Brownlow, Louis. (1958). *A Passion for Anonymity: The Autobiography of Louis Brownlow.* Chicago: University of Chicago Press.

Carnegie, Andrew. (1900). *The Gospel of Wealth.* New York: Century.

Donahue, John M. (1989). *The Privatization Decision.* New York: Basic Books.

Egan, Timothy. (1995). "Many Seek Security in Private Communities." *New York Times* (September 3).

Goodnow, Frank J. (1900). *Politics and Administration: A Study in Governments.* New York: Russell and Russell.

Gore, Al. (1993). *From Red Tape to Results: Creating a Government that Works Better and Costs Less.* Report of the National Performance Review. Washington: Government Printing Office.

Kaufman, Herbert. (1976). *Are Government Organizations Immortal?* Washington: Brookings Institution.

Kettner, P. M., and L. L. Martin. (1987). *Purchase of Service Contracting.* Beverly Hills, CA: Sage.

Lind, Michael. (1995). "To Have and Have Not: Notes on the Progress of the American Class War." *Harper's* (June).

Marlin, J. (1984). *Contracting for Municipal Services.* New York: Wiley.

McKenzie, Evan. (1994). *Privatopia: Homeowner Associations and the Rise of Residential Private Government.* New Haven, CT: Yale University Press.

Meriam, Lewis. (1939). *Reorganization of the National Government: What Does It Involve?* Washington: Brookings Institution.

Miller, Arthur. (1995). "To Newt on Art." *The Nation* (July 31/August 7).

Morgan, D. R., and R. E. England. (1988). "The Two Faces of Privatization." *Public Administration Review* 48.

Mosher, Frederick C. (1967). *Government Reorganization: Cases and Commentary.* Indianapolis: Bobbs-Merrill.

Nakashima, Ellen. (2001). "Bush Opens 40,000 Federal Workers' Jobs to Competition." *Washington Post* (June 8).

Osborne, David, and Ted Gaebler. (1992). *Reinventing Government.* Reading, MA: Addison-Wesley.

Pollitt, Christopher. (1996). "Antistatist Reforms and New Administrative Directions: Public Administration in the United Kingdom." *Public Administration Review* 56 (January–February).

Preer, Robert. (1986). "Town Meetings Don't Work." *Washington Post* (June 13).

Public Broadcasting System. (2005). *Frontline: Private Warriors.* Airdate, June 21, 2005

Rehfuss, J. A. (1989). *Contracting Out in Government.* San Francisco: Jossey-Bass.

Rosenbloom, David H. (1993). "Have an Administrative Rx? Don't Forget the Politics!" *Public Administration Review* 53 (November–December).

Ross, Bernard H. (1998). "Metropolitan Organization," *International Encyclopedia of Public Policy and Administration,* ed. Jay M. Shafritz. Boulder, CO: Westview Press.

Salant, Tanis Janes. (1998). "County," *International Encyclopedia of Public Policy and Administration,* ed. Jay M. Shafritz. Boulder, CO: Westview Press.

Savas, E. S. (1982). *Privatizing the Public Sector: How to Shrink Government.* Chatham, NJ: Chatham House.

Savoie, Donald J. (1994). *Thatcher Reagan Mulroney: In Search of a New Bureaucracy.* Pittsburgh: University of Pittsburgh Press.

Seidman, Harold. (1980). *Politics, Position, and Power: The Dynamics of Federal Organization,* 3rd ed. New York: Oxford University Press.

Szanton, Peter L., ed. (1981). *Federal Reorganization: What Have We Learned?* Chatham, NJ: Chatham House.

Weisband, Edward, and Thomas M. Frank. (1975). *Resignation in Protest.* New York: Viking Press.

Witte, Griff. (2005). "Democrats Criticize Payments to KBR. Pentagon Auditors Question More than $1 Billion in Iraq Costs." *Washington Post* (June 28).

Recommended Books

Downs, George W., and Patrick D. Larkey. (1986). *The Search for Government Efficiency: From Hubris to Helplessness.* Philadelphia: Temple University Press. An explanation of why efforts to reform government tend to operate in ignorance of previous reform efforts and why all such schemes have only "a minuscule chance of successful implementation."

Ingraham, Patricia W., James R. Thompson, Ronald P. Sanders, eds. (1998). *Transforming Government: Lessons from the Reinvention Laboratories.* San Francisco: Jossey-Bass. A collection of essays on the lessons for reform derived from the federal government's reinventing government effort.

Light, Paul C. (1997). *The Tides of Reform: Making Government Work, 1945–1995.* New Haven, CT: Yale University Press. The history of reforming the federal government in the 50 years after World War II.

Osborne, David, and Peter Plastrik. (1998). *Banishing Bureaucracy: The Five Strategies for Reinventing Government.* New York: Penguin Putnam. More stories of government organization turnarounds; touted as the "sequel" to the 1992 *Reinventing Government* because Osborne is the senior author of both books.

Smith, Steven R., and Michael Lipsky. (1993). *Nonprofits for Hire.* Cambridge, MA: Harvard University Press. The how and why of governmental use of nonprofit organizations.

Related Web Sites

Americorps
  www.americorps.org/
The Brookings Institution
  www.brookings.edu
Center for Local and State Solutions
  www.napawash.org/pc_local_state
Constitutions of the World
  www.psr.keele.ac.uk/const.htm#america
Federalist Papers
  www.yale.edu/lawweb/avalon/federal/fed.htm
International City/County Management Association
  www.icma.org

Library of Congress state and local governments page
  lcweb.loc.gov/rr/news/stategov/stategov.html
National Center for Charitable Statistics
  nccs.urban.org/
National Partnership for Reinventing Government
  www.govinfo.library.unt.edu/npr/
Privatization and contracting out
  www.afscme.org/about/resolute/1996/
  r32-019.htm
U.S. Government Manual Online
  www.www.gpoaccess.gov/gmanual/

CHAPTER 4

Intergovernmental Relations

•KEYNOTE: THE AGE OF DEVOLUTION

It was a disquieting time in the United States. Many of the states in the federal system were complaining that the central government in Washington was violating the spirit if not the letter of the Constitution. There was a resurgence in the concept of states' rights, strong feelings that federal involvement within the states was both oppressive and inefficient, and that republican ideals would be best served with a smaller, less-intrusive national government. These same conditions were occurring in the early 1860s, and they would emerge again in the mid-1990s. In the first instance this controversy over intergovernmental relations began its resolution with the election of Abraham Lincoln and was finally resolved by civil war. In the second instance the public sought to resolve these issues by voting for a Newt Gingrich–led Republican Congress.

Speaker of the House Gingrich was no Lincoln, but both men had to grapple with the core issues of the nature of the American federal system. Lincoln essentially said that devolution (returning powers to the states) can only go so far—and that secession by the 11 southern states of the confederacy was too far. More than 130 years later, Gingrich and company essentially said that centralization had gone too far—it was time to move decidedly in the other direction.

Wars, whatever else they might be (horrible, lethal, unnecessary!), are great centralizers. The world wars of the twentieth century, being total in the Clausewitzian sense (a mobilization of the entire society), have been the greatest engines of centralized governmental control of all time. Wartime governments not only told their conscripted soldiers when, where, and how they were to fight, but they also regulated their home fronts to such an extent that people were told, in detail, how they were to live: how much fuel they could burn, how much food they could eat, and even where they could work.

Over the past century, the response to crises, whether military or economic, most often has been an enlarged role for the central government. Sometimes the efforts were benign, as they were when Franklin D. Roosevelt presented the New Deal of the 1930s in the United States or when Clement Attlee led his Labour Party to socialized medicine by creating the National Health Service in the United Kingdom in the late 1940s. Often centralization has proved to be malignant, as it was with Hitler's Germany or Stalin's Soviet Union. The ending of a century that has been dominated by militarism—from the beginning of World War I in 1914 to the demise of the Soviet Union in 1991—is bringing with it renewed demands for decentralization. With the diminution of the threat from without, states throughout the world are giving more thought to demands for greater freedom within. It is a worldwide phenomenon fueled both by the end of the Cold War and the resurgence of a previously suppressed nationalism. The Soviet Union, Yugoslavia, and Czechoslovakia all disintegrated as political entities. They have been replaced by multiple smaller states that express the previously pent up tribal or nationalistic yearnings of their peoples.

On a less cataclysmic scale, similar nationalistic movements are visible even in the most stable states. Scottish and Welsh nationalists want greater autonomy from the British central government. Quebec has been talking for decades about seceding from Canada unless it gets greater autonomy. In the United States there has been a resurgence of demands for states' rights. Once a code word for opposition to federal civil rights legislation, the phrase is now political shorthand for those who seek to decrease the powers of the federal government and increase the powers of the states. This multifaceted international movement to reduce the power of national governments, to reduce the power of presidents and prime ministers, and to concomitantly increase the power of legislatures and subnational governments is a direct result of the reduction of external threats. In wartime, whether hot or cold, political leaders get extraordinary powers and deference. Peace diminishes both them and their office. Without the need to rally around the commander in chief, American national politics tends to return to a government dominated more by its legislative than by its executive branch—at least with domestic issues. The war on terrorism, being less than total, has yet to change this. This was the normal condition of American government during most of the nineteenth century (the Civil War being the major period of exception).

The key word in the new American thrust toward devolution is *mandate.* Normally this word refers to the perceived popular or electoral support for a public program, political party, or a particular politician. U.S. presidents who win elections by overwhelming majorities may rightly feel the vote was a "mandate" to carry out their proposed policies. But mandate has another equally important meaning: It is one level of government requiring another to offer—or pay for—a program as a matter of law or as a prerequisite to partial or full funding for either the program in question or other programs. It is the federal government ordering, by means of passing a law, state governments to reduce air pollution. Or it is a state government ordering, by means of passing a law, municipal governments to recycle trash collections. Mandates are orders pure and simple. And the movement toward devolution is spurred on by jurisdictions and constituencies that increasingly resent taking such orders. In the United States these jurisdictions cite the "fact" that they are sovereign states and shouldn't have to put up with this administrative tyranny.

Hypocrisy is what makes it possible for the states to demand federal action and funding on this or that program while complaining that federal regulations on their use of federal funds insult their sovereignty. It is like a grown child demanding his or her parents are obligated to pay for this and that, while at the same time insisting that he or she be treated like an independent adult. Neither the states nor such children can have it both ways. As Shakespeare's King Lear reluctantly learned, "How sharper than a serpent's tooth it is to have a thankless child." But who is the child here? The federal government is the creature (if not the child) of the states. Yet the states, like old King Lear, gave up their sovereign pretensions to "form a more perfect union." Now they complain when things are not perfect enough. But that was not the agreement. The deal made at the 1787 Constitutional Convention was "more perfect"—not perfect. Those who might say to the states, "Quit your whining and act your age" miss the point. The whining, the complaining, the hypocrisy is an inherent and beneficial part of a never-ending process of intergovernmental give and take. Besides, the complaining often leads to useful change.

Perhaps the best example of this give-and-take aspect of the federal system is that if a government function is not working at one level, it can be shifted onto another level to see if it can be done any better. A good example of a program that has bounced between the intergovernmental levels is welfare. When the Social Security Act was passed in 1935, it included a small program to help widows and orphans. This was the origin of Aid to Families with Dependent Children (AFDC), the program by which the federal government matched state spending on welfare. AFDC provided federal funds, administered by the states, for children living with a parent or a relative who met state standards of need. The program was controversial because of charges that it not only promoted illegitimacy but also encouraged fathers to abandon their families so they could become eligible for AFDC. In 1994 more than 14 million people were receiving AFDC, up from just over 2 million in 1955. (See Table 4.1)

Claiming that the system had produced "welfare queens"—women conceiving children out of wedlock to qualify for AFDC benefits—and a cycle of generational poverty encouraged by the welfare system, the Republican-controlled Congress in 1995 decided to act. It would change the system by giving the problem back to the states. Welfare was a local problem to begin with. The tradition of the county poor farm or workhouse can be traced back to sixteenth-century England. The money spent on AFDC would be converted to block grants with which the states in their 50 varieties of wisdom would decide who was worthy of the new-style welfare and under what conditions. In essence most of the federal strings would be removed, and the states would overall get less than before, but they would have far greater discretion on how to spend it. Thus a comprehensive welfare reform bill was passed by the Congress in 1996. This repealed the entitlement aspect of AFDC and was signed into law by President Clinton. The states—with the encouragement of the federal government—got busy simultaneously reinventing welfare programs while seeking to discourage the expansion of the welfare rolls by holding fathers more responsible for supporting their children. Simply put, the problem has proved so difficult that the Congress is giving up on it and seeking to dump it back on the states. Ah, federalism!

Even without reform we would expect welfare rolls to decrease when jobs are plentiful. But other, more lasting factors are at work as well—factors that suggest that the rolls will not "automatically" go up with a modest economic downturn. First, devolution means that welfare isn't what it used to be; most importantly, it is no longer an entitlement. According to Barbara Vobejda and Judith Havemann, in at least three dozen states welfare managers actively seek to prevent applicants from getting welfare once they apply. "Welfare offices are urging applicants to ask for help from relatives instead of signing up for government assistance, writing one-time emergency checks in place of monthly benefits, or requiring applicants to spend weeks searching for work before they receive their first welfare payment." This raises questions "of whether they have found jobs on their own, never truly needed them in the first place, or have been scared off or intimidated from applying for help that their children genuinely require."

Such diversion tactics are now commonplace. California, Kansas, Florida, Oregon, and New York, among other states, all seek to direct applicants into jobs or one-time cash payments (they cannot then reapply for a prescribed period). This leads to the second major new factor. The traditional welfare office is evolving into a new administrative animal. According to Rachel L. Swarns, in New York City "job centers are replacing welfare offices. Financial planners are replacing caseworkers. And the entire bureaucracy is morphing into the Family Independence Administration. In truth the same workers still do business in the same buildings, but the city has been infected by a

This 1937 picture, with its juxtaposition of rich and poor, has long symbolized welfare in a land of plenty. But the photo, taken in Louisville, Kentucky, is triply misleading. First, it is not about traditional welfare at all; the people waiting in the bread line were the victims of flooding. Second, it implies that most welfare recipients are black, when almost twice as many welfare recipients are white. This was as true in 1937 as it is today. According to the U.S. Census Bureau figures, 23 million whites receive welfare, while only 12 million blacks do. However, just about one-third of all blacks receive welfare, while only about 10 percent of whites do (*Charlotte Observer,* September 11, 1997). Finally, the United States does not have the "world's highest standard of living" when judged by overall social indicators such as infant mortality. A United Nations report ranked the United States fourth in overall quality of life (behind Canada, France, and Norway) and seventeenth in poverty levels behind almost all of the major industrialized states, despite the fact that the United States has the highest per capita income. It is just that this income isn't as evenly distributed as in the 16 other countries with lower poverty rates (*Pittsburgh Post Gazette,* September 9, 1998).

name-changing frenzy that has been sweeping the country. Massachusetts' Department of Public Welfare is now the Department of Transitional Assistance. Florida's welfare program is now the Work and Gain Economic Self-Sufficiency Program." Indicative of this major change in terminology is the 1998 decision of the American Public Welfare Association (which represents social service agencies) to change its name after 66 years to the American Public Human Services Association. Devolution may not yet have killed welfare in fact, but it has certainly killed it in name.

Welfare is just one example of how the age of devolution is bringing us back to the first principles of the age of revolution. Alexander Hamilton, the high priest of an energetic national government among the founding fathers, felt strongly that essentially local issues, as he wrote in *The Federalist,* No. 17 (1787), "can never be desirable

TABLE 4.1 Welfare Recipients (in millions) in the United States (1980 to 2003)

Year	Families on Welfare	Individuals on Welfare
1980	3.712	10.774
1985	3.701	10.855
1990	4.057	11.695
1995	4.791	13.418
1996	4.434	12.321
1997	3.740	10.376
1998	3.050	8.347
1999	2.554	6.828
2000	2.219	5.790
2001	2.110	5.420
2002	2.048	5.069
2003	2.048	4.932

SOURCE: *Statistical Abstract of the United States 2004–2005* (Washington, DC: Government Printing Office, 2005).

Note how the number of recipients dramatically declined after passage of the 1996 Welfare Reform Act.

cares of a general jurisdiction." Hamilton believed it "improbable that there should exist a disposition in the federal councils to usurp the [local] powers . . . because the attempt to exercise those powers would be as troublesome as it would be nugatory; and the possession of them, for that reason, would contribute nothing to the dignity, to the importance, or to the splendor of the national government." Will a rollback of the welfare state contribute to the "dignity" and "splendor" of the federal government? That depends if it is your welfare that is being rolled back! According to political analyst Gareth G. Cook, at least one thing is certain: "Devolution is the theme that runs through nearly all of the Republican's high-profile domestic initiatives. . . . Whether it's cops on the street, environmental protection, or school lunches for poor kids, the Republican solution is to devolve it."

For Discussion: *Why has devolution become a worldwide phenomenon in the wake of the Cold War? What are the major differences in welfare policy since the Reform Act of 1996 discontinued the entitlement aspect of welfare?*

The Evolution of Federal Systems

History indicates clearly that the principal factor in the formation of federal systems of government has been a common external threat. Tribes, villages, cities, colonies, or states have joined together in voluntary unions to defend themselves. However, not all systems so formed have been federal. A true federal system such as that in the United States must have the following features:

1. A written constitution that divides government powers between the central government and the constituent governments, giving substantial powers to each

2. Levels of government, through their own instrumentalities, exercising power directly over citizens (unlike a confederation, in which only subnational units act directly on citizens while the central government acts only on the subnational governments)

3. A constitutional distribution of powers that cannot be changed unilaterally by any level of government or by the ordinary process of legislation

Alliances and Confederations

In the beginning there was the alliance—a coalition of states agreeing to help each other in the event of war or crises. Alliances do not only involve cooperation and aggregation of capabilities; they are generally directed toward an actual or potential enemy and the actual or potential use of force. The agreement on which an alliance is based is often embodied formally in a treaty, but it can also be based on a tacit or informal understanding. Alliances can be between states that are relatively equal in power and involve mutual security guarantees, or they can be between unequal states—in which case the more powerful state generally extends a unilateral guarantee to the less powerful one. This is always a dangerous situation for the weaker state. Too often a willingness to protect and preserve has turned into a desire to take over and annex. Alliances differ in duration, number of members, and the extent to which there are common interests among the members. The greater the common interest, the stronger and more durable the alliance is likely to be.

Then came the confederation, a group of independent states that delegate powers on selected issues to a central government. In a confederation, the central government is deliberately limited, designed to be inherently weak, and has few independent powers. The United States was a confederation from 1781 to 1789. But the central government was so ineffectual in dealing with problems such as **Shays' Rebellion** and interstate commerce that the Constitutional Convention of 1787 was called to discuss the inadequacies of confederation government. To the great surprise of many who sent them to the convention, the delegates recommended not improvements in the confederation—which was expected—but a whole new form of national government.

Defining Intergovernmental Relations

Finally, when there was need for even stronger bonding among governments, along came federalism, a system of governance in which a national, overarching government

---

Shays' Rebellion A futile armed revolt (1786–1787) led by Daniel Shays (1747–1825), a Revolutionary War officer, in New England to protest the discontent of small farmers over debts and taxes. The rebellion was never a serious military threat, but it raised concern over the inadequacy of the Articles of Confederation to handle internal disorders and thus helped to create support for a stronger national government.

shares power with subnational or state governments. Intergovernmental relations is federalism in action. It is the complex network of day-to-day interrelationships among the governments within a federal system. It is the political, fiscal, programmatic, and administrative processes by which higher units of government share revenues and other resources with lower units of government, generally accompanied by special conditions that the lower units must satisfy as prerequisites to receiving the assistance.

In essence, intergovernmental relations are the sets of policies and mechanisms by which the interplay between different levels of government serving a common geographical area is managed. Such relations reflect the basic constitutional framework that links the levels of government, as well as dynamic contemporary factors including relative power, financial strengths, ethnic divisions, geographical factors, and so on. The essence of this constitutional framework is well captured by this famous 1763 statement by **William Pitt,** the elder, in the British House of Lords:

> The poorest man may in his cottage bid defiance to all the forces of the Crown. It may be frail—its roof may shake—the wind may blow through it—the storm may enter—the rain may enter—but the King of England cannot enter!—all his force dares not cross the threshold of the ruined tenement!

In the United States today, the "crown"—the federal government—may not interfere unless this "poorest man" commits the proverbial "federal offense" and federal officials obtain a search or arrest warrant. And only local officials can obtain warrants for local crimes. This is why the investigation of President John F. Kennedy's 1963 **assassination** was undertaken by the local police in Dallas, Texas. In the eyes of the law, Kennedy was just the victim of a local murder. In 1963 it was a federal crime to rob a bank if it was insured, as most are, by a federal agency, but it was not a federal crime to murder a president. (It is now!) After the local police so botched the investigation that they inadvertently spawned a conspiracy theory industry, Congress made it a federal offense to threaten or attack a president, vice president, or his or her immediate family. The point here is that within a federal system different levels of government often perform similar functions, law enforcement in this case, that are constitutionally separate. Each level has constitutional limitations.

An understanding of intergovernmental relations is essential for every public administrator, since this area defines the scope and territory of the administrative world in which he or she lives. It is not just a question of territorial boundaries, though the boundaries of all political units are established by laws, constitutions,

---

William Pitt (1708–1778) The First Earl of Chatham, known as the Great Commoner for his leadership in the House of Commons. The City of Pittsburgh is named in his honor. Historians call him "the elder" because his son with the same name was later prime minister.

assassination The deliberate murder of someone, especially of a politically prominent personage for political motives. The original assassins were thirteenth-century Muslims whose main goal was the murder of Christian Crusaders and other political rivals. Assassination is a time-honored though dishonorable way of removing people from public office. Presidents Lincoln, Garfield, McKinley, and Kennedy were assassinated; Presidents Theodore Roosevelt, Franklin Roosevelt, Truman, Ford, and Reagan all narrowly escaped death in various attempted assassinations.

and accords, the study of which is central to intergovernmental relations. It is equally a question of functional allocations, because most countries have found it necessary to distinguish among national, regional, and local issues and to allocate them in various ways to different levels of government. This allocation, the question of who does what and with what resources, is the essential core, the heart of intergovernmental relations.

The Fundamental Settlement

The most critical dimension of intergovernmental relations, that which forms and shapes the context of every government, is the fundamental settlement or accord by which the government was created. Such accords can never ultimately be unilateral—they must always involve a settlement between a plurality of communities. Federalism, like most institutional forms, is a solution of, or an attempt to solve, a certain kind of problem of political organization. Viable federal systems accommodate regional or subsystem diversity, thereby enhancing the strength of the greater federation. Both the United States and the European Community offer illustrations of settlements whose terms determine the nature, scope, and powers of the governments involved.

The Constitution

The 1789 Constitution of the United States is the oldest written constitution continuously in force and an enduring example to the rest of the world of the benefits and effectiveness of such a well-crafted document. Its famous beginning, "We the people," asserts that the source of its authority is the people as opposed to the states. It then assigns powers to the various branches of government and in doing so structures the government. It limits the powers that any branch may have and allows each branch to check and balance the others. Most significantly, it denies certain powers to the national government, reserving them for the states and the people. But aside from its legal force as law and its physical existence as a piece of fading parchment in the National Archives, the U.S. Constitution is the national icon, the premier symbol of American freedom and governance; above all, it represents the collective political will of the American people over two centuries to maintain their republican form of government. Nevertheless, because of the nature of judicial review, the Constitution is ultimately, as New York governor Charles Evans Hughes asserted in 1907, "what the judges [of the Supreme Court] say it is." It is as Thomas Jefferson angrily wrote in a September 6, 1819, letter to Judge Spencer Roane, "a mere thing of wax in the hands of the judiciary, which they may twist and shape into any form they please."

The 85 essays in *The Federalist,* published in 1787–1788, are the classic commentary on the U.S. Constitution and the theories behind it. They are considered by many political scientists to be the most important work of political theory written in the United States—the one product of the American mind counted among the classics of political philosophy. The papers were originally newspaper articles written by Alexander Hamilton, James Madison, and John Jay (all under the pseudonym

Publius) to encourage New York to ratify the new Constitution. The papers reflect the genius of the balance achieved in the American system between the views of Madison, an exponent of limited government, and Hamilton, an admirer of an energetic national government. It has been suggested that the papers reflected the thinking of the minority of Americans who wanted a more nationalist government than that desired by most of the postrevolutionary generation.

Jay wrote only a few of the Federalist papers, but he was the first chief justice of the United States—a job he considered so insignificant that he resigned to become governor of New York. His resignation had the beneficial effect of making room for a later chief justice, John Marshall, the Revolutionary War soldier who became the third chief justice of the Supreme Court and, by almost universal agreement, the one who did the most to establish the independent authority of the Court. From 1801 to 1835, he led the struggle for the Court to be the final arbiter of the Constitution and, by sheer force of will and legal cunning, made the federal judiciary a true check on the power of the other two branches.

Marshall, in a wide-ranging series of decisions, helped to create the American style of federalism. For example, in 1819 in *McCulloch v. Maryland* the Court upheld the implied powers granted to the Congress by the **necessary and proper clause** of the Constitution, upheld the supremacy of the national government in carrying out functions assigned to it by the Constitution, and established the doctrine of intergovernmental tax immunity. In stating that "the power to tax is the power to destroy," the Court held that the Bank of the United States was not subject to taxation by the State of Maryland. And "destroy" is exactly what the Maryland State Legislature wanted to do to the bank. It viewed the "Monster Bank" so much as the tool of the privileged elite and of the still hated British interests that it specifically passed a law taxing the bank's operations in Maryland in the hopes of crippling it.

The European Union

Sometimes the fundamental settlement occurs all at once, as it did with the creation of the American federal system by the U.S. Constitution. Sometimes it evolves over a series of accords, as it has with the European Union, which is still evolving. It may eventually become a "sort of United States of Europe" as Winston Churchill envisioned in 1946; or it could fracture in warring (both hot or cold) camps as it did so often in the twentieth century. Remember, the U.S. experience with federalism was not a ride in a continuous direction. The Civil War was a major setback. Of course, after the war the Union was stronger than ever. Historian James M. McPherson reminds us in his *Battle Cry of Freedom* (1988) that "before 1861 the two words 'United States' were generally rendered as a plural noun: 'the United States *are* a

---

Publius An ancient Roman who was famous for his devotion to republican government. It was common in the late eighteenth century for political writers to use a pseudonym of ancient lineage that reflected their political leanings.

necessary and proper clause That portion of Article I, Section 8, of the U.S. Constitution (sometimes called the elastic clause) that makes it possible for Congress to enact all "necessary and proper" laws to carry out its responsibilities.

republic.' The war marked a transition of the United States to a singular noun." Only after the Civil War were we "one nation under God, indivisible" as it says in the Pledge of Allegiance. The war had decided once and forever the issue of divisibility.

Political integration occurs as a result of a process, whether peaceful or force-ful, of joining together to create a new political community—one that is generally regarded as larger than the traditional nation-state. Foreign policy analyst Ernst Haas in *The Uniting of Europe* (1958) wrote of integration as a process "whereby political actors in several distinct national settings are persuaded to shift their loyal-ties, expectations, and political activities toward a new center, whose institutions possess or demand jurisdiction over the preexisting national states." This process has been at work in the European Union and is still going on as the community moves toward building a new political reality. To be viable, this new community must evoke loyalty from the populations of the individual units that have joined to-gether. One sign of the European Union's challenge in creating loyalty occurred dur-ing the summer of 2005 when French voters rejected a proposed European Union constitution. If similar acts of disunity follow, then disintegration will occur. What we do not know about the current movement toward European integration is how far it will go or if it will last. But without a formal overarching structure for Euro-pean integration, there can be no framework for intergovernmental relations.

The American Federal System

The U.S. Constitution is the fundamental settlement defining federalism and also defin-ing the permanent features of intergovernmental relations in the United States. Like the constitutions of many countries, the U.S. Constitution is capable both of amendment as to its formal terms and evolution as to its meaning as a result of such things as Supreme Court judgments. Yet, in essence, it represents a relatively unchanging ele-ment of the framework within which intergovernmental relations are conducted.

The most fundamental aspects include the Constitution's provisions in three areas:

1. Its creation of a federal system—that is, one in which there is both a national government and state governments

2. Its allocation of certain functions to the national government

3. Its embodiment of certain principles, particularly through the interpretation of the Constitution and the **Bill of Rights,** which provide scope for Supreme Court judgments that can profoundly alter the respective powers and functions of the national and state governments over time

If we grow up within a federal system and are used to belonging to a state as well as a nation, it is difficult to imagine what it would be like to live in a country without states. Yet this is the case in countries such as France and New Zealand, which have unitary governments, with all significant decisions being made at the national level.

Bill of Rights The first ten amendments to the U.S. Constitution. Only a few individual rights were specified in the Constitution that was ratified in 1788. Shortly after its adoption, however, ten amendments—called the Bill of Rights—were added to the Constitution to guarantee basic individual liberties.

Three Categories of Governments

There are three main categories into which we can allocate nations: unitary governments, federal governments, and confederations (see Table 4.2). Each has certain strengths and weaknesses, and it is interesting to consider what would be the effects of altering the system from one of these to another, as New Zealand did in 1879 when it abolished its federal system and moved to unitary government. In Australia today, a significant minority would like to abandon federalism, abolish state governments, and perhaps introduce a new level of less costly, more numerous regional administrations.

Sometimes the reform impetus goes in the other direction. For example, Great Britain, formally the United Kingdom, is on the verge of moving from a unitary government to a federal structure now that Scotland and Wales will have their own legislatures with broad powers.

Unitary Government Advantages   Unitary governments do have some significant strengths. The following are the four key advantages they usually have over a federal system or a confederation:

1. National direction is clear; policies can be made by a single government without the need for negotiation or conflict with subnational states.

2. There can be no confusion as to **accountability.** It is clear to voters which level of government is responsible for a particular problem or function. (Legislators

TABLE 4.2   Types of Governments

Type	Examples	
Unitary Governments		
There are no state governments; all important power lies with the national government.	Denmark France	Japan New Zealand
Federal Governments		
There is a national government and a number of state governments; power is shared between them.	Australia Brazil Canada Germany	India Mexico Switzerland United States
Confederations		
Power rests with "sovereign" state governments, and an overarching government has some defined powers.	European Union Commonwealth of Independent States (former USSR)	

accountability The extent to which one must answer to higher authority—legal or organizational—for one's actions in society at large or within one's particular organizational position. Elected public officials are theoretically accountable to the political sovereignty of the voters. In this sense, appointed officials—from file clerks to cabinet secretaries—are less accountable than elected officials. The former are accountable mainly to their organizational supervisors, while the latter must answer to their constituents.

who wish to spend money must raise it; it is not possible for legislators to seek to pass the **buck** for failure to another level of government.)

3. Duplication of legislatures, bureaucracies, and programs is avoided with significant savings in direct costs—and the more subtle but no less real costs of needless duplication.

4. Issues of fairness in raising and spending money between levels of government (vertical fiscal imbalance) simply do not arise.

Federal Government Advantages   Unitary governments also have major drawbacks, which in turn correspond to the major strengths of federal systems. These include the following:

1. A federal system has greater scope for diversity and experimentation in policy.

2. The need to debate issues rather than enact them instantly may provide a more considered and viable policy outcome. This tendency toward incrementalism is seen as integral to democracy.

3. A federal system must consider the different ethnic or cultural groupings that may predominate in a particular state and wish to pursue a distinct cultural or social policy—such as the French Canadians in Quebec. (As the cases of Quebec and Bosnia show, membership in a federation may still fail to fulfill the nationalist aspirations of many people.)

4. The danger always exists in a large country that a unitary government may be too remote for appropriate democratic participation by regional centers located away from the capital; a federal system encourages—indeed demands— regional participation in governance.

5. The danger exists in a unitary government that the stronger regions, the larger racial groups, or more powerful interests will provide insufficient allowance for the needs of minorities or weaker groups.

In *The Federalist*, No. 10, James Madison discusses the problem of such factions and the danger they pose to a political system. Madison feared that the interests of parties and pressure groups could destabilize a government, but he believed that an overarching representative government, with a functional as well as a territorial separation of powers, could prevent this.

Confederations   Confederal systems are inherently weak as central governments. The United States was originally a confederal system. The Articles of Confederation were the original framework for the government of the new United States; they went into effect in 1781 and were superseded by the U.S. Constitution in 1789. The Articles said that the states were entering into a "firm league of friendship" and a "perpetual union for the common defense, the

---

buck Responsibility. To avoid a problem or a responsibility is to *pass the buck*. President Truman was famous for having a sign on his desk that read "The Buck Stops Here." *Buck*, a term from poker, refers to the marker put in front of the player who next had to deal. Bureaucrats in many jurisdictions refer to the form memos that they use to direct paper from one to another as buck slips.

security of their liberties, and their mutual and general welfare." The Articles provided for a weak central government, which could not compel states to respect treaties, could not regulate interstate and foreign commerce, could neither collect taxes directly from the people nor compel the states to pay for the costs of the national government, and could not create a sense of national unity and national purpose. Such absence of central power directly contributed to problems such as a devalued national currency, trade wars between states, and an ineffectual foreign policy. It nonetheless provided the experience of state cooperation out of which the consciousness of the need for a stronger union could emerge.

All confederations such as the present European Union and the Commonwealth of Independent States (the former Soviet Union) pose the same question: Which way are they going? Will they evolve, as the United States did, into a strong federal system? Or will they follow the route of the **Confederate States of America** or the **Confederation of the Rhine** and simply disintegrate and be replaced by new governing structures?

The Structure of Intergovernmental Relations

There are eternal questions concerning the structure of intergovernmental relations: Which level of government will have overall responsibility for what functions? When functions are shared between levels of government, how will each function be divided among national, state, and local governments? Should the taxes needed to finance local government be raised by the government that is to spend them or by the higher level of government most successful at tax raising? Should a national government have an objective of redistributing revenues to reduce the differential between the richest and poorest regions of a nation?

As we said earlier, the Constitution itself is the best place to go for answers to these questions. For example, Article I, Section 8, of the Constitution gives the national government the authority to regulate trade "among the several states." Similarly, the Constitution makes explicit the limits of federal intervention in state matters, including restrictions on the federal government's ability to tax interstate commerce (Article I, Section 9). Such direction provides a framework for what governments can and cannot do in relation to each other.

While the Constitution does provide a framework for intergovernmental relations, the document does not provide all the details on how governments should relate to each other. In fact, the Constitution can be particularly vague in laying out the balance of power between the levels of government. Nowhere is this more obvious than in the Tenth Amendment. In this last amendment of the Bill of

---

Confederate States of America The short-lived confederation formed by the eleven states that sought to secede from the Union. That they could not do so was decided by the Civil War of 1861 to 1865. Those states, in alphabetical order, were Alabama, Arkansas, Florida, Georgia, Louisiana, Mississippi, North Carolina, South Carolina, Tennessee, Texas, and Virginia.

Confederation of the Rhine The 1806–1813 union of the smaller German-speaking states in the Rhine River region.

Rights we are told that "the powers not delegated to the United States by the Constitution, nor prohibited by it to the states, are reserved to the states respectively, or to the people." This amendment, commonly known as the reserved powers clause, has been at the heart of numerous debates on the balance of power between the national and state governments. For nearly two centuries a multitude of laws and court precedents have attempted to define exactly what the Tenth Amendment means, yet this single sentence continues to create as many questions as it answers. Even the Supreme Court has admitted that the Tenth Amendment's guidance regarding intergovernmental relations could be considered "tautological," or circular, in nature. Nevertheless, for individuals seeking constitutional justification for increased state power in relation to the national government, the Tenth Amendment can be seen as the Holy Grail. Just ask Bob Dole. During his 1996 presidential campaign, he carried with him a copy of the Tenth Amendment as a sign of his opposition to the growth of federal powers at the expense of the states.

Intergovernmental relations structures are almost always designed to accommodate differing communities of interest—social, ethnic, and political—as the boundaries of governments often possess, or soon acquire, symbolic meanings for communities that identify with them. This applies whether we are speaking of what it means to be a European or an American, a Luxemburger or a Texan, a Londoner or a San Franciscan. For example, localities in the United States often create fire, library, and school districts that for obvious reasons of **economies of scale** serve the citizens of a variety of small general-purpose jurisdictions such as boroughs or towns. These communities may develop a strong sense of identity that is focused on volunteer fire companies or high school sports teams.

The Effects of Pluralism

Sometimes a community is so dominated by one ethnic group that this impacts their relations—their intergovernmental relations—with other levels of government. Thus the people of Quebec, because of their strong French cultural identity, have been able to get special advantages from the Canadian national government. Alternatively, ethnically dominated communities in other countries have complained that they get fewer resources from their national governments because of their minority status. Sometimes national policies even encourage political ghettoization. For example, the United States has long practiced the art of gerrymandering, the reshaping of an electoral district to enhance the political fortunes of the party in power, as opposed to creating a district with geographic compactness. The term first arose in 1811, when Massachusetts Governor Elbridge Gerry reluctantly signed a redistricting bill, creating a district shaped like a salamander.

In 1986 the Supreme Court ruled in *Davis v. Bandemer* that partisan gerrymandering is unconstitutional "when the electoral system is arranged in a manner that

---

economies of scale Cost savings realized by doing things in larger rather than smaller units. This decreases the overall average cost.

will consistently degrade a voter's or a group of voters' influence on the political process as a whole." This encouraged a spate of affirmative gerrymandering, redistricting to consolidate minority votes so that a minority group member will most likely win the next election. This has resulted in more minorities, especially African-Americans, being elected to the U.S. Congress than ever before. The effect of this is to give them representation in numbers that approximate their percentage of the population. Just like all other members, they fight the political wars to bring resources to the myriad governments within their legislative districts. However, in the 1995 case of *Louisiana v. Hays,* the Supreme Court seemed to put severe inhibitions on this when it ruled that congressional district lines are unconstitutional if race is the "predominant factor" in drawing them. Nevertheless, the Court did not say that race could not be a factor at all.

The Marble-Cake Metaphor

People who have not worked in or studied public administration are often unaware of the complicated nature of intergovernmental relations. It is not simply a question of dividing the work between the levels: of assigning local issues to local government, and national issues to federal government. The majority of issues have national, regional, and local implications. The popular image of the federal system as a layer cake, each layer of government neatly on top of the other, is deceptive. The reality is more like a marble cake. This metaphor holds that the cooperative relations among the varying levels of government result in an intermingling of activities; this is in contrast to the more traditional view of layer-cake federalism, which holds that the three levels of government are totally or almost totally separate. Marble-cake federalism is usually associated with **Morton Grodzins,** who made a famous example out of the case of rural county health officials called sanitarians. Sanitarians are appointed by the state government under merit standards established by the federal government, and while their base salaries come from state and federal funds, the county provides them with offices and office amenities and pays a portion of their expenses.

> It is impossible from moment to moment to tell under which government the sanitarian operates. His work of inspecting the purity of food is carried out under federal standards; but he is enforcing state laws when inspecting commodities that have not been in interstate commerce; and somewhat perversely, he also acts under state authority when inspecting milk coming into the county from producing areas across the state border. He is a federal officer when impounding impure drugs shipped from a neighboring state; a federal-state officer when distributing typhoid immunization serum; a state officer when enforcing standards of industrial hygiene; a state-local officer when inspecting the city's water supply; and (to complete the circle) a local officer when insisting that the city butchers adopt more hygienic methods of handling their garbage.

The essential story of the sanitarian could be told of hundreds of other public sector jobs. Bus drivers, police officers, and teachers are all caught up in the

---

Morton Grodzins (1917–1964) A University of Chicago political scientist.

intergovernmental maze. Consequently, mass transit, law enforcement, and education policies, for example, must be the subject of attention at all levels of government. It takes wise legislators at each level to comprehend how their legislation will fit in with that being developed at other levels—and officials working at each level may find it a major task to see that their work is compatible with that of people working on similar topics in other levels of government. It is not surprising that modern nations have immensely complex sets of rules and procedures, innumerable committees, and frequent conferences designed to gain the best results from this immensely complex machine.

Dynamic Federalism

The formal structure of powers, roles, and relationships underlying the intergovernmental relations of a federal system is rather like the trunk and branches of an old tree. It sways in the wind, leaves come and go, and sometimes entire branches are lost in a storm. The more rigid the tree, the greater the possibility that a major storm (such as a civil war) may uproot it entirely. If the tree is more supple, it will adapt and change to withstand the storm—and may be all the stronger for the experience.

Some federations have collapsed entirely in recent political history. The Union of Soviet Socialist Republics and Yugoslavia are leading examples. Others such as Malaysia have lost a major branch (Singapore) but survived. Still others, like Canada, have been close several times to losing a very major branch (Quebec).

In the United States, there has been a series of major phases of intergovernmental relations.

Dual Federalism

This was the nineteenth-century concept, now no longer operational, that the functions and responsibilities of the federal and state governments were theoretically distinguished and functionally separate from each other. With this philosophy— which existed during the nineteenth century, when each level of the government could and did pretend the other level did not exist—rival lawmen rode through the Old West. In the absence of cooperation between jurisdictions, an outlaw could evade capture simply by "crossing the state line."

Some analysts suggest that this kind of federalism, which went out when the New Deal of 1933 came in, is what the Reagan administration sought, at least rhetorically, to eventually get back to. The basic idea of dual federalism was expressed succinctly in 1891 in *The American Commonwealth* by British historian James Bryce, who visited the United States in the 1880s to observe its political system:

> The characteristic feature and special interest of the American Union is that it shows us two governments covering the same ground yet distinct and separate in their action. It is like a great factory wherein two sets of machinery are at work, their revolving wheels apparently intermixed, their bands crossing one another, yet each doing its own work without touching or hampering the other.

Dual federalism has never really died out. It has just been extensively modified by two centuries of federal legislation and judicial precedents. Indeed, as recently as

1997 the Supreme Court in *Printz v. United States* held that "it is incontestable that the Constitution established a system of 'dual sovereignty.' "

Cooperative Federalism

This is the notion that the national, state, and local governments are cooperating, interacting agents, working jointly to solve common problems, rather than conflicting, sometimes hostile competitors pursuing similar or, more likely, conflicting ends. While some cooperation has always been evident in spite of the conflict, competition, and complexity of intergovernmental relations, cooperation was most prominent between the 1930s and the 1950s. The emergency funding arrangements of the Depression years, known collectively as the New Deal, and the cooperation among federal, state, and local authorities during World War II to administer civilian defense, rationing, and other wartime programs are noteworthy examples of cooperative federalism in the United States.

The New Deal's scheme of economic reconstruction involved many new federal grants to the states aimed at providing jobs. During this time, the concept of using federal spending to create demand—**pump priming**—led to an entirely new position for federal government as the shaper of programs in the states. This was the economic prescription of the British economist **John Maynard Keynes,** which called for stimulating the economy during a time of economic decline by borrowing money to spend on public works, defense, welfare, and so on. In theory, the prosperity generated by such expenditures would increase tax revenues, which in turn would pay for the borrowing.

Cooperative federalism also has a horizontal dimension: state-to-state interactions and relations. Such interstate relations take many forms, including **interstate compacts** and commissions established for specific purposes: river basin management, transportation, **extradition** of criminals, conservation of forests and wildlife, and administration of parks and recreation. Horizontal relations between local governments also are numerous. Cities frequently contract for services from various neighboring local governments (and even from private providers). The Lakewood plan, established in southern California in 1954, is the best-known example of interlocal contracting for services in the United States. Under this plan, the city of

---

pump priming Government spending to stimulate an economy during a time of economic decline.

John Maynard Keynes (1883–1946) The English economist who wrote the most influential book on economics of the last century, *The General Theory of Employment, Interest, and Money* (1936). Keynes founded a school of thought known as Keynesian economics, which called for using a government's fiscal and monetary policies to positively influence a capitalistic economy and developed the framework of modern macroeconomic theory.

interstate compacts Formal arrangements entered into by two or more states, generally with the approval of the U.S. Congress, to operate joint programs. While Article I, Section 10, of the Constitution requires that interstate compacts be approved by Congress, as a practical matter many agreements on minor matters ignore this requirement. The initial intent was to prevent states from forming regional alliances that might threaten national unity.

extradition The surrender by one nation or state to another of a person accused or convicted of an offense in the second nation or state.

> ### BOX 4.1   One Method of Pump Priming
>
> If the Treasury were to fill old bottles with bank notes, bury them at suitable depths in disused coal mines, which are then filled up to the surface with town rubbish, and leave it to private enterprise on well-tried principles of *laissez-faire* to dig the notes up again . . . there need be no more unemployment, and with the help of the repercussions, the real income of the community would probably become a good deal larger than it is. It would, indeed, be more sensible to build houses and the like; but if there are practical difficulties in the way of doing this, the above would be better than nothing.
>
> SOURCE: John Maynard Keynes, *The General Theory of Employment, Interest, and Money* (Cambridge: Cambridge University Press, 1936).

Lakewood contracted for a rather comprehensive package of services from Los Angeles County, where Lakewood is located.

Creative Federalism

This was the Lyndon B. Johnson administration's term for its approach to intergovernmental relations, which was characterized by joint planning and decision making among all levels of government (as well as the private sector) in the management of intergovernmental programs. Many new programs of this period had an urban-metropolitan focus, and much attention was given to antipoverty issues. Creative federalism sought to foster the development of a singular **Great Society** by integrating the poor into mainstream America. Its expansive efforts were marked by the rapid development of categorical grant programs to state and local governments and direct federal grants to cities, frequently bypassing state governments entirely. Great Society programs such as **Head Start** and the **War on Poverty** were all based on the concept of federal grants shaping activities and directions at the state and local levels. However, the idea that all wisdom rested in Washington was not always well received in state capitals or city halls. The Nixon administration's New Federalism sought to alter this balance.

Great Society The label for the 1960s domestic policies of the Johnson administration, which were premised on the belief that social and economic problems could be solved by new federal programs. This was Johnson's effort to revive the federal reform presence in social change represented in the Progressive movement, the New Deal, and the Fair Deal.

Head Start The federal program designed to provide early education opportunities for poor children prior to kindergarten. Head Start centers exist nationwide and offer not only preacademic instruction but also health, social, nutritional, and psychological services.

War on Poverty The phrase used by the Johnson administration for those 1960s Great Society programs designed to eliminate the causes and effects of poverty in the United States.

New Federalism

This was President Richard Nixon's attempt to return autonomy to the states while maintaining significant levels of federal funding. From 1972 onward, New Federalism entailed establishing aggregate grant levels by formula but allowing state and local governments substantial latitude in applying the funds in their own area. The term has its origins in the liberal Republican effort to find an alternative to the centralized state perceived as having been set up by the New Deal but an alternative that nonetheless recognized the need for effective national government. During the Nixon administration, New Federalism referred to the style of decentralized management at the federal level symbolized by such programs as general revenue sharing (see the next section) and the decentralization of federal regional management to ten coterminous regions, each with a common regional center.

New Federalism as developed by the Reagan administration disregarded the Nixon approach of decentralized federal regional management and turned to development of direct relations between the federal government and the state governments. The intent was to return power and responsibility to the states and to dramatically reduce the role of the federal government in domestic programs, ranging from community mental health to crime prevention. This was reminiscent of the dual federalism that prevailed in the United States in the nineteenth century.

New New Federalism

The Reagan administration imposed new policy objectives on intergovernmental arrangements. This was also called—in Nixon fashion—"new federalism." This made sense, however, in that it was basically an extension of the Nixon initiatives. Reagan and his advisers viewed much activity by the national government, especially many expenditures on social programs, as wasteful and unnecessary. Thus they turned their attention to cutting federal grants, attempting to transfer functions "back" to the states and away from Washington. In 1986 the Reaganites also destroyed general revenue sharing, the unrestricted distribution of a portion of federal tax revenues to state governments.

Because Reagan succeeded in making such large cuts in the funds available from Washington to state and local governments, the subnational jurisdictions had no choice but to curtail or close facilities and programs, or to look for energetic ways of funding those they wished to retain. In some respects, the entrepreneurship in state and local government documented by Osborne and Gaebler in *Reinventing Government* (1992) was the inventiveness mothered by the financial necessity imposed on them by Reagan administration policies. While the policy directions of the Reagan and Bush administrations, through their cuts in state and local aid, heavily impacted the poor in the United States, they failed to address the perception of **malaise** in Washington. Thus the Clinton administration began with public confidence in government at record low levels—especially with regard to intergovernmental issues such as welfare and crime.

---

malaise The medical term for a vague feeling of illness that is used in other contexts to express a lassitude or ineffectiveness not traceable to a specific source and not exhibiting a specific set of symptoms. "Malaise" was President Jimmy Carter's word for the political uneasiness he found in America.

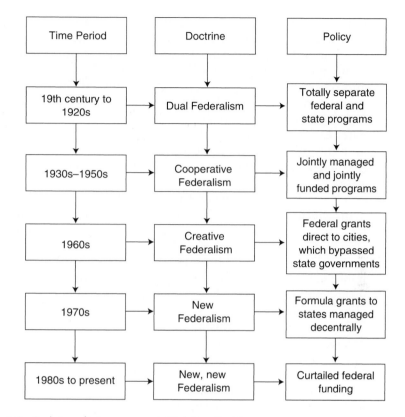

Figure 4.1 Evolution of Intergovernmental Relations Doctrine

Then history, as is its wont, repeated itself. The Republican Congress, elected in 1994, declared in 1995 that it was determined to create—what else—a new federalism. But according to political journalist Alan Ehrenhalt, "It would be more accurate to describe it as the New New New Federalism—the 1995 revival of the Reagan revival of the Nixon revival of some ideas that Dwight D. Eisenhower placed before the country almost 40 years ago." Ehrenhalt views the 1995 Republican version of federalism as "the fourth modern incarnation of the simple-enough notion that Washington ought to be doing less governing and the states ought to be doing more." You may well be thinking by now, "The more things change, the more they stay the same!." This now trite observation was first credited to Alphonse Karr, the nineteenth-century French journalist, in a January 1849 issue of *Les Guépes*, a satirical review of intergovernmental relations in Paris.

Intergovernmental Management

We cannot usually "see" intergovernmental relations, just as we cannot see other aspects of government machinery. But there are times when intergovernmental management bubbles to the surface and becomes visible. Unfortunately, these times usually involve great tragedies such as a major earthquake in California or a terrorist attack on the World Trade Center in New York or the federal building in Oklahoma City. In each case the various levels are literally on the scene. First to arrive are local police and fire personnel. They are backed up by appropriate state agencies such as the **National Guard**. The federal government is represented by the FBI (when a crime is suspected, as in a bombing) and the Federal Emergency Management Agency (FEMA), which plans for and coordinates emergency preparedness and response for all levels of government and for all kinds of emergencies—both civilian and military. FEMA is the organization that decides what the various governments should be doing after such a catastrophe.

The political dialogue in American politics is always full of intergovernmental management issues. Politicians running for president or Congress love nothing better than telling the voters what they are going to do about crime or education once elected. But these are only marginal concerns of the federal government. State and local police are responsible for law enforcement. The FBI, while highly visible in the public's crime-fighting imagery, is minuscule in comparison. State and local governments employ more than half a million uniformed police officers. The FBI has only about ten thousand special agents. Education is the province of local school boards. The bottom line is that aside from minor funding for special programs, there is practically nothing the federal government can do about these issues—nothing but talk. And federal officials, and would-be federal officials, spend so much time talking about such hot-button issues that the public often thinks there is something, usually something simple like mandating more homework for third-graders or telling teenagers not to become sexually active before marriage, that the federal government can do that will make a real difference. But while the politicians may think the public naive, there are no simple answers to the complex questions of intergovernmental management.

In the past, discussions of intergovernmental relations were very much preoccupied with legal and structural questions on the one hand and federal financial relations on the other. While these categories are, of course, fundamentally important, the structuring of various philosophies for, and types of, federal grants programs themselves set basic parameters of federal-state-local interaction. However, an additional strand of public administration studies in federalism emphasizes other dimensions of intergovernmental relations—namely, issues surrounding the management processes that are needed to make a federation work successfully.

Key issues from this perspective include a focus on implementation and problem solving in federal systems, the nature of coordination, accountability in a multiorganizational setting, and an interest in competence and capacity building (the development of both the physical and human infrastructure for economic advancement).

National Guard The military forces of the states, which often are used for civil emergencies, such as major fires or floods. Normally, under the command of each state's governor, any or all of the states' individual guard units may be called (by the U.S. Congress) into federal service at any time. Once a guard unit is called into federal service, it is no longer subject to state control. The National Guard was organized in 1916. Until that time, each state had a volunteer militia.

Any government servant who wishes to successfully manage a program that is intergovernmental in nature must come to grips with these issues. The most common danger with intergovernmental management is the tendency for each higher level to "micromanage" those below them. Congress has been accused of micromanagement when it writes detailed rules for program management into legislation, thus denying line managers any real administrative discretion. But any manager is a micromanager if he or she refuses to allow subordinates to have any real authority or responsibility. Even the federal courts play the micromanagement game. For example, according to *New York* magazine, they require New York City to provide inmates in municipal jails with free daily newspapers in both English and Spanish at a cost of $200,000 per year. They also require the windows of each city prison to be washed at least four times a year at an annual cost of $400,000.

Picket Fence Federalism

The human body depends on the interplay of a variety of comprehensive systems—from the cardiovascular system to the respiratory system to the nervous system—each of these as critical as the next one. It is similarly true that a federal system of government is built around several pervasive systems—systems a lot less predictable than those serving the human body but just as pervasive and critical. *Picket fence federalism* is the metaphor most commonly used for this systemic process. This concept implies that bureaucratic specialists at the various levels of government (along with clientele groups) exercise considerable power over the nature of intergovernmental programs. Bureaucratic or program specialists at national, state, and local government levels for such fields as public housing, vocational education, health and hospitals, and higher education represent the pickets in the picket fence. They communicate with each other in daily work, belong to the same professional organizations, and have similar professional training. They are likely to be in conflict with general-purpose government officials (mayors, governors, the president), who attempt to coordinate the vertical power structures, or pickets. The general-purpose officials are the crosspieces of the fence. The metaphor is credited to Terry Sanford, when he was governor of the state of North Carolina. It was initially presented in his *Storm Over the States*.

Councils of Governments and Intergovernmental Agreements

Any multijurisdictional cooperative arrangement to permit a regional approach to planning, development, transportation, environment, and other problems that affect a region as a whole tends to be known as a council of government (COG), even if the word *council* is not part of its formal title. COGs are typically substate regional planning agencies established by states. They are usually responsible for areawide reviews of projects applying for federal funds and for development of regional plans and other areawide special-purpose arrangements. They are composed of designated policymaking representatives from each participating government within the region. Some COGs have assumed a more enterprising role beginning in the 1980s by acting as contractors for, and service providers to, their local governments. For example, the COG for Lee and Russell counties in Alabama helped form a waste management authority to negotiate a single landfill contract with the private company that owns the landfills they use. According to journalist Eileen Shanahan, there is a tendency for COGs to be "transformed into regional entities that amount to multipurpose special districts, with real powers."

The value of councils of government and other cooperative agreements between local governments is becoming particularly noticeable in the area of land use management. As suburban sprawl has emerged as a significant challenge in many parts of the country, there has been a move on the part of state governments to use incentives to bring counties and municipalities into partnerships to manage growth. For example, local governments in Wisconsin are entitled to state grants for planning only if they enter into intergovernmental agreements with their neighbors. While the best way to effectively manage sprawl-related problems might be to simply merge local governments or shift land use management completely to the county level, such options are generally a political nonstarter. Thus states will likely continue to rely more on nudging local governments to join forces rather than shoving them together.

Finally, even if states can coax municipalities into councils of government, the voluntary nature of the partnerships makes them only advisory in nature. They have few, if any, independent sources of revenue. Bernard H. Ross has compared them to the General Assembly of the United Nations in that both institutions "can debate, discuss, and suggest, but they cannot enforce action" on any of their members.

Mandate Mania

Nothing sours intergovernmental relations faster than mandates. (The nature and scope of mandates were discussed in this chapter's Keynote.) It is difficult to even determine how many mandates impact any given jurisdiction. For example, according to journalist Eric Pooley, the New York State Governor's Office of Mandate Relief counted 1,700 state and federal mandates in 1992. But in 1994 the *New York Times* discovered that there were 3,200 from the state alone that affected local government. There is obviously a major problem of definition here. Different things were being counted.

The only way to comprehend the full scope of the mandates problem is to look at their different categories. First, are they direct orders (which imply civil or criminal penalties for disobeying) or merely conditions for receiving aid? If they are the latter, they may not be considered mandates at all, because they do not have any effect unless you want the aid. Then you must also take the strings—the mandates—that come with it. Second, are they programmatic or procedural? Programmatic mandates state the type and quality of program to be implemented—a school lunch program must meet specified national standards for nutrition. A procedural mandate requires jurisdictions to do what they were going to do anyway, but, according to new requirements, personnel must be hired according to equal opportunity provisions; formal meetings and records must be open to the public. While programmatic mandates may cost a great deal, many procedural mandates may cost little or nothing, or have a one-time-only cost.

BOX 4.2   Cyber Sales and Intergovernmental Relations

If you are like a growing number of college students, there is a good chance that you bought this book through an Internet company such as Amazon.com. According to the United States Department of Commerce, total Internet sales for 2004 were estimated at $69.2 billion, an increase of 23.5 percent from 2003. While only amounting to about 2 percent of all sales in the nation, the Internet is clearly becoming a cornerstone of the nation's economy. But what about Internet sales as a source of government revenue? When you purchase products or services in most states, you are charged a sales tax. However, when you make Internet purchases, you most likely pay no sales taxes at all. That's because the U.S. Supreme Court ruled in 1992 that online retailers did not need to collect taxes for sales to states where they did not have a physical presence. Thus, if a company doesn't have a store or shipping center in your state, your purchase online should be tax-free. While this scenario is good for you, it places a strain on most states' revenue streams. As of 2005, all but five states collected some form of sales tax. According to the National Governors Association and National Conference of State Legislatures, state and local governments lost between $15.5 billion and $16.1 billion in 2003 from untaxed Internet sales. Not surprisingly, states have be anxious to find a way to get their money back. However, the states' road to riches must travel through Washington, DC. That's because the Constitution gives the federal government control over interstate commerce. Without congressional action, or a change of heart by the federal judiciary, states cannot collect taxes on online sales. In 2000 and 2003 Congress considered legislation to allow state and local governments to tax Internet purchases, but the bills died before ever reaching the Senate or House floors. Given limited prospects for change in Washington, the states have embarked on a new strategy of intergovernmental cooperation

In 2005, 18 states joined together in a consortium under the Streamlined Sales Tax Project. Under this initiative the states have used their numerical strength to try and persuade online retailers to voluntarily collect sales taxes. Beginning in October 2005, a large number of Internet vendors will collect sales taxes based on the rates in effect in the buyer's home states and then remit the revenue to the states. In return, the e-businesses will receive a one-year amnesty for taxes they may owe on past online sales. While the states will benefit from the revenue generated from the new system, the project has a broader goal of pressuring Congress to create legislation that allows the states to directly tax online sales. Given the complexities that the Streamlined Sales Tax project will entail, Congress may be more likely to support some form of uniformity in the fastest-growing area of retail sales.

SOURCE: adapted from data found in http://www.streamlinedsalestax.org/.

Some mandates merely constrain. But the constraints can hurt, as they do when state laws specify the kinds of government, religious, and nonprofit organization property that is exempt from local property taxes or when states put limits on property taxes or tax increases for veterans or retired citizens.

Some mandates involve not one but large numbers of programs at once. These so-called crosscutting mandates are found in virtually all state and federal aid programs. For example, if you accept federal funds, you are subject to the Anti-Kickback Act of 1934 (the Copeland Act), which should inhibit you from extorting money from employees or contractors.

While it is possible to classify mandates, they are so integral to all of public policy and administration that it is virtually impossible to accurately count them—without first creating a classification scheme that defines what you mean by a mandate. There is no **czar** of mandates statistics. There are only countless studies by countless groups such as the U.S. Conference of Mayors and the **Advisory Commission on Intergovernmental Relations** that all conclude, essentially, that there are more mandates than you can shake a stick at!

Mandates and the War on Terrorism

The war on terrorism that started on September 11, 2001, has caused mandates to explode at the same time that state and local governments have had their revenues curtailed because of a poorly performing economy. The Transportation Security

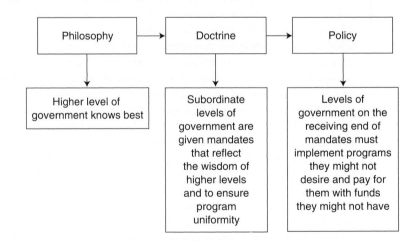

Figure 4.2 The Doctrine of Mandates

---

czar A former Russian absolute monarch; a nickname for any high-ranking administrator who is given great authority over something—for example, an energy czar, a housing czar.

Advisory Commission on Intergovernmental Relations A national, bipartisan organization created by the U.S. Congress in 1959. The commission sought to address itself to improve cooperation among the levels of government and the function of the federal system. Nevertheless, the ACIR became a victim of the budget wars in Congress. It was phased out and shut down by the end of 1996.

Agency, created in 2001, regularly tells airports to raise their security status. However, it hasn't been able to tell the airports where to find the funding to pay for overtime payments to local police. Dale Russakoff and Rene Sanchez reported in the *Washington Post* that when the Department of Homeland Security elevated the terror threat in early 2003, the city of Los Angeles, already spending $1 million a week on extra security and running a high deficit, sought to avoid the additional expense by asking its state to send National Guard troops to the airport. California, already suffering staggering deficits, sent 50 National Guard soldiers to the airport. While the city avoided the expense, the state was stuck with "$100,000 a week more to cut elsewhere."

This problem is hardly limited to California. At the February 2003 meeting of the National Governors Association, the governors voted unanimously that homeland security was the newest "unfunded mandate" with which the states need federal help—meaning money.

In order to address this problem, at least symbolically, Congress passed the Unfunded Mandate Reform Act of 1995. This law holds that any future **bill** might be out of order if it imposes a financial mandate of more than $50 million on any one state, local, or Native American tribal government. But this requirement could always be rescinded by a majority vote. The law did nothing to end current unfunded mandates. It was basically designed to force Congress to be more aware of the implications of possible future mandates. Thus the **Congressional Budget Office** has been assigned the task of developing estimates of the costs of all future mandates. The new CBO assignment amounted to an unfunded mandate in itself. So the then head of the CBO, Robert Reischauer, told a congressional appropriation subcommittee in February 1995 that the CBO would need $7.1 million in additional funds to carry out its new duties. No unfunded mandates for his agency!

Intergovernmental management, then, is the multiplicity of hourly relationships between governments, as well as the dynamic relationships with higher and lower levels of government and with peer governments on the same level. The currency of these relationships is broad; included are political negotiations and old-fashioned "horse trading," legal wrangling, and fiscal maneuvering. Over time, political acumen and economic power will alter the status of governments one to the other, and this dynamism will give rise to anguish—sometimes even to nostalgic attempts to restore past relationships. However, the student of public administration is well advised to begin with a detached assessment as to where his or her government stands in this regard, to acknowledge that the standing and independence of all governments wax and wane, and to demand managers who can administratively "sniff the wind" to ascertain the appropriate response.

---

bill A legislative proposal formally introduced for consideration; unfinished legislation. After a bill is passed and signed into law, it becomes an act.

Congressional Budget Office (CBO) A support agency of the U.S. Congress created in 1974 by the Congressional Budget and Impoundment Act to provide the Congress with basic budget data and with analyses of alternative fiscal, budgetary, and programmatic policy issues, independent of the executive branch and of the Office of Management and Budget.

The Transformation of Governance

In 1999, the National Academy of Public Administration (NAPA) established a Priority Issues Task Force to identify the key issues in public administration that would face the nation in the first years of the twenty-first century. What the task force found was that governance throughout the United States and around the world was "undergoing a fundamental transformation" that had huge implications for public administrators. In particular, the NAPA group suggested that public administrators would face (1) a growing complexity of relationships between government and society; (2) the shifting of national responsibilities both in the direction of international bodies and systems and in the direction of states, localities, and community-based institutions; and (3) the need for greater capacity to manage these relationships. According to Don Kettl, a leading scholar on the subject, "government at all levels has found itself with new responsibilities but without the capacity to manage them effectively." While government remains the only player in society that has formal authority to act in the name of the "people," it has seen its responsibility distributed to both nonprofit and profit-driven enterprises. Given the increasing importance of public-private partnerships, the already complex nature of intergovernmental relations becomes even more stressed. Not only must a local public administrator work with officials at the state and federal level, but he or she must also coordinate programs with nongovernmental organizations such as private contractors and nonprofit groups. Inevitably, such multidimensional relationships raise questions of accountability and responsiveness, with public administrators receiving blame and credit for actions they really do not have control of.

Fiscal Federalism—Following the Money

In the infancy of federalism in the eighteenth century, it may have been grandiose to think of the policy arrangements in national and state government as a system. Geographic separation, painfully slow systems of communication, and a relatively clear differentiation of functions gave each level of government a role that could be carried out with only limited interaction with other levels of government.

Several factors permanently changed this picture during the twentieth century. First, the galvanizing effect of the world wars and the Cold War saw national direction and planning emerge more thoroughly than had ever been necessary before. Second, a revolution occurred in transport and communications that has permanently ended the possibility for states to behave with the completely unilateral autonomy they once had. Third, there emerged with the 1930s New Deal, and with the 1960s civil rights and antipoverty programs, legislation embodying national values that needed to be uniformly implemented across the entire country. The cumulative effect of these fundamental changes gave rise to a concept of national policymaking and state policy implementation overlaid on the traditional and continuing functions of national and state government.

How could a national government bring about actions at the state level that state governments, left to themselves, might find neither palatable nor affordable?

TABLE 4.3   Federal Aid to State and Local Governments

Year	Total (in millions of dollars)	As a Percentage of Federal Outlays
1980	91,385	15.5%
1985	105,852	11.2
1990	135,325	10.8
1995	224,991	14.8
2000	284,659	15.9
2001	317,250	17.0
2002	351,550	16.9
2003	387,281	17.9
2004 (est)	418,091	18.0

SOURCE: *Statistical Abstract of the United States 2004–2005* (Washington, DC: Government Printing Office, 2005).

Certainly, at times, the federal courts have ordered state governments to adopt policies and actions based on judicial interpretations of the meaning of federal legislation or the Constitution. For example, the courts have ordered states to integrate schools (by **busing** if necessary) and to relieve prison overcrowding if it amounts to **cruel and unusual punishment**. However, the federal government, under the Tenth Amendment to the Constitution, does not have a general power to give directions to the states in their primary areas of power. Consequently, more often than not, financial inducement, through grants of money tied to a particular policy objective, has been the preferred instrument for achieving federal purposes. Financial arrangements have been the predominant vehicle within intergovernmental relations by which national policies have been implemented by and through the states.

The Theory of Fiscal Federalism

Fiscal federalism refers to the fiscal (financial) relationships that exist between and among units of government in a federal system (see Table 4.3). The theory of fiscal federalism, or multiunit governmental finance, addresses the question of the optimal design of governments in a multilevel (or federal) governmental system.

---

busing The transporting of children by bus to schools at a greater distance than those the children would otherwise attend to achieve racial desegregation. Busing has often been mandated by the federal courts as a remedy for past practices of discrimination. It has been heartily objected to by parents who want their children to attend neighborhood schools and has, in consequence, been a major factor in "white flight" from central cities. Busing is often used as an example of government by the judiciary, because busing, one of the most controversial domestic policies in the history of the United States, has never been specifically sanctioned by the Congress.

cruel and unusual punishment The criminal penalty prohibited by the Eighth Amendment, which not only bars government from imposing punishment that is barbarous but, as the U.S. Supreme Court has announced, forbids punishment that society's "evolving standards of decency" would mark as excessive.

The public sector has three principal economic problems to solve:

1. The attainment of the most equitable distribution of income
2. The maintenance of high employment with stable prices
3. The establishment of an efficient pattern of resource allocation

The theory of fiscal federalism postulates that a federal form of government can be especially effective in solving these problems because of the flexibility it has in dealing with some problems at the national or central level and some at the local or regional levels. It argues that, for a variety of reasons, the first two problems, equitable distribution of income and maintenance of high employment with stable prices, are problems that the national level of government is best equipped to handle. However, according to the theory, the decentralized regional or local units of government can more efficiently deal with the third problem, allocation of resources, because such units of government are more familiar than the central or national government with local needs and the desires of citizens for public services. Even so, grants-in-aid from the national level of government to local levels may be needed to stimulate local government spending for national purposes, to provide for uniform or minimum service levels (as in education), or to compensate citizens of one area for benefits from services they finance that spill over to residents of another area. Spillover benefits are especially frequent in such programs as clean water and air pollution control, health, and education.

In theory, an accountable government should involve representatives only voting for programs for which they have voted the taxes. The representatives would be accountable to the voters, who could directly assess whether the "purchase" of services and programs they had made at election time was what they wanted, and whether they got good value for their tax money. But in a large nation, need for services can vary greatly between communities, and the capacity to pay taxes also varies greatly among the categories of those who are taxed. This issue focuses attention on several of the central problems of the federal concept: the difficult notion of two or more governments overlaid on the same geographical territory; the difficulty of persuading voters that they need to pay their taxes twice (or more) to different levels of taxing authority; and the difficulty of persuading taxpayers that it is fair that some of their taxes should produce no direct benefit to them but be used to assist some other community or some ill-defined goal dear to an official in a remote office in another city.

Attitudes toward these issues illustrate the level of confidence citizens have in a democratic federation. If confidence is high, and a sense of common national purpose is high—as it was during a "popular" war such as World War II or during the early days of the Great Society programs, citizens are more prepared to trust politicians and bureaucrats to redistribute taxes to promote national goals elsewhere. If, however, confidence in politicians and the bureaucracy is low, citizens may well take some convincing that spending programs are fair and necessary. A confident, successful federal democracy that has confidence in its political leaders and has honest and efficient bureaucrats and well-articulated national aspirations will be one in which there is more room for redistributive programs—an admirable goal to strive for—or perhaps not!

All too often the same central question of fiscal federalism is asked in countless congressional and presidential elections: Why can't the citizens of the states just keep their money (meaning, have their federal taxes reduced) rather than paying it to the federal government so they can return it in grants and services? The answer is deceptively simple: Not all states are fiscally equal. If there are more poor people in one state, federal welfare funds from other states will in effect subsidize them. Would Delaware and Connecticut, for example, otherwise transfer tax dollars from their citizens to the overall poorer citizens of Mississippi and Alabama? Federal spending for military bases, while concentrated in more southern states for reasons of climate, benefit the entire nation—even if they benefit the local economy of Georgia more. While bases and ports may be concentrated in the South, defense contractors are widely distributed. Indeed, to gain support for many defense systems, the **Pentagon** quite consciously procures goods and services from companies in as many congressional districts as possible. Even NASA once boasted, in order to drum up congressional support, that the parts for the space shuttle were built in most of the 50 states.

TABLE 4.4   The Politics of Fiscal Federalism: The Case of Homeland Security Funding

Who wins and who loses in the game of fiscal federalism is often decided by raw politics. In Fiscal Year 2005, the Department of Homeland Security distributed over $2.5 billion to state and local governments. These two lists illustrate the role of raw politics in this distribution.

Overall Funding (Top Ten States)	Per Capita Funding (Top Ten States)
1. New York	1. District of Columbia
2. California	2. Wyoming
3. Texas	3. Alaska
4. Illinois	4. Vermont
5. Florida	5. North Dakota
6. District of Columbia	6. South Dakota
7. Pennsylvania	7. Delaware
8. Ohio	8. Hawaii
9. Michigan	9. Montana
10. Massachusetts	10. New York

Note that while the big states get the most money, the small ones get more per person. Why? Because the formula for the distribution favors the small states. Why? It might be, as economist Paul Krugman suggests, that "the small-state bias of the Electoral College is what allowed Mr. Bush to claim the White House despite losing the popular vote. It's hard not to suspect that the formula—which makes absolutely no sense in terms of national security—was adopted precisely because it caters to that same constituency" (*New York Times,* April 1, 2003). How else can you explain why each citizen of Wyoming is literally granted twice as much money for protection as each citizen of New York or three times as much money as a citizen of California?

SOURCE: The Department of Homeland Security, http://www.dhs.gov/interweb/assetlibrary/Grants_Summary; and the United States Bureau of the Census, http://www.census.gov/popest/states/tables/NST-EST2003-01.xls. Calculations of per capita spending were made by the authors.

Pentagon The building that has become the symbol of the U.S. Department of Defense.

Lobbying by defense contractors aside, the federal government justifies taking its measure of taxes from the states and distributing them in an uneven fashion because this furthers national policies for welfare, for defense, for conservation, for environmental protection, and so on. In this process, some states are winners and some losers. And while no one would deny that any given program could not be better managed or more economically operated, these redistribution programs all exist because lawmakers representing all the citizens thought them to be in the public interest. The members of Congress cannot have it both ways—they cannot argue that the federal government is too full of pork barrel programs for the congressional districts while at the same time kicking and clawing to bring home the bacon for their constituents. Fortunately this is becoming, though only gradually, a truth more universally acknowledged than before.

Grant Programs

Grants by formula or category are the most significant means by which federal moneys are transmitted to the states. A grant is simply an intergovernmental transfer of funds (or other assets). Since the New Deal, state and local governments have become increasingly dependent on federal grants for an almost infinite variety of programs. From almost the beginning of the republic to the present, a grant by the federal government has been a continuing means of providing states, localities, public (and private) educational or research institutions, and individuals with funds to support projects the national government considered useful for a wide range of purposes. In recent years, grants have been made to support the arts as well as the sciences. All such grants are capable of generating debate over what the public as a whole, acting through the grant-making agencies of the federal government, considers useful and in the national interest.

A "grant-in-aid" is the term used for federal or state payments to local governments for specified purposes and usually subject to supervision and review by the granting government or agency in accordance with prescribed standards and requirements. One function of a federal grant-in-aid is to direct state or local funding to a purpose considered nationally useful by providing federal money, on condition that the jurisdiction receiving it match a certain percentage of it. The federal government actively monitors the grantee's spending of the funds to ensure compliance with the spirit and letter of federal intent. Grants-in-aid have other public policy implications as well, because a jurisdiction that accepts federal money must also accept the federal "strings," or guidelines, that come with it. All federal grantees must comply with federal standards on equal employment opportunity in the selection of personnel and contractors, for example.

Historically, the most common grants have been "categorical"—those that can be used only for specified purposes. But there has been a trend, ever since the Nixon administration, to move toward block grants that give the states more discretion over the funds. This trend decidedly accelerated in the mid-1990s as the Republican-controlled Congress sought to reduce the size and role of the federal bureaucracy by reducing congressional oversight of grant programs—and at the same time permanently removing the federal employees who performed many of the oversight functions. For the public administrator, fiscal federalism refers, first and foremost, to the politics and administration of complex intergovernmental grant-in-aid systems.

BOX 4.3   What's in a Transportation Grant?

In August 2005 President George W. Bush signed the Safe, Accountable, Flexible, and Efficient Transportation Equity Act—Legacy for Users, or SAFETEA-LU. While the awkward name may not illicit excitement, the contents of this act are some of the most coveted resources in the federal government's financial relationship with state and local governments. In sum, SAFETEA-LU will send over $286 billion across the 50 states for a variety of transportation purposes. The vast majority of this allocation is geared toward road construction and public transit projects, with the money doled out over five years according to formulas designed to provide state and local governments considerable flexibility. But even as much of the funding in this bill will be distributed on the basis of a formula, there are plenty of specific "earmarked" projects that were added to the legislation as it passed through Congress. For example, the bill allocates $2.3 million for the beautification of the Ronald Reagan Freeway in California; $4 million for projects at the National Packard Museum in Warren, Ohio, and the Henry Ford Museum in Dearborn, Michigan; $2.4 million on a Red River National Wildlife Refuge Visitor Center in Louisiana; and $1.2 million to install lighting and steps and to equip an interpretative facility at the Blue Ridge Music Center. Perhaps the biggest winner in the distribution of the federal "pork" was Alaska. The Act directed $250 million for a bridge to connect the town of Ketchikan (pop. 14,000) to Gravina Island (pop. 50). And just for good measure, Congress threw in an additional $3 million to pay for a documentary film about how Alaska is spending money on its highways. In all, Citizens Against Government Waste estimated the transportation bill funded $24 billion of special projects, which translates into over 8 percent of the budget earmarked for pork.

SOURCES: Adapted from information found in *The Washington Post,* "Road Bill Reflects the Power of Pork: White House Drops Effort to Rein In Hill," Thursday, August 11, 2005, page A01; and Citizens Against Government Waste, http://www.cagw.org/site/PageServer?pagename=reports_highwaybill.

The federal government distributes money to the states through hundreds of grant programs, of which about half are related to **Medicaid.** Some 20 percent are for infrastructure, such as transportation (see Box 4.3), water, or sewage treatment, and the remainder relate to various social and labor market programs. During the 1970s, the Nixon administration introduced less-specific block grants to

---

Medicaid The federally aided, state-operated, and state-administered program that provides medical benefits for certain low-income people in need of health and medical care. Authorized by 1965 amendments to the Social Security Act, it covers only members of one of the categories of people who can be covered under the welfare cash payment programs—the aged, the blind, the disabled, and members of families with dependent children where one parent is absent, incapacitated, or unemployed. Under limited circumstances, states may also provide Medicaid coverage for children under 21 years of age who are not members of Congress. Subject to broad federal guidelines, states determine coverage, eligibility, payment to health care providers, and the methods of administering the program.

counter the criticism that overly restricting the ways federal moneys could be spent tended to reduce state governments to an extremely mechanical role not consistent with their status as governments in their own right. A block grant is distributed in accordance with a statutory formula for use in a variety of activities within a broad functional area, largely at the recipient's discretion. For example, the community development block grant program, administered by the Department of Housing and Urban Development, funds community and economic development programs in cities, counties, Indian reservations, and U.S. territories. The nature of the block grant allows these jurisdictions to allocate the funds to supplement other resources in ways they choose. The problem with block grants is that Washington loses control and the money may be spent even less wisely than it would if more federal strings were attached.

From Contractive to Coercive Federalism

Political scientist Deil S. Wright has developed a series of federalism metaphors—short descriptions for the intergovernmental administrative realities of each era in American federalism. He sees the United States leaving a period of Reagan administration–inspired "contractive federalism" known for its cuts in federal aid. Today he sees the United States as entering a period of "coercive-collage" federalism. The "coercive" refers to the continuing problems of unfunded mandates (just discussed); the "collage" refers to the fact that modern-day federalism is so much like a Salvador Dali painting (with melting clocks in surreal landscapes) in that both lack "thematic coherence." There are so many factors (so many reinventors) at work, so many conflicting political actors playing with the intergovernmental system, that "kaleidoscopic" may be the only way to describe the current situation.

This is made all the more complicated by the fact that some internal American federal issues have been internationalized. For example, the North American Free

TABLE 4.5   Phases of Intergovernmental Relations

Phase Description	Federalism Metaphor	Appropriate Time Period
Conflict	Layer-cake federalism	Nineteenth century to 1930s
Cooperative	Marble-cake federalism	1930s–1950s
Concentrated	Water taps (focused or channeled)	1940s–1960s
Creative	Flowering (proliferated and fused)	1950s–1960s
Competitive	Picket fence (fragmented federalism)	1960s–1970s
Calculative	Facade (confrontational federalism)	1970s–1980s
Contractive	De facto, telescope, and whiplash federalism	1980s–1990s
Coercive-collage	Kaleidoscopic federalism	1990s–?

SOURCE: Adapted from Deil S. Wright, *Understanding Intergovernmental Relations,* 3rd ed. (Pacific Grove, CA: Brooks/Cole, 1988), updated by Deil S. Wright in 1995.

Trade Agreement has allowed Canada to mount a successful legal challenge to state preferences (lower taxes) for in-state beer and wine. Now American six-packs and Canadian six-packs are equal in this regard. But the moral of this story is that state laws can be nullified by international agreement. This was a major surprise to American brewers, vintners, and state legislators.

The Devolution Revolution

The dilemmas of intergovernmental relations illustrated so clearly by the problem of federal-state financial relationships have always been critical issues in democratic federations. The only certainty here is that the states have become addicted to intergovernmental funding. The question remains whether their political leaders will gradually wean them from it or feed their habit. On this front there is good news and bad news. The good news is that many state governments seem genuinely caught up in the devolution revolution. In late 1994, all of the Republican governors and governors-elect met in Williamsburg, Virginia—the colonial capital of that state. Representing a clear majority of the states (30) with an overwhelming majority of the population (70 percent), they issued the "Williamsburg Resolve," which called for reversing the power that had been going to Washington since the New Deal. They said grandiose things appropriate to the place where Patrick Henry said in 1775, "Give me liberty or give me death!" California Governor Pete Wilson said that the "states are not colonies of the federal government." Governor Tommy Thompson of Wisconsin said they should no longer have to go to Washington "on bended knee to kiss the ring."

The bad news is that this is somewhat hypocritical. After all, what their "resolve" essentially calls for is the federal money without the federal strings. But these "strings" have important public policy implications—like ensuring the relatively equal treatment of all citizens no matter in which state they may reside. The current movement toward devolution is similar to the Sagebrush Rebellion. This term, first heard in the 1980s, covers any number of dissatisfactions—hardly a rebellion—that some people in the states of the American West have with the federal government's management and use of the federal lands within their borders. In general, they feel that the states should have more control over the lands and how they are used. The counterargument is that such lands are national trusts and can only legitimately be dealt with by representatives of the national government. According to historian Robert Hughes in *The Culture of Complaint*, the American West "is archetypally the place where Big Government is distrusted, the land of the independent man going it alone. Yet much of it—states like Arizona, for instance—has depended, not marginally or occasionally but always and totally, on federal money from Washington for its economic existence." Consequently, "the Southwestern states could never have been settled at their present human density without immense expenditure of government funds on water-engineering. They are less the John Wayne than the Welfare Queen of American development."

Yet these western states, mostly Republican at that, do not like to be reminded of the role that Washington played in creating and economically developing them. The federal lands within them belong just as much to the rest of the nation. While the political leaders of these western states are quick to assert their "rights" over federal lands, other citizens of other states are just as quick to note that these lands were paid for, indeed fought for, by the entire country.

The latest wrinkle in this Sagebrush Rebellion is to resurrect **Gifford Pinchot**'s definition of conservation as the "wise use" of resources. But this modern wise-use movement is not traditional conservation but a cover for those who advocate greater economic development of public lands. By asserting the legitimacy of multiple uses of public lands, they seek to roll back environmental protections now extant. One legal technique to achieve this rollback is to assert county supremacy by means of local land-use ordinances. This has engendered considerable conflict between local officials and federal land managers. The only certainty here is that as one contemplates the vast expanses of federal land in the West, much litigation can be seen on the horizon.

The web of intergovernmental relations is such a tangled one that there are no easy solutions to the understandable desire for devolution. Even a national administration completely sympathetic to the devolutionist will find it difficult to return powers and lands back to the states. It will take far more than a Williamsburg Resolve and a Sagebrush Rebellion to simply locate, let alone repeal, two centuries' worth of centralizing legislation. In fact, in some cases it may be the states themselves that spearhead campaigns against the weakening of central authority. In an interesting reversal of the dynamic of the Williamsburg Resolve and Sagebrush Rebellion, many state governments in the northeastern United States have joined together not to protest federal intervention but to instead fight against the lack of federal effort in the area of environmental protection. According to the *Christian Science Monitor*, New York, New Jersey, Pennsylvania, and Massachusetts, angered by the EPA's March 2005 mercury emission standards, brought suit against the federal government on the grounds that the new federal rules are not strong enough to meet the intent of the Clean Air Act. Just two years earlier, nine northeastern states banded together to challenge EPA rules that would exempt thousands of industrial air pollution sources, including coal-fired power plants, from the new Clean Air Act standards for emission. In these two instances the states joined forces to encourage the national government to increase its regulation of activities at the state and local levels.

The Public-Choice Solution

The Reagan Revolution of the 1980s, which was continued by the 1990s Republican Congress, coincided with public administration's increasing embrace of public-choice theory. This theory rejected the concept of welfare economics that emerged out of the New Deal: that when private markets failed, the government had to step in to effectively carry out the public interest, and the governmental level best suited to do this was the federal one.

Gifford Pinchot (1865–1946) America's first professional forester, who is credited with coining the term *conservation*. Twice governor of Pennsylvania (1923–1927; 1931–1935), he became internationally famous as President Theodore Roosevelt's partner in making conservation a national issue.

Public-choice theory seriously questioned whether such governmental decisions really represented the wishes of the majority of citizens. More emphatically, public choice denounced governments as being basically inefficient and completely lacking in incentives to perform well unless the expansion of their own programs and the increase of their budgets was involved. The better solution, public-choice advocates argued, was to place governmental action (and expenditures) at the lowest possible levels—that is, at the local government level. The feeling here was that local governments would provide more experimentation, true competition, and innovation. At the local level, citizens could "vote with their feet"—that is, if the citizens had access to appropriate information, they would be able to readily compare the levels of taxation to the quality of services they received. They could then reject inefficient or unresponsive governments by voting down budgets, by voting out big spenders, or even by moving elsewhere—or not moving in at all. Thus the solution to devolution offered by the public-choice advocates is to increase the discretion in the hands of the individual voter by maximizing "user-pay systems" (whether for trash collection or through fees at state park camping grounds) and by placing vouchers (for schools or housing) for spending in the hands of recipients rather than compelling them to use particular government services or institutions.

The Race to the Bottom

The ultimate devolution, of course, is to get government out of a particular activity altogether. Certainly, privatization, as discussed in Chapter 3, has a major role to play here. But those who would privatize many aspects of the welfare system are relying on private charitable giving to make up the difference between reduced government spending and the actual life-sustaining needs of the poor. But the very welfare programs that are being criticized were created in the first place because private charity proved insufficient.

Charity notwithstanding, the real issue in the devolution of welfare programs is that of a "race to the bottom." In this race states and their counties increasingly lower their welfare benefits to discourage the out-of-state poor from moving in to collect more generous aid than was possible where they were. "Generous" states increasingly resent the fact that "stingy" states are effectively exporting their poor. But as Minnesota Governor Arne Carlson said, "We do not want to be in the importing business. We will devise a range of policies to make sure we take care of Minnesotans, but we're not in the business of subsidizing Gary, Indiana." This is the crux of the intergovernmental welfare dilemma. A state designs a responsible welfare system to take care of its own only to become a welfare magnet to outsiders. But by "racing to the bottom" in terms of benefits, states discourage the out-of-state poor from moving in. Senator Daniel Patrick Moynihan offered this explanation: "The hidden agenda of the Devolution Revolution is a large-scale withdrawal of support for social welfare, no matter how well conceived. The result would be a race to the bottom, as states, deprived of federal matching funds, compete with one another to reduce spending by depriving their own dependent population of help."

There is already a major differential among the states. The block granting of federal welfare funding that withdraws the federal matching requirement (which was, in effect, an entitlement to the states) may make that differential far worse. Now that welfare eligibility is state (as opposed to nationally) determined, the differential in benefits can vastly increase. Many states now offer a low level of benefits. Conversely, some states have maintained fairly substantial benefits but have dramatically reduced the amount of time one can receive government support. The block grant reforms now allow them to offer no benefits. As this problem shows, the core issues of intergovernmental relations can be reduced to stark realities. It comes down to this: Intergovernmental fiscal arrangements ultimately determine—for a large class of citizens—who eats and who goes hungry.

◆ TWO CASE STUDIES: HOW INTERGOVERNMENTAL MANAGEMENT BECAME INTERGOVERNMETAL CHAOS: THE CASES OF UNITED FLIGHT 93 AND HURRICANE KATRINA

On September 11, 2001, United Airlines Flight 93, on its way from Newark, New Jersey, to San Francisco, California, was late. Scheduled for an 8:01 A.M. takeoff, it was stuck on the tarmac amid the usual airport congestion waiting for departure clearance. After a 41-minute delay, it became airborne. The delay is significant because when the plane was hijacked less than an hour into the flight, many of the passengers were able to call home and learn that similarly hijacked planes had just crashed into the World Trade Center. Assuming that their flight was on a similar mission—the hijackers had turned the plane toward Washington, DC—the passengers of the Boeing 757 decided to act.

Jeremy Glick, 31, told his wife in Hewitt, New Jersey, that some of the passengers had voted and decided to attack the hijackers. Sandy Bradshaw, 38, a flight attendant, told her husband in Greensboro, North Carolina, that passengers huddled in the rear of the plane were "in the back trying to get hot water to throw at them." Todd Beamer, 32, of Cranbury, New Jersey, failed to locate his wife by phone but was able to contact Lisa Jefferson, a GTE Airfone supervisor, and make her promise to call his wife with a final message of love. The last words Jefferson heard were at 9:58, when Beamer said to his fellow passengers, "Are you guys ready? Let's roll." Beamer's last words—"Let's roll"—have since become a famous phrase for defiance toward terrorists. The plane crashed eight minutes later in a rural area 80 miles southeast of Pittsburgh.

The heroism of the passengers speaks for itself. But what needs further explanation is the mess on the ground. The physical mess—aircraft and body parts spread over several square miles—was accompanied by a jurisdictional mess. Who was in charge and who was responsible for what?

If an airplane crash is caused by criminal acts, which was clearly the case with Flight 93, then the Federal Bureau of Investigation (FBI) is in charge of the crash site because it is a crime scene. If there is no suggestion of criminality, then the National Transportation Safety Board (NTSB) is in charge of the accident site. In the wake of the TWA Flight 800 crash off the coast of New York in July 1996, infighting among various agencies occasioned considerable confusion over who was to do what—especially in regard to the victims' families. They were rightly furious at the lack of support and communication from both the airline and government agencies. This led to the passage of the Aviation Disaster Family Assistance Act later that same year. This law clarifies the roles of the NTSB, the FBI, and the airlines in the event of a crash. Additionally, other agencies are designated specific responsibilities called "victim support tasks." For example, the American Red Cross is charged with family care and mental health. Grief counseling is notably important here. When the number of victims is more than the local medical examiner can cope with, the Department of Health and Human Services sends in forensic experts and portable mortuaries. If foreign nationals are among the dead, the Department of State is charged with assisting their families.

Meanwhile, the local authorities retain their jurisdictional obligations. Thus the state police, county sheriff, and district attorney all follow the lead of the FBI at a crime scene crash. Additionally a myriad of local, county, and state government offices have reason to be involved. At least 42 agencies of every governmental type and level were involved with the Flight 93 crash site. The Stoneycreek Township officials—those closest to the crash site—needed to interact with Somerset County officials and commonwealth agency officials up to and including the governor. Supplemental fire and rescue units from as far away as Pittsburgh also provided assistance. All these interacted with the various federal agencies. With body parts flung all over the site and distressed family members, as well as the news media, demanding information, both individual and organizational stress levels reached new highs. Opportunities abounded for both confusion and anger. The management of all of these intergovernmental issues and individuals is a difficult proposition at best. And people are often at their worst dealing with death in the glare of publicity.

While the cause—criminal or mechanical—of any given plane disaster may never be fully known, it is certain that any such crash will hit a morass of intergovernmental management issues.

Now the Department of Homeland Security (created in 2002) is supposed to alleviate some of these problems of jurisdictional conflict and intergovernmental confusion. One of the first big tests of the Department of Homeland Security's ability to coordinate intergovernmental management of a crisis came in 2005 when Hurricane Katrina devastated New Orleans. Given its primary mission, one might reasonably expect the DHS to deal with the disaster in an efficient and organized manner. Yet, almost four years to the day of the September 11 attacks, the Katrina disaster exposed the ongoing difficulties of intergovernmental relations in the area of emergency management. What happened?

Hurricane Katrina was not a surprise. The Gulf Coast had been hit by several powerful hurricanes in the preceding 100 years, and it was generally accepted that it was just a matter of time before a major hurricane would strike New Orleans. In fact, the city government, the state of Louisiana, and the Federal Emergency Management Agency (FEMA) had conducted numerous exercises on how to respond if a major hurricane hit New Orleans.

Nevertheless, when it happened, intergovernmental relations thoroughly broke down. To be sure, there were many mistakes on the parts of both the city and the state governments, but the failure of the Department of Homeland Security and FEMA in its biggest test since the September 11 attacks was especially troubling. In particular, the inability of FEMA to provide leadership and direction to the rescue efforts in the Gulf

Coast region left many Americans angry and disillusioned. While the list of FEMA's failures is quite extensive, *Time* magazine's account of the misuse of rescue personnel is particularly telling:

> As flames blazed 400 miles away in New Orleans on Labor Day, about 600 firefighters from across the nation sat in an Atlanta hotel, listening to a FEMA lecture on equal opportunity, sexual harassment, and customer service. The room, filled with many firefighters who, at FEMA's request, had arrived equipped with rescue gear, erupted in anger. "This is ridiculous!" one yelled. "Our fire departments sent us down here to save people, and you got us doing this?" The FEMA official climbed atop a chair and tried to restore order. "You are now employees of FEMA, and you will follow orders and do as you are told."

As you might expect, the firefighters got tired of the inactivity in Atlanta and simply went home. This occurrence demonstrates some of the key weaknesses in government coordination that were exposed by Katrina. How could badly needed emergency personnel from local agencies be kept away from the tragic scenes in New Orleans? The answer can be found in the same morass of intergovernmental confusion that plagued the response to Flight 93 in 2001. A major organizational restructuring and billions of dollars later, the federal government seems no more capable of coordinating reactions to major emergencies than it was in 2001.

For Discussion: *How has the war on terrorism increased the need for greater intergovernmental cooperation? How does the nature of federalism in the United States lead to the types of problems found in the government reactions to the crash of Flight 93 and Hurricane Katrina?*

Summary

The process of intergovernmental relations is federalism in action. It is the complex network of day-to-day interrelationships among the governments within a federal system. It is the political, fiscal, programmatic, and administrative processes by which higher units of government share revenues and other resources with lower units of government, generally accompanied by special conditions that the lower units must satisfy as prerequisites to receiving the assistance.

The U.S. Constitution created the permanent features of intergovernmental relations in the United States. The popular image of the federal system as a layer cake, with each layer of government neatly on top of the other, is deceptive. The reality is more like a marble cake, in which the cooperative relations among the varying levels of government result in an intermingling—not a layering—of activities.

The key word in the new American thrust toward decentralization or devolution is mandate: One level of government requires another to offer—or pay for—a program as a matter of law or as a prerequisite to partial or full funding for either the program in question or other programs. Mandates are orders. The movement toward devolution is spurred on by jurisdictions and constituencies that increasingly resent taking such orders.

Fiscal federalism refers to the financial relationships that exist between units of government in a federal system. A central question is frequently asked about fiscal federalism: Why can't the citizens of the states just keep their money (meaning have their federal taxes reduced) rather than paying it to the federal government so that it can be returned in grants and services? The only certainty here is that the states have become addicted to intergovernmental funding. The question remains whether their political leaders will gradually wean them from it or feed their habit.

Review Questions

1. What are the advantages and disadvantages of a federal system of government?
2. Why is the American federal system considered to be more like a marble cake than a layer cake?
3. Why are mandates such a cause of friction in intergovernmental relations?
4. Why are federal grant programs so important to state and local governments?
5. Is the movement toward devolution more of a threat or an opportunity for national governments in a federal system?

Key Concepts

block grant A grant distributed in accordance with a statutory formula for use in a variety of activities within a broad functional area, largely at the recipient's discretion.

categorical grant A grant that can be used only for specific, narrowly defined activities—for example, to construct an interstate highway.

council of government (COG) An organization of cooperating local governments seeking a regional approach to planning, development, transportation, environment, and other issues.

devolution The transfer of power from a central to a local authority.

federalism A system of governance in which a national, overarching government shares power with subnational or state governments.

federalism, cooperative The notion that the national, state, and local governments are cooperating, interacting agents jointly working to solve common problems, rather than conflicting, sometimes hostile competitors, pursuing similar or possibly conflicting ends.

federalism, dual The nineteenth-century concept, now no longer operational, that the functions and responsibilities of the federal and state governments were theoretically distinguished and functionally separate from each other.

federalism, marble-cake The concept that the cooperative relations among the varying levels of government result in an intermingling of activities; in contrast to the more traditional view of layer-cake federalism, which holds that the three levels of government are totally or almost totally separate.

Federalism, New The Republican efforts begun during the Nixon administration to decentralize governmental functions by returning power and responsibility to the states. This trend was continued in the 1980s by the Reagan administration and culminated in the 1990s movement toward devolution.

federalism, picket fence The concept that bureaucratic specialists at the various levels of government (along with clientele groups) exercise considerable power over the nature of intergovernmental programs.

fiscal federalism The financial relations between and among units of government in a federal system. The theory of fiscal federalism, or multiunit government finance, is one part of the branch of applied economics known as public finance.

grant An intergovernmental transfer of funds (or other assets). Since the New Deal, state and local governments have become increasingly dependent on federal grants for an almost infinite variety of programs.

intergovernmental relations The complex network of interrelationships among governments; the political, fiscal, programmatic, and administrative processes by which higher units of government share revenues and other resources with lower units of government, generally accompanied by special conditions that the lower units must satisfy as prerequisites to receiving the assistance.

mandating One level of government requiring another to offer—and/or pay for—a program as a matter of law or as a prerequisite to partial or full funding for either the program in question or other programs.

Bibliography

Arrandale, Tom. (1994). "The Sagebrush Gang Rides Again," *Governing* (March).

Boyle, Phillip, and Gordon P. Whitaker. (2001). "Educating for the New Public Service: Implications of the Transformation of Governance." *Journal of Public Affairs Education* 7 (October 2001).

Cannon, Angie. (2001). "Final Words from Flight 93," *U.S. News & World Report* (October 29).

Cohen, Richard. (1995). "States Aren't Saints, Either," *Washington Post National Weekly* (April 9).

Cook, Gareth G. (1995). "Devolution Chic: Why Sending Power to the States Could Make a Monkey Out of Uncle Sam," *Washington Monthly* (April).

Ehrenhalt, Alan. (1995). "The Locust in the Garden of Government," *Governing* (March).

Elazar, Daniel J. (1962). *The American Partnership: Intergovernmental Cooperation in the 19th Century United States*. Chicago: University of Chicago Press.

Furtwangler, Albert. (1984).*The Authority of Publius: A Reading of the Federalist Papers*. Ithaca, NY: Cornell University Press.

Grodzins, Morton. (1966). *The American System*, ed. Daniel J. Elazar. Chicago: Rand McNally.

Helvarg, David. (1994). *The War Against the Greens: The Wise Use Movement, the New Right, and Anti-Environmental Violence*. San Francisco: Sierra Club Books.

Hughes, Robert. (1993). *The Culture of Complaint*. New York: Oxford University Press.

Jones, Timothy, and Janine Tyne. (1994). "Printz v. United States: An Aassault upon the Brady Act or a Tenth Amendment Fortification?" *St. John's Journal of Legal Commentary* 10.

Kettl, Donald F. (2000). "The Transformation of Governance: Globalization, Devolution, and the Role of Government," *Public Administration Review* 60.

Larkin, John. (1995). "Mandate Protesters to Gain Limited Relief," *Public Administration Times* (March 1).

Lloyd, Alan. (1974). *The Scorching of Washington: The War of 1812*. Washington, DC: Robert B. Luce.

Marando, Vincent, and Patricia S. Florestano. (1990). "Intergovernmental Management: The State of the Discipline." In *Public Administration: The State of the Discipline*, eds. Naomi B. Lynn and Aaron Wildavsky. Chatham, NJ: Chatham House.

McCurdy, Howard E. (1984). "Public Ownership of Land and the 'Sagebrush Rebellion,'" *Policy Studies Journal* 12 (March).

McDonald, Forrest. (1985). *Novus Ordo Seclorum: The Intellectual Origins of the Constitution*. Lawrence: University Press of Kansas.

Miller, Sara B. (2005). "Northeast Battles Its Status as US 'Tailpipe,'" *Christian Science Monitor* (April 1).

Moynihan, Daniel Patrick. (1995). "The Devolution Revolution," *New York Times* (August 6).

Pooley, Eric. (1995). "Things That Make Rudy Nuts: The Mayor's Real Top Ten List: Unfunded Federal, State, and Judicial Mandates That Push the City into the Red," *New York* (January 30).

Popper, Frank J. (1984). "The Timely End of the Sagebrush Rebellion," *Public Interest* 76 (Summer).

Rainwater, Lee, and William Yancey. (1967). *The Moynihan Report and the Politics of Controversy*. Cambridge, MA: MIT Press.

Ross, Bernard H. (1998). "Metropolitan Organization." *International Encyclopedia of Public Policy and Administration,* ed. Jay M. Shafritz. Boulder, CO: Westview Press.

Russakoff, Dale, and Rene Sanchez. (2003). "Begging, Borrowing for Security: Homeland Burden Grows for Cash-Strapped States, Cities," *Washington Post* (April 1).

Sanford, Terry. (1967). *Storm Over the States.* New York: McGraw-Hill.

Shanahan, Eileen. (1991). "Going It Jointly: Regional Solutions for Local Problems," *Governing* (August).

Swarns, Rachel L. (1998). "A New Broom Needs a New Handle: Welfare as We Know It Goes Incognito," *New York Times* (July 5).

Swartz, Thomas R., and John E. Peck, eds. (1990). *The Changing Face of Fiscal Federalism.* Armonk, NY: M. E. Sharpe.

Thompson, Mark. (2005). "Why Did FEMA and Its Chief, Michael Brown, Fail Their Biggest Test?" *Time Magazine* (September 19).

Vobejda, Barbara. (1995). "Will There Be a Race to the Bottom on Welfare?" *Washington Post National Weekly* (September 18–24).

Vobejda, Barbara, and Judith Havemann. (1998). "States' Welfare Shift: Stop It Before It Starts," *Washington Post* (August 12).

White, Leonard D. (1948). *The Federalists.* New York: Macmillan.

Wikstrom, Nelson. (1985). *Councils of Governments: A Study of Political Incrementalism.* Chicago: Nelson-Hall.

Wills, Garry. (1981). *Explaining America: The Federalist.* Garden City, NY: Doubleday.

Wright, Deil S. (1988). *Understanding Intergovernmental Relations,* 3rd ed. Pacific Grove, CA: Brooks/Cole.

Recommended Books

Conlan, Timothy. (1998). *From New Federalism to Devolution: Twenty-five Years of Intergovernmental Reform.* Washington, DC: Brookings Institution. The history of American federalism from the 1970s through the 1990s.

Dilulio, John, and Donald F. Kettl. (1995). *Fine Print: The Contract with America, Devolution, and the Administrative Realities of American Federalism.* Washington, DC: Brookings Institution. The story of what happens when Republican party ideology seeks to cope with and reform the immutable facts of intergovernmental relations.

Filippov, Mikhail, Peter C. Ordeshook, and Olga Shvetsova. (2004). *Designing Federalism: A Theory of Self-Sustainable Federal Institutions.* Cambridge, England: Cambridge University Press. An analysis of the factors that led to the development of successful federalist systems.

Peterson, Paul E. (1995). *The Price of Federalism.* Washington, DC: Brookings Institution. A historical account and optimistic contemporary assessment of the intergovernmental fiscal relationships among the differing levels of government.

Posner, Paul L. *The Politics of Unfunded Mandates: Whither Federalism?* (1998). Washington, DC: Georgetown University Press. The origins and politics of congressional requirements for state and local governments to implement federal policies.

Rabe, Barry. (2004). *Statehouse and Greenhouse: The Emerging Politics of American Climate Policy.* Washington, DC: Brookings Institution Press. An examination of emerging state roles in dealing with international environmental policy.

Related Web Sites

Council of State Governments
  www.statesnews.org
Metropolitan Councils of Government
  www.nlc.org/about_cities/cities_101/167
National Academy of Public Administration
  www.napawash.org/
National Association of Counties
  www.naco.org
National Association of Regional Councils
  www.narc.org

National Association of Towns and Townships
  www.natat.org
National Conference of State Legislatures
  ncsl.org
National Governors Association
  www.nga.org
National League of Cities
  www.nlc.org
Publius: The Journal of Federalism
  http://ww2.lafayette.edu/~publius/

CHAPTER 5

Honor, Ethics, and Accountability

•KEYNOTE: NICCOLO MACHIAVELLI, THE PREEMINENT PUBLIC ADMINISTRATION ETHICIST

It has been more than five centuries since his birth, but Niccolo Machiavelli (1469–1527) remains the most quoted, most read, most interpreted, and most misunderstood public policy adviser who ever lived. By the time William Shakespeare wrote *Richard III* in 1592, he could assume that his audience would be familiar with Machiavelli's diabolical reputation. Thus Shakespeare could have his title character introduce himself as being so evil that he could "set the murtherous Machevil to school." Similar references to Machiavelli as the personification of evil doings abound in the plays and literature of Shakespeare's time and have continued ever since.

But it's a bum rap. Machiavelli was really a nice guy. Indeed, he is an exemplar as a public administrator and policy analyst. Born into a family of ancient nobility but persistent impoverishment, he was educated well enough to become a civil servant, sometime ambassador, for Florence beginning in 1498. He was an honest, truthful, and competent employee. But his was a patronage position (there being no merit system then), and he lost his job and nearly his life with a shift in the political winds of 1512. Thereafter, he eked out a living on a meager farm left to him by his father.

His greatest desire was to go back to work for his beloved Florence, now in the control of the Medici family. So, like many a high-level political appointee out of power, he wrote a book (indeed several) to demonstrate his usefulness to potential employers. In his most famous private letter (dated December 10, 1513), quoted by biographer Giuseppe Prezzolini, he expresses hope that "if it [his book *The Prince*] were read, they [the Medici] would see that for . . . fifteen years I have been studying the art of the state." He even offers proof of his honesty as a past and potential employee: "As a witness to my honesty and goodness I have my poverty."

Because Machiavelli, despite constant efforts, never did get the government job he so coveted, he, after working on his farm all day, spent his nights working on the most enduring books of political philosophy produced by the Italian Renaissance. *The Prince* (1532) and *The Discourses* (1531) were important political and military analyses that led to the use of the term <u>**Machiavellianism**</u> to refer to cunning, cynical, and ruthless <u>behavior based on the notion of the end justifying the use of almost any means.</u> What Machiavelli actually noted in *The Prince* was that a ruler would be judged by results: "So let a prince set about the task of conquering and maintaining his state; his methods will always be judged honorable and universally praised." Machiavelli, as one of the first policy advisers, developed a set of prescriptions and proscriptions for his prince that were designed to ensure that the prince would flourish politically. His introduction summarizes his methodology: "I have long pondered and scrutinized the actions of the

Machiavellian Referring to Niccolo Machiavelli (1469–1527), the Italian Renaissance political philosopher whose book of advice to would-be leaders, *The Prince* (1532), is the progenitor of all how-to-succeed books. Its exploration of how political power is grasped, used, and kept is the benchmark against which all subsequent analyses are judged. Machiavelli's amoral tone and detached analysis have caused him to be both soundly denounced as well as greatly imitated. While his <u>name has become synonymous with political deception,</u> no other writer has given the world such a brilliant lesson in how to think in terms of cold political power.

great, and now I offer the results . . . within the compass of a small volume." Machiavelli offers a set of axioms and ideas about obtaining power, holding on to power, and using power to advantage:

- Men should be either treated generously or destroyed, because they take revenge for slight injuries—for heavy ones they cannot. [Potential organizational or political rivals should be either made part of your team or "destroyed"—fired or killed—because if left in place, they will, like a snake, bite you in the rear when you least expect it.]

- Princes ought to leave affairs of reproach to the management of others, and keep those of grace in their own hands. [The good news a leader delivers with a maximum of publicity; the bad news is quietly announced by a low-level assistant.]

- It is necessary for him who lays out a state and arranges laws for it to presuppose that all men are evil and that they are always going to act according to the wickedness of their spirits whenever they have free scope. [It is as James Madison, a reader of Machiavelli, wrote in *The Federalist,* No. 51: "Ambition must be made to counteract ambition." To this extent the U.S. Constitution with its system of checks and balances is reflective of Machiavelli.]

- Princes who have achieved great things have been those who have given their word lightly, who have known how to trick men with their cunning, and who, in the end, have overcome those abiding by honest principles. [This advice may sound familiar to anyone who has been deceived by a leader, such as when President Richard Nixon said, "I am not a crook" or when president Bill Clinton told the nation, "I did not have sexual relations with that woman."]

If lying politicians have a patron saint, it must be Machiavelli, who wrote in *The Prince,* "It is necessary that the prince should know how to color his nature well, and how to be a great hypocrite and dissembler. For men are so simple, and held so much to immediate necessity, that the deceiver will never lack dupes." Machiavelli's ideal prince would not be a traditional man of honor; his word would not be his bond. Machiavelli's advice was "not to keep faith when by so doing it would be against his interest and when the reasons which made him bind himself no longer exist." This was the kind of thing that made people suspect that not only was Machiavelli not a gentleman, but his books were not fit reading for gentlemen either.

Machiavelli, in his advice, disregarded the issue of morality—apart from those circumstances where it was prudent or necessary for the prince to appear to be moral. Yet this was essentially ethical because the lying was for the good of the state. Machiavelli's theory of lying was a restatement of Plato's noble lie from Book 3 of *Republic,* in which he asserts that the guardians of a society may put forth untruths necessary to maintain social order.

But, alas, Machiavelli's books failed in their initial purpose to get him into a job and out of poverty. While his manuscripts circulated privately among his friends, *The Prince* was not published until five years after his death. Only then did it become a sensation. Posthumously Machiavelli has been a great success. Much as with a modern

Why is this man smiling? Princeton professor Maurizio Viroli titles his biography of Machiavelli *Niccolo's Smile* and then goes to great length—indeed, book length—to explain how the smile in this portrait is indicative of the subtlety of his mind. But since the portrait was painted several years after Machiavelli died, we may surmise that this is not necessarily his real smile. Enigmatic smiles are a hallmark of old portraits. (Remember the *Mona Lisa* by Leonardo da Vinci). Then remember the reason that practically none of these old portraits have toothy smiles as is common today: bad teeth. Until modern dentistry, even the richest people had terrible teeth—not to mention breath. So it is reasonable to conclude that Niccolo's smile is more dental than mental. •

rapper who becomes more and more famous as critics denounce his vile lyrics, Machiavelli became notorious because he was denounced by all three of the major political factions of his time: the Roman Catholics, the Protestants, and the Republicans.

Because it was so widely denounced, *The Prince* became all the more widely read—or, rather, misread. Readers seeking to find evil found it. But a more subtle and modern reading finds it less and less evil and more and more practical. Machiavelli's book of advice to would-be leaders is the progenitor of all "how-to-succeed" books that advocate practical rather than moral actions. In 1967, British Broadcasting Corporation executive Antony Jay reintroduced Machiavelli's concepts to a modern audience with his best-selling book *Management and Machiavelli,* which took Machiavelli's insights for managing a state and applied them to the problem of power and politics in organizations. Jay concluded that Machiavelli's principles are as valid now as they were 450 years ago because they are "rooted in human nature." According to Jay, "The new science of management is in fact only a continuation of the old art of government." Consequently, "when you study management theory side by side with political theory, and management case histories side by side with political history, you realize that you are only studying two very similar branches of the same subject."

For Discussion: *Why is Machiavelli still so critically important for understanding the mechanisms of power in public policymaking and administrative practices? What current public figures have followed Machiavelli's example and have written articles and books specifically so they could influence public policies and/or gain public office?*

The Origins and Nature of Honor

Our modern concepts of honor have their origins in ancient Greece and Rome. The classic example of honorable public service was Lucius Quinctius Cincinnatus, the Roman patrician who has become the symbol of republican virtue and personal integrity. In 458 B.C.E., when Rome was threatened with military defeat, Cincinnatus, a farmer, was appointed dictator by the Senate to deal with the emergency. Legend has it that he literally abandoned his plow in midfield to take command. Within 16 days he defeated the enemy, resigned from the dictatorship, and returned to his plow. Ever since, politicians have been insincerely asserting how much they yearn to give up power and return to the farm, as Cincinnatus did. This is a very strong theme in American political history. Until this century, it was thought politically indecent to publicly lust after political power. Politicians were expected to sit contentedly on their farms, metaphorically behind their plows, until they were called to service.

George Washington is one of the few genuine Cincinnatus figures in world history. Indeed, Lord Byron (George Noel Gordon) in his 1814 *Ode to Napoleon Bonaparte,* called Washington "the Cincinnatus of the West." Garry Wills writes in *Cincinnatus: George Washington and the Enlightenment* (1984), [On December 23, 1783, at the end of the Revolutionary War, General George Washington] "spoke what he took to be his last words on the public stage; 'Having now finished the work assigned me, I retire from the great theater of Action. . . . I here offer my commission, and take my leave of all the employments of public life.' At that moment, the ancient legend of Cincinnatus—the Roman called from his plow to rescue Rome, and returning to this plow when danger had passed—was resurrected as a fact of modern political life." The example of Cincinnatus is still with us today. It is even unconsciously evoked for a modern public that never heard of the ancient Roman. For example, Ronald Reagan is quoted by E. G. Brown in *Reagan and Reality:* "One thing our founding fathers could not foresee . . . was a nation governed by professional politicians who had a vested interest in getting reelected. They probably envisioned a fellow serving a couple of hitches and then looking forward to getting back to the farm." The modern term limits movement is at its core an effort to legislate Cincinnatus-type behavior—to send them back "to the farm." Of course, both Cincinnatus and Washington were not merely farmers. They both had major estates with slaves to do the heavy lifting. Modern political leaders not only lack slaves, but they do not even have farms anymore. Having no honorable and luxurious place to which to retreat when recalled from public life, they fight all the harder to stay in the game.

Shakespeare's Marc Antony was right. We are "all honorable men"—and women. Our culture inculcates us with concepts of honor from childhood. Much of our sense of honor comes from observing the actions of family and neighbors. The rest comes from the media. Many people get their first conscious lessons in honor from movies. Westerns directed by John Ford and others taught Americans the "code of the West." They taught you that one's word was sacrosanct and thus was not given lightly, taught you when an insult was so bad that it warranted violence, and taught you, above all, to protect the weak—all notions from medieval chivalry.

Later, space "westerns" like *Star Trek* and *Star Wars* taught a new generation the intergalactic concept of honor, which, of course, was no different from the medieval concept. Some things have not changed in a thousand years. Thus young people still learn what it means to be honorable by listening to (and watching) the sagas of their culture. *Star Trek* as a transmitter of notions of honor is just a modern version of the eighth-century *Beowulf* or the eleventh-century *Song of Roland*. Honor has been and remains one of the core influences of human behavior. It is often more important than life itself. The founders of the United States in the last sentence of their 1776 Declaration of Independence stated, "And for the support of this Declaration, with a firm reliance on the Protection of Divine Providence, we mutually pledge to each other our Lives, our Fortunes, and our sacred Honor." Their lives were not sacred. Their fortunes were not sacred. But their honor was.

National Honor

Once reserved for the nobility, honor has since the eighteenth century become increasingly democratized. As absolutist governments declined, national honor (once solely the concern of individual monarchs) became a factor that influenced whole peoples. No less a pragmatist than President Woodrow Wilson felt the pull of national honor. In 1916 he asserted that: "the nation's honor is dearer than the nation's comfort; yes, than the nation's life itself." Thus a collective democratic citizenry, no less than a defenseless maiden, may espouse the motto "death before dishonor." This notion is more than melodramatic hyperbole. During World War II, the French dishonored themselves by surrendering so quickly to the Germans in the spring of 1940. They were not willing to fight the Nazis in the streets of Paris and see their beautiful city destroyed. But the British, expecting an invasion soon afterward, were willing to sacrifice London. When Winston Churchill told the House of Commons on June 4, 1940, immediately after the Dunkirk evacuation that "we shall defend our island, whatever the cost may be, we shall fight on the beaches, we shall fight on the landing grounds, we shall fight in the fields and in the streets, we shall fight in the hills; we shall never surrender," he meant exactly that. Indeed, he later wrote in his postwar memoirs, *Their Finest Hour* (1949), that "we were prepared to go to all lengths. I intended to use the slogan 'you can always take one with you.' " Suicidal? Perhaps—but honorable all the same. When General Charles de Gaulle fled to England rather than surrender, he was asked why he was there. He replied, "I am here to save the honor of France." There is still debate about whether he succeeded or not. (At least he tried!)

The United State's involvement in the Vietnam War can also be viewed through the perspective of national honor. As the costs of the war became more than the American public was willing to bear, the nation's leaders struggled to find a way for the United States to leave Vietnam while maintaining its appearance as a strong and proud world power. Even when the chances of military success in Vietnam became remote, the United States continued to send troops into the field as diplomats tried to negotiate an acceptable peace. In 1973 President Richard M. Nixon addressed a national audience with his announcement that "we today have concluded an agreement to end the war and bring peace with honor in Vietnam and Southeast Asia."

Ultimately, it can be argued that Nixon's agreement brought neither real peace nor real honor to the United States, yet the importance of maintaining an appearance of honor was essential to any plan that extricated the United States from its involvement in Vietnam.

Why Honor Precedes Ethics

Honor comes before ethics because a person without honor has no moral compass and does not know which way to turn to be ethical. Honor goes to the essence of public affairs; since ancient times only individuals perceived to be honorable could be trusted with the public's business. Of course, honor always has a context, and it is always influenced by the prevailing organizational and political culture. Melvin M. Belli, the American attorney, relates a story that illustrates this point. In the early 1950s Belli traveled to Paris to represent his client, movie star Errol Flynn, who had a legal tangle with a French firm over the profits from a movie. When Belli arrived, the French lawyer on the case advised him that there was nothing to worry about: "We have given the judge 200,000 francs and the case is in the bag." When Belli wondered aloud what would happen if the other side were to give the judge 300,000 francs, his French associate became indignant and replied, "But Monsieur, we are dealing with a respectable judge. He is a man of honor. He would not think of taking from *both* sides." This French judge's concept of honor was quite unlike the apocryphal American judge who, after taking bribes from both sides in a dispute, decided to try the case on its merits. Which judge is more ethical?

Dimensions of Honor

Honor has many dimensions. The most obvious and superficial kind is *ex officio*. This is the Latin phrase meaning "by virtue of the office." Many people hold positions on boards, commissions, councils, and so on because of another office they occupy. For example, the mayor of a city may be an *ex officio* member of the board of trustees of a university in that city. Thus "honorable" is the form of address used for many public officials, such as judges, mayors, and members of the U.S. Congress. Here honorable does not necessarily imply personal honor or integrity; it merely signifies current (or past) incumbency. Consequently, even after Richard M. Nixon disgraced himself and was forced to resign as president in 1974, he was still formally "The Honorable" in terms of formal address. Other smaller crooks, temporarily in public office, are no less honorable.

Honor is also a function of the outward perception of one's reputation. Reputation in business, whether of an individual or an organization, is a highly valued asset. Indeed, when businesses are sold, they often sell for sums far in excess of their book value because of their intangible **goodwill** or reputation in the community.

---

goodwill The reputation and built-up business of a company. It can be generally valued as what a company would sell for over and above the value of its physical property, money owed to it, and other assets.

Shakespeare often addressed issues of professional reputation and honor. In *Richard II* (Act I, Scene 1) the Duke of Norfolk is accused of treason and responds with this exposition on how mere accusation hurts both reputation and personal honor:

> The purest treasure mortal times afford
> Is spotless reputation: take that away,
> Men are but gilded loam or painted clay.
> A jewel in a ten-times-barr'd-up chest
> Is a bold spirit in a loyal breast.
> Mine honour is my life; both grow in one;
> Take honour from me, and my life is done.

This is the origin of the phrase "spotless reputation." It is also a warning that an attack on someone's honor is also an attack on his or her life—professionally speaking. But outward perception is only one step removed from *ex officio* honor. True honor begins with personal integrity and honesty. It goes beyond Benjamin Franklin's famous admonition from his *Poor Richard's Almanac* that "honesty is the best policy." Think how cynical Franklin's statement is—which seems to have been derived from Cervantes's *Don Quixote* anyway. Honesty is not worthwhile for its own sake; it is simply the optimum policy—one choice from among many. But true honesty, as opposed to policy honesty, is the essence of a person of honor. Such people act with integrity. This is at the core of honor. Those who have integrity live up to their stated principles, values, and most importantly, their word. A person whose word is his or her bond gives the full faith and credit of his or her whole being to keeping commitments. Sometimes this is almost frivolous, as it was when the legendary Abraham Lincoln walked miles through the snow to return a book by a promised date. But far more often one's word is the coin of the administrative realm. Things happen because one person tells something to another. This integrity of communication is essential for the smooth functioning of organizations that, in essence, are merely information-processing structures. This is why codes of honor (of integrity) first evolved among the military. Because lives, indeed whole battles, depended on the accuracy of information sent up the chain of command, it was imperative that an ethic of honesty be instilled. This is still true today. If the word of an officer is not known to be good, that officer has lost his or her effectiveness to their superior.

A second but more subtle meaning of integrity is integrated strength or character. A building that holds together is said to have structural integrity. Individuals who have character, as demonstrated by an observable long period of acting with integrity, are said to have **gravitas,** or as the British put it, "bottom"—meaning that they are seated firmly enough in their convictions that they are not easily swayed. Thus those who have integrity have a sure sense of right from wrong; they know what their core beliefs are, and what they will or will not do, no matter what the pressure.

---

gravitas Intellectual weight. A politician must exhibit a certain degree of gravitas if he or she is to be taken seriously for high office.

Finally, if people feel that government officials have strong convictions and personal integrity, that can help them survive other political liabilities. This situation is clearly evident with the presidential administration of George W. Bush. Public opinion polls have consistently indicated that a majority of Americans believe Bush possesses strong convictions and beliefs. Even though a majority of the public may disagree with many of his decisions and policy positions (i.e., Iraq, Social Security), most Americans have had a generally favorable view of Bush as a person. Such public fondness for an official's personal integrity can allow that official to survive policy failures and other administrative weaknesses. In the wake of Clinton-era ethical challenges, Bush's reputation as a man of honor has helped him maintain a core of public support even when the public sours on many of his most important initiatives.

Regime Values

Administrators with integrity understand that they have a special moral obligation to the people they serve. They take seriously what John Rohr calls the "regime values" of their jurisdiction. In constitutional systems these values are established by the constitution, whether written, as in the United States, or unwritten, as in the United Kingdom. To a person of honor, an oath to "defend the Constitution of the United States against all enemies, foreign and domestic" is a serious matter. Thus, according to Rohr, the Constitution "is the moral foundation of ethics for bureaucrats." Those senior administrators who gain reputations for being ethical and honorable abide by a new-fashioned *noblesse oblige*. Originally the "nobility obliged" by leading in war and demonstrated their honor and valor by taking physical risks to prove their courage—to demonstrate on the field of honor (a battlefield) just how honorable they were.

Lacking a traditional nobility, republican governments give leadership roles to senior bureaucrats and elected officials. Once in office, their fellow citizens rightly expect them to take moral and career risks, parallel to the traditional risks of combat, to protect their fellow citizens, the regime, and their constitution. And they must be heroic enough to risk not just their lives but their livelihoods as well. Louis Brandeis, later to be an associate justice of the U.S. Supreme Court, argued in the 1910 *Glavis-Ballinger* case that public administrators "cannot be worthy of the respect and admiration of the people unless they add to the virtue of obedience some other virtues—virtues of manliness, of truth, of courage, of willingness to risk position, of the willingness to risk criticism, of the willingness to risk the misunderstanding that so often comes when people do the heroic thing." It is often said that managers are paid more than workers because they are paid to take risks, to make decisions that can cost them their jobs. Public managers live in an even riskier environment. Not only must they take normal management risks, but they must risk their careers, their reputations, sometimes even their lives, to protect the values of the regime. It is simply a matter of honor.

All too often managers and employees fall from honor—or it may be that they never had it in the first place. Lapses take many forms. The two most common lapses of honor and honesty are corruption and lying.

Corruption in Government

Recurrent **scandals** and instances of official mischief in government, no matter how much they threaten to cost, pose a great threat to the democratic notions of the rule of law. When a public official misuses his or her office for self-gain, then the rule of law no longer obtains, and there is, in effect, a return to tyranny. By engaging in such self-aggrandizement, corrupt representatives of the people illegally put themselves above the law. Moreover, a public official's act of wrongdoing is destructive of the claim that in a democracy all individuals are equal. Just like the pig in George Orwell's *Animal Farm* who cannot accept the idea that "all animals are equal," these self-interested officials in effect are saying, "but some of us are more equal than others." The porcine imagery continues when you think of them not only feeding at the public trough but "hogging" more than their share.

Bribery

Corruption also undermines economic rights. Consider bribery when it occurs within the competitive process of governmental purchasing. When contracts are awarded illegally by means of bribes, the losing competitors can be said to have had their rights to a fair and impartial bidding process abridged. The public's right to have purchases made in the most efficient and least costly fashion is also subverted. This kind of corruption makes a mockery of economic considerations. The few that greedily feed at the public trough deny the rights of others to enter a fair system of economic competition.

Of course, viewed systemically, bribery is an important element in any political system. It supplements the salaries of various public officials. This is especially true in societies where public sector salaries are unreasonably low. Some police officers, customs agents, and building inspectors, for example, would be unable to maintain their standard of living if it were not for such informal salary increments. Additionally, such income supplement programs forestall the need for politically unpopular, precipitous tax hikes that would bring the legal wages of such officers up to reasonable levels. Systematic bribery allows business operators, dependent on the discretionary powers of

TABLE 5.1 American Government Officials Convicted of Public Corruption under Federal Law

	1980	1985	1990	1995	1998	1999	2000	2001	2002
Federal Officials	131	470	583	438	414	460	422	414	429
State Officials	51	66	79	61	58	80	91	61	132
Local Officials	168	221	225	191	264	219	183	184	262

SOURCE: *Statistical Abstract of the United States* (Washington, DC: Government Printing Office, 2005).

---

scandal In religion, an offense committed by a holder of high office. The term has been popularized to cover the commission of any action considered a demeaning of the responsibilities of office by the holder of that office.

public officials for their livelihood, to stabilize the relationships essential for the smooth functioning of their businesses. After all, many regulations that govern safety or conditions of business operation may not be universally applicable, reasonably enforceable, or economically feasible. Bribery's occasional exposure by the press serves to foster the political alienation of the electorate, which in turn encourages cynicism and reduces support for the democratic processes of government. While it is possible to quibble over the particulars of any given instance or noninstance of bribery, its pervasiveness in too many communities is generally not contested except by the most naive or the most corrupt. Bribery is even an important and time-honored tool of foreign policy. Of course, the United States does not have to bribe a foreign government to influence its support on some international issue. It can achieve the same effect by granting or withholding military or economic aid.

Watergate

A society's humor is a good indicator of its political corruption. For example, many analysts predicted that President Nixon would eventually be forced from office because of the Watergate scandal once Johnny Carson, the most popular, most mainstream, and most middle-of-the-road of American comedians, started telling jokes on his *Tonight Show* that were premised upon the belief that the president of

---

BOX 5.1   The Difference Between Honest Graft and Dishonest Graft

"Everybody is talkin' these days about Tammany men growin' rich on graft, but nobody thinks of drawin' the distinction between honest graft and dishonest graft. There's all the difference in the world between the two. Yes, many of our men have grown rich in politics. I have myself. I've made a big fortune out of the game, and I'm gettin' richer every day, but I've not gone in for dishonest graft—blackmailin' gamblers, saloon-keepers, disorderly people, etc.—and neither has any of the men who have made big fortunes in politics.

There's an honest graft, and I'm an example of how it works. I might sum up the whole thing by sayin': "I seen my opportunities and I took 'em."

Just let me explain by examples. My party's in power in the city, and its goin' to undertake a lot of public improvements. Well, I'm tipped off, say, that they're goin' to lay out a new park at a certain place.

I see my opportunity and I take it, I go to that place and I buy up all the land I can in the neighborhood. Then the board of this or that makes its plan public, and there is a rush to get my land, which nobody cared particular for before.

Ain't it perfectly honest to charge a good price and make a profit on my investment and foresight? Of course, it is. Well, that's honest graft."

SOURCE: William Riordon, *Plunkitt of Tammany Hall* (New York: McClure, Phillips, 1905).

the United States was dishonest. The jokes were a bellwether because most of the audience—that is, most of mainstream America—accepted the premise. <u>Comedians do not lead public opinion, but they certainly reflect it.</u> The same is true today in Russia. *New York Times* columnist Thomas L. Friedman wrote that "corruption reaches right into the leadership." His indicator of this is the often told joke "about a man who drives into Moscow from the countryside and parks his new car right outside the Kremlin's Spassky Gate in Red Square. A policeman comes along and tells the man, 'Look, you can't park here. This is the gate all our leaders use.' The man answers, 'Don't worry. I locked my car.' "

TABLE 5.2   Watergate Chronology

1969	January 20	Nixon inaugurated.
1970	July 23	Nixon approves use of illegal methods to gather intelligence on demonstrators and political enemies.
1971	February	Nixon begins secret taping of all Oval Office conversations.
1972	March 30	John Mitchell, head of Nixon's reelection committee, approves plan for illegal entry into and wiretapping of the Democratic National Committee's Watergate headquarters.
	May 27	The first Watergate break-in takes place.
	June 17	The second Watergate break-in occurs; five agents of the Nixon campaign are arrested.
		Nixon's attorney, Herbert Kalmbach, begins making secret payments to Watergate burglars; over a year's time $450,000 in hush money is paid out of campaign contributions.
	August 29	Nixon announces that White House Counsel John W. Dean has conducted an investigation of the Watergate break-in: "I can state categorically that his investigation indicates that no one in the White House staff, no one in this administration, presently employed, was involved in this very bizarre incident. What really hurts is if you try to cover it up." Dean would later testify that he had not heard of his "investigation" until this announcement.
	September 15	Watergate burglars indicted.
	October 10	*Washington Post* reporters Bob Woodward and Carl Bernstein reveal that the Watergate break-in was part of a massive campaign of political spying and sabotage conducted on behalf of the president's reelection and directed by White House and reelection committee officials.
	November 7	Nixon reelected in a landslide; wins every state but Massachusetts. Shortly thereafter, bumper stickers appear reading, "Don't blame me: I'm from Massachusetts."
1973	January	Watergate burglars tried and convicted.
	February 7	Senate votes to investigate Watergate and other 1972 campaign abuses.
	March 22	Nixon tells John Mitchell, "I want you all to stonewall it—let them plead the Fifth Amendment, cover-up, or anything else."

(continued)

TABLE 5.2 Watergate Chronology (continued)

	April 30	Nixon announces resignations of White House Chief of Staff H. R. Haldeman; White House Domestic Affairs Advisor John D. Ehrlichman; the Attorney General Richard G. Kleindienst; and the firing of White House Counsel John Dean (who had just reported the cover-up to the Justice Department). Nixon tells the nation, "We must maintain the integrity of the White House. . . . There can be no whitewash at the White House."
	May 17	Televised Senate Watergate hearings begin.
	May 18	Archibald Cox named Special Prosecutor.
	June 25	John Dean tells the Senate Watergate committee, "I began by telling the president that there was a cancer growing on the presidency and that if the cancer was not removed . . . the president himself would be killed by it."
	July 16	White House aide Alexander Butterfield reveals existence of White House taping system.
	July 25	Nixon refuses to release tapes requested by special prosecutor because it would violate executive privilege.
	October 20	Nixon orders the firing of Special Prosecutor Cox.
	October 23	Yielding to public pressure, Nixon agrees to hand over some tapes after "firestorm" of criticism.
	October 30	The House Judiciary Committee begins its impeachment inquiry.
	November 1	Houston lawyer Leon Jaworski is appointed new Special Prosecutor.
1974	March 1	The grand jury indicts seven former White House aides for Watergate cover-up.
	May 24	Special Prosecutor Leon Jaworski appeals to the Supreme Court to rule on his subpoena for more tapes.
	July 24	The Supreme Court in *United States v. Nixon* rules that Nixon must release the tapes.
	July 27	House Judiciary Committee votes for impeachment.
	August 5	Nixon surrenders tapes proving he had approved cover-up from the beginning.
	August 9	Nixon resigns.
	September 8	Nixon is pardoned by his successor, President Gerald R. Ford.
2005	June 1	Former FBI Deputy Director Mark Felt acknowledges he was Woodward and Bernstein's informant, "Deep Throat."

Lying for Your Country

The public officials who have the greatest reputation for lying are ambassadors—the highest ranking of all diplomats, sent as the personal representatives of one head of state to another. Sir Henry Wotton (1568–1639), Queen Elizabeth I's ambassador to Venice, was the first of many wits to write that "an ambassador is an honest man sent to lie abroad for the commonwealth." Often ambassadors are not trusted to lie well enough, so their governments purposely misinform them to ensure that their false representations will seem all the more sincere. Thus the Japanese ambassador to the United States in 1941 did not know of the impending Pearl Harbor attack, the German ambassador to the Soviet Union in 1941 was not told of the coming invasion, and the U.S. ambassador to the United Nations in 1961, Adlai Stevenson, was not told of the Bay of Pigs landing.

Niccolo Machiavelli wrote in *The Prince* (1532) that "it is necessary that the prince should know how to color his nature well, and how to be a great hypocrite and dissembler." This was the kind of thing that made people suspect that Machiavelli was not a gentleman. A true gentleman had to absolutely keep his word. To not do so would "prove" that he was not a gentleman—and that he was without honor. Thus lying became as unforgivable an act of moral courage as cowardice was of physical courage. Of course, that was only if you got caught!

President Richard Nixon takes time out from subverting the U.S. Constitution (he had already approved illegal methods to gather information on his political enemies) to meet with Elvis Presley in the Oval Office on December 21, 1970. Elvis had a keen interest in public administration and came to offer his services to the country as a part-time, volunteer, federal narcotics agent. After all, few people had more experience with narcotics abuse. Not realizing the irony in this, Nixon was only too pleased to give the even then drug-saturated singer (who was destined to die of drug abuse) the badge and credentials of a special agent of the Bureau of Narcotics and Dangerous Drugs. Elvis was a strong supporter of the administration who had publicly criticized anti–Vietnam War entertainers such as the Smothers Brothers and Jane Fonda. He wanted the credentials so that he would have more credibility as a kind of ambassador to troubled young people. But alas, the only troubled young people with whom he met were teenage girls who had agendas other than politics. •

The Dirty Hands Dilemma

When do desirable public ends justify the lying means? When is doing evil acceptable to produce a greater political good? The "dirty hands dilemma" is a graphic phrase for this problem. Public officials dirty their hands when they commit an act generally considered to be a wrong to further the common good. This is a dilemma in the sense that doing bad seems to lead to something good. Thus public officials need to decide if they are willing to engage in wrongdoing for the sake of a perceived good deed. Of course, as a general rule they are prohibited from engaging in wrongdoing. Thus the dirty hands dilemma is the product of a tension between perceived professional obligations and long-standing moral obligations that are the standards of everyday life.

Machiavelli did not see this as a problem at all. He held that the rules of morality in everyday life should not be applied to the acts of public officials when they are carrying out their professional roles and responsibilities to further the common good. As Machiavelli expressed it in *The Discourses*, "When the act accuses, the result excuses." But can we divorce the person from his or her administrative role? If any moral judgment is to be made, it must be made about the office or the governmental unit in which the official is housed. We should not apply the ordinary standards of right and wrong to the extraordinary situation of a person who is acting only as a bureaucratic functionary. Others argue that it is a mistake to confuse the role of public official with the person who temporarily holds that role; moral rules are still applicable to the acts of the person who commits wrongs, whether that person be a public official or not. One cannot use one's position in an organization as an excuse to be exempted from basic morality. Wrongdoing is wrongdoing, no matter what the context. Public officials must be held accountable for their unethical acts, even if those acts were done in the name of the common good and performed by someone claiming to be a professional or a mere functionary.

There can be little doubt that the most common form of the dirty hands dilemma in public administration is lying. Lying can take many forms: direct falsehoods, exaggerations, omissions, evasions, deceptions, duplicity, and so on.

Do public officials have a special obligation to tell the truth? Do their offices permit them special excuses to depart from truth telling? It can be argued that since knowledge is the cornerstone of democracy, an informed public is a prerequisite for a democratic government. Hence, citizens have an inherent right to know the truth of public issues so that they can make intelligent decisions as voters and constituents. When public officials decide to dirty their hands, whether by direct falsehood or by omission, evasion, or whatever, they are abridging the public's right to know. There is, on this account, then, a special obligation for public officials to tell the truth based on this inherent need of democracy.

On the other hand, it also can be argued that public officials in a democracy may be excused at times from the general obligation of truth telling. There may be dire situations or times of crises that threaten the government and its people. Under such conditions it may be permissible for a public official to deceive the public for its own good. In other words, when public officials take their oaths of office, they are sworn to do everything in their power to ensure the survival of the government and the safety of the public. It is the very nature of public office, then, that excuses the public official who lies for the public good because the public good is essentially what the official is required to protect. If such protection in times of war or crises entails that officials engage in deception, then so be it. They are only fulfilling the responsibilities of their office. The argument for excusing lies by officials has a long history. The first instance of it appears in Plato's *Republic*, in which the term "royal lie"—referring to lies for the public good—was first coined.

Lying About Sex

When essayist Charles Dudley Warner (1829–1900) wrote in 1871 that "politics makes strange bedfellows," he was referring to the fact that political necessity so often forces unlikely pairs to work together for a common goal—not that politicians must necessarily end up in bed with strangers. Yet those who have a passion for politics all too often have a problem with their passions. American presidents are no exceptions. The multitudinous, miscellaneous trystings of Presidents John F. Kennedy and Lyndon B. Johnson are only the most recent examples that have been thoroughly documented by historians. Johnson even felt competitive with the deceased Kennedy about this. According to biographer Robert Dalleck, Johnson as president bragged that "I had more women by accident than he [Kennedy] ever had by design." President Bill Clinton is unique only in that he has been forced to admit to such infidelities while in office.

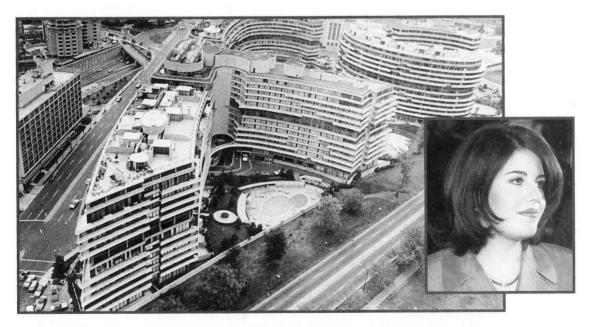

The Watergate Complex in Washington, DC. The Watergate once again became the center of an American political scandal in 1998 when Monica Lewinsky, the young woman with whom President Clinton had "an inappropriate relationship," resided there with her mother—who was also younger than the president. The affair was given a small-town flavor when it turned out the Lewinskys' next-door neighbor at the Watergate was Bob Dole, the former senator from Kansas who was Clinton's Republican opposition in the 1996 presidential election.

Until recently, lies about the sexual activities of consenting adults would not have been of concern to a textbook on public administration. But President Clinton changed that in 1998 when he told one lie after another about his Oval Office encounters with Monica Lewinsky, the White House intern with whom he eventually admitted having a relationship "that was not appropriate." And none of this would have come to public attention, no lies would have publicly been told, except for the involvement of the U.S. Supreme Court.

In what could turn out to be one of the most important modern Supreme Court decisions about the presidency, the Supreme Court ruled in 1998 *(William Jefferson Clinton v. Paula Corbin Jones)* that a sitting president could be sued by a private citizen seeking money damages in a civil suit for conduct alleged to have occurred before the president took office. Jones claimed that she was sexually harassed by Clinton while he served as governor of Arkansas years earlier. President Clinton urged the Court to delay the suit until he left office, claiming that the chief executive should not be burdened and distracted by having to defend against civil suits, except in far more exceptional circumstances.

Writing for the majority, Justice John Paul Stevens rejected Clinton's argument and concluded that that it would be highly unlikely that allowing the Jones case to proceed would generate a flood of other suits against this or other presidents, and, in any event, Stevens noted, the lower court judge could always defer such a case when it appears that to proceed would hamper a president's ability to do his job. What neither the members of the Court nor the public knew at the time was that President Clinton's testimony about Monica Lewinsky in a sworn deposition in the Jones case would set off a political firestorm powerful enough to threaten Clinton's presidency. Whether the Supreme Court's decision to permit civil actions against sitting presidents will result in future political and legal battles for presidents cannot be known. It is possible that the ever-present existence of powerful and well-funded political opponents anxious to "trap" presidents in sworn statements in civil suits was underestimated by the Court.

While Lewinsky's passion for President Clinton has been amply documented, she certainly seems to have lacked the "passion for anonymity" that the Brownlow Committee prescribed for White House assistants (see Chapter 3)—a passion that more mature presidential inamoratas have demonstrated by their silence. Because Lewinsky told so many people about her affair with Clinton, which began in 1995 when she was a 22-year-old unpaid White House intern, evidence began to appear that she lied in her sworn statement in the Jones case. Jones's lawyers had sought her statement to bolster their contention that Clinton was a persistent and consistent philanderer.

When audiotapes of Lewinsky's telephone conversations about the affair with President Clinton with her "friend" Linda Tripp surfaced early in 1998, two things happened: (1) a special prosecutor (Ken Starr), who had earlier been authorized by Congress to investigate alleged illegalities by the Clintons in other matters, sought and gained the permission of the Clinton-appointed attorney general to expand the investigation into possible perjury by the president in his Jones statements; and (2) many times and before many audiences, the president emphatically denied having had sexual relations with Lewinsky. There is little doubt that he would have continued to lie about the affair had not physical evidence become available that supported Lewinsky's testimony to a grand jury that both she and the president lied in their Jones case depositions. The evidence was a dress of Lewinsky's that was stained with presidential semen. Prior to the announcement of the existence of the physical evidence, the White House spin on the story was that Lewinsky was delusional about having an affair with the president—that she was just a politically starstruck kid who had lost a firm grasp on reality. But after the DNA of the dress stain was compared with freshly sampled presidential DNA, all doubts were over. After lying about this for seven months, the president, knowing of the DNA evidence of his lying, confessed before the grand jury, and then to the nation in a televised address, that he had had an "inappropriate relationship" with Lewinsky.

What got the president into legal trouble was not his multiple infidelities but the allegations of perjury about them. The party line from the White House after the confession was that since this whole scandal was about sex, it didn't rise to an impeachable offense. As with Watergate, it was not so much the initial "crime" as it was the cover-up—the lies—that forced Nixon from office and brought Clinton to impeachment. While some make the claim that lying about sex between consenting adults is only good manners, such matters are different affairs entirely once the parties have sworn to a grand jury to tell "the truth, the whole truth, and nothing but the truth." What does it say about the American legal system if the president of the United States is held exempt from that legal obligation—the violation of which has landed many of his fellow citizens in federal prison? This question was so troubling and Clinton's behavior was considered so reckless that in the fall of 1998 the House of Representatives impeached him for perjury and obstruction of justice. Clinton was tried by the Senate early in 1999 and was acquitted because there was nowhere near the constitutionally required two-thirds vote needed for his removal from office. Clinton remained president because many senators who believed he was guilty as charged felt that lying about sex was too petty a reason to remove a president.

Hierarchy of Ethics

The public administrator is frequently adrift in a sea of competing duties and obligations. This kind of conflict occurs when an individual is called upon to perform mutually exclusive acts by parties having legitimate "holds" on that person. For example, a rising young manager may not make it to the "big" meeting if he must at that moment rush his child to the hospital for an emergency appendectomy. When such conflicts arise, most individuals invoke a hierarchy of role obligation that gives some roles precedence over others. To most fathers, their child's life would be more important than a business meeting—no matter how "big." Real life is not always so unambiguous, however, and role conflict is a common dilemma in the world of work.

The "Nuremberg defense" is the often-used excuse of those caught performing illegal acts for their political or military superiors: "I was only following orders." The term and the tactic comes from war crimes trials in Nuremberg, Germany, of top Nazi leaders in the aftermath of World War II. The fallacy of this defense is that no soldier (or civilian employee) can be required to obey manifestly illegal orders. Indeed, as was even shown in the **My Lai** massacre during the Vietnam War, a soldier (or civilian employee) has a positive obligation to disobey such orders. Fortunately, few officials have to suffer angst over war crimes. But what about fixing traffic tickets, forcing a tax audit on someone, or pressuring employees to buy tickets to political dinners? Same issue, smaller stakes!

The Four Levels of Ethics

In public administration there is a hierarchy of levels of ethics, each of which has its own set of responsibilities. First, there is personal morality—the basic sense of right and wrong. This is a function of our past and is dependent on factors such as parental influences, religious beliefs, cultural and social mores, and one's own personal experiences.

Second in the hierarchy is professional ethics. Public administrators increasingly recognize a set of professional norms and rules that obligate them to act in certain "professional" ways. Such guidelines are codified by professional associations such as the American Society for Public Administration and the International City Management Association. However, occupations such as law and medicine, while operating within public administration, also have their own independent professional codes.

A third level of ethics is organizational. Every organization has an environment or culture that includes both formal and informal rules of ethical conduct. Public organizations typically have many such rules. Public laws, executive orders, and agency rules and regulations all can be taken as formal organizational norms for ethical behavior.

Finally, there are social ethics. The requirements of social ethics oblige members of a given society to act in ways that both protect individuals and further the progress of the group as a whole. Social ethics are formal to the extent that they can be found in the laws of a given society, informal to the extent that they are part of an individual's social conscience.

The Iran-Contra Affair

To illustrate the conflicting nature of responsibility and different levels of ethical obligations, let's consider the Iran-Contra affair in general and the actions of Oliver North in particular.

The Iran-Contra scandal arose in the fall of 1986, when it was revealed that the Reagan administration had secretly sold arms to the government of Iran (so Iran would use its **good offices** to gain the release of American hostages in Lebanon) at higher than normal prices and used the "profits" to fund the **Contras** in Nicaragua.

My Lai The South Vietnamese village where hundreds of old men, women, and children were murdered in 1968 by a U.S. Army unit commanded by Lieutenant William Calley Jr. Despite complaints by several soldiers, the U.S. Army sought to ignore or cover up this atrocity until congressional inquiries and press reports forced a comprehensive investigation that led to Calley's court-martial.

good offices The disinterested use of one's official position, one's office, to help others settle their differences; an offer to mediate a dispute.

Contras The U.S.-backed "democratic resistance movement" in Nicaragua. The Contras opposed the Communist Sandinista government. They disbanded in 1990 after the democratically elected government replaced the Sandinista regime.

The controversy grew into a scandal because it was illegal to sell arms to Iran, illegal to fund the Contras beyond limits set by the Congress, and against the expressed policy of the United States to negotiate for, let alone trade arms for, the release of hostages. Because the Iran-Contra operation was undertaken primarily by the National Security Council without the formal approval of the departments of Defense and State, the affair called into question the coherence of the Reagan administration's foreign policy.

As the major operative in the scheme, Lieutenant Colonel Oliver North of the U.S. Marine Corps, assigned to the White House National Security Council, serves as a case study in the conflict of responsibility. North has admitted that he found it necessary to lie to Congress about the Iran-Contra arms deal in order to further what he called national security goals. Thus, by overseeing the illegal sales of arms to Iran and channeling profits from the transactions to the Contras in violation of the law, North reached a decision that one set of responsibilities was higher than another. He justified his lies to Congress as necessary for national security. North violated the formal rules of organizational ethics and social ethics in illegally supplying military aid to the Contras and in lying to Congress to cover it up. However, he argued that he upheld his own personal morality and sense of duty to the country by acting as he did. Caught between his own interpretation of what is right and wrong on the personal level and that which his organization and society had deemed to be right and wrong, North chose the former over the latter. For many, he was a hero for doing so. Yet for many others, his actions were criminal and unconstitutional.

The Higher Law Defense

When North's secretary, Fawn Hall, was called to testify during the 1987 congressional hearings on the scandal, she asserted, "I felt uneasy but sometimes, like I said before, I believed in Colonel North, and there was a very solid and very valid reason he must have been doing this for and sometimes you have to go above the written law, I believe." In her pedestrian way Ms. Hall defended North by asserting the ancient idea of a higher law: the notion that no matter what the laws of a state are, there remains a higher law to which a person has an even greater obligation.

BOX 5.2   Thomas Jefferson on Higher Law

A strict observance of the written laws is doubtless one of the high duties of a good citizen, but it is not the highest. The laws of necessity, of self-preservation, of saving our country when in danger, are of higher obligation. To lose our country by a scrupulous adherence to written law, would be to lose the law itself, with life, liberty, property and all those who are enjoying them with us; thus absurdly sacrificing the end to the means.

SOURCE: Thomas Jefferson, letter to John B. Colvin, September 20, 1810.

A higher law is often appealed to by those who wish to attack an existing law or practice that courts or legislators are unlikely or unwilling to change. In a famous speech in the Senate on March 11, 1850, William Henry Seward of New York argued against slavery by asserting that "there is a higher law than the Constitution which regulates our authority." Martyrs throughout the ages have asserted a higher law in defiance of the state, thus earning their martyrdom. The classic presentation of this concept is in Sophocles' fourth-century B.C.E. play *Antigone,* in which the heroine defies the king, asserts a higher law as her justification, and "forces" the king to have her killed. Because the courts of any state will only enforce the law of the land, appealing to a higher law is always chancy business. Examples of Americans who have appealed to a higher law and wound up in jail as a result are Henry David Thoreau, Martin Luther King Jr., and Vietnam War resisters. Oliver North was convicted and would have gone to jail except that his conviction was overturned on a legal technicality. Thus he had all the glory of being a martyr with none of the pain of serving a prison sentence.

As the North case suggests, responsibilities can conflict because there are multiple levels of ethics and morality, each with its own set of obligations and duties. One of the most difficult aspects of being a public administrator is managing the conflict of responsibilities between the competing claims of stakeholders and the varying levels of ethics.

Codes of Honor, Conduct, and Ethics

It was a code of honor that forced Alexander Hamilton, one of the authors of *The Federalist* and the first U.S. secretary of the treasury, to face Aaron Burr, then the vice president of the United States, in an 1803 duel (pistols at ten paces) that ended with Hamilton's death. Duelists have often been occupants of the White House. Andrew Jackson was notorious for it—though not as president. Today, disagreements that once would have warranted duels are decided in the courts or the tabloids. Dueling over honor has not subsided; it has only taken new forms. The one constant factor in affairs of honor, as the Robert McNamara case at the end of this chapter demonstrates, is that they are still often matters of life and death.

The New Face of Dueling

Dueling has never abated. It has only taken on new forms, adapted to new circumstances and new technology. In the classic 1955 film *Rebel Without a Cause,* James Dean is challenged to a duel. The weapons are automobiles. He and the challenger drive the cars at high speed toward a cliff. The first one to jump out of his car is "chicken." Afterward, Dean explains to his father what happened: "Dad, I said it was matter of honor, remember? They called me chicken. You know, chicken? I had to go 'cause if I did not, I'd never be able to face those kids again. I got in one of those cars, and Buzz, that—Buzz, one of those kids—he got in the other car, and we had to drive fast and then jump, see, before the car came to the end of this bluff, and I got out okay, but Buzz did not and got killed."

Dueling by hotheaded teenage boys is the stuff of daily newspaper headlines. Teenage gang members, who once would have fought with fists or knives, now have cheap pistols or automatic weapons. A disrespectful comment or even a "look" is, as a matter of honor, all too often repaid with rapid fire. Those who do not act in accordance with gang codes of behavior suffer the consequences. Not all who kill for honor are gentlemen, but no one can be a gentleman if he is not prepared to die for honor.

Honorable Behavior

We still expect that our leaders will act honorably—meaning responsibly—and we disdain them when they do not. Almost everybody has heard of the 1912 *Titanic* disaster, in which many of the richest men in the world quietly went to their deaths when they could have taken the places of women and children in the lifeboats. The *Titanic* followed the tradition of the "Birkenhead Drill." When a British ship, the HMS *Birkenhead,* was sinking in 1852, the captain asked the men to "stand fast" so that the women and children could have the lifeboats. Over 400 men, including the captain, drowned. Ever since, "women and children first" has been the informal law of the sea because no man of honor could dispute it. And a ship's captain, responsible for all souls on board, was, as a matter of honor, traditionally expected to be the last one off of his sinking ship. Thus the world was appalled when Captain Yiannis Avranas was among the first to abandon his sinking Greek cruise ship, the *Oceanos,* off the coast of South Africa in 1991. Hundreds of passengers, many elderly, were left to shift for themselves. (The South African military eventually rescued everyone with helicopters.) As Captain Yiannis cravenly told reporters who asked him why he left his ship so soon, "When I order abandon ship, it does not matter what time I leave. Abandon is for everybody. If some people like to stay, they can stay." But his cowardly act was not morally different from the executive who arranges a golden parachute for himself while hundreds of employees who depended on his leadership are left with only pink slips and barren of financial windfalls. As you will see in this chapter's case study, Robert S. McNamara's dishonor was similar. He bailed out of the sinking ship of the Vietnam War, leaving thousands upon thousands of his country's children, 18- and 19-year-old drafted boys, to die. Leadership, as Shakespeare said of ambition, "should be made of sterner stuff."

More recently the behavior of members of the New Orleans Police Department in the wake of Hurricane Katrina left many considering the contemporary role of honor. As their city suffered through its bleakest days in September of 2005, many New Orleans police officers either turned in their badges or simply failed to report for duty. Given the police officers' oath to "protect the lives and property," of the citizens of New Orleans, their actions could only be seen as dishonorable in nature. One can only imagine how the officers who continued to work through the deplorable conditions felt when their comrades deserted them in such a time. Desertion in time of crisis is a form of dishonor that strikes at the very heart of a code of conduct. For some, including at least a few New Orleans police officers, their commitment to an ethical code is not strong enough to outweigh other personal interests.

However, those few who fail to live up to a code of honor seem to pale in comparison with those individuals who are willing to sacrifice everything to fulfill their duty.

Codes of honor have their origins in ancient precepts about how a person should behave in the face of danger, when confronted with temptation, or before authority figures. Much of what are still considered important elements of honorable behavior is contained in the Bible's Ten Commandments. Thus it is still honorable behavior to not kill, not steal, not bear false witness, and not covet thy neighbor's wife. As life grew more complicated, codes evolved for occupations as varied as clerics, masons, and warriors. The latter is both the most famous and most important, because those who feel a sense of traditional honor in their breasts today ultimately derive these emotions from medieval knights, eighteenth-century military and naval officers, and nineteenth-century British gentlemen.

But the honor of knights and gentlemen was highly stratified. Remember, they were gentlemen in the first place not because they were "gentle" (with women and horses!) but because of their genetic origin (Latin *gentilis*, "of a clan"), their breeding. Even today, polite people, those who ape upper-class manners, are called "well bred"—as if they were! Gentlemen were bound to act honorably only toward others in their own class. Consequently, if an ordinary citizen, having taken a dislike to Alexander Hamilton's face, had challenged him to a duel, he would not have been obligated to accept. There would have been no dishonor in declining. But a gentleman had always to defend his name, his reputation, his honor before members of his own class. According to Robin Gilmour, traditional honor to a gentleman "meant paying one's gambling debts, but not the tradesman's bill; deceiving a husband, if need be, but not cheating him at cards; insulting a servant with impunity, but one's equals only at the risk of a duel. The testing ground for one's courage, and therefore the justification for the whole bizarre code, was the gentleman's readiness to defend his honor with his life."

Was "Deep Throat's" Behavior Honorable?

Honorable behavior and ethical actions can sometimes seem at odds with one another. With the 2005 disclosure of Mark Felt as the informant "Deep Throat" in the Watergate scandal, the conflict between maintaining honor and acting ethically received increased public attention. During the investigation of the Watergate break-in, Felt, an FBI deputy director, provided *Washington Post* reporters Bob Woodward and Carl Bernstein with detailed information about the Nixon administration's efforts to cover up their involvement in illegal activities. The information Felt supplied proved essential in helping Woodward and Bernstein to expose the details of the White House's role in Watergate and helped lead to Nixon's unprecedented resignation from the presidency.

While many might think that Felt's role in this historic event was courageous and served the greater interest of the nation, Felt himself harbored misgivings about the honor of his actions. In the process of revealing his long-sought identity to the public, Felt expressed serious concern about how the FBI would regard his role in the Watergate episode. In the *Vanity Fair* article in which the identity of "Deep Throat" was revealed, author John D. O'Connor wrote that Felt "seemed to be struggling inside with whether he would be seen as a decent man or turncoat." He continued, "Deep in his psyche, it is clear to me, he still has qualms about his actions, but he also knows that historic events compelled him to behave as he did: standing up to an executive intent on obstructing his agencies pursuit of the truth."

Judging from the reaction of many of Felt's contemporaries to his revelation, his concern about being perceived as a "turncoat" was quite warranted. Former Nixon speechwriter and TV pundit Pat Buchanan stated, "I don't think he is a hero at all. . . . Here's a man who has been entrusted with a high honor, deputy chief of the FBI, sneaking around at night, handing out materials he got from a legitimate investigation to the *Washington Post.*" Conversely, Terry Lenzner, a senior counsel on the Senate Watergate committee, said, "The reason Felt turned into Deep Throat was that he had a sense that [FBI Director L. Patrick] Gray was participating in the cover-up and that it would destroy the reputation of the FBI. He was a classic FBI guy. His motives were that he had to protect the FBI. And he did." Clearly, one man's traitor is another's hero.

Standards of Conduct

Many civilian government agencies now have standards of conduct, formal guidelines, for ethical behavior. Their objective is to ensure that employees refrain from using their official positions for private gain. Typically, a variety of prohibited activities seek to ensure that employees conduct themselves in a manner that would not offer the slightest suggestion that they will extract private advantage from public employment. All too frequently, standards of conduct are used to say the obvious. For example, the British Cabinet Office created a document meant to be helpful to new cabinet ministers. Paragraph 55 of "Questions of Procedure for Ministers" offers the unsurprising advice that ministers "have a duty to refrain from asking or instructing civil servants to do things they should not do." Standards are often part of a state's formal legal code; thus violations can carry severe penalties—though never as draconian as articles of war. For example, the honest graft described by George Washington Plunkitt earlier in this chapter is now illegal in most jurisdictions in the United States. But since it was once both legal and quite common, we can surmise that ethical progress is being made.

While standards of conduct are always related to a specific organization, codes of ethics are wide in scope and encompass a whole profession or occupational category. A code of ethics is a statement of professional standards of conduct to which the practitioners of a profession say they subscribe. Codes of ethics are usually not legally binding, so they may not be taken too seriously as constraints on behavior. They sometimes become significant factors in political campaigns when questionable behavior by one side or the other is attacked or defended as being within or without a professional code. Professional groups also hide behind codes as a way of protecting (or criticizing) a member subject to public attack. President Ronald Reagan took the attitude "that people should not require a code of ethics if they're going to be in government. They should determine, themselves, that their conduct is going to be beyond reproach." Nevertheless, the problem remains that some people need help in determining just what constitutes ethical behavior. So codes are useful, but standards have the kind of teeth that can put you in jail.

The Challenge of Accountability

Accountability is the extent to which one must answer to higher authority—legal or organizational—for one's actions in society at large or within one's particular organizational position. Elected public officials are theoretically accountable to the political sovereignty of the voters. In this sense, appointed officials—from file clerks to cabinet secretaries—are less accountable than elected officials. The former are accountable mainly to their organizational supervisors, while the latter must answer to the people of their jurisdiction.

Administrative accountability is that aspect of administrative responsibility by which officials are held answerable for general notions of democracy and morality as well as for specific legal mandates. The two basic approaches to administrative accountability were first delineated by political scientists Carl J. Friedrich (1901–1984) and Herman Finer (1898–1969). Friedrich argued that administrative responsibility can be ensured only internally, through professionalism or professional standards or codes, because the increasing complexities of modern policies require extensive policy expertise and specialized abilities on the part of bureaucrats. Finer, on the other hand, argued that administrative responsibility could be maintained only externally, through legislative or popular controls, because internal power or control would ultimately lead to corruption. The tension between these two approaches continues today. Thus the challenge of accountability is to find a balance between completely trusting government officials to use their best professional judgment in the public's interest and watching them so closely through legislative committees or executive review agencies that it inhibits their ability to function.

Because we aspire to a democratic form of government, we need to consider how the links between democratic government and public administration work. What are the things we do, must do, and indeed must avoid if we are to be public administrators in a democracy rather than cogs in a despotic mechanism? Under the totalitarian communism of the former Soviet Union, the Russians had a word for people who served the apparatus of state without question. They were called apparatchiks—a term implying that the individual mindlessly follows orders. What stops us from being apparatchiks in all but name?

The answer to this question is that public administrators in a democracy work within the rule of law—a governing system in which the highest authority is a body of law that applies equally to all (as opposed to the rule of men, in which the personal whim of those in power can decide any issue). The idea of the desirability of a "government of laws, and not of men" can be traced back to Aristotle. The earliest American reference is in the 1779 Massachusetts Constitution. John Marshall also used this succinct legal description in *Marbury v. Madison* (1803): "The government of the United States has been emphatically termed a government of laws, and not of men. It will certainly cease to deserve this high appellation, if the laws furnish no remedy for the violation of a vested legal right." The rule of law and the concomitant

---

apparatchik This Russian word for a bureaucrat is now used colloquially to refer to any administrative functionary.

notion that no one is above the law have been continuously critical concepts. When Ford succeeded Nixon (who was forced to resign because of his illegal activities during the Watergate scandal), he told the nation right after taking the oath of office (August 9, 1974), "My fellow Americans, our long national nightmare is over. Our Constitution works; our great Republic is a government of laws and not of men." This was difficult for many citizens to reconcile with his **pardon** of Nixon one month later, so they voted Ford out of office the first chance they got. Now *that's* accountability!

In democratic societies, we require our administrators to work within a system of democratic accountability, respond to a complex system of checks and balances, and be subject to scrutiny by official auditors, by the media, and by community watchdogs and whistleblowers (as Finer advocated). But in the end, they are individually responsible for their own ethical and honorable behavior (as Friedrich believed). We often (but not always) remove from office those public administrators who seek to ignore their responsibilities to democracy. Occasionally, as in the case of J. Edgar Hoover of the FBI, there will be public administrators in democratic societies who seem to be above the law. But they, too, will fall from power in the end—if only because they eventually die.

Sometimes we purposely create public institutions that seem to have an "above the law" status. Security organizations sometimes seem to have this characteristic, best exemplified by the fictional British secret agent James Bond's "license to kill." Intelligence agencies have always had a certain mystical quality—perhaps because they are so associated with fictional exploits. This even affects presidents. Arthur M. Schlesinger Jr., in *A Thousand Days* (1965), quoted President John F. Kennedy: "If someone comes in to tell me this or that about the minimum wage bill, I have no hesitation in overruling them. But you always assume that the military and intelligence people have some secret skill not available to ordinary mortals." The review of the policies and activities of U.S. intelligence agencies by appropriate legislative review committees was not formally done by the Congress until the 1970s, when reports of FBI and CIA abuses of their operating mandates encouraged both houses of the Congress to create committees that would systematically and formally watch over the intelligence operations of the executive branch. Parliamentary systems, which are used in most of the world, have far less opportunity for comparable oversight because prime ministers, who ultimately direct intelligence agencies, lead both the executive and the legislative branches of government.

More generally, however, abuse of authority in public administration is a central target for condemnation in democratic societies and a likely route to disgrace and dismissal. Yet, in many societies around the world, to hold official office, to be

---

pardon An executive's granting of a release from the legal consequences of a criminal act. This may occur before or after indictment or conviction. The U.S. president's power to pardon people for federal offenses is absolute except for convictions in impeachment cases. A pardon prior to indictment stops all criminal proceedings. This is what happened when President Gerald Ford pardoned Richard M. Nixon in 1974 for all offenses that he "has committed or may have committed or taken part in while president."

a public administrator, is to be able to take **arbitrary** decisions, to confer benefits on family and friends, and to be open to corrupt, unethical—even inhuman—behavior. So we must ask, What legal and institutional arrangements, conventions, and ethical values essentially distinguish democratic from despotic public administration? In truly democratic societies—as opposed to those that are democratic in name only—there is a framework of constitutional, legal, and procedural requirements that subject public administrators to rigorous monitoring and oversight by a democratic legislature, independent courts, and other institutions at arm's length from the government. This leads to the expectation on the part of public administrators that, for the most part, they must work in the open, not only expecting but welcoming the scrutiny of elected representatives and the others whose task it is to make public accountability work.

Constitutional and Legal Constraints

Like it or not, public administrators always work within some kind of legal framework. In Europe, particularly in Germany, the legal setting of public administration is so all-encompassing that a senior official normally cannot be appointed without a formal law degree. In other parts of the world, a law degree is usually not required, but some understanding of constitutional and administrative law is. For American public administrators, the Constitution serves as an invisible fence surrounding their field of operation. Specific laws deriving from it delineate and regulate in finer and finer detail what public administrators can do to whom and when, and how, they can do it.

David H. Rosenbloom states that there are three reasons why public administrators should understand the Constitution:

1. Public administration must have democratic policy very much at heart so that managerial and political approaches are taken that are compatible with constitutional principles and values.

2. Many public administrators in America take an oath to support the Constitution, and this may be more important than routine administrative functions.

3. Public administrators may be personally liable for civil damages if they act in contravention to the Constitution.

As Rosenbloom emphasizes, it is no easy task to achieve the necessary understanding of the Constitution, since its contemporary meaning extends not only to the letter of the document but to **case law** and extensive interpretation, derived from legal, philosophical, moral, and political considerations as to how the law should be applied.

Public administrators in each policy domain—health, civil defense, education, or whatever it may be—need to maintain an awareness that the Constitution impacts what they can do by virtue of specific judgments and case law in the past, or alternatively because in a general sense what they propose to do may be seen to conflict

---

arbitrary Decided on the basis of individual judgments that do not meet commonly understood rules of procedure and hence may not appear justifiable to those seeking to explain them to others or to replicate them in similar circumstances.

case law All recorded judicial and administrative agency decisions.

with the Bill of Rights or some other fundamental constitutional precept. For example, in *Wood v. Strickland* (1975) the U.S. Supreme Court held that a school board member (and by implication other public employees) is not immune from liability for damages "if he knew or reasonably should have known that the action he took within his sphere of official responsibility would violate the constitutional rights of the students affected, or if he took the action with the malicious intention to cause a deprivation of constitutional rights or other injury to the student."

Apart from the general constraints and freedoms conferred on administrators by the Constitution, the laws creating governing institutions and regulating their particular policy domain must also remain foremost in administrators' minds. Sometimes this component of the framework of democratic oversight can involve the president and a committee of the Congress working with officials to design the legislation that will guide future administration. They all know that the **legislative history** may be used in writing rules, or by courts in interpreting the law, to ascertain the intent of the Congress if the act is ambiguous or lacking in detail. The history, particularly the committee reports, often contains the only complete explanation of the meaning and intent of the law. Thus members of Congress, their staffs, and other interested parties often try to influence a legislative history to help shape the way the law is eventually administered by agencies and interpreted by the courts. Sometimes, during the legislative debate on a bill, a member of the legislature will specifically talk about what is intended or not intended by the bill so that the ensuing legislative history will be a better guide to future interpretations of the **legislative intent**.

Arthur E. Morgan, the first chairman of the Tennessee Valley Authority, described how, after he had been chosen for the role, President Franklin D. Roosevelt gave him permission to meet and work with the **conference committee** of the House and Senate, which was designing the enabling legislation. The scope of the discussions extended to the composition of the board of the proposed agency and its powers and policies. In the course of the discussions, Morgan was able to make scores of suggestions for changes to the legislation within which he would have to work for many years. Few public administrators enjoy this rare privilege. For the most part, they must work within a framework laid down by others and hope that it provides scope for the needs that emerge—sometimes years later in very different contexts than originally anticipated.

Obsessive Accountability

It was Napoléon's foreign minister Charles-Maurice de Talleyrand who is usually credited with first saying of administrative affairs, "Above all, not too much zeal."

---

legislative history The written record of the writing of an act of the U.S. Congress.

legislative intent The supposed real meaning of a statute as interpreted from its legislative history.

conference committee A meeting between the representatives of the two houses of a legislature to reconcile the differences over the provisions of a bill. Unless all differences between the houses are finally adjusted, the bill fails. The conference committee process can sometimes have a dramatic effect on a bill. As President Ronald Reagan once said, "You know, if an orange and an apple went into conference consultations, it might come out a pear" (*New York Times,* December 18, 1982).

Yet it is an excess of zeal in the form of obsessive attention to minor details that so often leads to incompetence in modern organizations. Some of this dysfunctional zeal is caused by aberrant personalities, but the real culprit is the formally mandated zeal of governing rules and regulations. Much required zeal is good. No one can argue with requirements for punctuality. But once organization-wide standard procedures are established for major functions, there is an inevitable tendency for minutiae to be covered as well. These minutiae then, quite literally, take more time than they are worth.

For example, in 1993 the U.S. General Accounting Office reported that "each year the military spends some $20 million moving and storing a half-million items worth less than the cost of processing." Thus a U.S. base in Europe returns a few dollars' worth of metal bolts or nylon cord to a Defense Department warehouse in Ohio. But since it costs $40 to process these small items, it would have been far less expensive to give or throw away the stuff. However, there is no provision in the rules for disposing of unneeded items in this way. Such practices would give too much discretion to individual employees. The formal organization, in its zeal to prevent theft, mandates many such wasteful practices.

Peter Drucker maintains that organizations, most typically governments, that are obsessed with accountability are inherently less competent than they might be. New procedures are created in response to possible or previous abuses. Since individuals once showed themselves incapable of being responsible for specified organizational assets, discretion over them was taken out of their hands and given to unemotional, unbending, and, in some circumstances, irrational procedures. Accountability was placed in procedures rather than in individuals, the rationale being that the honest administration was too important a matter to leave to an individual's discretion. It is precisely because of governments' attempts to assign accountability for everything they control that public management operations grow to be outrageously expensive when compared to similar functions in private industry. According to Drucker, government must always tolerate this extra expense—not out of some unwarranted affection for red tape but because a "little dishonesty" in government is a corrosive disease that rapidly spreads to infect the entire polity. To fear such corruption is quite rational. Consequently, government "bureaucracy" and its attendant high costs cannot and should not be eliminated.

While the high costs of accountability can never be totally eliminated, some of the dysfunction of its associated procedures can be mitigated. Such mitigation frequently has organizations bending, ignoring, and subverting regulations in the interests of good management. The discretion that the regulations deny to the executive may be restored by the machinations of administrative operatives. When the flexibility deemed essential for mission accomplishment is formally denied to line managers, it is almost invariably obtained informally through administrative finesse. This is an idea that has not only been demonstrated in countless empirical studies, but also sanctioned and revered in American popular culture. The nation has a tremendous appetite for movies and television programs about war and other violent escapades. As any aficionado with sufficient exposure to this genre of entertainment can explain, you cannot have a successful military operation without a scrounger in your unit—at least not according to Hollywood's version of World War II. A scrounger was that member of the team who was assigned to obtain all the essential requirements of the mission that could not be obtained through official channels. It hardly mattered what methods the scroungers used to secure the needed supplies as long as they succeeded—and there were no official complaints. The war seems to have been won in large measure because our scroungers were better at overcoming organizational constraints than their scroungers.

The obvious danger of managers using excessive zeal in seeking to achieve an organization's mission, and thereby going beyond the proper range of discretion, is well recognized. This is an inherent and necessary risk in all managerial delegation. Unreasonable constraints only exacerbate the danger and increase the frustration. When mandates from on high reflect neither administrative wisdom nor experience, they are viewed as barriers to managerial effectiveness—which must be overcome. There is even significant evidence that organizational superiors discourage subordinates from reporting fully just how they have accomplished their missions because of concerns for formal or legal culpability. According to Herbert Kaufman, executives "may resort to the strategy of discouraging feedback about administrative behavior because they privately *approve* of the behavior they know they should, according to law and morality, prevent." Thus rookie police officers are told by their more experienced associates that they will have to forget what they learned at the police academy before they can operate effectively—and survive—in a real-world situation. Any new public manager must suffer through an on-the-job acquisition of administrative **realpolitik**. They learn by the unfortunate consequences of violating norms that are discovered only when they are breached. While this may seem at first to be an unnecessary and gratuitous bit of trauma to impose on innocent individuals, it is a critical rite of passage in the loss of administrative innocence and the learning of organizational norms and the inculcation of an organization's culture.

Avoiding Accountability

The public rightly expects an executive to be accountable for the actions of the subordinates he or she has selected, whether or not the executive had actual knowledge of the actions. It is based on the belief that the selection of subordinates and the monitoring of their behavior is an executive responsibility. Nowhere is primitive ritual or Machiavellian feigning more apparent than in the periodic assumption of full responsibility by an organization's chief executive. Although one of the advantages of delegating a problem is the ease with which the cunning leader can shift the blame for the situation if it sours, modern executives are seldom so crude as to lay blame. The appropriate tactic is to assume full responsibility for the situation. Paradoxically, in assuming full responsibility, the executive is seemingly relieved of it.

---

realpolitik A German word, now absorbed into English, meaning the politics of realism; an injunction not to allow wishful thinking or sentimentality to cloud one's judgment. At its most moderate, the word is used to describe an overcynical approach, one that allows little room for human altruism, that always seeks an ulterior motive behind another actor's statements or justifications. At its strongest, it suggests that no moral values should be allowed to affect the singleminded pursuit of one's own self-interest or patriotism. It also makes an absolute assumption that any opponent will certainly behave in this way.

Political scientist Murray Edelman observed that whenever this ritual is enacted, all of the participants tend to experience "a warm glow of satisfaction and relief that responsibility has been assumed and can be pinpointed. It once again conveys the message that the incumbent is the leader, that he knows he is able to cope, and that he should be followed." In reality, however, this ritual proves to have no substance. It "emphatically does not mean that the chief executive will be penalized for the mistakes of subordinates or that the latter will not be penalized."

This is the tactic that President Richard M. Nixon employed when he first addressed the nation concerning the Watergate scandal in the spring of 1973. He boldly proclaimed that all of the possibly illegal actions of the White House officials were his responsibility and that he fully accepted that responsibility. Certainly, Nixon did not mean to imply—at that point in time—that he should be punished for the transgressions of his underlings. Nor did Ronald Reagan in 1987 when he took full responsibility for the Iran-Contra affair. Bill Clinton, during an August 17, 1998, television address to the nation, took full responsibility for lying to his wife, his cabinet, his staff, and his nation about his affair with White House intern Monica Lewinsky. But his hopes that this would be enough to stop an impeachment inquiry were short-lived. Government officials of lesser rank are no less sophisticated with their manipulations of the ritualistic and symbolic aspects of their offices. Of course, the risk they take is that the legislature will investigate the situation thoroughly enough to expose any wrongdoing.

Legislative Oversight

While constitutional and legal frameworks themselves amount to a passive exercise of democratic control over the discretion of public administrators, there is no substitute for active control through energetic elected representatives. The main reason the U.S. Congress (or a state legislature or a city council) monitors the activities of executive branch agencies is to determine if the laws are being faithfully executed. After all, the president has the constitutional obligation (given in Article 2, Section 3) to "take care that the laws be faithfully executed." Congressional oversight is designed in our system of "checks and balances" to check that he does.

Hearings

Oversight takes many forms. The most obvious are the annual congressional hearings on agency budget requests, in which agency activities have to be justified to the satisfaction of the Congress. Both the House and the Senate hold budget hearings. But only the Senate holds hearings on the confirmation of major appointees such as cabinet secretaries and Supreme Court nominees.

Any member of Congress can instigate an investigation. Many of these investigations are small matters concerning the interests of a single constituent (see the section on casework following). But if something significant turns up worthy of a larger inquiry, an appropriate committee or subcommittee always has the right to initiate a further examination. The oversight function is primarily implemented through the process of hearings that often call for sworn testimony from officials, through consultancy reports, and through the publication of findings. Committees that have investigated scandals such as Watergate and the Iran-Contra affair, and issues such as whether gays should be permitted to serve in the military, illustrate how important and central a role this aspect of democratic government can be. In consequence, those who become chair of an influential committee of Congress occupy powerful positions indeed.

The entire Congress is in effect a permanently sitting **grand jury** always waiting to hear of improper acts by executive branch agencies so that **hearings** can be launched and witnesses called. Some members of Congress are so zealous in their oversight concerns that they will go to the trouble of traveling all over the world (at government expense) to see how federal programs and policies are operating. These visits are derisively called junkets, but they are an important part of the oversight process. Some members of Congress simply cannot understand why it is necessary to vote for money for American forces in NATO unless they first visit Europe and make a thorough investigation of the situation.

Of course, the oversight function may be abused, especially when it is done for partisan advantage. Such political oversight often happens when the executive and legislative branches of a government are controlled by opposing parties; then its purpose may be to embarrass the administration. Two famous examples of this are the Democratic Party–sponsored Watergate hearings of 1973–1974, which helped force Republican President Richard Nixon to resign in 1974, and the Republican Party–sponsored Whitewater hearings of 1995–1996, which were designed to embarrass the Democratic President Bill Clinton. Of course, whether an oversight action is simply in the interest of good government or whether it is a play in a game of partisan one-upmanship is in the eye of the beholder.

In 2005 congressional oversight of both the executive and judicial branches was on display for the nation. First, the resignation of Justice Sandra Day O'Connor and the death of Chief Justice William Rehnquist resulted in two presidential nominations to the Supreme Court. While Republican control of the Senate helped secure relatively smooth approval of John Roberts and Samuel Alito to the court, the confirmation process remains a key aspect of legislative oversight. Second, the failure of government agencies to adequately address the aftermath of Hurricane Katrina helped spawn demand for congressional hearings on the matter. As members of Congress came back to Washington from their summer recess, numerous congressional committees announced hearings on the government's response to Katrina. Senator John McCain of Arizona stated in a *Dallas Morning News* interview that "there's clearly a mood for

---

grand jury A group of citizens selected to review evidence against accused persons to determine whether there is sufficient evidence to bring the accused to trial—to indict or not to indict. A grand jury usually has from 12 to 23 members and operates in secrecy to protect the reputation of those not indicted. Grand juries have been both criticized for being easily manipulated tools in the hands of prosecutors and praised for protecting the rights of those falsely accused.

hearings A legislative committee session for hearing witnesses. At hearings on legislation, witnesses usually include specialists, government officials, and representatives of those affected by the bills under study. Subpoena power may be used to summon reluctant witnesses. The public and press may attend open hearings but are barred from closed (executive) hearings.

aggressive oversight on this issue because people are demanding it." What separates this situation from past hearings such as Watergate and Whitewater is that the Republican-controlled Congress directed its inquiry at one of its own: President Bush.

Casework

Casework is the term used for the services performed by legislators and their staffs at the request of and on behalf of constituents. For example, a U.S. representative may be asked to discover why a Social Security check has been delayed or why a veteran's claim for benefits has been denied. Casework is an important means by which legislators maintain oversight of the bureaucracy and solidify their political base with constituents.

Casework offers many advantages for legislators. First, it's cheap and noncontroversial. For the price of some minor staff time, a politician can make a voter happy. After dealing with thousands of cases over several years, this can pay back big on election day. Of course, there is always the danger that the legislator will not be able to solve the constituent's problem. But if the situation is handled with promptness and tactfulness, the case can still be a net gain from a public relations viewpoint. Even if the "customer" did not get what was wanted from the bureaucracy, a perception of fair treatment will still go a long way.

Agency administrators can also benefit from good casework service. The responsive handling of constituent problems will tend to make legislators more receptive to next year's budget requests. And a pattern of similar casework complaints could indicate administrative problems that need to be fixed before the numbers explode. Naturally, there is a thin line between administrative troubleshooting and special treatment. This is a line that astute administrators must walk straight—well, almost straight!

BOX 5.3 Casework in Action

I would relate to the crowds how I called on a certain rural constituent and was shocked to hear him say he was thinking of voting for my opponent. I reminded him of the many things I had done for him as prosecuting attorney, as county judge, as congressman, and senator. I recalled how I had helped get an access road built to his farm, how I had visited him in a military hospital in France when he was wounded in World War I, how I had assisted him in securing his veteran's benefits, how I had arranged his loan from the Farm Credit Administration, how I had got him a disaster loan when the flood destroyed his home, etc., etc.

"How can you think of voting for my opponent?" I exhorted at the end of this long recital. "Surely you remember all these things I have done for you!"

"Yeah," he said, "I remember. But what in hell have you done for me lately?"

SOURCE: Alben W. Barkley, *That Reminds Me* (Garden City, NY: Doubleday, 1954). Barkley was vice president under Truman.

✦ A CASE STUDY: THE BLOOD ON ROBERT McNAMARA'S HANDS—AND CONSCIENCE

Robert S. McNamara offers a clear example of a government official in an ethical quandary. His resolution of it will forevermore be a case study on the ethics of loyalty. The question here is, to whom must the official be ultimately loyal—to the administration or to the people? Is a patronage appointee's expected loyalty to a mayor, governor, or president greater or lesser than a competing loyalty to the overall interests of the citizenry?

Before World War II, McNamara taught statistics at Harvard Business School. During the war, he served honorably and rose to the rank of lieutenant colonel in the U.S. Army Air Corps, where he helped develop statistical control systems. A civilian again in 1946, he joined the Ford Motor Company, rising to become its president in 1961. It would be only a few months later that President John F. Kennedy would make him secretary of defense. In that position he energetically pursued what was to be by his own admission a futile war in Vietnam. He served as the principal administrative instrument in the deaths of tens of thousands of Americans and more than a million Vietnamese. He consequently was viewed as such a moral and intellectual coward by virtue of his hypocrisy and silence that the *New York Times,* in an unusually personal April 12, 1995, editorial, damned him as someone "who must not escape the lasting moral condemnation of his countrymen."

How did this man, this Eagle Scout who volunteered for World War II service when he had two legitimate deferments (he was an instructor at an officer training facility—Harvard—and he was a married man with a child), who only wanted to do good in government service, end up doing bad on such a massive scale? What he did was so bad that he was soundly condemned by many on both sides of the issue of whether the war itself was worthy of U.S. involvement. What is undisputed is that McNamara, the archetypal bureaucratic policy analyst and number cruncher, was the architect of American military strategy in Vietnam and the strongest advocate of the war—first for President Kennedy and then, after Kennedy's assassination in 1963, for President Lyndon B. Johnson. In 1964 he even publicly boasted that he was pleased when critics called it "McNamara's War." But gradually, as the war wore on, McNamara became disenchanted with the slaughter, so much so that he began to believe that the war could never be won.

Neil Sheehan wrote in his Pulitzer Prize–winning history of the war, *A Bright Shining Lie* (1988), that by the end of November 1967 President Johnson would complain that "McNamara's gone dovish on me" and had deteriorated into "an emotional basket case" because of the burdens of the war. Thus "McNamara learned through a press leak of his appointment as the new president of the World Bank." According to Senator Max Cleland of Georgia, who lost both legs in the war, "McNamara went to the World Bank, while a lot of other people went to their graves."

For the next quarter-century, McNamara, despite more than a dozen years as head of the World Bank and numerous writings on the inherent evil of nuclear war, was off the public's radar screen. Then in 1995 he published his memoir on the war, *In Retrospect,* which brought a firestorm of condemnation upon him. The book essentially said that he knew the war was unwinnable long before he left office and that he continued to pour American blood and treasure into a policy rathole out of loyalty to President

Johnson. Yet this was well known. For more than two decades, history books by the score acknowledged McNamara's disenchantment. And who was the source for all this information on McNamara's true feelings? Why, the man himself! He frequently poured out his anguish to his many influential friends. McNamara's tearful emotions over his role in Vietnam were an open secret. According to David Halberstam, McNamara "carefully fended off [on-the-record] questions on what he really thought by pointing out that as head of the World Bank, he had no viewpoints, no politics."

More than a quarter-century too late to do any real good, McNamara admitted two explosive things in his book: (1) The Johnson administration did not possess superior knowledge of the situation that was not available to the public (this "you don't know what we know" stance had been used in demanding public deference to their war policies), and (2) he, the secretary of defense, essentially had agreed with the antiwar protesters' belief that the war was futile and unwinnable. If he had said this at the time he left office, if not sooner, it surely would have had a significant effect on the situation and could have saved tens of thousands of American lives.

It is hard today to appreciate the deference in which the American public and members of Congress once held executive branch pronouncements about foreign policy and military issues. The modern cynicism and often-expressed attitude that the government, indeed the president, is lying largely came about because of the lies told during the Vietnam War. If McNamara had rallied the opposition with a timely confession, he could have given political cover to many opinion leaders and officeholders who had doubts but were too fearful to express them. It was literally a matter of life and death. And McNamara chose to sit in his office at the World Bank and let those who were at risk—American soldiers as well as countless Vietnamese—die.

Senator John McCain of Arizona was in Hanoi, Vietnam, on a mission to recover the remains of U.S. servicemen when McNamara's book came out. McCain, a Navy pilot who spent seven years as a prisoner of war in Hanoi, said, "I think it's about 25 years too late to save those Americans who would be alive if he hadn't pursued a policy that was doomed to failure. . . . I can only assume that McNamara's doing it now because he's trying to assume some place in history." Many questioned McNamara's motives for the book. Some were angered by the thought that he did it for the money. But he was already wealthy enough that money could not possibly have been a motivator. McNamara's motives can best be compared to those of Lady Macbeth trying to wash the blood off her murderous hands ("Out, damned spot!"). Both had a need to come psychologically clean, a need to assuage the guilt for all the spilled blood that was their responsibility ("Who would have thought the old man to have had so much blood in him?"). So Lady Macbeth went mad ("a mind diseas'd"), and McNamara published a *mea culpa,* a public confession, saying that "we were wrong, terribly wrong." Instead of the forgiveness he sought, he got condemned by virtually all sides. Those who protested the war at the time condemned him for not publicly joining their ranks when he first gave them his heart. Those who supported the war condemned him for attacking their strong belief that the war was winnable if only this or that were done. Those who were veterans and families of veterans condemned him for saying in effect that the sacrifices he so often called on them to make were for nothing.

When McNamara was pointedly asked by *Newsweek* (in an April 17, 1995, interview that accompanied an excerpt from his book) whether he put his loyalty to President Johnson over loyalty to the American people, he replied, "I don't think that's the case. We are not a parliamentary government, where ministers can overthrow the prime minister. A minister in our government is there solely as the representative of the president. Therefore, every cabinet officer must do as the president says, or get the hell out. And if he got out, my view is that he cannot attack the president from outside the cabinet, essentially using the power given to him by the president. I recognize this is not a widely accepted view, but I believe it's the correct view—grounded in the Constitution."

However, there is nothing in the Constitution that says former cabinet secretaries lose their rights as citizens to complain about—indeed "attack"—the president they previously served. William Jennings Bryan, President Woodrow Wilson's first secretary of state, resigned in 1915 over Wilson's policy toward Germany. They disagreed on the best way to keep the United States out of the war then raging in Europe. Not only was the policy dispute public at the time, but Bryan continued for months to attack Wilson's policies at every opportunity. There was much noise and debate about who was correct but never a hint of a constitutional crisis. But McNamara did not even have to think back to the Wilson administration for an example of a dissenting former cabinet member. His close friend Robert F. Kennedy, to whom he often confessed his misgivings about the war, resigned his position in the Johnson cabinet as attorney general in 1964 and then proceeded to criticize Vietnam policy as a senator from New York.

There was no constitutional issue that prevented McNamara from speaking out. So why didn't he? Was he so egocentric that his primary loyalty was to himself as opposed to the nation because he wanted to remain a player in the game of power? Or did he, as Colonel David H. Hackworth suggests, "confuse loyalty to his president with a higher loyalty to the country"? As a public official, he was charged with sending fellow citizens to their deaths in a cause he first championed but then labeled both unworthy and impractical. But despite the Lincolnesque "last full measure of devotion" that he had demanded from thousands of Americans, he was unwilling to risk the sacrifice of his public career in an effort to stop the carnage. This is the essence of his moral cowardice and personal dishonor.

Aside from the vital lessons learned about the limitations of mathematical models and systems analysis as aids in decision making, there are two reasons why McNamara's legacy of deceit is important to modern public administration.

First, McNamara's case offers a clear-cut example of one of the most common ethical quandaries facing public officials at all levels—whether political appointees, as McNamara was, or career civil servants. Who deserves our ultimate loyalty—the individual who, by virtue of a public office, employs us or the greater interests of the state? Loyalty is allegiance, but to whom? Mark Twain wrote, "My kind of loyalty was loyalty to one's country, not to its institutions or its officeholders." McNamara's loyalty was bureaucratic—not patriotic. Thus he did not publicly complain about President Johnson's policies. As a good organization man, he did not believe in going over the head of his administrative superior. He silently acquiesced to a policy he knew, and history has proved, to be wrong. This is the kind of loyalty that President Lyndon B. Johnson referred to when he told his staff, according to Larry Berman, what he meant by loyalty over Vietnam: "I want him to kiss my ass in Macy's window at high noon and tell me it smells like roses." The strange thing here is that McNamara continued to "smell the roses" long after Johnson was out of office and long after Johnson was dead. It must have been a powerful perfume!

Second, McNamara's most lasting contribution is the cynicism and disaffection so many citizens have toward their governments at all levels in the United States. The Vietnam War made presidential lying to the American public if not normal, then at least an expected part of government. The lying and disinformation machine that McNamara created to "inform" the news media and the American public about the war was continued by and brought into domestic politics and made bipartisan by President Richard M. Nixon. The Nixon administration's lying about the Watergate scandal was just a continuation and extension of Vietnam policy cover-ups. Yet McNamara asserts in his book that one of the reasons he wrote his memoir was because he had "grown sick at heart witnessing the cynicism and even contempt with which so many people view our political institutions and leaders." He should know! It is his legacy to his country—that and many of the names of the dead on the inscribed slabs of the Vietnam War Memorial.

For Discussion: *Was McNamara ethically justified in keeping silent about his disillusionment with the Vietnam War policies for so many years? Is there ever adequate justification for allowing loyalty to one's administrative superior to outweigh one's overall loyalty to one's country—especially considering that officeholders have usually taken an oath to defend the interests of their country?*

Summary

Honor comes before ethics because a person without honor has no moral compass and does not know which way to turn to be ethical. Honor goes to the essence of public affairs. Since ancient times only individuals perceived to be honorable could be trusted with the public's business.

Recurrent government scandals, no matter how much they cost, pose a great threat to the democratic notions of the rule of law. When a public official misuses his or her office for self-gain, then the rule of law no longer obtains, and there is, in effect, a return to tyranny.

Do public officials have a special obligation to tell the truth, or do their offices permit them special excuses to depart from truth telling? Since knowledge is the cornerstone of democracy, an informed public is a prerequisite for a democratic government. Hence, citizens have an inherent right to know the truth of public issues. On the other hand, there may be times of crisis when it may be permissible for a public official to deceive the public for its own good.

In public administration there is a hierarchy of levels of ethics: personal morality, professional ethics, organizational ethics, and social ethics. This last level obliges members of a given society to act in ways that both protect individuals and further the progress of the group as a whole.

Codes of honor have their origins in ancient precepts about how a person should behave in the face of danger, when confronted with temptation, or before authority figures. Many civilian government agencies now have parallel standards of conduct, formal guidelines for ethical behavior, which seek to ensure that employees refrain from using their official positions for private gain.

Administrative accountability is that aspect of administrative responsibility by which officials are held answerable for general notions of democracy and morality as well as for specific legal mandates. In democratic societies administrators are required to respond to a complex system of checks and balances and to be subject to scrutiny by official auditors, the media, and community watchdogs and potential whistleblowers.

While a government's constitutional and legal frameworks are a passive exercise of democratic control over the discretion of public administrators, there is no substitute for the active control of energetic elected representatives. This control, known as legislative oversight, takes many forms. The most obvious form is the annual congressional hearings on agency budget requests, in which agency activities have to be justified to the satisfaction of the Congress.

Review Questions

1. Why is honor, both national and personal, such a critical aspect of public administration?

2. Is corruption in government any worse than in the private sector, or is it just more visible?

3. Is it ever appropriate for a government official to lie to the public?

4. How does a hierarchy of ethics govern the behavior of people holding public office?

5. What means do all legislators have to hold their government's bureaucracy accountable to its legislature?

Key Concepts

accountability   The extent to which one must answer to higher authority—legal or organizational—for one's actions in society at large or within one's particular organizational position.

big lie   An untruth so great or so audacious that it is bound to have an effect on public opinion.

bribery   The giving or offering of anything of value with intent to unlawfully influence an official in the discharge of duties; a public official's receiving or asking for anything of value with the intent to be unlawfully influenced.

casework   The services performed by legislators and their staffs at the request of and on behalf of constituents.

code of ethics   A statement of professional standards of conduct to which the practitioners of a profession say they subscribe. Codes of ethics are usually not legally binding, so they may not be taken too seriously as constraints on behavior.

common law   The totality of judge-made laws that initially developed in England and continued to evolve in the United States. Whenever this kind of law—which is based on custom, culture, habit, and previous judicial decisions—proved inadequate, it was supplanted by statutory laws made by legislatures. But the common law tradition, based on precedent, is still the foundation of the American legal system, even though much of what was originally common law has been converted into statutes over the years.

congressional oversight   The total means by which the U.S. Congress monitors the activities of executive branch agencies to determine if the laws are being faithfully executed.

corruption   The unauthorized use of public office for private gain. The most common forms of corruption are bribery, extortion, and the misuse of inside information.

dirty hands dilemma   A graphic phrase for the tendency of public officials to commit an act generally considered to be a wrong to further the common good. This is a dilemma in the sense that doing bad seems to lead to something good.

higher law   The notion that no matter what the laws of a state are, there remains a higher law to which a person has an even greater obligation. A higher law is often appealed to by those who wish to attack an existing law or practice that courts or legislators are unlikely or unwilling to change.

honor   The internalized moral compass by which individuals ascertain correct behavior in public and private life; the perception by others of one's reputation for integrity.

integrity   The core of honor. Those who have integrity live up to their stated principles,

values, and most importantly, their word. A person whose word is his or her bond gives the full faith and credit of his or her whole being to keeping commitments.

rule of law   A governing system in which the highest authority is a body of law that applies equally to all (as opposed to the traditional "rule of men," in which the personal whim of those in power can decide any issue).

standards of conduct   A compendium of ethical norms promulgated by an organization to guide the behavior of its members. Many government agencies have formal codes (or standards) of conduct for their employees.

Watergate   The scandal that led to the resignation of President Richard M. Nixon. Watergate itself is a hotel-office-apartment complex in Washington, DC. When individuals associated with the Committee to Reelect the President were caught breaking into the Democratic National Committee Headquarters (then located in the Watergate complex) in 1972, the resulting cover-up and national trauma was condensed into one word: Watergate. The term has grown to refer to any political crime or instance of bureaucratic corruption that undermines confidence in governing institutions.

Bibliography

Belli, Melvin M. (1973). Review of *The Finest Judges Money Can Buy* by Charles Ashman in the *New York Times Book Review* (November 18).

———. (1976). *My Life on Trial.* New York: Morrow.

Berman, Larry. (1982). *Planning a Tragedy: The Americanization of the War in Vietnam.* New York: Norton.

Brown, E. G. (1970). *Reagan and Reality.* New York: Praeger.

Dallek, Robert. (1998). *Flawed Giant: Lyndon Johnson and His Times.* New York: Oxford University Press.

Downs, G., and P. D. Larkey. (1986). *The Search for Government Efficiency.* New York: Random House.

Drucker, Peter F. (1969). "The Sickness of Government," *Public Interest* 14 (Winter).

Dynes, Michael, and David Walker. (1995). *The New British State.* London: Times Books.

Finer, Herman. (1941). "Administrative Responsibility in Democratic Government," *Public Administration Review* 1.

Friedrich, Carl J. (1940). "The Nature of Administrative Responsibility." In Carl J. Friedrich, ed., *Public Policy.* Cambridge, MA: Harvard University Press.

Gillman, Todd J., and Robert Dodge. (2005). "Congress Quick to Demand Answers on Response to Katrina," *Dallas Morning News* (September 6).

Gilmour, Robin. (1981). *The Idea of the Gentleman in the Victorian Novel.* London: George Allen and Unwin.

Halberstam, David. (1972). *The Best and the Brightest.* New York: Random House.

Howard, Philip K. (1995). *The Death of Common Sense.* New York: Random House.

Jos, Philip H., Mark E. Tompkins, and Steven W. Hays. (1989). "In Praise of Difficult People:

A Portrait of the Committed Whistleblower," *Public Administration Review* 49 (November–December).

Kaplan, Fred. (1983). *The Wizards of Armageddon.* New York: Simon and Schuster.

Kearns, Doris. (1976). *Lyndon Johnson and the American Dream.* New York: Harper and Row.

Madsen, Peter, and Jay M. Shafritz, eds. (1992). *Essentials of Government Ethics.* New York: Meridian Books.

Miceli, Marcia, and Janet Near. (1992). *Blowing the Whistle.* New York: Lexington Books.

Miller, Merle. (1973). *Plain Speaking: An Oral Biography of Harry S. Truman.* New York: Berkeley.

Morgan, Arthur E. (1974). *The Making of the TVA.* New York: Prometheus Books.

Mustafa, Husain, and Anthony A. Salomone. (1971). "Administrative Circumvention of Public Policy," *Midwest Review of Public Administration* 5, No. 1.

O'Connor, John D. (2005). "I'm the Guy They Called Deep Throat," *Vanity Fair* (June).

Orwell, George. (1946). *Animal Farm.* New York: Harcourt, Brace.

Popkin, James. (1993). "Wasteline: By the Book," *U.S. News & World Report* (May 24).

Rohr, John. (1986). *Ethics for Bureaucrats,* 2nd ed. New York: Marcel Dekker.

Romzek, Barbara, and Melvin J. Dubnick. (1987). "Accountability in the Public Sector," *Public Administration Review* (May–June).

Rosenbloom, David H. (1993a). "Have an Administrative Rx? Don't Forget the Politics!" *Public Administration Review* 53 (November–December).

———. (1993b). *Public Administration,* 3rd ed. New York: McGraw-Hill.

Sayre, W. (1948). "The Triumph of Techniques Over Purpose," *Public Administration Review* 8 (Spring).

Slater, Philip E., and Warren Bennis. (1964). "Democracy Is Inevitable," *Harvard Business Review* 42 (March–April).

Steffens, Lincoln. (1904). *The Shame of the Cities.* New York: Sagamore Press.

Stevenson, Richard. (1992). "U.S. Judge Orders $7.5 Million Award to Whistleblower," *New York Times* (July 7).

Thompson, Dennis F. (1985). "The Possibility of Administrative Ethics," *Public Administration Review* (September–October).

Twain, Mark. (1899). *A Connecticut Yankee in King Arthur's Court.* New York: Harper.

Williams, Charles. (1993). *The Last Great Frenchman.* New York: Little, Brown.

Wills, Garry. (1984). *Cincinnatus: George Washington and the Enlightenment.* New York: Doubleday.

Recommended Books

Adams, Guy B., and Danny L. Balfour. (1998). *Unmasking Administrative Evil.* Thousand Oaks, CA: Sage. Finally, a book that seeks out the evil that lurks within government bureaucracies; explains how ordinary people doing their normal professional duties can take part in evil without even being aware of it.

Callahan, David. (2004). *The Cheating Culture: Why More Americans Are Doing Wrong and Getting Ahead.* Fort Washington, PA: Harvest Books. What happens in government is often an extension of the broader culture. This book nicely examines the types of unethical behavior Americans will embrace in order to succeed.

Emery, Fred. (1994). *Watergate: The Corruption of American Politics and the Fall of Richard Nixon.* New York: Random House. A history of the scandal that forced a president to resign in disgrace.

Kearns, Kevin P. (1996). *Managing for Accountability: Preserving the Public Trust in Public and Nonprofit Organizations.* San Francisco: Jossey-Bass. A strategic management approach to organizational accountability; accountability should not be undertaken as an afterthought—it must be integrated with all aspects of management.

Light, Paul C. (1995). *Thickening Government: Federal Hierarchy and the Diffusion of Accountability.* Washington, DC: Brookings Institution. A study of how the federal government has constantly expanded the number of its high-level positions (during the period 1935–1992) to increase efficiency and accountability.

Madsen, Peter, and Jay M. Shafritz. (1992). *Essentials of Government Ethics.* New York: New American Library. A collection of writings on government ethics from ancient times to the present.

McMaster, H. R. (1997). *Dereliction of Duty: Lyndon Johnson, Robert McNamara, the Joint Chiefs of Staff, and the Lies that Led to Vietnam.* New York: HarperCollins. The history of the lies and dishonor of America's top military and civilian leadership during the Vietnam War.

Rohr, John A. (1989). *Ethics for Bureaucrats: An Essay on Law and Values.* New York: Marcel Dekker. The original presentation of the concept of regime values, which holds that the most fundamental principles of a polity—such as its constitution—should be the primary guide to ethical behavior.

Rosen, Bernard. (1998). *Holding Government Bureaucracies Accountable,* 3rd ed. Westport, CT: Praeger. A survey of the mechanisms of accountability in the federal government, with excellent coverage of 1990s accountability legislation such as the Government Performance and Results Act of 1993.

Related Web Sites

Annenberg Political Fact Check
   www.factcheck.org
Center for the Study of Ethics
   www.iit.edu/departments/csep
Centre for Applied Ethics
   http://www.ethicsweb.ca/resources/business/
Citizens' Circle for Accountability
   www.accountabilitycircle.org
Congressional Accountability Project
   http://www.congressproject.org/
Council for Excellence in Government
   http://www.excelgov.org/

Ethics and Public Policy Center
   www.eppc.org/
Government Accountability Project
   www.whistleblower.org
Institute for Business and Professional Ethics
   http://commerce.depaul.edu/ethics
New York Times Web page on Watergate
   www.nytimes.com/library/cyber/week/061797watergate.html
U.S. Office of Government Ethics
   www.usoge.gov/index.html

CHAPTER 6

The Evolution of Management and Organization Theory

Systems Theory
Cybernetics • The Learning Organization • Complex Adaptive Systems
A Case Study: The Critical Importance of Administrative Doctrine

•KEYNOTE: MOSES MEETS THE FIRST MANAGEMENT CONSULTANT

The scene is set as in the Bible: Moses (in Exodus 18) has led the Israelites out of the land of Egypt. Now . . .

Moses sat to judge the people: and the people stood by Moses from the morning unto the evening.

And when Moses' father-in-law saw all that he did to the people, he said, "What is this thing that thou doest to the people? Why sittest thou thyself alone, and all the people stand by thee from morning unto even?"

And Moses said unto his father-in-law, "Because the people . . . when they have a matter, they come unto me; and I judge between one and another. . . ."

Moses, while certainly an effective and charismatic leader, could not delegate. "The system" he created would not let him let go. He literally had thousands of people reporting to him. The managerial workload became overwhelming, The ancient Israelites by the hundreds were unhappily standing in line "from the morning unto the evening" to confer with him. Finally, Jethro, Moses' father-in-law, became the first-known management consultant when he gave Moses the reengineering advice he needed to create a more competent organization. First he assessed the problem:

And Moses' father-in-law said, "The thing that thou doest is not good. Thou wilt surely wear away, both thou, and this people that is with thee: for this thing is too heavy for thee: thou art not able to perform it thyself alone.

Hearken now unto my voice, I will give thee counsel. . . . Thou shalt teach them ordinances and laws, and shalt show them the way wherein they must walk.

Here is the beginning of modern bureaucratic structures. A body of laws, a book of regulations, that apply to everyone means that all similar problems are treated alike; the organization does not have to "reinvent the wheel" each time a common problem reoccurs. Jethro next lays out the most basic principles of all hierarchical organizations, the very same principles that are today used in literally all large organizations whether they be military or civilian, private or public.

Moreover thou shalt provide out of all the people able men . . . to be rulers of thousands, and rulers of hundreds, rulers of fifties, and rulers of tens:

And let them judge the people at all seasons: and it shall be, that every great matter they shall bring unto thee, but every small matter they shall judge: so shall it be easier for thyself, and they shall bear the burden with thee.

If thou shalt do this thing, . . . then thou shalt be able to endure. . . ."

In those three verses we have the origins of all large-scale enterprises. Jethro's advice of putting able people to be "rulers of thousands, and rulers of hundreds, rulers of fifties, and rulers of tens" was followed by the ancient Roman army, the early Catholic Church, and every major organization since. Early in the twentieth century, Frederick Taylor, the so-called "father of scientific management," called bringing "every great matter" to the head of the organization "management by exception"—meaning that if all was going well, there was no reason to bother the next-higher layer of management. This is exactly what Jethro advised. He then stated the main advantage of abiding by this advice: "If thou shalt do this thing, . . . then thou shalt be able to endure." The essential problem of the nondelegating manager is not that he or she is not able and wise, but that in large organizations no one person "is able to endure" without delegating. Thus an otherwise extremely competent manager becomes incompetent by seeking to be supercompetent—by trying to do it all.

But what did Moses do with all this good advice?

> So Moses hearkened to the voice of his father-in-law, and did all that he had said.
>
> And Moses chose able men out of all Israel, and made them heads over the people, rulers of thousands, and rulers of hundreds, rulers of fifties, and rulers of tens.
>
> And they judged the people at all seasons: the hard causes they brought unto Moses, but every small matter they judged themselves.

Moses took his consultant's advice and became a more competent leader. He had to deal only with "the hard causes" because he adopted a system by which "every small matter" would be dealt with by others. Not only did Moses make himself more competent, but his structural reforms made all of his lieutenants better managers as well. Moses had, to use a modern term, reinvented tribal management.

Now, what happened to Jethro, the consultant who turned Moses from an over-controlling to an empowering manager? All we know is that Moses "let his father-in-law depart; and he went his way into his own land." He then disappeared from the Bible and from history. It just goes to show that even in biblical times, it was true that all management consultants eventually wear out their welcome. But it gets worse as far as Jethro's reputation is concerned. Later on in the Bible (Deut. 1:9–18), Moses is giving a kind of annual report to the Israelites. He recounts the reorganization plan he adopted with Jethro's advice and, like many a modern executive, does not give any credit at all to the person who had the ideas that he successfully implemented. And this is not unjust. After all, the job of the consultant—the reason he or she is hired in the first place—is to make the person who hires them look good. A consultant's final task is to take the money he or she has earned—and run.

For Discussion: *Are the organizing principles spelled out by Jethro still valid today? Is it always true that an overcontrolling manager who refuses to delegate authority is destined to fail?*

Charlton Heston as Moses in the 1956 film *The Ten Commandments*. Here he demands that Pharaoh (played by Yul Brynner) stop reading his book about Egyptian public administration and "let my people go!" Ever since playing Moses in one of the most successful films of all time, Heston's voice has been the patriarchal voice of authority. This was reinforced by many subsequent films in which he played strong historical characters such as El Cid, Cardinal Richelieu, and Andrew Jackson. Thus, when in 1998 he was elected president of the National Rifle Association, the preeminent gun lobby, his denunciation of President Clinton in his inaugural speech as head of the NRA had a resonance far beyond these damning words: "Mr. Clinton, America didn't trust you with our health care system, . . . America doesn't trust you with our 21-year-old daughters, and we sure, Lord, don't trust you with our guns!" Heston was particularly annoyed that during the course of the Lewinsky affair, the president seemed to have violated at least three of the Ten Commandments. (See Chapter 5 for more on this.) Consequently, Heston turned the full resources of his organization against Clinton's Democratic Party in the election of 2000 and deserves substantial credit for helping to elect the Republican presidential candidate, George W. Bush.•

The Origins of Public Management

Civilization and administration have always gone hand in hand. Since ancient times, a city was defined by the walls created for its defense. Even today many **municipalities** will award someone a key to the city in symbolic remembrance of when the only way into a city was through a locked gate in the wall. This meant that once primitive tribes

---

municipalities Local governments. The word and concept comes from the Latin in which *municipium* referred to any self-governing body within the Roman Empire.

gathered in cities—when they literally became civilized (meaning to live in cities)—they had to be sufficiently organized for war to build their stronghold and defend it from attackers. This necessitated a sophisticated system of administration. Cities without walls only became possible in relatively recent times, when an overarching state authority was able to impose peace over a large area.

Thus the profession of **management** began and developed as the **profession of arms**. To the extent that the history of the world is the history of warfare, then it is also the history of public administration—because war at the state level is quite literally not possible without an effective system of public administration behind it. Military officers were the first public administrators. Societies beyond the extended family only became possible with the rise of an officer class. Thus the first armies were mobs with managers.

Only gradually did these mob managers develop the organizational skills to command large armies and rule large areas. These early martial skills constitute the most basic elements of all administrative processes. **Hierarchy**, line and staff personnel, **logistics**, and communications were all highly developed by ancient armies. Even *reform* is of military origin. After all, it means to once again (the "re") organize the ranks (the "form") for an additional assault—whether on another army or on a difficult management problem. And there is hardly any core concept in modern strategic thought that had not been anticipated by **Sun-Tzu** in ancient China. The word *strategy* itself comes from the ancient Greek, meaning "the art of the general."

The vocabulary of public administration is so heavily indebted to its military origins that the field would be literally tongue-tied without it. Next time you see an organization's slogan (such as New Hampshire's "Live Free or Die") printed on a sheet of its letterhead, remember that "quality first" or some other inane would-be motivator had its beginnings as a war cry of the Highland clans of Scotland. If you don't get what you initially want and go for your fall-back position, remember that fall-backs were prepared fortified sites that soldiers ran to once the enemy broke through their first line of defense. If you are in an organization's rear echelon, console yourself with the fact that the French are to blame because they used their word for the rung of a ladder—*échelon*—to describe parallel military formations. And if you cherish a particular tax loophole, remember that a loophole was a small opening in a fort for soldiers to shoot out of, or use as a means of escape, depending on the circumstances. They are still a means of escape—from taxes.

---

management A term that can refer to both (1) the people responsible for running an organization and (2) the running process itself—the utilizing of numerous resources to accomplish an organizational goal.

profession of arms The practice of the art and science of war; the occupation of a career military officer.

hierarchy Any ordering of persons, things, or ideas by rank or level. Administrative structures are typically hierarchical in that each level has authority over levels below and must take orders from levels above.

logistics Traditionally the art and science of moving military forces and keeping them supplied; those inventory, production, and traffic-management activities that seek the timely placement of materiel and personnel at the proper time and in the appropriate quantities.

Sun-Tzu (fourth century B.C.E.) The ancient Chinese writer whose essays, traditionally published as *The Art of War*, have influenced all Western military analysts since they were first available in European editions in the late eighteenth century.

> ### BOX 6.1   Listen Up!
>
> The ancient Egyptians were highly skilled administrators—how else could they have built the pyramids? Here is an example of their wisdom—4,000-year-old advice for supervisors that could be found in any industrial psychology text today:
>
> > Be calm as thou listenest to what the petitioner has to say. Do not rebuff him before he has swept out his body or before he has said that for which he came. . . . It is not [necessary] that everything about which he was petitioned should come to pass, [for] a good hearing is soothing to the heart.
>
> Some things haven't changed much in the last four millennia!
>
> SOURCE OF QUOTE: John A. Wilson, *The Culture of Ancient Egypt* (Chicago: University of Chicago Press, 1951).

The Continuing Influence of Ancient Rome

In his landmark 1941 book *The Managerial Revolution*, James Burnham contended that as the control of large corporations passes from the hands of the owners into the hands of professional administrators, the society's new governing class would be the possessors not of wealth but of technical expertise. But Burnham was two millennia off in his analysis because this managerial changeover from those of wealth and power to those of professional expertise first occurred in the ancient Roman army. According to military historian John Keegan, "The Roman centurions, long-service unit leaders drawn from the best of the enlisted ranks, formed the first body of professional fighting officers known to history." This middle-management class transmitted from generation to generation the technical skills and discipline by which Rome dominated the world for five centuries. They were the managers who allowed the **patrician** governing class to exercise actual command. They were motivated by loyalty to their legion, pride in their profession, regular pay, and retirement payments that were an additional inducement to good behavior. Here is the beginning of the modern **merit system**. The West would not see its like again until **Napoléon**, espousing the best in French revolutionary idealism, announced "careers

---

patrician A member of the upper class in ancient Rome; by analogy, a member of any high-ranking group or governing class. The opposite was a plebeian, a member of the lower class.

merit system A public sector concept of staffing that implies that no test of party membership is involved in the selection, promotion, or retention of government employees and that a constant effort is made to select the best qualified individuals available for appointment and advancement.

Napoléon Bonaparte (1769–1821) The Corsican-born French general and dictator who dominated the political and military affairs of Europe from the time he seized control of France in a coup d'état in 1799 until his final defeat at the Battle of Waterloo in 1815.

open to talent" in both the civilian and military spheres. The regulating of pay and pensions in ancient Rome was the key to maintaining the army—and to this end the first civil service was created (by the Emperor **Augustus Caesar**) to raise the taxes necessary to support the legions. Thus <u>out of military necessity was born civilian public administration</u>. The same Augustus would boast that "I found Rome a city of bricks and left it a city of marble." While spoken by an emperor, these are also the words of a proud municipal **public works** administrator.

While many ancient kingdoms, such as Egypt and China, had sophisticated administrative institutions, the core features of modern public administration in the Western world were first found in the Roman Empire. The Roman state was depersonalized. It had existed independent of any political leader or king; it was not "owned" by anyone. Significantly, the state's public finances were separate from the private funds of its leadership. Second, it made use of a centralized hierarchical structure. At the top was the central government, then the province, and finally the diocese. These structures are still familiar, still in use. Finally, the Romans introduced several units of functional specialization that form the heart of most modern public administrative systems. They had organizational units for military affairs, finance, justice, and **police**. This last function was so broadly conceived that it included transportation, health, education, agriculture, and commerce.

Ever since the time of ancient Rome, young men have viewed a stint of service as a military officer as a logical prelude to larger public service or to greater political office. Indeed, during the days of the Roman Republic it was a condition of elective office that a candidate have a decade of military service. Not only was this a seasoning period for youths, it was the only social institution that offered systematic training in administration. It was thought reasonable that those who could demonstrate the ability to command and administer should be considered legitimate candidates. This is still true today. Most U.S. presidents and countless lesser politicians have used their military experience as a springboard for their political careers. Has your member of Congress served in the armed forces?

When Governor Bill Clinton of Arkansas announced he would be running in the 1992 presidential race, the very legitimacy of his candidacy was called into question because he not only lacked military experience but conspicuously sought to avoid it during the Vietnam War. While many who opposed the war thought that Clinton's legal avoidance of the draft was a more honorable course of action than serving in this unpopular war, the depth of reaction to his lack of prior military

---

Augustus Caesar (63 B.C.E.–14 C.E.) The nephew of Julius Caesar who became the first Roman emperor after defeating his rivals Mark Anthony and Marcus Brutus in the civil war that followed his uncle's assassination in 44 B.C.E.

public works A general term for government-sponsored construction projects.

police Paramilitary state and local government organizations whose most basic responsibilities include maintaining public order and safety (through the use of force if necessary), investigating and arresting persons accused of crimes, and securing the cooperation of the citizenry. But a state's police power goes far beyond the criminal justice system; it is the legal basis by which governments regulate such areas as public health, safety, and morals.

service continued to make it difficult for him to function as **commander in chief** well into his presidency. Even those who did serve in the military may fall prey to criticism regarding the quality of their service. John Kerry's bid for the presidency was undermined by a group of his fellow Vietnam veterans, who called his valor into question. Thus the ancient Roman attitude toward the desirability of youthful military service as preparation for later public office still strongly affects modern American politics and administration.

The Military Heritage of Public Administration

The history of the world can be viewed as the rise and fall of public administrative institutions. Those ancient empires that rose and prevailed for a while were those with better administrative institutions than their competitors. Brave soldiers have been plentiful in every society, but they are ultimately wasted if not backed up by administrators who can feed and pay them. **Marcus Tullius Cicero**, the ancient Roman orator, is usually credited with first saying that "the sinews of war are infinite money." And this was already a trite sentiment when he said it!

Rome, like Egypt, Persia, and other empires before it, conquered the ancient world because it had an organizational doctrine that made its soldiers far more effective than competing forces—and because its legions were backed up by a sophisticated administrative system of supply based on regular if not equitable taxes. The Roman Empire only fell when its legions degenerated into corps of mercenaries and when its supply and tax bases were corrupted. Napoléon was wrong. Armies do not "march on their stomachs," as he said; they march on the proverbial backs of the tax collectors and on the roads built by administrators. Regular pay allows for discipline. Strict discipline is what makes a mob an army. And a disciplined military, obedient to the leaders of the state, is a precondition for civilization. This is the classic chicken-and-egg problem. Which comes first—effective public administration or an effective military? The rise and fall of ancient Rome proved that you could not have one without the other.

Early bureaucrats in ancient Rome and modern Europe literally wore uniforms that paralleled military dress. After all, the household servants of rulers traditionally wore **livery**. It indicated that the wearer was not free but the servant of another. Government administrators are still considered servants in this sense; they are public servants because they, too, have accepted obligations, which means they are not

---

commander in chief The authority granted under Article III, Section 2, of the U.S. Constitution that "the president shall be commander in chief of the army and the navy of the United States and of the militia of the several states when called into the actual service of the United States."

Marcus Tullius Cicero (106–43 B.C.E.) The Roman senator who was killed by henchmen of Augustus Caesar because Cicero was a republican and Augustus was a murderous dictator. This in no way diminishes Augustus's reputation as a fine administrator. Public administrators throughout the ages have used murder as an administrative tool. Only relatively recently has this become less fashionable.

livery The uniform of a servant; any identical and identifying item of dress—such as a necktie, scarf, or blazer—worn by members of the same organization.

completely free. Indeed, until early in the twentieth century, many otherwise civilian public officials in Europe—most notably diplomats—had prescribed uniforms.

Both victorious soldiers and successful managers tend to be inordinately admired and disproportionately rewarded as risk takers. True, the specific risks and rewards are different, but the phenomenon is the same. They both may have to put their careers, and sometimes significant parts of their anatomy as well, "on the line" to obtain a goal for their state or organization. Notice again the military language, for "the line" originally referred to the line of battle where you faced the enemy. This is why line officers today are still those who perform the services for which the organization exists. This is the direct link between the Roman centurion and the modern fire captain, chief of detectives, or elementary school principal. Life on the line is still a daily struggle.

The Evolution of Management Principles

Authoritarian or traditional management is the classic model of military governance applied to civilian purposes. Managers under an authoritarian doctrine value order, precision, consistency, and obedience. To them, the power that flows from structure is supreme. Relationships are hierarchical, based on dominance and dependence. This authoritarian style has gradually given way to less centralized, more participative management styles—not because management developed an altruistic desire to be nice to the workers but because participation has proved to be more competent than authoritarianism when dealing with sophisticated workers. This change takes nothing away from the fact that at an earlier time authoritarianism was the most competent management posture. Thus, in judging the competence of an organization at any given time, you must, as with a stock market, learn whether the level of competence (as with the price of a stock) is high or low relative to others in the market.

Since antiquity, the military has evolved principles about how their authoritarian organizations are best managed. While there are many versions of the principles of war that reflect local conditions, they all contain the same basic elements. Those elements having civilian applications have been incorporated into principles of management. Thus concepts once military—such as **span of control** and **unity of command**—are now thoroughly civilian as well.

Comparing Military and Civilian Principles

There is no **royal road** to administrative wisdom. There are no generally accepted principles of management, no one list on which there is general agreement. However, there is a principles approach that has its origins in the principles of war.

---

span of control The extent of an administrator's or agency's responsibility. The span of control has usually been expressed as the number of subordinates that a manager should supervise.

unity of command The concept that each individual in an organization should be accountable to a single superior.

royal road An easy way. The Greek mathematician Euclid in about 300 B.C.E. supposedly told the mathematically challenged Ptolemy I of Egypt that there was no royal road to geometry. There still isn't!

While these precepts can be traced back to ancient times, for comparison's sake it is convenient to use the nine principles of war currently used by the U.S. Army:

1. *Objective:* Direct every military operation toward a clearly defined, decisive, and attainable objective.
2. *Offensive:* Seize, retain, and exploit the initiative.
3. *Mass:* Concentrate combat power at the decisive place and time.
4. *Economy of force:* Allocate minimum essential combat power to secondary efforts.
5. *Maneuver:* Place the enemy in a position of disadvantage through the flexible application of combat power.
6. *Unity of command:* For every objective, ensure unity of effort under one responsible commander.
7. *Security:* Never permit the enemy to acquire an advantage.
8. *Surprise:* Strike the enemy at a time and/or place and in a manner for which he is unprepared.
9. *Simplicity:* Prepare clear, uncomplicated plans and clear, concise orders to ensure thorough understanding.

All nine principles are not always important. But in any large-scale operation they are always all there. Which ones dominate at any given time is a function of context, of the evolving situation. These principles are inherently interrelating and reinforcing. They represent the distilled science of war as it has evolved over thousands of years. But they are merely the colors with which the commander paints. If he or she is artful in execution, then victory, promotion, and acclaim will follow. If clumsy, then removal by death or disgrace will. Note that the principles of war (and management) are not really designed for experienced officers. These are instructions for the inexperienced. Military historian John Keegan even called them "words to the unwise."

There are a large number of formulations of the principles of management from which to choose. The following are from **Catheryn Seckler-Hudson**, who wrote them in 1955 when she was dean of the School of Government and Public Administration at the American University. Her 12 principles, distilled from the literature of business and public administration and presented in her book *Organization and Management,* came with a warning label: "It should never be assumed that principles of organization are immutable laws to be applied automatically."

1. Policy should be defined and imparted to those who are responsible for its achievement.
2. Work should be subdivided, systematically planned, and programmed.
3. Tasks and responsibilities should be specifically assigned and understood.

Catheryn Seckler-Hudson (1902–1963) A pioneer in developing the "nuts and bolts" of public management technology, she was the author of many groundbreaking works on public sector planning, budgeting, and organization.

4. Appropriate methods and procedures should be developed and utilized by those responsible for policy achievement.

5. Appropriate resources (men, money, material) in terms of availability and priority should be equitably allocated.

6. Authority commensurate with responsibility should be delegated and located as close as possible to the point where operations occur and decisions need to be made.

7. Adequate structural relationships through which to operate should be established.

8. Effective and qualified leadership should head each organization and each subdivision of the organization.

9. Unity of command and purpose should permeate the organization.

10. Continuous accountability for utilization of resources and for the production of results should be required.

11. Effective coordination of all individual and group efforts within the organization should be achieved.

12. Continuous reconsideration of all matters pertaining to the organization should be a part of regular operations.

These principles represent the received wisdom of public administration at mid-century by one of its most acknowledged scholars. Yet when they are compared with the principles of war, they seem mushy and vacillating—hardly any guidance for leadership at all. (True, in the book from which these are taken the author includes many pages of additional explanation.) Part of the reason for this is that these are guidelines for administrators, not for leaders. Her guidelines and principles try to be so all-encompassing that they defeat themselves by their complexity. **Herbert Simon** gained much of his early reputation by attacking the principles approach in his 1946 article condescendingly titled "The Proverbs of Administration." He denounced the whole principles approach to public administration that then dominated administrative thinking. He found the management principles of his era inconsistent, conflicting, and inapplicable to too many of the administrative situations facing managers. He concluded that they were little more than proverbs. Simon would later write in his memoirs that this article, which "secured my instant and permanent visibility in public administration," came "almost purely from the logical structure and internal inconsistency of the principles themselves. No experience of organization was required to detect it."

Simon's criticism of these "proverbs" was valid only to a point. Principles of either kind—military or management—were never meant to be dogma. Even Napoléon warned that "no rule of war is so absolute as to allow no exceptions." But rules can be, nevertheless, very useful. As **Bernard Brodie** wrote, "It may be well that the

---

Herbert Simon (1916–2001) The winner of the 1978 Nobel Prize in economics for his pioneering work in management decision making.

Bernard Brodie (1910–1978) The American who was the first major academic theorist of nuclear warfare.

consideration of a catalog of numbered principles (usually fewer than a dozen) with the barest definition of the meaning of each may be necessary to communicate to second-order minds (or minds too busy with the execution of plans to worry much about the specific validity of the ideas behind them) some conception of what the business is all about."

What is striking about the two lists is how the military list is more policy oriented, more leadership directed, than the civilian list. The latter seems obsessed with the routines of administration—as opposed to breaking new ground with innovation. The military principles are far more proactive and appropriately aggressive. But strangely enough, aggression is back in fashion in contemporary management thinking. The thrust of the military approach with its emphasis on strategy can be found, for example, in the philosophic underpinnings of the reinventing government and total quality management movements of the 1990s. Far from being of mere historical interest, they seem almost fresh when compared with the staid principles of management—and certainly relevant. When used with common sense and attention to experience, the principles of war can be extremely useful to those public managers who would join the never-ending battle against the evil trinity of waste, fraud, and abuse. This is all the more true for those public sector organizations forced to compete with private sector competitors. Competition by creating "enemies" clarifies objectives. The difference between a lean, mean fighting machine, as the U.S. Marine Corps aspires to be, and a lean, mean management machine is, in essence, one of objectives.

The Principles Approach

The principles approach to management, whether of the civilian or military variety, was a pivotal development in the advancement of management as a profession. Why? Because it seeks to make a science out of what was once considered only art. Antoine-Henri Jomini was the Swiss bank clerk turned Napoléonic era general who wrote dozens of books explaining why some generals (mainly Napoléon) and some armies (mainly the French) were consistently more successful than their rivals. The answer was to be found in scientific principles of strategy. Jomini proved in literally dozens of major books that victory went to those who instinctively followed the principles that he had distilled from historical accounts and years of experience campaigning with Napoléon—simply put, victory went to the general who used massive forces in an offensive action against a decisive point. Yet Jomini was keenly aware that art had a major role to play in this science. As he wrote in *The Art of War,* "It is almost always easy to determine the decisive point of a field of battle, but not so with the decisive moment; and it is precisely here that genius and experience are everything, and mere theory of little value."

While simple enough and mostly common sense, Jomini's principles were enormously influential. Because Jomini was *the* military theorist of the nineteenth century, his ideas were widely disseminated. His basic teaching, his doctrine, was that the management of war could be taught—just study the principles and how they are applied in specific situations. (Today this technique is known as the **case study** method.) Since so

---

case study A research design that focuses on the in-depth analysis of a single subject. It is particularly useful for the understanding of dynamic processes over time.

many of the activities of war—planning, training, logistics, and so on—are more management than fighting, it was not much of a leap of the imagination to apply similar principles to management. The timing was certainly right, because the mid-nineteenth century saw the beginning of large-scale industrial enterprise, especially railroads, the scope of which was similar to managing a large army.

By the time business administration emerged as an academic field toward the end of the nineteenth century, it seemed only natural to take a principles approach to teaching management. But these early efforts at developing and teaching principles were authoritarian in that they were premised on the notion that all direction and innovation came from the top—that the people in power, while not necessarily having a monopoly on brains in the organization, had the only brains that mattered. Thus success or failure was a function of how smart the boss was. Bosses would certainly be more effective if they adopted principles, but they were inherently limited by their own abilities.

The explosion of textbooks and self-improvement and "how-to-succeed" books on management that take a principles approach began early in the twentieth century and has never abated. Next time you see a best-seller offering a new management system, remember that while the author may never acknowledge it, he or she is an intellectual disciple of Jomini—because the authors of these best- and would-be best-sellers all premise their works on the belief that management is a skill that can be taught.

What Is Organization Theory?

An "organization" is a group of people who jointly work to achieve at least one common goal. A "theory" is a proposition or set of propositions that seeks to explain or predict something. The something in the case of organization theory is how groups and individuals behave in differing organizational arrangements. This is critically important information for any manager or leader. It is not an exaggeration to say that the world is ruled by the underlying premises of organization theory. This has been true ever since humankind first organized itself for hunting, war, and even family life. Indeed, the newest thing about organization theory is the study of it.

Only since the twentieth century has intellectual substance and tradition been given to a field that was the instinctual artistic domain of adventuresome entrepreneurs and cunning politicos. It was artistic in the sense that it was done naturally without formal learning. Leaders in every field during every age used organization theory as naturally as they used their oratorical powers. In neither case did they need to intellectualize about it. Thus the pirate captain in the seventeenth-century Caribbean, the revolutionary leader in eighteenth-century colonial America, and the suffragist leader in late-nineteenth-century America were all organization theorists—because none of them could have made it as leaders without understanding, if only subliminally, how to structure and motivate a group.

Organization theory was always there in the authoritarian model offered by the military. While many of its premises were understood by the ancients, it did not coalesce as a self-conscious field of knowledge until society found a practical use for it—to help manage the ever-burgeoning national (as opposed to local) industries and institutions brought about by the **industrial revolution**. When the problems of managing an organization grew to be more than one head could cope with, the search for guidance on how to manage and arrange large-scale organizations became as noble a quest as the secular world of business could offer. If a commercial society ever had prophets, it was those pioneers of industrial engineering who claimed that the path to ever-greater prosperity was to be found in the relentless search for the "one best way." They were offering society a theory—abstract guidance for those who knew where they wanted to go but did not quite know how to get there. They already knew what social psychologist Kurt Lewin would assert years later: "There is nothing so practical as a good theory." What was once said of the first atomic bomb has also been said of the first U.S. voyage to the moon: It was as much an achievement of organization as it was of engineering and science. Have our more recent theories of organization kept pace with our industrial and technical achievements? Maybe. But certainly yes when they are compared with the "primitive" authoritarian management. Yet many of the basics remain the same—remain as givens. The laws of physics and gravity do not change with intellectual fashions or technological advances, nor do the basic social and physical characteristics of people. Just as those who would build spaceships have to start by studying the physics of Isaac Newton, those who would design and manage organizations must start with Frederick Taylor, Scottish economist Adam Smith, and French executive engineer Henri Fayol. The future will always build upon what is enduring from the past.

It was T. E. Lawrence (of Arabia) who wrote, "With 2,000 years of examples behind us, we have no excuse when fighting, for not fighting well." The same, even double, can be said of organization theory: With 4,000 years of examples behind us, we have no excuse when organizing, for not organizing well.

While it is always great fun to delve into the wisdom of the ancients, most analysts of the origins of organization theory view the beginnings of the **factory system** in Great Britain in the eighteenth century as the birth point of complex economic organizations and, consequently, of the field of organization theory.

Classical Organization Theory

Classical organization theory, as its name implies, was the first theory of its kind, is considered traditional, and continues to be the base on which other schools of organization theory have been built. Its basic tenets and assumptions, however, which were rooted in the industrial revolution of the 1700s and the professions of mechanical engineering, industrial engineering, and economics, have never changed. They were only expanded upon, refined, and made more sophisticated. Thus an understanding of classical organization theory is essential not only because of its historical

---

industrial revolution A very general term that refers to a society's change from an agrarian to an industrial economy. The Industrial Revolution of the Western world is considered to have begun in England in the eighteenth century.

factory system Any production process that has individual workers specializing in the varying aspects of a larger task.

interest but also, more importantly, because subsequent analyses and theories presume a knowledge of it.

The fundamental tenets of organization theory can be summarized as follows:

1. Organizations exist to accomplish production-related and economic goals.
2. There is one best way to organize for production, and that way can be found through systematic, scientific inquiry.
3. Production is maximized through specialization and division of labor.
4. People and organizations act in accordance with rational economic principles.

The evolution of any theory must be viewed in context. The beliefs of early management theorists about how organizations worked or should work were a direct reflection of the societal values of their times. And the times were harsh. It was well into the twentieth century before the industrial workers of the United States and Europe began to enjoy even limited "rights" as organizational citizens. Workers were not viewed as individuals but as the interchangeable parts in an industrial machine whose parts were made of flesh only when it was impractical to make them of steel.

The advent of power-driven machinery and hence the modern factory system spawned our current concepts of economic organizations and organization for production. Power-driven equipment was expensive. Production workers could not purchase and use their own equipment as they once had their own tools. The memorable phrase for being fired—"get the sack"—comes from the earliest days of the industrial revolution, when a dismissed worker literally was given a sack in which to gather up his tools. Increasingly, workers without their own tools and often without any special skills had to gather for work where the equipment was—in factories. Expensive equipment had to produce enough output to justify its acquisition and maintenance costs.

Under the factory system, organizational success resulted from well-organized production systems that kept machines busy and costs under control. Industrial and mechanical engineers—and their machines—were the keys to production. Organizational structures and production systems were needed to take best advantage of the machines. Organizations, it was thought, should work like machines, using people, capital, and machines as their parts. Just as industrial engineers sought to design "the best" machines to keep factories productive, industrial and mechanical engineering-type thinking dominated theories about "the best way" to organize for production. Thus the first theories of organizations were concerned primarily with the anatomy or structure—of formal organizations. This was the milieu, or the environment, the mode of thinking, that shaped and influenced the tenets of classical organization theory.

Adam Smith and the Pin Factory

Centralization of equipment and labor in factories, division of specialized labor, management of specialization, and economic paybacks on factory equipment all were concerns identified by the Scottish economist Adam Smith (1723–1790) in his work *An Inquiry into the Nature and Causes of the Wealth of Nations*. Smith and James Watt

> **BOX 6.2 The Invisible Hand**
>
> Every individual endeavors to employ his capital so that its produce may be of greatest value. He generally neither intends to promote the public interest, nor knows how much he is promoting it. He intends only his own gain. And he is in this led by an invisible hand to promote an end which was no part of his intention. By pursuing his own interest he frequently promotes that of society more effectually than when he really intends it.
>
> SOURCE: Adam Smith, *The Wealth of Nations* (1776).

(1736–1819), the inventor of the steam engine, are the two people who are most often named as being responsible for pushing the world into industrialization.

Smith, considered the "father" of the academic discipline of **economics**, provided the intellectual foundation for **laissez-faire** capitalism. But Smith's *The Wealth of Nations* devotes its first chapter, "Of the Division of Labour," to a discussion of the optimum organization of a pin factory. Why? Because specialization of labor was one of the pillars of Smith's "invisible hand" market mechanism in which the greatest rewards would go to those who were the most efficient in the competitive marketplace.

Traditional pin makers could produce only a few dozen pins a day. When organized in a factory with each worker performing a limited operation, they could produce tens of thousands a day. Smith's chapter, coming as it did at the dawn of the Industrial Revolution, is the most famous and influential statement on the economic rationale of the factory system, even though factory systems had been known since ancient times. For example, in 370 B.C.E., Xenophon described the division of labor in a shoe factory. But it was not until centuries later that the popularity of Smith's 1776 book revolutionized thinking about economics and organizations. Hence, 1776 is the year that is traditionally considered the starting point of organization theory as an applied science and academic discipline. Besides, 1776 is easy to remember as it was a good year for other events as well.

All formal organizations, whether Smith's eighteenth-century factory or the most sophisticated modern corporation, are *force multipliers* in the sense that they allow the combined individual efforts to be far greater than the sum of their parts. Smith's pin makers acting individually could make a few dozen pins a day at best; as a team, they could make many thousands. Proper organization thus means that two plus two does not equal four; it probably equals 100.

---

economics The study of how people or states use their limited resources to satisfy their unlimited wants; how scarce resources are allocated among competing needs.

laissez-faire A hands-off style of governance that emphasizes economic freedom so the capitalist invisible hand can work its will.

BOX 6.3   Adam Smith on the "Division of Labour"

The way in which this business [pin making] is now carried on, not only the whole work is a peculiar trade, but it is divided into a number of branches. . . . One man draws out the wire, another straights it, a third cuts it, a fourth points it, a fifth grinds it at the top for receiving the head; to make the head requires two or three distinct operations; to put it on, is a peculiar business, to whiten the pins is another; it is even a trade by itself to put them into the paper; and the important business of making a pin is, in this manner, divided into about 18 distinct operations. . . . I have seen a small manufactory of this kind where ten men only were employed, and where some of them consequently performed two or three distinct operations. But though they were very poor, and therefore but indifferently accommodated with the necessary machine, they could, when they exerted themselves, make among them about 12 pounds of pins in a day. There are in a pound upwards of 4,000 pins of a middling size. Those ten persons, therefore, could make among them upwards of 48,000 pins in a day. Each person, therefore, making a tenth part of 48,000 pins, might be considered as making 4,800 pins in a day. But if they had all wrought separately and independently, and without any of them having been educated to this peculiar business, they certainly could not each of them have made 20, perhaps not one pin in a day. . . . In every other art and manufacture, the effects of the division of labour are similar to what they are in this very trifling one.

SOURCE: Adam Smith, *The Wealth of Nations* (1776).

This phenomenon is also illustrated by a story playwright George Bernard Shaw tells in *Everybody's Political What's What:* "More than 50 years ago I was marching in a procession which numbered at least a thousand men. It was broken up and scattered in hopeless confusion and terror by 20 pale nervous policemen armed with nothing more deadly than their clubs. Not one of the thousand knew what to do or what any of the others would do; so they all ran away, except those who were overtaken and knocked on the head." The policemen, because they were effectively organized, had their force multiplied. "Each of the 20 policemen knew what the other 19 were going to do, and had the law on his side. He had a uniform, a helmet, and a weapon, and could depend on the cooperation of 19 uniformed, helmeted, weaponed comrades. It was a triumph of expected behavior over mistrust and anarchy." It was a triumph of good organization over bad organization. The leaders of the demonstration organized their men to march but did not provide any guidance on what to do when the police arrived. In the absence of leadership, in the absence of organization, they ran away.

The military uses the term *force multiplier* to refer to any new technology that makes a soldier more effective on the battlefield. Thus the machine gun is a force multiplier because it means that one soldier with it is as effective as, say, a hundred soldiers with traditional rifles. Modern computers and word processors are force multipliers in a civilian context because one word processor operator can be as effective as dozens of traditional typists. But as both Smith and Shaw have shown, it is not just technology that can be a force multiplier. Good organization is a technology in its own right, is as powerful a force multiplier as any machine—and far cheaper, too!

The Origins of Scientific Management

The basic problem with the traditional hierarchical organization was that it was dependent on the proper enculturation of individual supervisors at every level for its success. Under stable conditions, properly trained military officers and factory supervisors performed well. But as military affairs and factory production became increasingly unstable during the **French Revolution**, the Age of Napoléon, and the industrial revolution, mechanisms had to evolve to compensate for the inherent rigidity of the traditional hierarchy. Individual officers and supervisors, competent enough under stable conditions, became less competent under revolutionary conditions. Whether on the "field of honor" or the factory floor, they could not cope with the competition—organizations that adopted the major structural innovation of that era, the staff concept.

While traditional hierarchical organizations allowed leaders to extend their reach, the organization was still dependent on the necessarily limited intellectual energy at the top. But even the greatest mind with the best advisers has limits. The staff concept evolved to overcome the inherent limitations of a single mind and ever-fleeting time.

The Staff Concept

"Staff" refers to two mutually supporting ideas that gradually evolved in both military and civilian contexts. As the management function becomes increasingly complex and differentiated, managers started using assistants—secretaries and clerks at first, later personnel and purchasing specialists. This traditional use of staff was followed by the staff principle (or staff concept), which created a specific unit in the larger organization whose primary responsibility was to think and plan, to ponder over innovations and plan for their implementation. Under the factory system that emerged from the industrial revolution, business success resulted from well-organized production systems that kept machines busy and costs under control. Industrial and mechanical engineers—and their machines—were the keys to production. Organizational structures and production systems needed constant tinkering and refining to take best advantage of ever-evolving technology. Organizations, it was thought, should work like machines, using people as their parts. Just as industrial engineers sought to design "the best" machines to keep factories

---

French Revolution The political convulsions that began in Paris when the citizens stormed the Bastille (a prison) on July 14, 1789. These convulsions have continued ever since.

productive, industrial and mechanical engineering-type thinking dominated theories about "the best way" to organize people for their role as part of the overall industrial machine.

Beginning with the industrial revolution (and Napoléonic era military organizations) the staff concept has made ever-increasing inroads into the public and private sector. The concept was first formally instituted in the military, and it can be traced back to the ancient Greek armies of Alexander the Great. While generals have always had **aides-de-camp**, the modern military general staff principally originates from the Prussian military reforms that transformed an inefficient army into the foremost military machine in Europe by the middle of the nineteenth century. The Prussian, later German, general staff has been admired for its efficiency (if not its ethics), though seldom fully imitated, by military analysts ever since. It consisted of a small group of the most intellectually able officers, drawn from the main officer corps relatively early in their careers, who then spent their professional lives in the central planning unit known as the general staff. The general staff then developed the strategies and tactics that Germany would use in future wars. By the end of the nineteenth century, all of the major military powers, including the United States and Japan, had adopted a variant of the German general staff for their militaries.

The general staff concept, modified to reflect local conditions, was increasingly adopted by burgeoning industrial and governmental organizations. In the latter part of the nineteenth century, American industrial engineers began asserting that factory workers could be much more productive if their work was designed scientifically. And who would these designers be? They would be the civilian counterparts of the military general staff. Their job was to conduct the research and do the planning that would make the organization more competitive relative to other organizations. Thus scientific management grew out of engineering—which brings up another connection to our old friend Jomini. The greatest single source of the nineteenth-century American engineers who built the railroads, canals, harbors, and bridges was one school, West Point, where the principles espoused by Jomini were and are still taught. The professional paper that management historians considered to be the first call for scientific management was entitled "The Engineer as an Economist," and it was presented by **Henry R. Towne** at the 1886 meeting of the American Society of Mechanical Engineers. Those nineteenth-century engineers, whether educated at West Point or not, tended to know good principles when they saw them.

The Influence of Frederick W. Taylor

Frederick Winslow Taylor became the acknowledged father of the scientific management movement. He pioneered the development of **time-and-motion studies**, originally under the name "Taylorism" or the "Taylor system." Taylorism, or its

---

aide-de-camp A young officer serving as a personal assistant to a general.

Henry R. Towne (1844–1924) An early scientific management advocate whose efforts predated and influenced Frederick W. Taylor.

time-and-motion studies Various techniques for establishing time standards for the performance of manual work.

successor, scientific management, was not a single invention but rather a series of methods and organizational arrangements designed by Taylor and his associates to increase the efficiency and speed of machine shop production. Premised upon the notion that there was "one best way" of accomplishing any given task, Taylor's scientific management sought to increase output by using special staff to discover the fastest, most efficient, and least-fatiguing production methods.

Scientific management emerged as a national movement in the United States during a series of events in 1910. Some eastern railroads filed for increased freight rates with the **Interstate Commerce Commission**. Louis D. Brandeis, the populist lawyer who would later be a Supreme Court justice, took the case against the railroads. He called in **Harrington Emerson**, a consultant who had "systematized" the Santa Fe Railroad, to testify that the railroads did not need increased rates: They could "save a million dollars a day" by using what Brandeis initially called "scientific management" methods. According to historians Harold Smiddy and Lionel Naum, this "sudden realization among business leaders everywhere that the then proudest industrial achievement, the system of railroads, was actually something less than the flawless gem of American enterprise, brought at last the needed widespread attention and support the management movement had lacked." It was a managerial epiphany similar to, but less nationwide in effect than, the shock of *Sputnik* in 1957. It was, as the saying went, "a hell of a way to run a railroad!"

At first Taylor was reluctant to use the phrase "scientific management" because it sounded too academic. But the ICC hearings meant that the national scientific management boom was under way, and Taylor was its leader. Taylor had a profound—indeed revolutionary—effect on the fields of business and public administration. His work and fame gave ever-increasing credence to the notion that organizational operations could be planned and controlled systematically by staff experts using scientific principles.

Taylor echoed Jomini when he asserted that "the remedy for . . . inefficiency lies in systematic management, rather than in searching for some unusual or extraordinary man." Jomini's goal was to make any would-be Napoléon as skillful as the legendary general if they adopted Jomini's principles. Taylor sought "to prove that the best management is a true science, resting upon clearly defined laws, rules, and principles, as a foundation." Taylor—indeed all the scientific managers of his generation—took Jomini's approach to teaching war and applied it to management.

Many people unfamiliar with Jomini think that Clausewitz was *the* greatest nineteenth-century theoretician of war. After all, his classic *On War* was published in 1832. Yes, but being published is not the same as being read. Clausewitz had to wait for the beginning of the twentieth century and good translators to become influential. Fortunately, Taylor had better luck. His classic book *The Principles of Scientific Management* was an instant success when it was published in 1911 and has

---

Interstate Commerce Commission (ICC) The federal agency that regulated interstate surface transportation. Established in 1887, it was abolished in 1996.

Harrington Emerson (1853–1931) One of the first management consultants in the United States; known as the "high priest of efficiency" because of his advocacy of eliminating "wanton, wicked waste."

Frederick W. Taylor, a strange man. Born to wealth, he graduated from Phillips Exeter Academy in Exeter, New Hampshire, and passed the entrance exam to Harvard with honors but declined to go. Instead, he had family friends arrange a job for him as an apprentice pattern maker and machinist at the Enterprise Hydraulic Works of Philadelphia. In the following years he led a double life: a genuine member of the working class by day, who, on any night he wished, could be found in Philadelphia's most exclusive clubs. Indeed, in 1881 he won (with his brother-in-law) the first U.S. Lawn Tennis Association doubles championship—at a time when tennis was the most upper-class of sports. Meanwhile, he earned an engineering degree through correspondence at the Stevens Institute of Technology of Hoboken, New Jersey. As he advanced into management jobs, he never lost his understanding of workers, his hostility to poor supervision, and his profound belief that labor should be paid for performance, not mere attendance. Thus was formed his religious zeal to measure output as a means toward greater productivity and more equitable pay.•

been in print ever since. Unfortunately, Taylor died in 1915, so he had only a few years to enjoy his success. Still, he fared better than Clausewitz, whose great book was published a year after he died. Posthumous publication is a much overrated joy!

Taylor's greatest public sector popularity came in 1912 after he presented his ideas to a Special Committee of the House of Representatives to Investigate the Taylor and Other Systems of Shop Management. Taylor's comprehensive statement of scientific management principles was focused on what he called the "duties of management":

1. Replacing traditional, rule-of-thumb methods of work accomplishment with systematic, more scientific methods of measuring and managing individual work elements

2. The scientific study of the selection and sequential development of workers to ensure optimal placement of workers into work roles

3. Obtaining the cooperation of workers to ensure full application of scientific principles

4. Establishing logical divisions within work roles and responsibilities between workers and management

Taylor's duties seem so obvious today, but they were revolutionary in 1912. Taylor himself even insisted in his *Principles of Scientific Management* that "scientific management does not necessarily involve any great invention, nor the discovery of new or startling facts." Nevertheless, it did "involve a certain combination of elements which have not existed in the past, namely, old knowledge so collected, analyzed, grouped and classified into laws and rules that it constitutes a science."

BOX 6.4   Sherlock Holmes Makes the Case for Scientific Management

A *consultant* was originally an expert in an obscure area of the law. By the late 1800s the term had been extended to medical specialists. At that time Arthur Conan Doyle (1859–1930) was a struggling English physician with few patients and a lot of time on his hands. His marginal medical practice gave him the free time to write a story about a new kind of detective, one who would treat crime as physicians treated disease: by combining modern science with ancient logic. He used as his model one of his medical school professors at the University of Edinburgh, Dr. Joseph Bell, a consultant well known for deducing the occupations of patients just by looking at their clothes, posture, complexion, and deformities.

Thus was born Sherlock Holmes—the world's first consulting detective. Not a member of the police force, he was available for hire to private individuals or to advise—consult for—the police. He explains his unique occupation when he is introduced to the world in *A Study in Scarlet* (1887): "Here in London we have lots of government detectives and lots of private ones. When these fellows are at faults, they come to me, and I manage to put them on the right scent. They lay all the evidence before me, and I am generally able, by the help of my knowledge of the history of crime, to set them straight."

The first escapades of Sherlock Holmes and his friend Dr. John H. Watson, purportedly the author of all the Holmes stories, appeared at just about the same time—the late 1880s—that the theory of scientific management was first being presented. To fully appreciate the significance of this happy coincidence, one must first appreciate the impact of Sherlock Holmes in his time. He was *big*. He was as great a phenomenon in his time as Elvis or the Beatles or Harry Potter. He captured the attention of the international public so much that when Conan Doyle allowed Holmes to die after several dozen stories, he was force to resurrect him by popular demand.

Because Sherlock Holmes shone the spotlight on the job description of a consulting detective, he extended the notion of what a consultant was and could do. If the fictional police could call in the fictional Holmes to help solve a case, then it was that much more acceptable for a real company to call in a real consultant to solve a management problem. And these management consultants were every bit as enamored of scientific methods as was Holmes. The scientific managers who plied their trade in the shadow of Holmes's notoriety were very much in his debt for making their mutual profession—generic consulting, if you will—acceptable to the public and their customer base. Behold the role of the management consultant as envisioned by Frank B. Gilbreth! In their family remembrance, *Cheaper by the Dozen* (1948), two of his children (Frank Jr. and Ernestine) described this apostle of scientific management as someone "who'd walk into a factory like the Zeis works in Germany or the Pierce Arrow [automobile] plant in this country and announce that he could speed up production by one-fourth. He'd do it too."

Just as Frederick W. Taylor, the preeminent apostle of scientific management, was able to demonstrate that workers using different-sized shovels were more efficient at moving different weights of coal, Holmes delights us with his ability to solve mysteries also by pointing to the obvious. By telling the reader in *A Scandal in Bohemia* (1891) that "you see, but you do not observe," and "it is a capital mistake to theorize before one has data," Holmes developed a science for solving crimes. His techniques bypassed his colleagues in the police department who were still using old-fashioned detective methods such as a roundup up the usual suspects. As Holmes asserted in *The Sign of the Four* (1889), "Detection is, or ought to be, an exact science and should be treated in the same cold and unemotional manner." Similarly, both Taylor and Gilbreth eschewed informal rules for a scientific approach in solving the problems of organization and production.

Looking at the illustrious career of Sherlock Holmes, it can be deduced, as only Holmes might do, that Conan Doyle's fictional consulting detective paved the way for the introduction of the theories of scientific management and birth of the management consultant as we know the position today. It was Sherlock Holmes's enormous popularity that helped blaze the trail for the acceptance of scientific management. That this connection has not been made before is much like "the curious incident of the dog in the night-time," as Holmes said in "Silver Blaze" from *The Memoirs of Sherlock Holmes* (1894).

Replied Colonel Ross, "The dog did nothing in the night-time."

Holmes concluded, "That was the curious incident."

So it is with this connection. Without the pipe-smoking man in the deerstalker hat, it seems certain that the independent management consultant selling modern scientific management methods would have taken much longer to become an essential part of business and public administration.

SOURCE: Written for this edition by Jeffrey K. Guiler (of Robert Morris University) and Jay M. Shafritz

Fayol's General Theory of Management

While the ideas of Adam Smith, Frederick Winslow Taylor, and others are still dominant influences on the design and management of organizations, it was Henri Fayol (1841–1925), a French executive engineer who developed the first comprehensive theory of management. While Taylor was tinkering with the technology employed by the individual worker, Fayol was theorizing about all of the elements necessary to organize and manage a major corporation. Fayol's major work, *Administration Industrielle et Générale* (published in France in 1916), was almost ignored in the United States until Constance Storr's English translation, *General and Industrial Management,* appeared in 1949. Since that time, Fayol's theoretical contributions have been widely recognized, and his work is considered fully as significant as that of Taylor.

Fayol believed that his concept of management was universally applicable to every type of organization. While he had six principles—(1) technical (production of goods); (2) commercial (buying, selling, and exchange activities); (3) financial (raising and using capital); (4) security (protection of property and people); (5) accounting; and (6) managerial (coordination, control, organization, planning, and command of people)—Fayol's primary interest and emphasis was on his final principle: managerial. His managerial principle addressed such variables as division of work, authority and responsibility, discipline, unity of command, unity of direction, subordination of individual interest to general interest, remuneration of personnel, centralization, **scalar chains**, order, equity, stability of personnel tenure, initiative, and **esprit de corps**.

Fayol was the first to explain why principles beyond the golden rule and other moral precepts were needed: "Surprise might be expressed at the outset that the eternal moral principles . . . are not sufficient guide for the manager. . . . The explanation is this: the higher laws of religious or moral order envisage the individual only, or else interests which are not of this world, whereas management principles aim at the success of associations of individuals and at the satisfying of economic interests. Given that the aim is different, it is not surprising that the means are not the same."

The Period of Orthodoxy

It is hardly possible to exaggerate the influence that scientific management has had and continues to have on the intellectual development of public administration. Those who have traced the historical evolution of public administration, such as Dwight Waldo, Vincent Ostrom, Nicholas Henry, and Howard McCurdy, would describe the pattern of development within public administration between the world wars as a "period of orthodoxy." The tenets of this orthodox ideology held that the

---

scalar chain The chain of supervisors from the top of an organization to the bottom.
esprit de corps The spirit or morale of a group; traditionally, the pride that soldiers take in their military units.

work of government could be neatly divided into decision making and execution (the politics–administration dichotomy of Woodrow Wilson) and that administration was a science with discoverable principles (scientific management). This dichotomy, which played such an important part in the historical development of public administration, would hardly have been possible if scientific management had not evolved when it did.

The notion that politics could, let alone should, be separated from administration was quickly disposed of by the New Deal and World War II. While those wars against depression and oppression were primarily economic and military operations, they were also immense managerial undertakings. The experience of those years called into question much of what was then the **conventional wisdom** of public administration. The politics–administration dichotomy of the progressive reform movement lost its viability amid the New Deal and the war effort because it was increasingly seen that it simply was not possible to take value-free processes of business and apply them to government. Government, in spite of the best efforts of many reformers, was not a business and was not value-free.

The attack on the politics–administration dichotomy came from many quarters at once. David E. Lilienthal, writing of his experiences as chairman of the Tennessee Valley Authority—the federal government's flood control and electric power corporation for the Tennessee River Valley—found the planning process of government to be a blatantly political enterprise. One that was, not incidentally, both healthy and beneficial for a democratic society.

Paul Appleby's Polemic

But it remained for Paul Appleby, a prominent New Deal administrator and dean of the Maxwell School at Syracuse University, to write the most skillful polemic of the era, which asserted that this theoretical insistence on apolitical governmental processes went against the grain of the American experience. In his book *Big Democracy* Appleby emphatically shattered public administration's self-imposed demarcation between politics and administration. He held that it was a myth that politics was separate and could somehow be taken out of administration. This was good—not evil, as many of the progressive reformers had asserted—because this political involvement in administration acted as a check on the arbitrary exercise of bureaucratic power. In the future, those who would describe the political ramifications and issues of administration would not begin by contesting the politics–administration dichotomy as incorrect or irrelevant, but they would begin from the premise, as Appleby put it so succinctly, that "government is different because government is politics."

---

conventional wisdom That which is generally believed to be true. However, any writer who uses the phrase is setting something up to be knocked down; so conventional wisdom really means that which most people believe to be true but is not. The phrase first gained currency after John Kenneth Galbraith used it in *The Affluent Society* (1958): "Only posterity is unkind to the man of conventional wisdom, and all posterity does is bury him in a blanket of neglect."

Luther Gulick's POSDCORB

The second tenet of the interwar "orthodoxy," that administration was a science with discoverable principles, has never left us. The influence of scientific management continues to be pervasive. Taylor's scientific management sought to increase output by discovering the fastest, most efficient, and least-fatiguing production methods. The job of the scientific manager, once the "one best way" was found, was to impose this procedure upon his or her organization. Classical organization theory derives from a corollary of this proposition. If there was one best way to accomplish any given production task, then correspondingly, there must also be one best way to accomplish any task of social organization—including organizing firms. Such principles of social organization were assumed to exist and to be waiting to be discovered by diligent scientific observation and analysis. Thus the methodology used to divine the "one best way" to accomplish physical tasks was increasingly applied to the problem of social organization.

Luther Gulick's "Notes on the Theory of Organization" is without doubt the best-known statement of this "principles" approach to managing organizations. In 1937, he and Lyndall Urwick edited a collection entitled *Papers on the Science of Administration*. Originally this was intended to be a staff report for the Brownlow Committee (see Chapter 3). Overall, these *Papers* were a statement of the "state of the art" of organization theory. It was here that Gulick introduced his famous mnemonic, POSDCORB, which stands for the seven major functions of management:

Planning, that is working out in broad outline the things that need to be done and the methods for doing them to accomplish the purpose set for the enterprise

Organizing, that is the establishment of the formal structure of authority through which work subdivisions are arranged, defined, and coordinated for the defined objective

Staffing, that is the whole personnel function of bringing in and training the staff and maintaining favorable conditions of work

Directing, that is the continuous task of making decisions and embodying them in specific and general orders and instructions and serving as the leader of the enterprise

Coordinating, that is the all important duty of interrelating the various parts of the work

Reporting, that is keeping those to whom the executive is responsible informed as to what is going on, which thus includes keeping himself and his subordinates informed through records, research, and inspection

---

Luther Gulick (1892–1993) Perhaps the most highly honored reformer, researcher, and practitioner of public administration in the United States. Often called the dean of American public administration, Gulick was intimately involved with the pioneering development and installation of new budget, personnel, and management systems at all levels of government. He was a founder of the Institute of Public Administration, the American Society for Public Administration, and the National Academy of Public Administration.

Budgeting, with all that goes with budgeting in the form of fiscal planning, accounting, and control

Gulick helped shape a critical distinction in orthodox public administration: that the study of management and administration was to be focused on the role of upper-level management. Its organizational outlook, as demonstrated by POSDCORB, took the point of view of the top. But this narrow focus was to be increasingly challenged. Even as Gulick wrote, his "scientific" approach to management was being confronted by the more humanistic focus that would increasingly challenge it. Although this was not immediately apparent, the theoreticians of the human relations and **behavioral science** approaches to management were very much contemporaries of Gulick; they were simply prophets before their time.

The Many Meanings of Bureaucracy

The bureaucratic institutions of the modern state with their hierarchies of officials have their origins in ancient times, as the keynote story about Moses illustrated. Ever since, most large organizations, both in the public and private sectors, have been hierarchical structures. Thus bureaucracy has always been one of the central concerns of organization theory. But before we can deal with this concern, we must explore the many meanings of the word itself.

All Government Offices

First, "the bureaucracy" is the totality of government offices or *bureaus* (a French word meaning "office") that constitute the permanent government of a state—that is, those public functions that continue irrespective of changes in political leadership. Modern Western-style bureaucracies originated in Europe when the governing affairs of centralized autocratic regimes became so complicated that it became necessary to delegate the king's authority to his representatives. American bureaucracy has never fully recovered from its nondemocratic European origins. This has allowed politicians to continually rejoice in attacking the "unresponsive" bureaucracy. At the same time, "good government" groups often contend that, once in office, politicians make the bureaucracy all too responsive to special **interests** instead of leaving it alone to impartially administer the programs for which it was originally established.

---

behavioral science A general term for all of the academic disciplines that study human and animal behavior by means of experimental research. The phrase was first put into wide use in the early 1950s by the Ford Foundation to describe its funding for interdisciplinary research in the social sciences and by faculty at the University of Chicago seeking federal funding for research—and concerned in an era of McCarthyism that their social science research might be confused with socialism.

interests A group of persons who share a common cause, which puts them into political competition with other groups or interests. Thus the oil interests want better tax breaks for the oil industry, and the consumer interests want new laws protecting consumer rights vis-à-vis the business interests, who want fewer laws protecting consumer rights.

All Public Officials

Second, "the bureaucracy" refers to all of the public officials of a government—both high and low, elected and appointed. Thus the secretary of the treasury is a bureaucrat, but so is a lowly secretary in the Treasury Department. We typically think of a bureaucrat sitting at a desk shuffling papers on behalf of the citizenry. But most bureaucrats lead far more active lives. They are police officers, teachers, firefighters, scientists, and astronauts. While many fit the image and do sit behind a desk all day—somebody has to shuffle the papers—they are no more representative of bureaucrats as a whole than are other major categories such as trash collectors and street maintenance workers. However, the paper shufflers often finish the day cleaner.

A General Invective

Third, bureaucracy is often used as a general invective to refer to any inefficient organization encumbered by **red tape**. We've all heard the jokes. There was the malfunctioning rocket that was named "the civil servant" because it would not work and you could not fire it. When a voter registration card arrived in the mail for her recently deceased husband, the bereaved widow dutifully informed the Bureau of Elections of his passing and promptly received an absentee ballot for him. Then there is the story of the spy sent to discover which Washington agencies could be sabotaged. He reports back, "Suggested plan hopeless. Americans brilliantly prepared. For each agency we destroy two more are already fully staffed and doing exactly the same work." There is a germ of truth in all these stories and their ilk. Some rockets do not work. Some agencies send letters (and even checks) to the dead. And duplication of efforts is not uncommon. This does not mean that the government organization involved is always inefficient. Many government agencies have long-standing reputations for efficient operations. We do not hear much about them because normal everyday efficiency does not generate much publicity—and bad publicity is a long-lasting stain. For example, NASA (as the case study in Chapter 2 showed) has an an extraordinary reputation for efficient operations. But the space shuttle disasters of 1986 and 2003 have been long-lasting stains. Nevertheless, efficient operations, whether in NASA, the Postal Service, or your municipality, are the norm in government. But widespread perceptions of inefficiency have given an additional meaning to the word *bureaucracy*.

Max Weber's Structural Arrangements

Fourth, bureaucracy refers to a specific set of structural arrangements. The dominant structural definition of bureaucracy—indeed, the point of departure for all further

---

red tape A symbol of excessive formality and attention to routine. It has its origins in the red ribbon with which clerks bound official documents in the nineteenth century. The ribbon has disappeared, but the practices it represents linger on. Herbert Kaufman, in *Red Tape: Its Origins, Uses and Abuses* (1977), found that the term "is applied to a bewildering variety of organizational practices and features." After all, "one person's 'red tape' may be another's treasured procedural safe-guard." Kaufman concluded that "red tape turns out to be at the core of our institutions rather than an excrescence on them."

analyses on the subject—is that of the German sociologist **Max Weber**, who used an "ideal type" approach to extrapolate from the real world the central core of features that would characterize the most fully developed bureaucratic form of organization. This ideal type is neither a description of reality nor a statement of normative preference; it is merely an identification of the major variables or features that characterize bureaucracy. The fact that such features might not be fully present in a given organization does not necessarily imply that the organization is not bureaucratic. It may be an immature rather than a fully developed bureaucracy. At some point, however, it may be necessary to conclude that the characteristics of bureaucracy are so lacking in an organization that it could neither reasonably be termed bureaucratic nor be expected to produce patterns of bureaucratic behavior.

Weber's ideal type of bureaucracy possesses the following characteristics:

1. The bureaucrats must be free as individuals; they can only be bossed around with respect to the impersonal duties of their offices.

2. The bureaucrats are arranged in a clearly defined hierarchy of offices, the traditional scalar chain wherein every bureaucrat has an unambiguous place—and knows his or her place!

3. The functions of each office are clearly specified in writing.

4. The bureaucrats accept and maintain their appointments freely—without duress. Slave bureaucrats, while once fashionable in the Ottoman Empire and Imperial China, are an inherent contradiction except within military or prison organizations.

5. Appointments to office are made on the basis of technical qualifications, which ideally are substantiated by examinations administered by the appointing authority, a university, or both.

6. The bureaucrats receive money salaries and pension rights, which reflect the varying levels of the hierarchy. While the bureaucrats are free to leave the organization, they can be removed from their offices only under previously stated, specific circumstances.

7. The office must be the bureaucrat's sole or at least major occupation.

8. A career system is essential; while promotion may be the result of either seniority or merit, it must be premised on the judgment of hierarchical superiors.

9. The bureaucrats do not have property rights to their office nor any personal claim to the resources that go with it.

10. The bureaucrat's conduct must be subject to systematic control and strict discipline.

While Weber's structural identification of bureaucratic organization (first published in 1922) is perhaps the most comprehensive statement on the subject in

Max Weber (1864–1920) The German sociologist who produced an analysis of an ideal-type bureaucracy that is still the most influential statement—the point of departure for all further analyses—on the subject. Weber also pioneered the concepts of the Protestant ethic, charismatic authority, and a value-free approach to social research.

the literature of the social sciences, it is not always considered satisfactory as an intellectual construct. For example, Anthony Downs, in *Inside Bureaucracy,* argued that at least two elements should be added to Weber's definition. First, the organization must be large. According to Downs, "Any organization in which the highest-ranking members know less than half of the other members can be considered large." Second, most of the organization's output cannot be "directly or indirectly evaluated in any markets external to the organization by means of voluntary **quid pro quo** transactions." This latter element is what economist Ludwig von Mises meant when he said that the work of a government bureaucracy had "no cash value." It is not that the "successful handling of public affairs has no value, but that it has no price on the market, that its value cannot be realized in a market transaction and consequently cannot be expressed in terms of money."

Definitions of bureaucracy apply equally to organizations in the public as well as the private sector. However, public sector bureaucracies tend to operate in a somewhat different climate from those in the private sector. What has come to be known as the "third sector"—not-for-profit organizations such as hospitals, universities, and foundations—would analytically be classed with public organizations because of the lack of free-market forces upon them. In short, bureaucracy is best conceptualized as a specific form of organization, and public bureaucracy should be considered a special variant of bureaucratic organization. Yet in the popular imagination a bureaucracy is any organization in which people arranged in hierarchical ranks have to obey lots of rules.

Neoclassical Organization Theory

There is no precise definition for *neoclassical* in the context of organization theory. The general connotation is that of a theoretical perspective that revises and/or is critical of classical organization theory—particularly for minimizing issues related to the humanness of organizational members, coordination needs among administrative units, internal-external organizational relations, and organizational decision processes. The major writers of the classical school did their most significant work before World War II. The neoclassical writers gained their reputations as organization theorists by attacking the classical writers after the end of the war. They sought to "save" classical theory by introducing modifications based on research findings in the behavioral sciences.

The neoclassical school was important first because it initiated the theoretical movement away from the oversimplistic mechanistic views of the classical school. The neoclassicists challenged some of the basic tenets of the classical school head on—and they did so when the classical school was the only school. Organization theory and classical organization theory were effectively synonymous.

Second, in the process of challenging the classical school, the neoclassicalists raised issues and initiated theories that became central to the foundations of most of the schools or approaches to organization theory that have followed. Thus the

---

quid pro quo A Latin phrase meaning "something for something"—initially meaning the exchange of one thing for another. In politics it suggests actions taken because of some promised action in return.

neoclassical school was a critically important forerunner to the "power and politics" and the "organizational culture" perspective discussed in Chapter 2 and the "systems theory" school discussed next.

Herbert A. Simon's Influence

Herbert A. Simon was the most influential of the neoclassical organization theorists. He was the first to seriously challenge the principles approach proposed by Fayol, Gulick, and others. (His assertion that those principles were more like proverbs was discussed earlier in this chapter.) Simon was also a firm believer that decision making should be the focus of a new "administrative science." He wrote that organization theory is, in fact, the theory of the **bounded rationality** of human beings who **satisfice** because they do not have the intellectual capacity to maximize. He was also the first analyst to draw a distinction between "programmed" and "unprogrammed" organizational decisions; he highlighted the importance of the distinction for management information systems. His work on administrative science and decision making went in two major directions: First, he was a pioneer in developing the "science" of improved organizational decision making through quantitative methods such as operations research and computer technology. Second, and perhaps even more important, he was a leader in studying the processes by which administrative organizations make decisions.

The Impact of Sociology

One of the major themes of the neoclassical organization theorists was that organizations did not—indeed, could not—exist as self-contained islands isolated from their environments. As might be expected, the first significant efforts to "open up" organizations (theoretically speaking) came from analysts whose professional identity required them to take a broad view of things—from sociologists. One such analyst was Philip Selznick, who in his 1948 *American Sociological Review* article, "Foundations of the Theory of Organization," asserted that while it is possible to describe and design organizations in a purely rational manner, such efforts can never hope to cope with the nonrational aspects of organizational behavior. In contrast with the classical theorists, Selznick maintained that organizations were made up of individuals whose goals and aspirations might not necessarily coincide with the formal goals of the organization—as opposed to consisting of just a number of positions for management to control. Neoclassical writers such as Simon and Selznick opened up the field of organization theory. Thereafter, it would be inherently interdisciplinary and open to the perspectives of sociology, cultural anthropology, political science, business administration, economics and, of course, public administration.

---

bounded rationality The "bounds" that people put on their decisions. Because truly rational research on any problem can never be complete, humans make decisions on satisfactory as opposed to optimal information.

satisfice Accept a satisfactory and sufficient amount of information on which to base a decision. Herbert Simon invented this word to help explain his theory of bounded rationality.

TABLE 6.1   Classical Organization Theory: A Chronology

1776	Adam Smith's *The Wealth of Nations* discusses the optimal organization of a pin factory. This becomes the most famous and influential statement on the economic rationale of the factory sytem and the division of labor.
1832	Charles Babbage's *On the Economy of Machinery and Manufactures* anticipates many of the notions of the scientific management movement, including "basic principles of management" such as the division of labor.
1855	Daniel C. McCallum, in his annual report as superintendent of the New York and Erie Railroad Company, states his six basic principles of administration; the first was to use internally generated data for managerial purposes.
1885	Captain Henry Metcalfe, the manager of an army arsenal, publishes *The Cost of Manufactures and the Administration of Workshops, Public and Private,* which asserts that there is a "science of administration" that is based on principles discoverable by diligent observation.
1886	Henry R. Towne's paper "The Engineer as an Economist," read to the American Society of Mechanical Engineers, encourages the scientific management movement.
1903	Frederick W. Taylor publishes *Shop Management.*
1904	Frank B. and Lillian M. Gilbreth marry; they then proceed to produce many of the pioneering works on time-and-motion study, scientific management, and applied psychology, as well as 12 children.
1910	Louis D. Brandeis, an associate of Frederick W. Taylor (and later a U.S. Supreme Court justice), coins and popularizes the term "scientific management" in his Eastern Rate Case testimony before the Interstate Commerce Commission by arguing that railroad rate increases should be denied because the railroads could save "a million dollars a day" by applying scientific management methods.
1911	Frederick W. Taylor publishes *The Principles of Scientific Management.*
1912	Harrington Emerson publishes *The Twelve Principles of Efficiency,* which put forth an interdependent but coordinated management system.
1916	In France, Henri Fayol publishes his *General and Industrial Management,* the first complete theory of management.
1922	Max Weber's structural definition of bureaucracy is published posthumously; it uses an "ideal type" approach to extrapolate from the real world the central core of features that characterizes the most fully developed form of bureaucratic organization.
1931	James Mooney and Alan Reiley in *Onward Industry* (republished in 1939 as *The Principles of Organization*) show how the newly discovered "principles of organization" have really been known since ancient times.
1937	Luther Gulick's "Notes on the Theory of Organization" uses a mnemonic device (POSDCORB) to draw attention to the functional elements of the work of an executive.

SOURCE: Adapted from Jay M. Shafritz and J. Steven Ott, *Classics of Organization Theory,* 5th edition (Fort Worth, TX: Harcourt Brace, 2001).

"Modern" Structural Organization Theory

Usually when someone refers to the structure of an organization, that person is talking about the relatively stable relationships among the positions and groups of positions (units) that comprise the organization. Structural organization theory is concerned with vertical differentiations—hierarchical levels of organizational authority and coordination, and horizontal differentiations between organizational units—for example, between product or service lines, geographical areas, or skills. The organization chart is the ever-present "tool" of a structural organization theorist.

Basic Assumptions

The label "modern" is used to distinguish the more recent writers of structural organization theory from the pre–World War II classical theorists such as Taylor and Weber. Management analysts Lee Bolman and Terrence Deal identified the basic assumptions of the "modern" structural school:

1. Organizations are rational institutions whose primary purpose is to accomplish established objectives; rational organizational behavior is achieved best through systems of defined rules and formal authority. Organizational control and coordination are key for maintaining organizational rationality.

2. There is a "best" structure for any organization—or at least a most appropriate structure—in light of its given objectives, the environmental conditions surrounding it (for example, its markets, the competition, and the extent of government regulation), the nature of its products and/or services (the "best" structure for a management consulting firm probably is substantially different than for a certified public accounting firm), and the technology of the production processes (a coal mining company has a different "best structure" than the manufacturer of computer microcomponents).

3. Specialization and the division of labor increase the quality and quantity of production—particularly in highly skilled operations and professions.

4. Most problems in an organization result from structural flaws and can be solved by changing the structure.

Mechanistic and Organic Systems

The most immediate issue in the design of any organization is the question of structure. What should it look like? How should it work? How will it deal with the most common structural questions of specialization, departmentalization, span of control, and the coordination and control of specialized units? A famous example of structural organization theory in action was provided by two British researchers: Tom Burns and G. M. Stalker of the Tavistock Institute in London. They developed a widely cited theory of "mechanistic" and "organic systems" of organization, while examining rapid technological change in the British and Scottish electronics industry.

Burns and Stalker found that stable conditions may suggest the use of a mechanistic form of organization, where a traditional pattern of hierarchy, reliance on formal rules and regulations, vertical communications, and structured decision making is possible. However, more dynamic conditions—situations in which the environment changes rapidly—require the use of an organic form of organization where there is less rigidity, more participation, and more reliance on workers to define and redefine their positions and relationships. For example, technological creativity, an essential ingredient in an organic system, requires an organizational climate and management systems that are supportive of innovation. The impacts of these two organizational forms on individuals are substantially different. Supervisors and managers find that the mechanistic form provides them with a greater sense of security in dealing with their environment than the organic form, which introduces much greater uncertainty. Thus either form may be appropriate in particular situations.

Systems Theory

Since World War II, the social sciences have increasingly used **systems analysis** to examine their assertions about human behavior. The field of management, which to the extent that it deals with human resources can be said to be a social science, has been no exception.

Systems theory views an organization as a complex set of dynamically inter-twined and interconnected elements, including its inputs, processes, outputs, feedback loops, and the environment in which it operates and with which it continuously interacts. Any change in any element of the system causes changes in other elements. The interconnections tend to be complex, dynamic (constantly changing), and often unknown. Thus, when management makes decisions involving one organizational element, unanticipated impacts usually occur throughout the organizational system. Systems theorists study these interconnections, frequently using organizational decision processes and information and control systems as their focal points for analysis.

Whereas classical organization theory tends to be one-dimensional and some-what simplistic, systems theories tend to be multidimensional and complex in their assumptions about organizational cause-and-effect relationships. The classicalists viewed organizations as static (unchanging) structures; systems theorists see organizations as continully changing processes of interactions among organizational and environmental elements. Organizations, not being static, are in constantly shifting states of dynamic equilibrium. The maintenance of this dynamic equilibrium was the task referred to in the title of the 1938 classic *The Functions of the Executive*, by **Chester I. Barnard**. Barnard viewed organizations as cooperative systems where "the function of the executive" was to maintain the dynamic equilibrium between the needs of the organization and the needs of its employees. In order to do this,

---

systems analysis The methodologically rigorous collection, manipulation, and evaluation of data on social units (as small as an organization or as large as a polity) to determine the best way to improve their functioning and to aid a decision maker in selecting a preferred choice among alternatives.

Chester I. Barnard (1886–1961) The Bell System executive closely associated with the Harvard Business School, best known for his sociological analyses of organizations that encouraged and foreshadowed the post–World War II behavioral revolution.

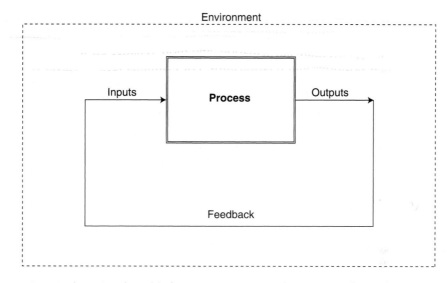

Figure 6.1 Norbert Wiener's Model of an Organization as an Adaptive System, from *Cybernetics*.

management had to be aware of the interdependent nature of the formal and informal organization. Barnard's analysis of the significance and role of informal organizations provided the theoretical foundations for a whole generation of empirical research.

Cybernetics

Because organizations are adaptive systems that are integral parts of their environments, they must adjust to changes in their environment if they are to survive; in turn, virtually all of their decisions and actions affect their environment. Norbert Wiener's model of an organization as an adaptive system, from his 1948 book *Cybernetics,* epitomizes the basic theoretical perspectives of the systems perspective. *Cybernetics,* from a Greek word meaning "steersman," was used by Wiener to mean the multidisciplinary study of the structures and functions of control and information processing systems in animals and machines. The basic concept behind cybernetics is self-regulation—biological, social, or technological systems that can identify problems, do something about them, and then receive feedback to adjust themselves automatically. Wiener, a mathematician, developed the concept of cybernetics while working on antiaircraft systems during World War II. Variations on this simple model of a system have been used extensively by systems theorists for many years— particularly around the development and use of management information systems.

The search for order among complex variables has led to an extensive reliance on quantitative analytical methods and models. The systems approach is strongly cause-and-effect oriented (logical-positivist) in its philosophy and methods. In these respects, systems theories have close ties to Taylor's scientific management approach. Whereas Taylor used quantitative scientific methods to find "the one best way," the systems theorist uses quantitative scientific methods to identify cause-effect relationships and to find optimal solutions. In this sense, the conceptual approaches and purposes between the two perspectives are strikingly similar. Thus systems approaches are often called management sciences or administrative sciences. However, one should never make the unpardonable error of calling them scientific management!

Systems thinking is critically important because the whole world, in essence, is a collection of interrelated systems. Nothing happens in isolation. Your reading of this page is made possible by your visual system. Your turning to the next page is a function of your nervous system and muscular system—which is also related to your visual system. How else would you know when to turn the page? The systems of the world seem so infinite that another theory—chaos theory—has evolved to explain why they are often unexplainable. This theory postulates that the tiniest change in the smallest part of a system can eventually produce enormous effects. In weather forecasting this has become known as the Butterfly Effect. According to James Gleick, this is "the notion that a butterfly stirring the air today in Peking can transform storm systems next month in New York." All of chaos theory seeks to explain how the smallest elements of a system, whether weather or organizational, can have the biggest consequences. Yet all this was summed up by Benjamin Franklin in a 1758 issue of *Poor Richard's Almanac:*

> For the want of a nail the shoe was lost,
> For the want of a shoe the horse was lost,
> For the want of a horse the rider was lost,
> For the want of a rider the battle was lost,
> For the want of a battle the kingdom was lost—
> And all for want of a horseshoe-nail.

The Learning Organization

MIT Professor Peter Senge's *The Fifth Discipline* became one of the most influential "systems" books of the 1990s. Senge sought to destroy the "illusion that the world is created of separate, unrelated forces. When we give up this illusion—we can then build 'learning organizations.' " This phrase is Senge's term for "organizations where people continually expand their capacity to create the results they truly desire, where new and expansive patterns of thinking are nurtured, where collective aspiration is set free, and where people are continually learning how to learn together." Thus Senge's particular variant of the systems approach builds on the doctrines of participation. He, too, builds on the work of Abraham Maslow (discussed in Chapter 7). Indeed Senge's **yellow brick road** to the "learning organization" is in essence the route to Maslow's concept of **self-actualization.**

---

yellow brick road A clearly marked path such as the one provided for Dorothy in the 1939 film *The Wizard of Oz.*

self-actualization The apex of Abraham Maslow's needs hierarchy, where an individual theoretically reaches self-fulfillment and becomes all that he or she is capable of becoming. The importance of the concept of self-actualization was established long before Maslow gave it voice. The nineteenth-century poet Robert Browning described its essence when he said, "A man's reach should exceed his grasp, or what's a heaven for?"

Senge argues that five new "component technologies" are gradually converging that will collectively permit the emergence of learning organizations. He labels these component technologies the "five disciplines": (1) personal mastery—how people approach life and work; (2) mental models—our deeply ingrained assumptions or mental images "that influence how we understand the world and how we take action"; (3) building shared vision—because "when there is a genuine vision . . . people excel and learn, not because they are told to, but because they want to"; (4) team learning—where team members engage in true dialogue with their assumptions suspended; and (5) systems thinking—the integrative discipline that fuses the others into a coherent body of theory and practice. Thus, without an understanding of systems, we can neither grow nor thrive as an organization or as an individual.

Complex Adaptive Systems

While Franklin, Weiner, Gleick, and Senge have pushed the theory that one small change can have much larger ramifications, contemporary public administrators are increasingly turning to the study of Complex Adaptive Systems (CAS). In the wake of the terrorist attacks on September 11, 2001, public administration scholars have become increasingly interested in thinking about organizations as systems capable of reacting to very quickly changing circumstances and threats. As noted earlier, at the heart of complex systems are the nonlinear relationships between variables. This means that a small change in one part of an organization may have a very great effect on another part (i.e., the butterfly effect). In the area of homeland security, removing a well-liked field agent from a counterterrorism assignment may damage morale in that agent's unit. With lower morale, that unit does not perform its investigations as well, thus missing critical leads that could have uncovered a terrorist plot that caused major loss of life. This example demonstrates how a relatively minor and well-meaning act can end up causing significant negative results. But how can we foresee such seemingly unpredictable outcomes? While difficult, methods such as laboratory experiments and computer modeling have showed promising results in predicting what will happen when even the smallest changes occur. Of course, such approaches to organization management are not easy to complete, so their use in many organizations may just have to wait.

◆ A CASE STUDY: THE CRITICAL IMPORTANCE OF ADMINISTRATIVE DOCTRINE

All organizations are guided by a doctrine of management that reflects basic values. Doctrines and values may be stated or unstated, conscious or unconscious, advertent or inadvertent, but they are always there. Without a guiding doctrine and compatible behavioral techniques for implementing it, no management program can be viable. The first administrative doctrine was that contained in the brutality of military discipline: "Do this or die." Indeed, one of the main reasons officers traditionally carried pistols was to shoot their own men if they were not sufficiently enthusiastic about obeying an order—especially one involving great danger. As Edward Gibbon wrote in *The Decline and Fall of the Roman Empire* (1776), "It was an inflexible maxim of Roman discipline that a good soldier should dread his own officers far more than the enemy."

A more modern example of a doctrine is **Henry Ford**'s famous simplistic dictum: "All that we ask of the men is that they do the work which is set before them." With Ford there was an underlying assumption that employees who do not respond adequately to the "work which is set before them" should be dismissed. (A much better alternative than being shot!) The behavioral technique used here is the same as that applied to those small experimental animals who have spent generations running through mazes for psychologists. The more work, the more cheese.

More sophisticated doctrines are needed when meaningful and fulfilling work for its employees is a central goal of the organization. Here the underlying assumptions are radically different. Wages are not the only reason for working! Strategies that emerge from this management value and philosophy are more conducive to long-term organizational **effectiveness** and **productivity**. Just as religious doctrine often defines an individual's attitude toward life, a managerial doctrine defines management's values and attitude toward work and people at work. By the exercise of its doctrinal philosophy, management earns a reciprocal attitude from others toward their responsibilities. This is why doctrines, values, and attitudes on the part of management so often become self-fulfilling prophecies. Employees and managers, like students and teachers, tend to live up (or down) to expectations.

But doctrine and attitudes do far more than affect the **morale** and performance of individual employees; they are part of the culture of the organization, and the organizational culture affects the overall competence or incompetence of an organization. When managers are heavily constrained by official doctrine, by standard operating procedures, and by "the book," they cannot use discretion to respond to changing circumstances. Faced with an obvious right decision that is contrary to formal policy, they all too often dutifully make the wrong decision, feeling that they have no choice. This is a faulty conception of managerial responsibility. Any organization that does not allow its managers to appropriately respond to changing conditions is headed for a fall. It is this conception, this philosophy, this doctrine of leadership as expressed by the organization's culture and as manifest in the organization's policies that ultimately determines success or failure, victory or defeat, competence or incompetence.

Henry Ford (1863–1947) The founder of Ford Motor Company, which first mass-produced automobiles on a moving assembly line.

effectiveness Traditionally, the extent to which an organization accomplishes some predetermined goal or objective; more recently, the overall performance of an organization from the viewpoint of some strategic constituency. Effectiveness is not entirely dependent on the efficiency of a program because program outputs may increase without necessarily increasing effectiveness.

productivity The measured relationship between the quantity (and quality) of results produced and the quantity of resources required for production. Productivity is, in essence, a measure of the work efficiency of an individual, a work unit, or a whole organization.

morale The collective attitude of the workforce toward their work environment and a crude measure of the organizational climate.

Administrative doctrines resemble the paradigms of Thomas S. Kuhn. In his land-mark 1962 book *The Structure of Scientific Revolutions,* Kuhn explained that as the natural sciences progressed, they amassed a body of ever-changing theory. Scientific advances were based not on the accumulation of knowledge and facts but rather on a dominant paradigm (or model) used in any specific period to explain the phenomena under study. Rather than refuting previous theories, each paradigm would build on the body of relevant knowledge and theories. Once a paradigm was accepted by consensus among current scholars, it would last as long as it was useful. Ultimately, it would be replaced by a more relevant and useful paradigm; this process of replacement was Kuhn's "scientific revolution."

While paradigms have their own timeframes and contents, they overlap both in time and content because they are constantly evolving. In a parallel sense, doctrinal development in administration has been inherently cyclical. A successful innovation by reformers is followed by a period of increased effectiveness, at least until competing organizations adopt similar reforms. But over time, advancing technologies and changing environments allow the innovation to deteriorate relative to other arrangements—first to become less competent, then to become incompetent. After an innovative change remedies the problem, the cycle of competence and incompetence repeats. This "time lag" phenomenon is similar to the traditional boom-and-bust business cycle with incompetence occurring when the cycle is in recession. Thus maintaining organizational competence is a never-ending struggle.

This is why competing organizations tend to look like each other over time. Whenever an innovation earns a reputation for being successful, it is copied by others wishing to be equally successful. But equality in structure and equipment is not always enough to ensure being a successful competitor. A famous example will illustrate. During the spring of 1940, Nazi Germany conquered France using tanks and troops in a **blitzkrieg** formation. Germany won despite the fact that France not only had more troops but significantly more tanks that were of better quality. What made the difference was the fact that the Germans had a better tactical doctrine for the use of their tanks—in massed assaults as opposed to piecemeal support for infantry.

Remember that the military, the seminal administrative institution of all societies, only has to be led in battle a relatively few days of any year. But it has to be adminis-tered every day. Societies may be protected by their standing armies or navies, but armed forces cannot stand or float without administrative institutions to support them. It is often true, as Mao Zedong famously said, that "political power grows out of the barrel of a gun." But political power is empty and meaningless without concomitant economic and administrative power. Historian Paul Kennedy in his *The Rise and Fall of the Great Powers* demonstrated how in modern times ultimate victory went to the

---

blitzkrieg German for "lightning war," the tactical method used by the German army in the invasion of Poland, France, and the Soviet Union during World War II. The classic blitzkreig campaign involves swift strikes with tanks and planes and a series of army columns exploiting weak spots in the enemy line. Advance units pass behind the enemy, destroying its lines of communication and disrupting unit cohesion.

state that was economically strong. Those that were merely militarily strong—Austria, France, Great Britain, Germany, Spain, and the Soviet Union—all suffered from "imperial overstretch" and declined as great powers. *Is the U.S. next?*

Revolutionaries with their guns can start a revolution, but only the administrators that follow in their wake can solidify and complete it. Thus all conquering armies have necessarily been followed by hordes of bureaucrats. Napoléon solidified the French Revolution of 1789 with the administrative reforms embodied in the Code Napoléon and the creation of a merit-based civil service. The U.S. Constitution of 1787, which followed the Revolution of 1776, still provides the administrative framework of American government. The Russian Revolution of 1917 led to the administrative apparatus of a socialist state that, with its **command economy**, was so cumbersome and inefficient that a subsequent revolution in 1991 replaced it with a regime that had greater hopes for efficiency. All the political revolutions in Eastern Europe during the late 1980s, while initially politically motivated, increasingly became administrative revolutions to secure for their people the blessings of a new administrative doctrine that allows a state's economy to function with the greater efficiency offered by a free market.

Every major political revolution—from the American to the French to the Russian—can be said to have been caused by the same thing—poor public administration. Remember that the large middle section of the American Declaration of Independence is a list consisting largely of administrative complaints against George III, the British king. For example, the Declaration asserted that the king "has obstructed the administration of justice," has imposed "taxes on us without our consent," and "has erected a multitude of new offices and sent hither swarms of officers to harass our people, and eat out their substance." Simply put: Happy and prosperous people do not revolt. Revolutions are caused by incompetent public administration, and they are made by disgruntled consumers of government services. This is why an effective public administration doctrine is so important—because no society can live in peace and prosperity, or prevail in war, without it. It is a matter of national security!

---

command economy The traditional economic model offered by communism wherein all industry is controlled by a central government that makes all decisions and appoints all managers.

For Discussion: *Why is an effective administrative doctrine essential for the successful public administration of a state? Why is the competence/incompetence cycle of large organizations so much like the boom and bust of the traditional business cycle?*

Summary

Modern management has its origins in the military institutions of the ancient world. While many ancient kingdoms, such as Egypt and China, had sophisticated administrative institutions, the core features of modern public administration in the Western world were first found in the Roman Empire. *?*

civilization first began in Africa.

The Roman Empire derives its traditions from earlier civilizations, —i.e, Africa

All organizations are guided by a doctrine of management that reflects the basic values of the cultural environment. No management program can be viable without such guiding doctrines and compatible behavioral techniques for implementing them. The first doctrines were authoritarian and paralleled the brutality of military discipline. Since antiquity the military has evolved principles about how their authoritarian organizations were best managed. Those elements having civilian applications have been incorporated into principles of management. Thus concepts once military—such as span of control and unity of command—are now thoroughly civilian as well.

Advances in organization theory are not based on the accumulation of knowledge and facts but rather on a dominant paradigm (or model) used in any specific period. Rather than refuting previous theories, each paradigm builds on the body of relevant knowledge and theories. Once a paradigm is accepted by consensus, it lasts as long as it is useful. Ultimately, it is replaced by a more relevant and useful paradigm.

Classical organization theory (which includes bureaucracy), as its name implies, was the first theory of its kind, is considered traditional, and continues to be the base on which other schools of organization theory have been built.

In the latter part of the nineteenth century, American industrial engineers began asserting that factory workers could be much more productive if their work was designed scientifically; their job was to conduct the research and do the planning that would make the organization more competitive relative to other organizations. Thus scientific management grew out of engineering. The progressive reformers were able to use scientific management as the core rationale for their call to separate politics from administration.

The pattern of development within public administration between World Wars I and II became known as a "period of orthodoxy." This ideology held that the work of government could be neatly divided into decision making and execution (the politics–administration dichotomy) and that administration was a science with discoverable principles (scientific management). This dichotomy would hardly have been possible if scientific management had not evolved when it did.

All the subsequent perspectives on organization theory—for example, the neoclassical, the "modern" structuralists, and systems theory—are essentially revisions and expansions of the classical writers. There is no consensus on what constitutes knowledge in organization theory. Anyone who studies this subject is free to join the school of organization theory of his or her choice and is free to accept the philosophic boundaries of one group of serious thinkers over another. No single perspective may deserve your loyalty because each contains important information and insights that are useful in differing circumstances.

Review Questions

1. Why is it that so many of the principles and practices of public administration have their origin in military organizations?

2. Why are classical organization theory and scientific management still relevant today?

3. What is the essence of Max Weber's concept of bureaucracy?

4. How can systems theory be used to explain the workings of a government organization?

5. How does the concept of administrative doctrine help to explain the success or failure of any given organization?

Key Concepts

administrative doctrine   The rules, procedures, and ways of doing things that reflect the basic values of an organization.

bureaucracy   The totality of government officers; all of a government's employees; a general invective to refer to any inefficient organization encumbered by red tape or a specific set of structural arrangements.

classical theory   The original theory about organizations that closely resemble military structures.

learning organization   Peter Senge's term for organizations in which new patterns of thinking are nurtured and people are continually learning together to improve both the organization and their personal lives.

neoclassical theory   Theoretical perspectives that revise, expand, or are critical of classical organization theory.

organization   A group of people who jointly work to achieve at least one common goal.

organization theory   A set of propositions that seeks to explain or predict how groups and individuals behave in differing organizational arrangements.

paradigm   An intellectual model for a situation or condition.

POSDCORB   The mnemonic device invented by Luther Gulick in 1937 to call attention to the various functional elements of the work of a chief executive.

principles of management   Fundamental truths or working hypotheses that serve as guidelines to management thinking and action.

scientific management   A systematic approach to managing that seeks the "one best way" of accomplishing any given task by discovering the fastest, most efficient, and least fatiguing production methods.

systems theory   A view of an organization as a complex set of dynamically intertwined and interconnected elements, including its inputs, processes, outputs, feedback loops, and the environment in which it operates and with which it continuously interacts.

Bibliography

Appleby, Paul. (1945). *Big Democracy*. New York: Knopf.

Barker, Ernest. (1944). *The Development of Public Services in Western Europe, 1660–1930*. London: Oxford University Press.

Bolman, L. G., and T. E. Deal. (1984). *Modern Approaches to Understanding and Managing Organizations*. San Francisco: Jossey-Bass.

Brodie, Bernard. (1973). *War and Politics*. New York: Oxford University Press.

Burnham, James. (1941). *The Managerial Revolution*. New York: John Day.

Burns, T., and G. M. Stalker. (1961). *The Management of Innovation*. London: Tavistock Publications.

Byrne, John A. (1993). *The Whiz Kids: The Founding Fathers of American Business—and the Legacy They Left Us*. New York: Doubleday.

Downs, Anthony. (1967). *Inside Bureaucracy*. Boston: Little, Brown.

Drucker, Peter F. (1950). *The New Society: The Anatomy of the Industrial Order*. New York: Harper.

Gerth, H. H., and C. Wright Mills, eds. (1946). *From Max Weber: Essays in Sociology*. New York: Oxford University Press.

Gladden, E. N. (1972). *A History of Public Administration*, 2 vols. London: Frank Cass.

Gleick, James. (1987). *Chaos: Making a New Science*. New York: Viking.

Grant, Michael. (1991). *The Founders of the Western World: A History of Greece and Rome*. New York: Charles Scribner's.

Gulick, Luther, and Lyndall Urwick. (1937). *Papers on the Science of Administration*. New York: Institute of Public Administration.

Handel, Michael I. (1992). *Masters of War: Sun-Tzu, Clausewitz, and Jomini*. London: Frank Cass.

Henry, Nicholas. (1975). *Public Administration and Public Affairs*. Englewood Cliffs, NJ: Prentice Hall.

Jomini, Antoine-Henri. (1862). *The Art of War*. Philadelphia: Lippincott.

———. (1805). *Treatise on Great Military Operations*. New York: Van Nostrand.

Keegan, John. (1993). *A History of Warfare*. New York: Knopf.

Kennedy, Paul. (1987). *The Rise and Fall of the Great Powers*. New York: Random House.

Kuhn, T. S. (1970). *The Structure of Scientific Revolutions*, 2nd ed., enlarged. Chicago: University of Chicago Press.

Lilienthal, David E. (1944). *TVA: Democracy on the March*. New York: Harper & Bros.

Livingston, J. Sterling. "Pygmalion in Management." *Harvard Business Review* (July–August 1969).

Marini, Frank E. (1971). *Toward a New Public Administration*. San Francisco: Chandler.

Marrow, Alfred J. (1969). *The Practical Theorist: The Life and Works of Kurt Lewin*. New York: Basic Books.

McCurdy, Howard E. (1986). *Public Administration: A Bibliographic Guide to the Literature*. New York: Marcel Dekker.

Mises, Ludwig von. (1944). *Bureaucracy*. New Haven, CT: Yale University Press.

Osborne, David, and Ted Gaebler. (1992). *Reinventing Government*. Reading, MA: Addison-Wesley.

Ostrom, Vincent. (1974). *The Intellectual Crisis in American Public Administration*, rev. ed. Tuscaloosa: University of Alabama Press.

Ott, J. Steven. (1989). *The Organizational Culture Perspective*. Pacific Grove, CA: Brooks/Cole.

Seckler-Hudson, Catheryn. (1955). *Organization and Management: Theory and Practice*. Washington, DC: The American University Press.

Senge, Peter M. (1994). *The Fifth Discipline: The Art and Practice of the Learning Organization*. New York: Doubleday.

Shaw, George Bernard. (1944). *Everybody's Political What's What*. New York: Dodd, Mead.

Simon, Herbert A. (1991). *Models of My Life*. New York: Basic Books.

———. (1946). "The Proverbs of Administration." *Public Administration Review* (Winter).

Smiddy, Harold F., and Lionel Naum. (1954). "Evolution of a Science of Managing in America," *Management Science* 1 (October).

Taylor, Frederick W. (1911). *The Principles of Scientific Management*. New York: Harper.

Waldo, Dwight. (1948). *The Administrative State: A Study of the Political Theory of American Public Administration*. New York: Ronald Press.

Wiener, Norbert. (1948). *Cybernetics*. Cambridge, MA: MIT Press.

Wilson, John A. (1951). *The Culture of Ancient Egypt*. Chicago: University of Chicago Press.

Wren, Daniel A. (1987). *The Evolution of Management Thought*, 3rd ed. New York: Wiley.

Recommended Books

Kanigel, Robert. (1997). *The One Best Way: Frederick Winslow Taylor and the Enigma of Efficiency*. New York: Viking. More than you ever wanted to know about the man, his times, his movement, and his continuing influence.

Merkle, Judith A. (1980). *Management and Ideology: The Legacy of the International Scientific Management Movement*. Berkeley: University of California Press. A highly readable historical analysis of the continuing influence of Frederick Taylor and scientific management in business and public administration.

Shafritz, Jay M., and J. Steven Ott, eds. (2001). *Classics of Organization Theory*, 5th ed. Fort Worth, TX: Wadsworth. A comprehensive collection of the most important writings on organization from ancient times to the present, from Socrates to postmodernism.

Wren, Daniel A., and Ronald G. Greenwood. (1998). *Management Innovators: The People and Ideas That Have Shaped Modern Business*. New York: Oxford University Press. A collection of minibiographies of all the major thinkers on and experimenters with management techniques, from Eli Whitney to Peter Drucker.

Related Web Sites

Adam Smith's *Wealth of Nations*
    www.bibliomania.com/NonFiction/Smith/Wealth/
    index.html
Frederick W. Taylor archive
    www.melbecon.unimelb..edu.au/het/taylor/
    sciman.htm
Herbert A. Simon
    www.psy.cmu.edu/psy/faculty/hsimon/hsimon.html
International Society for Performance Improvement
    www.ispi.org/

Management history
    www.ollie.dcccd.edu/mgmt1374/book_contents/
    1overview/management_history/
    mgmt_history.htm
Max Weber's home page
    www.faculty.rsu.edu/~felwell/Theorists/Weber/
    Whome.htm
Napoléon Bonaparte Internet guide
    www.iselinge.nl/napoleon/

CHAPTER 7

Organizational Behavior

•KEYNOTE: ORGANIZATION DEVELOPMENT IN HOLLYWOOD: FROM *THE SANDS OF IWO JIMA* TO *G.I. JANE*

Demi Moore and John Wayne may not appear to have much in common. However, they have both played roles in feature films that deal with organizations behavior. In the 1997 film *G.I. Jane* Moore takes a disparate group of would-be Navy SEALS (sea-air-land teams) and forges them into a competent combat team—just in time to see "real" action on a fictional mission off the coast of Libya. What she did was not much different from what John Wayne did in the World War II films *The Sands of Iwo Jima* (1949) and *Flying Leathernecks* (1951). In the former, Wayne is the sergeant of a Marine infantry squad; in the latter, he is the commanding officer of a Marine fighter squadron. In both cases he forges his unruly and high-spirited young charges into an effective, highly disciplined fighting force. He, as an older, more mature character, teaches them by example and instruction. And when someone inevitably dies because one of his men failed the group, Wayne is ready (in *The Sands*) with the kind of after-action fatherly consolation that makes his charges determined not to screw up again. "A lot of guys make mistakes, I guess, but every one we make, a whole stack of chips goes with it. We make a mistake, and some guy don't walk away—forevermore, he don't walk away." He says this with his eyes welling up with moisture and his voice choking to give it greater poignancy. Wayne was always most effective as here, when he gets almost to the point of crying but manfully holds it in.

Taking a cue from the John Wayne school of acting, Demi Moore also "manfully" holds in her tears throughout much of *G.I. Jane*—especially during a brutal mock prisoner-of-war interrogation. She is finally accepted by the SEALs as one of the guys when she, hands tied behind her back, attacks her sadistic interrogator with a brutal kick to the groin (thus denying him—at least temporarily—his masculine advantage) and lets forth with a blue streak of verbal abuse that shows once and for all that she can use the foul language of the barracks like the toughest of the guys. After this, the men she commands are ready to follow her anywhere. The point is that her actions—her example—like Wayne's, forge them into an effective team, whereas before they lacked group cohesion. *G.I. Jane* and many other war movies, such as those of John Wayne, demonstrate how organization development is, and always has been, an inherent part of military training.

Of course, Moore, even with her hair in a crew cut, is not *really* the new John Wayne. After all, she has not made a career of war movies and become the symbol of an aggressive American military. Wayne first became that symbol in a major way in 1949 when he played Sergeant Stryker in *The Sands*. Wayne earned his first Academy Award nomination with his portrayal of a tough disciplinarian whose men hated him for his rigorous training methods until the end of the film, when they realize that his toughness saved many of their lives by making them an effective combat team. According to Lawrence Suid, in *Guts and Glory: Great American War Movies*, Wayne himself described the plot of *The Sands* as "the story of Mr. Chips [a benevolent English boarding school teacher] put in the military. A man takes eight boys and has to make men out of them." But Randy Roberts and James Olson, in *John Wayne: American*, add, "If one can imagine Mr. Chips cracking the jaw of one of his students with the butt of a rifle, the comparison is an apt one."

This film, made with the complete cooperation of the U.S. Marine Corps (the "cast of thousands" are mostly real Marines), has often been derided by "serious" critics but has nevertheless become one of the more influential films of the twentieth century. It taught a whole generation of Americans what it meant to be a leader—especially of small groups. Stryker's hallmark shouts of impending action—"saddle up" and "lock and load"—are still commonly heard in both military and civilian contexts. For example, journalist Pat Buchanan, who never served in the military, often used those phrases during his ill-fated political campaign for the 1996

Republican presidential nomination. The speaker of the House of Representatives, Newt Gingrich of Georgia, told Elizabeth Drew in *Showdown* that *The Sands* was "the formative movie of my life." Stryker's style of leadership—make them tough and effective even if they hate you for it—was Gingrich's self-confessed tactic for shaping up his Republican insurgents for their successful 1994 assault on the House of Representatives.

Wayne played similar roles, outwardly tough but inwardly caring older leaders of younger men, in *Flying Leathernecks* (1951) and director John Ford's U.S. Cavalry trilogy: *Fort Apache* (1948), *She Wore a Yellow Ribbon* (1949), and *Rio Grande* (1950). But only his *The Cowboys* (1971) was a reprise of his role as Sergeant Stryker in a different guise. Here he is a Texas rancher who must use untrained boys to drive his cattle herd to the railhead many hundreds of miles away. But the plot, the organization development effort, is essentially the same: make these boys men enough for the job at hand. In both cases the boys dislike him at first but then learn to love him because they realize his way will see them through. In both cases Wayne is killed—by a Japanese sniper as the U.S. flag is raised on Iwo Jima in *The Sands* and by a despicable cattle rustler played by Bruce Dern in *The Cowboys*. In both cases the team can now carry on without him because he has trained, nurtured, and developed them so well. In *The Sands* the squad goes on to secure the island as the Marine Corps hymn reminds us that this same kind of thing has been going on "from the halls of Montezuma to the shores of Tripoli." In *The Cowboys* the group realizes that they—because of *him*—are now strong enough to go it alone, to take back the herd from the rustlers and kill the villains for good measure. In both cases Wayne, much like the Old Testament Moses, gets his people close to the "promised land" but then dies before reaching the goal. They must go on without him, and they can do it because of what they learned from him. It is just this patriarchal aspect of Wayne that makes him, his characters, and his movies so sublimely moving and ultimately lasting.

But, alas, the real John Wayne was no "John Wayne." The archetypal hero of so many movies and of America's popular imagination, far from being a hero, was quite the opposite. As a warrior he was a complete phony. Unlike many of his contemporary film stars, such as Clark Gable, Robert Taylor, James Stewart, Tyrone Power, Henry Fonda, Glenn Ford, and Sterling Hayden, to name a few, who gave up established Hollywood careers to serve in World War II with distinction—Wayne made every effort to avoid military service during the war. He was, more than any other major public figure, an active, artful, and successful draft dodger many times over. He simply arranged for the movie studios to say he was in a job essential to the war effort. However, by 1943 Wayne decided he would serve his country if he could get the assignment he wanted: working for director (but now naval officer) John Ford's naval photography unit. But Ford couldn't get him in because all such billets were frozen at that time. According to Ford's grandson, Dan Ford, "Wayne tried other avenues but couldn't get a commission. The only way he could get in the service was to enlist in the army as a private." Wayne explained, "I felt that it would be a waste of time to spend two years picking up cigarette butts. I thought I could do more for the war effort if I stayed in Hollywood."

Wayne's career thrived during the war when so many other leading men were in uniform facing the enemy while he faced the cameras. Many in the film industry never forgave Wayne for refusing to serve. Political analyst Garry Wills wrote, "A few even claim that Wayne did not forgive himself—that the compensatory superpatriotism of later years, when he urged the country on to wars in Korea and Vietnam, was a form of expiation. If so, it was not enough. This is a man who called on other generations to sacrifice their lives, and called them 'soft' if they refused."

Wayne's personal honor and patriotism notwithstanding, in the postwar era he became—and remains—the national icon of organization development. Wayne's performance in *The Sands*, while excellent in its own right, was a movie cliché even then. The stern fatherly taskmaster who takes error-prone "boys" under his wing and makes men out of them is a dramatic device that can be found as far back as the works of Homer in ancient Greece. It became the standard plot device for so many war movies because it lent itself so well to a story line needing a neat beginning, middle, and end. *The Sands* is simply the leading example of this genre. Other films with almost identical plot structures include *Gung Ho!* (1943), starring Randolph Scott; *Battle Cry* (1954), starring Van Heflin; *Cockleshell Heroes* (1956), starring José Ferrer; *Darby's Rangers* (1958), starring James Garner; *The Dirty Dozen* (1967), starring Lee Marvin; *The Devil's Brigade* (1968), starring William Holden; *Gallipoli* (1981), starring Mel Gibson; *Heartbreak Ridge* (1986), starring Clint Eastwood; and *The Last Samurai* (2003), starring Tom Cruise.

The formula used by these films has three acts. In the first, the disparate group is assembled and seen as a bunch of individualists not capable of functioning as a team. Almost always, the group is ethnically diverse to represent the tensions and composition of the larger society. Thus there is often the college boy, the lumberjack, the "dead-end" kid, the farmer, and the urban ethnics (characters that are obviously meant to be Polish, Italian, or Jewish). Later, as U.S. society became more inclusive, Hispanic, Asian, and African-Americans would appear. The first "act" always has the various types gradually lose their "street" identities and, under the harsh but benevolent guidance of the father-figure drill instructor, mold themselves into a team whose motto might well be that of Alexander Dumas's *Three Musketeers* (1844): "All for one, one for all."

The second act has the group performing as a team in training exercises and, often equally important, while on leave. For the purposes of the plot, it is equally valid for the group to realize they are a team in a barroom brawl or on field maneuvers. It's the group adventure, the sharing of mutual stress and danger, that finally cements the individuals into a team. (For the same reason, retreats and outdoor adventures are still popular means of developing civilian groups. The team that drinks together and climbs mountains together will perform the mundane duties of their everyday work in a more cooperative manner.) Once team status is achieved and the young soldiers realize how good the tough training they initially hated has been for them, they are ready for the third act: combat.

The third act validates the first two. It "proves" that the training works. While lives are inevitably lost, discipline and teamwork are shown to save lives and save the day. The father figure—whether John Wayne or Randolph Scott—is never more fatherly than when he leads them into danger and helps them fulfill their destiny as soldiers or cannon fodder.

One of the reasons films that follow this three-act formula have been so popular is that they ring true. While they have been decidedly sanitized for the mass public, they are true in that this *is* how the military—of all countries for seemingly all times—has indoctrinated and readied new soldiers for service. Thus the genre represents a time-tested method of organization development. The problem, of course, is that this particularly brutal method cannot be universally applied. First-line supervisors (the industrial equivalent of sergeants) cannot demand an instant 50 push-ups from an errant worker. In the industrial world the punishments must be more psychological than physical.

So far we have discussed the low end of war movie organization development. While such small unit plots offer the greatest opportunity for character development and audience identification, there is also a high end: organization development at the command level. This is best illustrated by films such as *Patton* (1970), starring George C. Scott, and *Twelve O'Clock High* (1949), starring Gregory Peck. In both instances new generals take charge of large units whose performance has been deficient. Yet, even though they are generals, not sergeants, they use the same techniques as John Wayne's Sergeant Stryker to change the dysfunctional organizational culture that has led to failed operations and the sacking of the previous commanders. When Scott and Peck use their general's stars to impose a harsh disciplinary regime on their errant outfits, they are following Stryker's example and techniques but on a higher organizational level. And they get the same results: an effective team that yields high morale and successful operations.

The essence of this little essay has been to demonstrate that the military throughout the ages—and American war movies in particular—has evidenced a sophisticated understanding of organization development long before this became a formal element of modern management education. Wayne's Sergeant Stryker may not have been anyone's ideal of your friendly organization development facilitator or consultant, but he—quite literally—knew the drill. Even without an advanced degree in applied behavioral science or public administration, he and his brothers-in-arms, going back to the legions of ancient Rome and beyond, knew how to instill planned organizational change. Higher education is a wonderful thing, but sometimes you can learn just as much by staying home and watching a bunch of old war movies.

For Discussion: *Why are each of the "three acts" of organization development so essential to understanding how the process works both in a military and civilian context? Is organization development limited to war movies, or can examples of it be found in other films as well?*

Hollywood continues the tradition of employing war films to illustrate the utility and methods of organization development using variants of the formula described in this keynote. In *Master and Commander* (2003) (right), Russell Crowe as a British Navy captain spends less time fighting than teaching his crew of disparate characters to develop their skills as team players. The proof of his success as an organization developer is that his small ship (meaning small team) defeats a ship and team twice as large in the end. In the photo Crowe is confident that his team will follow him as he jumps aboard an enemy ship. He, meaning his character, is literally betting his life on his team development efforts.

Similarly, in *The Last Samurai* (2003) (left), Tom Cruise is part of a group of nineteenth-century U.S. Army officers hired by the Japanese government to change a traditional hand weapon–wielding army into a modern one using firearms. In the photo Cruise's character disdains modernity and demonstrates the futility of baring your teeth and charging into machine gun fire. The inexperienced machine gunners only manage to kill all the attackers but Cruise. After the usual developmental problems, the newly developed higher-tech organization triumphs. This is a trend that will never end—because social improvements, whether military or civilian, are almost always premised upon successful organization development interventions. This is even more true in real life than in the movies. Unfortunately, in real life the process inevitably takes longer than two hours.•

Organizational Behavior

The study of organizational behavior includes those aspects of the behavioral sciences that focus on the understanding of human behavior in organizations. Students of public administration have always been interested in the behavior of people in government organizations. But fundamental assumptions about the behavior of such people at their work did not change dramatically from ancient efforts at organization until only a few decades ago. Using the traditional authoritarian, militaristic, and "papa knows best" set of attitudes toward work organizations,

Hugo Münsterberg pioneered the application of psychological findings from laboratory experiments to practical matters. He sought to match the abilities of new hires with a company's work demands, to positively influence employee attitudes toward their work and their company, and to understand the impact of psychological conditions on employee productivity. Münsterberg's pre–World War I approach was typical of how the behavioral sciences tended to be applied in organizations well into the 1950s.

In contrast to Münsterberg's traditional perspective on organizational behavior, a new style of applied behavioral science emerged in the 1960s. It focused attention on seeking to answer questions such as how organizations could encourage their workers to grow and develop. The belief was that organizational creativity, flexibility, and prosperity would flow naturally from employee growth and development. The essence of the relationship between organization and people was redefined from dependence to codependence. In contrast, managers in Münsterberg's day did not believe (assume) that codependence was the "right" relationship between an organization and its employees.

There has long been considerable interest in the behavior of people inside bureaucracies. After all, the whole purpose of organization theory, as discussed in the previous chapter, is to create mechanisms for regulating the behavior of people in organizations. However, it was not until about 1960, with the publication of Douglas McGregor's *The Human Side of Enterprise,* that our basic assumptions about the relationship between organizations and people truly began to change. This new approach to analyzing organizations focused on people, groups, and the relationships among them and the organizational environment. It was built around the following assumptions:

1. Organizations are created to serve human ends.

2. Organizations and people need each other (organizations need ideas, energy, and talent; people need careers, salaries, and work opportunities).

3. When the fit between the needs of the individual and the organization is poor, one or both will suffer: Individuals may be exploited or may seek to exploit the organizations, or both.

4. A good fit between individuals and organizations benefits both because people gain meaningful and satisfying work—and organizations receive the talent and energy they need to thrive.

It is instructive to contrast these assumptions with the paternalistic authoritarian attitudes that preceded them. Previously, when new technology was to be introduced, new orders were given for its installation and operation. There was no concern about what the workers would think about such changes. They simply had no say. Once in a while some **Luddites** might surface, but they were quickly suppressed. Compare this

---

Hugo Münsterberg (1863–1916) The German-born psychologist whose later work at Harvard would earn him the title of "father" of industrial or applied psychology.

Luddites Originally English workers in the early nineteenth century who destroyed new textile machinery that was displacing them in factories; now the term, after the legendary Ned Ludd, refers to anyone who sabotages high-tech equipment to protect jobs.

"orders is orders" approach to how modern organizational behaviorists contemplate the introduction of a new technology. They immediately start thinking about and planning a specific approach:

1. Minimize fear of change by involving people at all levels in designing the introduction of the changes.
2. Minimize the negative impacts of the change on groups of workers at risk (such as older, less-skilled, or younger workers).
3. **Co-opt** informal and formal (usually union) leaders, especially those who might become antagonistic.
4. Find alternatives for employees who do not see the changes as consistent with their personal goals.

Because the modern perspective places a high value on the individual, employees are provided with maximum amounts of accurate information, so they can make informed decisions about their future.

The assumptions of the Münsterberg traditional perspective continue to be alive and well in many less-sophisticated organizations—where it is still assumed that people should be fitted to the organization. With the classical organization theory of Frederick Taylor and others, the organizational role of the applied behavioral sciences largely consisted of helping organizations find and shape people to serve as human replacement parts for the organizational machine.

Yet, under the right circumstances, people and organizations will grow and prosper together. Individuals and organizations are not necessarily antagonists. Managers can learn to unleash previously stifled energies and creativities. Two of the most important "tools" for doing this are group dynamics and organization development.

Group Dynamics

Since the earliest days of the Industrial Revolution, workplace organizations have been constructed on the foundation principles of specialization and division of labor (remember Adam Smith's pin factory). In our complex organizations of today, few jobs can be done from start to finish by one person. Specialization allows an organization to use people's skills and efforts more systematically and to focus their knowledge and energy on a limited number of tasks. Employee **learning curves** are minimized.

Most employees who perform sets of specialized functions are organizationally clustered in work groups, which are organized into units or branches, which are organized into divisions or departments, which are organized into agencies, and so forth. Work groups attract people with like backgrounds—for example, professional

---

co-opt To include potentially dissident group members in an organization's policymaking process to prevent such elements from being a threat to the organization or its mission. The classic analysis of co-optation is found in Philip Selznick's *TVA and the Grass Roots* (1949).

learning curve The time it takes to achieve optimal efficiency in performing a task. When workers repeatedly do a new task, the amount of labor per unit of output initially decreases according to a pattern that can be plotted as a curve on a graph.

training, socialization, and experience as accountants, teachers, engineers, or computer programmers. All such shared backgrounds involve the socialization of people into common value/belief/behavior systems. We learn how to think and act like lawyers, teachers, or accountants—and like Virginians or Southern Californians.

Practically all groups, and particularly purposeful, specialized, organizational groups, develop their own sets of norms of behavioral assumptions about things like the nature of their organizational environment and appropriate relations with other groups. All groups expect their members to conform to their norms. By rewarding activities the organization wants done and punishing counterproductive behavior, managers engineer the accomplishment of organizational goals. Virtually all organizations attempt to motivate employees through combinations of rewards and punishments. **Reinforcement** theories of motivation assume that people at work seek rewards and try to avoid punishments.

Acceptance of and adherence to group norms permits people to know what to expect from each other and to predict what other members will do in different circumstances. Norms cause people to behave in patterned and predictable ways. Thus, by institutionalizing common expectations, they stabilize the organization. Always remember, though, that too much adherence to norms causes overconformity. This can hurt or destroy individualism—and even lead to groupthink (see the section on groupthink in this chapter). The potential damage here is not limited to individuals who work in organizations. Excessive conformity may result in so much organizational rigidity that the organization's overall ability to achieve its mission is degraded.

When a group becomes institutionalized in an organization, such as a production unit or a branch office, these shared beliefs, values, and assumptions—these norms—become the essence of a cohesive group and of an organizational subculture. Most group subcultures have a resemblance to the overall organizational culture but also contain unique elements that form through the impacts of events, circumstances, and personalities. Considering the normal loyalties that groups demand and the affiliational needs they meet, it becomes easy to understand why ingroups and outgroups and feelings of we-and-they and we-versus-they are so characteristic of life in organizations.

Group dynamics is the subfield of organization behavior concerned with the nature of groups, how they develop, and how they interrelate with individuals and other groups. Usually the term "group" refers to what is more technically known as a primary group—a group small enough to permit face-to-face interaction among its members that remains in existence long enough for some personal relations, sentiments, and feelings of identification or belonging to develop. There are two basic kinds of primary groups: formal and informal.

Formal groups are officially created by a larger organization, usually for the purpose of accomplishing tasks. Employees are assigned to formal groups based

---

reinforcement An inducement to perform in a particular manner. Positive reinforcement occurs when an individual receives a desired reward that is contingent upon some prescribed behavior. Negative reinforcement occurs when an individual works to avoid an undesirable outcome.

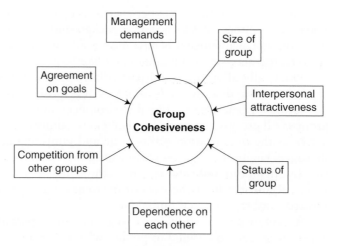

Figure 7.1   Factors Contributing to Group Cohesiveness

on their position in the organization. There are two basic types of formal groups. First, there are command groups that are specified in a formal organization chart. These include both supervisors and the people who report directly to them. Groups of this type are the essential building blocks of organizational structure. They vary from a mail room staff to the employees of a small branch office to an entire head-quarters staff. Second, there are task groups, formally sanctioned job-oriented units with short lives. Here you will find employees who work together to complete a particular project or task and then are disbanded. Any ad hoc ("for this") **task force** or temporary ("for this") committee is an example.

Informal groups are made up of individuals who have spontaneously developed relationships and patterns of interactions in work situations. Included here are employees who associate voluntarily, primarily to satisfy social needs. Although informal groups at work may have goals and tasks (for example, ethnic support groups, bowling clubs, and luncheon speaker groups), their primary reasons for existence are friendship, affiliation, and shared interests. Although informal groups seldom are formally sanctioned, they are extremely important to the working of organizations. Their norms, values, beliefs, and expectations have significant impacts on work-related behavior and attitudes. Chester I. Barnard in *The Functions of the Executive* has provided the classic statement on the vital significance of informal groups:

> Informal organization, although comprising the processes of society which are uncon-scious as contrasted with those of formal organization which are conscious, has two important classes of effects: (a) it establishes certain attitudes, understandings, customs, habits, institutions; and (b) it creates the condition under which formal organization may arise.

---

task force A temporary interdisciplinary team within a larger organization charged with accomplishing a specific goal. Task forces are typically used in government when a problem crosses departmental lines.

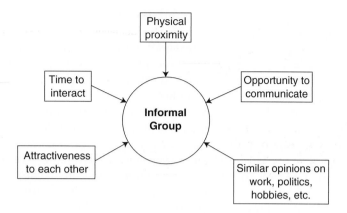

Figure 7.2 Factors Leading to the Creation of Informal Groups

Groups in organizations of all types are of high importance and interest to students and practitioners of organizational behavior, both for what happens in them (and why) and what happens between them.

Organization Development

The French Foreign Legion, when it occupied most of the North African desert early in the twentieth century, had the slogan "march or die"—which meant that a legionnaire could not survive unless he kept his place in the moving column. A similar slogan should be on the walls of all organizations: "Change or die." The message here is that without constant change, renovation—indeed reinventing—this social organism will die just as surely as the solitary legionnaire of old.

Organization Development (OD) is planned organizational change. Organizations exist in a dynamic environment, both internally and externally, to which they must respond or become ineffectual. The responsibility of OD advisers, specialists on applied behavioral science, is to facilitate change—to use their knowledge of the behavioral sciences for organizational improvement. These advisers can be internal in that they already work for the organization or external independent consultants. A frequently desired change is the installation of a beneficent managerial philosophy. More modest goals might be the creation of an atmosphere of trust in order to facilitate communications or the development of participatory mechanisms that would stimulate productivity. Any organization that wishes to survive or simply to remain healthy must periodically divest itself of those parts or characteristics that contribute to its malaise.

OD itself is not a philosophy. It is an approach or strategy for increasing organizational effectiveness. As a process, it has no value biases, but it is usually associated with the idea that effectiveness is found by integrating the individual's desire for growth with organizational goals. There is no universal OD model that can easily be plugged into a troubled organization. The basic task of the OD adviser is to adapt appropriate portions of the generally available OD technology to the immediate demands of his or her organizational problem. This is why the OD adviser must be thoroughly conversant with the findings of the behavioral technology of modern management. Since no textbook will have a case study of the exact organizational problem to be remedied, these advisers must be prepared to draw upon their backgrounds to improvise. OD advising, like much of the rest of public administration, contains a large element of art.

The OD process is made all the more difficult to implement in the public sector because top management, which must first be sold on the OD process, is fractured, consisting of political and career executives, legislative committees, client groups, and so on. Hostility can also be expected from line management. As an OD role for the personnel department implies a greater involvement with management's traditional line prerogatives, it may take some time before personnel's agitation in this regard is viewed as supportive instead of threatening.

A decision on the part of top management to suddenly replace a highly structured authoritarian organizational climate with an atmosphere of greater employee participation and collaboration probably would create a great sense of shock and suspicion among employees. All changes in organizational climate or culture must be well planned in advance and implemented gradually. OD is not something that can be accomplished in an afternoon. It is a slow process that extends, at the very least, over many months and requires the commitment and cooperation of all of the principal actors in the organizational drama. The first phase of almost all OD models is the education of top management in basic OD objectives and strategies. OD as a process is one that must flow from the top down. As leadership sets the tone of organizational life, it is futile to seek to change the pace and quality of that life without uninhibited cooperation from the top down.

OD is concerned with deep, long-lasting organization-wide change or improvement—not in superficial changes in isolated organizational pockets. This concern for broad-based and long-term change led OD practitioners to an interest in the concept of organizational culture long before it became a fashionable management topic in the 1980s. OD advisers have developed numerous strategies and techniques for improving organizations: Most of them utilize **interventions** facilitated by outsiders (often called change agents). Some of the most common strategies include organizational diagnosis, **process consultation**, team building (in many forms), action research, data feedback, **job enlargement**, **job enrichment**, and conflict management. But each adviser has his or her own preferred tactics.

The origins of the organization development movement can be generally traced to the Hawthorne studies (discussed later in this chapter). But the specific understandings of organizational behavior-oriented change processes came out of the sensitivity

---

intervention The entering of an outsider into an ongoing system of relationships, such as an organization, to help make it perform better.

process consultation The interventionist activities of an organization development adviser.

job enlargement Adding additional but similar duties to a job.

job enrichment Adding different kinds of duties so that the work is both at a higher level and more personally satisfying.

training (or **T-group**) movement that started in 1946 when Kurt Lewin and associates collaboratively conducted a training workshop to help improve racial relations and community leadership in New Britain, Connecticut. During their evening staff meetings, they discussed the behavior of workshop participants and the dynamics of events. Several workshop participants asked to join the night discussions, and the results of the process eventually led to the initiation and institutionalization of T-group technology. Although the early T-groups focused primarily on individual growth and development, they quickly were adapted for organizational application. T-groups became the method by which organizational members learned how to communicate honestly and directly about facts and feelings. (From the human relations perspective, feelings are facts.) Thus T-groups became a keystone strategy for increasing organizational effectiveness by improving interpersonal communications (e.g., feedback), reducing defensiveness (and thus rigidity), and otherwise helping organizations achieve greater effectiveness through the development of coping processes. The meaning of coping here is twofold: coping with the job and coping with fellow workers.

But the T-group needed to be part of a larger overarching methodology. Survey research methodology, when combined with feedback/communication (T-group) techniques and applied to planned organizational change, resulted in the development of the action research model of organizational change—the mainstay of OD practitioners and theorists. The action research model is a process for identifying needs for organizational improvement through the use of external consultation but also through fostering **psychological ownership** of problems and solutions by organizational members. Briefly, action research involves the following:

1. Collecting organizational diagnostic data (ascertaining the problem) usually either through written questionnaires or interviews
2. Systematically feeding back information to the organization members who provided input
3. Discussing what the information means to members and its implications for the organization in order to be certain if the "diagnosis" is accurate and to generate psychological ownership of the need for actions to improve the situation
4. Jointly developing an improvement plan, using both the knowledge and skills of the consultant and the insider perspective of members
5. Repeating all of the preceding as needed

The key to long-term OD success is this very last step: repeat as needed. Lewin is well known for his assertion that social change must be viewed as a three-step process of unfreezing, change, and refreezing. If one focuses only on the change

---

T-group A training group. According to Chris Argyris, a leading authority on OD techniques, the T-group experience is "designed to provide maximum possible opportunity for the individuals to expose their behavior, give and receive feedbacks, experiment with new behavior, and develop everlasting awareness and acceptance of self and others."

psychological ownership Emotional involvement with, and commitment to, an intangible something such as an organizational reform effort.

process per se, change will be short-lived at best. The organization must put the change in place to see if it takes. The process is called action research because the thing being experimented on, the organization, is constantly in action. When Lewin says "unfreezing," he means opening up the organization to change. The "refreezing" process is installing the new change, then watching it to see if the "refreezing" is an improvement. This OD effort toward continuous improvement is a precursor to the total quality management (TQM) movement discussed in Chapter 8.

The ultimate question here is not whether organizations should change. They are constantly changing in response to the dynamic environments in which they all exist. Of course, some environments are more dynamic than others. But change, fast or slow, is inexorable. The best line Thomas Wolfe ever wrote was the title of his 1940 novel *You Can't Go Home Again*. The home you left, because of the simple passage of time, is no longer the home to which you return. The home in which you once lived, just like the office in which you once worked, changes every day.

Figure 7.3 The Organization Development Action Research Model

SOURCE: Adapted from J. Steven Ott, ed., *Classic Readings in Organizational Behavior,* 2nd ed. (Belmont, CA: Wadsworth, 1996).

People get older, attitudes evolve, and new skills are learned no matter what we do. So the question for would-be managers of organizations is not change: yes or no, but unplanned change or planned change. OD as planned change is just a tool for managers to gain control of and give direction to the inevitable changes within their organizations.

The Impact of Personality

Chris Argyris, a preeminent analyst of organizational phenomena for over four decades, first became noteworthy with the publication of his 1957 book *Personality and Organization*. In it he claimed that there was an inherent conflict between the mature adult personality and the needs of modern organizations. The problem, simply put, was that most organizations were treating adults like children. As the truth of this finding was made increasingly evident, ways of treating employees changed. A new dogma evolved that organizations should give their citizens all the responsibilities they could handle—and then some.

While this nicely dovetailed with concerns for greater productivity and effectiveness, the inherent problem of personality was not so much superseded as ignored. After all, in the era of equal employment opportunity and workforce diversity, efforts to address the impact of individual personalities on organizations could be dangerous. Who needs lawsuits claiming that an employee's cultural heritage is being "attacked" by an inherently oppressive organization and a supervisor insensitive to the subtleties of managing in a multicultural environment?

Nevertheless, organizational analysts have once again begun, despite the diversity issue minefield, to look anew at the impact of personality. And they are beginning to say things that will make some people uncomfortable. They are not rejecting what Argyris said about adults and organizations. But they are saying that different kinds of adults fit organizations differently, that individuals who might have been heroes in an earlier age because of their inherent aggressiveness and disdain for established authority are too often misfits in a contemporary bureaucratic culture.

The issue here is inherent temperament. According to Winifred Gallagher, there is still much to be said for the validity of four basic human temperaments first described in ancient Greece by Hippocrates 2,500 years ago. His four "humors" are still commonly used today to informally describe personality types. We have all seen people who are sanguine (optimistic and energetic), melancholic (moody and withdrawn), choleric (irritable and impulsive), and phlegmatic (calm and slow). Indeed, many people have displayed all of these "humors" or moods at one time or another.

Even if we discard Hippocrates' "humors" as a classification system, it is just common sense that a "Dirty Harry" (the archetypal aggressive police officer portrayed by Clint Eastwood in a series of films) should not be placed in charge of the police department's computer system. Similarly, an extremely shy, soft-spoken person would not usually be the best individual to represent your organization on radio and TV. And someone prone to constant anxiety and worry will probably not do well in a high-stress position. Yet such mismatches are so commonplace that they are a leading cause of organizational incompetence.

The Impact of Bureaucratic Structure on Behavior

The impact of bureaucratic structure on the behavior of its denizens results from their unique personalities interacting with the organizational structures in which they must function. Each organization has structures that define the unique ways labor is divided, how specialized roles and functions are coordinated (related to each other and to other organizational levels and functions), how information flows among people and groups, and how the system of controls (how tasks are measured, evaluated, and altered) is to work. These structures, often visualized in the form of an **organization chart**, establish how roles, expectations, and resource allocations are determined for people and groups in any given organization. Structure is a primary reason why organizational behavior differs from behavior in everyday life and thus why organizational behavior developed as a separate field of study within the applied behavioral sciences. Structure, however, is only one of a variety of forces that affect the behavior of people in organizations. Attitudes and behaviors are also shaped by **peer group** pressure, shared group norms of behavior, social and technical aspects of work tasks, and the organization's internal and external cultures (discussed in Chapter 2).

The structures of a large bureaucracy are inherently conservative in that they are slow to change. Thus one of the perennial complaints about bureaucracy is its lack of responsiveness to changing conditions. But this notorious slowness to change is very often a function of its legal mandate. No public bureaucracy in a democratic government does anything that is not provided for by its enabling legislation. This alleged slowness, from another point of view, is simply its obedience to the law. What a chief executive would streamline and make more efficient, the power brokers of the legislature would just as often keep bloated and inefficient. And if government jobs for their constituents are at stake, efficiency and economy in government suffer even more. This is exactly what members of the U.S. Congress must confront every time the Department of Defense seeks to close military bases. Congressional **doves** suddenly turn into defense **hawks** when the jobs of the voters in their district are at stake.

As organizations grew from small offices and shops into large corporations and government agencies, the disciplined hierarchies and unambiguous functional assignments of bureaucracy evolved as the ideal structural form. This structure allowed for pervasive control from the top of an organizational pyramid. But tight control is a good news/bad news story. The good news is that it is possible to centrally monitor and regulate the behavior of the employees. The bad news is that there are high costs involved with excessive control and the line between tight control and excessive control is a thin one. Employees in organizational straitjackets

---

organization chart The visual representation of the structure of an organization, usually in the form of a diagram.

peer group People at the same organizational level in terms of rank, title, or salary.

dove A peaceful bird in metaphor; a symbol of peace since ancient times.

hawk Person inclined toward military action. Its antithetical term is *dove*.

are unlikely to exercise initiative. Like automatons—human robots—they perform their prescribed duties until appropriate bureaucratic authority tells them otherwise. A properly designed bureaucratic organization can be impressively efficient even though none of its individual bureaucrats are in any way exceptional individuals. This is why Herman Wouk in his 1951 novel *The Caine Mutiny* called the U.S. Navy "a machine invented by geniuses, to be run by idiots." These machines, whether governmental or industrial, can be extraordinarily impressive in performance even when run by mediocre people. Thus the French novelist Honoré de Balzac called bureaucracy "the giant power wielded by pygmies." In this sense bureaucracy, far from being incompetent, is a bastion of super-competence—its overall performance far exceeding the quality that could otherwise be expected from its miscellaneous human parts.

Bureaucratic Dysfunctions

Unfortunately, bureaucracies often have within them the seeds of their own incompetence, like a bad genetic inheritance. Contemporary writers such as Robert K. Merton and Victor A. Thompson have argued that bureaucracies have inherent dysfunctional and pathological elements that make them inefficient in operations. Merton found that bureaucracies have a "trained incapacity." This refers to a "state of affairs in which one's abilities function as inadequacies or blind spots. Actions based on training and skills that have been successfully applied in the past may result in inappropriate responses under changed conditions." According to Merton, bureaucracy exerts constant pressures on people to be methodical and disciplined, to conform to patterns of obligations. These pressures eventually cause people to adhere to rules as an end rather than a means—as a matter of blind conformance.

It is this blind conformance that gives bureaucracy its catch-22 quality, its trained incapability to respond to contradictory requirements. This "catch," from Joseph Heller's 1961 novel of the same name about American bomber crews in World War II, meant that you could get out of flying combat missions if you were insane. All you had to do was ask. But if you asked, you were not insane because seeking to avoid combat was a rational, not an insane, act. In Heller's words a pilot "would be crazy to fly more missions and sane if he didn't, but if he was sane, he had to fly them. If he flew them, he was crazy and didn't have to, but if he didn't, he was sane and had to." The "catch" is beautifully circular in its perversity. Because the book was such an enormous best-seller, "catch-22" entered the language as the code word for the essence of bureaucratic dysfunctionalism, for being trapped between contradictory bureaucratic regulations. A common example of catch-22 is this double bind: A person can't get a job without experience but can't get experience without first having a job.

Bureaucratic structure also stresses depersonalized relations, and power and authority gained by virtue of organizational position rather than by thought or action. Thus ideas and opinions are valued not according to their intrinsic merit but according to one's rank. This would be perfectly fine if the bosses truly were always smarter than the workers. Without question, Merton sees bureaucratic structure as more than affecting organizational behavior and thinking: It also determines and controls. It determines that not all of the organization's brain power will be used and that the objectively less deserving may remain in control. Of course, there is always the bright, aspiring bureaucratic leader who holds his tongue or her brains in check while they climb the bureaucratic career ladder. But the danger here is that they suffer from "evaporation." Historian B. H. Liddell Hart observed in his *Why Don't We Learn from History?* that "ambitious officers when they came in sight of promotion" to high rank, "would decide that they would bottle up their thoughts and ideas, as a safety precaution, until they reached the top and could put these ideas into practice. Unfortunately the usual result, after years of such self-repression for the sake of their ambition, was that when the bottle was eventually uncorked the contents had evaporated."

As a form of organization, bureaucracy has many advantages: order, predictability, stability, professionalism, and consistency. Nevertheless, the behavioral consequences of bureaucratic structure are often negative. To illustrate this, Thompson combined "bureaucracy" with "pathological" to describe the all-too-familiar "bureaupathic official." Such a person "usually exaggerates the official, nontechnical aspects of relationships and suppresses the technical and the informal." Being insecure he or she "may be expected to insist on petty rights and prerogatives, on protocol, on procedure—in short, on those things least likely to affect directly the goal accomplishment of the organization." This is the classic stereotype of "the bureaucrat." Thus an otherwise "functionless reviewing officer will often insist most violently on his right to review and scream like an injured animal if he is bypassed." Moreover, "if he has a counterpart at a higher organizational level, he will probably insist on exclusive contact with that higher clearance point. By controlling this particular communication channel, he protects his authority and influence." This stereotype has been around, quite literally, for ages. In *Measure for Measure* (Act II, Scene 2) Shakespeare writes of the "petty officer," the "proud man, dress'd in a little brief authority, most ignorant of what he's most assur'd." This "petty officer" with his or her "little brief authority" is also probably performing at a bureaucracy near you—right now!

Bureaucratic Impersonality

Max Weber referred to bureaucracy's "special virtue" as "dehumanization." Hardly anyone would argue that bureaucracy does not have dehumanizing consequences for its employees and, to a lesser extent, for its clients as well. By dehumanization, Weber meant the elimination "from official business [of] love, hatred and all purely personal, irrational, and emotional elements." In Weber's view, formalization, hierarchy, and the other central features of bureaucracy render the individual bureaucrat "only a single cog in an ever-moving mechanism which prescribes to him an essentially fixed route of march." Consequently, "the individual bureaucrat is forged to the community of all functionaries who are integrated into the mechanism." He cannot "squirm out of the apparatus in which he is harnessed." Today the term *impersonality* is generally used in referring to this aspect of bureaucratic behavior. Viewed against a historical background of administrative organizations characterized by such "irrational" elements as

nepotism, personal subjugation, and capricious and uninformed judgment, impersonality can be seen as a step in the direction of greater rationality; a step further in the direction of Aristotle's ideal of "**a government of laws**; not of men."

Bureaucratic impersonality has three major advantages. First, it increases organizational effectiveness by enabling administrators to do things that are otherwise difficult for people to do. In the course of their normal functioning, organizations may create considerable hardships for individuals. This is especially true of public organizations, which are often engaged in punishment, taxation, and the withholding of benefits such as food stamps, unemployment compensation, or welfare funds. Impersonality creates a desirable moral insensitivity. For example, it is much easier—emotionally speaking—for military planners on a general staff to select targets for bombardment than it is for a rifleman to shoot an enemy soldier who is a few yards ahead of him and whose face is clearly visible. Similarly, it is far easier for welfare agency budget analysts to cut school lunch funding for poor students than for a food service worker at a school cafeteria to see children go hungry when they cannot pay for lunch.

A second advantage of impersonality flows from the fact that as Peter Blau and Marshall Meyer observed in *Bureaucracy in Modern Society,* "Efficiency also suffers when emotions or personal considerations influence administrative decisions." If, for example, recruitment and promotions within an organization are based on personal preference, or ascriptive criteria (such as race or class), rather than competence, that organization's administrative processes will over time become less efficient.

Finally, impersonality tends to produce relatively evenhanded rule application. Thus procedural, if not necessarily actual, justice is ensured. "By the book" behavior requires equal treatment of those in the same categories, regardless of their social status. While this attitude may cause hardship for some, there has long been great philosophic support for it. For example, eighteenth-century philosopher Jean Jacques Rousseau denied that it was an abridgment of anyone's freedom to do the **general will**. Rousseau defined freedom in this context as simply being treated the same as everyone else. He would have loudly applauded modern bureaucracy's institutionalized lack of respect for a person's station in life.

---

nepotism Any practice by which officeholders award positions to members of their immediate family. It is derived from the Latin *nepos,* meaning "nephew" or "grandson." The rulers of the medieval church were often thought to give special preference to their nephews in distributing churchly offices—at that time, "nephew" being a euphemism for an illegitimate son.

government of laws A governing system in which the highest authority is a body of law that applies equally to all (as opposed to the rule of men, in which the personal whim of those in power can decide any issue). The idea of the desirability of a "government of laws, and not of men" can be traced back to Aristotle. The earliest American reference is in the 1779 Massachusetts Constitution. John Marshall also used this succinct legal description in *Marbury v. Madison* (1803): "The government of the United States has been emphatically termed a government of laws, and not of men. It will certainly cease to deserve this high appellation, if the laws furnish no remedy for the violation of a vested legal right."

general will Jean Jacques Rousseau's ideal from *The Social Contract* (1761) that there is a collective will or consensus among the people, which is the ultimate locus of all political power.

Although impersonality may further procedural justice, it may at the same time fail to provide substantive or actual justice. The decisions bureaucrats reach may fail to fit the individual cases in terms of providing a just resolution. Many people fail to accept that their case is no different from those of others. They resent being treated on the basis of categories to which they do not feel they rightly belong. This tendency of bureaucracy has often aroused considerable hostility—sometimes even violence—on the part of clients. But the nature of impersonal organization is such that bureaucrats must apply established rules and procedures, even when they realize that these will not provide a reasonable or just resolution of a specific problem. Consequently, it has frequently been argued that a characteristic pathology of bureaucracy is an inversion of ends and means whereby the rules become more important than the objectives underlying their creation.

While impersonality is acknowledged as a central feature of bureaucratic behavior, there is disagreement over its desirability. Given that it has both advantages and dysfunctions, it would appear that the most sensible approach is to try to maximize the former while minimizing the latter. At the very least, this requires that students and practitioners of public administration avoid sweeping generalizations about bureaucratic behavior. The focus of concern ought to be the operations of individual bureaucratic units. By the same token it is imperative that the serious student recognize that some popular analyses of bureaucratic behavior—for example, **Parkinson's Law** that "work expands so as to fill the time available for its completion" and the **Peter Principle** that "in a hierarchy every employee tends to rise to his level of incompetence"— are generally more amusing than descriptive of reality.

Bureaucrat Bashing

Bashing is extreme and public criticism (often unwarranted and irrational) of a person, policy, or nation. Domestically, bashing has often followed the word *bureaucrat.* During the 1980s, the constant complaints and jokes about the competence of government employees—led by President Ronald "Government Is the Problem" Reagan—helped to create an acceptance of bureaucrat bashing. Following his 1964 campaign for governor of California, Reagan was constantly complaining that "government is like a big baby—an alimentary canal with a big appetite at one end and no sense of responsibility at the other."

The term *bureaucrat bashing* has been used so frequently in so many contexts that it has taken on two meanings that are the opposite of each other. Those on the

---

Parkinson's Law The title of a 1957 best-seller by C. Northcote Parkinson (1909–1993), an otherwise serious British naval and economic historian. Parkinson also "discovered" that any public administrative department will invariably increase its staff an average of 5.75 percent per year. In anticipation of suggestions that he advise what might be done about this problem, he asserted that "it is not the business of the botanist to eradicate the weeds. Enough for him if he can tell us just how fast they grow."

Peter Principle The 1969 best-seller of the same name by Laurence J. Peter (1919–1990), then an obscure professor of education, who offered the corollary that "in time, every post tends to be occupied by an employee who is incompetent to carry out its duties."

ideological right who tend to oppose big government use it to refer to justified criticism of "lazy and incompetent" government employees. At the same time, those on the ideological left, who tend to be more supportive of big government, use it to refer to the political right's "unnecessary and inappropriate" condemnation of public employees. But the meaning goes beyond rhetoric. The term now also refers to widespread support for specific policies that adversely impact or demean public employees. For example, monitoring phone calls to prevent personal use, reducing office sizes, and curtailing free parking privileges all reduce the quality of bureaucratic life on the job.

Perhaps no bureaucrat in recent memory has received as much bashing as Federal Emergency Management Agency (FEMA) Director Michael Brown.
In the aftermath of Hurricane Katrina's devastation of the Gulf Coast in 2005, Brown became the lightning rod for public anger over the mismanagement of government efforts to protect the public from the disaster. As the scope of the disaster became apparent, the media and Congress began to look closely at Brown's background and management of the crisis. What the examination of Brown uncovered fueled public outcry for his dismissal.

First, attention was called to Brown's preparation to serve as the federal government's chief emergency manager. Before being appointed to FEMA as a deputy chief in 2001, Brown served as the judges and stewards commissioner of the International Arabian Horse Association. According to a *Time Magazine*

investigation, the only emergency management experience Brown had before coming to FEMA was a largely fabricated 1975 to 1978 stint as an assistant city manager in Edmond, Oklahoma, in which he claimed to have "emergency services oversight." The *Time* investigation found his work in Edmond was largely an internship in which he had little to no contact with emergency services.

Second, Brown's lack of awareness of the severity of the situation on the Gulf Coast baffled many. Most notably, as thousands of residents of New Orleans sat for days at their city's convention center without food and water, Brown apparently was unaware that this situation was even taking place as late as three days after the hurricane struck. Similarly, e-mails released through the congressional investigation demonstrated that Brown did not know key aspects of the federal efforts to evacuate individuals from the coast.

Finally, Brown's cavalier attitude as the hurricane was wreaking havoc contributed to public anger at his behavior. According to those e-mails collected by Congress, Brown was e-mailing friends about his fashion selection at the very time Katrina was passing over New Orleans. In particular, on the morning of the hurricane's arrival, Brown was e-mailing his press secretary that he was a "fashion god."

Such a "perfect storm" of factors made it easy for the public to bash Brown to the point that he became a political liability. Despite President Bush's insistence that "Brownie" was "doing a heck of a job," Brown stepped down as FEMA director on September 12, 2005, and simultaneously entered into the hall of fame of bashed bureaucrats.•

SOURCES: Derived from articles in *Time Magazine*, September 8, 2005; and the *Washington Post*, November 4, 2005.

And being asked to take a urine test to detect drug use or to sign an antileak (of information) pledge may be personally demeaning.

The problem with bureaucracy from the point of view of the cultural conservatives is that the values they most cherish seem to be under attack by bureaucratic institutions. They see a **red** flag in both the literal (meaning danger) and political senses when a government agency such as the National Endowment for the Arts subsidizes works of art they consider to be obscene or when a government welfare agency takes the social stigma out of illegitimacy by making no distinction between widowed (or divorced) women with dependent children in financial need and never-married mothers. The bureaucratic grouping of them together as simply "single mothers" is morally offensive to many cultural conservatives who view it as a policy

Ronald Reagan cheerfully bashing the bureaucracy at the National Press Club in 1966. Three of his favorite bashes were (1) "Government is like a big baby—an alimentary canal with a big appetite at one end and no sense of responsibility at the other"; (2) "Government does not solve problems; it subsidizes them"; and (3) "The nine most terrifying words in the English language are 'I'm from the government and I'm here to help.'" Ironically, the most expensive federal building ever constructed is now named after this critic of the bureaucracy. The huge Ronald Reagan Building and International Trade Center cost $818 million. Only the Pentagon houses more federal workers. According to Gloria Borger, the behemoth is "an embarrassment to Republicans who believe that it represents everything Reagan fought against: big-spending government, inefficient bureaucracy, waste, fraud, and abuse. Reagan himself authorized the building, which makes it awkward for his flock to openly abandon it. And guess who will work there? Employees of the Environmental Protection Agency, one of Reagan's favorite targets." (*U.S. News,* December 15, 1997)•

---

red A Communist; the red flag is the international symbol of communism. This is why someone thought to be leaning toward communism might be called *pink* or a *pinko*.

that only encourages a continual rise in the number of children born outside of marriage (30 percent of all U.S. births in 1995). Thus the bureaucracy with its subsidizing of single motherhood is castigated by conservatives as seeking to destroy the traditional family, the indispensable weaver of the social fabric.

There is really nothing new in American politics about attacking the bureaucracy. Indeed, the middle of the Declaration of Independence of 1776 contains a major assault on the bureaucracy of King George's colonial government. But what is new is that the people running the bureaucracies, not just their political opposition, are also on the attack. Ronald Reagan won election in 1980 by running against the federal bureaucracy. After four years of being responsible for it, he successfully ran against it again in 1984. Bill Clinton pledged in his successful 1992 presidential campaign to reinvent federal bureaucracy. His reinventing cost 200,000 federal bureaucrats their jobs by 1996. The bureaucracy is an easy political target to bash because, being largely politically neutral, it does not bash back.

The Case for Bureaucracy

Despite widespread berating of "the bureaucracy" and a constant stream of jokes about the efficiency of government employees, Americans often like their bureaucrats and think highly of the quality of the services they recieve. Charles T. Goodsell, a professor of public administration at Virginia Polytechnic Institute and State University, got so enraged about the popular "vision of a failed bureaucracy" that he wrote a book, *The Case for Bureaucracy,* exploring what he called "the great falsehood about American government." After reviewing a wealth of research reports, he found "satisfactory citizen treatment as the *norm* rather than the *exception.*"

BOX 7.1 How Bureaucracy Is "Set Up"

A major cause for chronic underestimation of American bureaucratic performance is our tendency to hold unrealistic expectations for it. Belonging to a culture accustomed to optimism and habituated to progress, we Americans tend to assume that if bureaucracies do not succeed in changing the world in the ways we wish, they have somehow failed. But in reality we often "set up" bureaucracy in such a way as to make complete success impossible. We give administrative organizations inconsistent or contradictory goals, creating disappointments no matter what happens. We make effective implementation of laws unduly difficult in many policy areas by holding several different organizations responsible for the job. . . . Bureaucracy is further handicapped by the tendency of Americans to expect it to solve any and all problems, no matter how solvable or unsolvable they may be, even when the bureaucrats have no control whatsoever over the causes of the problems.

SOURCE: Charles T. Goodsell, *The Case for Bureaucracy,* 3rd ed. (Chatham, NJ: Chatham House, 1994).

Moreover, Goodsell argued, "The commonly accepted view of political conservatives that government never performs as well as business is also shown to be a patent falsehood." In addition, "a comparison of American bureaucracy to that of other countries reveals that we experience one of the best levels of service in the world, light years ahead of that endured by most national populations." Goodsell's book is a perennial rebuttal to all those misguided or malicious bureaucrat bashers.

Motivation

Theatrical lore has it that as a famous actor struggled to find just the right characterization for a scene, he turned to his director and asked, "What's my motivation?" The director sarcastically replied, "To keep your job!" And so it is with most work done off the stage as well. "Keeping the job" has been the primary goal of industrial workers ever since they abandoned their farms to find work in the factories of the city. The perennial problem for managers is to motivate the workers to do more than is minimally necessary to keep that job.

While there always has been consensus about the need for motivated employees, the same cannot be said for beliefs about how to induce higher levels of motivation—and concomitant productivity. Not only have prevailing views (or theories) of motivation changed radically over time, but incompatible theories usually have competed with each other at the same points in time. Some theories assume that employees act rationally: Managers simply need to manipulate rewards and punishments logically, fairly, and consistently. Other theories start from the position that managerial assumptions about employees—which undergird such systems of rewards and punishments—actually stifle employee motivation. This section summarizes some of the more important theories.

The Hawthorne Experiments

It was during the late 1920s and early 1930s that the Hawthorne experiments were undertaken at the Hawthorne Works of the Western Electric Company near Chicago. This study, consisting of the most famous management experiments ever reported, was conducted by Elton Mayo and his associates from the Harvard Business School. The decade-long series of experiments started out as traditional scientific management examinations of the relationship between work environment and productivity. But the experimenters, because they were initially unable to explain the results of their findings, literally stumbled upon a finding that today seems so obvious: that factories and other work situations are first of all social situations. The workers, as **Mary Parker Follett** had suggested a decade earlier, were more responsive to peer pressure than to management controls. The Hawthorne studies are generally considered to be the genesis of the human relations school of management thought, providing the first

---

Mary Parker Follett (1868–1933) An early social psychologist who anticipated, in the 1920s, many of the conclusions of the Hawthorne experiments of the 1930s and of the post–World War II behavioral movement.

major empirical challenge to the scientific management notion that the worker was primarily an economic animal who would work solely for money.

It is important to note that the Mayo team began its work trying to fit into the mold of classical organization theory thinking. The team phrased its questions in the language and concepts that industry was accustomed to using in order to see and explain certain problems, among them productivity in relationship to such factors as the amount of light, the rate of flow of materials, and alternative wage payment plans. The Mayo team succeeded in making significant breakthroughs in understanding only after it redefined the Hawthorne problems as social psychological problems—problems conceptualized in such terms as interpersonal relations in groups, group norms, control over one's own environment, and personal recognition. It was only after the Mayo team achieved this breakthrough that it became the "grandfather"—the direct precursor—of the field of organizational behavior and human resource theory. The Hawthorne experiments were the emotional and intellectual wellspring of modern theories of motivation. They showed that complex, interactional variables make the difference in motivating people—things like attention paid to workers as individuals, workers' control over their own work, differences between individuals' needs, management's willingness to listen, group norms, and direct feedback.

A particularly notable discovery that came out of the Hawthorne experiments was the Hawthorne effect: the discovery that production increases were due to the known presence of benign observers. The researchers' concern for and attention to the workers led the workers, who naturally wanted to be reciprocally nice, to increase production. This "effect" caused great confusion at first because the changing physical conditions (lighting, rest breaks, etc.) seemed to make no difference. Output just kept going up. Once they realized that the workers' perception of participation was the true "variable," the effects of the "effect" were understood.

The Needs Hierarchy

Abraham H. Maslow, a psychologist, took the basic Hawthorne finding that workers are as much social as economic creatures a step further when he first proposed his famous "needs hierarchy" in his 1943 *Psychological Review* article, "A Theory of Human Motivation." Maslow asserted that humans had five sets of goals or basic needs arranged in a hierarchy of prepotency: (1) physiological needs (food, water, shelter, etc.), (2) safety needs, (3) love or affiliation needs, (4) esteem

Figure 7.4 Maslow's Needs Hierarchy

needs, and (5) self-actualization needs. After fulfilling these needs, an individual theoretically reaches self-fulfillment and becomes all that he or she is capable of becoming. Once the lower needs are satisfied, they cease to be motivators of behavior. Conversely, higher needs cannot motivate until lower needs are satisfied. Simply put—a person will risk being eaten by a hungry lion if that risk is the only way to get food and water. Only after the body is sustained can thoughts turn to safety and the other higher needs.

According to Maslow, "It is quite true that man lives by bread alone—when there is no bread. But what happens to man's desires when there is plenty of bread and when his belly is chronically filled? At once other (and higher) needs emerge, and these, rather than physiological hungers, dominate the organism." When these in turn are satisfied, new, even higher needs will emerge. Maslow's psychological analysis of motivation proved to be the foundation for much subsequent research. While other researchers, such as Herzberg, McGregor, and Bennis (all discussed on the following pages), would take Maslow's concepts and develop them into more comprehensive theories of motivation and organizational behavior, Maslow's work remains the point of departure.

The Motivation-Hygiene Theory

One of the first extensive empirical demonstrations of the primacy of internal worker motivation was the motivation-hygiene theory put forth by Frederick Herzberg, Bernard Mausner, and Barbara Snyderman, in a landmark 1959 study entitled *The Motivation to Work*. Five factors were isolated as determiners of job satisfaction: (1) achievement, (2) recognition, (3) work itself, (4) responsibility, and (5) advancement. Five factors associated with job dissatisfaction were similarly realized: (1) company policy and administration, (2) supervision, (3) salary, (4) interpersonal relations, and (5) working conditions. The satisfying factors were all related to job content, the dissatisfying factors to the environmental context of the job. The factors that were associated with job satisfaction were quite separate from those factors associated with job dissatisfaction. Herzberg later made this observation in "The Motivation-Hygiene Concept" in *Personnel Administration:*

> Since separate factors need to be considered depending on whether job satisfaction or job dissatisfaction was involved, it followed that these two feelings were not the obverse of each other. The opposite of job satisfaction would not be job dissatisfaction, but rather NO job satisfaction; and similarly the opposite of job dissatisfaction is NO job dissatisfaction—not job satisfaction.

Because the environmental context of jobs, such as working conditions, interpersonal relations, and salary, served primarily as preventatives, they were termed hygiene factors, as an analogy to the medical use of hygiene meaning preventative and environmental. The job-content factors such as achievement, advancement, and responsibility were termed motivators because these are the things that motivate people to superior performance. Herzberg wrote this in *Work and the Nature of Man:*

> The principal result of the analysis of this data was to suggest that the hygiene or maintenance events led to job dissatisfaction because of a need to avoid unpleasantness; the motivator events led to job satisfaction because of a need for growth or

self-actualization. At the psychological level, the two dimensions of job attitudes reflected a two-dimensional need structure: one need system for the avoidance of unpleasantness and a parallel need system for personal growth.

Since its original presentation, a considerable number of empirical investigations by a wide variety of researchers has tended to confirm the motivation-hygiene theory. Its chief fault seems to be its rejection of the view that pay is a unique incentive capable, in differing circumstances, of being a hygiene factor as well as a motivator. But the theory's main holding—that worker motivation is essentially internal—remains largely unchallenged.

Toward a Democratic Environment

According to Warren Bennis, a preeminent sage of organizational futures, democracy in an organization context "is inevitable." Its inevitability has been determined by its empirically proven effectiveness when compared with the more traditional, autocratic methods of organizational management. While the evidence is not complete, the whole thrust of behavioral research concerning employee motivation and productivity supports the notion of extending democracy to the lowest levels of the organizational hierarchy. That extension includes sharing power and policy decisions.

Three basic stratagems have evolved to meet the demands for a more democratic environment in the workplace. First—and historically the most common in the public as well as the private sector—top management tries to meet an expressed need for greater participatory management with a symbolic sop rather than with a meaningful program. When an employee "crisis" erupts because of the general **alienation** of the workforce or because of some specific reason such as perceived racism or the dehumanizing nature of the work, management seeks to mollify the situation. If it is unable to make any substantial changes, it can often defuse a present crisis by providing a limited upward mobility program or employee representation on the decisional councils of the organization. However, this tactic can only mitigate or alleviate the current problem; there is no real change. There is only an increase in what Frederick Herzberg has called the "hygiene" factors of work—salary, working conditions, interpersonal relations, and so forth. These in turn lead to an insatiable appetite for still more "hygiene." Like heroin, it soon takes more and more to produce less and less effect. In such a context, a manager is called upon to play the morally corrupt role of a narcotics pusher, rather than the more beneficial role of an organizational physician.

Yet this is not all dysfunctional. It is a gross misunderstanding to view symbolic rewards as mere deception. In redressing a real or imagined grievance with a symbolic gesture, management, perhaps unwittingly, is taking its first step toward actually

---

alienation A term adopted by Marxism to describe the inevitable feeling of dissociation of industrial workers because of their lack of control over their work (thus making them ripe for revolution). The word has largely lost its Marxist meaning and now refers to any feelings of estrangement from one's work, family, government, society, and the like. In the context of politics and voting behavior, alienation refers to a voluntary dropping out of the political process, to nonvoting, to feelings of contempt or indifference toward government.

resolving the grievance. Responding to an employee demand with a symbolic reward simultaneously acknowledges the appropriateness of the demand and establishes its legitimacy. Once the legitimacy of a demand is established, its eventual achievement is practically preordained, though it may be many years in coming.

To attempt to deal with the question of employee participation in decision making on the plane of symbolic action, however, is not to deal with the question at all. It is merely a delaying tactic, and delay becomes less and less of an option as public sector unions take ever-increasing interest in participatory management. Therefore, the manager sincerely interested in increasing productivity and decreasing **turnover** will adopt one of the remaining two stratagems: participation implemented by management from above or participation implemented in cooperation with an employee organization such as a union.

Theory X and Theory Y

Psychologists have long been noted for their studies of human and animal motivation. Why else have so many rats gotten so lost in so many mazes? But the operative discipline in organizational motivation is philosophy. The sincerity and rigor of the motivation of employees toward their duties is a direct reflection of management's philosophy toward them. That an operative philosophy is neither written down nor formally stated is irrelevant to its existence. Many organizations have commendable formal managerial philosophies. Reams upon reams of paper have been dedicated to espousing an official view of what an idyllic place the jurisdiction is in which to work. The only problem with these fine-sounding philosophies is that they are seldom operational, tending to exist only on paper. Subordinates soon perceive the reality of the situation.

All managerial philosophies are premised upon a set of assumptions about human behavior. Douglas McGregor, through his 1960 book *The Human Side of Enterprise*, popularized the contending concepts of managerial philosophy with his now famous Theory X and Theory Y sets of assumptions. McGregor hypothesized that a manager's assumptions about human behavior predetermined his administrative style. Because of the dominance of traditional theory in managerial thought, many managers had long accepted and acted upon a set of assumptions that are at best true of only a minority of the population. McGregor labeled as Theory X the following assumptions:

1. The average human being has an inherent dislike of work.
2. Most people must be coerced or threatened with punishment to get them to put forth adequate effort.
3. People prefer to be directed and wish to avoid responsibility.

Theory X sounds very much like a traditional military organization, which is in fact where it comes from. While McGregor's portrait of the modern industrial citizen can be criticized for implying greater pessimism concerning human nature on the part

---

turnover The rate at which employees leave an organization—usually expressed as a percentage of all workers who resign or are fired each year.

of managers than is perhaps warranted, Theory X is all the more valuable as a memorable theoretical construct because it serves as such a polar opposite of Theory Y, which assumes the following:

1. The expenditure of physical and mental effort in work is as natural as play or rest.
2. A person will exercise self-direction and self-control in the service of objectives to which he is committed.
3. Avoidance of responsibility, lack of ambition, and emphasis on security are generally consequences of experience, not inherent human characteristics.
4. The capacity to exercise a relatively high degree of imagination, ingenuity, and creativity in the solution of organizational problems is widely, not narrowly, distributed in the population.

Of course, these differing philosophic orientations are extremes for purposes of example. Most work situations would require a mix rather than a simplistic acceptance of either construct. Nevertheless, assumptions shape destiny; they tend to create self-fulfilling prophecies. Just as it has been shown in experiments with schoolchildren that a teacher's attitude toward any given child helps to determine that child's classroom performance, so it has been shown in similar studies that management's attitude toward workers has the same effect. Simply put, if management assumes that employees are "no damn good" and acts upon these assumptions, their employees are going to live down to management expectations.

Different philosophies are appropriate to differing organizational environments and work situations. The philosophy appropriate to a military combat unit would hardly be suitable for a research program in computer science. Unfortunately, the environment in which a public sector personnel program tends to operate frequently mitigates against the development of a coherent managerial philosophy. The most basic reason for this is external to the nature of the individuals comprising the organization. While private organizations typically exist in response to a specific goal, the objectives of public organizations are seldom as definite. It has frequently been shown that the professed objectives of a public organization are only vaguely related to its actual mission. For example, the goal of a correctional institution may be reform, but the organization's specific mission is more likely to be simply that of detention. The goal of a police department may be to enforce all of the laws of the community, but its specific mission is more likely to be the maintenance of public order. One goal of a public personnel unit may be to find the best qualified managers for its agency, but its specific mission in some cases may be limited to processing the papers of those candidates with prior **political clearance**. When the public policy process is so schizophrenic, it is little wonder that it is difficult or impossible for coherent managerial philosophies to emerge.

---

political clearance The process by which qualified applicants for both patronage and merit system appointments are hired only after there is an appropriate indication of partisan political sponsorship. While it is illegal to require political clearance for merit system appointments, it remains a common practice.

How can organizational policies premised on one set of rhetorical conditions be implemented in a real world operating on contradictory premises? It is a gross understatement to assert that this aspect of public management tends to severely hinder the development of comprehensive managerial strategies and objectives. This is one of the reasons that management by objectives (see Chapter 9) has not been able to provide a comprehensive answer to the need to set direction in the public sector. Objectives in public administration tend to fall victim to expediencies. Many organizational objectives in government tend to be inherently unstable in reaction to the dynamics of the political process.

By the end of the 1960s, the basic relationship between people and the organizations they work in was being redefined from the old world of dependence to the new world of codependence. The whole focus of organization management began to shift from executive control to executive nurturing of the people, groups, and relationships in the organizational environment. The new goal of management was less leadership than the unleashing of the previously stifled energies and creativities of the organization. This trend was fine as far as it went. But a happy organization is not necessarily the most productive one.

In this scene from *Ben-Hur*, the Roman officers discuss using a kind of Theory X management style to motivate the galley slaves. Later in this scene, the Roman general played by Jack Hawkins (standing left) walks over to slave number 41—Charlton Heston, in the title role—and offers this eternal bit of motivational advice: "There is hate in your eyes, Number 41. That's good. Hate keeps a man alive." Unfortunately, getting your subordinates to hate you is a much-used, if inadvertent and too often ineffectual, management technique.•

The Future of Organizations

Be assured—organizations have a future. What that future will be is far more difficult to predict. But change is inevitable. Here are the major trends that will have impact on government organizations in the years ahead.

Postbureaucratic Organizations

In 1952 administrative historian Dwight Waldo prophesied a future society in which "bureaucracy in the Weberian sense would have been replaced by more democratic, more flexible, though more complex, forms of large-scale organization." Waldo called such a society "postbureaucratic." However, it remained for Warren G. Bennis, in the 1960s, to make the term particularly his own with a series of articles and books predicting the "end of bureaucracy." In its place, Bennis wrote in *The Temporary Society*, "There will be adaptive, rapidly changing temporary systems. These will be task forces composed of groups of relative strangers with diverse professional backgrounds and skills organized around problems to be solved." The various task forces would "be arranged in an organic, rather than mechanical, model, meaning that they will evolve in response to a problem rather than to present, programmed expectations." Thus employees would "be evaluated not vertically according to rank and status, but flexibly according to competence. Organizational charts will consist of project groups rather than stratified functional groups."

Bennis wasn't a voice in the wilderness. Many other organization analysts of the time (such as Leonard Sayles, George Berkley, and Victor Thompson) were making similar noises. But it remained for **future shock** theorist Alvin Toffler, in his 1970 worldwide bestseller *Future Shock*, to give the popular name to the postbureaucratic

TABLE 7.1   Alternatives to the Bureaucratic Paradigm

The Bureaucratic Agency	The Customer-Driven Agency
Focuses on own needs	Focuses on customer needs
Defined by the resources it controls	Defined by results it achieves for customers
Controls costs	Creates value
Sticks to routine	Responds to changing customer demands
Fights for turf	Competes for business
Follows standard procedures	Builds choice into operating systems
Separates thinking from doing	Empowers all front-line employees

SOURCE: Adapted from Michael Barzelay, *Breaking Through Bureaucracy* (Berkeley: University of California Press, 1992).

---

future shock Alvin Toffler's term, from his book *Future Shock*, for the "distress, both physical and psychological, that arises from an overload of the human organism's physical adaptive systems and its decision-making processes. Put more simply, future shock is the human response to overstimulation."

lack of structure: "ad hocracy"—a contraction of **ad hoc** and bureaucracy—for "the fast-moving, information-rich, kinetic organization of the future, filled with transient cells and extremely mobile individuals."

Is the bureaucratic form of organization on an inevitable road to extinction? Is it being replaced by systems of temporary democratic networks or structures without hierarchical layers of authority, responsibility, and accountability? If so, the trend is not apparent yet. The announcement of bureaucracy's death seems, once again, to be premature—or at the very least, as in Mark Twain's case, "greatly exaggerated." Actually, bureaucracy appears to be holding its own quite well in practice—even if not in the mainstream literature of organization theory. Within the discipline of public administration, defenders (such as Kaufman, Krislov, and Goodsell) have emerged who justify the bureaucratic form of organization both for its efficiency as well as for its promotion of equity and representativeness.

Elliot Jaques emerged as the foremost defender of the hierarchical-bureaucratic form of organization in the 1990s. Jaques contends that those who argue against hierarchy are "simply wrong, and all their proposals are based on an inadequate understanding of not only hierarchy but also human nature." Hierarchical layers add value to organizations by separating tasks into manageable series of steps: "What we need is not some new kind of organization. What we need is managerial hierarchy that understands its own nature and purpose." According to Jaques, hierarchy is *the* best alternative for large organizations: "We need to stop casting about fruitlessly for organizational Holy Grails and settle down to the hard work of putting our managerial hierarchies in order." Well said!

The enduring strength of the hierarchical structure is elegantly illustrated by Leon E. Panetta, a U.S. representative from California who became President Clinton's first director of the Office of Management and Budget. After the president realized that there was much validity in the widespread criticism about how the White House was managed, he promoted Panetta to chief of staff in 1994. Panetta thereupon set about creating the most ancient of organizational structures for the White House. According to *New York Times* reporter Alison Mitchell, "Panetta set about creating a hierarchy, with himself and his two deputies . . . at the top. He instituted a 7:30 A.M. meeting for a handful of senior staff members—the restrictiveness of the meeting sending a message about the chain of command." There's nothing like a chain of command for creating organizational order out of chaos—even at the White House.

So if the traditional hierarchy (which is all that most people think of when they hear the word "bureaucracy") continues to hold its own, what will happen to all these highly structured government agencies aching for reinvigoration? After the polemical bashing of bureaucracies by angry politicos and "end of bureaucracy" futurists subsides, what will remain is a kernel of reform that calls for traditional bureaucracies to be transformed into customer-driven service organizations. In *Breaking Through Bureaucracy,* Michael Barzelay outlines the new-style government organization that offers "responsive, user-friendly, dynamic, and competitive providers of valuable

---

ad hoc A Latin term meaning "temporarily, for this one time." It is sometimes used to criticize methods that substitute for standard procedures.

services" as the alternative to traditional Weberian bureaucracy. In essence, modern government bureaucracies are fighting a two-front war. They are being denounced from without at the same time they are being reformed from within.

Postmodernism

Nothing is changing bureaucracies—both public and private—faster than postmodernism, an "ism" that embraces constant change and accepts as a new fact of life that large organizations today are living on the edge, on the boundary between order and chaos. In this context, however, "chaos" is not synonymous with "anarchy." Instead, it refers to a pervasive condition of unpredictability and complexity. The chaos and uncertainty of this approaching postmodern era has been accompanied by—and accelerated by—rapidly advancing information technology, particularly information networks. In the space of only a few years, information technology has evolved from mainframes to personal computers, local area networks, remote bulletin boards, information networks, and the Internet—the "information superhighway."

We have been experiencing technological advancement, however, almost since time began. Is something different happening now? The answer is a resounding yes. Information—and information technology—can extend human mental capability. We are not certain, though, what effects information technology will have on interpersonal relations, working teams, and thus organizations as we know them. Emerging forms of communication technology already are spanning time and space. The differences between information technology in premodern, modern, and postmodern organizations can be illustrated by examining the changing nature of the passport. This ubiquitous document is of ancient origins. It is essentially an instruction from the ruler (the state) to allow the bearer to "pass" through the "port"—the gateway to a city whether on a waterway or a highway. In the modern period it became a small printed book with pages for visa stamps and personal information about the bearer (address, next of kin, etc.). A suspicious-looking traveler might have his or her passport closely inspected to see if the seals on it were authentic or forgeries. The traveler's name might be checked against a list of undesirables. But today's postmodern passports may contain encrypted information on an attached plastic strip allowing immigration officials access to much of the bearer's life and medical history. Or the document can be matched with information from a worldwide network of data that reveal even more about the bearer. What do officials do with all this information? What implications are here for the abuse of civil liberties? The postmodern passport illustrates both the potentialities as well as the dangers of a total information age.

Information networks that tap into (and simultaneously update) real-time databases are providing empowered, self-managing work teams with the information they need to schedule and coordinate their own tasks as well as discipline their own members. Layer upon layer of supervisors and middle managers that are no longer needed are being eliminated. The traditional hierarchy (remember Moses in Chapter 5) was created in the first place so that information could be efficiently communicated up and down the line (often, the line of battle). If all of the organization members now (because they are each online in the computer sense) instantly have the same information, the traditional communicators—the hoards of middle managers—are, at the very least, less necessary if not totally superfluous.

Information networks in the postmodern era are raising vexing questions that tax existing theories of organization. Those postmodernists who consider themselves deconstructionists (because they intellectually take things apart to analyze their parts) like to think of organizations not as entities in their own right but just simply as a web of relationships. To them an organization can have no goals; it is simply the vehicle by which individuals pursue their personal goals.

Technology and postmodernism also raise questions about the experience of people who work in—or around—organizations. Will Warren Bennis's prediction finally come true? Will bureaucratic organizations as we know them disappear because they are unable to adapt to rapidly changing environments? Will working at home and "telecommuting" become the norm for some public service occupations? If so, how will government employees be held accountable for their time? Can trusting relations be established through interpersonal communications along the information highway in cyberspace?

Old, familiar machine analogies of organization simply do not apply in the postmodern era. The texture of the relationships between individuals, their work, and their organization is changed irreversibly by information technology. Shoshana Zuboff, in her book *In the Age of the Smart Machine,* describes this irreversible change in the texture of work relationships in her account of a visit to a large bank's offices: "I witnessed a sight that would eventually become so familiar as to defy notice—an entire floor of people seated at their partitioned workstations, staring into the screens of desktop terminals. . . . Many [of these] people voiced distress, describing their work as 'floating in space' or 'lost behind the screen.' They complained that they were no longer able to see or touch their work." Zuboff "saw that a world of sensibilities and expectations was being irretrievably displaced by a new world."

The Problem of Technocracy

Organizations today must wrestle with complex dilemmas about participating in this "new world" where the workers who once interacted face to face with other people now "float in space" and stare at computer screens instead of faces. In 1965 Don K. Price formulated a new hypothesis on the impact of decisional authority. In his book *The Scientific Estate,* he posited that decisional authority inexorably flowed from executive to technical offices. Consequently, a major distinction had to be made between the legal authority to make a policy decision and the technical ability to make the same decisions. Price's work predated John Kenneth Galbraith's *The New Industrial State* (1967), in which Galbraith made a similar claim for the decisional processes of the large corporations. This theme is destined to be a continuing one in the study of public administration, involving the dilemmas of control of power, information, and technical expertise—what many writers have called the problem of technocracy.

Zuboff, in newly expanding upon this old problem of technocracy, coined the term *informate* to highlight a duality that is central to the issues and dilemmas of this postmodern world. Technology can be used to automate operations using the same logic that was in place before the automating was initiated. This use of technology, to "automate," enables a task to be performed with more control and predictability than when it was performed by humans. Automation, then, is a logical, evolutionary extension of the work begun by Frederick Taylor and the scientific management movement early in the twentieth century.

Although "automating" represented an information technology revolution in the 1960s, it does not now. In contrast, "informating" is concerned with "radical changes as it alters the intrinsic character of work" and requires the adoption of new concepts of authority. Zuboff contends that the coming of the "information age" will require us to critically revisit our notions of systems, power, authority, accountability, and the role of people in organizations. An organization that merely automates is locked into the predictability and control system logic of the modern era. An organization that informates has the potential to adapt to the changes and uncertainties of the postmodern era.

The Core Themes of Postmodernism

Organization theorist William Bergquist has analyzed postmodernism extensively: "In many ways, postmodernism is a fad—and is at the same time about fads. Even though postmodernism is characterized by superficial, facile, and often internally contradictory analyses, it must not be dismissed, for these analyses offer insightful and valuable (even essential) perspectives on and criticisms of an emerging era." Bergquist identifies the four core themes of postmodernism:

1. *Objectivism versus constructivism:* "Objectivism"—which predominated in the modern era—is "rational." It assumes that there is an objective reality that can be discovered. "Constructivism," which is a postmodern phenomenon, "believe[s] that we construct our own social realities. . . . There are no universal truths or principles, nor are there any global models of justice or order. . . . Ways of knowing may themselves change over time and in differing situations."

2. *Language as reality:* Language, and the use of verbal symbols and signs, is more than a means for communicating information about reality. It is (at least a part of) reality. "The language being used to describe . . . elusive and changing reality is itself a major source of this social construction."

3. *Globalization and segmentalism:* "According to the postmodernists, our world is becoming progressively more global, while at the same time becoming progressively more segmented and differentiated." At the same time that information technology is allowing us to know more about our commonalties with people around the world, we seem to have lost our sense of community and organization. Thus perhaps we live in an era of "contradiction between globalism and localism in many aspects of our daily lives."

4. *Fragmented and inconsistent images:* "Postmodernists are enthralled with the superficial and the trendy." Virtual-reality machines "convey the sense of depth, yet like holographic devices, they actually replicate only the surface, never the depth of the experience. We are tricked into believing that we have experienced depth or virtual reality when in fact we have seen only the surface."

These four themes represent the central realities of a fragmented and inconsistent postmodern world. "The modern manager sees systems as the ultimate tool for making sense out of chaos." In contrast, "the postmodern manager sees chaos as what is to be managed and systems, though very useful, as merely one aspect of the chaotic environment. To the postmodern manager chaos is not bad. It is what is."

The postmodern world can be extremely frightening to people of traditional bureaucratic sensibilities. There is something comforting about knowing, quite literally, where you stand in your organizations and what your duties are. The premodern, modern, and postmodern organizational worlds will continue to live side by side for the foreseeable future—sometimes even in the same overall organization. The post office, for example, has premodern door-to-door mail delivery, it has modern automated mail-sorting operations, and somewhere in the depths of its research and development operations it has postmodern units trying to discover a role for the Postal Service on the Internet. In the premodern world land was the dominant form of capital. In modern times money and buildings became more important. In the postmodern world information is the new capital. This is why Bill Gates of Microsoft, the world's leading computer software company, is now the richest person in America.

Postmodern Public Administration

So far we have been discussing postmodernism within the context of organizations. But there also exists another context for postmodernism under the rubric of postmodern public administration. This perspective takes the view that the **logical-positivism** of the social sciences that has evolved since the **enlightenment** is, according to H. George Frederickson and Kevin Smith "simply misguided." After all, facts, the building blocks of logical-positivism, are mute. They do not really speak for themselves. "Facts represent propositions or hypotheses derived from observation. In the telling of facts, therefore, the observer is not only an active shaper of the message sent but also an active shaper of the likely image received." This frame of reference whereby a fact exists on two planes at the same time, in reality and in the mind of the person perceiving it, is known as phenomenology. This is why the essence of postmodern public administration is a concern for the semantics of a situation (or the "text," both as written and as perceived). This means that postmodernists must study both the real facts and the facts as perceived—which may be unreal but real to the observer.

Postmodern public administration represents a bundle of theories about perceptions and the social construction of reality. It offers a unique way of thinking about social and administrative problems rather than a bundle of techniques for resolving them. Such issues as the transformation of governance structures that we discussed

---

logical-positivism An approach to scientific explanation that emphasizes empirical methods and uses quantitative analysis wherever appropriate to logically create formal explanations for the phenomena under study.

enlightenment The seventeenth- and eighteenth-century European intellectual movement that advocated reason, as opposed to God, as the prime means by which the human condition could be understood and improved.

in Chapter 3 are a prime focus of postmodern public administration. Given the complexities of relationships between multilevel governments and nongovernmental organizations, postmodern public administration attempts to provide resolution to the problems brought on by transforming systems. But understanding is the first step in resolution.

A Feminist Perspective

Viewing organizational behavior from a feminist perspective is important for two reasons. First, there is an ever-increasing body of literature on the different ways that the genders operate in organizations. Any managers, whether male or female or from the private or public sector, who are ignorant of this perspective are figuratively walking into an unmarked minefield. No matter how careful they try to be, they will eventually step on something that will do them great harm. Reinforcing the importance of this first reason is the simple fact that women in the United States are an ever-increasing majority of public sector workers. Women constituted 24 percent of all public officials and administrators in 1970. By 1990 they constituted 59 percent. The growth of women in government is not only at low-level positions, but also in professional and administrative capacities. The Office of Personnel Management (OPM) found that between 1992 and 2002 the percentage of women in management-level jobs increased by 15 percent. While the current gender makeup of government employment demonstrates the increasing role of women, the future appears to hold even greater promise for the presence of women in the field of public administration. According to U.S. Department of Education data published in the *Chronicle of Higher Education* (June 9, 1995), women are earning bachelor's degrees in public administration and related service areas at more than three times the rate of men. More recently, the Council of Graduate Schools found that in 2001, three out of every four public administration graduate students were women. However, if you deduct the number of foreign students in these degree fields, who are almost all men, then the percentage of female predominance in America is even greater. So we may conclude that a feminist perspective on public administration is important because this profession is being feminized in the most literal sense possible.

Feminist organizational analysts such as Joan Acker have argued that long-standing male control of organizations has been accompanied and maintained by male perspectives of organization theory. Thus it has been mainly through male lenses that we see and analyze organizations. At least four sets of gendered processes perpetuate this male reality of organizations:

1. Gender divisions that produce gender patterning of jobs

2. Creation of masculine organizational symbols and images

3. Interactions characterized by dominance and subordination

4. "The internal mental work of individuals as they consciously construct their understandings of the organization's gendered structure of work and opportunity and the demands for gender-appropriate behaviors and attitudes"

Ordinary activities in organizations are not gender-neutral. They perpetuate the "gendered substructure within the organization itself and within the wider

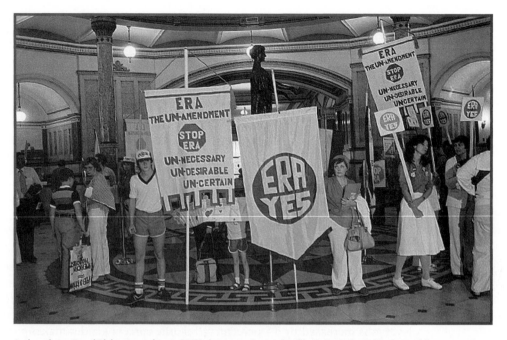

Anti–and pro–Equal Rights Amendment (ERA) demonstrators at the Illinois State Capital in 1980. This proposed amendment to the U.S. Constitution was passed by Congress in 1972. It said in part: "Equality of rights under the law shall not be denied or abridged by the United States or any state on account of sex." At first, the ERA seemed headed for quick passage. By the end of 1972, over 22 states had ratified it. But when it became apparent that the ERA would eventually become law, a conservative opposition organized against it. It argued that the ERA would not only subject women to a potential military draft but also to combat duty, and that women would lose the legal advantages they hold under many state domestic-relations law and labor codes. As the ERA became more controversial, fewer states moved to ratify it. On March 27, 1982, the final deadline, three states were still needed for ratification, and the ERA was dead. The women's movement thought that the ERA was essential for legal equality at work. But so many barriers have been broken down by the sex discrimination prohibition of the Civil Rights Act of 1964 as amended that, in retrospect, the ERA seems far less essential than it did at first.•

society"—as well as in organization theory. So what do we do about this? One option is to do nothing. Just wait—and consider lung cancer. It used to be that lung cancer was pretty much a male problem. Then women started smoking as much as men. Since lung cancer takes a few decades to develop, it takes a while to catch up. But "progress" is slowly being made. Complete equality, thanks to continued cigarette advertising and government subsidies of tobacco farmers, is approaching ever nearer.

What happened with women and lung cancer is also happening today in organizations. As women increasingly climb the organizational ladders, they leave their mark—they gradually change the culture. Substantial research has already shown that women tend to have different management styles from men. For example, Judy B. Rosener, an expert in the area of women and men at work, has shown women to be more cooperative and to share leadership; they are less apt to use the traditional authoritarian "command and control" militaristic style so favored by men. The

> ### BOX 7.2 The Assertions of Feminist Theory
>
> Feminist theory asserts that women's influence in the workforce will result in significant changes in the workplace:
>
> - Organizational hierarchies will become less rigid.
> - Organizational climates will become more cooperative, less competitive, and less aggressive.
> - Values of trust, openness, and acceptance will replace the quest for individual power.
>
> SOURCE: Mary E. Guy, "The Feminization of Public Administration," in *Public Management in an Interconnected World*, eds. Mary Timney Bailey and Richard T. Mayer (New York: Greenwood Press, 1992).

greatest beneficiaries of the last three decades of affirmative action hiring policies have been women. The seed has been planted. Organizations, as they are increasingly impacted by feminine management styles, will gradually change their operating styles to reflect ever-increasing female influences. The alternative hypothesis is that instead of making their organizations more hospitable to feminine management culture, the women managers—subject to the same stimuli for increased production as men have traditionally been—will become more like the men, will adapt more masculine attitudes because that is the way to thrive in the competitive environment of organizational life.

According to Camilla Stivers, in her book *Gender Images in Public Administration*, "As long as we go on viewing the enterprise of administration as genderless, women will continue to face their present **Hobson's choice**, which is either to adopt a masculine administrative identity or accept marginalization in the bureaucratic hierarchy." So the leaders of today's organizations have three options: (1) do nothing and wait for the problem to resolve itself over time, (2) intervene to consciously create organizations more hospitable to women, or (3) hope that managerial women will be content to become more like men. These options are not mutually exclusive. Time inexorably moves on. Considerable progress is constantly being made. In the end, the best hope is that women will not necessarily become the organizational infighters that men traditionally have been but that a mutual accommodation will evolve.

For a point of reference on the role of gender in public administration, Stivers examines the effect of strict gender roles during the progressive era in her book *Bureau Men, Settlement Women: Constructing Public Administration in the Progressive Era*. During the government reform movement of the early twentieth century, the

---

Hobson's choice A dilemma; a difficult decision; a choice of only the lesser of two evils. No choice at all is the original meaning. Thomas Hobson (1544–1631) ran a stable in England. When someone came to rent a horse, Hobson made him take the next horse in line.

policy innovativeness of women social workers was not brought into the emerging field of public administration, thus making the field unnecessarily rigid. Stivers argues that the reliance on the scientific management approach that was part of the traditional male-dominated public administration limited the growth of the field and we should be careful not to let such situations repeat themselves.

✦ A CASE STUDY: THE DANGERS OF GROUPTHINK FROM PEARL HARBOR TO THE WAR IN IRAQ

In a classic 1951 article "Effects of Group Pressure upon the Modification and Distortion of Judgments," Solomon Asch described his investigations into the ways individuals cope when a group's majority opinion is contrary to the facts of a situation. Asch put lone experimental subjects in rooms with people who had been instructed to give blatantly wrong answers to factual questions—for example, saying a chair was green when it was obviously blue. Only the experimental subjects did not know what was going on. Although a slim majority of subjects retained their independence and reported the facts accurately, a sizable minority of them altered their judgment to match that of the majority. When faced with a group opinion that was obviously wrong, they were not willing to report what they saw. They changed their minds.

Asch's experiments provided dramatic evidence of group impacts on people in organizations. From a managerial perspective, they showed why it is extremely important to focus attention on a work group's beliefs, values, and composition. But for the most part, informal groups are outside of the formal organization's direct sphere of influence.

Twenty years after Asch's experiments, Irving Janis published his now even better-known study on "groupthink." Like Asch, Janis explored pressures for conformance—the reason why social conformity is encountered frequently in groups. But unlike Asch's experimental use of college students, Janis looked at high-level decision makers at the time of the following major fiascoes:

- The 1941 failure to prepare for the Japanese attack on Pearl Harbor. This brought the United States into World War II.
- The 1950 decision during the Korean War to send General Douglas MacArthur to the Yalu River, the boundary between North Korea and China. This provoked Chinese intervention and expanded the war.
- The 1961 decisions to allow an American-sponsored invasion of Cuba by expatriate Cubans trained by the CIA to overthrow the government of Fidel Castro. The landing at the Bay of Pigs was a total failure and a major embarrassment to the Kennedy administration.

Groupthink is "the mode of thinking that persons engage in when concurrence seeking becomes so dominant in a cohesive in-group that it tends to override realistic appraisal of alternative courses of action." Thus a "desperate drive for consensus at any cost . . . suppresses dissent"—and information that might encourage or support dissent as well. The organizational culture that allows groupthink also stifles information.

Janis identified eight easily observable symptoms of groupthink that lead to incompetent—and sometimes disastrous—decisions:

1. An illusion of invulnerability
2. Collective construction of rationalizations that permit group members to ignore warnings or other forms of negative feedback
3. Unquestioning belief in the morality of the in-group
4. Strong, negative, stereotyped views about the leaders of enemy groups
5. Rapid application of pressure against group members who express even momentary doubts about virtually any illusions the group shares
6. Careful, conscious, personal avoidance of deviation from what appears to be a group consensus
7. Shared illusions of unanimity of opinion
8. Establishment of mind guards—people who "protect" the leader and fellow members from adverse information that might break the complacency they shared about the effectiveness and morality of past decisions

The groupthink phenomenon is hardly limited to high-level decision makers in the government. Groupthink tends to occur when individuals value membership in a group and identify strongly with their colleagues. It may also occur because the group leader does not encourage dissent or because of stressful situations that make the group more cohesive. In essence, group members suppress doubts and criticisms about proposed courses of action, with the result that the group chooses riskier and more ill-advised policies than would otherwise have been the case. Groupthink, because it refers to a deterioration of mental efficiency and moral judgment due to in-group pressures, has now developed an invidious connotation.

Janis concluded that groupthink has a negative influence on executive decision making because it leads to an overestimation of the group's capabilities and a self-imposed isolation from new or opposing information and points of view. Note that there is nothing new about groupthink. For example, what happened at the Bay of Pigs in 1961 is in groupthink essence no different from what happened to the Spanish Armada's attempted invasion of England in 1588. In both cases leaders (John F. Kennedy and Philip II of Spain) expected small landings of hostile forces to lead to a general uprising against the established regime. False intelligence led to false premises that, in turn, led to failed invasions. In the cases concerning the Pearl Harbor attack and the Korean War, false intelligence was not the issue. Here there was plenty of intelligence. The failure was to accurately interpret and act upon it.

What's really new about groupthink is that we can now label it with an official social science word. Kennedy speechwriter Theodore C. Sorensen, in his biography of his old boss, quotes the president in assessing his judgment on the Bay of Pigs: "All my life I've known better than to depend on the experts. How could I have been so stupid, to let them go ahead?"

Groupthink seems to have played a major role in the decision to go to war with Iraq. The major justification for the war was the fallacious assumption that Iraq had weapons of mass destruction. This was something that "everybody" believed. The few dissenting voices were ignored or dismissed as uninformed. Nevertheless, after it became evident that the dreaded weapons did not exist, the Bush administration simply took the view that while it was wrong on this point, the war was still more than justified on other grounds. This attitude, as well as the ever-increasing number of American dead and wounded in the war, has led to a steady decline in public opinion support of the war as well as a concomitant decline in the president's personal popularity.

For Discussion: *What are the major factors that lead to groupthink in any organization? Is groupthink only of historical interest, or is it still a common occurrence in government?*

Summary

Organizational behavior examines individuals, groups, and the relationships among them within their organizational environments. Typically, people are clustered in work groups; when a group, such as a branch office, becomes institutionalized in an organization, it evolves shared beliefs, values, and assumptions—norms that become the essence of a cohesive group and of an organizational subculture. Formal groups are officially created by a larger organization. Informal groups are formed through spontaneously developed relationships.

Organization development is planned organizational change necessitated by the fact that organizations exist in a dynamic environment, both internally and externally, to which they must respond or become ineffectual. This process is especially difficult to implement in the public sector because top management, which must first be committed to the process, is so fractured.

As a form of organization, bureaucracy has many advantages; nevertheless, the behavioral consequences of bureaucratic structure are often negative. Because structure stresses depersonalized relations and authority gained by virtue of position, individual ideas and opinions are often valued not according to their intrinsic merit but according to rank.

While there always has been consensus about the need for motivated employees, the same cannot be said for beliefs about how to induce higher levels of motivation. The Hawthorne experiments provided the first major empirical challenge to the scientific management notion that the worker was primarily an economic animal who worked solely for money. Abraham H. Maslow took these findings a step further with his "needs hierarchy." Based on this, Douglas McGregor developed his Theory X and Theory Y sets of managerial assumptions.

Postbureaucratic organizational theorists predict a future society in which traditional bureaucracy is replaced by more flexible forms of large-scale organization. Nevertheless, the hierarchical-bureaucratic form of organization is still highly defended because of its ability to add value to organizations by separating tasks into manageable series of steps.

Two new forces are rapidly changing the organizational world. Postmodernism, with its acceptance of unpredictability and complexity, is being accelerated by rapidly advancing information technology. And as women increasingly climb organizational ladders, they are changing organizational cultures, causing them to be more cooperative and less militaristic.

Review Questions

1. How does an understanding of group dynamics help managers motivate their subordinates more effectively?
2. How do the organizational change techniques called for by the action research model facilitate more capable organizational arrangements?
3. What are the pros and cons of bureaucratic impersonality?
4. Why is Maslow's needs hierarchy considered to be the foundation for all subsequent research on organizational motivation?
5. In terms of overall policy and management practices, how much difference would it make if women were in charge of all major government organizations?

Key Concepts

bureaucrat bashing Either justified criticism or inappropriate condemnation of public employees.

bureaucratic dysfunctions The pathological elements of bureaucratic structures that often make them inefficient in operation; the pressures on workers to conform that cause them to adhere to rules as an end rather than a means.

bureaucratic impersonality The dehumanizing consequences of formal organizational structures eliminating personal and emotional consideration from organizational life so that the individual bureaucrat functions only as a cog in an ever-moving machine.

group cohesion The shared beliefs, values, and assumptions of a group that allow it to function as a team.

group dynamics The subfield of organization behavior concerned about the nature of groups, how they develop, and how they interrelate with individuals and other groups.

Hawthorne experiments The late 1920s and early 1930s management studies undertaken at the Hawthorne Works of the Western Electric Company near Chicago. Conducted by Elton Mayo and his associates from the Harvard Business School, they became the most famous management experiments ever reported.

motivation An amalgam of all of the factors in one's working environment that foster (positively or negatively) productive efforts.

needs hierarchy Abraham H. Maslow's five sets of goals or basic needs arranged in a hierarchy of prepotency: physiological needs (food, water, shelter, etc.), safety needs, love or affiliation needs, esteem needs, and the need for self-actualization.

organization development An approach or strategy for increasing organizational effectiveness. As a process it has no value biases, but it is usually associated with the idea that effectiveness is found by integrating the individual's desire for growth with organizational goals.

postbureaucratic organization Constantly changing temporary organizational systems; task forces composed of groups of relative strangers with diverse skills created in response to a special problem rather than to a continuing need.

postmodernism The belief that constant change is a new fact of life for large organizations that are living on the edge, on the boundary, between order and chaos.

technocracy A contraction of "technical" and "bureaucracy," which refers to the high-tech organizational environments of the postmodern world.

Theory X The assumptions that the average human being has an inherent dislike of work, that most people must be threatened to get them to put forth adequate effort, and that people prefer to be directed and to avoid responsibility.

Theory Y The assumptions that work is as natural as play, that workers can exercise self-direction and self-control, and that imagination, ingenuity, and creativity are widespread.

Bibliography

Acker, Joan. (1992). "Gendering Organizational Theory." In *Gendering Organizational Analysis*, A. J. Mills and P. Tancred, eds. Newbury Park, CA: Sage.

Argyris, Chris. (1964). "T-Groups for Organizational Effectiveness." *Harvard Business Review* (March–April).

———. (1957). *Personality and Organization*. New York: Harper and Row.

Asch, S. E. (1951). "Effects of Group Pressure upon the Modification and Distortion of Judgments." In *Groups, Leadership, and Men*, H. S. Guetzkow, ed. Pittsburgh, PA: Carnegie Press.

Barnard, Chester I. (1938). *The Functions of the Executive*. Cambridge, MA: Harvard University Press.

Barzelay, Michael. (1992). *Breaking Through Bureaucracy*. Berkeley: University of California Press.

Bennis, Warren G. (1966). *Changing Organizations*. New York: McGraw-Hill.

Bennis, Warren G., and Philip E. Slater. (1969). *The Temporary Society*. New York: Harper Colophon Books.

Bergquist, William. (1993). *The Postmodern Organization: Mastering the Art of Irreversible Change*. San Francisco: Jossey-Bass.

Berkley, George E. (1971). *The Administrative Revolution*. Englewood Cliffs, NJ: Prentice Hall.

Bernstein, R. J. (1992). *The New Constellation: The Ethical-Political Horizons of Modernity/Postmodernity*. Cambridge, MA: MIT Press.

Blau, Peter, and Marshall Meyer. (1971). *Bureaucracy in Modern Society*. New York: Random House.

Clegg, S. (1990). *Modern Organizations: Organizational Studies in the Postmodern World*. Newbury Park, CA: Sage.

Drew, Elizabeth. (1996). *Showdown*. New York: Simon and Schuster.

Drucker, Peter F. (1988). "The Coming of the New Organization." *Harvard Business Review* (January–February).

Ford, Dan. (1979). *Pappy: The Life of John Ford*. Englewood Cliffs, NJ: Prentice Hall.

Fox, Charles J., and Hugh T. Miller. (1995). *Postmodern Public Administration: Toward Discourse*. Thousand Oaks, CA: Sage.

Frederickson, H. George, and Kevin B. Smith. (2003). *The Public Administration Theory Primer*. Boulder, CO: Westview Press.

Gallagher, Winifred. (1994). "How We Became What We Are." *Atlantic Monthly* (September).

Goodman, P. S., and L. S. Sproull, eds. (1990). *Technology and Organizations*. San Francisco: Jossey-Bass.

Goodsell, Charles T. (1994). *The Case for Bureaucracy*, 3rd ed. Chatham, NJ: Chatham House.

Guy, Mary. (1992). "The Feminization of Public Administration." In *Public Management in an Interconnected World*, Mary Timney Bailey and Richard T. Mayer, eds. New York: Greenwood Press.

Hayles, N. I., ed. (1991). *Chaos and Order: Complex Dynamics in Literature and Science*. Chicago: University of Chicago Press.

Herzberg, Frederick. (1964). "The Motivation-Hygiene Concept." *Personnel Administration* (January–February).

———. (1966). *Work and the Nature of Man*. Cleveland, OH: World.

Hoesterey, I., ed. (1991). *Zeitgeist in Babel: The Post-Modernist Controversy*. Bloomington: Indiana University Press.

Janis, Irving L. (1972). *Victims of Groupthink*. Boston: Houghton Mifflin.

Jaques, Elliot. (1990). "In Praise of Hierarchy." *Harvard Business Review* (January–February).

Kaufman, H. (1977). *Red Tape*. Washington: Brookings Institution.

Keil, L. Douglas. (1995). *Managing Chaos and Complexity in Government*. San Francisco: Jossey-Bass.

Kellert, Steven H. (1993). *In the Wake of Chaos: Unpredictable Order in Dynamical Systems*. Chicago: University of Chicago Press.

Krislov, S., and D. H. Rosenbloom. (1981). *Representative Bureaucracy and the American Political System*. New York: Praeger.

Kurtz, Howard. (2005). "Dressed for Success, Primed for Failure." *Washington Post* (November 4).

Liddell Hart, B. H. (1972). *Why Don't We Learn from History?* New York: Hawthorn Books.

Mayo, Elton. (1933). *The Human Problems of an Industrial Civilization*. New York: Viking.

McGregor, Douglas M. (1960). *The Human Side of Enterprise*. New York: McGraw-Hill.

Merton, Robert K. (1957). *Social Theory and Social Structure*. New York: Free Press.

Mitchell, Alison. (1995). "Panetta's Sure Step in High-Wire Job." *New York Times*, (August 17).

Osborn, Alex F. (1953). *Applied Imagination*. New York: Scribner's.

Price, Don K. (1965). *The Scientific Estate*. Cambridge, MA: The Belknap Press of Harvard University Press.

Rheingold, H. (1993). *The Virtual Community*. Reading, MA: Addison-Wesley.

Roberts, Rand, and James S. Olson. (1995). *John Wayne: American*. New York: Free Press.

Rosener, Judy B. (1995). *America's Competitive Secret: Utilizing Women as a Management Strategy*. New York: Oxford University Press.

Sayles, Leonard R., and Margaret Chandler. (1971). *Managing Large Systems*. New York: Harper and Row.

Schein, Edgar H. (1969). *Process Consultation: Its Role in Organization Development*. Reading, MA: Addison-Wesley.

Sorensen, Theodore C. (1965). *Kennedy*. New York: Harper and Row.

Sproull, L. S., and P. S. Goodman. (1990). "Technology and Organizations: Integration and Opportunities."
In *Technology and Organizations*, P. S. Goodman and L. S. Sproull, eds. San Francisco: Jossey-Bass.

Stivers, Camilla. (1993). *Gender Images in Public Administration: Legitimacy and the Administrative State*. Newbury Park, CA: Sage.

———. (2002). *Bureau Men Settlement Women: Constructing Public Administration in the Progressive Era*. Lawrence, KS: University of Kansas Press.

Suid, Lawrence. (1978). *Guts and Glory: Great American War Movies*. Reading, MA: Addison-Wesley.

Thompson, Victor A. (1961). *Modern Organization*. New York: Knopf.

Toffler, Alvin. (1970). *Future Shock*. New York: Random House.

Truman, David B. (1951). *The Governmental Process*. New York: Knopf.

Villa, D. R. (1992). "Postmodernism and the Public Sphere." *American Political Science Review* 86.

Waldo, Dwight. (1952). "Development of Theory of Democratic Administration." *American Political Science Review* 44 (March).

Weick, Karl E. (1990). "Technology as Equivoque: Sensemaking in New Technologies." In *Technology and Organizations*, P. S. Goodman and L. S. Sproull, eds. San Francisco: Jossey-Bass.

Wills, Garry. (1977). *John Wayne's America*. New York: Simon and Schuster.

Wilson, James Q. (1989). *Bureaucracy*. New York: Basic Books.

Zuboff, Shoshana. (1988). *In the Age of the Smart Machine: The Future of Work and Power*. New York: Basic Books.

Recommended Books

French, Wendell L., and Cecil H. Bell. (1995). *Organizational Development: Behavioral Science Intervention for Organization Improvement*, 5th ed. Englewood Cliffs, NJ: Prentice Hall. Everything you always wanted to know about how to do organizational development.

Kaufman, Herbert. (1977). *Red Tape: Its Origins, Uses and Abuses*. Washington, DC: Brookings Institution. A very engaging account of the bureaucratic origins of red tape; after defining this elusive term, Kaufman assesses its pros and cons.

Lipsky, Michael. (1980). *Street-Level Bureaucracy: Dilemmas of the Individual in Public Services*. New York: Russell Sage Foundation. Many were genuinely surprised when the author first asserted that public employees who interacted directly with the public—police, social workers, etc.—were also, by default, the makers of bureaucratic policy, albeit on a small scale but with vast implications for accountability.

Ott, Steven J., Sandra J. Parks, and Richard B. Simpson. (1996). *Classic Readings in Organizational Behavior*. New York, NY: Wadsworth. A thorough collection of the key works in the field of organizational behavior.

Wilson, James Q. (2000). *Bureaucracy: What Government Agencies Do and Why They Do It*. New York: Basic Books. A now classic analysis of bureaucratic behavior in a wide variety of institutional settings; might have been retitled "everything Max Weber would have said about modern bureaucracy if he were still alive and working as an American professor of public administration."

Related Web Sites

Abraham Maslow
www.nidus.org/
American Society for Quality
www.asq.org.
Center for Collaborative Organizations
www.workteams.unt.edu/
Journal of Managerial Psychology
www.mcb.co.uk/cgi-bin/journal1/jmp
People management
www.peoplemanagement.co.uk/index.html

Performance Management Network
www.pmn.net/
Society for Industrial and Organizational
Psychology
www.siop.org/
Section for Women in Public Administration
www.carbon.cudenver.edu/public/gspa/swpa/
archives.html

CHAPTER 8

Managerialism and Performance Management

•KEYNOTE: SOCRATES DISCOVERS UNIVERSAL MANAGEMENT

In ancient Greece, Socrates was busy establishing the intellectual foundations of modern educational testing when he discovered that "the unexamined life is not worth living." Still, he found time to argue for the universality of management, that a successful business leader could be an equally effective general. Universal or generic management refers to management practices that are equally applicable in the public, private, and

nonprofit sectors. The underlying doctrine holds that a properly trained manager will be effective in any type of organization, whether public or private, whether in service or manufacturing.

In a dialogue recorded by Socrates' disciple Xenophon, an experienced soldier named Nicomachides complains to Socrates about being passed over for promotion to general despite "having received so many wounds from the enemy" [as he says this, he opens his cloak to reveal his scars] in favor of a businessman "who has never served in the heavy-armed infantry and who indeed knows nothing but how to get money."

Socrates tells the brave soldier that a leader who "knows what he needs, and is able to provide it, [can] be a good president, whether he have the direction of a chorus, a family, a city, or an army."

"By Jupiter, Socrates," cried Nicomachides, "I should never have expected to hear from you that good managers of a family [business] would also be good generals."

"Come, then," proceeded Socrates, "let us consider what are the duties of each of them, that we may understand whether they are the same, or are in any respect different."

"By all means."

"Is it not, then, the duty of both," asked Socrates, "to render those under their command obedient and submissive to them?"

"Unquestionably."

"Is it not also the duty of both to intrust various employments to such as are fitted to execute them?"

"That is also unquestionable."

"To punish the bad, and to honor the good, too, belongs, I think to each of them."

"Undoubtedly."

"And do you think it for the interest of both to gain for themselves allies and auxiliaries or not?"

"It assuredly is for their interest."

"Is it not proper for both also to be careful of their resources?"

"Assuredly."

"And is it not proper for both, therefore, to be attentive and industrious in their respective duties?"

"All these particulars," said Nicomachides, "are common alike to both; but it is not common to both to fight."

"Yet both have doubtless enemies," rejoined Socrates.

"That is probably the case," said the other.

"Is it not for the interest of both to gain the superiority over those enemies?"

"Certainly; but to say something on that point, what, I ask, will skill in managing a household avail, if it be necessary to fight?"

"It will doubtless in that case, be of the greatest avail," said Socrates, "for a good manager of a house, knowing that nothing is so advantageous or profitable as to get the better of your enemies when you contend with them, nothing so unprofitable and preju-dicial as to be defeated, will zealously seek and provide everything that may conduce to victory, will carefully watch and guard against whatever tends to defeat, will vigorously engage if he sees that his force is likely to conquer, and, what is not the least important point, will cautiously avoid engaging if he finds himself insufficiently prepared."

Socrates, in listing and discussing the duties of all good leaders—of public as well as private institutions—emphasized their similarities. He then states that "the conduct of private affairs differs from that of public concerns only in magnitude; in other respects they are similar." Socrates concludes that "those who conduct public business make use of men not at all differing in nature from those whom the managers of private affairs employ; and those who know how to employ them conduct either public or private affairs judiciously, while those who do not know will err in the management of both." His is the first known statement that managerial competence was transferable. Thus a manager who could cope well with one type of organization would be equally adept at coping with others, even though their purposes and functions might be widely disparate. Ever since, the generalist manager has been an ideal.

Socrates was not the only ancient Greek to provide significant insights into modern management. Plato, a student of Socrates, is often considered to be the first political scientist. His *Republic* (360 B.C.E.) is the Western world's first systematic analysis of the political process. There he provided an intellectual rationale for the "divine right of kings" even before Christianity sanctioned the notion. To Plato, only an elite of philosopher kings or "guardians" had the political wisdom necessary to govern; he would not have been an equal opportunity employer. His just society was one where each person had a predetermined place—with the guardians on top. Yet, in essence, Plato's elitism is a call for professionalism—a challenge to his contemporaries who thought that no training or aptitude was necessary to manage public affairs.

In his *Politics,* Aristotle, a student of Plato, wrote of the division of labor, departmentalization, centralization, decentralization, and delegation of authority. But most importantly he presented the first comprehensive analysis of the nature of a state and any other political community. To Aristotle, the state was a natural development because "man is by nature a political animal." The state was even more important than family because, while a family exists for comfort, the state can be a vehicle for glory and the good life.

Perhaps Aristotle's most famous analytical construct is his classification of the three basic forms of government. He found that every political community had to be governed by either the one, the few, or the many. This corresponds to his three governing types: kingship, aristocracy, and polity (majority rule). Unfortunately, each of these had its perversions, the conditions to which it degenerated when the rulers ceased ruling in the interests of the whole community. Kingship often degenerated into tyranny; aristocracy (rule by a talented and virtuous elite) into an oligarchy (rule by a small group in its own interest); and a polity or constitutional system (where a large middle class rules for the common interest) into democracy (mob rule in the interests of the lower classes). Overall, Aristotle favored a mixed constitution—one in which all citizens "rule and are ruled by turn," where no class monopolizes power and a large middle class provides stability.

It is only in this last situation that administrative institutions evolve to be responsive to the needs of the mass of the citizenry. Still the Greeks limited citizen participation. Manual workers, merchants, and other "disreputable" types (including large numbers of slaves) were excluded from citizenship. Because work itself was disdained, no professional corps of administrators emerged. The relatively few citizens, competent or not, took turns managing the public's business. As Pericles said in his funeral oration over the Athenians who died in the Peloponnesian War, "We are called a democracy, for the administration is in the hands of the many and not of the few." The Athenians assumed that all citizens would participate in government. Pericles proudly asserted that "we are the only people to regard the man who takes no interest in politics not as careless, but as useless." Thus it made sense to them that most offices were filled by lot for short terms. Effectively, the gods decided who did what. However, some offices such as treasurer or military commander were elected—they were simply too important to give the gods free rein. As any student of Greek mythology knows, the gods often proved to be perverse.

In the Bible it is written that "greater love hath no man than this, that a man lay down his life for his friends" (John 15:13). In this 1787 depiction of *The Death of Socrates* by French artist Jacques-Louis David, Socrates is explaining to his followers why he is expressing love for them by laying down his life (by drinking hemlock, a poison) for the public administrative institutions of his state, the city of Athens. Socrates, as the inventor of the Socratic method of seeking truth by a constant, nagging questioning of facts and values, had so annoyed most of his fellow citizens that they condemned him with the expectation that he would then voluntarily exile himself—and pester citizens of another city with his questions. Socrates always took pride in his service to the state as a soldier in the famous battle of Marathon and as a citizen gadfly and critic. He was too respectful of the institutions of his government to disdain them by exiling himself. So he tells his distraught followers that he is about to drink the hemlock as his final duty as a citizen. Or maybe he was just ravaged by the illnesses of old age and tired of living. All we know for sure is that Socrates remains the archetype of a great teacher—even when he quite literally (as in this picture) points out his final lesson: that government-mandated suicide is an acceptable way of dealing with adverse administrative edicts. •

Aristotle's most famous student was Alexander the Great. He did not write any books; he just used what Aristotle taught him and conquered the world. But because he never created an institutional foundation for his empire, it dissipated shortly after his death. The Greeks simply lacked the knack—lacked the doctrine—for large-scale administrative structures. They never got beyond the city-state. So it was relatively easy for the better organized Romans to take them over in the middle of the second century B.C.E. It just goes to show that in the game of chutes and ladders that is the rise and fall of civilizations, the better organized—those who have the best public administration doctrine—win. And it has been that way since the beginning of recorded history. Aristotle might just as well have said that "man is an administrative animal" because states do not get very far politically or militarily unless they also develop administratively.

For Discussion: *What is the validity of Socrates' core argument in favor of the universality of management? Is management as universal and generic today as it was at the time of Socrates?*

Managerialism

In the 1960s and 1970s there was a vast expansion in the intellectual development and technical capabilities of public administration. The new tools of program evaluation and policy analysis, with quantitative precision, called into question the efficacy and utility of long-standing public programs—especially those having to do with social services and education. New budgeting techniques—from **PPBS to zero-based budgeting**—meant that political executives and legislators could better see, if not better control, where money was spent. The traditional management focus was expanded to include greater emphasis on strategic planning (see Chapter 9), and **internal control** and ethical responsibility (see Chapter 5). Nevertheless, in spite of all these advances in the art and science of public administration, the 1980s became a period of decline in the public service—declining budgets, declining productivity, declining quality of services, and the declining reputation of the public service itself. In response a new doctrine—managerialism—would emerge and ride, if not to the rescue, then at least into the fray.

PPBS Planning, programming, budgeting systems; a budgeting process that requires agency directors to identify program objectives, to develop methods of measuring program output, to calculate total program costs over the long run, to prepare detailed multiyear program and financial plans, and to analyze the costs and benefits of alternative program designs.

zero-based budgeting A budgeting process that is, first and foremost, a rejection of the incremental decision-making model of budgeting. It demands a rejustification of the entire budget submission (from ground zero), whereas incremental budgeting essentially respects the outcomes of previous budgetary decisions (collectively referred to as the budget base) and focuses examination on the margin of change from year to year.

internal control The sum of the many diverse procedures that management uses to administer an agency, from accounting systems to training programs.

Managerialism as a term has long been used by sociologists as referring to the economic and bureaucratic elites that run an industrial society. **James Burnham**, in his 1941 *The Managerial Revolution,* announced that the world was in transition *"from* the type of society which we have called capitalist or bourgeois *to* a type of society which we shall call *managerial."* Burnham asserted that as control of large businesses moved from the original owners to professional managers, society's new governing class would be not the traditional possessors of wealth—but those who have the professional expertise to manage, to lead, those large organizations. The same phenomenon was occurring at roughly the same time in the Communist world. **Milovan Djilas** wrote in his 1957 *The New Class* that instead of producing a classless society, the Communists had developed a new class system consisting of party officials, managers of the nationalized industries, and bureaucrats. These people, especially those near the top, were the only ones in the Communist states to have any power. They used the repressive forces of the state, especially the secret police, to ensure total obedience. This enabled them to enjoy a standard of living vastly higher than ordinary members of society. And they were able to pass on this privilege to their children. Even though they could not legally own much more than ordinary citizens, access to high-quality education and easy entrance to prestige jobs guaranteed their children the same status that they possessed themselves. Thus they constituted an upper social class, albeit a nontraditional one.

In the 1980s managerialism, now a well-established sociological "ism," took on new connotations. When Margaret Thatcher began her 11-year stint as British prime minister in 1979, she immediately sought to refocus the civil service from policy toward management. Thus she tried to force the bureaucracy to be more responsive to the needs of its customers (into which citizens were to be transformed). Managerialism, entrepreneurial management that goes beyond participative management to unleash the creative abilities of public managers at all levels, became the prevailing public sector doctrine. As a philosophy of continuous reform, it seeks to prevent an organization from ever degenerating into incompetence. Paradoxically, managerialism is also a retreat from participative management in that it romantically assumes that a managerial elite can radically change and control the direction, culture, and purpose of organizations. The romance of managerialism would not be possible if there were not heroes to romanticize. Who are these new-style heroes? The answer is, the managers themselves, who have come to revitalize the public service by slaying the dragons of self-serving unions and inefficient bureaucrats. Plato would have felt right at home with these modern philosopher-kings.

A New Managerial Revolution

The core theme of managerialism is management rights—giving managers enough room to maneuver so that they can accomplish their goals. This additional managerial

---

James Burnham (1905–1987) The professor of philosophy at New York University who, after an early career as a Communist of the anti-Stalinist, Trotsky type, became a leading conservative writer who advocated defeating and rolling back the Soviet Empire.

Milovan Djilas (1911–1995) The Yugoslavian vice president whose writings attacking European Communism cost him his job and earned him a lengthy stay in jail.

room is necessarily taken from the **rank and file**. Thus managerialism is quite comfortable with authoritarian management styles and a new version of scientific management—except the search for the "one best way" has been updated to the constant installation of the latest in behavioral and mechanistic technologies. In an effort to gain maximum control of personnel costs, and minimal problems with introducing labor-saving technologies, managerialism seeks to contract out to the private sector as much of the public's business as it can. The techniques of administrative improvement advocated by managerialism, such as management audits and program evaluations, are comparatively old. What's new is that these same old techniques, like the same old tanks (remember the 1940 blitzkrieg discussed in Chapter 6), are being reinvigorated by a new doctrine or guiding philosophy.

It is no longer sufficient for a public manager to be the traditional "neutral gun for hire" passively performing the tasks set by political masters. In 1923 Charles G. Dawes, the first modern budget director of the U.S. government (and later vice president from 1925 to 1929), explained the traditional concept of neutral competence thusly: "If Congress . . . passed a law that garbage should be put on the White House steps, it would be our regrettable duty, as a bureau, in an impartial, nonpolitical and nonpartisan way to advise the Executive and Congress as to how the largest amount of garbage could be spread in the most expeditious and economical manner."

Policy Entrepreneurs

Today such an attitude by a senior administrator would find him or her in bad odor—and not just because of the garbage. Modern public managers are expected to be policy entrepreneurs who forcefully develop, argue for, and yes, sell, creative solutions to vexing problems. Current thinking calls for the most aggressive actions on the part of administrators to fight the never-ending threats of waste, fraud, and **abuse**. These modern crusaders go into the administrative battles shouting their slogans in the same manner that the French revolutionaries of 1789 chanted, "Liberty, Equality, Fraternity." But today's administrative chant, also of French etymological origin, is reengineering, empowerment, and entrepreneurialism.

The current horde of administrative revolutionaries preach as if they are the first to ever see the light of divine bureaucratic guidance. But none of this is new. Franz Kafka, the preeminent novelist of bureaucratic oppression, warned us that "every revolution evaporates, leaving behind only the slime of a new bureaucracy." In a parallel sense, every revolution in management thinking and dogma leaves in its wake only the slime of a new vocabulary.

---

rank and file A colloquial expression for the masses. When used in an organizational context, it refers to those members of the organization who are not part of management; those who are the workers and have no status as officers. *Rank and file* was originally a military term referring to the enlisted men who had to line up in ranks, side by side, and files, one behind the other. Officers, being gentlemen, were spared such indignities.

abuse The furnishing of excessive services to beneficiaries of government programs, violating program regulations, or performing improper practices—none of which involves prosecutable fraud. Fraud, a more serious offense, is the obtaining of something of value by unlawful means through willful misrepresentation.

Reengineering

Reengineering is an old-fashioned reorganization with a college education. Traditional reorganization calls for changes in the administrative structure or formal procedures of government that do not require fundamental constitutional change or the creation of new bodies not previously established by the legislature. Many reorganizations are undertaken for the purposes of departmental consolidation, executive office expansion, budgetary reform, and personnel administration—primarily to promote bureaucratic responsiveness to central executive control and, second, to simplify or professionalize administrative affairs. Of course, all those contemplating a major reorganization should first heed John Kenneth Galbraith's timeless advice: "When things are not good, it is usually imagined that a review, or possibly a reorganization, will make things better. No one ever asks whether the best is being made of a lousy situation."

Radical as Opposed to Incremental Change

The "message" of reengineering is that all large organizations must undertake a radical reinvention of what they do, how they do it, and how they are structured. There is no room for incremental improvement—for small and cautious steps. Organizations need to quit asking, "How can we do things faster?" or "How can we do our current work at the lowest cost?" The question needs to be "Why do we do what we do—at all?" In *Reengineering the Corporation*, reengineering proselytizers Michael Hammer and James Champy claim that reengineering "is to the next revolution of business what the specialization of labor was to the last." It is the process of asking, "If I were recreating this company today, given what I know and given current technology, what would it look like?" More formally, reengineering is the "fundamental rethinking and radical redesign of business processes to achieve dramatic improvements in critical, contemporary measures of performance, such as cost, quality, service, and speed." Thus reengineering is the search for new models for organizing work.

Reengineering takes reorganization beyond its traditional focus by seeking to totally rethink and refocus how programs are managed and to take maximum advantage of new technology—especially computers. Laudable intentions indeed! But neither reorganization nor reengineering happens in a political vacuum. Harold Seidman, in *Politics, Position, and Power,* warns that all potential reengineers should be aware of the strong relationship between the organization of a legislature and its executive branch. "One could as well ignore the laws of aerodynamics in designing an aircraft as ignore the laws of congressional dynamics in designing executive branch structure. What may appear to be structural eccentricities and anomalies within the executive branch are often nothing but mirror images of jurisdictional conflicts within the Congress." Legislative and executive branch organizations are "interrelated and constitute two halves of a single system."

The most famous warning on reorganization applies equally to reengineering. It is usually attributed to Petronius Arbiter, a Roman writer of the first century: "I was to learn later in life that we tend to meet any new situation by reorganizing;

and a wonderful method it can be for creating the illusion of progress while producing confusion, inefficiency, and demoralization."

Note that Hammer and Champy's best-seller contains a reformulation of what has been known since ancient times. Remember the story of the Trojan horse, about how the besieging Greeks finally defeated the defenders of Troy in Asia Minor? For years the Greeks used conventional siege tactics to no avail. Then Ulysses said that the besieging Greeks had to completely rethink what they were doing. With the help of Minerva—the goddess of wisdom, no less—Ulysses reengineered the siege. The new approach was to feign abandoning the siege while leaving behind a wooden horse large enough to contain a squad of Greek soldiers inside. The Trojans, thinking the horse was a tribute from the fleeing Greeks, took it within their city's walls and had a party. Later that night the Greeks who were hiding inside the horse came out and opened the gates for their returning comrades. Then they sacked and looted Troy in the classic manner. Hammer and Champy could not offer a better example of a "fundamental rethinking and radical redesign" of a business effort. Ever since, Ulysses the reengineer has retained his reputation for cunning.

Becoming a Reengineer

Reengineering is as much a mental discipline and a philosophy as it is a process. The reengineer's primary skill is an ability to look at things such as work processes and organizational structures with new eyes. Reengineering is a radical change strategy, not an incremental "grass-roots" employee involvement approach. Reengineering literally means what its name implies. According to Hammer and Champy, "When someone asks us for a quick definition of business reengineering, we say that it means 'starting over.' It *doesn't* mean tinkering with what already exists or making incremental changes that leave basic structures intact. . . . It involves going back to the beginning and inventing a better way of doing work."

While there are various paths to reengineering, they all usually include the following three steps:

1. *Process mapping:* The flowcharting of how an organization presently delivers its services and products as a process. This emphasis on process is why reengineering is often called "process reengineering."

2. *Customer assessments:* The evaluation of the organization's customers' needs, both presently and in the future, by means of **focus groups**, surveys, and meetings with consumers of the organization's products and services.

3. *Process visioning:* A total rethinking of how the work processes ought to function, keeping in mind the latest available technology.

---

focus group A relatively small number (6 to 20) of people with a common characteristic brought to a neutral setting to participate in a discussion on products or politics led by a trained researcher. Focus groups are a major tool of marketing research. They allow analysts to delve deeply into the motivations for buying a product or voting for a politician.

The key to successful reengineering efforts is the ability to challenge the assumptions underlying the current system. Just as there are **barriers to entry** that face all new business ventures, there are a parallel set of barriers to reengineering. They include bureaucratic turf concerns, employee resistance to change, lack of incentives, and general skepticism about just another in a long line of reform efforts. But with a strategic commitment from top management, these barriers can be overcome. For example, a 1994 International City/County Management Association report illustrates how Charlottesville, Virginia, reengineered their process for issuing new business licenses to take less than a half-hour instead of two days; how Merced County, California, reengineered their social service eligibility process to take less than 3 days instead of the previous 40 days; and how Phoenix, Arizona, reengineered the time it took to get city property maps from five days to five minutes.

Robert M. Melia, as first deputy commissioner of the Massachusetts Department of Revenue, became a famous reengineer to many "deadbeat dads" in the early 1990s when he reengineered how past-due child support payments are collected. According to John Martin, because "there was no money for throwing more caseworkers at the problem . . . [Melia] forced the department to rethink child-support enforcement from the ground up—the essence of reengineering." Consequently, "these days, it's a computer, rather than expensive caseworkers, that handles the bulk of the commonwealth's child-support cases. The computer issues a single warning before proceeding to collect overdue child support anywhere it can: garnishing wages, raiding bank accounts and intercepting tax refunds, unemployment benefit checks, and lottery winnings." Collections have gone up 30 percent. But, more important, the average number of families leaving the welfare rolls because of improved child support is now double its previous monthly rate.

Reengineering, thinking from the ground up, is hardly new. In the nineteenth-century operetta *The Mikado* by Gilbert and Sullivan, the Mikado's (the emperor of Japan's) efforts at reengineering the Japanese judicial system are explained in Act 1: "Our logical Mikado, seeing no moral difference between the dignified judge who condemns a criminal to die, and the industrious mechanic who carries out the sentence, has rolled the two offices into one, and every judge is now his own executioner." Then as now, reengineering is merely a combination of applied logical and strategic will.

Empowerment

Power is the fuel of organizational life. It is what makes things go. It is relatively easy for managers to get the traditional authoritarian powers of domination that allow them to control and punish subordinates. What is far more difficult is obtaining the power needed for positive accomplishment. This kind of power is less formally given than informally earned—often by empowering others. Thus the paradox that

---

barriers to entry Impediments to further competition in an industry, whether they be legal (critical patents owned by others), economic (start-up costs too high), political (unstable government), or social (the market has established brand preference).

managers can often make themselves more powerful by giving power away. By empowering others, leaders actually acquire more "productive power"—the power truly needed to accomplish organizational goals.

Managers who cannot delegate, who will not trust or empower subordinates, become less and less powerful, and correspondingly more and more incompetent, as they increasingly seek to hoard power. Remember power, much as with money—a variant of power—is like manure: you have to spread it around for it to do any good. Perhaps the most common example of the dysfunctional withholding of power concerns the way managers are punished for not spending all of their budgeted funds. The typical punishment is to take away the money by reallocating the funds and then, to add insult to injury, budget less money during the next budget cycle. No wonder managers have become adept at spending their allocations down to virtually the last penny. Not only is this wasteful, but it discourages cost-cutting to achieve real savings and greater productivity. Empowering managers to control their budget savings is one of the main thrusts of the entrepreneurial management movement in the United States.

Nor are universities immune from this problem. University administrators seem constantly surprised when academic departments vote tenure for mediocre or marginally competent professors. This tends to happen when the administration maintains a policy of automatically taking budget authority for professional positions away from departments whenever a position becomes vacant. Thus, from the point of view of the department, a faculty slot filled by a mediocrity is better than being understaffed. So the department's tenure decision all too often is based not on merit or competence but on whether the individual in question is better than nothing.

Empowering Teams

Virtually all of the "new" approaches to management that are being advocated—the attempts to find solutions to the "productivity problem"—have blended traditional management methods with new forms of employee involvement and participative management. For the past two decades, we have witnessed a never-ending series of "new" management approaches, particularly approaches that emphasize organizational flexibility through the development and **empowerment** of individuals and work groups.

All of these team-based approaches assume that groups provide individuals with opportunities for personal and professional growth and self-expression and **job satisfaction**. They also assume that these opportunities cannot become available to workers in traditional hierarchical organizations. Groups provide structure and discipline for individuals at work. Therefore, organizations that permit empowerment do not need multiple levels of supervisors to coordinate, control, and monitor production.

---

empowerment Giving a person or organization the formal authority to do something.
job satisfaction The totality of an employee's feelings about the various aspects of his or her work; an emotional appraisal of whether a job lives up to an employee's values.

While empowerment is a proven means of enhancing productivity, Marc Holzer warns, "One danger in employee involvement, especially within the **TQM** envelope, is the extent to which it will parallel or bypass the union. In those cases the gains to be made through participation may run up against the losses resulting from political alienation of the union hierarchy." It is reasonable to conclude that the "most effective systems might involve both union and workplace committees. In both sectors the most effective organizations are those which treat unions as real partners, not imagined enemies. Excellent union relationships are especially important in the more heavily unionized public sector."

Entrepreneurialism

The last and potentially the most powerful element of the revolutionary credo is entrepreneurialism. This calls for managers to be transformational leaders who strive to change organizational culture. Each must develop a new vision for the organization—and then convert that vision into reality.

President George H. W. Bush was not a man to inadvertently create many new phrases. But "the vision thing" inadvertently became uniquely his own after he first complained about it in 1988 because he seemed to lack it, knew he seemed to lack it, and couldn't get it. This lack of vision created an image of domestic-policy incompetence that greatly contributed to his failure to win reelection in 1992. Perhaps President Bush should have paid more attention to the biblical Moses. There was a man with vision. He took a people who were slaves in Egypt and transformed them into an independent nation. Now we cannot all be a Moses and get our vision from a burning bush, but we can all avoid being a Bush with no vision. *AMEN!*

Entrepreneurial vision cannot and should not be limited to the top. At every organizational level managers need vision and dreams, need the ability to assess the situation and plan for a better future. Those who cannot do this, who cannot visualize and plan for change, are by definition incompetent. After all, organizations that do not change must eventually die—even in the public sector. Besides, if you don't have a dream—if you don't have a vision—how will you ever know if it comes true?

But be aware that the true believers of any philosophic system or ideology are often headed for a fall. This is nowhere more true than with theories of management. We constantly fool ourselves into thinking we're onto something really new until we discover that, for example, Socrates in ancient Greece espoused the merits of generic management, that Aristotle anticipated the underlying premises of organizational culture, and that during the Italian Renaissance Niccolo Machiavelli wrote *The Prince*, the first of an endless series of "how-to-succeed" books of management advice.

Too many organizations become infatuated with each new management fad and slick-talking consultant that comes along. They buy books for their managers, send

---

TQM Total quality management; processes to ensure that all aspects of an organization are performing at an optimal level.

them to training programs—and then expect them to manage by **MBO, OD, ZBB, QC, TQM,** and a host of other acronyms submerged in a bowl of alphabet soup.

But be careful of swallowing any of this soup whole. Both you and your organization could get a bad case of indigestion because management philosophy taken to extremes is one of the leading causes of incompetence. For example, the scientific management of Frederick Taylor was premised upon the notion that there was "one best way" of accomplishing any given task. The job of the line manager, then—once the "one best way" was found by the staff—was to impose this procedure upon the organization. The problem with traditional scientific management is its paternalistic "papa knows best" attitude. It presupposes that the managers have a monopoly on brains, that input from the workers is a distraction to be avoided. But every worker comes with a brain. Only an incompetent organization wastes or ignores this resource. Thus scientific management, a good idea in principle, becomes scientific incompetence when taken to extremes.

Public administration, and management in general, is newly concerned—indeed, newly obsessed—with an issue variously described as quality, competence, more bang for the buck, or meeting the needs of your customers. The whole thrust of this trend toward managerialism is with instilling a newfound sense of competence in organizations—to ward off the evils of incompetence. Unfortunately, competence and incompetence are two sides of the same trick coin. It is a trick coin because there is no common agreement on which side wins—no universal agreement on what constitutes either competence or incompetence. This problem is much like Supreme Court Justice Potter Stewart's famous dilemma over defining pornography. He asserted that while he could not define it, he nevertheless knew it when he saw it. Competence suffers from a similar problem of perception. After all, while one person may see obstructing red tape, another, looking at the same thing, may see a treasured procedural safeguard.

Perhaps the greatest example of the dangers associated with the entrepreneurial spirit in public administration can be found in Orange County, California, during the 1990s. Back in the soaring days of the stock boom, Orange County Treasurer Robert Citron attempted to cash in on the vibrant market through investing public funds in a particularly risky form of investments called derivatives. While Citron was responsible for the decision to invest in derivatives, he did so with the tacit consent of the county government. Citron had established a strong track record of robust returns from his investments. Those earnings had become an increasingly important

---

MBO Management by objectives; an approach to managing, the hallmark of which is a mutual setting—by both organizational subordinate and superior—of measurable goals to be accomplished by an individual or team over a set period of time.

OD Organization development; a process for increasing an organization's effectiveness. As a process it has no value bias, yet it is usually associated with the idea that maximum effectiveness is to be found by integrating an individual's desire for personal growth with organizational goals.

ZBB Zero-based budgeting.

QC Quality circles; small groups of employees working in the same organizational unit who, with the approval of management, voluntarily meet on a regular basis to identify and solve problems that directly affect their work.

part of the Orange County budget since the late 1970s, With such success at raising funds without raising taxes, it's not surprising that there came a relaxation of the rules surrounding how funds could be invested. For local government officials, the steady supply of investment revenue allowed them to "have their cake and eat it, too." However, in 1994 Citron's investment strategies began to fail, eventually leading to a loss of $1.6 billion and the bankruptcy of one of the most prosperous counties in the nation. In essence, the county was relying on Citron's entrepreneurial skills in making money and ignoring the risks that such entrepreneurial behavior entails.

Toward a Competitive Public Administration

The great flaw in managerialism is the logic by which it approaches reform. The problem is not so much the fine people who populate the public service but the systems under which they must work. Just bring in hardheaded managers, presumably with considerable private sector experience, and they will whip things into shape in no time. While it is always true that public service operations can be improved, it does not necessarily follow that the wholesale adoption of private sector tactics will do the job. What the would-be reformers so often forget is that government operations are not inefficient because stupid people work there; they are inefficient because they have been designed by the legislature to reflect the competing interests of patronage, representativeness, and due process. Efficiency has to take its turn with these other factors. And no upstart executive most recently from some hotshot corporation is going to push these other factors out of line—because they are just as much a part of the agency's legal mandate as efficiency.

This is why the managerialist impulse initially rode into town on the back of conservative or right-of-center governments such as the Reagan (U.S.) and Thatcher (U.K.) administrations of the 1980s. They both talked a better managerial game than they played. Nevertheless, their influence has been both lasting and ultimately bipartisan in that politically center and left-of-center governments in the early 1990s in the United States, Australia, and New Zealand, for example, have also adopted the essence of managerialism. As the guru of managerialism Christopher Pollitt has argued, "Managerialism is the 'acceptable face' of new-right theory concerning the state. . . . [It] provides a label under which private sector disciplines can be introduced to the public services, political control can be strengthened, budgets trimmed, professional autonomy reduced, public service unions weakened, and a quasi-competitive framework erected to flush out the 'natural' inefficiencies of bureaucracy."

The myriad managerialist intiatives have been favorably received by the public because of the general antipathy toward "the bureaucracy," the increasing reluctance of citizens to pay more taxes, the widespread belief (which is often erroneous) that privatization will cost the public less, and the fact that reform of whatever ilk is often good politics.

Practically all the managerialists' goals can be achieved by what has come to be known as **competitive public administration**. At all levels of government under regimes

---

competitive public administration Public sector policies that force different organizations to compete with each other for the opportunity to do the public's work. Thus private contractors compete with a government agency, government agencies compete with each other, and so on.

of vastly differing political philosophies, self-standing bureaucratic components such as building-maintenance staffs or trash-collection operations are being forced to compete in price with private sector contractors that are ready and willing to put the jobs in question into the private sector. Various **voucher systems** allow this same strategy to be applied to public education and housing—even free meals for the homeless. This Darwinian atmosphere of the "survival of the cheapest" is indeed introducing private sector discipline, strengthening political control, trimming budgets, and curtailing unionism and professionalism. What was once right wing is now mainstream. In the United States this is often referred to as the "reinventing government" movement after the book of that same title by David Osborne and Ted Gaebler.

A perennial theme in American politics is that government's administrative problems will be solved just as soon as some successful business leaders show those bureaucrats what's what. Yet managerialism's doctrine of transferability, this genericism that goes back to Socrates, when tried, has usually been far less successful than initially anticipated. Within private corporations, a parallel genericism has been equally destructive. As managers skilled in finance increasingly gained control of manufacturing corporations, products and eventually sales suffered. This problem of a top-management cadre skilled in juggling numbers but ignorant of how their products are made has become so great as to call into question the core beliefs of genericism. Indeed, there is now talk of what economist Robert Samuelson calls the "death of management," the death of the notion that a manager with an MBA (master of business administration) degree "should be able to manage any enterprise, anywhere, anytime."

The New Public Management

As a doctrine, managerialism continues to evolve, its essence having been distilled under the label "the new public management," which according to Christopher Pollitt has four main aspects:

1. A much bolder and larger-scale use of marketlike mechanisms for those parts of the public sector that could not be transferred directly into private ownership (quasi-markets)
2. Intensified organizational and spatial decentralization of the management and production of services
3. A constant rhetorical emphasis on the need to improve service "quality"
4. An equally relentless insistence that greater attention be given to the wishes of the individual service user/"consumer"

The new public management is ambitious. It is far more ambitious than the traditional management aspects of public administration (which can be called the

---

voucher systems A government program that issues redeemable vouchers to eligible citizens to purchase services on the open market. For example, housing vouchers have been suggested as an alternative to public housing, and education vouchers have been suggested as an alternative to public education. The idea of using vouchers was popularized by economist Milton Friedman in *Capitalism and Freedom* (1962).

BOX 8.1   The Ten Principles for Reinventing Government

1. Catalytic government: steering rather than rowing
2. Community-owned government: empowering rather than serving
3. Competitive government: injecting competition into service delivery
4. Mission-driven government: transforming rule-driven organizations
5. Results-oriented government: funding outcomes, not inputs
6. Customer-driven government: meeting the needs of the customer, not the bureaucracy
7. Enterprising government: earning rather than spending
8. Anticipatory government: prevention rather than cure
9. Decentralized government: from hierarchy to participation and teamwork
10. Market-oriented government: leveraging change through the market

SOURCE: David Osborne and Ted Gaebler, *Reinventing Government* (Reading, MA: Addison-Wesley, 1992).

"old" public management), and, according to Owen Hughes in *Public Management and Administration,* it is a "new paradigm" that heralds a major change in the role of government in society. Like any good paradigm, it seeks to replace the earlier model of public administration because that model "has been discredited theoretically and practically." While one can admire Hughes's intensity of feeling, it is difficult not to figuratively shout, "Don't throw out the baby with the bathwater!"

All reform movements seek vehicles for proselytizing, for educating new converts. The most prominent vehicle for this has been Osborne and Gaebler's *Reinventing Government.* This 1992 surprise best-seller has become the bible of the new public management movement. And just as the original Bible warns us that "there is no new thing under the sun" (Ecclesiastes), the Osborne and Gaebler bible preaches its gospels using ten principles. The ghost of Jomini reasserts itself! (See Chapter 6.)

Will these new principles "solve the major problems we experience with bureaucratic government," as their authors intend? To find out, stay tuned to another exciting chapter in the history of public administration! There is no official "new public management." No government has formally sanctioned a group of practices with that title. There only exists a disparate group of structural reforms and informal management initiatives that reflect the doctrine of managerialism and can usefully be grouped under the rubric of the "new public management."

Subsequent chapters will constantly return to these themes not because they are supplanting a "discredited" public administration, but because they are an almost expected revitalization of public administration in the tradition of the progressive movement that started more than one hundred years ago. The progressives got their name from the fact that they believed in the doctrine of progress—that governing institutions could be improved by bringing science to bear on public problems. It was a disparate movement, with each reform group targeting a level of government, a particular policy, and so on. Common beliefs were that good government was possible and that "the cure for democracy is *more* democracy." To achieve this, they only had to "throw the rascals out." And it was the progressive influence that initially forged the fledgling discipline of public administration.

Doctrines come and doctrines go, but public administration is always and inherently progressive. Managerialism, the new public management, and the reinventing government movements are just the latest landmarks on the yellow brick road of progressivism. All these reforms are like Macbeth's "poor player that struts and frets his hour upon the stage and then is heard no more." In 1933 Leonard D. White, the preeminent historian of American public administration, published *Trends in Public Administration,* in which he devoted several chapters to "the new management" that had evolved since 1900. In 1971 Frank E. Marini published his highly influential edited volume *Toward a New Public Administration.* New! New! New! But all this new stuff is just the reaffirmation of the progressive doctrine. There can be no end to the doctrine of public administration; there is only continuous doctrinal reform.

What Is Performance Management?

Performance management is what leaders do; it is the primary responsibility of an organizational leader. It is the systematic integration of an organization's efforts to achieve its objectives. What makes performance management different from mere management is this emphasis on systematic integration. Thus it includes the comprehensive control, audit, and evaluation of all aspects of organizational performance. The components of performance management are long-established management tools that encompass most of the other senses in which the term *performance* is used in the language of public sector management. These components include the following:

1. The specification of clear and measurable organizational objectives (i.e., management by objectives), which is the essence of strategic management (discussed in Chapter 9)

2. The systematic use of performance indicators, measures of organizational performance, to assess organizational output (this is closely linked to concepts of performance standards to allow the performance measured in one organization to be compared with industry averages, **best practice**, and benchmarking—the systematic comparison of performance between or among organizations)

3. The application of the performance appraisal of individual employees to assist in harmonizing their efforts and focusing them toward organizational objectives

4. The use of performance incentives, such as **performance pay**, to reward exceptional personal efforts toward organizational goals

5. The linking of human and financial resource allocation to an annual management or budget cycle

---

best practice The generally recognized optimal way of performing a task.
performance pay Extra compensation for extraordinary efforts on the job.

6. Regular review at the end of each planning cycle of the extent to which goals have been achieved and the reasons for performance that is better or worse than planned. This creates the feedback that helps start the cycle anew.

Most organizations operate within a calendar or management cycle. This, in its simplest terms, plots against a calendar the main management actions that must be taken in the coming year. As a minimum, such calendars normally record the meeting dates of the governing board of the body, if there is one, and dates surrounding the preparation, consideration, and finalization of the budget. This reflects the de facto role of the budget in many organizations as the central focus of decision making concerning resource allocation for the coming year. A management cycle not only forces decisions to be made with a calendar in mind, but it also serves as a conceptual

Figure 8.1   The Performance Management Cycle

diagram, which implies a logical interaction, sequencing, and, above all, linking of related categories of management activity. Moreover, a logical performance management cycle will indicate which classes of decisions must be made by which management actors—and when they must be made.

The Politics of Performance Management

Performance management begins with a plan. It is tempting to think of planning as a rational, linear, straightforward process of collecting and analyzing data, establishing and assigning priorities to strategic targets, assessing alternative methods for achieving ends, designing implementation programs, and evaluating programs so as to use the information to improve program and agency impact and performance. However, this is an illusion. Planning is neither straightforward nor linear. Planning never occurs in a vacuum; it is an inherently political process. Consequently, the success of a plan of any kind is often a function of the political astuteness of the planner. Things are still the same as they were in 1788, when Alexander Hamilton advised in *The Federalist*, No. 70, "Men often oppose a thing merely because they have had no agency in planning it, or because it may have been planned by those whom they dislike."

In the public sector, plans often begin out of political necessity. The citizens literally vote for the plans espoused by elected political executives in their campaign promises. For example, Jimmy Carter promised, if elected president, to implement zero-based budgeting. He was, and he did—but then his successor, Ronald Reagan, used an executive order to abolish zero-based budgeting for the federal government on his first day in office. Rudolph W. Giuliani ran for mayor of New York in 1993 and promised to reduce crime. During his first year in office, crime—especially the murder rate—declined. Whether this was caused by changing demographics or better police management, nobody really knows. What is certain is that the mayor—as any mayor would—took credit for the decrease. In 1994 the Republican Party offered a "contract with America" that would radically affect federal budgeting practices. Because of their electoral victory, many federal agencies had to begin planning for downsizing. And opposition party President Bill Clinton was no less ambitious with his reinventing government plans to significantly reduce federal employment.

Performance management plans do not have to wait upon elected officials. In the early 1990s the postmaster general did not have to run for office to hear the political winds blowing. All he had to do was read the newspaper accounts of increasing criticisms of mail services, of members of Congress calling for the dismemberment of the Postal Service, and of business leaders calling for an end to the government's first-class-mail monopoly. He got the message. Performance, meaning on-time mail delivery, started going up; complaints and calls for dismemberment started going down.

The most comprehensive adoption of performance management by the U.S. government to date has been the Government Performance and Results Act of 1993—sometimes known as just the "Results Act." This legislation is a typical performance management system in that it seeks to link resource allocations and results; improve program performance; provide better information for congressional policymaking;

force agencies to specify their missions, objectives, and strategies; and require them to advise Congress on just how they've gone about this.

A recent focus of performance management at the federal level has been toward the area of human resources. For many of the previously discussed areas of government performance it is necessary to retain quality employees. It has always been difficult for government to retain its most talented workers because of higher salaries found in private industries. While not able to compete in terms of salaries, government may be able to compete on issues such as flexible schedules and benefits. In 2005 comittees in Congress began work on the "Workforce Flexibility Act." This act is designed to provide government more flexibility in setting pay rates for employees, providing bonuses for recruitment and retention, and improving the management of training activities of government.

Management Control

Management information and **control** systems are instituted in public agencies for two primary reasons: (1) to allow administrators to find out what is going on in an organization (and in the environment as the result of an agency's activities) and thereby to manage the activities of others and (2) to respond to the need to report (to be accountable) to external groups. Control systems are employed to see whether plans are being executed as intended, to monitor goal-oriented behavior, and to make corrections when behavior or results veer from planned goals. This monitoring is essential because organizational goals, quite simply, often get lost. This happens in part because organizations, as artificial entities, cannot have true goals; only people can. And people, despite the fact that they create or join organizations with professed goals, all too often have goals of their own that do not coincide with the ostensible goals of the organization.

The more an organization's stakeholders, the people affected directly or indirectly by the organization's activities, work toward their own separate goals, as opposed to the "official" goals of the organization, the more incompetent the organization must necessarily become. Organizational goals get displaced when employees become more concerned with what they can get out of, as opposed to what they must contribute to, the organization. Thus, the most essential task of a manager—indeed, the "function of the executive," as Chester I. Barnard asserted—is to maintain the "dynamic equilibrium" between the needs of the organization and the needs of its employees.

Productivity Improvement

Productivity in private and public sector organizations has become the overriding issue in top-management suites as well as in the legislative corridors of power. The

---

control That aspect of management concerned with the comparison of actual versus planned performance as well as the development and implementation of procedures to correct substandard performance. Control, which is inherent to all levels of management, is a feedback process that ideally should report only unexpected situations.

ultimate aim of all performance management efforts is greater productivity. Productivity is a measured relationship between the quantity (and quality) of results produced and the quantity of resources required for the production of goods or services. Productivity is, in essence, a measure of the work efficiency of an individual, a work unit, or a whole organization.

Productivity Measurement

Measuring the productivity of any jurisdiction, organization, program, or individual is particularly problematic in the public sector because of the problem of defining outputs and of quantifying measures of efficiency, effectiveness, and impact.

Organizations that provide public services often have multiple and sometimes intangible outputs. In evaluating efficiency, selecting from among the many possible input/output ratios is troublesome. A considerable danger exists in selecting only certain input and output variables because a single efficiency measure may be, in truth, a meaningless or oversimplified measure of performance.

The productivity measurement issue is further complicated by the fact that different efficiency and effectiveness measures must be selected, depending on certain organizational variables: highly routine work versus nonroutine work, high or low degrees of employee discretion, and outputs that are standard, novel, or simple, as opposed to complex work processes. Another way of stating this problem is that from the variety of available productivity measures, those selected must differentiate between intermediate outputs (outputs used by other members of the organization) and final outputs (those absorbed by the outside environment) and between staff and line functions (some individuals/units perform support functions whose impact can be assessed only in terms of increased performance of line departments). Productivity measurement is beset by many obstacles, not the least of which is the insecurity felt by managers attempting to undertake productivity assessments.

And none of this is new. In 1776 Adam Smith in his *Wealth of Nations* wrote, "The labor of some of the most respectable orders in the society is, like that of menial servants, unproductive of any value, and does not fix or realize itself in any permanent subject or vendible commodity, which endures after that labor is past." The eternal problem is that in some areas, when government produces a service, the labor that goes into it cannot be measured as to impact and evaluated as to quality as if it were a manufactured product. Thus it is easy to measure and even improve government productivity when factory-like operations lend themselves to engineered **work measurement standards.** But service workers such as police officers, social workers, and grade school guidance counselors do not always create a product that is directly measurable except by broad **social indicators.**

---

work measurement standard A numerical value applied to the units of work an employee or group can be expected to produce in a given period of time.

social indicators Statistical measures that aid in the description of conditions in the social environment (e.g., measures of income distribution, poverty, crime, health, physical environment).

Barriers to Productivity Improvement

The barriers to increased public employee productivity are legion. They can often appear insurmountable: cumbersome and rigid civil service procedural rules that prevent management from reallocating and reorganizing work; a public personnel management approach that has created endless, cumbersome, inflexible systems of position descriptions, job classifications, testing, and equal employment opportunity and affirmative action requirements, which in combination have resulted in what Wallace Sayre called a "triumph of techniques over purpose"; union intransigence; and combinations of procedural and structural rules that inhibit management's ability to reward and punish workers for performance or lack thereof.

The public sector productivity problem also ties directly into the privatization debate. Again, there are assumptions about inferior public sector versus private sector productivity rates. Although researchers such as George W. Downs and Patrick D. Larkey have gone to great lengths to explain why these comparisons cannot be made, are not made correctly, and should not be made in the first place, the simple truth remains that the burden is on public sector organizations to demonstrate that they are not inferior in terms of their productivity. This is doubly difficult because productivity in the public sector frequently involves multiple client groups and conflicting objectives and priorities. In comparison, private sector counterparts like to make single horizontal comparisons and to stack one set of products or services against another.

Public sector organizations can certainly be faulted for not being willing to do productivity measurements, but one should be clear about both the context and reasons for that unwillingness. There are far too many system "disincentives" built into productivity measurement—from fears of having budgets cut, personnel levels trimmed, or other penalties for producing above budgeted levels to the serious measurement problems that are inherently biased against public sector goods and products.

There is yet another major difference to be considered. There is a common assumption that private sector organizations use productivity measurement and improvement in the same way public sector organizations do. They do not. Most private sector organizations use productivity measurement systems to assign more work, more responsibility, more financial reward, more capital resources, and more power to the units that demonstrate the highest levels of productivity. They do not cut the most productive units. Instead, they tend to give them more resources or more rewards. This also affects the investment strategy that goes into productivity improvement efforts. Most public sector organizations commission productivity efforts by assignment without up-front investment. In other words, staff members are reassigned or reprogrammed to take on productivity responsibilities. In short, productivity improvement endeavors must be financed internally. In contrast, private sector organizations expect to pay up-front costs to start a productivity measurement or participative management effort and then evaluate the results against total costs.

Because it traditionally has been so difficult for government organizations, already fiscally strapped, to find the funds to invest in productivity improvement efforts (especially new technology), many jurisdictions have created "innovation funds" to finance such ventures. For example, both the Internal Revenue Service and the state of Florida use this approach. The city of Philadelphia uses savings from

> ## BOX 8.2   The Emperor Caligula Finds a "Double Economy" in Government
>
> [In ancient Rome] the money went faster and faster and at last Caligula decided to make economies. He said one day, for instance, "What is the use of putting men in prison for forgery and theft and breaches of the peace? They don't enjoy themselves there and they are a great expense for me to feed and guard; yet if I were to let them go they would only start their career of crime again. I'll visit the prisons today and look into the matter." He did. He weeded out the men whom he considered the most hardened criminals, and had them executed. Their bodies were cut up and used as meat for the wild beasts waiting to be killed in the amphitheatre: which made it a double economy.
>
> SOURCE: Robert Graves, *I, Claudius* (New York: Modern Library, 1934).

cost-cutting for productivity improvement. Mayor Ed Rendell told the National Performance Review Staff, "We tell a department, 'You go out there and do good work. You produce more revenue. You cut waste. And we'll let you keep some of the savings of the increased revenue.'"

Traditionally, the mayor said, "Every nickel that they would have saved would have gone right back to the general fund. . . . They would have gotten a pat on the back, but nothing else." Now municipal departments can keep some of the money they save to finance productivity improvement projects. For example, when Philadelphia's Department of Licenses and Inspection generated $2.8 million more than expected in 1992, the city let the department keep $1 million of the savings to hire more inspectors, which in turn led to increased collections in subsequent years.

Total Quality Management

Although comprehensive productivity improvement movements have taken different shapes, developed much jargon, and took off in many directions in the 1980s and 1990s, the origins of all of them can be traced back to **W. Edwards Deming** and his 1950 trip to Japan. Deming, a New York University professor, was invited by Japanese executives to teach them his approach to **statistical quality control**. Joseph

---

W. Edwards Deming (1900–1993) The professor of management who developed his philosophy of customer service and statistical quality control while working at AT&T's Hawthorne plant (see Chapter 7) in the 1920s and 1930s.

statistical quality control A statistical technique for maintaining product quality at the desired level without 100 percent inspection. Statistical quality control uses acceptance sampling to determine whether a large lot of finished products meets preset quality levels. Using statistical techniques, a random sample is taken from a lot of goods and the sample is inspected. From this analysis, an inference as to the quality level of the entire lot is made. This technique is often used in conjunction with periodic inspection along the production line that permits corrective action to be taken before finally assembly of the product.

Juran, who emphasizes the "management" part of "quality," followed Deming to Japan in 1954. In turn, Armand V. Feigenbaum followed Juran with "total quality control" (TQC), a management approach that required all employees to participate in quality improvement activities—from the chair of the board to hourly workers.

By 1975, Japan had developed into the world leader in quality and productivity. In contrast, "quality teachings" were mostly ignored in the United States. According to Keki Bhote in *World Class Quality,* "Deming's popularity in Japan was in contrast to an almost total ignorance about him in the United States. . . . Deming remained in the quality wilderness of America for a whole generation."

If any one event can be said to have triggered the total quality movement in the United States, it was a June 24, 1980, NBC television documentary, "If Japan Can . . . Why Can't We?" The program documented Deming's experiences and successes in Japan. The response was overwhelming. Within months, hundreds of major U.S. corporations and government agencies had scrambled aboard the quality bandwagon. Quality circles—voluntary work groups that cut across organizational layers and boundaries to analyze and recommend solutions to organizational problems—appeared everywhere as if by magic.

In 1991 the U.S. Government Accounting Office defined "quality management":

> A leadership philosophy that demands a relentless pursuit of quality and the stamina for continuous improvement in all aspects of operations: product, service, processes, and communications. The major components of quality management are leadership, a customer focus, continuous improvement, employee empowerment. . . .

"How to Do It" TQM materials are now abundant, but Deming's 14 points of management is its most famous formulation. Note how Deming's "theory of TQM" is the intellectual descendant of Jomini's (see Chapter 6) principles of war—a road map for organizational, as opposed to military, victory. In *Out of the Crisis* Deming provides this 14-point guide, which we have paraphrased, for would-be quality managers:

1. Create constancy of purpose for improvement of product and service. (A long-term focus is thus essential.)

2. Adopt the new philosophy. (Be prepared for a total transformation.)

3. Cease dependence on mass inspections. (Quality must be built in; defects must be prevented rather than detected.)

4. End the practice of awarding business on the basis of price tag alone. (Low bids lead to low quality. Long-term relationships must be established with single suppliers.)

5. Improve constantly and forever the system of production and service. (Continuous improvement becomes a philosophy, not just a goal.)

6. Institute training. (Training at all organizational levels is a necessity, not an option.)

7. Adopt and institute leadership. (Managers must lead, not supervise.)

8. Drive out fear. (All employees must feel secure enough to express ideas and ask questions.)

9. Break down barriers between staff areas. (Work in organizations is inherently teamwork.)

10. Eliminate slogans, exhortations, and targets for the workforce. (Problems are caused by the system, not by individuals. Posters and slogans tend to create resentment.)

11. Eliminate numerical quotas for the workforce and numerical goals for people in management. (Production quotas yield defective products; replace work standards with intelligent leadership.)

12. Remove barriers that rob people of pride of workmanship. (The individual performance appraisal is a barrier, not an aid, to productivity.)

13. Encourage education and self-improvement for everyone. (Education never ends—for anybody at any level of the organization.)

14. Take action to accomplish the transformation. (Both top management and employee commitment is essential.)

Deming, being a quantitative type, loved to make lists. So while he offered 14 points to transform an organization, he also warned of 7 deadly diseases and 16 obstacles that tended to inhibit or altogether prevent such transformation. As Steve Wall, the director of Ohio's Office of Quality Services, told Jonathan Walters in *Governing,* "This [TQM] isn't about hitting home runs. This is about hitting single after single after single after single. You score a lot more runs that way." The problem is that too many managers want to use TQM just to hit a few home runs so they can look good and go on to higher positions.

TQM is further hampered by an emphasis on short-term profits (in the private sector) or short-term "looking good" results (in the public sector). The whole thrust of TQM is to change the organizational culture to one that values long-term, long-lasting effectiveness. This is why Deming finds short-term numerical ratings of productivity or individuals to be ineffective. Deming believes the effects of annual performance appraisals or management by numbers to be devastating. "Management by fear would be a better name." Such systems force managers to manage defects rather than lead toward constant quality.

Still the question must be asked, as Albert C. Hyde of the Brookings Institution puts it, "Is it a fad, or is it for real?" Hyde laments the fact that "for over two decades the public management experience seems to replicate one management fad after another, each promising more and delivering less. Little wonder that there is so much cynicism about quality management." Yet quality seems to be a major movement now. *Quality Is Free* shouts the title of a book by Philip Crosby, urging organizations to constantly do their best and focus on the needs of the customers. It's "free" because it doesn't really cost any more to do your best as an individual or as an organization.

It's the Customer, Stupid!

Bill Clinton's 1992 presidential campaign headquarters had what became a famous sign on its wall: "It's the economy, stupid!" This was designed to keep the campaign focused. Similarly, all public managers might well keep a sign on their walls that

> ### BOX 8.3 The Management Fad Cycle
>
> The average management fad, like the average love affair, goes through a fairly predictable cycle from infatuation to disillusionment. First, a management guru comes up with an idea, coins a buzzword, and sweet-talks the press. Next, one or two big companies, threatened with bankruptcy or desperate to seem with it, give the idea a go. Stories are published about sensational results, the corporate world clamors for advice, and the guru forms a million-dollar consultancy. Finally, some business-school professor produces an authoritative report arguing that the fad is a fraud; the press discovers a raft of sensational failures; and the guru, muttering that he was misunderstood, comes up with another idea.
>
> SOURCE: The *Economist,* July 2, 1994.

reads "It's the customer, stupid!" The customer is government's new focus. And governments at all levels would be "stupid" to forget it.

A customer service orientation is inherently part of the workplace quality movement. And, in line with TQM theory, it means not just good service in the present but a constant striving for continuously better service. The 1993 National Performance Review listed the following eight principles to govern the provision of customer service:

1. Survey customers frequently to find out what kind and quality of services they want.
2. Post standards and results measured against them.
3. Benchmark performance against "the best in business."
4. Provide choices in both source of service and delivery means.
5. Make information, services, and complaint systems easily accessible.
6. Handle inquiries and deliver services with courtesy.
7. Provide pleasant surroundings for customers.
8. Provide redress for poor services.

All federal agencies dealing directly with the public, in line with aforementioned principle 2, must now issue standards of performance that the public can expect of them. For example, the Postal Service standards include the following:

1. Your first-class mail will be delivered anywhere in the United States within three days.
2. Your local first-class mail will be delivered overnight.
3. You will receive service at post office counters within five minutes.
4. You can get postal information 24 hours a day by calling a local number.

You may well snicker at standard number 3—especially if you have gone to any big-city post office at lunch time. But at least now there is a standard about which you can complain. A standard violated is better than no standard at all. Besides, most people are happy with their mail service. According to a U.S. News/CNN poll reported in *U.S. News & World Report* on March 13, 1995, eight out of nine Americans are basically satisfied with their mail services. About 10 percent of all citizens give their individual mail carriers cash presents at Christmas. Can you think of any other group of public employees who are so regularly given such "tips"? Actually it is quite dangerous to offer cash to other public employees—especially police officers who stop you for a traffic violation or an Internal Revenue Service auditor examining your tax returns. They and the local district attorney may think you are offering them a bribe instead of showing them the kind of affection so many Americans reserve for their mail carriers at Christmas.

In the 1950s when Ronald Reagan, then an actor, was hosting the TV program *General Electric Theater,* he would close each episode by reminding the audience, on behalf of the sponsor, that "progress is our most important product." Many governments today are picking up on this product orientation by asserting, in effect, that "service is our most important product." Service for whom? The citizens. That is why the purveyors of these services are historically and rightly called public servants. The only thing really new here is that the public sector has picked up a word more traditionally used in private business: *customer.* So the public is now the customer. And a customer service orientation simply means that all activities are focused on pleasing the customer. That has always been known by the best businesses, and governments are increasingly becoming aware of it.

✦ A CASE STUDY: FROM E-COMMERCE TO E-GOVERNMENT

E-commerce has arrived. The simple proof of this is that you can now buy almost anything over the Web—from automobiles to zippers. And things that can't be bought directly on the Web, such as real estate, can be researched so that any eventual purchase is made by a better-informed buyer. And e-commerce is not only retail; it is also wholesale—business to business. While there are quibbles over which e-commerce activities and individual businesses will thrive and which will decline, there is no doubt that e-commerce is BIG and is here to stay.

Another major aspect of e-commerce is the ease with which the Internet facilitates conveying information to customers about their accounts. On any given day millions of citizens can access their accounts with various vendors and see the exact status of their orders—when they were shipped, what has been back-ordered, and how much is owed or has been charged to a credit card. Similarly, clients can access their checking and retirement accounts to see what checks have cleared and how their 401(k) stock portfolios are faring in a volatile market. This technological wonder begs a very serious question: If a mutual stock fund holding many hundreds of different securities can at the close of each business day tally up the values of all its assets and within several hours tell (on the Web) each client the value of their accounts to the penny, why can't governments do the same with their myriad accounts? The answer is, of course, that they could. But, as we know, for the most part they don't. So the question to be answered is "Why don't they?"

Government organizations are inherently and properly conservative—not necessarily in the political sense of tending toward the political right but in the legal sense of having a **fiduciary** responsibility to manage government assets and programs in a prudent manner. Consequently, governments cannot undertake the kinds of risks with evolving technologies that businesses routinely do. Governments cannot "bet the firm" on a new technology because, quite literally, it wouldn't be prudent. Therefore, in terms of customer service, government will always tend to offer older technologies because they must wait until the newest technologies have proven themselves. Only then can a "prudent" public manager pay for and install them. This is why e-government is much later in arriving than e-commerce. So the answer to the question "Why don't they?" is "They will—it just takes a bit longer to institutionalize innovations in government."

E-government is already a reality in a vast number of jurisdictions at all levels of government. In North Carolina citizens can use their credit cards to pay for their automobile registration renewals. In Miami those unfortunate enough to have earned parking tickets can now pay for them online 24 hours a day, seven days a week. In Riverside County, California, you can pay your property taxes online. You can even download all of the Internal Revenue Service's income tax forms from the Web and then file your federal income tax return online. The whole point of this is to allow citizens to conduct their government business, as the e-government battle cry says, "online rather than in line." The question is not "Is e-government here?" It clearly is. The question to be asked is "How big will it get?"

There are two faces to e-government: internal and external. The internal face refers to the operations of government itself—for example, using the Web for electronic procurement, electronic forms, and Web-based management information systems. The external face refers to the online services offered to citizens and businesses—for example, community calendars, bill payment portals, and application forms for employment. While there are two distinct faces to e-government, they seldom represent independent initiatives. *E-government,* then, is in essence the overarching term for all efforts to use the Internet to simplify governmental activities for both the public and the public's employees.

Just as the Internet is changing the way public policy is made, its e-government applications are changing the way programs are implemented and managed. The great increases in productivity enjoyed by the American economy in the 1990s were made possible in large part due to the investments made in computer technology. Will there be a corresponding increase in government productivity because e-government operations, while expensive to install, offer the potential of enormous savings down the online line?

Just consider the potential savings from having citizens pay their taxes and user fees online. If a jurisdiction needs fewer clerks at front-office windows where citizens can walk in to pay their bills, and fewer back-office clerks to open envelopes and process checks, their personnel costs go way down. And if you need fewer clerks, then

---

fiduciary A person who manages money or property for others. For example, anyone who has discretionary authority or responsibility for the administration of a pension plan is a fiduciary.

you also need fewer staff supporting them, such as guards and cleaning staff. Again—a cut in personnel staff. And with fewer staff comes less necessary office support needed and more savings.

But bill paying online is just the tip of the proverbial iceberg. Big savings are also to be had in a great variety of other areas. For example, occupational licenses can be renewed online. Architectural review of building plans can be done without having to send blueprints across town. Health and building inspection reports can be sent to those concerned the moment they are written—saving on postage and handling. E-government does not, cannot, and will not replace human interaction. But with less interaction come more savings and a greater increase in productivity. And when government increases its productivity, that means stable or lower taxes. This is why President George W. Bush in his 2002 federal budget proposal recommended $20 million as the first installment on a $100 million fund for an intra-agency e-government initiative to be managed by the General Services Administration. Despite the fact that Bush wants to cut taxes and reduce the size of government, he recognizes that this increase in spending is seed money that will rebound "big time." The president's recommendations helped with the passage of the E-government Act of 2002. This Act formally established federal infra-structure to assist in the evolution of e-government throughout the nation.

Just as e-government has grown at the federal level, state and local governments may be even more impressive in terms of shifting to e-based governance. For example, the increased use of Geographic Information Systems (GIS) has allowed municipalities to provide citizens with geographic-based information about the environment, public safety matters, and government resources. E-government programs at the local level have also facilitated citizen-to-citizen interaction through community discussion boards and chat rooms. Such measures may increase citizen participation in government by creating oppor-tunities for citizens that are traditionally challenged by time and geographic barriers.

But, as in many areas of service delivery, the question of equity arises when consid-ering the use of e-government. The "digital divide" that separates rich and poor and young and old requires government to not abandon traditional means of doing business. This is especially true given the fact that much of what government does is directed at groups such as the poor and elderly who are least likely to have Internet access.

To critics who assert that e-government has failed to live up to its potential, one must answer with a paraphrase of **John Paul Jones**'s comment when he was asked to surrender his ship during a 1779 sea battle: "I have not yet begun to fight." With simi-lar irony, modern governments struggling with the new technology of e-government Web sites might well say, "We have not yet begun to site."

John Paul Jones (1747–1792) The Revolutionary War captain who is considered the "father" of the U.S. Navy.

For Discussion: *Why is e-government so important as a means of generating cost savings and productivity improvements? What are the implications of e-government for program implementation and customer (meaning citizen) satisfaction?*

Summary

Managerialism as a term has long been used by sociologists as a reference to the economic and bureaucratic elites that run an industrial society. In the 1980s this well-established sociological "ism" took on new connotations when the British government sought to refocus the civil service from policy toward management. Now managerialism is used worldwide to refer to efforts to force the bureaucracy to be more responsive to the needs of its customers. Thus it is no longer sufficient for public managers to be the traditional "neutral guns for hire." They are now expected to be policy entrepreneurs who forcefully develop creative solutions to vexing problems.

There are three major aspects to managerialism: (1) reengineering, which takes reorganization beyond its traditional focus by seeking to totally rethink and refocus how programs are managed and to take maximum advantage of new technology—especially computers; (2) empowering others, which reflects the paradox that managers can often make themselves more powerful by giving power away; and (3) entrepreneurialism, which calls for managers to be transformational leaders who strive to change organizational culture—to develop a new vision for the organization and then convert that vision into reality.

Performance management, the primary responsibility of an organizational leader, is the systematic integration of an organization's efforts to achieve its objectives. It includes the comprehensive control, audit, and evaluation of all aspects of organizational performance. Closely associated with this is the concept of contracting, because individual or organizational goals are often embodied in quasi-commercial contracts.

Measuring the productivity of any jurisdiction, organization, program, or individual is particularly problematic in the public sector because of the problem of defining outputs and of quantifying measures of efficiency, effectiveness, and impact. Total quality management programs require all employees to participate in quality improvement activities; the thrust is to change the organizational culture to one that values long-term, lasting effectiveness. A customer service orientation is inherently part of the workplace quality movement. This means not just good service in the present but a constant striving for better service.

Review Questions

1. Does managerialism represent a new managerial revolution or a sophisticated new version of scientific management?

2. Why is the reengineering of an organizational unit considered a radical rather than an incremental approach to making it more efficient?

3. How do competitive public administrations and the new public management seek to deal with the traditional inefficiencies of public bureaucracies?

4. Will the total quality management movement become a long-standing management approach, or will it fade away as the latest management fad?

5. What are the forces encouraging the implementation of e-government operations within established government bureaucracies?

Key Concepts

e-commerce   Selling and buying over the Internet, whether wholesale or retail.

e-government   Conducting any aspect of government business operations over the Internet—from providing information by government to paying bills to government.

empowerment   Giving a person or organization the formal authority to do something.

management control   That aspect of management concerned with the comparison of actual versus planned performance, as well as the development and implementation of procedures to correct substandard performance.

managerial revolution   James Burham's concept that as control of large businesses moved from the original owners to professional managers, society's new governing class became not the traditional possessors of wealth but those having the professional expertise to manage, to lead, large organizations.

managerialism   An entrepreneurial approach to public management that emphasizes management rights and a reinvigorated scientific management.

new public management   A disparate group of structural reforms and informal management initiatives that reflects the doctrine of managerialism in the public sector.

performance management   The systematic integration of an organization's efforts to achieve its objectives.

productivity   A measured relationship between the quantity (and quality) of results produced and the quantity of resources required for production. Productivity is, in essence, a measure of the work efficiency of an individual, a work unit, or a whole organization.

reengineering   The fundamental rethinking and redesign of organizational processes to achieve significant improvements in critical measures of performance, such as costs or quality of services.

self-directed work team   A work group that will accept responsibility for their processes and products—as well as for the behavior of other group members.

total quality management (TQM)   A new phrase for quality control in its most expanded sense of a total and continuing concern for quality in the production of goods and services.

Bibliography

Abramson, Mark A., and Grady E. Means, eds. (2001). *E-Government 2001*. Latham, MO: Rowman & Littlefield.

Aristotle. (1952). *Politics*, trans. B. Jowett. Chicago: Great Books, Encyclopedia Britannica.

Barnard, Chester I. (1938). *The Functions of the Executive*. Cambridge, MA: Harvard University Press.

Barzelay, M. (1992). *Breaking Through Bureaucracy: A New Vision for Managing in Government*. Berkeley: University of California Press.

Bhote, Keki R. (1991). *World Class Quality*. New York: Amacom.

Borick, Christopher. (1998). "Going to Market: The Realtionship Between Fiscal Constraints and State Investment Management Policies." *State and Local Government Review*, 30, No. 3.

Bowen, D. E., and E. E. Lawler III. (1992). "The Empowerment of Service Workers: What, Why, How, and When." *Sloan Management Review* (Spring).

Burnham, James. (1941). *The Managerial Revolution*. New York: John Day.

Coates, Breena E. (2001–02). "Smart Government Online, Not Inline." *The Public Manager*, 30, No. 4 (Winter).

Congressional Research Service. (2003). A Primer on E-Government: Sectors, Stages, Opportunities and Challenges of Online Government. http://www.fas.org/sgp/crs/RL31057.pdf (January 28).

Crosby, P. B. (1979). *Quality Is Free*. New York: McGraw-Hill.

———. (1984). *Quality Without Tears*. New York: McGraw-Hill.

Dawes, Charles G. (1923). *The First Year of the Budget of the United States*. New York: Harper & Brothers.

Deming, W. E. (1986). *Out of the Crisis*. Cambridge, MA: MIT Press.

———. (1993). *The New Economics*. Cambridge, MA: MIT Press.

Djilas, Milovan. (1957). *The New Class*. New York: Praeger.

Downs, G., and P. D. Larkey. (1986). *The Search for Government Efficiency*. New York: Random House.

Dynes, Michael, and David Walker. (1995). *The New British State*. London: Times Books.

Feigenbaum, Armand V. (1983). *Total Quality Control*. New York: McGraw-Hill.

Galbraith, John Kenneth. (1998). *Letters to Kennedy*, ed. James Goodman. Cambridge, MA: Harvard University Press.

Halachmi, Arie, and Geert Bouckaert, eds. (1995). *Public Productivity Through Quality and Strategic Management*. Amsterdam: IOS Press.

Hammer, Michael, and James Champy. (1993). *Reengineering the Corporation*. New York: HarperCollins.

Holzer, Marc. (1955). "Productivity and Quality Management." In *Handbook of Public Personnel Administration*, Jack Rabin, et al., eds. New York: Marcel Dekker.

Hughes, Owen. (1994). *Public Management and Administration*. London: Macmillan.

Hyde, Albert C. (1991). "Productivity Management for Public Sector Organizations." In *Public Management: The Essential Readings*, J. S. Ott, A. C. Hyde, and J. M. Shafritz., eds. Chicago: Lyceum Books/Nelson-Hall.

———. (1992). "Implications of Total Quality Management for the Public Sector." *Public Productivity and Management Review* 16 (Fall).

International City Management Association. (1986). 1985 *Municipal Year Book*. Washington: ICMA.

Juran, J. M. (1992). *Juran on Quality by Design*. New York: Free Press.

Juran, J. M., and F. M. Gryna, eds. (1988). *Juran's Quality Control Handbook*, 4th ed. New York: McGraw-Hill.

Katzenbach, J. R., and D. K. Smith. (1993). *The Wisdom of Teams: Creating the High-Performance Organization*. Boston: Harvard Business School Press.

Lawler, E. E. III, S. A. Mohrman, and G. E. Ledford Jr. (1992). *Employee Involvement and Total Quality Management*. San Francisco: Jossey-Bass.

Lemov, Penelope. (1995). "Managing Cash in a Post-Orange County World." *Governing* 8, No. 8.

Linden, Russ. (1994). *MIS Report: Re-Engineering Local Government*. Washington: International City/County Management Association.

Marini, Frank E. (1971). *Toward a New Public Administration*. San Francisco: Chandler.

Martin, John. (1994). "Robert M. Melia: The Soul of a Child Support Machine." *Governing* (December).

M.I.T. Commission on Industrial Productivity. (1989). *Made in America: Regaining the Productive Edge*. Cambridge, MA: MIT Press.

Mitroff, I. I. (1987). *Business Not as Usual*. San Francisco: Jossey-Bass.

Orsburn, J. D., L. Moran, E. Musselwhite, J. H. Zenger, with C. Perrin. (1990). *Self-Directed Work Teams: The New American Challenge*. Homewood, IL: Business One Irwin.

Osborne, D., and T. Gaebler. (1992). *Reinventing Government: How the Entrepreneurial Spirit Is Transforming the Public Sector*. Reading, MA: Addison-Wesley.

Pascale, R. T., and A. G. Athos. (1981). *The Art of Japanese Management*. New York: Simon and Schuster.

Peters, T. J., and R. H. Waterman Jr. (1982). *In Search of Excellence*. New York: Harper and Row.

Plato. *The Republic*. (1925). Oxford: Clarendon Press.

Pollitt, Christopher. (1993). *Managerialism and the Public Services*, 2nd ed. London: Blackwell.

Pollitt, Christopher, and Geert Bouckaert, eds. (1995). *Quality Improvement in European Public Services*. London: Sage.

Samuelson, Robert J. (1993). "The Death of Management." *Newsweek* (May 10).

Sayre, Wallace S. (1948). "The Triumph of Techniques Over Purpose." *Public Administration Review* 8 (Spring).

Seidman, Harold. (1980). *Politics, Position, and Power*, 3rd ed. New York: Oxford University Press.

Tichy, N. M., and D. O. Ulrich. (1984). "The Leadership Challenge—A Call for the Transformational Leader." *Sloan Management Review* 26.

U.S. General Accounting Office. (1997). "Performance Budgeting: Past Initiatives Offer Insights for GPRA Implementation." Washington: GAO (March).

Walters, Jonathan. (1994). "TQM: Surviving the Cynics." *Governing* (September).

Weisbord, M. R. (1991). *Productive Workplaces: Organizing and Managing for Dignity, Meaning, and Community*. San Francisco: Jossey-Bass.

White, Leonard D. (1933). *Trends in Public Administration*. New York: McGraw-Hill.

Xenophon. (1859). *The Anabasis or Expedition of Cyrus and the Memorabilia of Socrates*, trans. J. S. Watson. New York: Harper and Row.

Recommended Books

Hammer, Michael. (1996). *Beyond Reengineering: How the Process-Centered Organization Is Changing Our Work and Our Lives.* New York: HarperCollins. What to do after you reengineer, by the author who first popularized the concept.

Hilmer, Frederick G., and Lex Donaldson. (1996). *Management Redeemed: Debunking the Fads That Undermine Our Corporations.* New York: Free Press. An exposé on how the latest management trends all too often lead managers down "false trails."

Holzer, Marc, and Kathe Calahan. (1998). *Government at Work: Best Practices and Model Programs.* Thousand Oaks, CA: Sage. After presenting a model for comprehensive productivity improvement, the authors offer a number of good examples in which such "best practices and model programs" are succeeding every day.

Pollitt, Christopher. (1993). *Managerialism and the Public Services,* 2nd ed. London: Blackwell. The first major work applying managerialism to public administration; unfortunately, it has decidedly difficult diction—a book more to be aware of than to read.

Related Web Sites

American Productivity and Quality Center
www.apqc.org

E-commerce
ecommerce.internet.com/

E-government
www.whitehouse.gov/omb/egov/

History of the Internet
www.netvalley.com/intval.html

John Paul Jones
www.seacoastnh.com/jpj/

Managerialism
www.vusst.hr/Encycopedia/managerialism.htm

National Center for Public Productivity
www.nccp.us

National Institute of Standards and Technology Quality Program
www.quality.nist.gov

The Performance Institute
www.performanceweb.org

Quality Network
www.quality.co.uk/

W. Edwards Deming Institute
www.deming.org

CHAPTER 9

Strategic Management in the Public Sector

•KEYNOTE: WHEN SHORT-TERM LEADERS DO LONG-TERM PLANNING

Strategic management—the achievement of long-term organizational goals—is not a tidy business. It is not that managers do not want to be neat; it is just that the managerial environment, especially in the public sector, is inherently and notoriously lacking in neatness. It is not exactly what the Scottish poet Robert Burns had in mind when he said that the "best laid schemes of mice and men" often go awry; it is instead that these plans are seldom comprehensive documents—if they exist at all. Often the overall strategy exists only as a vague document or unwritten philosophy. The full implementation of a strategic plan usually takes many years—sometimes decades or even more. The usefulness of a strategic plan is that it provides the long-term doctrine, the overall guidance, so essential for short-term, or tactical, management decisions.

Ancient Rome was into strategic management in a big way. Of course, there was no one single document entitled "The Strategic Plan for the Roman Empire," but all of its elements lay scattered about in various laws, policies, and proclamations. It was much like the British Constitution of today, unwritten but nevertheless thoroughly understood by all those with the responsibility for its implementation. Indeed, the process of strategic planning has always been done—especially in a military context where it began. However, the Romans of old were among the first to apply strategic concepts to the large-scale nonmilitary aspects of government as well.

Julius Caesar espoused a strategic doctrine that so enraged the Roman aristocracy they assassinated him in 44 B.C.E. Nevertheless, his successors implemented the plan that became known as the Pax Romana. This established relatively stable borders and co-opted possible opposition to Roman governance by expanding Roman citizenship. The several centuries of mostly peace that followed were made possible by a relatively small military establishment that was so well trained and managed that disturbances within the empire could be suppressed with the utmost efficiency and ruthlessness. An unremitting management discipline was the critical element in the tactical doctrine that provided for the peace and prosperity envisioned by the strategic plan.

In the twentieth century arguably the most significant single strategic plan was the Truman Doctrine, the policy of President Harry S. Truman's administration of extending military and economic aid to those countries (originally Greece and Turkey) seeking to resist "totalitarian aggression." The Truman Doctrine became the cornerstone of the U.S. policy of containing (restricting the influence of) the Soviet Union, the underlying basis of U.S. foreign, military, and much of domestic policy after World War II. The demise of the Soviet Union in 1991 can be seen as the ultimate vindication of the containment strategy.

While there was broad agreement on the objective of containment, at least until the reaction against American involvement in Vietnam in the late 1960s, different strategies were used to implement this objective. From 1947 until 1950, the emphasis was on rebuilding allies in Western Europe; this massive infusion of economic aid became known as the Marshall Plan—so named by Truman to honor Secretary of State George C. Marshall Jr., who headed the U.S. Army during World War II. During the Korean War, the emphasis moved to actual fighting on the borders of the free world to prevent the spread of communism. The Eisenhower administration emphasized the possibility of nuclear retaliation. Then the Kennedy and Johnson administrations used containment as the rationale for massively escalating the limited war in Vietnam. The Nixon administration did not abandon containment but tried instead to uphold it through greater reliance on allies and on détente (a lessening of military and diplomatic tensions) with the Soviet Union. The Carter administration initially tried to ignore containment but embraced it after the Soviet invasion of Afghanistan. The Reagan administration not only pursued a highly military containment policy but tried to go beyond it and roll back some of the Soviet gains of the 1970s in the Third World through support for anti-Communist revolutionary movements. The Bush administration saw containment come to an end with the demise of the Soviet Union—a development that vindicated the logic of the initial architects of containment.

The Truman Doctrine provided the vision, the overall philosophy for all of these efforts. Its strategic vision guided all of the details of the Cold War that followed—from the Marshall Plan to the Korean and Vietnam Wars. President Truman made this statement to a joint session of Congress, on March 12, 1947:

> At the present moment in world history nearly every nation must choose between alternative ways of life. The choice is too often not a free one.
>
> One way of life is based upon the will of the majority, and is distinguished by free institutions, representative government, free elections, guarantees of individual liberty, freedom of speech and religion, and freedom from political oppression.
>
> The second way of life is based upon the will of a minority forcibly imposed upon the majority. It relies upon terror and oppression, a controlled press and radio, fixed elections, and the suppression of personal freedoms.
>
> I believe that it must be the policy of the United States to support free peoples who are resisting attempted subjugation by armed minorities or by outside pressures.
>
> I believe that we must assist free peoples to work out their own destinies in their own way.
>
> I believe that our help should be primarily through economic and financial aid which is essential to economic stability and orderly political processes.

The domestic implications of the Truman Doctrine were equally important. For example, the communist threat justified the Federal Aid Highway Act of 1956 (which built the U.S. interstate road network—the National Defense Highway System), the National Defense Education Act of 1958 (which provides loans and fellowships for students and grants to schools and colleges), and the National Aeronautics and Space Administration Act of 1958 (for the peaceful exploration of space).

Of course, Truman never envisioned his doctrine supporting local public works or graduate student education. But the Cold War goal of defeating communism meant that anything that could be presented as part of this international struggle would get a more sympathetic legislative reception. Thus graduate student fellowships and academic research in almost every field were justified as aiding the national defense effort. As more and more people got with the plan, it turned out that there was hardly any worthwhile government project that could not be designed, however farfetchedly, to defeat communism. It turned out that every single member of Congress was willing, indeed eager, to fight the worldwide communist menace by bringing pork barrel projects home to his or her district.

This combination of limited wars on the perimeter, interstate highways, and fellowships for graduate students was more than the Soviet Union could bear. When the great communist experiment finally failed, credit was given to the containment policies of the Truman administration and its successors and more recently to the Reagan administration's massive arms buildup that the Soviets could not match. But no direct credit was given to the overall strategic plan. That's because there was no plan as such. There was the Truman strategic vision and all that followed. Thousands of programs and millions of people each played their part in an effort to achieve a goal that often seemed impossible. It was messy. Only retrospectively can we behold all the

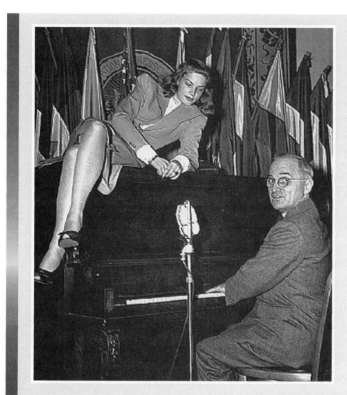

Then Vice President Harry Truman playing the piano for actress Lauren Bacall. This February 1945 photo illustrates how good intentions can easily turn into political embarrassment. Truman, an accomplished amateur piano player, agreed to perform at a variety show for 800 servicemen at the Washington Press Club. Sensing an ideal photo op, Bacall's press agent perched her atop the piano. The crowd of soldiers roared their approval, and Truman kept on playing. The photos became a minor scandal. Truman's wife, Bess, was said to be furious and forbade Truman from making any more public performances. Two months later, President Franklin Roosevelt died, and President Truman had less time to play the piano •

oars in the water rowing to the same philosophy. All the warriors, diplomats, highway builders, and scholars rowed out of faith, out of self-interest, or out of the simple desire to have a job. But in the end and because of the overall philosophy, they rowed in the same direction. What more could you ask of a plan?

For Discussion: *What were the major elements of the two basic aspects of the Truman Doctrine: domestic and international? What are the parallels between the Truman Doctrine to fight communism and the Bush doctrine to fight terrorism?*

What Is Strategic Management?

Strategy, the ancient art of generalship, is the employment of—the management of—overall resources (classically soldiers) to gain an objective. Tactics are the use of a subset of these resources to gain a part of the overall objective. Strategic management is the modern application of this ancient art to contemporary business and public administration. It is the conscious selection of policies, development of capability, and interpretation of the environment by managers in order to focus organizational efforts toward the achievement of preset objectives. These objectives necessarily vary. In the private sector it could be the doubling of annual dividends to stockholders within so many years. In the nonprofit sector it could be the creation of a repertory theater or a significant increase in attendance at symphony orchestra concerts. In the public sector it could be a reduction in the crime rate, an increase in the high school graduation rate, or, as we have seen in the keynote, the defeat of worldwide communism.

All strategic management efforts take an essentially similar approach to planning where an organization wants to be by a future target date. These are the six features that identify a strategic, as opposed to a nonstrategic, management approach:

1. The identification of objectives to be achieved in the future (these are often announced in a vision statement)
2. The adoption of a time frame (or "planning horizon") in which these objectives are to be achieved
3. A systematic analysis of the current circumstances of an organization, especially its capabilities
4. An assessment of the environment surrounding the organization—both now and within the planning horizon
5. The selection of a strategy for the achievement of desired objectives by a future date, often comparing various alternatives
6. The integration of organizational efforts around this strategy

The overall strategy chosen is in essence the package of actions selected after analyzing alternatives, assessing the outside environment, and determining the internal capabilities of an organization to achieve specified future objectives through the integration of organizational effort. The strategic management process is often conducted by a strategic planning unit within the organization. Eventually, its findings are presented in a detailed document known as the strategic plan. Many of the core elements of strategic management just listed have unique considerations when they are applied to public sector organizations.

Objectives

Objectives-based thinking in management has become so pervasive that it is as hard to think of management without objectives as living rooms without television sets. Originally, objectives were part of military thinking. The Swiss-born Napoléonic era general Henri Jomini, in his 1838 book *The Art of War,* taught how battles should be conducted, with soldiers' moves being planned either for strategic benefit (a qualitative improvement in the long-term position, particularly vis-à-vis the enemy) or tactical benefit (that is, a shorter-term move designed to win the problems—the fighting—of the day and create a better position for the next day's battle).

In this context, we can think of a tactical objective such as "Hill 45"—a specific location that must be taken from the enemy to further the purpose of the overall plan of battle. A strategic objective might be victory on the whole of a battlefront or theater of war. This military vocabulary is now commonly applied to business. For example, when Honda, the Japanese company, started selling motorcycles in the United States in

Figure 9.1   The Strategic Management Process

the early 1960s, it secured a tactical objective. When it forced British motorcycles out of the American market, however, it secured a strategic victory.

The public sector was slower than the private sector in embracing strategic management notions. This is because, traditionally, public administrators were expected to focus not on their objectives—what they were trying to achieve—but on their functions and responsibilities—that is, the duties assigned to them by law. Indeed, public administration was traditionally defined as the enforcement or implementation of public policy—that is, the law. This emphasis on the responsibility to discharge ongoing functions set down by law has been the focus of traditional public administration. The seniority principle in promotions often accompanied this attitude. After all, if detailed knowledge of how to administer the laws in a certain functional area were critical, it logically followed that it must be better to have a more senior—and therefore more knowledgeable—employee than to hire someone fresh, who might take

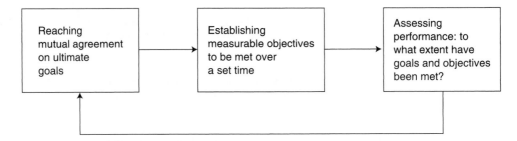

Figure 9.2 The Management by Objectives Process

years to acquire a parallel level of knowledge. Job descriptions even emphasized knowledge of laws and regulations as a key selection criterion.

In contrast, today's most sophisticated selection officers tend to look for a record of achievement, as opposed to highly specific knowledge of this kind. A world in which public administrators take responsibility for unchanging functions still exists in some corners of the public sector in most countries, but it is increasingly being replaced by a focus on objectives. No longer do we begin by asking a public administrator, "What do you do?" (i.e., "What is your function?"). Today the question is more likely to be "What are you trying to achieve?" (i.e., "What are your objectives?"). While there are many reasons for this change in perspective, three are paramount.

The first is the popularization of the concept of management by objectives (MBO) by **Peter Drucker** through his pioneering 1954 work *The Practice of Management.* MBO as espoused by Drucker and, by now, countless others is an approach to managing whose hallmark is the mutual—by both organizational subordinate and superior—establishment of measurable goals to be accomplished by an individual or team over a set period of time. The widespread adoption of the MBO concept across the world has aided in the distinction between a function and an objective. It is now widely understood that an emphasis on the latter can stimulate a focus on performance and effort as opposed to the more traditional custodial focus toward one's organizational obligations.

Second, the ever more rapid pace of change in the communities served by the public sector is such that there are now few functions that can go on unchanged from year to year and decade to decade. The public organizations of today must generally fight and compete in a less-sheltered environment—where the luxury of just "administering" timeless functions rarely exists. The objectives of public sector organizations have become moving targets—and public sector managers must move with them.

Third, the ideas of strategic management and the use of objectives are pervasive in the private sector. Since there is no **Berlin Wall** dividing the sectors, and staff move

---

Peter Drucker (1909–2005) The preeminent philosopher of management during the post–World War II era.
Berlin Wall The concrete and barbed-wire wall built by East Germany in 1961 to divide East and West Berlin. The wall became the symbol of the division of Eastern and Western Europe. It was dismantled in 1989.

increasingly in and out of each sector, there is an ever-increasing unification of language, concepts, and standards between the sectors.

Nonetheless, many public sector organizations still produce separate statements of their functions (or responsibilities) and objectives. You can broadly distinguish the language of each. Since a statement of functions is about what an organization is responsible for under law, it broadly answers the question "What do we do?" The answer is normally a static description, timeless and without directionality. A statement of objectives (often called a mission statement), however, answers the question, "What are we trying to achieve?" Instead of a static description, this normally implies a direction being pursued, along with specific measures so that we will know when we get there. A statement of functions might say "we are in charge of child care"; a statement of objectives might say "we intend to provide a preschool place for every child in the community by 2008." A statement of objectives should be the following:

1. Succinct, and limited to the organization's sphere of influence
2. Directional, with specific future states to be achieved
3. Time limited, with indications when each objective is to be achieved
4. Measurable, so that achievement or progress can be evaluated

The Planning Horizon

Sometimes when you apply for a job, the recruitment officer or selection committee may say to you, "Where do you see yourself in ten years' time?" This is often perceived to be a silly question to ask an individual, and, with respect to the structure of women's careers, it is possibly a discriminatory one. But in asking this question, a selection committee is trying to see whether the applicant for the job has a personal career strategy or is drifting in an opportunistic way without a strategy, without personal objectives, and without a career plan.

The same question is most decidedly not silly when addressed to public sector organizations. It is of the utmost importance to assess whether or not they have strategic intent—that is, the will to shape their future, rather than merely reacting to changes driven by others. Any organization's planning horizon, the time limit of organizational planning beyond which the future is considered too uncertain or unimportant to waste time on, is an important factor in assessing its short- as well as long-term viability. While private corporations have the luxury of determining their own planning horizons, severe obstacles are put in the path of those who advocate the most rational possible planning in the public sector. The inherently political nature of public administration can place a premium on short-term thinking. It was the late British Prime Minister Harold Wilson who said, "A week is a long time in politics." By this he was drawing attention to the fickle nature of the public's awareness, to the fact that an issue of premier significance one week may be forgotten the next. Political leaders may lose power—and even office—in a very short time, often unexpectedly. "Today a rooster, tomorrow a feather duster" sums up the uncertain job prospects of those who would lead the political barnyard. Thus the reigning administrations in developed democracies feel they must be very sensitive to the results of very

Figure 9.3   The Essence of Planning

short-term opinion polling. These factors and all others that bring a short-term focus to bear on public policymaking work—and work very hard—against strategic management efforts.

Public budgeting procedures, because of their annual nature, reinforce this tendency toward short-term thinking. National, state, and local legislators are accustomed to exercising oversight authority during the annual rituals of the budget formulation and review process. To them, biennial and multiyear budgeting represent immediate threats to their political powers and patronage prerogatives. Aaron Wildavsky discussed this problem in a famous article, "A Budget for All Seasons: Why the Traditional Budget Lasts." It lasts because it is the basis of the political power of so many legislators. Otherwise, rational reforms leading to multiyear budgets are simply not in their personal political interests. Despite the many efforts that have been made over the years to introduce longer budget cycles, success has been limited. Thus short-term budgeting continues to reinforce short-term policymaking and inhibit the inherently long-term nature of strategic planning.

Despite the preceding constraints, long-term planning is inescapable in some areas of public sector activity. Some endeavors clearly require long-term planning horizons because they need both gradual development and enormous capital investment. Publicly owned power, water, and transit utilities must operate in this way. They must have long forward plans and multiyear lead times to complete a new transit system, power station, or water purification plant. Here, the constraints of traditional short-term government planning cannot apply. Often, such utilities, if they are not already in the private sector, are placed in semiautonomous public corporations or commissions. There they have more freedom to think, plan, and operate within a longer-term time horizon than if they were to operate as traditional government departments. Government-owned utilities, with their heavy investment and long lead times, illustrate areas of the public sector where long-term strategy and concomitant long-term planning are inescapable.

Longer-term strategic planning can occur close to the heart of power. If a government wishes to bring about a fundamental change in community attitudes or lifestyle, a national strategy of some kind may be needed. A national energy strategy may be desirable to persuade citizens, over time, to be more responsible in the way they use finite energy resources. But ever since the **oil embargo** of 1973–1974, successive national administrations in the United States have tried but failed to develop a politically acceptable comprehensive energy policy. As happened with the Clinton

---

oil embargo The 1973–1974 effort by the Arab members of OPEC to change Western policies toward the Middle East by refusing to export oil to those countries that supported Israel during the October 1973 Yom Kippur War.

administration's comprehensive health care reform efforts, much planning was done but little was actually implemented. Sometimes such planning efforts are an end in themselves. Many a planning effort is undertaken by an agency or by a presidential or royal commission to assuage a political constituency. It is just because long-term national strategies are notoriously difficult to achieve in developed economies that strategies are often developed for the crassest political motives.

In developing and less-democratic countries, longer-term strategy may come naturally. In Indonesia, for example, the country has proceeded since independence in 1945 through a series of five-year plans that have helped it to modernize and industrialize despite many difficulties. Attitudes to national strategy may differ significantly between developed and developing countries in large measure because so many developing countries offer their citizens only the minimum of political freedoms. Consequently, there is less need to consult obstreperous interest groups seeking to influence the policy process. The problem with democratic government is that planning is inherently messy when so many interests must be accommodated. The "neatness" of planning in authoritarian regimes may be admirable in technique—but at what cost?

Policy analyst Charles E. Lindblom, in his classic 1959 article "The Science of Muddling Through," argued that in pluralistic democracies, step-by-step decision making—muddling through toward an acceptable decision—was a more appropriate model for public decision making than leaping forward toward a desired strategic objective chosen as part of a rational planning process. Lindblom views a rational model as unrealistic. The policymaking process is above all, he asserts, complex and disorderly. Interestingly, policy analyst Yehezkel Dror made the point that incremental, step-by-step muddling through might be all right for a wealthy and confident democracy such as the United States, but developing nations with massive problems needed the certainty of rational planning and confident movement toward a known set of goals. Incremental decision making is in many respects highly compatible with the pluralistic compromise typical of the American political system. But it is important to note in these times of international economic competition how countries more attuned to rational planning, such as the economies of Southeast Asia, have used rational planning successfully.

When strategic management is adopted in a corporation, municipality, or bureau, or in a presidential initiative, a choice is made for rational decision making. In this sense, there is now a greater commitment to rational planning in American institutions than ever before. For example, the Government Performance and Results Act of 1993 requires that "federal agencies must prepare and submit strategic plans to the Office of Management and Budget and Congress." The states are increasingly passing similar legislation. For example, according to House Bill 2009, passed by the Texas State Legislature in 1991, all state agencies must use strategic plans as the basis for developing their "requests for legislative appropriations, and measure agency effectiveness by the outcomes and outputs they achieve."

Capabilities

Strategic management has been described, most notably by H. Igor Ansoff, as "a matching process" in which the variables of strategy, capability, and environment

> ## BOX 9.1   Strategic Planning Is Now Compulsory for Federal Agencies
>
> The strategic approach to management is no longer just an option, but it's compulsory if you work in a U.S. federal agency. The Government Performance and Results Act (GPRA) of 1993 requires every federal agency to ask itself, "What is our mission?" "What are our goals?" and "How will we achieve them?" The GPRA requires each agency's strategic plan to have six components:
>
> - A comprehensive mission statement
> - Agency-wide, long-term goals and objectives for all major functions and operations
> - Approaches (or strategies) to achieve the goals and objectives
> - A relationship between the long-term goals/objectives and the annual performance goals
> - An identification of key factors, external to the agency and beyond its control, that could significantly affect achievement
> - A description of how program evaluations were used to establish or revise strategic goals
>
> An important feature of the approach to strategic planning required by GPRA is that agencies cannot "go it alone"—they must consult with Congress and other stakeholders. They are required by an Office of Management and Budget Circular (A-11 of September 1995) to send their proposed plans to Congress with a letter explaining how they've consulted with stakeholders, including consultants, customers, contractors, and state governments.

are matched as the organization seeks to manage change through strategy. As the environment moves from stable to turbulent, Ansoff argues, the required capability moves from "custodial" toward "entrepreneurial." In a stable environment, a custodial, unchanging capability may suffice. But as the environment becomes surprising and turbulent, a more entrepreneurial and risk-taking capability is needed.

When mismatch exists between environment and capability, management must take action to better match its human resources capability with the emerging environment. The actions required may include hiring new employees who are better oriented by disposition or training to a new entrepreneurial environment. Existing employees could be given additional training. Unfortunately, it is often the case that some employees may no longer be suited to what the present environment requires. For example, a juvenile correctional institution moving toward a counseling and support model may find difficulties if its staff capability exclusively consists of tough custodial officers. Similarly, many organizations in the public sector whose strengths have traditionally been in technical or professional excellence may find that new requirements for customer orientation require, at the very least, extra training programs, but more likely the hiring of some new staff with new attitudes and skills.

Strengths	Weaknesses
Delivery network that reaches virtually all possible customers Established branch office in every significant locality An ongoing capability to complete its core mission (deliver the mail) every day	Inferior top-management core Poorly motivated and alienated workforce Large organization with difficulties maintaining service of consistent quality Public perception of massive incompetence
Opportunities	**Threats**
Every citizen a potential customer Expand services into new technologies Alliances with private deliverers	Forced privatization by Congress Competition from private sector (Federal Express, United Parcel Service, etc.) Hostile labor unions

Figure 9.4   SWOT Analysis for the U.S. Postal Service

What is true of human resources capability is also likely to be the case with systems capability, or financial capability—indeed, capability in whatever dimension is critical to the organization's ability to adapt to an emerging environment. For example, years ago, the task of servicing lighthouses—traditionally a public sector function—was viewed as requiring a capability to maintain a fleet of tough little ships that could reach remote areas. This capability later gave way to a capability to service remote locations by helicopter. Eventually, as global positioning systems developed, that capability in turn became obsolete.

The SWOT analysis—a review of an organization's Strengths, Weaknesses, Opportunities, and Threats—is a technique widely used to provide another test of strategic viability. SWOT analysis is often conducted by consultants or senior management groups in an interactive, brainstorming mode, in which the group turns its attention sequentially to each aspect of the organization's position. Analysis of strengths and weaknesses highlights capability issues, while attention to opportunities and threats turns attention to the opportunistic as well as the predatory aspects of organizational survival. A SWOT analysis is often undertaken as part of a situation audit, an assessment of an organization's performance in absolute terms or in comparison to a competing or parallel organization.

Game Theory

In recent years public administrators have begun to embrace game theory as a key component of strategic management. Game theory has been a major tool for scholars for many decades, with applications in fields such as international relations, business management, and economics. It has recently gained popular appeal because of Ron Howard's film A *Beautiful Mind* (which won the Oscar for Best Film in 2001), in which prominent game theorist John Nash's life was examined. At its core, game theory deals with cooperation and conflict in the context of decision making. It assumes that individuals who behave rationally will seek to maximize their benefits whenever they make a decision. Thus if one can identify the goals of the other players in the game, they can strategically adapt their decisions. For example Russell Crowe, the actor portraying Nash in the film, explains to his male friends at a bar how they can use game theory to pick up girls. He says, "If we all go for the blonde and block each other, not a single one of us is going to get her. So then we go for her friends, but they will all give us the cold shoulder because no one likes to be second choice. But what if none of us goes for the blonde? We won't get in each other's way and we won't insult the other girls. It's the only way to win. It's the only way we all get . . . [what we want]."

For managers in public agencies and organizations this approach to decision making may have many applications. One area where a public manager may apply game theory is in budget negotiations with elected officials. By recognizing that the primary goal of most politicians is to be reelected to political office, a public administrator can craft budget requests in a way that puts pressure on the elected officials. For example, through framing of a budget request in an "all-or-nothing" form, a manager may place the members of Congress in a difficult situation. If Congress supports full funding of a program, government resources will be strained. However, no funding of a program (i.e., Amtrak rail service) may cause anger among constituents depending on a service. By making the decision an all-or-nothing proposition, the public manager is structuring the "game" between himself and Congress in a manner that seeks to optimize the probability of full funding.

Four Strategic Factors

Strategic management, in its focus on measurable objectives to be achieved, contrasts with the older form of functional management, which emphasizes responsibilities to be discharged and things to be done, without a primary focus on what is to be achieved. Strategic management may embrace strategic leadership, strategic direction, and strategic planning, but it is broader than any of these. Strategic management requires the deployment of all the organization's managerial functions toward getting results. Strategic planning, for example, while it is an important and logical precondition, should not be equated with strategic management. After all, strategic management often occurs without formal strategic planning, but strategic planning is impotent and meaningless without strategic management.

Are policy and strategy different? We know that strategic management is a central concern of virtually all large organizations. Since the 1970s, the study of strategic management has assumed a central role in both the teaching and practice of management. Every major management school—both public and private sector—now has its experts in strategic management. The word *policy* does not seem as natural coming from the lips of private business executives. *Policy* has always been a looser word than *strategy*. As used in the context of government, it usually refers to a statement of goals that can be translated into a plan or program by specifying the objectives to be obtained. Goals are a far more general statement of aims than are objectives. Goal-objective ambiguity may exist for a variety of reasons. The original sponsors of the policy or program may not have had a precise idea of the end results desired. Formal statements of objectives may be intentionally ambiguous if such vagueness makes it easier to obtain a consensus on action. After all, value judgments underlying the objectives may not be shared by influential groups. Consequently, the result intended may be perceived by some as implying ill effects for them. So explicit statements of objectives, which tend to imply a specific assignment of priorities and commitment of resources, may be purposely avoided.

Consequently, it is hardly a surprise that in many MBA programs, the course unit that used to be called "business policy" is now called "strategic management." The public sector has been as uncomfortable with the word *strategy* as the private sector has been with *policy*. While all administrative and political analysts are obsessed with policy—its formulation, its direction, and its implementation—many elected political executives and appointed agency administrators feel reluctant to use the word "strategy" for fear of its Machiavellian and militaristic connotations.

But clearly it is not the case that strategic management concepts are inapplicable or even foreign in many parts of the public sector. From the national administration through to the smallest local governments, the concepts and language of strategic management are in ever-growing use. To understand this, we need to appreciate four important factors that affect the use of strategic management concepts in the public sector:

1. The public–private paradox
2. The importance of being close to the center
3. Organizational language and culture
4. Organizational place

A review of these factors will establish bearings on the road map of strategic management, which will help to explain how organizations use strategic management concepts and how these concepts are constantly encountered in the daily lives of virtually all public administrators.

The Public–Private Paradox

Over the years, scholars and managers have come to appreciate two interconnected propositions about the relationship between business and government—and thus about the relationships between business management and public administration. The first is that business and government are ultimately different; the second is that business administration and public administration have very much in common. This paradox lies at the heart of public administration as a discipline. There is much that is unique about government and about the work of the public administrators within it that distinguishes public sector from private sector management. In modern democracies, the work of government has the mandate of political **legitimacy**—no private company, however important, can claim this. The work of government can be embodied in law and, if necessary, implemented by force. Government is owned by all, is responsible to all, and must be equitable to all. So the work of its officials

---

legitimacy A characteristic of a social institution, such as a government or a family, whereby it has both a legal and a perceived right to make binding decisions for its members.

must be fair and defensible, based on the principle of fear and favor to no one. Modern administrative states contain many groups and interests, so the work of government necessarily involves accommodation, compromise, and incremental decision making. Political leaders and public administrators work in a complex web of interconnections and make unilateral decisions at their peril. Finally, bottom-line profit in itself is almost never the test of success.

In contrast, managers in private corporations live in a world ruled by different fundamental principles. They are there to pursue the interests of their shareholders, not those of the public as a whole. They must pursue a designated private interest and may at times ignore or even act against the public interest in doing so. The most famous statement on this was made by William Henry Vanderbilt, the executive of the New York Central Railroad, who in 1882 answered a reporter's question about whether the railroad would maintain a particularly unprofitable train service "for the benefit of the public." Vanderbilt's response was "the public be damned"— which seemed to epitomize the **robber baron** attitude toward social responsibility and helped create the climate for greater public regulation of the railroad industry. Yet most of those who have complained about Vanderbilt's callous remark have also ignored the inherent sensibleness of what he went on to say—that "railroads are not run on sentiment but on business principles." And those principles may force a business sometimes to act against the public interest. This is essentially the attitude of **Milton Friedman**, who has long argued that the resolution of social problems is the task of governments, not businesses, and managers who so spend money on them act irresponsibly.

Rather than focusing on equity and fairness to all, private corporation executives often focus on differentiating products and markets to "position" themselves selectively and advantageously for their bottom lines. The leadership, the boards of directors of private corporations, though they may have strategic alliances and a conglomerate structure, have far greater autonomy and capability to make strategy unilaterally than is generally the case for their public sector counterparts. The bottom line, the stock exchanges, the possibility of mergers and acquisitions, sales and profit margins—in short, the signals of the competitive market—rule the priorities of business executives. Their public sector counterparts are more focused on political promises, election and issue polling, budget making, inter- and intragovernmental power plays, media attention, and citizen perceptions.

Thus at the extremes, public management leadership and business management leadership seem to be marching to different tunes. So the question must be asked: Can we expect a common language and approach in the way they approach setting

---

robber barons The label first applied to the big-business titans of the United States toward the end of the nineteenth century. Now it is an invidious term for corporate leadership in general.

Milton Friedman (1912–) A conservative economist of the Chicago school, generally considered the leading proponent of a return to laissez-faire economics. A 1976 Nobel Prize winner, Friedman has been a major influence on thinking about monetary policy, consumption, and government regulation. He is generally considered to be the intellectual godfather to the movement toward government deregulation.

directions for their organizations? To begin to answer this, we must return to the other side of the public–private paradox: that there is very much in common at the heart of both business and public administration.

Both the public and private sectors possess large bureaucracies and comparatively small leadership structures. Both possess professional elements (such as hospitals and research units), as well as mass production and transportation organizations. Many features of organizational culture and decision making are more a product of the type of organization and its place in "the system" than whether it exists in a public or private context. While it is true that there are special languages and cultures peculiar to organizations in each sector, it is also true that the same people and overall culture are shared by both. After all, both sectors recruit from the same pool of college and university graduates. Individuals move in their careers from private to public and back again, even more so than in the past—and, significantly, they bring their ideas with them. So while there is no impenetrable cultural wall dividing the two sectors, there are some significant differentiations.

Today the public sectors in all modern nations are focusing on bringing in the best of private sector management ideas, including **competitiveness**, customer orientation, contracting out, strategic management, and so on. There is an increasing recognition that because of the profit incentive, the private sector is more efficient at generating, experimenting with, and rapidly installing new management techniques. The public sector is inherently and necessarily more conservative in this sense. Corporate executives rightly and regularly, with the support of their boards of directors, risk the firm if they believe a new product or process will offer appropriate gains. But it would be irresponsible for public sector managers to take similar risks. Thus the public sector constantly benefits from the inherently more experimental nature of private sector management. Additionally, an increasing proportion of public programs are delivered via private corporations or not-for-profits. So while there are barriers, there is also daily cooperation and interaction between the sectors.

Technology presents a common basic language for many of the daily tasks in each sector. The software a clerk in a public organization is using today will almost certainly be the same essential product that his or her private sector counterpart is using. And standard medical procedures are no different in public as opposed to private hospitals even though the food and quality of hotel-type services may vary considerably. And all sectors now ride the information superhighway via the Internet.

Thus it is fair to conclude that both the public and private sectors have very much in common—and that the public–private paradox remains very true today. Strategic

---

competitiveness The ability of the United States to compete economically with other developed nations—especially Japan. In the late 1980s, the term became an abbreviated way of referring to the concern for a comprehensive national industrial policy, to the persistent problem of lagging productivity of American workers, and to an increasingly unfavorable U.S. balance of trade. Competitiveness goes beyond the concerns of international trade to a concern for—indeed, a reevaluation of—the entire American business structure. This is because the countries with which the United States mainly competes—ironically, its closest military allies in most cases—play the competitiveness game by radically different rules using business-government partnership (corporatism) in ways that are for all practical purposes unknown in the United States.

management concepts, largely developed in the private sector, are now applied daily in public sector organizations. But how they are applied is heavily influenced by organizational role, size, and structure—and by the political environment.

The Importance of Being Close to the Center

Many of the key phrases in Osborne and Gaebler's book *Reinventing Government* have become familiar arguments in public debate, but none more so than the subtitle of the first chapter, "Steering Rather Than Rowing." This proposes that governments should direct their attention more to shaping and ensuring the outcomes of programs (the steering) rather than being preoccupied with their delivery (the rowing). This in effect is a call for governments to center themselves, to focus, on setting overall strategy rather than on the tactical details of delivery. Trash collection, schooling, or water supply may—perhaps should—be privatized, this argument goes, as long as government ensures that the outcomes are those that meet the public's needs.

However, there is an equally strong proposition that, with respect to many services that they have traditionally provided, governments should be neither steering nor rowing—that strategy itself can be set by those who deliver programs and that there may be no role for government in the steering process. Many jurisdictions in privatizing particular assets (such as railroads), services (such as telephones), or functions (such as trash collection) are implicitly accepting that they should neither steer nor row. Strategy making, if it happens at all, will occur in the boardrooms of corporations, presumably on commercial criteria. In such a context the "will of the people" is made evident by customer demand.

Sweden has long made the most emphatic distinction between steering and rowing in designing its machinery of government. There a separation exists between "policy ministries," which decide what is to be done, and "executive agencies," which do not make policy but deliver set programs for which they are responsible. In Britain, a major reform of the machinery of government in the 1990s has involved the emulation of aspects of the Swedish model through the creation of what are termed the "Next Steps" agencies, which, like executive agencies in Sweden, are there to deliver set programs in an autonomous way but not to deliberate on policy. In federal systems, such as that in the United States, another variant on this problem occurs: Policies are determined nationally—in Washington—but are designed to be delivered through state or local government agencies. Here again a conceptual distinction is made between steering or strategy making as the center's role and delivery as the role of the periphery. Jeffrey Pressman and Aaron Wildavsky, in their classic study *Implementation*, documented how easy it is for the best centrally made plans to be subverted, misunderstood, or bungled by service deliverers with limited ownership of the plans they are given to implement. More recently, not-for-profit organizations have often been substituted for state or local governments in the role of program deliverers for the central government, usually with the aim of cost savings in program delivery.

Yet in assigning the role of strategy making to the center, we face another significant issue. At the center, the predominant form taken by the machinery of government is the bureau or department. Such organizations lie deep at the heart of decision making. But according to management analyst Nancy Roberts, there are at least four key reasons why it may be difficult to adopt strategic management in such organizations:

1. Bureau managers must share power with other important actors as they seek to make decisions. These actors can be nearby, within the organization; far-flung, in another branch of government (the legislature or judiciary); or in an outside interest group.

2. Because bureaus function in a political as opposed to a rational environment, they often do not concur as to measures of adequate performance. After all, what one group of taxpayers perceives to be an overly generous bureaucratic effort to ameliorate a social program, another group of service recipients may see as too meager to do any lasting good.

3. Government managers have far less overall autonomy and control than their private sector counterparts. This makes it far more difficult for government to implement and coordinate any plan of action.

4. Strategic decision making in government, because of the preceding factors, is far more complex and difficult than in the private sector environment.

In the industrialized states of the Western world, strategy making generally has been the role of the national or state capital, while delivery has been the role of the **grass roots**. But there is an equally strong tradition that values the role of local decision making. National programs are often designed to provide for or even maximize local or individual discretion. The American tradition of local choice goes back to the **town meetings** of colonial New England and to the tradition of electing many officials (like judges and **sheriffs**) who would be appointed public servants in other administrative traditions. School boards, university councils, and many other locally elected public boards have a capacity to plan their own operations and to make strategy themselves, limited only by the constraints that may be attached to grant funding received from governments. More recently, the teachings of public choice economics have promoted the values of local choice and advocated voucher systems for financing various types of public projects. Such voucher systems maximize the opportunity for individuals to influence what is funded by government and provide scope for strategy making to be pushed down into smaller and smaller autonomous providers of services.

Organizational Language and Culture

The application of the behavioral sciences to management studies has heightened our awareness that issues of language and style, of culture, are central to how an

---

grass roots The rank and file of a political party or of a large bureaucracy.

town meeting A method of self-government, suitable for only the smallest jurisdictions, where the entire citizenry meets to decide local public policy. The town meeting is still the governing body for 88 percent of all New England municipalities.

sheriff In all states but Rhode Island, the elected chief officer of a county law enforcement agency, usually responsible for law enforcement in unincorporated areas of the county and for the operation of the county jail.

organization approaches its task (see Chapter 2). Quite simply, the special language of strategic management—however widespread in many public organizations—does not fit with the culture of all of them. Some years ago, one of the authors of this book visited Whitehall in London to ask a senior British civil servant about strategic management and how the concepts of objectives, strategies, and performance measurement were used. "Objectives?" was the reply. "My dear chap, we don't bother about objectives. Good chaps know what good chaps ought to do!" It is highly likely that this "good chap" is now gone from the Whitehall scene (and not just because of advancing age). Beginning with the conservative Thatcher administration in 1979, the British public sector has radically changed its organizational culture. One manifestation of this is its embrace of strategic management. This has been more difficult to achieve in the United States because as both a federal system with independent levels of government and a presidential system with a separation of powers, it is far more difficult for any one actor to mandate the implementation of systematic strategic management. Nevertheless, strategic management is well on its way to becoming the norm rather than the exception in American governments.

Strategic management entails a special culture and language. It is easier to adopt this language and develop this culture in environments where staff members are likely to have undergone postgraduate training in management. Also, the more open government organizations are to new talent, the more likely strategic management is to be adopted. Executives who move to and from the various organizational sectors are worker bees who bring about the pollination of new ideas. Finally, strategic management is more likely to be adopted in an organization where there has been a successful culture of change rather than one where new approaches to management are viewed with skepticism and reserve.

Organizational Place

The old saying in real estate is that three factors determine the price of a property: location, location, and location. The same can be said of strategic management. The most important single factor in the effectiveness of public sector strategic management efforts is location. The closer an organization is to the center of national decision making, the more difficult it is to sustain a successful strategic management effort. President Bill Clinton's attempt to reform the American health care system during his first two years in office, 1993 and 1994, was a massive strategic effort—and a massive failure. Nothing was accomplished despite the fact that impressive resources were devoted to the problem by the executive, the legislature, and a host of health care industry lobbies. The problem was so large and aroused such competing interests that the national ability to cope, even to reach a compromise, was paralyzed. This is why strategic management is so difficult with the really big issues.

While strategic management can succeed at the presidential level, it is often displaced by the hurly-burly of politics and horse-trading that properly occupies much time at all levels in Washington. On the other hand, local school districts, public hospitals, or state departments of highways are more likely to be consistently successful in using strategic management.

As rules of thumb, we can say that strategic management approaches in the public sector can more readily be adopted under these conditions:

1. The further a public organization is from the heart of political leadership in its nation, state, or local government
2. The more the organization undertaking strategic management is self-contained and autonomous as to its funding, personnel decisions, and overall destiny
3. The smaller it is (providing that it has the minimum critical mass needed to manage, plan, and operate independently)
4. The more its results are consistently measurable
5. The greater the proportion of its income is raised directly from its customers (from **user charges/user fees**, for example)

In short, strategic management approaches fit better if an organization has a reasonable amount of autonomy in its decision making—a prerequisite if strategic management is to be adopted and successfully implemented. If the organization is highly dependent, and inseparably tied into the workings of a political administration, it may not in truth be able to make independent strategic decisions at all or, if it can make them, not do so well. For some organizations, this problem can be overcome by "commercializing" them—that is, changing structural arrangements to give them substantial autonomy and freedom over key decisions, such as pricing, staffing, and budgets. Others may be so bound up in the central work of government that such commercialization is neither feasible nor proper. Yet even these public-policy-dominated organizations can benefit from and employ strategic management techniques, albeit in a more limited context.

Strategic Management Tools

The level of analysis is one of the classic issues in the study of politics because it poses an eternal question: Should the focus of political analysis be the individual political actor, a local government, a national government, or the international political system as a whole? The forces at play and the linkages that are made within and between these levels make single-level analysis problematic at best. Thus there is no point in undertaking a political analysis of a political actor in isolation—because that actor is never in isolation. He or she is always a citizen of a state and/or a member of other large groups. Thus there are always a large number of linkages and interactions among the various levels of government and other social groupings.

Strategy presents a similar level of analysis problem. It is inherently hierarchical. The most general notions come down from the top to be implemented at various stages leading to the bottom. When the president orders "justice" for America's enemies, that order travels down the chain of command until a soldier pulls the

---

user charges/user fees Specific sums that users or consumers of a government service pay to receive that service. For example, a homeowner's water bill, if based on usage, would be a user charge. Other examples include toll roads and bridges and charges to use public swimming pools.

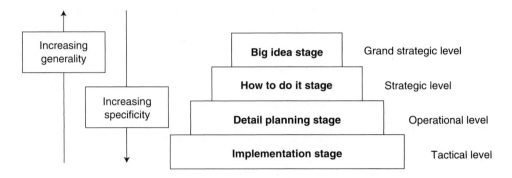

Figure 9.5   The Hierarchy of Strategy

trigger on his rifle and administers a full measure of such justice to a deserving per-son. Strategy sets into action the ways and means by which people are ultimately shot, or given food stamps, or provided health care. Whether the end result is bullets or bedpans, the strategy involved will travel a similar route toward implementation—from the grand strategic (the national policymaking) level to the strategic (the highest organizational level) to the operational (the planning or administrative) level to the tactical (the service delivery) level. Each level accepts strategy from above but uses dis-cretion to create substrategies or level-specific strategies that facilitate implementation. At the same time each level develops measurement and reporting techniques to assess how well the overall strategy is being implemented. Three of these tools for measuring effectiveness are best practices, benchmarking, and management scorecards.

Best Practices

This may be the oldest idea in war and management—look at what your competi-tors are doing and imitate their successful innovations. Long before the age of patents and copyrights, organizations—whether military or industrial—would simply steal, borrow, or copy the best ideas of others. Remember the whole thrust of the scientific management movement (see Chapter 6) was to find the "one best way." But "best" is inherently temporary. A successful innovation by reformers is followed by a period of increased effectiveness—at least until competing organizations adopt similar reforms. But over time advancing technologies and changing environments allow the innovation to deteriorate relative to other arrangements, first to become less competent and then to become incompetent. Thus installing and maintaining best practices is quite literally a matter of organizational life and death.

This critical question must always be asked: Is this organization efficient by industry standards? For public sector managers, the challenge to maximize opera-tional efficiency is critical because public organizations may lose their credibility or even their right to exist if their managers cannot operate them in such a way as to demonstrate acceptable standards of competence. In past years, managers could some-times obfuscate discussion of the efficiency of public sector organizations by references to unique characteristics, measurement difficulties, and the complexity of public sector life. While there is a measure of truth in all of these as reasons for why assessing the efficiency of public sector organizations is difficult, it is also true that we now have, through benchmarking and studies of comparative performance, a good deal more data to consider—especially in those parts of the public sector where measurements and comparisons are easiest—that is, where "hard," measurable outputs exist.

Despite the problems and subtleties of measuring performance and productivity in the public sector, an objective baseline is indispensable if any manager or government wishes to bring about better performance. Almost as indispensable is a systematic way of comparing how you are doing with the efforts of others working in the same sphere. This latter problem is not unique to public sector management; it is a problem all managers face. This technique of comparison, known as benchmarking, was developed by the Xerox corporation just for this purpose. It has now spread around the world and is widely used in the public sector.

Benchmarking

Benchmarking systematically compares work processes with those of competitors or with best practices in an industry. It involves choosing and studying key performance areas in an organization and often involves entering into cooperative arrangements with partner organizations. The process may be carried out internally (perhaps comparing how the organization's regional offices perform); it may be carried out externally (for example, a study of local tax collection efficiency comparing two municipalities); or it may involve like functions (such as customer service) in unlike organizations. Whatever the scope or focus, benchmarking should not be carried out in isolation. It must be linked to the strategic plans of the organization (to ensure that the most relevant areas are chosen for study) and to formal quality improvement efforts, since any shortfall in performance, once pinpointed, must be attacked and improved.

One of the most creative applications of benchmarking in the public sector has been in the state of Oregon, where the Oregon Benchmarks Project is run by the governor's office. Each agency is required to define long-term goals, benchmarks, mission statements, and performance measures. In aggregate, the process achieves integrated strategic planning for the state. (You can see these benchmarks on the Internet at www.econ.state.or.us\opb.) Oregon has used this concept very creatively; it even has detailed (and quantified) benchmarks for "civic engagement."

In Australia, benchmarking was first promoted heavily within industry in the 1980s by the federal government as a means of encouraging private enterprise to become more internationally competitive. Then it was used in the struggle to make public enterprises more efficient. In the 1990s, a number of benchmarking studies compared the performance of Australian public enterprises (like railroads, ports, and electricity undertakings) with each other and with those overseas. Then benchmarking was extensively applied in local government. Benchmarking can be a valuable aid in judging the efficiency of a public organization. However, the technique is susceptible to misuse and poor application if inappropriate comparisons are made and if sufficient explanation of variances is not provided in published results.

Focus

How public, private, and nonprofit organizations compare with each other. Strategic benchmarking is seldom industry focused. It moves across industries and cities to determine the best-in-class strategic outcomes.

Strategic benchmarks

How public, private, and nonprofit organizations compare with each other in terms of product and service. Performance benchmarking usually focuses on elements of price, technical quality, ancillary product or service features, speed, reliability, and other performance features.

Performance benchmarks

How public, private, and nonprofit organizations compare, through the identification of the most effective operating practices of many organizations that perform similar work processes.

Progress benchmarks

Figure 9.6 Three Types of Benchmarks

SOURCE: Adapted from Anthony H. Rainey, "Benchmarking to Become Best in Class," *Government Finance Review* (February 1997).

Where public and private sector organizations are able to compete with one another on a "level playing field"—that is, under circumstances where regulatory controls, policy latitude, and other key determinants are impartial—public sector organizations often compare well with private sector counterparts. This has been demonstrated in Australia, where public/private competition in the airline and banking industries existed for many years and where the large public operators often defeated large private operators under comparable operating conditions. Such examples reinforce the proposition that competition is a more important precondition of organizational efficiency than ownership as such.

Management Scorecards

In essence, a management scorecard is a tally sheet, just as are scorecards in golf or bowling. However, what is being tallied is the performance, not of individual players but of the individual units or functions of a large organization. This allows the managers at the top to get an overview of how well their tactical managers are playing the "game." The whole point of the scorecard approach was to allow executives to instantly scan, by looking at the scores, the status of their organization units.

In the early 1990s "balanced scorecards" first became fashionable in the private sector as a means to evaluate a company's performances from several perspectives simultaneously. Traditionally the emphasis had been on financial performance (the bottom line), but a balanced scorecard complemented financial performance with data on customer satisfaction, internal processes, and ability to learn—among other measures. While report cards of this nature are as old as school, the scorecard approach suddenly became "hot" in government once they were introduced in 2002 as part of the President's Management Agenda. All of the major federal agencies (more than fifty in all) are now being graded on their progress in these five government-wide management initiatives:

1. Strategic management of human capital
2. Competitive sourcing
3. Improving financial performance
4. Expanded electronic government
5. Budget and performance integration

The grades are color coded so each department is rated red, yellow, or green for the level of success in implementing each of the preceding initatives. The first scorecard, the 2001 Baseline Evaluation, gave out mostly red circles. As the Office of Management and Budget explained, "The initial scorecard shows a lot of poor scores, reflecting the state of government this Administration inherited." Every six months, acting for the president, OMB issues new grades. At the end of June 2005 the OMB report showed that the Department of Labor under Secretary Elaine Chao was the first and only department to have met the standards for all five management initiatives. Meanwhile, the Departments of Defense (DoD) and Veterans Affairs (VA) ranked at the low end of federal performance, with the DoD possessing unsatisfactory scores in three areas and the VA failing to meet standards in four of five rating categories. Table 9.1 lists the scores for all 15 federal departments, as well as the Environmental Protection Agency.

So what's the point of this exercise? It is mainly a way of artificially creating the competitive forces inherent in the private sector. To a large degree this is management by shame—no organization wants to be ashamed of its rankings. Not surprisingly, the scores have been going up. OMB has also introduced directional arrows within the circles. Thus a yellow circle with an upward-pointing arrow is like a B-plus. While the red, yellow, and green circles may seem silly on the surface, underneath they facilitate three key objectives:

1. To focus attention on what top management considers its key priorities
2. To motivate organizational units to improve
3. To provide timely assessments of progress

It would be hard to argue against the Bush administration's five government-wide initiatives. Worthy goals all! But will they be achieved with a management scorecard system that employs "getting to green"? Or will managers, like students, work mainly for the grade at the expense of real learning or real reform? Only two things are certain: (1) nothing will be reinvented, as that was the goal of the previous administration, and (2) the next administration will have a new set of strategic management tools.

TABLE 9.1 Federal Government Department Management Scorecards—June 2005

	Human Capital	Competitive Sourcing	Financial Management	E-government	Budget Performance
Agriculture	Mixed	Mixed	Not Met	Mixed	Mixed
Commerce	Met	Mixed	Met	Mixed	Mixed
Defense	Mixed	Not Met	Not Met	Not Met	Mixed
Energy	Met	Met	Met	Mixed	Met
EPA	Mixed	Mixed	Met	Met	Mixed
Health and Human Services	Met	Met	Not Met	Mixed	Mixed
Homeland Security	Mixed	Mixed	Not Met	Not met	Mixed
Housing and Urban Development	Mixed	Mixed	Not Met	Mixed	Mixed
Interior	Mixed	Met	Not Met	Mixed	Mixed
Justice	Mixed	Mixed	Not Met	Mixed	Mixed
Labor	Met	Met	Met	Met	Met
State	Met	Mixed	Met	Met	Met
Transportation	Met	Met	Not Met	Met	Met
Treasury	Mixed	Met	Not Met	Not Met	Mixed
Veterans	Mixed	Not Met	Not Met	Not Met	Not Met

SOURCE: The White House, http://www.whitehouse.gov/results/agenda/scorecard.html.

Met = Met standards

Mixed = Partially met standards

Not Met = Failed to meet standards

✦ A CASE STUDY: HOW MILITARY GENERAL STAFFS BECAME THE FIRST STRATEGIC THINK TANKS

On January 20, 1953, Dwight D. Eisenhower, the general who led the Allies to victory against Nazi Germany in World War II, took the oath of office as president of the United States. A few hours later he was handed a sealed envelope. According to Eisenhower biographer Geoffrey Perret, "Eisenhower was annoyed." He told the man who gave him the envelope, "Never bring me a sealed envelope again." Perret wrote that this sealed envelope was "concrete proof of something he already believed—that this place [the White House] was badly organized, badly run. Hundreds of letters addressed to him arrived each day. Just opening them would have been a chore. More than that, though, they had to be screened so that only those that he had to read, whether to conduct government business or to keep old friendships in good repair, were placed before him." To deal with the problem that was symbolized by the sealed envelope, Eisenhower adopted a variant of the system—the general staff system—that was pioneered and perfected by the army he had so recently defeated.

As an organizational model to be copied and adapted to local conditions, the German general staff has no peer in the history of administration and policymaking. While large military organizations as far back as the armies of Alexander the Great (336–323 B.C.E.) had staff elements for logistics and intelligence, the birth of the modern staff system can be traced to a specific time and place: eastern Germany, October 14, 1806. In a single day a smaller French army led by Napoléon destroyed (killed, wounded, or captured) virtually the entire Prussian army at the battles of Jena and Auerstadt. In the wake of this disaster and occupation of their country by the French, two of Prussia's brighter officers, Gerhard Scharnhorst (1755–1813) and August Gneisenau (1760–1831), convinced their king that there was a way to eventually defeat Napoléon. But to do it the Prussians had to copy some of the French military reforms and come up with a few new ones of their own. The Prussian Army then began to imitate the French by selecting officers on the basis of merit as opposed to social rank in a new emphasis on field maneuvers instead of parade grand drill and in the creation of a citizen's as opposed to a mercenary army. Then they bettered the French by inventing the general staff—a think tank for the army.

Napoléon had plenty of staff but no real general staff because he, being a military genius, didn't need one. But true geniuses are rare. Thus a general staff, who brings together the brightest officers to plan future operations, is in effect a collective substitute for individual genius. In 1806 the Prussian Army was so incompetently organized and led that it deserved to lose to Napoléon. By 1813 the Prussians had so reformed their army that they defeated Napoléon and helped to force his initial abdication and exile to Elba. When Napoléon surfaced again in 1815 it was the Prussians who joined the British under the Duke of Wellington at Waterloo to defeat Napoléon again. The two most famous battleships of the 1930s were named in honor of Scharnhorst and Gneisenau; both, fortunately, were destroyed during World War II.

By the beginning of the twentieth century all of the major military powers adopted a variant of the German general-staff system. Of course, it sometimes took a large-scale demonstration of incompetence for the military to see the wisdom in reform. For example, both the United States and Great Britain created general staffs only after the demonstrably poor management of major wars: the Spanish-American War of 1898 and the Boer War of 1899–1902. Elihu Root, as U.S. secretary of war, wrote in his annual report for 1902 that "the most important thing to be done now for the regular army is the creation of a general staff." He didn't have to remind his readers that this was necessary because of the poor management of the last war—that soldiers sent to fight in the heat of Cuba had only wool shirts to wear, that the famous charge up San Juan Hill by cavalry troops led by Colonel (later President) Theodore Roosevelt was on foot because no horses were sent with them, and that only 300 of the 3,000 U.S. soldiers who died in the war were killed in combat. Root's report complained, "Our system makes no adequate provision for the directing brain which every army must have to work successfully. Common experience has shown that this cannot be furnished by any single man without assistants, and that it requires a body of officers working together under the direction of a chief and entirely separate from and independent of the administrative staff of an army. . . . This body of officers, in distinction from the administrative staff, has come to be called a general staff."

The following year the U.S. Army was ordered to create a general staff by an act of Congress. The president who signed the bill into law was Theodore Roosevelt—the same colonel whose men, because of poor staff work, lacked horses when they had to charge up San Juan Hill. Root's description of the duties of the general staff, while written in English in his report, were in essence a translation from the German: "Such a body of men doing general staff duty is just as necessary in time of peace as it is in time of war. It is not an executive body; it is not an administrative body; it acts only through the authority of others. It makes intelligent command possible by procuring and arranging information and working out plans in detail, and it makes intelligent and effective execution of commands possible by keeping all separate agents advised of the parts they are to play in the general scheme."

But it took a while for the general staff concept to be widely understood. For example, D. Clayton James tells of the time in 1914 when President Woodrow Wilson read in the *Baltimore Sun* that the general staff of the U.S. Army was working on plans for a war with Germany. World War I had just started in Europe, and Wilson was determined at that time to keep the United States out of it. So he directed the secretary of war to launch "an immediate investigation, and if it proved true, to relieve at once every officer of the general staff." Once it was explained to Wilson that preparation of theoretical war plans is a continuing and primary function of the staff, the president quietly allowed the matter to drop.

In order to train officers to work on the new general staff, the Army created a staff school at Fort Levenworth, Kansas, which has evolved into the Command and General Staff College. President Eisenhower was not only a graduate of this school but during World War II commanded perhaps the largest military staff in the history of warfare. So Eisenhower, whom General Douglas MacArthur called "the best clerk I ever had," knew about staff and knew that he, as president, shouldn't have to open envelopes. Of course, when President Eisenhower was inaugurated, the White House had plenty of both personal and professional staff for the president. But it was largely a spoke-and-wheel administrative structure. Thus all senior staff had direct access to the president. Eisenhower immediately supplanted this with a hierarchical structure by which all staff reported to a chief of staff who became the gatekeeper to the president. This protected the president's time and ensured that all proposals were adequately "staffed out" before being presented to him.

While both Presidents Kennedy and Johnson, who followed Eisenhower, reverted to the spoke-and-wheel approach, the White House staff got increasingly involved with departmental policy reviews and independent policy development. Richard Nixon was vice president under Eisenhower. For eight years he watched and learned from Eisenhower's staff system. So when Nixon became president in 1969, he immediately appointed a chief of staff for the White House, as has every president since. Despite the fact that Nixon's chief of staff and several dozen of his henchmen went to jail for Watergate-related crimes, the White House staff remains the de facto national think tank whose job, in addition to helping the president to oversee the federal bureaucracy, is to develop national policy and the president's legislative agenda.

A chief of staff was once a rarity and strictly military. This is no longer the case. The influence of the German general staff model is now so pervasive that you can hardly walk into a government office without bumping into a chief of staff. Most governors and mayors and county administrators have them. So do major department heads from police chiefs (yes, the chief has a chief!) to school superintendents. Increasingly, even individual legislators have them. The point is that you as a public manager are not very important unless you have one—even if your chief of staff is really not much more than a chief of a few clerks.

Just as the chief-of-staff concept has developed many variations, so too has the notion of a think tank. The phrase itself, while used here to describe the function of a true general staff, is really just a colloquial term for an organization, or organizational segment, whose sole function is research. The purpose of civilian think tanks is to identify options, assess policies, and generally contribute to the debate over public policies. Although they began, at least on a large scale, after World War II as a particularly American phenomenon, other countries have emulated the American experience. Now think tanks are pervasive throughout the world. Many are associated with universities, others with government. More recently there has been a trend toward partisan think tanks. The U.S. tax code encourages any eccentric with enough money to establish a foundation to fund research on virtually anything. So what was once solely the tool of nations to deal with the great issues of war and peace is now also a vehicle for social reformers and crackpot millionaires. Blame Napoléon!

For Discussion: *How did the general-staff concept and its associated practices travel from military to civilian institutions? How can you tell if a chief of staff is for real or is just a puffed-up job title for an administrative assistant?*

Summary

Strategy is the employment of resources to gain an objective. Tactics are the use of a subset of these resources to gain a part of the overall objective. Strategic management is the application of this ancient art to contemporary business and public administration. Strategic planning should not be equated with strategic management because strategic management often occurs without formal strategic planning. Strategic planning, however, is meaningless without strategic management.

All strategic management efforts entail all the following:

1. The identification of objectives to be achieved
2. The adoption of a time frame
3. An assessment of organization capabilities
4. An assessment of the organization's environment
5. The selection of a strategy from among alternatives

Overall, strategic management approaches in the public sector can more readily be adopted (1) the further a public organization is from the heart of its political leadership, (2) the more the organization undertaking strategic management is self-contained and autonomous, (3) the smaller it is (providing that it has the minimum critical mass), and (4) the more its results are consistently measurable.

Strategic management has become an indispensable perspective for many public sector managers. Such perspectives do not displace traditional management concerns but rather add a new dimension.

Review Questions

1. What are the differences between strategy and tactics for an overall national government or for an individual government agency?
2. Why must strategic planning be fully integrated with strategic management?
3. Is management by objectives more of a planning technique or more of a management control technique, or is it both?
4. Select any major government agency and explain how a SWOT analysis of it would usefully contribute to its strategic planning processes.
5. How has benchmarking proven to be such a successful technique for analyzing the comparative efficiency of organizations?

Key Concepts

chief of staff   The military title for the officer who supervises the work of the other officers on a commander's staff; civilian supervisor of an overall management team who reports directly to the chief executive officer.

general staff   A group of officers in a military's headquarters who assists their commanders in planning, coordinating, and supervising operations.

objective   A short-term goal; something that must be achieved on the way to a larger overall achievement.

planning horizon   The time frame during which the objectives of a strategic plan are to be achieved.

staff principle   That a unit of a larger organization should have primary responsibility to think and plan, to ponder over innovations and plan for their implementation.

strategic management   A philosophy of management that links strategic planning with day-to-day decision making. Strategic management seeks a fit between an organization's external and internal environments.

strategic plan   The formal document that presents the ways and means by which a strategic goal will be achieved.

strategic planning   The set of processes used by an organization to assess the strategic situation and develop strategy for the future.

strategy   The overall conduct of a major enterprise to achieve long-term goals; the pattern to be found in a series of organizational decisions.

SWOT analysis   A review of an organization's Strengths, Weaknesses, Opportunities, and Threats. This technique is widely used to examine the viability of strategic plans.

tactics   The short-term immediate decisions that in their totality lead to the achievement of strategic goals.

think tank   A colloquial term for an organization, or organizational segment, whose sole function is research, usually in the policy and behavioral sciences.

vision   A view of an organization's future. The purpose of strategic management is to make such a vision a reality.

vision statement   The identification of objectives to be achieved in the future.

Bibliography

Ansoff, H. Igor. (1965). *Corporate Strategy*. New York: McGraw-Hill.

Bryson, John M. (1995). *Strategic Planning for Public and Nonprofit Organizations*, 2nd ed. San Francisco: Jossey-Bass.

Dickson, Paul. (1971). *Think Tanks*. New York: Atheneum.

Dror, Yehezkel. (1964). "Muddling Through—'Science' or Inertia." *Public Administration Review* 24 (September).

Drucker, Peter F. (1954). *The Practice of Management*. New York: Harper.

Gordon, Gerald C. (1993). *Strategic Planning for Local Government*. Washington: International City Management Association.

Keegan, John. (1993). *A History of Warfare*. New York: Knopf.

Kennan, George F. ("X") (1947). "The Sources of Soviet Conduct." *Foreign Affairs* (July).

Lindblom, Charles E. (1959). "The Science of Muddling Through." *Public Administration Review* 19.

Luttwak, Edward N. (1976). *The Grand Strategy of the Roman Empire*. Baltimore: Johns Hopkins University Press.

McMillan, John. (1996). *Games, Strategies, and Managers*. Oxford, England: Oxford University Press.

Mintzberg, Henry. (1994). *The Rise and Fall of Strategic Planning*. New York: Free Press.

Osborne, David, and Ted Gaebler. (1992). *Reinventing Government*. Reading, MA: Addison-Wesley.

Pascale, Richard T. (1993). "The Honda Effect." In *The Strategy Process*, James Brian Quinn, Henry Mintzberg, and Robert M. James, eds. Englewood Cliffs, NJ: Prentice Hall.

Perret, Geoffrey. (1999). *Eisenhower*. New York: Random House.

Porter, Michael E. (1980). *Competitive Strategy*. New York: Free Press.

Pressman, Jeffrey L., and Aaron Wildavsky. (1973). *Implementation: How Great Expectations in Washington Are Dashed in Oakland; Or, Why It's Amazing that Federal Programs Work at All. . . .* Berkeley: University of California Press.

Roberts, Nancy C. (1993). "Limitations of Strategic Action in Bureaus." In *Public Management: The State of the Art*, Barry W. Bozeman, ed. San Francisco: Jossey-Bass.

Rumelt, Richard. (1992). "The Evaluation of Business Strategy." In *The Strategy Process*, James Brian Quinn, Henry Mintzberg, and Robert M. James, eds. Englewood Cliffs, NJ: Prentice Hall.

Seward, Desmond. (1988). *Napoleon and Hitler: A Comparative Biography*. New York: Viking.

Smith, Bruce L. R. (1968). *The RAND Corporation*. Cambridge, MA: Harvard University Press.

Smith, James A. (1993). *The Idea Brokers: Think Tanks and the Rise of the New Policy Elite*. New York: Free Press.

Toffler, Alvin. (1970). *Future Shock*. New York: Random House.

Weigley, Russell F. (1984). *History of the United States Army*, enlarged edition. Bloomington: Indiana University Press.

Wettenhall, Roger, and Colm O. Nuallain, eds. (1990). *Public Enterprise Performance: Seven Country Studies*. Brussels: International Institute of Administrative Studies.

Wildavsky, Aaron. (1978). "A Budget for All Seasons: Why the Traditional Budget Lasts." *Public Administration Review* 38, No. 6 (November–December).

Recommended Books

Bryson, John M. (1995). *Strategic Planning for Public and Nonprofit Organizations*, rev. ed. San Francisco: Jossey-Bass. A comprehensive guide to all aspects of strategic leadership, with an emphasis on planning, implementation, and strategy evaluation.

Dale, Ernst, and Lyndall F. Urwick. (1960). *Staff in Organization*. New York: McGraw-Hill. The classic study of staff throughout history.

Dixit, Avinash, and Barry Nalebuff. (1993). *Thinking Strategically*. New York: W. W. Norton. An accessible introduction to game theoretical approaches to decision making.

Koteen, Jack. (1997). *Strategic Management in Public and Nonprofit Organizations in Managing Public Concerns in an Era of Limits*, 2nd ed. Westport, CT: Praeger. A comprehensive how-to-do-it manual on creating, installing, and evaluating strategic management systems.

Mitchell, Jerry. (1998). *The American Experiment with Government Corporations*. Armonk, NY: M. E. Sharpe. A survey of the organizational form that incorporates the best features of public and private management to accomplish tasks that are deemed unsuited for commercialization or traditional bureaucracy.

Moore, Mark, H. (1995). *Creating Public Value: Strategic Management in Government.* Cambridge, MA: Harvard University Press. A call for public managers to go beyond being competent bureaucratic technicians; they must retool as strategic managers who "search for public value"—that is, more bang for the buck, better quality or quantities for each dollar spent.

Stone, Diane, Andrew Denham, and Mark Garnett, eds. (1998). *Think Tanks Across Nations: A Comparative Approach.* Manchester, England: Manchester University Press. A tour of think tank antics and influences in the industrialized world.

Related Web Sites

Center for Strategic and International Studies (CSIS)
www.csis.org/
Center for Strategic Management
www.csmweb.com
Contingency analysis
www.contingencyanalysis.com/
Council on Foreign Relations
www.cfr.org/p/
Government Performance and Results Act
www.whitehouse.gov/omb/mgmt-gpra/ gplaw2m.html
Hoover Institution on War, Revolution and Peace at Stanford University
www-hoover.stanford.edu/

Milton Friedman
http://www.hoover.stanford.edu/bios/ friedman.html
National Strategy Forum
www.nationalstrategy.com
Peter Drucker
www.peter-drucker.com
Rand Corporation
www.rand.org/
Strategic planning in Canada
www.cityofgp.com/Default.htm
Strategic Planning Institute
http://pimsonline.com/

CHAPTER 10

Leadership

•KEYNOTE: THE HEDGEHOG, THE FOX OR HENRY V

The hedgehog is a small animal similar to a porcupine. When threatened, it rolls up into a ball so it is protected by the sharp quills covering its body. The fox is a notoriously clever, shrewd, and ingenious creature—so much so that "foxy" has become a synonym for these traits. One fine day in ancient Greece the poet Archilochus wrote, "The fox knows many things, but the hedgehog knows one big thing." Twenty-six hundred years later Isaiah Berlin (1909–1997), the British political philosopher, used Archilochus's brief poetic fragment as the basis for *The Hedgehog and the Fox*, his now famous essay on intellectual style, on how leaders think, and on the utility of animal similes for describing human traits.

Berlin's essay has inspired a popular parlor game in political circles: classifying leaders as either hedgehogs or foxes. Hedgehogs are those who are single-minded about a concept. They know, like the hedgehog, "one big thing." President Ronald Reagan was a hedgehog. He knew that capitalism was better for the prosperity of the peoples of the world than socialism. This basic belief guided both his domestic policies (lower taxes, less government regulation) and his foreign policies (defeat communism wherever possible). As a hedgehog he was notorious for not bothering with the details of policy implementation. But that, of course, was what helped define him as a hedgehog. Hedgehogs are big-picture, not small-detail, leaders.

Now contrast Reagan with the Democratic presidents who preceded and followed him. Both Jimmy Carter and Bill Clinton were policy wonks obsessed with the details. They were both brilliant foxes. They knew all the excruciating details on all the policies before them. The problem was that they were men who knew too much. They were so obsessed with details that they never gave their subordinates in the administration, let alone the American people, a clear vision to follow. They thought and acted too much tactically and not enough strategically. Foreign policy to them was essentially a collection of improvisations. In contrast, Reagan's foreign policy could be summed up in two words: beat communism. And he did!

A hedgehog leader is one who imbues the organization with his or her overall philosophy of action. It is Elizabeth I heaping "foul scorn" on the 1588 Spanish armada that unsuccessfully sought to invade England. It is Admiral Horatio Nelson telling his captains before the 1805 Battle of Trafalgar, "No captain can do very wrong if he places his ship alongside that of the enemy." It is President Abraham Lincoln in 1863 dedicating the cemetery at Gettysburg, Pennsylvania, and demanding of the nation "that from these honored dead we take increased devotion to that cause for which they gave their last full measure of devotion; that we here highly resolve that these dead shall not have died in vain." Fancy words for "Let's win the war." It is President Franklin D. Roosevelt telling the nation in a radio address (December 19, 1940) that "we must be the great arsenal of democracy." And it is President Ronald Reagan telling a Republican congressional dinner (May 4, 1982), "We're the party that wants to see an America in which people can still get rich."

Hedgehogic visions all. These are calls to action that, while simple, are not simplistic, that offer specific instructions, and that are ultimately inspirational. After all, the job of a leader is to inspire—and hedgehogs do it better than foxes because they are more focused, more on target. People will not rally around a laundry list of little things no matter how worthy each item may be. Foxes may be brilliant managers and organizers of all the policy details, but management is not leadership. The original managers, etymologically speaking, were horse trainers. The word's meaning was gradually extended to any kind of skillful handling. So while a fox's skill in handling situations is generally acknowledged, handling is not leadership. All the attention to details may not add up to "Follow me!" A leader with a hedgehogic vision inspires others, while a manager merely delegates.

The presidential election of 2000 offered a direct contrast between a hedgehog and a fox. Then Governor George W. Bush knew a few big things: cut taxes, strengthen the military, and reform education and Social security. His opponent, then Vice President Al Gore, wallowed in details like the class know-it-all. Despite Gore's obviously better grasp of the facts at hand, Bush seemed to win the presidential debates because he stayed on message with his hedgehogic vision. According to columnist Dick Morris, "It wasn't that Bush didn't know the details, but that he didn't much care. He knows, instinctively, that details don't matter as much as big ideas do" (*New York Post,* January 2, 2001). Now President Bush gets to be a hedgehog in the White House. He shows every sign of following in the hedgehogic tradition of Ronald Reagan—except that while the elderly Reagan sought a nap every afternoon, the energetic Bush heads off to the gym for a workout. Remember that leaders may have a detached management style and still be strongly focused on objectives. They just see things differently. They see to it that their staff deals with the foxy details.

Note that it is Reagan that Bush is imitating here, not his father. The first President Bush, despite being understudy to hedgehog Reagan for eight years, became too foxy for his own good. He got off his own message domestically ("Read my lips—no new taxes") when he raised taxes. Then his foreign policy of forging a "new world order" was so vague and complicated—not to mention reminiscent of Nazi phraseology—that what he meant by it remains elusive to this day. The best proof that the son will not imitate the father is the glaring fact that the father lost his 1992 bid for reelection to the fox from Arkansas. Bill Clinton was the ultimate fox. He put forth one detail after another with no overarching vision. So the public is all the more ready to follow a presidential hedgehog—especially if there are no sex or financial scandals that demean the presidential office.

BOX 10.1   The Lion and the Fox

Beastly descriptions of leaders have a long lineage in political analysis. Perhaps the best known is Niccolo Machiavelli's comparison of the lion and the fox in *The Prince* (1532):

> A prince being thus obliged to know well how to act as a beast must imitate the fox and the lion, for the lion cannot protect himself from traps, and the fox cannot defend himself from wolves. One must therefore be a fox to recognize traps and a lion to frighten wolves.

The most famous recent political leader with both of these animalistic traits was President Franklin D. Roosevelt (1882–1945). Roosevelt reached the height of political power despite the fact that, after 1921 when he contracted polio, he was basically confined to a wheelchair. Yet, because he was able to stand (with braces) to give speeches and because reporters were not allowed to take pictures that made him appear to be disabled, much of the American public was unaware of his handicapped condition—even though it was not a secret. His critics attacked him and his wife, Eleanor, as being either socialist or fascist. But he was just being pragmatic in response to his times. He was the president of the United States (1933–1945) whose New Deal policies are often said to have saved the capitalistic system; who led the nation through the Great Depression of the 1930s and to victory in World War II; and who is on every leading historian's list, along with Abraham Lincoln and George Washington, as one of the best U.S. presidents ever. So it was not surprising that historian James MacGregor Burns entitled his 1956 biography of him *Roosevelt: The Lion and the Fox.*

There is no better example in the world's literature of tactical rhetoric supporting a strategic objective than Shakespeare's *Henry V*. President George W. Bush is often analyzed as a modern Henry V. While still a prince young Henry led a degenerate life as a hard-drinking associate of fun loving ne'er-do-wells—thieves, prostitutes and worse. His father despairs that his son, destined to inherit the throne, will never amount to much. As he approaches death, King Henry IV advises the prince to cope with his forthcoming domestic problems by making an effort to "busy giddy minds with foreign quarrels." The youthful Prince Hal, when crowned Henry V on his father's death, takes exactly that advice. Shakespeare has the new king order his officials to find a legal justification for waging war on France. Henry then assembles his "band of brothers" and forces them to listen to some of the most famous, most inspirational and most quoted lines in all of Shakespeare. With poetry he rallies them to go "once more into the breach," compares them to "greyhounds in the slips, straining upon the start," and has them attack upon the shout of "the game's afoot!" Thanks to Shakespeare's stirring words and to the 1415 Battle of Agincourt, Henry conquers France; thus becoming history's and literature's greatest example of how someone turns out to be a great national hero after a misspent youth.

Ever since George W. Bush became a serious contender for president, political commentators have compared him to Henry V as a leader. (Nobody has ever compared him to Henry for eloquence.) Bush has a father who led a great nation, a misspent youth replete with frequent alcoholic binges and ascension to power. All this links the 43rd President with the legendary English ruler. Yet the question remains, will Bush end up as much of a hero as Henry V? He certainly followed Henry in busying "giddy minds with foreign quarrels" with wars in Afghanistan and Iraq. However, will George W. Bush continue his parallel with Henry V by achieving the same kind of decisive victory won by the historical Henry? Decisive or not, one aspect of this parallel is particularly disquieting. Henry V's great victory was but one battle fought in the middle of what history calls the Hundred Years' War.

For Discussion: *Why are the hedgehog and fox analogies so useful as shorthand ways of referring to leadership styles? Have you seen leaders in organizations with which you are familiar who fit the hedgehog and fox analogies?*

Leading for Performance

There are many characteristics of public sector management that call for knowledge and skills somewhat distinct from those required in private sector management. We have seen how the political context and governance arrangements that exist in the public sector present constraints and frameworks of decision making that must be understood and in many respects "managed" by public officials. We have discussed the special problems in public sector strategic management of converting political programs and managerial imperatives into a well-sequenced path to be followed. We have examined how the external and internal structures through which government is managed—intergovernmental relations and the machinery of government—give a framework that public sector managers must acknowledge and accommodate if they are to work effectively.

All of these areas, however fundamental, really amount to parts of the context in which the public sector manager is to operate. It is as though we have examined a theater—its lighting, its marketing arrangements, its ownership, the way the supporting cast of actors and dancers are hired and fired. But we have now to turn to the heart of the question: how good is the performance going to be? What do the producer and director, the managers, have to do to exact from the cast the best performances of which they are capable?

The word *performance* is shared here by the world of management and the theatrical world—it also permeates the sporting world. There, too, the task is to exact a personal best from an athlete or a supreme performance from a team. There, too, issues like training, team functioning, leadership, comparison with the best, total quality in the sense of trying never to miss a trick, and of course strategy are central ideas. *Performance*, above all, means the demonstration of a skill, the display of competence. In public sector management there are now many senses in which the term is applied. There are so many because knowing what kind of performance we are getting and setting up means for individuals and teams to do better are central concerns of public sector leaders. Thus performance management really does begin with leadership.

Defining Leadership

As a callow youth, one of the authors of this book took an undergraduate course in medieval history. Having seen dozens of films in which castles were stormed by a cast of thousands, this student asked the professor, "How do they get large numbers of men in real life to storm castles and the like when it appears to be, and indeed often is, certain death?" The professor's answer was memorable: "That's leadership for you!"

And so it is. The job of the leader of any organization is to get people to do things they have never done before, to do things that are not routine, and to take risks—and sometimes even to die—for the common good. Once the organization accepts the credo of Alexander Dumas's three musketeers—"one for all and all for one"—then they have been led, and only then have they been molded into an organization. In essence, that is the most basic task of a leader—to create organization out of disorder, to make people more capable as a cohesive group than they are as unorganized individuals.

Leadership is the exercise of authority, whether formal or informal, in directing and coordinating the work of others. The best leaders are those who can simultaneously exercise both kinds of leadership: the formal, based on the authority of rank or office, and the informal, based on the willingness of others to give service to a person whose special qualities of authority they admire. It has long been known that leaders who must rely only on formal authority are at a disadvantage when compared with those who can also mobilize the informal strength of an organization or nation. Shakespeare observed this when in *Macbeth* (Act V, Scene 2) he has Angus describe Macbeth's waning ability to command the loyalty of his troops:

> Those he commands move only in command,
> Nothing in love: now does he feel his title
> Hang loose about him, like a giant's robe
> Upon a dwarfish thief.

Macbeth had become the very definition of an incompetent leader. Once he lost the respect and admiration of his followers, his organization was as doomed as he was.

The power that a leader possesses implies a hierarchy of control of stronger over weaker. J. R. P. French and B. Raven, in "The Bases of Social Power," suggest that there are five major bases of power: (1) expert power, which is based on the perception that the leader possesses some special knowledge or expertise; (2) referent power, which is based on the follower's liking, admiring, or identifying with the leader; (3) reward power, which is based on the leader's ability to mediate rewards for the follower; (4) legitimate power, which is based on the follower's perception that the leader has the legitimate right or authority to exercise influence over him or her; and (5) coercive power, which is based on the follower's fear that noncompliance with the leader's wishes will lead to punishment. Subsequent research on these power bases has indicated that the first two (expert and referent power) are more positively related to subordinate performance and satisfaction than the last three (reward, legitimate, and coercive power).

Leadership and Management

We need to distinguish between leadership and management. The two functions and roles overlap substantially. Management involves power (usually formal authority) bestowed on the occupant of a position by a higher organizational authority. With the power of management comes responsibility and accountability for the use of organizational resources. In contrast, leadership cannot be bestowed upon a person by a higher authority. Effective managers must also be leaders, and many leaders become managers, but the two sets of roles and functions differ.

The subject of leadership raises many complex issues that have plagued the behavioral sciences for generations. For example, what gives a manager or a leader legitimacy? Simply put, legitimacy is a characteristic of a social institution, such as a government, a family, or an organization, whereby it has both a legal and a perceived right to make binding decisions. Thus managers presumably have legitimacy because of the legal and perceived rights that accompany their organizational positions. In contrast, the legitimacy of a leader—separate and distinct from the legitimacy of a manager—cannot be addressed without introducing the concept of charisma, leadership based on the compelling personality of the leader rather than on formal position.

This last concept was first articulated by our old friend Max Weber—he wasn't called a universal genius for nothing—who distinguished charismatic authority from the traditional authority of a monarch and the legal authority one receives by virtue of law, such as the authority that legitimizes organizational executives. The word *charisma* is derived from the Greek word for divine grace. Charismatic leadership, if it is to survive, must eventually be institutionalized or routinized. Thus the founder of a movement or organization may be a charismatic spellbinder, but his or her successors are often, of necessity, comparatively dull bureaucrats.

Despite the differences and the unresolved questions, two things are evident: First, leadership involves a relationship between people in which influence and power are unevenly distributed on a legitimate basis; and second, a leader cannot function in isolation. In order for there to be a leader, someone must follow.

Perhaps the most accepted pure definition of the organizational leadership function comes from Chester I. Barnard. In his 1938 study *The Functions of the Executive,* he defines three essential functions of leaders or executives:

1. To provide a system of communication
2. To promote the securing of essential efforts
3. To formulate and define the purposes and goals of an organization

Note how he was decades ahead of his time in arguing that the most critical function of a chief executive is to establish and communicate a system of organizational values among organizational members. "The formulation and definition of purpose is then a widely distributed function only the more general part of which is executive. In this fact lies the most important inherent difficulty in the operation of cooperative systems: the necessity for indoctrinating those at the lower levels with general purposes." Here Barnard is referring to the necessity for top management to develop and instill a strategic vision for the organization. "Without that up-and-down-the-line coordination of purposeful decisions, general decisions and general purposes are mere intellectual processes in an organization vacuum, insulated from realities by layers of misunderstanding. The function of formulating grand purposes and providing for their redefinition is one that needs sensitive systems of communication, experience in interpretation, imagination, and delegation of responsibility." Barnard knew, in part because he was a real executive, that if the value system of the organization was clear and strong, the day-to-day concerns would take care of themselves.

Trait Theories

The trait approach to leadership assumes that leaders possess traits—personality characteristics—that make them fundamentally different from followers. Advocates of trait theory believe that some people have unique leadership characteristics and qualities that enable them to assume responsibilities not everyone can execute. Therefore they are "born" leaders.

It is no longer fashionable to contend that people will be effective leaders because they possess certain traits—without also considering other variables that influence leadership effectiveness. The arguments against trait theory are persuasive and come from a number of points of view. First, trait theory has largely fallen out of favor because reality never matched the theory. Instead, starting in the late 1950s, it has become standard practice to view leadership as a relationship, an interaction between

BOX 10.2   Leading Through Public Relations

Napoléon Bonaparte (1769–1821) was a master of modern propaganda. The horsey example in this picture has Napoléon gloriously pointing the way to victory in Italy. Life-sized pictures such as this were commissioned for public display to influence popular feelings and perceptions of Napoléon. Of course, this picture by Jacques-Louis David (1748–1825) is a lie. Note that the rider has a great-looking long leg. But if Napoléon had legs that size, he would not have been the subject of so many "short" jokes. And, unlike generals such as George Washington and Ulysses S. Grant, who were among the best horsemen of their age, Napoléon was a notoriously poor rider—often falling off his horse, especially if it had reared up as in the picture. This is why he much preferred traveling by coach. But the greatest misrepresentation here is that Napoléon crossed the Alps not on a fleet-footed steed but on a sure-footed mule. Thus this picture is a good example of Napoléon's policy of never telling the truth when a lie would do him more good. After all, a diminutive Napoléon on a rearing mule would hardly have had the same emotive punch. The French wouldn't have it. The only people ever to be inspired by mules are members of the Democratic Party in the United States.

Of course, American presidents don't do propaganda. They do photo opportunities. This President George W. Bush action figure toy was not authorized by the White House. But it was inspired by President Bush's visit to the aircraft carrier *Abraham Lincoln* on May 1, 2003. He landed on the flight deck as a passenger in a military aircraft so all the world would see him exit in full "top gun" regalia—just like the action figure. While the photos were optimal, he was severely criticized for imitating a real warrior when it was totally unnecessary. After all, the carrier was within sight of the California coast and his regular helicopter could have transported him without the need of a photogenic costume. While he also gave an internationally televised speech to the crew of the carrier, the "warrior" photos of the commander in chief in wartime were the major reason for the trip. Unfortunately, the photos also reminded his critics that when Bush had the opportunity to be a real warrior as a young man during the Vietnam War, he conspicuously avoided combat by joining the National Guard. Nevertheless, both Bush and Napoléon knew that whatever their critics said, all that mattered was their posturing pictures. And pictures never lie—or do they?

BOX 10.3   When a Leader Is Best

A leader is best
When people barely know he exists,
Not so good when people obey and acclaim him.
Worse when they despise him.
But of a good leader, who talks little,
When his work is done, his aim fulfilled,
They will say:
We did it ourselves.

SOURCE: Lao-tzu, a sixth-century B.C.E. Chinese philosopher, reprinted in Charles C. Manz and Henry P. Sims Jr., "SuperLeadership: Beyond the Myth of Heroic Leadership," *Organizational Dynamics* (Spring 1991).

individuals. The interaction was called a transaction, so that the term *transactional leadership* has become the umbrella label encompassing many theories of leadership. Second, the situation strongly influences leadership. The situation is now viewed as an enormous influence in determining the qualities, characteristics, and skills needed in a leader. There is even a **law of the situation** that deals with this.

Probably the most damaging criticism of trait theory, however, has been its lack of ability to identify which traits make an effective leader. Even among the traits that have been most commonly cited—intelligence, energy, achievement, dependability, and socioeconomic status—there is a lack of consensus across studies. The most obvious proof that leadership involves more than possessing certain traits is the simple fact that a leader may be effective in one setting and ineffective in another. It all depends on the situation.

Transactional Approaches

While the central question for the trait approach was who was a leader, transactional approaches sought to determine how leadership was established and exerted. Leadership-style-oriented **transactional approaches** all follow in the tradition of the famous K. Lewin, R. Lippitt, and R. K. White (1939) studies of the effectiveness of leadership styles on the group efforts of ten-year-old children engaged in hobby activities. The leader in each group was classified as having an authoritarian, a democratic, or laissez-faire orientation.

---

law of the situation A notion developed by social psychologist Mary Parker Follett (1868–1933) that one person should not give orders to another person, but both should agree to take their orders from the situation. If orders are simply part of the situation, the question of someone giving and someone receiving does not come up.

transactional approaches Any means of analyzing leadership style that focuses on how leaders interact and how they treat those they seek to lead.

Authoritarian leaders determined all policies, set all work assignments, were personal in their criticisms, and were product (or task) oriented. Democratic leaders shared decision-making powers with subordinates, left decisions about assignments up to the group, and participated in group activities but tried not to monopolize. They exhibited high levels of consideration for others. Laissez-faire leaders allowed freedom for individual and group decision making, provided information (or supplies) only when requested, and did not participate in the group except when called upon. They functioned more as facilitators.

Groups with democratic leaders were the most satisfied and productive. The authoritarian-led groups showed the most aggressive behavior and were the least satisfied, but they were highly productive (possibly because of fear of the leader). The groups with laissez-faire leaders showed low satisfaction and low production, and they were behaviorally aggressive toward group members and other groups. Thousands of subsequent studies have essentially presented the same findings. Democracy, meaning participative management, works.

Managers with authoritarian personalities and styles value order, precision, consistency, obedience, rules, law, and organization. To them, the power that flows from structure is supreme. Relationships are hierarchical, based on dominance and dependence. Authoritarianism, control through structure, is rigidly unbending. Yet authoritarians, while often initially successful, cannot survive over the long term. Whether large scale (such as Hitler or Stalin) or pint sized (such as an oppressive supervisor), authoritarians will ultimately fail because "democracy is inevitable." It is inevitable not just because it is good but because it is more effective—especially in the modern world, with its high-tech workforce. In the meanwhile, however, authoritarians cause considerable psychic damage in individuals and generate lost productivity in the internal organizational polity while often sustaining **authoritarianism** in the outside polity.

Because it is so easy and tempting for authoritarian personalities to rise to power, they must be all the more resisted because of their inherent tendencies toward destruction. People, groups, and organizations must evolve and adapt to their environment. Authoritarians do not adapt willingly to changing circumstances and new ideas. They are conservative in the worst sense of the word. Thus their need to protect and preserve the past and to inhibit constructive change leads to organizational rigidity and incompetence. Authoritarians dominate; their disciples obey. Organizational authoritarians and democrats cannot coincide; they are mutually exclusive.

---

authoritarianism Rule by an individual whose claim to sole power is supported by subordinates who sustain control of the system by carrying out the ruler's orders and by a public that is unwilling or unable to rebel against that control. The ruler's personality may be a significant element in maintaining the necessary balance of loyalty and fear. Authoritarianism differs from totalitarianism only in that the latter may have a specific ideology that rationalizes it, although it may require a leader who embodies that ideology to sustain public support. An authoritarian state may be further distinguished from a totalitarian one by the fact that under some circumstances an authoritarian state could allow limited freedom of expression and political opposition, as long as the regime does not feel threatened.

Democracy, whether it takes the form of representative government or participative management, is in marked contrast. It allows for a peaceful evolution and change. Dissent is not suppressed; it is instead used as a creative force leading to greater effectiveness and less incompetence. The Soviet Union and its Communist party disintegrated in 1991 because its authoritarian command economy was increasingly unable to provide its citizens an adequate standard of living. Democratic institutions are more competent because they allow for inevitable mistakes to be corrected in an evolutionary manner—before they lead to revolution.

Authoritarian rigidity is an important structural cause of organizational incompetence. It inhibits an organization's ability to learn and adapt to its environment. It concentrates decision making and responsibility in too few places and individuals. It denies others the right and opportunity to influence or to grow as employees and as people. Rigidity is illustrated by the British contingent of soldiers continuing to march in formation between Lexington and Concord, Massachusetts Colony, in 1775 despite colonial sharpshooters diminishing their ranks. Why did the dedicated targets keep on marching in file? Because the structure (the rules, lines of authority, the policies and procedures) said that was how wars were to be fought and soldiers were to behave. British structural rigidity—in all aspects of its eighteenth-century relationships with its American colonies—not only caused the American Revolution but led to the British defeat as they tried to suppress it.

Transactional leadership approaches assumed that leaders could be trained to act in the appropriate way as called for by their organization. This has proved to be wishful thinking. When leaders return to their organization after leadership training sessions, they seldom exhibit behavior changes. Despite training, department heads will not necessarily act considerately toward subordinates if their own supervisors

---

BOX 10.4   Oligarchic Leadership

"Who says organization says oligarchy." This is Robert Michels's "iron law of oligarchy," stated in his *Political Parties,* which holds that organizations are by their nature oligarchic because majorities within an organization are not capable of ruling themselves:

> Organization implies the tendency to oligarchy. In every organization, whether it be a political party, a professional union, or any other association of the kind, the aristocratic tendency manifests itself very clearly. The mechanism of the organization, while conferring a solidity of structure, induces serious changes in the organized mass, completely inverting the respective position of the leaders and the led. As a result of organization, every party or professional union becomes divided into a minority of directors and a majority of the directed.

SOURCE: Robert Michels, *Political Parties* (Glencoe, IL: Free Press, 1915, 1949).

do not act supportively toward them. One obvious implication is that changes must be introduced into an organization as a whole—not just to certain employees. In practice, leaders apply different styles in different situations. Thus the "pure" leadership style emphasis has given way to contingency approaches.

Contingency Approaches

We have all seen examples of the heroic leader: The general who leads troops from the front lines is the managerial cousin to the supervisor who leads from the assembly line. Each finds it almost impossible to delegate responsibility and, by trying to do it all alone, ultimately fails. This inherently theatrical style of leadership was appropriate for ancient armies when an Alexander the Great, sword in hand, would be the first to engage the enemy. This lead worker (or lead killer) approach had by the middle of the twentieth century become discredited. True, there will always be organizational heroes, but their heroism will be more situational, a response to an urgent need or crisis—not a way of organizational life.

Heroic-style managers are stress carriers. They create high levels of stress for themselves and transmit it to others around them. Such managers typically will give a secretary a handwritten letter to type and then stand there and *watch,* with ever-increasing nervousness, as it is typed. He will give an assignment to subordinates and then tell them exactly how to do it. She will insist on being the center and controller of all organizational communications, creating information bottlenecks and corresponding organizational incompetence. When heroic leadership is allowed by the organization's top managers, it is reinforced and imitated by lower-level managers. While no organization would advocate self-destructive leadership styles, tolerating them amounts to the same thing. Modern organizational leadership is inherently more situational or contingent than heroic.

Unlike the trait theory and transactional leadership approaches, contingency approaches take into consideration the many factors that may influence a leader's style. There is a recognition that a successful leader in one type of organization may not be successful in another simply because it differs from the previous one. Its situation (or context) is different, and the choice of a style needs to be contingent upon the situation. As leadership historian Ralph Stogdill notes, the contingency theories stress:

1. The type, structure, size, and purpose of the organization
2. The external environment in which the organization functions
3. The orientation, values, goals, and expectations of the leader, his superiors, and subordinates
4. The expert or professional knowledge required of the position

The contingency approaches assert that different leadership styles will differ in their effects in different situations. The situation (not traits or styles themselves) determines whether a leadership style or a particular leader will be effective. Thus, contingency theorists maintain that there is no "one best way"—as in the scientific management of Frederick Taylor—of effective leadership. Just think of Ulysses S. Grant, the victorious general of the American Civil War. On the basis of his war record, he was elected president in 1868, but as good as he was a general, he was bad as president. He is rated among the best generals in American history, but historians almost universally concede that he was one of the very worst presidents. Other American generals were able to make the leap from military to civilian leadership: George Washington, Andrew Jackson, and Dwight D. Eisenhower being the most famous examples. But poor President Grant just did not have it in him. He wasn't able to spontaneously retool his mind as a civilian leader. While Grant himself was honest, he consistently showed blind loyalty to corrupt friends.

Robert Tannenbaum and Warren Schmidt conducted one of the first studies that actually indicated a need for leaders to evaluate the situational factors prior to the implementation of a particular leadership style. They concluded that "the successful manager . . . can be primarily characterized neither as a strong leader nor as a permissive one." Indeed, he or she "is one who maintains a high batting average in accurately assessing the forces that determine what his most appropriate behavior at any given time should be and in actually being able to behave accordingly."

While Tannenbaum and Schmidt assert that leaders should adjust their styles to accommodate followers, University of Washington professor Fred Fiedler found that the opposite was often true. It is sometimes easier to change the work environment, the situation, to fit a leader's style. The underlying leadership style depends on personality. According to Fiedler, a leader's personality is not likely to change because of a few lectures or a few weeks of intensive training. Therefore, an organization should not choose a leader who fits a situation but should change the situation to mesh with the style of its leader. But this is easier said than done. The choices are clearly expressed by the new boss who tells the staff, "We can do things my way, your way, or the company's way. If you do things my way, we'll get along just fine."

Transformational Leadership

A transformational leader is one with the ability to change an embedded organizational culture by creating a new vision for the organization and marshalling the appropriate support to make that vision the new reality. The best-known transformational

---

BOX 10.5   Machiavelli on Leadership Style

From this arises the question whether it is better to be loved more than feared, or feared more than loved. The reply is, that one ought to be both feared and loved, but as it is difficult for the two to go together, it is much safer to be feared than loved, if one of the two has to be wanting. . . . And men have less scruple in offending one who makes himself loved than one who makes himself feared; for love is held by a chain of obligation which, men being selfish, is broken whenever it serves their purpose; but fear is maintained by a dread of punishment which never fails.

SOURCE: Niccolo Machiavelli, *The Prince* (1513).

leader is General George S. Patton Jr., who during World War II took charge of a defeated and demoralized American Army in North Africa and transformed it into a winning team. The task was different but no less difficult for Lee Iacocca when he took charge of a Chrysler Corporation on the verge of bankruptcy and disintegration in the late 1970s and brought it back into profit. Similar challenges faced the leadership of AT&T when it went from a monopoly public utility to a company that had to change its corporate culture to compete in the open market.

Edward G. Rendell faced a similar problem (but different in its content) when he became mayor of Philadelphia in 1992. Philadelphia was a "loser"—in just about every way—in the eyes of employees, potential employers, bondholders, suppliers, and citizens. It was simply *assumed* that the city could not compete head-on with comparable cities. Rendell had to change not only an organizational culture, but also just about *everybody's perception* of that culture. He effectively told the municipal unions to get with the plan or "kiss off." After a brief strike that was notable for its lack of public support, they got with the plan. Philadelphia needed and got in Rendell a transformational leader, a person who could totally transform an embedded organizational culture by creating a new vision of and for the organization, and successfully selling that vision—by rallying commitment and loyalty to make the vision become a reality.

Just as Ed Rendell played the role of a transformational leader in Philadelphia, Donald Rumsfeld has attempted to transform the way the Department of Defense (DoD) operates. Almost from the time he was sworn in as secretary of defense in 2001, Rumsfeld has made an explicit goal of moving the mammoth military structures of the United States in a new direction. In particular, Rumsfeld inherited a federal department that he felt was designed to fight the Cold War, while the types of threats faced by the nation had dramatically evolved. In particular, he believed the U.S. military needed to be less cumbersome and much more agile in an age of quickly emerging threats throughout the world. The events of September 11, 2001, only served to strengthen Rumsfeld's determination to change the makeup of the DoD, with fighting terrorism the major focus of a retrofitted Defense Department. As is the case with most transformational leaders, Rumsfeld came up against a well-entrenched bureaucracy that made transformation of the Defense Department a daunting task. Needless to say, the transformation of a federal department with a budget of nearly $400 billion and 1 million civilian employees would have a major impact on the careers and livelihoods of many people. In particular, Rumsfeld's goals for transforming the DoD involved flattening the department's organizational hierarchy, thus reducing the number of midlevel management positions that are always popular among aspiring bureaucrats.

Despite resistance from entrenched employees and members of Congress opposed to his budget priorities, Rumsfeld has had success in substantially reorganizing the DOD that other leaders have been unable to achieve. According to Brookings Institution analyst Paul Light, "There has been plenty of rhetoric in past administrations about revolutions in military affairs, but few secretaries have given transformation much attention until Rumsfeld. He may yet accomplish the unthinkable by turning one of the world's greatest bureaucracies into one of its lightest, leanest, and most robust." However, the ultimate transformation of the Defense Department depends greatly on Rumsfeld's standing with the American public. As he began his transformational agenda, Rumsfeld received high approval ratings from the nation's citizens. Such public support provided him with the leverage to take on individuals and groups that were resistant to the types of changes he was seeking. But as Rumsfeld's standing with the American public plummeted with the increasing problems in Iraq, his ability to convince Congress and DoD employees of his vision started to be compromised. As with the president that he serves, Rumsfeld's legacy as a leader may rest with the ultimate outcome of the war in Iraq.

Noel Tichy and David Ulrich describe transformational leaders as those rare individuals who can lead employees through their fears and uncertainties to the realization of the new vision. This requires strategic leadership that successfully changes people's perceptions of the organization. Transformational change is more than a rational, technical, incremental approach to change. The leader's primary function is to lead and support through carefully conceived change stages, acting as a cheerleader and as a belief model—verbally and nonverbally communicating belief in the benefits to all that will accrue from the changes.

Whereas the transactional theories of leadership apply primarily to leadership roles, functions, and behavior within an existing organizational culture, transformative leadership is about leadership to change a culture. Transactional leadership focuses on incremental change. Transformative leadership is about radical change. Sometimes the radical changes call for co-optation, the inclusion of new, potentially dissident group members into an organization's policymaking process to prevent such elements from being a threat to the organization or its mission. More often it is the implementation of a new strategic vision.

It is interesting to observe that transformational leadership theories have many similarities with the trait theories of leadership. Transformational leadership borders on "great man" theory—the belief that leaders are born, not made. In many ways, leadership theory is once again involved in seeking to find the basis of leadership in traits—rather than in relational and cultural factors. We have come full circle!

The Importance of Optimism

At the beginning of the World War II **Battle of the Bulge,** Americans were reeling from a German counterattack, and things seemed quite desperate. As matters went from bad to worse, General Dwight D. Eisenhower (later to be president) called a meeting of his leading commanders and announced, "The present situation is to be regarded as one of opportunity for us and not of disaster. There will only be cheerful faces at this conference table." His newly "cheerful" commanders went on to win the battle.

Battle of the Bulge The final German offensive on the Western Front in World War II. The attack came along the French-German border in December 1944. Parts of the American lines were pushed back as far as 50 miles (this penetration was the "bulge"). As the Allied forces concentrated their forces on the "bulge," the Germans were either killed, captured, or forced to withdraw. By late January 1945 the "bulge" was gone—and so were the last of the German army's effective reserves in the West.

Historian Stephen E. Ambrose wrote that Eisenhower felt it was critical that he, no matter what his personal feelings at the time, maintain an air of absolute confidence. He knew that confidence, or "cheerleading," at the top would permeate down through every level of his immense organization. Eisenhower instinctively knew, as social science now proves, that a confident organization is far more likely to succeed than a doubtful one—even if its leader in reality has doubts. Optimism or positive thinking works—even when the leader has to fake it.

Throughout history the most successful leaders—whether generals, managers, or football coaches—have been those who were the most optimistic. Was there ever a more optimistic politician than President Franklin D. Roosevelt, who, in the depths of the **Great Depression,** told the nation in his 1933 **inaugural address** that "the only thing we have to fear is fear itself"? Here was a man who in his prime was crippled by polio. Yet he only succumbed to physical paralysis. He didn't let his affliction prevent him from becoming governor of New York and then president of the United States. His optimism was infectious. People around him caught it, and it was a "communicable disease" that was good for the country.

Effective leaders have long known the importance of instilling a winning optimism in their followers. Even though it may not be warranted by circumstances, it is a far more potent force in leading than logic would dictate. What is certain is that the opposite of optimism, pessimism, depression, or what social psychologist Martin E. P. Seligman has called "learned helplessness," will tend to lead to failure, both of the mission at hand and eventually of health. When people find themselves in situations where they feel that they have no control and that their best efforts are futile, they "learn" from this repeated experience that they are "helpless" and thus become pessimistic and depressed. Seligman uses the example of American prisoners of war in Korea. Those who retained an optimistic outlook were far more likely to survive their ordeal. Those who felt helpless and consequently depressed were far more likely to die in captivity even though they got the same food and treatment as the others.

Optimistic attitudes on the part of leaders often become self-fulfilling prophecies. This **Pygmalion** effect, causing something to happen by believing it will, has often been demonstrated with both teacher/student and manager/worker relationships. If the teacher or manager believes his or her students or workers are capable (or not capable), they will tend to live up (or down) to expectations. This helps to explain why optimistic leaders are more likely to have successful followers and why pessimistic leaders tend to wind up with a bunch of losers.

Great Depression The period between the stock market crash of October 29, 1929, and World War II, when the United States and the rest of the Western world experienced the most severe economic decline in the twentieth century.

inaugural address The speech that a political executive makes upon being sworn into office. These speeches are often used to set a tone for an administration.

Pygmalion A legendary sculptor in ancient Greece who so loved a statue of a woman he had created that his prayers gave it life so that he could then marry her. This theme of willing something into existence that you then learn to love was explored by George Bernard Shaw in his play *Pygmalion* (1913), which was later made into the musical *My Fair Lady* (1956).

BOX 10.6   The Confident Leader

Anyone who accomplishes anything of significance has more confidence than the facts would justify. It is something that outstanding executives have in common with gifted military commanders, brilliant political leaders, and great artists. It is true of societies as well as of individuals. Every great civilization has been characterized by confidence in itself.

Lacking such confidence, too many leaders add ingenious new twists to the modern art which I call "How to reach a decision without really deciding." They require that the question be put through a series of clearances within the organization and let the clearance process settle it. Or take a public opinion poll and let the poll settle it. Or devise elaborate statistical systems, cost-accounting systems, and information-processing systems, hoping that out of them will come unassailable support for one course of action rather than another.

This is not to say that leadership cannot profit enormously from good information. If the modern leader doesn't know the facts he is in grave trouble, but rarely do the facts provide unqualified guidance. After the facts are in, the leader must in some measure emulate the little girl who told the teacher she was going to draw a picture of God. The teacher said, "But Mary, no one knows what God looks like"; and Mary said, "They will when I get through."

SOURCE: John W. Gardner, "Some Maladies of Leadership," *Annual Report 1965,* Carnegie Corporation of New York.

Remember the advice traditionally given to actors: Always be sincere—once you can fake that, you've got it made. It's the same with leadership. Always be optimistic, and fake it if you don't feel it. New York City Mayor Rudy Giuliani admitted as much when discussing his inspiring leadership after the terrorist attacks that destroyed the twin towers of the World Trade Center on September 11, 2001: "I wonder how much of it [his leadership] was bluff. A lot of it had to be bluff. . . . Look, in a crisis you have to be optimistic. When I said the spirit of the city would be stronger, I didn't know that. I just hoped that" (*Time,* December 31, 2001). And do you think President Franklin D. Roosevelt *really* thought that the only thing we had "to fear was fear itself"? All who knew him agree that he was a great actor. Of course, all politicians are actors. Some just get better reviews than others.

Too Much Leadership

Structural rigidity often causes managers to overmanage—to lead too much. *Micromanage* is the pejorative term for supervising too closely. Any manager may be guilty of micromanagement for refusing to allow subordinates to have any real authority or responsibility, thereby ensuring that subordinates can neither function as, nor grow into, effective managers. Furthermore, the managers are kept so busy micromanaging that they never have time to do what managers are supposed to do—like develop long-term strategy and overall vision. Legislators at all levels of government are frequently practitioners of micromanagement. By writing detailed rules for programs into legislation, by demanding that particular items be procured from suppliers in their districts, or by mandating that certain employees be hired or promoted for patronage purposes, they deny public managers a large measure of the real administrative discretion that all effective managers need.

Micromanagement

An apt example of legislative micromanagement is provided by Philip Howard. In *The Death of Common Sense,* his denouncement of governmental micromanagement, he recounts the story of Mother Teresa's Missionaries of Charity's attempts to build a homeless shelter in New York City. A group of nuns from the organization proposed refurbishing an abandoned four-story building that would house 64 residents. But all four-story buildings in New York must, by law, have an elevator—which would have added $100,000 to the cost. This lack of amenities did not deter the nuns, who shun modern conveniences and did not want an elevator anyway. It was to be a no-frills basic shelter. But regulations are regulations. When the Mother Teresa group could not find anyone who had the authority to waive the elevator requirement after 18 months of navigating the hallways of the municipal bureaucracy, they gave up and went on to other good works.

While there is some legitimate justification for micromanagement by legislators and directors (after all, they are the legitimate representatives of the owners of the government or corporation), there is no justification for micromanagement along the traditional chain of hierarchical authority. While close supervision is appropriate for a trainee, it is insulting and disabling for any employee who is presumably able. And it can be dangerous. Micromanagement can drive employees over the edge into violence. For example, in recent years the U.S. Postal Service has had a spate of enraged workers going berserk and murdering their supervisors. These tensions are common in many industries. But according to Peter Kilborn, in post offices they "fester[ed] within an archaic, Army-like culture in which many top managers communicate by directive, and front-line supervisors often hover over their charges, waiting for a mistake and timing workers' trips to the bathroom." Shootings have killed three dozen people in U.S. post offices from the mid-1980s to the mid-1990s. In 1994 the Federal Centers for Disease Control and Prevention found that murder was the second leading cause of death on the job for postal workers.

Micromanagement will not make a competent employee more competent; it only makes things worse by wasting time, by damaging interpersonal relationships, by demonstrating that the micromanagers themselves are not competent supervisors, and by distracting managers from the kinds of activities that can prevent organizational incompetence. Instead, micromanagement—and overmanagement—lead to overcommitment and bureaucratic overcontrol, two of the classic symptoms of organizational incompetence.

Overmanagement

Having too many managers for the nature of the organization or task—overmanagement—is related to and inevitably leads to micromanagement and organizational rigidity. Overmanagement has become a particularly important problem in recent years as computer-driven information systems render once-useful layers of middle management obsolete. These threatened managers struggle to find new roles for themselves and ways to retain their long-standing sources of authority, which have depended on their exclusive control of organizations' knowledge bases. They get in the way of more productive organizational units until periodic downsizing efforts permanently remove them. But until they are sought out and expelled, they are among the major structural causes of organizational incompetence.

Moral Leadership

Garry Wills in the *Atlantic Monthly* warns that "if the leader is just an expediter of what other people want, a resource for their use, the people are not being *led* but *serviced*." Thus it is moving people in new directions—taking them to places where they did not know they wanted or needed to go—that is the essence of leadership and has been since ancient times. Thucydides, in his *History of the Peloponnesian War*, describes Pericles, the leader of ancient Athens, as someone who, because he was so "clearly above corruption, was enabled, by the respect others had for him and his own wise policy, to hold the multitude in a voluntary restraint." Thus "he led them, not they him; and since he did not win his power on compromising terms, he could say not only what pleased others but what displeased them, relying on their respect."

The Bully Pulpit

Pericles exercised moral leadership. He was able to send people in new directions of action and thought because it was the right and decent thing to do. During the presidential campaign of 1932, then New York Governor Franklin D. Roosevelt spoke for all political executives when he said, "The presidency is not merely an administrative office. That's the least of it. It is more than an engineering job, efficient or inefficient. It is preeminently a place of moral leadership. All our great presidents were leaders of thought at times when certain historic ideas in the life of the nation had to be clarified." Presidents have traditionally used what President Theodore Roosevelt called their "bully (meaning "first-rate") pulpit" to provide this clarification.

Rhetorical Leadership

Political scientists James Caeser, Glen Thurow, Jeffrey Tulis, and Joseph Bessette, in their article *The Rise of the Rhetorical Presidency,* argue that, historically, leadership through rhetoric was suspect, that presidents rarely spoke directly to the people, and that, in any event, presidents relied much more heavily on party and political leadership in the Congress for their electoral and programmatic support. But today's presidents attempt to move mass opinion by speeches that exhort the public to support

The "inventor" of the bully pulpit, President Theodore Roosevelt. He was such an energetic speaker—really a civil preacher—that once in 1912, when a would-be assassin shot him in the chest, he refused medical treatment until he had finished his speech. He told his Milwaukee audience, "I have just been shot, but it takes more than that to kill a Bull Moose!" They looked on in shocked admiration as he continued to bleed and talk. What saved Roosevelt's life was the fact that the bullet went into his breast pocket and through a folded piece of paper on which his speech was written and a metal eyeglass case before hitting him. While the event was dramatic and bloody, Roosevelt, with his extensive experience during the Spanish-American War, knew that he had suffered only a flesh wound. And why let that ruin a good speech on an otherwise fine day?

their policies and programs. Presidents are obliged to do this for three reasons: (1) the modern doctrine of the presidency, which avers that the presidency is a place of moral leadership and should employ rhetoric to lead public opinion; (2) the advent of the modern mass media, especially television, which facilitates the use of rhetoric; and (3) the modern presidential campaign, which blurs campaigning and governing.

According to Caeser, et al., "Popular or mass rhetoric, which presidents once employed only rarely, now serves as one of their principal tools in attempting to govern the nation. Whatever doubts Americans may now entertain about the limitations of presidential leadership, they do not consider it unfitting or inappropriate for presidents to attempt to 'move' the public by programmatic speeches that exhort and set forth grand and ennobling views." But just as it was with ancient Pericles, their views are only accepted as "grand and ennobling" if they themselves are perceived as noble, worthy, and above corruption.

The "two presidencies" phenomenon is telling here. This is Aaron Wildavsky's division of the presidency into two differing spheres of influence: foreign policy and domestic policy. Wildavsky contended that presidential leadership in foreign policy will, generally speaking, find greater support among the public than leadership in domestic policy. To test his hypothesis, Wildavsky examined congressional action on presidential proposals from 1948 to 1964. For this period, the Congress approved 58.5 percent of the foreign policy bills; 73.3 percent of the defense policy bills; and 70.8 percent of general foreign relations, State Department, and foreign aid bills and treaties. During this same period, the Congress approved only 40.2 percent of the president's domestic policy proposals. Thus the two-presidencies thesis was confirmed. Wildavsky's work has spawned a bevy of research articles. While Wildavsky himself in "Reconsidering the Two Presidencies" would in 1989 concede that his thesis was decidedly "time and culture bound," nothing has materially diminished the essence of his original thesis put forth in 1966. The reason the president is so much more successful in foreign policy is that he comes to the table with cleaner hands. He is less the conniving politician and more the noble statesman.

But more people than presidents can offer moral leadership. For example, Secretary of Health and Human Services Louis W. Sullivan was considered one of the most ineffectual members of the Bush administration until 1990, when he started attacking cigarette companies for targeting the marketing of cigarettes to minorities and women. His popularity and stature immediately soared. More important, he was effective. R.J. Reynolds, one of the largest U.S. tobacco companies, was test-marketing a new brand called "Uptown," which was specifically aimed at African-Americans. Sullivan said, "This brand is cynically and deliberately targeted toward black Americans. . . . At a time when we must cultivate greater responsibility among our citizens, Uptown's slick and sinister advertising proposes instead a great degree of personal irresponsibility." After Sullivan's attack, the brand was withdrawn. While moral leadership may not move mountains, it can sometimes move cigarette companies.

✦ A CASE STUDY: TRANSFORMING THE POSTAL SERVICE

Ever since the nineteenth century when stamps were first used as postage on letters, people have collected them for their artistic merit and their investment value. The United States first issued adhesive postage stamps in 1847. These stamps had portraits of Benjamin Franklin and George Washington. Governments have conscientiously produced a multitude of commemorative stamps for the collectors' market. After all, a stamp purchased and saved is almost pure profit to the post office.

When the U.S. Postal Service decided to issue a stamp commemorating the rock 'n' roll star Elvis Presley, it created publicity by asking Americans to "vote" on stamp designs featuring either the young or old Elvis. When the "polling" was complete, the young Elvis design won by four to one. More importantly, this created a ready audience—a ready market—for the stamp when it was released in 1992. Nevertheless, the Postal Service was surprised at the depth of the public's enthusiasm. People who had never saved stamps before suddenly become collectors—at least of this stamp. The Postal Service could barely keep up with the initial demand for the Elvis stamp. Since hardly anyone bought the first Elvis stamps to use on letters, the Postal Service, from its point of view, was almost literally printing money.

Taken by surprise by the public's tremendous response to the Elvis stamp, the Postal Service was determined that the next time they would be ready—ready with more stamps to sell. But stamps of what? Most commemorative stamps are issued, bought by collectors or people who prefer stamps with some distinction, and then forgotten. The Postal Service searched for another dead national icon with a following comparable to Elvis's. "Dead" was an important consideration here. Contrary to the philatelic policies in monarchies and dictatorships, only the likenesses of the deceased are allowed on American stamps. Marilyn Monroe, dead since 1962, had never faded from the public's mind. As with Elvis, her face and persona were instantly recognizable. Both had died prematurely of drug overdoses when they were still enormously popular.

Realizing the market potential, the Postal Service gave the Marilyn stamp a lavish publicity send-off. Postmaster General Marvin Runyon made the rounds of the TV and radio talk shows as if he were hawking a book. He scheduled visits to shopping malls where he would judge Marilyn Monroe look-alike contests. They even advertised her on TV. Over old news clips of Marilyn, an announcer asks, "When is a stamp not just a stamp? The Marilyn stamp [picture of stamp replaces news film] now at your post office." Many people give great patriotic service to their government when they are alive; to do so after death as Marilyn has done—and is still doing—is patriotism indeed.

Today's Postal Service was created by the Postal Reorganization Act of 1970. This federal statute converted the Post Office Department into an independent establishment—within the executive branch of the government—to own and operate the nation's postal system, thereafter known as the U.S. Postal Service. The old Post Office Department was "reinvented" (before this term was in common usage in government) as a public enterprise because the Nixon administration was unhappy with its poor management and constant need for public subsidies.

Amid a dramatic postal strike in the spring of 1970, the government for the first time in history agreed to allow wages, which hitherto had always been set through the legislative process, to be negotiated between union and government representatives. That ended the strike. Subsequently, the Postal Reorganization Act was passed, establishing the corporate framework sought by Nixon and providing for collective bargaining with postal employees in the future. The Postal Service remains the only federal agency whose employees are governed by a collective-bargaining process that permits negotiations over wages.

The chief executive officer of the Postal Service, the postmaster general, is appointed by the nine governors of the Postal Service, who are appointed by the president, with the advice and consent of the Senate, for overlapping nine-year terms. The ambiguous legal status of the Postal Service has been the source of political controversy since it was established in 1970. It does not report to the president and is only indirectly responsible to Congress. Even though it is an "independent" government corporation, it cannot even set its own prices for services. A Postal Rate Commission, created by the 1970 Reorganization Act, must approve all postage rates, fees, and mail classifications. The commission also has appellate jurisdiction to review Postal Service determinations to close or consolidate small post offices. There have been a number of bills introduced in recent congresses to return the Postal Service to the status of a regular executive department—and to greater political control. Such proposals tend to increase dramatically whenever local post offices are forced to merge or close.

Despite perennial criticism, what the Postal Service does is impressive: In 2004 more than 206 billion pieces of mail were delivered to 140 million residences and businesses by almost 800,000 employees in 38,000 post offices. With annual revenues of more than $65 billion, it delivers more than 40 percent of the world's mail each day. And while most Americans do not realize it, their daily mail is cheap, comparatively speaking. The United States has the lowest first-class postage of any industrialized state. For the price of a first-class stamp, even one with Marilyn or Elvis on it, the Postal Service will take your letter—if properly addressed—to the bottom of the Grand Canyon by mule, to the Arctic Circle in Alaska by bush pilot, or to ships on America's remote rivers by mailboat. The current motto of the Postal Service is "We Deliver for You." They know that if they do not, that if there are too many complaints, Congress may change its mandate.

The Postal Service's worst nightmare is that Congress will jeopardize the service's solvency by allowing others—maybe Federal Express or United Parcel Service—the right to deliver first-class mail. Such totally private corporations could then easily skim off the easy and profitable urban delivery routes and leave the Postal Service with all the unprofitable and difficult ones. Fearful of losing its monopoly and viability, the Postal Service is hustling to improve its core services, to create new products, such as the 2005 Muppet stamps and self-adhesive stamps, and to match the competition. Thus "express mail" overnight delivery was created in 1977 specifically to compete with Federal Express, and the Postal Service has conducted quarterly performance evaluations since 1990 to monitor the timeliness of its first-class mail delivery.

The Marilyn and Elvis stamps are indicators of a major new trend in public administration in general, and the Postal Service in particular: the concern for marketing. Marketing, entrepreneurship, and promotional management are relatively new areas of interest in the public and nonprofit sectors. The first published argument (that we have been able to locate) that nonprofit organizations should engage in marketing even though they face somewhat unique circumstances is in Philip Kotler and Sidney Levy's 1969 article "Broadening the Concept of Marketing." The first textbook on the subject, also by Kotler, was not published until 1975. Although some nonprofit organizations have engaged in business-enterprise-type activities at least since the beginning of the twentieth century—for example, the Metropolitan Museum of Art in New York City opened its first official sales store in 1908—only scattered attention was paid to such income-generating activities prior to 1980.

Entreprenurial-type business ventures by agencies of the public sector are not limited to the Postal Service. Creating and capitalizing on chances to make money—the core of entrepreneurship—are becoming increasingly fashionable. Thus organizations as diverse as the Chicago Public Library and the Los Angeles County coroner's office sell a wide range of memorabilia.

The result of entrepreneurial forays by the Postal Service and other public sector entities is to raise revenue through nontraditional methods rather than increasing taxes or user fees (or stamp prices). Entrepreneurship is a frame of mind, a willingness to create and to be receptive to opportunities, an orientation toward risk-taking ventures. But nonprofit organizations cannot allow the current interest in entrepreneurship to allow them to forget their traditional purposes. Business ventures can be dangerous when they compromise the organization's original mission. Marilyn and Elvis stamps, pins, and other souvenir items are like best-selling books. They generate tremendous income when first offered for sale and even have comfortable backlist sales, but they are no substitute for the organization's core function: selling a service.

So what's the lesson here? The public sector can benefit from some entrepreneurial techniques. If stamps with Washington, Franklin, and other dignitaries do not sell well enough as collectibles, then sell what sells. Sell Marilyn, Elvis, and even Miss Piggy. The Postal Service, by being made a public enterprise, has simply used its discretion to branch out into the entertainment industry. In so doing, it has found a way to improve its financial health so as to better fulfill its primary purpose: delivering the mail.

For Discussion: *What steps has the U.S. Postal Service taken to transform itself? How has the fear of increased competition from FedEx and UPS motivated the Postal Service to reform?*

Summary

Leadership is the exercise of authority, whether formal or informal, in directing and coordinating the work of others. The best leaders are those who can simultaneously exercise both kinds of leadership: the formal, based on the authority of rank or office, and the informal, based on the willingness of others to give service to a person with special qualities of authority.

There is a difference between leadership and management: management involves power (formal authority) bestowed on the occupant of a position by a higher organizational authority. Leadership, in contrast, cannot be bestowed by a higher authority but must be earned.

Review Questions

1. What is the difference between leadership and management?
2. Which leadership style is more likely to be successful over the long term: authoritarian or democratic?

3. Why are transformational leaders so essential in times of organizational crisis?
4. Why is micromanagement a trap into which so many leaders fall?
5. Under what circumstances can moral leadership be effective?

Key Concepts

charisma   Leadership based on the compelling personality of the leader rather than on formal position. The word *charisma* is derived from the Greek word for divine grace. The concept was first developed by Max Weber, who distinguished charismatic authority from both the traditional authority of a monarch and the legal authority given to someone by law.

contingency theory   An approach to leadership asserting that leadership styles will vary in their effects in different situations. The situation (not traits or styles themselves) determines whether a leadership style or a particular leader will be effective.

leadership   The exercise of authority, whether formal or informal, in directing and coordinating the work of others.

moral leadership   Leading people in specific directions of action and thought based on morals and decency.

rule of law   A governing system in which the highest authority is a body of law that applies equally to all (as opposed to the traditional "rule of men," in which the personal whim of those in power can decide any issue).

trait theory   An approach to leadership that assumes leaders possess traits that make them fundamentally different from followers. Advocates of trait theory believe that some people have unique leadership characteristics and qualities that enable them to assume responsibilities not everyone can execute. Therefore they are "born" leaders.

transformational leadership   Leadership that strives to change organizational culture and directions. It reflects the ability of a leader to develop a values-based vision for the organization, to convert the vision into reality, and to maintain it over time.

Bibliography

Ambrose, Stephen E. (1994). *D-Day*. New York: Simon and Schuster.

Barnard, Chester I. (1938). *The Functions of the Executive*. Cambridge, MA: Harvard University Press.

Berlin, Isaiah. (1953). *The Hedgehog and the Fox*. New York: Simon and Schuster.

Caeser, James, Glen Thurow, Jeffrey Tulis, and Joseph Bessette. (1981). "The Rise of the Rhetorical Presidency," *Presidential Studies Quarterly* (Spring).

Cohen, Jeffrey E. (1982). "A Historical Reassessment of Wildavsky's 'Two Presidencies,'" *Social Science Quarterly* (September).

Dynes, Michael, and David Walker. (1995). *The New British State*. London: Times Books.

Edelman, Murray. (1967). *The Symbolic Uses of Politics*. Urbana: University of Illinois Press.

Edwards, George C., III. (1986). "The Two Presidencies: A Reevaluation," *American Politics Quarterly* (July).

Fiedler, Fred. E. (1967). *A Theory of Leadership Effectiveness*. New York: McGraw-Hill.

Fielder, F. E., and M. M. Chemers. (1974). *Leadership Style and Effective Management*. Glenview, IL: Scott, Foresman.

Fielder, F. E., M. M. Chemers, and L. Mahar. (1976). *Improving Leadership Effectiveness: The Leader Match Concept*. New York: Wiley.

Fink, S. L. (1992). *High Commitment Workplaces*. New York: Quorum Books.

French, J. R. P., and B. Raven. (1959). "The Bases of Social Power." In D. Cartwright and A. Zander, eds., *Studies in Social Power*. Ann Arbor: University of Michigan, Institute of Social Research.

Howard, Philip K. (1995). *The Death of Common Sense*. New York: Random House.

Ignatieff, Michael. (1998). *Isaiah Berlin: A Life*. New York: Henry Holt.

Kilborn, Peter T. (1993). "Inside Post Offices, the Mail Is Only Part of the Pressure," *New York Times* (May 17).

Kotler, Philip. (1982). "The Responsive Organization: Meeting Consumer Needs." In D. Gies, ed., *Marketing for Nonprofit Organizations*, 2nd ed. Englewood Cliffs, NJ: Prentice Hall.

Kotler, Philip, and Sidney J. Levy. (1969). "Broadening the Concept of Marketing," *Journal of Marketing* (January).

Lewin, K., R. Lippitt, and R. K. White. (1939). "Patterns of Aggressive Behavior in Experimentally Created Social Climates," *Journal of Social Psychology* 10.

Light, Paul C. (2005). "Rumsfeld's Revolution." *Govexec.com* (August 8). http://www.govexec.com/dailyfed/0805/080805ol.htm.

Livingston, J. Sterling. (1969). "Pygmalion in Management," *Harvard Business Review* (July–August).

Marinucci, Carla. (2001). "Gingrich Says GOP Has a Handle on High Tech," *San Francisco Chronicle* (January 27).

Metcalf, Henry C., and Lyndall Urwick, eds. (1940). *Dynamic Administration: The Collected Papers of Mary Parker Follett*. New York: Harper.

Morgan, Arthur E. (1974). *The Making of the TVA*. New York: Prometheus Books.

Mustafa, Husain, and Anthony A. Salomone. (1971). "Administrative Circumvention of Public Policy," *Midwest Review of Public Administration* 5, No. 1.

Myers, Steven Lee. (1995). "City Hall's Going Retail in Wholesale Fashion," *New York Times* (July 9).

Oldfield, Duane M., and Aaron Wildavsky. (1989). "Reconsidering the Two Presidencies," *Society* 26 (July–August).

Peterson, Christopher. (1993). *Learned Helplessness: A Theory for the Age of Personal Control*. New York: Oxford University Press.

Popkin, James. (1993). "Wasteline: By the Book," *U.S. News & World Report* (May 24).

Riccucci, Norma M. (1995). *Unsung Heroes: Federal Execucrats Making a Difference*. Washington: Georgetown University Press.

Rosenbloom, David H. (1993a). "Have an Administrative Rx? Don't Forget the Politics!" *Public Administration Review* 53 (November–December).

———. (1993b). *Public Administration*, 3rd ed. New York: McGraw-Hill.

Sayre, W. (1948). "The Triumph of Techniques Over Purpose," *Public Administration Review* 8 (Spring).

———. (1991). *Learned Optimism*. New York: A. A. Knopf.

Seligman, Martin E. P. (1992). *Helplessness: On Depression, Development, and Death*. New York: W. H. Freeman.

Slater, Philip E., and Warren Bennis. (1964). "Democracy Is Inevitable," *Harvard Business Review* 42 (March–April).

Stogdill, Ralph M. (1974). *Handbook of Leadership: A Study of Theory and Research*. New York: Free Press.

Tannenbaum, Robert J., and Warren H. Schmidt. (1973). "How to Choose a Leadership Pattern," *Harvard Business Review* 51 (May–June).

Tichy, N. M., and D. O. Ulrich. (1984). "The Leadership Challenge—A Call for the Transformational Leader," *Sloan Management Review* 26.

Wildavsky, Aaron. (1966). "The Two Presidencies," *Trans-Action* (December).

Wills, Garry. (1994). "What Makes a Good Leader?" *Atlantic Monthly* (April).

Recommended Books

Barnard, Chester I. (1968). *The Functions of the Executive*, 30th anniversary ed. Cambridge, MA: Harvard University Press. The classic analysis of organizations as cooperative systems wherein the function of the executive was to maintain the "dynamic equilibrium" between the needs of the organization and the needs of its employees.

Burns, James MacGregor. (1978). *Leadership*. New York: Harper & Row. Uses history and biography to distill the essential elements of leadership.

Goleman, Daniel, Richard Boyatzis, and Annie McKee. (2002). *Primal Leadership*. Boston: Harvard Business School Press. A demonstration of how current behavioral science research validates the doctrine of optimism for leaders.

Harari, Oren. (2002). *The Leadership Secrets of Colin Powell*. New York: McGraw-Hill. How-to-do-it advice from one of America's most successful leaders.

Klitgaard, Robert, and Paul Light. (2005). *High-Performance Government: Structure, Leadership, Incentives*. Washington, DC: Rand Corporation. An examination of the contemporary role of leadership in relation to organizational structure.

Wren, J. Thomas. (1995). *The Leader's Companion: Insights on Leadership Through the Ages*. New York: Free Press. Sixty-four selections of the best writing on leadership, from ancient classicists to modern social scientists.

Related Web Sites

Center for Creative Leadership
 www.ccl.org/
Hartwick Leadership Institute
 www.hartwick.edu/hhmi/seminars/
Academy of Leadership University of Maryland
James MacGregor Burns Academy of Leadership
 www.academy.umd.edu/
Jepson School of Leadership Studies
 www.oncampus.richmond.edu/academics/
 leadership/
 www.richmond.edu/academics/leadership

The Leadership ForumCenter
 www.learnleadership.com/
Leadership development
 www.leadership.opm.gov/
NTL Institute for Applied Behavioral Science
 www.ntl.org/index.html
U.S. Postal Service
 www.usps.gov

CHAPTER 11

Personnel Management and Labor Relations

•KEYNOTE: THE ADVENTURES OF A YOUNG MAN AS A PERSONNEL TECHNICIAN

I didn't mean to discover the netherworld of personnel administration in 1965. I was just looking for a job. This was complicated by the fact that I had no skills. A bachelor's degree in English from Temple University and a decidedly undistinguished academic record did not suggest any immediate directions. I thought it might be fun to be a librarian, so off I went to the Free Library of Philadelphia. I asked a bored circulation clerk, "Could you please tell me whom to see about becoming a librarian?" She sent me to Mr. Greenberg in the personnel office.

I bounded into his office and politely inquired if he could advise me on how to get a job as a librarian. Never in 30 subsequent years of going in and out of other people's offices have I been greeted with such genuine warmth and solicitude. And I didn't even have an appointment! But I had something going for me that Mr. Greenberg needed very badly—my gender; that is, I was a male college graduate and thus met all of his needs in a new librarian trainee. Even today, careers as professional librarians attract a disproportionate number of females. It was much more so in the mid-1960s. This caused a very particular staffing problem for the library because it had recently purchased a new bookmobile. But the female librarians were exceedingly reluctant to work on a bookmobile that traveled through Philadelphia's poorer neighborhoods. They felt, and with good reason, that it was too dangerous. This accounts for Mr. Greenberg's immediate warm regard for me. He was very much in need of a brave young man to take literacy into the neighborhoods of the inner city.

There was just one minor technicality to attend to before I could gain the command of a municipal bookmobile. I had to pass a civil service examination. Mr. Greenberg was almost apologetic about the inconvenience as he told me where in City Hall I would find the continuous testing room of the Civil Service Commission. There I would take a general entrance examination for new college graduates desiring a variety of entry-level professional positions. The test, he assured me, would be scored immediately after I completed it, and he would be able to formally put me on the payroll and in the bookmobile within a few days. He was very pleased to have solved a personnel problem using the much unappreciated but classic technique of sitting at his desk waiting for someone to walk in the door.

But I was fated never to be a librarian, never to ride the bookmobile, and never to see Mr. Greenberg again. Yet this was my start in the world of personnel. The examination I took was used by the city for a dozen different professional trainee positions. On the first page I was asked to check off the names of all the jobs for which I wished to be considered. I checked every one. After being told by the examinations proctor that I had easily passed the hour-long, multiple-choice examination, I went home to await my call to the bookmobile. Instead it was Mrs. Margolis, a certification clerk for the Civil Service Commission, who called. It was her job to take the names of job applicants who passed various civil service examinations and officially certify them as eligible for appointment. Whenever a municipal department had a vacancy in a given job category, she would contact the highest scorers on the list of eligibles to see if they were still interested in employment with the city. If so, she would arrange a job interview. I told her of my meeting with Mr. Greenberg and how anxious I was to get started on my new career on the bookmobile. She immediately and emphatically responded with these immortal words of career advice: "Don't be an idiot! That's not for you."

She went on to explain that I ought to take the highest paying of all the entry positions for which my test score now qualified me. The job for me, she insisted, was management trainee. This paid a whopping 20 percent more than librarian trainee, $6,000 a year as opposed to $5,000. I told her that I didn't know anything about management but knew lots about books. She assured me that it didn't matter. They would train me; that's why the job was called management *trainee*. A 20 percent raise even before I started working for the city and not being an idiot were pretty powerful inducements. So I agreed.

"Good," she said. "I'll schedule you for an oral exam at three o'clock tomorrow afternoon."

"What oral exam?" I asked in amazement.

"All management trainee applicants must take an oral exam. You put on your suit and come to the sixth floor of the Municipal Services Building at three," she demanded of me as if she were my mother. To this day I still wonder how she knew that I had only one suit.

The next day I put on that suit, as ordered, and having never taken an oral exam before, and not knowing what to expect, I also brushed my teeth very carefully. Upon my arrival at the designated place at the designated time, a receptionist ushered me into a small room in which three men were seated behind a table. I would later learn they were all personnel officers for the city. They each wore a dark suit with a thin tie atop a white shirt. They could easily have been mistaken for the FBI agents or IBM salesmen of those days who were all required to wear white shirts, thin ties, and short hair. After a round of handshakes, they offered me a chair and proceeded to ask me a series of questions that I could not possibly answer. I had never given any thought to the problems of perpetually tardy employees and clogged typing pools. I didn't even know that typists were allowed to swim! So I responded to their questions by just making up stuff off the top of my head all the while thinking: "Bookmobile, here I come."

To make matters worse, one of my examiners took an immediate dislike to me. He was unusually rude and kept badgering me with questions phrased in a hostile manner. He would constantly interrupt my sentences and often call my answers stupid. I soon realized that the situation was hopeless; so I relaxed and took what Californians would call a mellow approach to the examination. I calmly answered all questions as best I could and didn't let the badgerer upset me no matter what his antics. Consequently, I exhibited a degree of self-confidence that was as convincing as it was artificial.

A few weeks later I would learn that the oral exam had no purpose except to size up the physical deportment and extemporaneous speaking ability of the applicant. One member of the examining board was always hostile to see if the examinee could be emotionally shaken by a disagreeable exchange. My badgerer didn't dislike me after all; it was simply his turn to be the bad guy. Nevertheless, I left the Municipal Services Building confident that the bookmobile was my destiny. Shortly after nine the next morning Mrs. Margolis called again. Before I could tell her how sorry I was that I did so poorly on the oral exam, she said, "Congratulations, you've passed the oral."

"You've got to be kidding," I said in contradiction. "I was terrible."

"No. You got a very high score. They even want you for personnel. You have to come to an interview this afternoon at two."

"But I did the interview yesterday," I complained.

"No, that was the oral exam. The job interview is today. Put your suit back on."

The subsequent job interview was my first introduction to position classification. Two nice but seemingly elderly senior supervisors in the Department of Personnel (which is administratively under the Civil Service Commission) spent an hour asking me about my whole life. At 21 there was not much to tell. When they seemed on the verge of ending the discussion and offering me a position, I bluntly asked what the duties would be. They said I would start in the Division of Position Classification and Pay doing reports that would ultimately determine how much city employees would be paid.

"But I thought the mayor did that," I explained in honest ignorance.

"No," I was corrected, "the city has over 30,000 employees. He couldn't possibly do it all. That's why we have position classification."

"Oh," I responded, still not really sure what they meant by *classification*.

They seemed to understand my discomfort about the strange nature of the work they were describing. To conclude, they said they had only one final question, "If we forced you to state the one area that you really know well, what would it be?"

I quickly thought about all that I had studied in college and replied with great seriousness and complete honesty, "The only thing I really know well is modern American fiction."

They thereupon hired me to write job descriptions for the employees of the City of Philadelphia. I would report to work on the following Monday and be a management trainee in the personnel technician series, meaning that I would later be eligible for promotion to Personnel Technician I, Personnel Technician II, and so on. By going to the library to seek a job that would allow me the leisure to write fiction, I stumbled upon a job for which I would be paid to write fiction—although I wouldn't be allowed to call it that.

I started my new job with every intention of doing well and pleasing my superiors. It was my first real job after college, and I was determined to be a success. Unfortunately, within eight weeks I had become such a problem for my employers that I was about to be dismissed.

The Division of Classification and Pay occupied one-quarter of the sixth floor of the Municipal Services Building. There were two private offices for the division chief and his deputy. Everyone else, a dozen professionals and four clerk-typists, had desks in one large, open area whose walls were lined with file cabinets. Promptly at 8:30 Monday morning I reported to Mrs. L., the deputy chief, who introduced me to everyone and assigned me a desk directly in front of her door. She then told me that my first week would be spent in training. She handed me a very thick book with small print that she described as "the bible" of position classification—Ismar Baruch's *Position Classification in the Public Service,* written in 1940. This was my training—to sit at my desk under the helpful eye of Mrs. L. and read. It was just like the library except that I could read only one book.

The theory underlying position classification is quite rational and logical. In the bad old days the salaries of public employees were determined by whatever entity had authority over the budget, usually the legislature. Any individual salary was a function of that individual's influence with the legislature. Vast disparities in pay grew up over the years as public servants worked the political system; one clerk would often be paid twice as much as another in the same job, all because an uncle or sugar daddy was on an appropriate legislative committee. Position classification was put forth by reformers early in this century as a way of curbing the corruption inherent in the old system. Jobs would be grouped according to their duties and responsibilities so that all similar positions would be paid the same.

After a week of reading "the bible" of classification, I spent another week following an experienced classifier around as he did desk audits—that is, as he traveled to the "desk" or workstation of an employee to interview him or her about his or her job to ascertain if it was properly classified. After talking to the incumbent and the incumbent's supervisor, the classifier would write an elaborate report, which was technically a memorandum to the Civil Service Commission. Only one of three recommendations was possible: that the job be reclassified to a higher level or a lower level, or that it remain the same. Since the whole point of classification was ultimately to determine salary levels, everybody wanted to be reclassified upward. Consequently, much of the work of the Division of Classification and Pay consisted of dealing with reclassification requests by means of desk audit reports.

Finally, my several weeks' training complete, I was let loose to play in the fields of municipal administration. Assigned to do a desk audit on a variety of relatively uncomplicated junior clerk-typists who wanted to be senior clerk-typists, I became the boy investigative reporter I was fated to be.

A few days later, Mrs. L. was quite annoyed. She held up my report and asked in a tone of controlled fury, "Just what do you think you are doing?"

"What do you mean by 'just what do you think you are doing?'" I asked back in all innocence. But this only agitated her further.

"You know very well what I mean," she insisted in a loud voice.

"No, I don't," I replied, suddenly realizing I must be in a lot of trouble for something.

"Where did you get the information that went into your desk audit report?"

"I did just what you told me to do. I spoke to the incumbent and to the incumbent's supervisor."

"But they didn't tell you all this?"

"No. Much of the information came from coworkers and other people around the office such as the security guards, the mail room guy, and the other secretaries."

"But you weren't supposed to speak to them," she lamented.

"Whom was I supposed to speak to?"

"Just to the incumbent and to the supervisor."

"But they lied," I said in explanation.

"That's none of your business," she responded in exasperation.

"You mean I'm just supposed to take down their lies and write them up as if they were the truth? You've got to be kidding!"

"I never joke about classification."

"And I don't write lies, with all due respect, for you or anyone."

"No one's asking you to lie," she explained. "We just don't want you talking to the wrong people and getting the wrong idea about things."

"But it's a good thing that I did speak to those additional people. Otherwise I would never have been able to write up the whole story."

"You just don't understand. Your job is to interview just the people we tell you to. Then write up what they say."

"But what if they lie?" I asked.

"That's not for you to determine."

"Then who does?"

"This is getting us nowhere. Please wait outside."

"Should I continue with my work?"

"No. Just sit at your desk."

I sat and tried to figure out what went wrong. As an idealistic youth I genuinely wanted to do well by my city but had only managed to get myself fired. A short while later the ax fell. The deputy director of personnel came by and told me that it had been decided that I wasn't quite ready for the arduous life of a position classifier. I assumed that his next words would herald the end of my life in municipal administration. I wondered if the bookmobile was still available. But to my astonishment he offered to transfer me to the Division of Recruitment and Examinations. So I was only half fired. What a break! My budding career in public administration had been salvaged by the kindness of strangers. For my sins, such as they were, I would spend the next year writing civil service examinations for such exciting jobs as morgue attendant and sewer crawler.

It would be several years before I fully realized what had happened to me in classification. I had stumbled upon the netherworld, but hadn't seen it. Of course nobody calls it that. "The netherworld" is just my term for the underground or black market in personnel decision making that exists in all large governmental organizations. It was just an accident that I first discovered it in Philadelphia. It exists almost everywhere. It exists whenever a government manager wants to reward an unusually productive employee but cannot because the system denies managers any real discretion over salaries. So they play the position classification game to informally win the discretion that they are formally denied.

Suppose you have a secretary who is the best ever. You are going to lose her if you cannot get her salary raised. What's worse, she would then be replaced by someone not half as good. That was the quality of secretary—"not half as good"—that you could typically expect to come from civil service lists. Consequently you'll do anything to keep your current secretary happy—even lie, cheat, and steal. Fortunately, that is exactly what you must do to win the position classification game.

But all this I would discover later. At the time, all I knew was that I had bumped into some strange ethics. And I felt extremely fortunate to be exiled into the world of civil service examinations, where I would spend the next year writing multiple-choice tests and avoiding the moral mazes of position classification. But it was a dull life for an adventurous soul. The library would have been more exciting. I yearned for something more and found it in the *New York Times*. I came upon an advertisement that graduate assistantships were available at the Baruch School of Business and Public Administration of the City University of New York. I applied in October 1966. Before Christmas I received a letter congratulating me on the scholarly attainments that had earned me a research assistantship beginning in January. I felt like a fraud. But I was equally determined to take full advantage of my ill-deserved appointment. So off I went to the Big Apple to earn a master's degree in public administration.

Years later, after I had earned my Ph.D. and was a new assistant professor attending a professional conference, I chanced to come upon Professor Samuel Thomas, then still dean of the Baruch School. It was he who awarded me the graduate research assistantship that started my academic career. We exchanged a few pleasantries, and when the moment seemed right, I popped the question: Why had I been awarded the assist-antship when my record was so undistinguished and comparatively undeserving? "Oh, that's easy to recall," he said with an impish grin. "You, Dr. Shafritz, were the only one to apply." It seems that Woody Allen was right: "Eighty percent of success is showing up."

For Discussion: *Why is the public personnel netherworld such an important, and often beneficial, part of public personnel practices? Have you seen the netherworld in operation, for good or ill, in organizations with which you have been associated?*

The Personnel Function

The function of a personnel staff, or even an entire personnel agency, is service to line management. Typical services include recruiting, selection, training, evaluation, compensation, discipline, and termination. *Personnel* is a collective term for all of the employees of an organization. The word is of military origin—the two basic components of a traditional army being materiel and personnel. Personnel is also commonly used to refer to the personnel management function or the organizational unit responsible for administering personnel programs. While the terms *personnel administration* and *personnel management* tend to be used interchangeably, there is a distinction. The former is mainly concerned with the technical aspects of maintaining a full complement of employees within an organization, while the latter concerns itself as well with the larger problems of the viability of an organization's human resources—how motivated and productive they are.

Not very long ago, it would have been absurd to refer to the occupation of the public personnel administrator as a *professional* practice. The traditional professions all presupposed a large measure of formal training in preparation for the ensuing professional practice—a practice that was highlighted by the personal autonomy and independent judgments of the practitioner. Just as the repugnant caterpillar evolves into the graceful butterfly, personnel management is undergoing a similar metamorphosis. From its origins as a clerical function, it has gradually been evolving into an in-house consultant to management on labor relations, job redesign, Equal Employment Opportunity (EEO) provisions, organization development, productivity measurement, and other pressing concerns. Top management values and seeks out the professional opinion of the personnel practitioner because that opinion is backed up by expertise that is essential if the organization is to thrive. Unfortunately, in the majority of U.S. jurisdictions this metamorphosis is only just beginning. The in-house expertise either does not yet exist or is ignored by political executives. Butterfly status is many years away. All the more reason to now begin raising the consciousness of the occupation.

As with many questions in public administration, the issue of how the overall public personnel function should be organized has been plagued by an attempt to realize several incompatible values at once. Foremost among these values have been those of "merit" or neutral competence, executive leadership, political accountability, managerial flexibility, and representativeness. The main problem of the structure and policy thrusts of central personnel agencies has been that maximizing some of these values requires arrangements ill-suited for the achievement of others. Thus achieving neutral competence requires the creation of a relatively independent agency to help insulate public employees from the partisan demands of political executives. Yet the same structural arrangement will tend to frustrate executive leadership and the ability of political executives to manage their agencies. To facilitate executive leadership, on the other hand, the central personnel agency should be an adjunct of the president, governor, or other chief executive. Similarly, maximizing the value of representativeness may require less emphasis on traditional merit concepts and examinations, and the placement of personnel functions having an impact on EEO in an equal employment or human rights agency. So doing, however, will also complicate the possibilities of achieving a high degree of executive leadership and neutral competence, as traditionally conceived.

Matters are further confused by the rise of public sector collective bargaining, which emphasizes employee–employer **codetermination** of personnel policy and the creation of independent public sector labor relations authorities. The desire to maximize simultaneously these incompatible values accounts for many of the problematic aspects of the organization of the central personnel function. Arrangements satisfying some values inevitably raise complaints that others are being inadequately achieved.

Recruitment

Recruitment is the process of advertising job openings and encouraging candidates to apply. It is designed to provide an organization with an adequate number of viable candidates from which to make its selection decision. One indicator of the economic health of a community is the number of applicants for public employment. In poor economic times, government agencies are flooded with applications from the qualified and unqualified alike.

The main objective of recruitment is the generating of an adequate number of qualified applicants. An applicant is any individual who submits a completed application form for consideration. Indeed, it is often said that the first phase of the examining process consists of filling out the application form. If applicants do not provide the necessary information documenting their minimum qualifications, they are not given any further consideration—they are not permitted to take the formal examination. However, it is not uncommon for applicants who qualify in every respect for a position to be refused consideration. Many positions above the entry level are open only to individuals already employed within the jurisdiction. Outsiders, no matter how qualified, may not be admitted to such promotional examinations. For example, only currently employed police officers may be permitted to take the police sergeant's examination; only police sergeants may take the police lieutenant's examination.

---

codetermination Union participation in all aspects of management, even to the extent of having union representatives share equal membership on an organization's board of directors.

Merit Selection

Selection is the oldest function of public personnel administration. The 1883 Pendleton Act, which put the federal government on the road to widespread, merit-system coverage, foreshadowed the character of the examinations process when it mandated that "examinations shall be practical in their character." As the British civil service was the greatest single example and influence upon the U.S. reform movement, there was considerable concern that a merit system based on the British system of competitive academic examinations would be automatically biased in favor of college graduates. Because higher education in the United States was essentially an upper-class activity at that time, this was reminiscent of the aristocratic civil service that the Jacksonian movement found so objectionable only 50 years earlier. Mandating that all examinations be "practical in their character" presumably neutralized any advantage that a college graduate might have, for in those days there was little that was "practical" taught in most U.S. colleges. Indeed, it would not be until 1934 that the U.S. Civil Service Commission offered its first entrance examination designed especially for liberal arts graduates.

Over the years, the primacy of examination practicality was often breached. However, that primacy was loudly reaffirmed by the U.S. Supreme Court in the *Griggs v. Duke Power Company* decision of 1971—the most significant single decision concerning the validity of employment examinations. The Court unanimously ruled that Title VII of the Civil Rights Act of 1964 "proscribes not only overt discrimination but also practices that are discriminatory in operation." Thus, if employment practices operating to exclude minorities "cannot be shown to be related to job performance, the practice is prohibited." The ruling dealt a blow to **restrictive credentialism,** stating that, while diplomas and tests are useful, the "Congress has mandated the commonsense proposition that they are not to become masters of reality." In essence, the court held that the law requires that tests used for employment purposes "must measure the person for the job and not the person in the abstract." The *Griggs* decision applied only to the private sector until the **Equal Employment Opportunity Act of 1972** extended the provisions of Title VII to cover public employees.

Job relatedness is now the paramount consideration in developing a selection device. The legality of any test hinges on its capability in predicting job success, and validation is the process of demonstrating how well the testing device actually can predict success on the job. While examinations were once simply technical and administrative problems of the personnel department, they are now of equal concern to a jurisdiction's legal office. The thrust of the Equal Employment Opportunity Act of 1972 is to stop, by providing legal remedies for, acts of discrimination

---

restrictive credentialism A general term for any selection policy adversely affecting disadvantaged groups because they lack the formal qualifications for positions that, in the opinion of those adversely affected, do not truly need such formal qualifications.

Equal Employment Opportunity Act of 1972 An amendment to Title VII of the 1964 Civil Rights Act strengthening the authority of the Equal Employment Opportunity Commission and extending antidiscrimination provisions to state and local governments and labor organizations with 15 or more employees, and to public and private employment agencies.

in hiring, assignments, promotional opportunities, or any other benefits or conditions of employment. Theoretically, there is no inherent conflict between a merit selection program and EEO laws. Each requires selection without regard to race, color, religion, sex, quotas, or compensatory hiring (although the courts retain discretion to impose remedies for proved past patterns of discrimination). While there are no legal limits on an organization's use of tests, all examining tools may now be challenged as discriminatory in effect. Job success is a complex matter and not generally attributable to any single factor. To ensure job relatedness, organizations must identify the appropriate criteria that "contribute" to job success and must ensure that the testing devices used accurately measure those criteria. Those responsible for the preparation of examinations have no choice but to develop their testing techniques on the assumption they will have to be defended in a court challenge.

In the United States every important public issue becomes a legal problem. Such an issue is the central question of civil service examinations—test validity. While the validity of such exams could be theoretically determined by psychologists and other social scientists who could offer their professional opinions, the opinion of a federal judge provides binding social legitimacy. When the historians of personnel operations look back at the last few decades, they no doubt will write that the courts markedly accelerated the sophistication of aptitude examinations, which became so sophisticated and valid they were able to withstand considerable litigation.

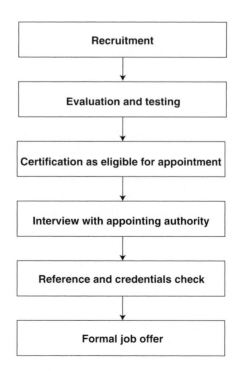

Figure 11.1   The Selection Process

Position Classification and Pay

A fable is sometimes told about position classification. Once upon a time a new tiger was brought to a municipal zoo. He was put into a habitat, cages being passé, next to another tiger. At mealtime, 10 pounds of raw red meat was thrown into the habitat of the tiger next to him. "Yummy," thought the new tiger as he eagerly awaited the first meal in his new home. You can imagine his surprise, however, when the zookeeper tossed him not the decaying portions of a bloody carcass but 20 pounds of bananas. After a few days of enforced vegetarianism, the tiger finally asked the zookeeper why his neighbor got meat and he only got yellow finger food. "Well," said the zookeeper, "this is a government zoo, and we didn't have money in our budget that was authorized for another tiger. But we did have approval to buy more monkeys. Because we bought you instead, you get the food for six monkeys."

While this is but a fable, it does contain a large germ of truth. For example, it is true that a large municipal hospital on the East Coast of the United States once employed a janitor to perform brain surgery. Just as with the tiger/monkey story, the hospital was authorized to hire an additional full-time janitor, but it really needed a part-time brain surgeon. So they hired the brain surgeon to work one day a week but paid him the full-time salary of the janitor—and kept him on the official books as a janitor. While the personnel staff thought it was a very funny way of solving a very real management problem, it also illustrates—and reinforces our keynote adventure about—how position classification systems create much dysfunctional and some-times silly activity. Position classifications are formal job descriptions that organize all jobs in a civil service merit system into classes on the basis of duties and responsi-bilities, for the purposes of delineating authority, establishing chains of command, and providing equitable salary scales. The principles and practices of position classi-fication that are generally used in the public service are throwbacks to the heyday of the scientific management movement. They were conceived at a time—before 1920—when this school of management thought held sway, and they have never really adapted to modern currents of management thought. Reduced to its essentials, a classification plan is nothing more than a time-and-motion study for the govern-mental function. The duties of the larger organization are divided into positions in order to prevent duplication and promote efficiency. In this schema, a position merely represents a set of duties and responsibilities, not a person. While position classifications tend to be universally recognized as essential for the administration of a public personnel program, their allegiance to notions of the past causes them to be frequently denounced as unreasonable constraints on top management and sappers of employee morale, or for being little more than polite fictions in substance.

Because the most basic doctrines of position classification were established prior to World War II, current practices ignore many of the advances in management science and theory that have occurred since then. In addition, the kind of workforce that clas-sification plans were originally designed to accommodate no longer exists. Classifica-tion principles assume, in the best scientific management tradition, that work can most efficiently be organized by imitating industrial machinery and creating a system of human interchangeable parts. Thus one person in any given class was considered absolutely equal to any other person in that class. However, because of advances in the social sciences and radical changes in the nature of the workforce, conventional

BOX 11.1 Position Classification Principles

Here are basic principles of position classification that constitute the foundation of most position classification systems in government. They were promulgated by the 1919 Congressional Joint Commission on Reclassification of Salaries:

1. Positions and not individuals should be classified.
2. The duties and responsibilities pertaining to a position constitute the outstanding characteristics that distinguish it from, or mark its similarity to, other positions.
3. Qualifications in respect to education, experience, knowledge, and skill necessary for the performance of certain duties are determined by the nature of those duties. (Therefore, the qualifications for a position are an important factor in the determination of the classification of a position.)
4. The individual characteristics of an employee occupying a position should have no bearing on the classification of the position.
5. Persons holding positions in the same class should be considered equally qualified for any other position in that class.

SOURCE: *Report of the Congressional Joint Commission on Reclassification of Salaries,* 66th Cong., 2nd sess., 1920, H. Doc. 686.

classification systems are obsolete for many categories of employees, in terms of simply not being as efficient as other modes of organization. They have also proved themselves to be frequently counterproductive in achieving the organizational mission.

Because of the ever-increasing rise in U.S. educational levels, the bulk of the labor force now consists of highly skilled technical and professional employees. Such workers should not be treated as if they were semiskilled laborers, menials, or clerical functionaries. Yet classification systems, designed to meet the needs of these latter employees, are being imposed upon administrative, professional, and technical employees for reasons that are hardly defensible in light of what is known today about organizing and motivating a workforce. The old dichotomy between managers and workers is no longer valid. Workers in the traditional sense are an ever-decreasing minority. They are being replaced by technical and professional employees. This group is more likely to consider itself part of management than of the oppressed proletariat.

Even employees at the bottom of the organizational hierarchy are at such a level of education and consciousness that they cannot be casually treated as so many human, interchangeable spare parts. Relying on a management tool—position classification—that has not changed in two generations is akin to relying on a pre–World War I Model T Ford for transportation in the supersonic age. Is there another field of endeavor in the United States that is so backward? An engineer or architect could not design very much for today's world if limited to the technology of the 1930s. This is exactly what public personnel administrators are doing to the employees of their jurisdictions: engaging in a presumably professional practice using a technology that predates World War II.

Performance Appraisal

Performance appraisal is the title usually given to the formal method by which an organization documents the work performance of its employees. An employee evaluation process is essential for managerial decisions on retention, advancement, and separation. Lamentably, most performance evaluation systems have not been very successful. The main reason may be that supervisors have a great deal of difficulty writing useful and objective performance reports. They submit appraisals that tend to be very subjective, impressionistic, and noncomparable with the reports of other raters.

Performance appraisals are designed to serve a variety of functions, among them (1) changing or modifying dysfunctional work behavior, (2) communicating to employees managerial perceptions of the quality and quantity of their work, (3) assessing the future potential of an employee in order to recommend appropriate training or developmental assignments, (4) assessing whether the present duties of an employee's position have an appropriate compensation level, and (5) providing a documented record for disciplinary and separation actions.

There are five basic types of appraisals.

1. *Supervisory ratings:* This is the most common type of appraisal, whereby the supervisor evaluates the performance of subordinates.
2. *Self-ratings:* Individuals rate themselves by completing a standard form, writing a narrative report on their work, or submitting a work product as documentation of performance.
3. *Peer ratings:* Each individual rates every employee in his or her division or office at a parallel level in the organization.
4. *Subordinated ratings:* Subordinates rate the performance of a supervisor.
5. *Group ratings:* An independent rater, usually a qualified expert, rates the performance of an entire work unit based on selected interviews or on-the-job visitations.

When significant numbers of employees must be evaluated, rating forms often offer multiple choices to the evaluator. Then all the evaluator must do is check the appropriate boxes. Typically, these forms are behaviorally anchored—that is, they are premised upon varying levels of performance. Here is an example of a behaviorally anchored numerical rating scale for tennis players:

Rating	Behavioral Anchor
1	Knows rules of tennis, can bounce ball and hit it over the net
2	Hits forehand strokes with consistency, backhand weak
3	Hits both forehand and backhand strokes with consistency
4	Can place ball accurately, including serves, volleys, and half volleys
5	All strokes are accurate, firm, and consistent; topspin and underspin strokes can be employed as required

Strong-minded supervisors with very high standards will do their better employees an injustice when their reports are compared with those of supervisors who have low standards or are less professional. The result is a vast quantity of inflated reports filled with superlatives so that any review of performance appraisals will boil down to a consideration of who wrote the report, what other reports they have prepared, and what was left unsaid. More often than not, reports submitted on employees will primarily reflect the strengths and weaknesses of the rater. The impact of this factor substantially limits the validity and use of an individual performance appraisal. To complicate matters even further, supervisors are often not sure of "what" is really being rated—their subordinates' work performance, or their own ability to use the **critical-incident method** of evaluative narration. Nevertheless, appraisal systems will always be with us if only because so many civil service laws and regulations require them as a precondition to annual salary increases. Employees without at least a satisfactory rating may be denied even "automatic" wage increases based on longevity.

The question remains: Why do so few employees receive poor evaluations—the first step toward dismissing them? The answer is that there is seldom adequate incentive for a line supervisor to be held accountable for his or her lack of punitive action toward deserving employees. Why should a supervisor risk creating a difficult interpersonal situation with all other subordinates for some vague notion of the public interest? Unless there is some extraordinary pressure for productivity, there is simply no incentive to take the hard action that is occasionally the duty of all managers. The public manager is not, after all, the proprietor of his or her own small business; the actions or inactions of employees, unless they exhibit some gross misconduct, do not directly affect his or her own interests. Why should he or she be the one manager in the jurisdiction to take the waste of public funds seriously enough to take concrete action? Does it not take an individual of intense ideological conviction to act upon his or her beliefs when all others indicate contrary attitudes? Before interfering with a system that tolerates marginally performing employees, a reasonable person would have to be sure of the legitimacy of his or her actions. Precedence creates legitimacy. To upset what has evolved as the natural order of things may be socially and morally illegitimate, and simultaneously legally appropriate.

Training

Training has frequently been a victim of organizational neglect. In a budget squeeze, training funds have tended to be cut in favor of the examination and the classification functions frequently mandated by legislation or charter. Training was considered to be an option, a luxury, or, even worse, illegal. Prior to the 1950s, many jurisdictions operated on the premise that employees hired via the merit system were fully qualified for their duties. Training almost by definition was superfluous. Why should a jurisdiction suffer the expense of training individuals to do a job that they had to have

---

critical-incident method Identifying, classifying, and recording significant examples—critical incidents— of an employee's behavior for purposes of performance evaluation. The theory behind the critical-incident approach holds that there are certain key acts of behavior that make the difference between success and failure. After the incidents are collected, they can be ranked in order of frequency and importance and assigned numerical weights. Once scored, they can be as useful for employee development and counseling as for formal appraisals.

Figure 11.2   The Training System

a proven capability of performing before they were employed? Attitudes changed as merit systems grew stronger, as more and more occupations became limited to the public service, and as public jobs came to be thought of as career positions requiring continuous upgrading rather than as sets of static duties.

It was not until 1958 that Congress passed the Government Employees Training Act that required federal agencies to provide for employee training. It would be yet another decade before the U.S. Civil Service Commission would be authorized to create the federal government's first in-residence management training facility: the Federal Executive Institute in Charlottesville, Virginia. And it was not until the Intergovernmental Personnel Act of 1970 that the federal government was able to provide any funds for state and local government training programs. But this was only temporary. The Reagan administration discontinued such grants in the mid-1980s. With such a recent history as a serious concern for personnel, it is no wonder that the state of the training art is, at the very least, immature.

A training program is not complete without an evaluation of its effectiveness and usefulness. Yet most government training efforts that do not simply stop at the training itself are given only the most cursory of evaluations. While evaluation is the last phase of a training program, preparations for it must be made prior to the commencement of the program. If base points of performance are not established prior to training, subsequent attempts to measure progress are likely to yield spurious results.

The essential question is whether or not a training effort has met its objective. While this is relatively easy when you are dealing with word processors, the matter becomes vastly more complicated when your training population consists of police officers, research scientists, or administrators. The measurement and evaluation of training programs for these latter classes require a great deal of subtlety, technical skill, and time. A word processor training program can be evaluated immediately thereafter, but it could easily take months and in some cases years to objectively measure the effectiveness of training for police officers, administrators, and scientists.

Although there is a great variety of training formats, almost all will fall into one of the following categories:

1. *Skills training:* Teaching specific skills such as word processing, welding, or computer operation
2. *Coaching:* Personal instruction in which an expert oversees the efforts of a learner and provides continual advice

3. *Formal or informal classroom instruction:* Traditional classroom instruction, including courses at nearby academic institutions, whereby groups of employees are instructed (with jurisdictions often providing subsidies for job-related college courses)

4. *Sensitivity or "T-group" training:* Assembling small groups of employees to deal with the problems of interpersonal relationships (usually requiring a professional "facilitator" and relying heavily on the willingness of individuals to confront the emotional aspects of their behavior)

5. *Job rotation:* Providing employees with differing work activities in order to increase their experience (a variant of this being cross-training, where each job, and thus the entire work of an office, is learned by each employee)

6. *Special conferences and seminars:* Meetings of employees or professional groups to discuss and exchange ideas about common processes, problems, and techniques

7. *Modeling, games, and simulation training:* Simulated real-life situations providing employees with various experiences

8. *Exchange and sabbatical programs:* Getting the individual out of the organizational environment and into a totally different one for a substantial period of time—several months to a year

All the training options listed above are limited by the availability of funding. While all large organizations have training budgets, these are among the most tempting targets to cut during times of financial strain. Nevertheless, annual reports frequently boast of the number of employees who have been trained during the past year. But such statistics must be looked upon with great suspicion. It is a common mistake to assume that the number of people who have been subjected to training is equal to the number that have actually been trained. No statement of training accomplishment can honestly be made unless it is supported by sophisticated measures of evaluation.

Management Development

Management development is a hybrid of training and selection. Any conscious effort on the part of an organization to provide a manager with the skills needed for future

TABLE 11.1   Training and Development Compared

	Training	**Development**
Time Frame	Short term	Long term
Goals	To learn specific techniques, behaviors, and processes	To understand the context of management, develop judgment, and enlarge personal abilities
Measures of Effectiveness	Performance appraisals, testing, and/or certification	Promotion of those developed; an overall organization with a competent managerial corps

duties such as rotational assignments or formal educational experiences constitutes management development. The semantic difference between *training workers* and *developing managers* is significant. Workers are trained so that they can better perform their present duties; managers are developed so that they can be of greater organizational value in both present and future assignments. In such a context, the development investment made by the organization in a junior manager may pay off only if and when that individual grows into a bureau chief. One common method of developing managers is to provide them with the kinds of assignments and experiences that will allow them to grow professionally. Unfortunately, rank-in-position personnel systems—the norm in the U.S. public service—very much inhibit such efforts.

The secondary focus of management development is selection. The range of experiences, both on and off the job, that managers are exposed to over the years leaves records in terms of specific scores or subjective evaluations on which future advancements may be based. While it is not overly difficult to make promotional decisions based on this array of information, what criteria should an organization use in selecting relatively inexperienced managers in whom to invest its development resources? **Assessment centers** have proved to be an increasingly popular way of establishing the criteria on which to base management-development program selection. The assessment-center process typically consists of the intense observation of a subject undergoing a variety of management simulations and stress situations over a period of several days. The resulting evaluations have proved to be remarkably accurate in indicating capability and potential.

The assessment-center concept is far from new. Assessment-center techniques were used by the German army for selecting officers in World War I, and the Office of Strategic Services used them for selecting secret agents in World War II. However, the assessment-center concept did not reach U.S. industry until the mid-1950s, when AT&T pioneered a program. The practice spread during the 1960s, but it was not until 1969 that a U.S. government agency, the Internal Revenue Service, used assessment-center methodology on a large scale. Today such techniques are being rapidly adopted by government agencies at all jurisdictional levels.

The Bittersweet Heritage of Civil Service Reform

The perversion of most civil service merit systems for private, administrative, and especially partisan ends is one of the worst kept, yet least written about, secrets in government. It is one of the dirty little secrets of life. ("Dirty" because it is less than honorable, and "little" because it is not really a secret at all—just a much-neglected topic of conversation.) Books on government management tend to deal with this subject as if it were an abnormal malignancy instead of an inherent and frequently beneficial part of civil service systems. But this is a faulty perspective. The perversion of merit systems is a normal, even healthy, condition. Indeed, such perversions are essential if actual merit is often to be rewarded within the merit system.

---

assessment center Not a particular place but a process consisting of the intense observation of a person undergoing a variety of simulations and stress situations over a period of several days.

"Civil service" and "merit system" are concepts that are frequently confused. A civil service consists of all those civilians who work for a government. Any government employee who is not in the military is part of the civil service. A jurisdiction's merit system, if it has one, consists of all those members of the civil service who are selected by a formally established merit process. Of course, to be intellectually honest, "merit system" should always be proceeded by the phrase "so-called" because merit may or may not be an integral part of any given "so-called merit system." Because of the netherworld of personnel administration, determining the true level of merit in any given merit system is almost impossible.

The Netherworld of Public Personnel Administration

Throughout the United States, public personnel merit systems tend to operate on three different planes within the same jurisdiction. In effect, parallel administrative universes, invisible to the untrained eye, occupy the same physical space. This notion of parallel universes was a plot device used on the *Star Trek* television series during the late 1960s. It seemed that the "good" starship *Enterprise* had a parallel but "evil" twin operating in a hidden dimension. The personnel netherworld is much the same in that both good and bad occupy the same space but on different planes. The vast majority of civil service employees within the merit system enter, perform, and advance on the basis of their own talents and the design of the system. However, at the same time and within the same system there are two groups of employees who enter the system and advance according to criteria other than those provided for by merit system regulations.

The first group consists of all those employees who were appointed for considerations other than personal fitness. Here are hidden the political appointees in excess of those policymaking and confidential positions that are legally the chief executive's prerogative. These positions are obtained only after months of diligent effort performing political good works such as aiding the mayor's, the governor's, or the president's election campaign or playing up to some other influential political actor. *Washington Post* columnist Mike Causey wrote that both the White House and the Congress "all too often defend the career civil service system up to the point where a friend or brother-in-law needs a job badly." The same can be said of governors and state legislators, of mayors and city councils.

It is a time-honored practice for a limited number of such politicos to be fudged into presumably merit system positions. "Fudge," meaning to cheat or grossly exaggerate, is one of the most important words in personnel management. Indeed, it can be said that the whole public personnel netherworld only exists because of the ability of personnel administrators to produce a seemingly endless supply of fudge. The extent of such placements depends on such factors as the strength and longevity of the merit system, the political culture of the community, and the personal integrity of a chief executive who, having taken an oath to uphold all of the laws of the jurisdiction, can only make such appointments in violation of the spirit, if not the letter, of that oath.

While the merit system is frequently perverted for traditional political purposes, it is similarly abused for more scrupulous purposes. The excessively rigid procedures

TABLE 11.2 A Few Examples of How Civil Service Systems Are "Fudged"

Model	Process
"Tailoring"	"Preferred" candidate is identified. Qualifications for position in vacancy announcement tailored to skills of preferred candidate. Preferred candidate hired or promoted. This practice is technically legal but it goes beyond the spirit of civil service law.
"Bridging" a permanent appointment	Agency targets highly qualified (i.e., "preferred") candidate. To avoid a hiring delay, candidate is hired on a temporary line, which is later converted, or bridged, to a permanent line. This practice is technically legal, but it goes beyond the spirit of civil service law.
Provisional appointment	This practice is technically legal, but it goes beyond the spirit of civil service law.
"Soliciting" a declination	Convince persons ranked high on civil service list to turn job offer down. To do so, candidate must be convinced that the work is undesirable and unpleasant. Or a bargain will be made whereby the candidate is promised a "helping hand" for some other current or future job vacancy. This practice is clearly illegal.

NOTE: This represents just a sample of techniques, all of which have been employed at least at the federal level of government.

SOURCE: Adapted from Carolyn Ban, "The Realities of the Merit System." In *Public Personnel Management: Current Concerns, Future Challenges,* eds. Carolyn Ban and Norma M. Riccucci (White Plains, NY: Longman Press, 1991).

for entering and advancing in most merit systems have long been recognized as being hindrances to effective management practices. In order to compensate for the lack of management discretion caused by these rigidities, career civil servants as well as other highly qualified individuals from outside the system have been advanced or initially installed through a fudging of the civil service regulations similar to the processes by which politicos are foisted on the merit system. The formal system with its attendant procedural morass simply does not allow for the timely promotion or placement of such meritorious individuals.

Consequently, what frequently exists in fact, although nowhere is it officially recognized, is a first-class and a second-class civil service. This is not an indicator of the quality of any individual or of the productive value of each class; it is merely a reference as to how people are treated by the merit system. While the politically uninfluential who comprise the civil service proletariat must be content with careers bounded by the full force of the frequently unreasonable and always constraining regulations, others—fortunate enough to be recognized for their talents or in spite of their talents—benefit markedly by having these same regulations waived, fraudulently complied with, or simply ignored.

From Spoils to Merit

Of course, all this—the formal merit system and the informal netherworld—was brought about by the civil service reform movement. While federal civil service reform is generally dated from the post–Civil War period, the political roots of the reform effort go back much earlier—to the beginning of the republic. Thomas Jefferson was the first president to face the problem of a philosophically hostile bureaucracy. While sorely pressed by his supporters to remove Federalist office-holders and replace them with Republican partisans, Jefferson was determined not to remove officials for political reasons alone. He maintained that only "malconduct is a just ground of removal: mere difference of political opinion is not." With occasional defections from this principle, even by Jefferson himself, this policy was the norm rather than the exception down through the administration of Andrew Jackson. President Jackson's rhetoric on the nature of public service was far more influential than his administrative example. In claiming that all men, especially the newly enfranchised who did so much to elect him, should have an equal opportunity for public office, Jackson played to his plebeian constituency and put the patrician civil service on notice that they had no natural monopoly on public office. The spoils system, used only modestly by Jackson, flourished under his successors. The doctrine of rotation of office progressively prevailed over the earlier notion of stability in office.

Depending on your point of view, the advent of modern merit systems is either an economic, a political, or a moral development. Economic historians would maintain that the demands of industrial expansion—a dependable postal service, a viable transportation network, and so on—necessitated a government service based on merit. Political analysts could argue rather persuasively that it was the demands of an expanded **suffrage** and democratic rhetoric that sought to replace favoritism with merit. Economic and political considerations are so intertwined that it is impossible to say which factor is the true midwife of the merit system. The moral impetus behind reform is even more difficult to define. As moral impulses tend to hide economic and political motives, the weight of moral concern undiluted by other considerations is impossible to measure. Nevertheless, the cosmetic effect of moral overtones was of significant aid to the civil service reform movement, because it accentuated the social legitimacy of the reform proposals.

With the ever-present impetus of achieving maximum public services for minimum tax dollars, business interests were quite comfortable in supporting civil service reform, one of a variety of strategies they used to have power pass from the politicos to themselves. The political parties of the time were almost totally dependent for financing on

---

suffrage The right to vote. Property ownership was commonly required for voters in the early years of the United States, but, by the time Andrew Jackson became president in 1829, universal white male suffrage had been effectively achieved. Since then, various constitutional amendments have been devoted to expanding the suffrage. In 1870, the Fifteenth Amendment held that suffrage shall not be denied "on account of race, color, or previous condition of servitude." In 1920, the Nineteenth Amendment held that citizens of either sex had the right to vote.

assessments made on the wages of their members in public office; with the decline of patronage, the parties had to seek new funding sources, and American business was more than willing to assume this new financial burden—and its concomitant influence.

The Pendleton Act

There is no doubt that civil service reform would have come about without the 1881 assassination of President James A. Garfield; there is also no doubt that the assassination by a disappointed office seeker helped. Garfield was shot by Charles Guiteau, an insane, self-styled attorney who had worked for Garfield's election and was angry about not receiving a patronage appointment. While the twentieth president's death was certainly instrumental in creating the appropriate climate for the passage of the Pendleton Act, historians maintain that the Republican reversals during the midterm elections of 1882 had the more immediate effect on enactment. Civil service reform had been the deciding issue in a number of congressional contests. Thus, when President Chester A. Arthur signed the Pendleton Act into law on January 16, 1883, and created the U.S. Civil Service Commission, it was essentially a gesture by reluctant politicians to assuage public opinion and the reform elements.

The Pendleton Act or "An Act to Regulate and Improve the Civil Service of the United States" has been a remarkably durable piece of legislation. Within it is the framework for personnel management that is still the heart of the federal civil service system. The act created the U.S. Civil Service Commission as the personnel management arm of the president. While it was termed a **commission,** it was by no means independent. It was an executive agency that for all practical purposes was subject to the administrative discretion of the president. Written into the act were requirements for open competitive examinations, probationary periods, and protection from political pressures. While the personnel program was to remain decentralized and in the control of the departments, the commission was authorized to supervise the conduct of examinations and make investigations to determine the degree of departmental enforcement of its rules.

The Pendleton Act was hardly a total victory for the reformers. It only covered just over 10 percent of the federal service. Actually the reformers were not at all anxious for near universal merit system coverage. They recognized the problems of creating the appropriate administrative machinery and were concerned that the reform program would be overburdened and subject to failure if complete reform were attempted all at once. Over the years, federal employees were brought more and more under the jurisdiction of the Civil Service Commission or of other federal merit systems, such as those of the Foreign Service, Tennessee Valley Authority, and so forth.

---

assessment The contributions to political parties determined according to a schedule of rates and made in order to retain a civil service patronage appointment.

commission A group charged with directing a government function, whether on an ad hoc or a permanent basis. Commissions tend to be used (1) when it is desirable to have bipartisan leadership, (2) when their functions are of a quasi-judicial nature, or (3) when it is deemed important to have wide representation of ethnic groups, regions of the country, differing skills, and so on.

American presidents during the reform period typically entered office taking full advantage of their patronage prerogatives and left office with extensions of the merit system to their credit. This was the case with every president from Arthur to Wilson. Merit system coverage went from 10 percent in 1884 to more than 70 percent by the end of World War I. Generally, lame-duck presidents being succeeded by someone of a different party would **blanket-in** large numbers of employees in order to reduce the amount of patronage available to the opposition party. One of the ironies of civil service reform brought about by such blanketing-in is that such initial reforms had a tendency to benefit employees who were the least meritorious.

State and Local Reform

Influenced by the example of the 1883 Pendleton Act, state and local jurisdictions began to institute civil service commissions. But this was a very slow process. While New York adopted a merit system that same year and Massachusetts did so during the following year, it was more than 20 years before another state did so in 1905. By 1935, only 12 states had formally instituted merit systems. These early efforts were not all successes. Connecticut had its first civil service law repealed, while Kansas kept the statute as law but "made it innocuous by refusing to vote appropriations." Nor were these laws necessarily effective even when kept on the books. For example, New York State, which since 1883 had the most stringent prohibitions against political assessments on the salaries of public employees, had widespread "voluntary" contributions to the party at least through the 1930s. It wouldn't be until well after World War II that most states would install merit systems—initially, in many cases, only to qualify for federal grants. Today almost all states have general merit system coverage for their employees.

Only 65 cities had created civil service commissions by 1900. By 1930, that number had risen to 250. Today less than 12 percent of cities with populations exceeding 50,000 do not have merit systems. The percentage lacking merit system coverage is almost double that for all cities in the 25,000 to 50,000 population range. Only 6 of the more than 3,000 counties had adopted merit systems by 1933. Even today less than half of all county government have instituted general merit systems.

It is important to note that all statistics concerning merit system coverage are inherently deceptive. While such figures may be numerically accurate, they merely indicate that merit systems are "on the books," not that they exist in practice. The surveys of merit system coverage that are annually undertaken by a variety of good-government groups are typically administered by mailed questionnaire. These statistics are by no means ascertained by empirical investigation. Consequently, while the arithmetic of these surveys may be impeccable, the resulting summaries frequently belie the true extent of merit system coverage. Remember, the city of Chicago has an

---

blanket-in A term for the large-scale importation of previously noncareer jobs into the regular civil service merit system. In the short run, blanketing-in can be (and has been) used to protect political favorites from the next administration. In the long run, blanketing-in is one of the major means through which the civil service merit system has been enlarged.

> ## BOX 11.2   George Washington Plunkitt on "The Curse of Civil Service Reform"
>
> This civil service law is the biggest fraud of the age. It is the curse of the nation. There can't be no real patriotism while it lasts. How are you goin' to interest our young men in their country if you have no offices to give them when they work for their party? Just look at things in this city to-day. There are ten thousand good offices, but we can't get at more than a few hundred of them. How are we goin' to provide for the thousands of men who worked for the Tammany ticket? It can't be done. These men were full of patriotism a short time ago. They expected to be servin' their city, but when we tell them that we can't place them, do you think their patriotism is goin' to last? Not much. They say: 'What's the use of workin' for your country anyhow? There's nothin' in the game.' And what can they do? I don't know, but I'll tell you what I do know. I know more than one young man in past years who worked for the ticket and was just overflowin' with patriotism, but when he was knocked out by the civil service humbug he got to hate his country and became an Anarchist.
>
>   This ain't no exaggeration. I have good reason for sayin' that most of the Anarchists in this city to-day are men who ran up against civil service examinations. Isn't it enough to make a man sour on his country when he wants to serve it and won't be allowed unless he answers a lot of fool questions about the number of cubic inches of water in the Atlantic and the quality of sand in the Sahara desert? There was once a bright young man in my district who tackled one of these examinations. The next I heard of him he had settled down in Herr Most's saloon smokin' and drinkin' beer and talkin' socialism all day. Before that time he had never drank anything but whisky. I knew what was comin' when a young Irishman drops whisky and takes to beer and long pipes in a German saloon. That young man is to-day one of the wildest Anarchists in town. And just to think! He might be a patriot but for that cussed civil service.
>
> SOURCE: William C. Riordon, *Plunkitt of Tammany Hall* (New York: McClure Phillips, 1905).

excellent merit system on the books, yet it manages to retain its well-earned reputation as the American city with the most notorious patronage abuses.

The Rise and Fall of the Civil Service Commission

Subnational jurisdictions followed the federal merit system example in many respects: Bipartisan civil service commissions became common, examining methods and related administrative detail were frequently similar, and prohibitions concerning assessments and other varieties of political interference were legally binding many years before a general pattern of compliance appeared. In some areas, such as position classifications programs and retirement provisions, a variety of local jurisdictions were many years ahead of the federal service. However, at the local level the pattern of reform that evolved contained a crucial difference—the civil service commission was made administratively and presumably politically independent of the jurisdiction's chief executive officer.

The commission format was mandated by political, not administrative, considerations. Then, as now, the illogic of divorcing the control of personnel from programmatic authority was recognized. Nevertheless, the more immediate goal of defeating the influences of spoils was paramount. With this in mind, the rationale for the commission device was quite reasonable. Not only would it be independent from the party-controlled government, but its three- or five-part membership would be in a better position to resist political pressures than could any single administrator. **Appellate** functions, especially, are better undertaken by a tribunal than by a solitary judge. Not insignificantly, a commission provides a political safety valve by making room for representatives of special interests such as racial or employee groups.

It was not very long before the rationale for the independent commission was seriously challenged. As the city manager movement developed early after World War I, managers—nonpartisan reform-type managers at that—found themselves burdened with the same kinds of restrictions on their authority over personnel that had been designed to thwart the spoilsmen. They felt, quite reasonably, that the personnel function should be integrated with the other administrative functions under the executive.

While this line of reasoning made considerable headway where the city manager concept was firmly entrenched, it had little applicability for most of the larger cities where merit system provisions implemented only a few years earlier had degenerated into a sham. This was achieved by the dual process of appointing persons unsympathetic to merit system ideals as civil service commissioners and by restricting the work of the commission by denying adequate appropriations. In response to such "starve 'em out" tactics, many jurisdictions later enacted **ordinances** providing that a fixed percentage of each year's budget would be for the administration of the merit system.

Despite these rather inauspicious beginnings, the merit system has now taken a firm hold on most sizable public jurisdictions. Two basic factors have accounted for the continued growth of merit systems at the state and local level. First, as the scope and nature of state and local employment changed, it was almost inevitable that patronage appointees would have to give way to those with greater technical training and an interest in public service careers. It should be remembered in this context that even in the federal government at its worst, the spoils system never substantially abused positions requiring technical skills. For the most part, then, the complex functions of government, rather than the ideals of civil service reformers, have led to the relative demise of spoils practices.

Second, the federal government threw its weight in favor of the development of forceful merit systems at the state and local levels. Beginning in the 1930s, it has adopted a variety of measures to coerce or induce states to use merit procedures

---

appellate Any court that considers appeals concerning a lower court's actions.

ordinances Regulations enacted by a local government that have the force of law but must be in
compliance with state and national laws. They are issued under the authority derived from
a grant of power (such as a city charter) from a sovereign entity (such as a state).

where federal funding is involved. Federal standards for this purpose were first issued in 1939 and have been periodically revised ever since.

Ironically, at the same time that the federal government has been pressuring state and local governments to adopt and strengthen merit systems, the commission form of administering them has been on the wane for reasons similar to the abolition of the commission format at the federal level. Put simply: Independent, structurally and politically isolated personnel agencies of a regulatory nature have great difficulty in serving the needs of elected executives and public managers.

The advent of the civil service commission as a political device was not synonymous with the development of personnel administration as such. The commission impetus was decidedly negative and heavily moralistic. Its goals were to smite out "evil" as personified by the spoils system. Viewed historically and dispassionately, one could argue that considerable good in the guise of executive discretion also got washed away with the evil. Administrative historian Frederick C. Mosher saw two lasting efforts from the widespread implementation of civil service commissions. They not only "perpetuated the association of public personnel and its administration with morality," but they also "divorced personnel administration from general management—from the executives responsible for carrying out the programs and activities of governments." Unlike its private sector counterpart, the personnel function in government has two frequently conflicting roles. Of necessity, it must attend both to service and to control. Is it possible to be both an integral member of the management team and the organization's policeman at the same time? In its various manifestations, this is the central dilemma of public personnel administration today.

The Civil Service Reform Act of 1978

On March 2, 1978, President Jimmy Carter, with the enthusiastic support of his Civil Service Commission leadership, submitted his civil service reform proposals to Congress. On that same day, before the National Press Club, he further called his

A woman exiled to a turkey farm. Turkeys may be good eating, but they are among the dumbest of farm animals. Thus a "turkey farm" has come to mean a government office with little work and slight, if any, responsibility. Government managers frequently find it easier to place troublesome or incompetent employees on turkey farms, rather than go through the hassle of adverse action proceedings to have them removed. •

proposals to the attention of the Congress by charging that the present federal personnel system had become a "bureaucratic maze which neglects merit, tolerates poor performance, and permits abuse of legitimate employee rights, and mires every personnel action in red tape, delay, and confusion."

The reform bill faced considerable opposition from federal employee unions (which thought the bill was too management oriented) and from veterans' groups (which were aghast at the bill's curtailment of veterans' preferences). The unions lost. The veterans won. The bill passed almost intact, thanks in great measure to the efforts of Alan K. "Scotty" Campbell, the last chairman of the U.S. Civil Service Commission, who was both the architect of the reform act and its most fervent advocate before Congress. (Campbell would then serve as the first director of the new Office of Personnel Management during 1979–1980.)

The Civil Service Reform Act of 1978 mandated that the U.S. Civil Service Commission would be divided into two agencies: an Office of Personnel Management (OPM) to serve as the personnel arm of the chief executive and an independent Merit Systems Protection Board (MSPB) to provide recourse for aggrieved employees. In addition, the act created the Federal Labor Relations Authority (FLRA) to oversee federal labor–management policies.

Was the OPM nothing more than the old commission with a facelift? A case can be made that the whole Civil Service Reform Act was not much more than reorganization for cosmetic effect—that is, much changed on the surface but essentially the same underneath. While some criticize the act as too little too late, others concede their misgivings and say "better a symbolic act than no act." The show must go on! For if the act fails in substance, it is an overwhelming success as a symbol. Because of the scandals that arose during the Nixon-Ford years, the U.S. Civil Service Commission grew to symbolize corruption and incompetence. Of course, only a minority of individuals engaged in corrupt behavior or exhibited incompetent tendencies. But that was enough to ruin a reputation.

The commission's "good name" could not be salvaged. Only a new name could remove the stigma of past indiscretions. The stigma was so great that the reformers went so far as to formally assert that it was not the giant Office of Personnel Management that would be the successor agency to the commission but the little Merit Systems Protection Board. OPM would be a totally new entity—an organization without a history starting with a clean slate. It's a nice thought. But quite untrue except as a symbolic purging of the evils of the past. Yet on this plane of symbolic action it has been a considerable success. Alan K. Campbell and company deserve a lot of credit. You cannot help but admire a federal manager who, upon inheriting a troubled and demoralized agency, destroys it only to find himself and practically all of his previously troubled agency born again on the White House organization chart.

Reinventing Public Personnel Administration

Personnel management in government has been heavily impacted by the reinventing government movement. Indeed, civil service reform was a major theme of the 1993 National Performance Review (the Gore Report), which stated that "to create an effective federal government, we must reform virtually the entire personnel system: recruitment, hiring, classification, promotion, pay, and reward systems." If one word sums up the overall focus of the reform agenda, that word is *decentralization.* Accordingly, the federal government did the following:

1. Deregulated personnel policy by phasing out the 10,000-page Federal Personnel Manual and all agency implementing directives
2. Gave all departments and agencies authority to conduct their own recruiting and examinations for all positions, and abolished all central registers and standard application forms
3. Dramatically simplified the current classification system to give agencies greater flexibility in how they classify and pay their employees
4. Allowed agencies to design their own performance management and reward systems, with the objective of improving the performance of individuals and organizations
5. Sought to reduce by half the time required to terminate federal managers and employees for **cause.**

For over 100 years, the concept of merit employment progressively spread across U.S. governments. However, in 1996, Georgia introduced Senate Bill 635 to "eliminate" the merit system the state had introduced in 1943. In practice, the legislation drew on common themes of increasing decentralization, employment flexibility, and ease of hiring and firing. But it went further and abolished the state's merit system as well, including employment protections and grievance appeal processes.

Was this an aberration or a turning point? Advocates of the change noted greater simplicity and ease of personnel action by management, especially simplicity of firing. But the way was opened for the return of a political spoils system, and it is doubtful whether a regime with no due process rights for employees and a capacity to diminish minority rights will withstand constitutional scrutiny.

Nevertheless, it is difficult to usher in the brave new world of reinvented government in an era of downsizing and privatization. Downsizing is reducing the total number of an agency's employees by **attrition,** buy-outs (financial incentives to retire or resign), and layoffs—often called "reductions-in-force." Privatization entails sending both a function and the employees who performed it to a private company. With this, the U.S. Office of Personnel Management has led the way. [The Clinton administration's first major privatization of a federal program took place in 1995, when about 125 former employees of the Office of Personnel Management's Workforce Training Service started work for the U.S. Department of Agriculture's Graduate School. While affiliated with the Department of Agriculture, this "graduate school" is a nonprofit organization that receives no federal funds; it supports itself through tuition fees.]

---

cause The reason given for removing someone from an office or job (short for just cause). The cause cited may or may not be the real reason for the removal.

attrition The reduction in the size of a workforce that naturally occurs through voluntary resignations, retirements, and deaths.

The ultimate goal of the reinventors of public personnel administration is to force government personnel offices to always remember the customer, as stated in the Gore Report: "Personnel officers must shift from reactive processors of paperwork to responsive consultants and advisors." This new focus requires personnel officers to look at the federal manager "as a customer" with needs that must be anticipated and met with responsive service.

Note the significant change here. The manager is the customer, the manager is the priority. The traditional public personnel agency concerns of protecting the rights of employees and maintaining the integrity of the merit system have been relegated to the appeals agencies such as the Merit Systems Protection Board and to the public employees' unions.

Privatizing Public Personnel

The push to make government personnel more efficient and responsive to "customer" demands has produced an increased government reliance on the practice of privatization. Privatization entails sending both a function and the employees who performed it to a private company. With this, the U.S. Office of Personnel Management has led the way. This harkens back to the romance of managerialism discussed in Chapter 8. Starting in a limited way with the Clinton administration's reinventing government efforts spearheaded by then Vice President Al Gore, this romance has become even more torrid during the George W. Bush administration because the Republicans are so much more enamored of anything that smells of privatization and reduces the total number of government employees.

Since 1995 privatization has become a much more common practice at all levels of government in the United States. Ironically, one of the most significant privatizations of government services and personnel has come in the area of human resource management. In 2004 the OPM awarded a contract to the company TMP Worldwide Government Services to operate the federal career Web site "USAJobs." This company is best known for its service Monster.com, the largest and most popular online job search site. TMP personnel, and not OPM staff, are now responsible for managing the "help wanted" needs of the federal government. These needs amount to about 17,000 job postings each month. The reasoning behind the shift of USAJobs to a private firm rested in the belief that the services could be performed both cheaper and better in the hands of a private company. The same reasoning has been behind the privatization of jobs in the areas of education, corrections, and security.

While growing in popularity, the practice of hiring nongovernment employees to perform government functions is not without controversy. First, contracting out jobs to private firms has taken on qualities of a new political patronage system. Contracts for public services may be used as rewards for campaign supporters, just as political jobs once were. Second, it is unclear if contracting out government jobs to private firms really saves the taxpayer money. Numerous studies have tried to measure the cost effectiveness of contracting out policies, with significantly varied findings. A detailed GAO examination of contracting out during the 1990s provided no conclusive evidence of the financial benefits of this practice. As the GAO report noted, "We cannot convincingly prove nor disprove that the results of federal agencies' contracting out decisions have been beneficial and cost-effective." Finally, questions of accountability have surrounded the privatization of government employees. More specifically, while government employees work directly for the taxpayer, contracted employees are only indirectly linked to the citizens whose interest they are supposedly serving.

Even with the controversy that surrounds privatization of personnel, the practice has found a strong supporter in the administration of George W. Bush. The Bush administration introduced its Competitive Sourcing Initiative upon taking office in 2001, establishing a policy in which government agencies had to provide evidence that their functions are better off being carried out by government employees rather than contracted out to private employees. Under competitive sourcing, the OMB classified over 800,000 federal government positions as "commercial," thus requiring government agencies to provide evidence that their employees could do their work more efficiently than private contractors or risk having the work outsourced. In 2004 the OMB released a report on competitive sourcing that showed federal agencies completed 662 job competitions, putting over 17,000 full-time federal jobs up for competition from contractors. The OMB calculated that those contests produced a net savings of $1.1 billion for the federal government. These savings were realized despite the fact that 89 percent of the time an agency's employees were found to be a more efficient option than the private contractors they were competing against.

While Bush's Competitive Sourcing Initiative has led to many agencies increasing their use of outsourcing, it as been seemingly ignored by many more. The OMB's 2004 report found that over one out of four major federal agencies didn't complete any studies at all in 2003. How could agencies ignore a directive that came from the president himself? The answer is, things move slowly in federal personnel management. Government employee unions have been strong adversaries of competitive sourcing, helping to prevent its adoption. Even the Bush administration itself recognized the difficulties in bringing competition to the federal bureaucracy, abandoning the aggressive overall goal for competitive sourcing tests, and allowing agencies to set more modest targets. In the end, even this glacial change in federal personnel policy that has occurred under this initiative may be considered an accomplishment. As Bush's former head of competitive sourcing at OMB, Angela Styles, noted in an interview with Government Executive magazine, "If you get some, then you've made progress. In some respects, that's better than anyone else has done in 50 years."

Patronage Appointments

At exactly noon on January 20, 2001, George W. Bush took the oath of office as president of the United States. That same day a memorandum was sent to all the heads and acting heads of executive departments and agencies by Andrew H. Card Jr., the new president's chief of staff. Card observed that "the President's appointees have the opportunity to make personnel decisions consistent with his goals." Therefore, he ordered, "Effective immediately, no decision relating to hiring shall be made unless and until such decision is reviewed and approved by a department or agency head appointed by the President after noon on January 20, 2001." This was the new administration's first step in taking control of the federal bureaucracy. But the same order could have been issued by a new governor or mayor—because the way any new administration takes control of its bureaucracy is to first control its patronage positions.

Patronage is the power of elected and appointed officials to make partisan appointments to office or to confer contracts, honors, or other benefits on their political supporters. While subject to frequent attack from reformers, patronage has traditionally been the method by which political leaders ensure themselves a loyal support system of people who will carry out their policies and organize voters for their continued political control. The patronage appointments process is more commonly known as the spoils system. The spoils system got its name in 1832 when Senator William L. Marcy (1786–1854) asserted in a Senate debate that "that the politicians of the United States . . . see nothing wrong in the rule, that to the victor belongs the spoils of the enemy."

While modern civil service reforms have curtailed many of the excesses of the spoils system, there remains at the top of all government bureaucracies a thin veneer of spoils that goes by the name of "policy and supporting positions" or "policy and confidential positions." Whenever there is a change of administration—whether in Washington, a state capital, or a city hall—there is a concomitant patronage feeding frenzy over these positions. When the national government changes administrations, this frenzy is encouraged by "the Plum Book." Formally *United States Government: Policy and Supporting Positions,* this book is published by the Government Printing Office every four years, right after the presidential election. It lists most of the jobs that a new president can fill at his or her discretion.

The 2000 edition of the Plum Book, for the first time sporting a plum-colored cover, lists 6,722 high-level policy jobs for both political and career appointees. Fewer than half of this number are clearly available to the new administration. The rest are either part of the merit-based Senior Executive Service or are of such a scientific or technical nature that traditional political considerations cannot apply to them. However, that still leaves a healthy number of jobs for the party faithful. And, according to *Washington Post* reporter Stephen Barr, many Senior Executive Service jobs that are filled by career federal employees "can be flipped to political status when a career employee leaves the position, if an administration wants to expand the number of patronage slots."

The man President George W. Bush designated to determine just how faithful and deserving the party faithful have been is Clay Johnson. His qualifications: He was the president's college roommate at Yale and his chief of staff when Bush was governor of Texas. As director of Presidential Personnel, Johnson candidly told *New York Times* reporter Mark Lacey, "I didn't know anything about government or politics when I joined the governor in Austin. I didn't know anything about the federal government when I came up here. I know I don't have very good political instincts, but I know people who do, and I'm not here to be the political manager. I'm here to help identify people and let others make sure the politics are right." Here is a man happy in his ignorance. Effectively, what he has said is that he gets to consider an applicant only if the "politics are right," if the candidate has already been politically vetted.

The process Johnson so obliquely describes is the same with every new administration. In response to the fact that jobs such as "Confidential Assistant to the Executive Assistant to the Secretary of Agriculture" and "Commissioner, Inter-American Tropical Tuna Commission" are now open, thousands of patriotic citizens send their résumés to the White House. For most it will be a totally futile effort. In 1993, according to *Washington Monthly* editor Charles Peters, "The Clinton administration dumped 25,000 unread, unprocessed résumés out of the 40,000 it received from citizens hoping to serve as a part of the new administration." And the earlier Bush and Reagan administrations did the same. Despite the fact that every new administration states it is seeking to hire the best people the nation can offer, don't think that just submitting a résumé—however impressive it might be—will land you a plum job from the Plum Book. The brutal political fact is that no one will even look at unsolicited credentials for high-level patronage jobs unless they are politically sponsored. Only phone calls and letters from influential people will get you seriously consideration. The reason they call it *patronage* is that you need a *patron*.

The Constitutionality of Patronage

Patronage has always been one of the major tools by which executives at all levels in all sectors consolidate their power and attempt to control a bureaucracy. In the 1990 case of *Rutan v. Republican Party,* the U.S. Supreme Court ruled that traditional patronage in public employment is unconstitutional. Writing the majority opinion, Justice William J. Brennan Jr. said, "To the victor belongs only those spoils that may be constitutionally obtained." In earlier cases, *Elrod v. Burns* (1976) and *Branti v. Finkel* (1980), the Court held that the First Amendment forbids government officials to discharge or threaten to discharge public employees solely for not being supporters of the political party in power, unless party affiliation is an appropriate requirement for the position involved.

In the *Rutan* case the Court was asked to decide the constitutionality of several related political patronage practices—"whether promotion, transfer, recall and hiring decisions involving low-level public employees may be constitutionally based on party affiliation and support. We hold that they may not." In a stinging dissent, Justice Antonin Scalia said, "The new principle that the Court today announces will be enforced by a corps of judges (the members of this Court included) who overwhelmingly owe their office to its violation. Something must be wrong here, and I suggest it is the Court." The Supreme Court notwithstanding, patronage will turn out to be like prostitution: It can be outlawed, but it cannot be stopped. Laws barring either will merely drive the practice underground—into the netherworld.

Veterans Preference

Patronage appointments are essentially a means of implementing a society's values. The United States has always sought to advance the interests of its military veterans. Thus veterans preference—special influence earned by honorable military service— has become a special variant of patronage. While veterans have always been given special benefits by their governments, the formal concept dates from 1865, when the Congress, toward the end of the Civil War, affirmed that "persons honorably discharged from the military or naval service by reason of disability resulting from wounds or sickness incurred in the line of duty, shall be preferred for appointments to civil offices, provided they are found to possess the business capacity necessary for the proper discharge of the duties of such offices." The 1865 law was superseded in 1919, when preference was extended to all "honorably discharged" veterans, their widows, and wives of disabled veterans. The Veterans Preference Act of 1944 expanded the scope of veterans preference by providing for a five-point bonus on federal examination scores for all honorably separated veterans (except for those with a service-connected disability, who are entitled to a ten-point bonus). Veterans also received other advantages in federal employment (such as protections against arbitrary dismissal and preference in the event of a reduction in force).

All states and many other jurisdictions have veterans preference laws of varying intensity. New Jersey, an extreme example, offers veterans absolute preference; if a veteran passes an entrance examination, he or she must be hired (no matter what the score) before nonveterans can be hired. Veterans competing with each other are rank-ordered, and all disabled veterans receive preference over other veterans. Veterans preference laws have been criticized because they have allegedly made it difficult for government agencies to hire and promote more women and minorities. Although the original version of the Civil Service Reform Act of 1978 sought to limit veterans preference in the federal service, the final version contained a variety of new provisions strengthening veterans preference.

In *Personnel Administrator of Massachusetts v. Feeney* (1979), the Supreme Court held that a state law operating to the advantage of males by giving veterans lifetime preference for state employment was not in violation of the equal protection clause of the Fourteenth Amendment. The Court found that a veterans preference law's disproportionate impact on women did not prove intentional bias.

Patronage Gone Bad

While patronage is almost as old as the nation itself—and a useful tool for rewarding political loyalty—it can be damaging to elected officials when patronage appointments go bad. The 2005 case of Federal Emergency Management Agency Director Michael Brown reminded the nation that patronage can come with both political and performance costs. Brown's less than impressive handling of the Hurricane Katrina disaster, coupled with his vastly limited experience in the field of emergency management, drew high levels of scrutiny from both the media and Congress in the wake of the destruction along the Gulf Coast. While this scrutiny was bad for Brown himself (he resigned under pressure), it also ended up damaging President Bush. After all, it was Bush who personally appointed Brown to the position, and it's the president who is ultimately accountable for the performance of the federal bureaucracy. While the case of Michael Brown may not end the long history of ill-prepared political appointees, it may serve as a cautionary tale that leads future elected officials to place their least-skilled patronage appointments in offices that don't have substantial responsibilities.

Public Sector Labor Relations

Unions are groups of employees who create a formal organization (the union) to represent their interests before management. *Labor relations* is the term for all of the interactions between the union leaders (representing the employees) and management (representing the corporation or jurisdiction). The importance of labor relations in the public sector is painfully evident to anyone who has ever sniffed through a garbage strike, walked through a transit strike, or suffered through the **blue flu.** A reasonable person would seem to have adequate cause to be alternately optimistic or pessimistic concerning the emergence of militant public employee unions. Job actions notwithstanding, the extraordinary ability of such unions to gain fiscally crippling pay raises from their jurisdictions without exchanging corresponding increases in productivity is certainly adequate cause for pessimism. On the other hand, the future of unions as vehicles to replace part of the merit system's worn-out regalia and as a source of leadership in the fight for greater productivity is exceedingly hopeful.

Why have the unions been so successful in so many instances? Simply put, union leaders have been better politicians than the elected political executives. Their acceptance of a militant posture directly followed their recognition that nontraditional forms of political behavior had been exceedingly productive for other interest groups—especially the civil rights advocates of the early 1960s whose use of civil disobedience was exceedingly effective.

Public personnel departments have traditionally had the dual function of simultaneously representing management while enforcing and interpreting civil service regulations. This institutionalized degree of conflict over what role personnel should play on what occasion has often been noted, but the problem is reaching its resolution. Unions, opting for the pluralistic conflictive model of ascertaining the public interest, reject the proposition that personnel departments in the public sector have as equal a responsibility to employees as they do to management. No less an authority than the longtime public employees union chief Jerry Wurf has flatly stated that the "civil service is nothing more—and not much less—than management's personnel system." The unions see their prime role as representing the public employee. Any remaining pretensions on the part of personnel that this is not the case will eventually be negotiated away. Even the sacrosanct, independent civil service commission will gradually see its duties considerably narrowed by the more vigilant and better staffed unions. This situation begs a significant question. If the civil service commissions are not to play a role in the collective bargaining process, how are they to remain relevant? The National Civil Service League—the organization that drafted the original 1883 Pendleton Act, which established the U.S. Civil Service Commission—has concluded that other forces have so lessened the significance of the independent civil service commission that the league's current Model Public Personnel Administration Law now recommends the abolition of such commissions.

---

blue flu An informal strike by police officers, who all call in sick on the same day; the "blue" refers to their uniforms.

The AFL-CIO

The American Federation of Labor-Congress of Industrial Organizations is a voluntary federation of more than a hundred national and international labor unions operating in the United States and representing in total more than 13 million workers. The AFL-CIO is not itself a union; it does no bargaining. It is perhaps best thought of as a union of unions. The affiliated unions created the AFL-CIO to represent them in the creation and execution of broad national and international policies and to coordinate a wide range of joint activities. The American Federation of Labor (organized in 1881 as a federation of craft unions, the Federation of Organized Trade and Labor Unions) changed its name in 1886 after merging with those craft unions that had become disenchanted with the more idealistic national labor organization, the Knights of Labor. In 1955, the AFL merged with the Congress of Industrial Organizations to become the AFL-CIO. Each member union of the AFL-CIO remains autonomous, conducting its own affairs in the manner determined by its own members. Each has its own headquarters, officers, and staff. Each decides its own economic policies, carries on its own contract negotiations, sets its own dues, and provides its own membership services. Each is free to withdraw at any time. Such was the case in July 2005 when three of the AFL-CIO's largest unions—Service Employees International Union (SEIU), International Brotherhood of Teamsters (IBT), and United Food and Commercial Workers (UFCW)—officially split from the AFL-CIO. While it is unclear what effect the split will have on the bargaining position of labor in the United States, the AFL-CIO shakeup has raised questions about the future of organized labor groups in representing the interests of workers. But through such voluntary participation, the AFL-CIO, based in Washington, plays a role in establishing overall policies for the U.S. labor movement, which in turn advances the interests of every union.

Almost all major public sector unions are members of the AFL-CIO. Among these unions are the American Federation of Government Employees (AFGE), with 600,000 employees, and the American Federation of State, County, and Municipal Employees (AFSCME), with 1.4 million employees. The National Education Association, representing teachers, is the largest, with 1.7 million members. While the International Association of Firefighters, with 150,000 members, may seem small in comparison, a greater percentage of firefighters are union members than workers in any other public sector occupation. The one major public sector union that is not part of the AFL-CIO is the mammoth National Education Association (NEA), which represents 2.7 million American teachers and education workers.

Administrative Agencies

In the context of labor relations, an administrative agency is any impartial private or government organization that oversees or facilitates the labor relations process. The contemporary pattern of labor relations in both the public and private sectors relies on administrative agencies to provide ongoing supervision of the collective bargaining process. While generally headed by a board of three to five members, these agencies make rulings on unfair labor practices, on the appropriateness of bargaining units, and sometimes on the proper interpretation of a contract or the legitimacy of a scope of bargaining. They also oversee **authorization elections** and certify the winners as the exclusive bargaining agents for all of the employees in a bargaining unit. The National Labor Relations Board (NLRB), created in 1935 by an act of Congress, is the prototype of administrative agencies dealing with labor relations. The NLRB seeks to protect the rights of employees and employers, to encourage collective bargaining, and to eliminate practices on the part of labor and management that are harmful to the general welfare. The NLRB establishes procedures by which workers can exercise their choice at a secret ballot election and determines whether certain practices of employers or unions are unfair labor practices. The NLRB model has been adapted to the public sector by the federal government and several states.

The equivalent agency for federal employees is the Federal Labor Relations Authority (FLRA), created by the Civil Service Reform Act of 1978 to oversee the creation of bargaining units, supervise elections, and otherwise deal with labor–management issues in federal agencies. The FLRA is headed by a three-member panel—a chair and two members—who are appointed on a bipartisan basis to staggered five-year terms. The FLRA replaced the Federal Labor Relations Council (FLRC). A general counsel, also appointed to a five-year term, investigates alleged unfair labor practices and prosecutes them before the FLRA. Also, within the FLRA and acting as a separate body, the Federal Service Impasses Panel (FSIP) acts to resolve negotiation impasses.

In the states, such agencies are generally called Public Employment Relations Boards (or PERBs). Typically, their functions parallel those of the NLRB, as do the methods by which they are appointed, their terms of office, and their administrative procedures. One important difference in the public sector is that binding arbitration over questions of contract interpretation may be used instead of strikes as the final

TABLE 11.3 The Labor Relations Legal System

Sector	Legal Base	Administrative Agency
Private industry	National Labor Relations Act, as amended	National Labor Relations Board
Railroads and airlines	Railway Labor Act, as amended	National Mediation Board
Postal Service	Postal Reorganization Act of 1970	National Labor Relations Board
Federal government	Civil Service Reform Act of 1978	Federal Labor Relations Authority
State and local government	Public employees relations acts	Public employment relations boards

SOURCE: Jay M. Shafritz, *Facts on File Dictionary of Public Administration* (New York: Facts on File, 1985).

---

authorization election Polls conducted by the National Labor Relations Board (or other administrative agency) to determine if a particular group of employees will be represented by a particular union or not. Authorization election is used interchangeably with certification election (because, if the union wins, it is certified as the representative of the workers by the administrative agency) and representative election (because a winning union becomes just that: the representative of the workers).

means of resolving disputes. When this is the case, the PERB may have a role in overseeing the use of arbitration and even the substance of the arbitrators' rulings when they raise serious issues about the scope of bargaining or public policy.

Collective Bargaining

Collective bargaining is bargaining on behalf of a group of employees, as opposed to individual bargaining, in which each worker represents only himself or herself. Collective bargaining is a comprehensive term that encompasses the negotiating process that leads to a contract between labor and management on wages, hours, and other conditions of employment as well as to the subsequent administration and interpretation of the signed contract. Collective bargaining is, in effect, the continuous relation between union representatives and employers. There are four basic stages of collective bargaining:

1. The establishment of organizations for bargaining
2. The formulation of demands
3. The negotiation of demands
4. The administration of the labor agreement

Collective bargaining is one of the keystones of the **National Labor Relations Act** (the Wagner Act) of 1935, which declares that the policy of the United States is to be carried out

> by encouraging the practice and procedure of collective bargaining and by protecting the exercise by workers of full freedom of association, self-organization, and designation of representatives of their own choosing, for the purpose of negotiating the terms and conditions of their employment or other mutual aid or protection.

The predominant public sector labor relations model comes from the private sector. But this fit has been long recognized as far from perfect. This is one reason why public sector labor relations were at first opposed and then organized as **meet-and-confer discussions** rather than as a collective bargaining process. The term "collective negotiations" was often used to further avoid the suggestion of actual bargaining. But today those jurisdictions with well-developed labor relations programs rely on the private sector model. The ramifications are considerable.

Instead of accepting the "public interest" or some equally saccharine goal as the watchword of the negotiating process, they have tended to adopt the adversary model of negotiations so common in the private sector. This model assumes that for

---

National Labor Relations Act In common usage, the National Labor Relations Act refers not just to the act of 1935 but to the act as amended by the Labor-Management Relations (Taft-Hartley) Act of 1947 and the Labor-Management Reporting and Disclosure (Landrum-Griffin) Act of 1959.

meet-and-confer discussions A technique used mostly in the public sector for determining conditions of employment whereby the representatives of the employer and the employee organization hold periodic discussions to seek agreement on matters within the scope of representation. Any written agreement is in the form of a nonbinding memorandum of understanding. This technique is often used where formal collective bargaining is not authorized.

one side to win the other must lose. Essentially, each party is haggling over its share of the organization's profits. There being no legal profits as such in government, has the private sector model based on conflict and individual acquisitiveness been appropriately applied to the public sector?

This private sector model of labor relations was consolidated by the National Labor Relations Act. It provides for negotiations between workers and management on the assumption that the outcome will reflect the inherent **bargaining strength** of each. Rules for fair labor relations practices were established, and the **National Labor Relations Board** was created to adjudicate disputes over their application. Workers retain the right to strike and to bargain as equals with management over virtually all employment-related issues not constrained by law. Although relations are assumed to be adversarial, the model is based on the belief that the free market imposes an ultimate harmony of interest between employer and employee: Neither party favors the economic demise of the employer.

Employing this basic model in the public sector is problematic because some of its crucial assumptions do not fit. It is difficult to assume equality between the parties in public sector collective bargaining. What does it mean to say that a union is equal to the government or to the people as a whole? Elected legislative bodies and elected executives are generally considered the appropriate policymaking bodies in American government. Public managers bargaining with organized employees are not. The basic adjustment to the inequality of the parties in labor disputes has been to recognize the government's greater authority by restricting the **scope of bargaining.**

Since it is not assumed that the parties in public sector collective bargaining are equal in principle, it follows that the outcome of disputes should not depend on their relative strengths; consequently, there should be no need to strike. But public sector strikes are not necessarily intended to harm the employer economically. They tend to do more political than economic damage, at least in the short run. This is because the governmental employer is likely to derive its revenues from taxation, rather than exclusively from user fees. Yet when a strike interrupts a government service, tax dollars are not refunded, nor are they paid out in compensation to striking employees. So a strike may temporarily enhance a government's economic position. In short, the function of a strike in the public sector is substantially different from that in the private sector.

Overall, the public sector is incredibly fragmented in terms of collective bargaining. There is no national law on the subject. States and cities vary widely in their practices. The law differs from one to another, placing substantial burdens on

---

bargaining strength The relative power each party holds during negotiation. Management has greater bargaining strength than labor if it believes that a short strike would be desirable. Final settlements often reflect the bargaining power of each side.

National Labor Relations Board The federal agency created by the National Labor Relations Act of 1935 that administers the nation's laws relating to labor relations in the private and nonprofit sectors. (Also under its jurisdiction is the U.S. Postal Service.) The NLRB is vested with the power to safeguard employees' rights to organize, determine through elections whether workers want unions as their bargaining representatives, and prevent and remedy unfair labor practices.

scope of bargaining Those issues over which management and labor negotiate during the collective bargaining process.

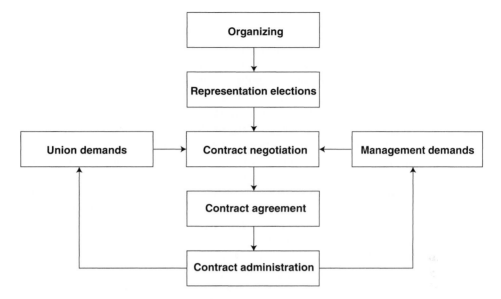

Figure 11.3   An Overview of the Collective Bargaining Cycle

national labor unions and dispute-resolution personnel who work in different jurisdictions. While the opportunity to experiment and to adapt to local conditions is valuable, such fragmentation makes it hard to speak of "public sector collective bargaining" without engaging in overgeneralization.

Impasse Resolution

An impasse is a condition that exists during labor–management negotiations when either party feels that no further progress can be made toward a settlement—unless the negotiation process changes. The most common techniques used to break the impasse are mediation, fact-finding, and arbitration.

Mediation or conciliation is any attempt by an impartial third party to help settle disputes. A mediator has no power but that of persuasion; the mediator's suggestions are advisory and may be rejected by both parties. Mediation and conciliation tend to be used interchangeably to denote the entrance of an impartial third party into a labor dispute. However, there is a distinction. *Conciliation* is the less active term. It technically refers just to efforts to bring the parties together so they can attempt to resolve their problems themselves. *Mediation,* in contrast, is a more active term. It implies that an active effort will be made to help the parties reach agreement by clarifying issues, asking questions, and making specific proposals. However, the usage of the two terms has been so blurred that the only place where it is absolutely necessary to distinguish between them is in a dictionary.

Fact-finding is an impartial review of the issues in a labor dispute by a specially appointed third party, whether it be a single individual, panel, or board. The fact-finder holds formal or informal hearings and submits a report to the administrative agency and/or parties involved. The fact-finder's report, usually considered advisory, may contain specific recommendations.

Arbitration is the means of settling a dispute by having an impartial third party (the arbitrator) hold a formal hearing and render a decision that may or may not be binding on both sides. The arbitrator may be a single individual or a board of three, five, or more (usually an uneven number). When boards are used, they may include, in addition to impartial members, representatives from both of the disputants. In the context of labor relations, arbitrators are selected jointly by labor and management, or recommended by the Federal Mediation and Conciliation Service, a state or local agency offering similar referrals, or the private American Arbitration Association.

Compulsory arbitration is a negotiating process whereby the parties are required by law to arbitrate their dispute. Some state statutes concerning collective bargaining impasses in the public sector mandate that parties who have exhausted all other means of achieving a settlement must submit their dispute to an arbitrator. The intent of such requirements for compulsory arbitration is to induce the parties to reach agreement by presenting them with an alternative that is certain, even though it may be unpleasant in some respects to everyone involved.

Final or last-offer arbitration is a negotiating stratagem that has an arbitrator choose from among the disputing parties' final or last offers.

The most common effort to adjust public sector collective bargaining in the absence of the legalized strike has been to introduce some form of binding arbitration. But this raises a host of different problems. Arbitration inherently undercuts the bargaining process itself. If both sides are convinced a dispute will go to arbitration, they will tend to spend most of their time posturing rather than negotiating or compromising. Moreover, arbitration cannot resolve the concern that the sovereign—the state and not its employees—makes public policy. And arbitrators' decisions are not automatically sensible or in the public interest. Sometimes, they may even disregard a jurisdiction's ability to pay for the awards they authorize.

The nature of the arbitration of public sector labor disputes is also related to the remoteness of the "market" as a constraint on the total compensation of employees. In fact, the economic aspects of public sector labor relations tend to work best when cities are on the threshold of bankruptcy and therefore the "market" is not so remote. Since the market does not serve as a constraint as directly in the public sector as in the private sector, some substitute for it must be devised to resolve labor disputes. Unfortunately, arbitration has not always fared well in this context. Often, arbitrators will look to comparable jurisdictions to determine what is equitable. But there is a built-in redundancy in this approach and the selection of "comparable" jurisdictions is always somewhat arbitrary. In the private sector, an arbitration award is sometimes based on the relative strength of the parties, but this approach is not very meaningful in the public sector, since the parties are fundamentally so unequal. In other words, the remoteness of the market has required arbitrators to develop other standards for reaching their awards—standards that are fraught with difficulty.

Strikes

A strike is a mutual agreement among workers (whether members of a union or not) to a temporary work stoppage to obtain—or to resist—a change in their working conditions. The term is thought to have nautical origins because sailors would stop work by striking or taking down their sails. A strike or potential strike is considered an essential element of the collective bargaining process. Many labor leaders claim that collective bargaining can never be more than a charade without the right to strike. Major strikes have been declining in frequency in recent years, as unions in both the public and private sectors have lost a large measure of economic clout and political support. Public employee strikes also have been declining for another reason as well. A great percentage of public sector strikes in the 1960s and early 1970s were over one issue: recognition of the union for purposes of collective bargaining. Because recognition strikes tend to be one-time issues and because many states have in the last three decades passed comprehensive public employee relations laws, public sector labor strife has been less than it once was.

The use of strikes is becoming somewhat outmoded. The use of economic force can be too damaging and unpredictable in today's economy, and, consequently, the strike is viewed as a last-resort means of producing an agreement. Moreover, it is sometimes argued that the fundamental character of the strike is changing due to the maturing of collective bargaining relationships. Violence is sometimes incidental to strikes nowadays, but physical force no longer plays a central role. Rather, the parties tend to view the strike as a continuation of the bargaining process. Indeed, negotiations may avidly continue during the entire length of a strike. Again, it is important to remember that both sides have an overriding interest in common—the economic vitality of the employer and the concomitant maintenance of the employees' jobs. Another general factor affecting strike behavior is what singer Bob Dylan refers to as "Union Sundown." Because the public's image of unions has changed, they are no longer considered weak underdogs struggling for justice in the workplace. In contrast, many segments of the population see them as too powerful and too greedy. Since organized labor now seeks to achieve many of its goals through political means such as lobbying and electioneering, it cannot be oblivious to its public standing.

Why Strikes Occur

Strikes do occur, and it is possible to identify at least five sets of concerns that promote them. First, it is often the case that workers will not work after a contract has expired. "No contract, no work" remains fundamental to the system of collective bargaining, since the purpose of negotiations is to arrive at agreements to govern the workplace. Sometimes, as negotiations reach the hour for the termination of the existing contract, the "clock is stopped" and marathon, all-night/all-day, bargaining sessions take place. There is no doubt that "no contract, no work" places a great deal of pressure on both sides to arrive at an agreement.

Second, the union leader is often in a complicated political position. A strike and the solidarity it promotes may be necessary for the leader to maintain his or her position. Union leaders tend to oversell their ability to dictate conditions to management. In order to justify their leadership and the exclusive representative position of the union, they tend to generate very high expectations. Eventually, the gap between these expectations and reality leads the membership to think it has been "sold out" by the union leader. (Many readers will notice a parallel with the election and subsequent performance of U.S. presidents in this regard.) Subsequent contract rejection by the

membership can be viewed as a technique to compel management to further concessions. In the public sector, this ploy raises an interesting problem because management's
concessions to labor may also be subject to outside ratification by a legislative body.
In some cases, the legislature has used the city's negotiators as "surface bargainers,"
intending later on to reject the contract and force further concessions from the union.
This practice is a breach of **good faith** and illegal in many jurisdictions, but if used
with sophistication, it is hard to identify and challenge.

Third, a strike may be used as a political weapon against public officials. It may
be intended to embarrass an official, such as a mayor, who is running for reelection.
It may also be intended to show public officials "who's boss." Municipal strikes
have resembled urban guerrilla warfare: tons of garbage left in the streets, buildings
allowed to burn, drawbridges left in a raised position, and sewage spewed into
waterways and on public beaches. One of the acute problems in public sector labor
relations is the tendency for unions to play a major role in a candidate's election,
only to find later on that all their economic demands will not be met. This too leads
to frustrations caused by a gap between expectations and reality.

A fourth general factor contributing to strikes has been management's efforts
to provoke them at a time when unions are relatively weak. It may be too evocative
and emotive to call this a "union busting" technique. Perhaps "union taming"
would be a better term. However, today a failed strike can lead to a decertification
election, and unions are now losing such elections (and the right to represent workers) with greater frequency than ever before. A tame union will be an aid to the
employer in selling management's view of what conditions in the workplace should
be left to the employees. It will also be more willing to engage in givebacks, demands
that a union accept lower salaries or benefits, ostensibly to preserve jobs. The most
common giveback of recent years is union agreement that its members will pay a
larger portion of the cost of health insurance than before.

Finally, strikes are related to the economic positions of the two sides. An economic
weapon can backfire if it cannot be afforded. Unions with limited membership may
have difficulty developing large and sufficient strike funds to aid the workers during
the length of a strike. The timing of strikes can also be of great importance. Strikes
during periods of economic recession and high unemployment are very risky because
they make it easier for the employer to find **scabs** and replacement workers, and
because the public's sympathy is hardly likely to be extended to those people fortunate enough to have jobs but unwilling to work them.

---

good faith Honesty; in the context of equal employment opportunity, good faith is the absence of dis-
criminating intent. Good-faith bargaining is a requirement of the National Labor Relations Act,
which makes it illegal for an employer to refuse to bargain in good faith about wages, hours, and
other conditions of employment with the representative selected by a majority of the employees in
a unit appropriate for collective bargaining.

scab Generally, an employee who continues to work for an organization while it is being struck by
coworkers. Since the 1500s, *scab* has been used as a term for a rascal or scoundrel. Early in the
1800s, Americans started using it to refer to workers who refused to support organized efforts on
behalf of their trade. A scab should be distinguished from a *fink* or a *strikebreaker,* who is brought
into an organization only after a strike begins.

✦ A CASE STUDY: THE AIR TRAFFIC CONTROLLERS STRIKE

Strikes are often compared to warfare—never more so than when the strike results in the complete destruction of the union. This is understandably rare, but the Professional Air Traffic Controllers Organization (PATCO) was the rarest of unions. Not only was it one of the very few unions to support the Republican Party candidate, Ronald Reagan, for president in 1980, but it was the first major union to make job stress and burnout major collective bargaining issues.

On July 29, 1981, 95 percent of PATCO's 13,000 members went on strike. PATCO had rejected the federal government's final offer. The union's position was that it wanted twice-a-year cost-of-living increases that would be one and a half times greater than inflation; a four-day, 32-hour workweek without a compensating salary cut; and retirement after 20 years at 75 percent of base salary. As one striking controller put it, "Where are they going to get 13,000 controllers and train them before the economy sinks? The reality is, we are it. They have to deal with us."

In response, the U.S. government cut back scheduled flights and reduced staff at smaller airports. Then it brought supervisors and retired controllers into service and ordered military controllers to civilian stations. Then the ghoulish wait began. It would only take one midair collision and the deaths of hundreds for the situation to radically change to the union's favor. PATCO was loudly critical of the safety of the nation's "fill-in" air traffic control system. The union's president menacingly suggested, "I hope that nothing happens!" He told the secretary of transportation, "If passengers are killed, it'll be your responsibility." Luckily, while there were some near misses, no one was hurt.

Finally, President Ronald Reagan addressed the nation on television. After reminding viewers that it is illegal for federal government employees to strike and that each controller signed an oath asserting that he or she would never strike, he proclaimed, "They are in violation of the law, and if they do not report for work within 48 hours, they have forfeited their jobs and will be terminated." Just over 1,000 controllers reported back. Most thought that the president was bluffing, but he wasn't. The union's assets were frozen by the courts, some PATCO leaders were literally hauled away to jail in chains, and the Department of Transportation started formal proceedings to decertify the union.

With its members fired, with practically no public support, and with the "fill-in" system working better every day, PATCO—the union that had broken ranks with labor to support Republican presidential candidate Reagan—called for labor solidarity. The response was lip service. All of the major labor leaders verbally supported the strike and deplored the president's efforts at "union busting," but they did nothing else. United Auto Workers President Douglas Fraser said that the strike "could do massive damage to the labor movement. That's why PATCO should have talked to the AFL-CIO council"—before the strike. Had any of the other major airline unions joined in the strike, the system would surely have been shut down. But none of these unions felt that they had any obligation to support the controllers in any way that mattered.

In late October, the Federal Labor Relations Authority formally decertified PATCO—the first time that it had ever done so to any union of government workers. In

December PATCO filed for bankruptcy. In the end more than 11,000 controllers, who stayed on strike, lost their jobs permanently.

The strike and subsequent firing of the controllers has had a chilling effect on public sector strikes for more than two decades. If the federal government would fire practically all of the controllers (who must undergo one year of training), there is no doubt that other workers requiring less training would be fired just as fast. Before the PATCO strike, the leaders of the postal workers unions, facing upcoming contract talks, were making noises about how they did not know if they could "control" the membership. *Control* here is a code word for a possible illegal wildcat strike—one that breaks out without an appropriate vote. After the PATCO strike, not a word has been heard about "controlling" the postal workers. They and all the other federal unions had been tamed by the only president of the United States who was also a union leader (Reagan was president of the Screen Actors Guild during the 1950s).

For Discussion: *Why were the PATCO members so foolishly confident that they could "win" a blatantly illegal strike? Why did the fate of PATCO have such a chilling effect on public sector strikes?*

Summary

The function of a personnel agency is service to line management. Typical services include recruiting, selection, training, evaluation, compensation, discipline, and termination.

Selection is the oldest function of the public personnel administration. Job relatedness is now the main consideration in developing a selection device because the legality of any test hinges on its validity, on its ability to predict job success. Those responsible for the preparation of examinations now have no choice but to develop them on the assumption that they will have to be defended in a court challenge.

The perversion of most civil service merit systems for private, administrative, and especially partisan ends is one of the worst kept, yet least written about, secrets in government. While the vast majority of civil service employees within the merit system enter, perform, and advance on the basis of their own talents and the design of the system, at the same time and within the same system there are other employees who enter the system and advance according to criteria other than those provided for by merit system regulations.

The advent of the civil service commission as a political device was not synonymous with the development of personnel administration as such. The commission impetus was decidedly negative and heavily moralistic. Its goals were to smite out "evil" as personified by the spoils system. Viewed historically and dispassionately, one could argue that considerable good in the guise of executive discretion also got washed away with the evil.

The ultimate goal of the current reinventors of public personnel administration is the expectation that government personnel officers must always remember the customer—that they shift from being reactive processors of paperwork to responsive consultants and advisers.

Public personnel departments have traditionally had the dual function of simultaneously representing management while enforcing and interpreting civil service regulations. This institutionalized degree of conflict over what role personnel should play on what occasion is reaching resolution because public sector unions reject the proposition that personnel management in the public sector has an equal responsibility to employees and to management.

Collective bargaining encompasses both the negotiating process that leads to a contract between labor and management on wages, hours, and other conditions of employment as well as the subsequent administration and interpretation of the signed contract. However, the public sector is incredibly fragmented in terms of collective bargaining. There is no national law on the subject. States and cities vary widely in their practices. Because the law differs so widely, substantial burdens are placed on national labor unions and dispute resolution personnel who work in different jurisdictions.

Review Questions

1. What is the difference between a civil service system and a merit system?
2. Why do netherworld operations tend to evolve in so many aspects of public personnel administration?
3. Why is civil service reform a never-ending process of which the reinventing personnel movement is just the latest manifestation?
4. What has the U.S. Supreme Court said about the constitutionality of patronage appointments?
5. How do labor relations practices in the public sector differ from those in the private sector?

Key Concepts

civil service   A collective term for all nonmilitary employees of a government. Paramilitary organizations, such as police and firefighters, are always included in civil service counts in the United States. Civil service employment is not the same as merit system employment because all patronage positions (those not covered by merit systems) are included in civil service totals.

civil service reform   Efforts to improve the status, integrity, and productivity of the civil service at all levels of government by supplanting the spoils system with the merit system; efforts to improve the management and efficiency of the public service; or the historical events, the movement, leading up to the enactment of the Pendleton Act of 1883.

collective bargaining   Bargaining on behalf of a group of employees, as opposed to individual bargaining, in which each worker represents only himself or herself.

competitive sourcing   The act of exposing government activities to competition with the private sector. The objective is to focus on the most effective and efficient way to accomplish the agency's mission, regardless of whether it is done by civil servants or contractors.

impasse resolution   A condition that exists during labor–management negotiations when either party feels that no further progress can be made toward a settlement—unless the process of negotiating changes. The most common techniques used to break an impasse are mediation, fact-finding, and arbitration.

management development   Any conscious effort on the part of an organization (such as rotational assignments or formal educational experiences) to provide a manager with the skills needed for future duties.

merit system   A public sector concept of staffing that implies that no test of party membership is involved in the selection, promotion, or retention of government employees and that a constant effort is made to select the best-qualified individuals available for appointment and advancement.

patronage   The power of elected and appointed officials to make partisan appointments to office or to confer contracts, honors, or other benefits on their political supporters. Patronage has always been one of the major tools by which political executives consolidate their power and attempt to control a bureaucracy.

performance appraisal   The formal methods by which an organization documents the work performance of its employees. Performance appraisals are typically designed to change dysfunctional work behavior, communicate perceptions of work quality, assess the future potential of employees, and provide a documented record for disciplinary and separation actions.

personnel   A collective term for all of the employees of an organization. The word is of military origin—the two basic components of a traditional army being materiel and personnel. *Personnel* is also commonly used to refer to the personnel management function, or the organizational unit responsible for administering personnel programs.

position classification   The use of formal job descriptions to organize all jobs in a civil service merit system into classes on the basis of duties and responsibilities, for the purposes of delineating authority, establishing chains of command, and providing equitable salary scales.

spoils system   The practice of awarding government jobs to one's political supporters, as opposed to awarding them on the basis of merit.

strike   A mutual agreement among workers (whether members of a union or not) to a temporary work stoppage to obtain—or to resist—a change in their working conditions.

unions   Groups of employees who create a formal organization (the union) to represent their interests before management.

Bibliography

Argyris, Chris. (1964). "T-Groups for Organizational Effectiveness," *Harvard Business Review* (March–April).

Ban, Carolyn, and Norma Riccucci, eds. (1991). *Public Personnel Management.* New York: Longman.

Barr, Stephen. (2000). "A Barrel of Plum Jobs for One Side or the Other," *Washington Post* (November 9).

Government Accountability Office. (2004). *Competitive Sourcing: Greater Emphasis Needed on Increasing Efficiency and Accountability.* (February)

Gruber, Amelia. (2004). "George Bush's Ambitious Management Reforms Agenda Is Only Beginning to Show Results," *Government Executive Magazine* (July 15, 2004).

Hays, Steven W., and Richard C. Kearney, eds. (1995). *Public Personnel Administration: Problems and Prospects,* 3rd ed. Englewood Cliffs, NJ: Prentice Hall.

Ingraham, Patricia, and Carolyn Ban, eds. (1984). *Legislating Bureaucratic Change: The Civil Service Reform Act of 1978.* Albany: State University of New York Press.

Kearney, Richard. (2000). *Labor Relations in the Public Sector,* 3rd ed. New York: Marcel Dekker.

Kingsley, J. Donald. (1944). *Representative Bureaucracy: An Interpretation of the British Civil Service.* Yellow Springs, OH: Antioch Press.

Krislov, Samuel. (1967). *The Negro in Federal Employment.* Minneapolis: University of Minnesota Press.

Lacey, Marc. (2001). "Public Lives: Old Ties Give Bush Aide Cachet; Job Gives Him Power," *New York Times* (February 19).

Mosher, Frederick. (1982). *Democracy and the Public Service,* 2nd ed. New York: Oxford University Press.

Mosher, William E., and J. Donald Kingsley. (1936). *Public Personnel Administration.* New York: Harper.

Office of Management and Budget. (2004). *Report on Competitive Sourcing: Fiscal Year 2004.*

Peters, Charles. (1993). "Tilting at Windmills," *The Washington Monthly* (May).

———. (1994). "Tilting at Windmills," *The Washington Monthly* (November).

Rosenbloom, David H. (1971*a*). *Federal Equal Employment Opportunity.* New York: Praeger.
———. (1971*b*). *Federal Service and the Constitution.* Ithaca, NY: Cornell University Press.
Rosenbloom, David H., and Jay Shafritz. (1985). *Essentials of Labor Relations.* Reston, VA: Reston.
Shafritz, Jay M. (1973). *Position Classification: A Behavioral Analysis for the Public Service.* New York: Praeger.
———. (1975). *Personnel Management in Government: The Heritage of Civil Service Reform.* New York: Praeger.

Shafritz, Jay M., Norma Riccucci, David H. Rosenbloom, Katherine Naff, and Al Hyde. (2001). *Personnel Management in Government,* 5th ed. New York: Marcel Dekker.
Tompkins, Jonathan. (1995). *Human Resource Management in Government.* New York: Harper-Collins.
Van Riper, Paul P. (1958). *History of the United States Civil Service.* Evanston, IL: Row, Peterson.
Wurf, Jerry. (1966). "Personnel Opinions," *Public Personnel Review* (January).

Recommended Books

Bissinger, Buzz. (1997). *A Prayer for the City.* New York: Random House. An insider's account of Edward Rendell's first term as mayor of Philadelphia; includes an extensive account of how Rendell tamed the municipal unions and thus brought the city back from the brink of bankruptcy.

Condrey, Stephen E., and Robert Maranto, eds. (2001). *Radical Reform of the Civil Service.* Lanaham, MD: Lexington Books. A collection of assessments of current public personnel reinventing efforts.

Freedman, Anne. (1994). *Patronage: An American Tradition.* Chicago: Nelson-Hall. An engaging historical analysis of the rise and modest fall of political patronage, from the spoils system of the nineteenth century to the most recent Supreme Court decisions curtailing it.

Heclo, Hugh. (1977). *A Government of Strangers: Executive Politics in Washington.* Washington: Brookings Institution. The now classic analysis of how political appointees and career executives cope with each other in the federal bureaucracy.

Kearney, Richard C. (2000). *Labor Relations in the Public Sector,* 3rd ed. New York: Marcel Dekker. The rules of the game in governmental collective bargaining, at all levels of government.

Mosher, Frederick C. (1982). *Democracy and the Public Service,* 2nd ed. New York: Oxford University Press. The best short history of the U.S. Public Service and the impact that an ever-increasing professionalism has had on it.

Related Web Sites

American Federation of Government Employees
http://www.afge.org/
American Federation of State, County, and Municipal Employees
www.afscme.org/
American Society for Training and Development
www.astd.org
Classification and Compensation Society
www.classandcomp.org
Federal government jobs
www.jobsfed.com/
Federal Mediation and Conciliation Service
www.fmcs.gov
International Public Management Association for Human Resources
www.ipma-hr.org/

National Education Association
www.nea.org
National Labor-Management Association
www.nlma.org/lbr-link.htm
Public employment statistics
www.census.gov/govs/www/apes.html
U.S. National Labor Relations Board
www.nlrb.gov
U.S. Office of Personnel Management
www.opm.gov/html/topics.htm
World Federation of Personnel Management Associations
www.wfpma.com/

CHAPTER **12**

Social Equity

•KEYNOTE: THREE THOUSAND YEARS OF SEXUAL HARASSMENT

Joseph, the Bible tells us, was sold into slavery by his older brothers for "twenty pieces of silver" (Genesis 37:28). Taken to Egypt by a slave merchant and sold to Potiphar, the captain of Pharaoh's guards, Joseph's talents served his master so well that Potiphar "made him overseer over his house."

Joseph, a natural administrator, was on the fast track, as slavery goes, until his career was derailed by an unfounded claim of sexual harassment. Potiphar's wife "cast her eyes upon Joseph." One day when they were alone in the house, "she caught him by his garment, saying lie with me." Joseph immediately fled, leaving "his garment in her hand."

442

Poor Joseph. He goes to work one day, and the next thing he knows he's running away. But where to? In those days there was no Equal Employment Opportunity Commission to whom Joseph could complain about workplace sexual harassment. Besides, slaves did not have the right to complain about anything anyway—least of all a workplace free of sexual intimidation. While it is bad enough to be harassed, it is worse to be framed and jailed—which is just what happened next to Joseph. Potiphar's wife claimed that Joseph had approached her and had run away when she cried out, leaving his garment behind as evidence. When Potiphar heard this false accusation, "his wrath was kindled." And Joseph was put into prison.

Fortunately, this particular story of sexual harassment has a happy ending. While in prison, Joseph's skills in long-range business forecasting came to the attention of the Pharaoh, who needed a dream interpreted—something about seven thin cows eating seven fat cows. Joseph's warning of a coming famine so impressed Pharaoh that Joseph began his rise to the top of the Egyptian bureaucracy. It just goes to show that sometimes an ex-convict can be a very effective employee.

More than three thousand years later, Joseph's problem with sexual harassment at work arrived on the docket of the U.S. Supreme Court. While too late to help Joseph, the Court ruled in 1986 on a similar case. In *Meritor Savings Bank v. Vinson,* sexual harassment that creates a hostile or abusive work environment, even without economic loss for the person being harassed, was declared illegal—because it was in violation of Title VII of the Civil Rights Act of 1964. (Title VII is that portion of the act that prohibits employment discrimination because of race, color, religion, sex, or national origin.)

This case sought to establish ways by which to judge whether or not sexual harassment exists in any given set of circumstances. Thus the court held that Title VII is violated when the workplace is permeated with discriminatory behavior that is sufficiently severe or pervasive to create a discriminatorily hostile or abusive working environment. The standard laid down by the Court is that of an objectively hostile or abusive environment—one that a reasonable person would find hostile or abusive. Whether an environment is "hostile" or "abusive" can be determined only by looking at all the circumstances: the frequency of the discriminatory conduct, its severity, whether it is physically threatening or humiliating (or only an offensive utterance), and whether it unreasonably interferes with an employee's work performance. The effect on an employee's psychological well-being is also relevant in determining whether the environment is abusive.

But this standard was not detailed or clear enough to provide sufficient guidance to employers and the lower federal courts. So the Supreme Court had to expand upon the 1986 standard in the 1993 case of *Harris v. Forklift Systems.* Teresa Harris worked as a manager at an equipment rental company for more than two years. Throughout Harris's time of employment, the male president of Forklift Systems often insulted her because of her gender and often made her the target of unwanted sexual innuendos. For example, he said to Harris on several occasions, in the presence of other employees, "You're a woman. What do you know?" and "We need a man as the rental manager."

Again in front of others, he suggested that the two of them "go to the Holiday Inn to negotiate [Harris's] raise." He even asked Harris and other female employees to get coins from his front pants pocket. When Harris complained about this conduct, the company president said he was surprised that Harris was offended, claimed he was only joking, and apologized. He also promised he would stop. Based on this assurance, Harris stayed on the job. But a few weeks later the problem began anew. Harris quit, and then she sued Forklift Systems, claiming that the president's conduct had created an abusive work environment for her because of her gender. The lower federal courts held that the situation had not created an abusive environment. The courts found that the comments would offend any reasonable woman but that they were not "so severe as to be expected to seriously affect [Harris's] psychological well-being."

The Supreme Court agreed to hear this case to resolve the conflict over just what constituted a "sexually abusive" work environment. Associate Justice Sandra Day O'Connor, in writing the majority opinion of the Court, asserted that Title VII's protections necessarily had to "come into play before the harassing conduct leads to a nervous breakdown." Victims do not have to prove "concrete psychological harm," only that the offending conduct "would seriously affect a reasonable person's psychological well-being." Thus the new standard holds that "so long as the environment would reasonably be perceived, and is perceived, as hostile or abusive, there is no need for it also to be psychologically injurious." In effect, there is no need to wait for it to lead "to a nervous breakdown." O'Connor concluded that "while psychological harm, like any other relevant factor, may be taken into account, no single factor is required" because this is not, and by its nature cannot be, "a mathematically precise test."

The story of Joseph may be the first recorded instance of on-the-job sexual harassment. More than three millennia later, the issue is still being debated within the courts. Progress has certainly been slow. But the quest for social equity at the office seems to be finally passing into a phase of resolution.

For Discussion: *How has it come about that the sex discrimination prohibition of the Civil Rights Act of 1964 has been applied to sexual harassment? What are the Supreme Court's rulings about the minimal obligations of employers regarding sexual harassment?*

What Is Social Equity?

Social equity is fairness in the delivery of public services; it is egalitarianism in action—the principle that each citizen, regardless of economic resources or personal traits, deserves and has a right to be given equal treatment by the political system. Even though the United States has not lived up to this ideal, and has not provided equality to all its men and women throughout its history, it has nevertheless been constantly moving in that direction. Political theorist Jean-Jacques Rousseau warned in *The Social Contract* (1762), "It is precisely because the force of circumstances tends always to destroy equality that the force of legislation must always tend to maintain it." The United States has a long tradition of using legislation to mitigate the "force of circumstances" that so often inhibits equality. For example, in the early nineteenth century, free public schools made education gradually available to all classes. In 1862 the Homestead Act made it possible for any citizen to own 160 acres of public land if he or she would live on it for five years. The Civil War of 1861–1865 can be viewed alternatively as conflict over the nature of intergovernmental relations or a moral crusade to bring "equality" to those in bondage. The twentieth century witnessed an outpouring of legislation that gave new rights to workers, women, and minorities. This has gone so far that social equity, in addition to efficiency, is now a major criterion for evaluating the desirability of any public policy or program.

Government organizations have a special obligation to be fair—to pursue social equity both with their employees and the public—because they represent the citizenry. This is in distinct contrast to business organizations, which represent private interests such as stockholders. It is often asserted that corporations have a social responsibility, that they have a moral and ethical duty to contribute to society's well-being—obligations far beyond just seeking a profit in a legal manner. But others, such as economist Milton Friedman, feel that the resolution of social problems is the task of governments, not businesses, that managers who spend money to alleviate social problems act irresponsibly.

Mandating Social Equity

There is a long tradition of government forcing private organizations to better treat their employees. Better treatment was inhibited by social Darwinism, Charles Darwin's (1809–1882) concept of biological evolution applied by others to the development of human social organization and economic policy. American social Darwinism applied Darwin's concepts of "natural selection" and "survival of the fittest" to society in general. Thus practices such as child labor, the employment of children in a manner detrimental to their health and social development, were justified. Efforts by the labor movement and social reformers to prevent the exploitation of children in the workplace date back well into the nineteenth century. As early as 1842, Connecticut and Massachusetts legislated a maximum ten-hour workday for children. In 1848, Pennsylvania established a minimum working age of 12 years for factory jobs. But it would be 20 more years before any state had inspectors to enforce child labor laws. And it would not be until the late 1930s that federal laws would outlaw child labor (mainly through the Fair Labor Standards Act of 1938). The practice was so entrenched that earlier federal attempts to outlaw child labor were construed by the Supreme Court as being unconstitutional infringements on the power of the states to regulate conditions in the workplace. So achieving social equity for children was an uphill battle that lasted more than a century because, in large measure, of the social Darwinist belief that the "fit" children would survive and that this was all part of a normal process of "natural selection."

Child labor is just one example of how government regulation has been used to further social equity. The whole thrust of the labor and women's movements that began in the nineteenth century and the post–World War II civil rights movement was to obtain legislation that would equalize the employment and social prospects of unions, women, and minority group members. The fine-tuning of those public policies is an ongoing process. The Supreme Court cases discussed in the keynote dealt with sexual harassment, a variant of sexual discrimination. While it is impossible to predict future cases, it seems certain that the Court will be ruling on the subject well into this century. The quest for social equity is never-ending. While legislation seeks to cope with gross abuses, the subtleties are left to the courts.

The New Public Administration

By the late 1960s, serious questions were being raised concerning the state of the discipline and profession of public administration. Dwight Waldo, having noted that public administration was "in a time of revolution," called a conference of younger academics in public administration, through the auspices of his position as editor-in-chief of *Public Administration Review* and with funds from the Maxwell School of Syracuse University. Held in 1968 at Syracuse University's Minnowbrook conference site, the event produced papers that were edited by Frank Marini, then managing editor of *Public Administration Review,* and published in 1971 under the title *Toward a New Public Administration: The Minnowbrook Perspective.* The goal of the meeting was to identify what was relevant about public administration and how the discipline had to change to meet the challenges of the 1970s. H. George Frederickson, now a professor at the University of Kansas, contributed a paper, "Toward a New Public Administration," which called for social equity in the performance and delivery of public services.

Frederickson's new public administration called for a proactive administrator with a burning desire for social equity to replace the traditional, impersonal, neutral, gun-for-hire bureaucrat. While this call was heeded by few, it was discussed by many. The basic problem with the new public administration's call for social equity was that it was also a call for insubordination—something that is not lightly tolerated in bureaucracies. **Victor Thompson** immediately attacked the new public administration movement in his aptly titled *Without Sympathy or Enthusiasm* as an effort by left-wing radicals to "steal the popular sovereignty."

Thompson need not have worried. All these "radicals" did was talk—and write. From the 1970s to the present day, and still led by Frederickson, they have produced an endless stream of conference papers and scholarly articles urging public administrators to show a greater sensitivity to the forces of change, the needs of clients, and the problem of social equity in service delivery. This has had a positive effect in that now the ethical and equitable treatment of citizens by administrators is at the forefront of concerns in public agencies. Reinforced by changing public attitudes, the reinventing government movement, and civil rights laws, the new public administration has triumphed after a quarter century. Now it is unthinkable (as well as illegal), for example, to deny someone welfare benefits because of his or her race or a job opportunity because of his or her sex. Social equity today does not have to be so much fought for by young radicals as administrated by managers of all ages.

Victor Thompson (1912–) One of the most gifted stylists in the literature of public administration. Thompson is best known for dealing deftly with bureaucratic interactions and dysfunctions. In his most influential work, *Modern Organization,* he reminds us that "one must not forget that clients are notoriously insensitive to the needs of bureaucrats."

The Challenge of Equality

Equality is an American ideal. In 1776 the Declaration of Independence proclaimed that "all men are created equal, that they are endowed by their Creator with certain unalienable rights." These are rights derived from natural law, which all people have and which cannot be taken away or transferred. Yet the Declaration as well as the subsequent Constitution denied these rights to a large group of residents. Because the Constitution was initially oblivious to the plight of African Americans, Supreme Court Associate Justice **Thurgood Marshall** pointedly rejected the view that Americans should celebrate the Constitution as the source of all that is good in the nation. On the contrary, he said of the founders that "the government they devised was defective from the start, requiring several amendments, a civil war, and momentous social transformation to attain the system of constitutional government, and its respect for individual freedoms and human rights, we hold as fundamental today." Marshall's harsh rhetoric notwithstanding, all discussions of equality in the United States must begin with the issue of race.

Racism

Race can be defined as a large group of people with common characteristics presumed to be transmitted genetically. Which characteristics are properly included has been a subject of debate. They range from physical characteristics that are immediately observable, such as color of hair, skin, and eyes, to the subtler aspects of emotions and aptitudes. Some races even have genetic susceptibility to certain diseases or physical disorders. Rational people of all races are often uncomfortable talking about race. There is a depth of feeling about past injustices that is dangerous to bring to the surface in polite conversation. Yet no subject is more important in administering the public affairs of a multiracial society. The issues must be faced and discussed even if they cannot be immediately resolved.

Up to the middle of the twentieth century, race was used as a way of distinguishing among national groups. This practice is traceable to eighteenth-century distinctions among people according to language. It became a method of attempting to define a hierarchy of races, with the so-called Anglo-Saxons at the top and others arranged along supposedly developmental lines. In recent times, in American political language, race has come to designate issues or attitudes concerning citizens of African origin. Other minority groups are called *ethnics*. Originally, the term applied only to European ethnics. The term is now more likely to refer to the new ethnics, both those who have long been here and those who are more recent arrivals—for example, the Hispanics and the Vietnamese. Technically, every American except for white Anglo-Saxon Protestants is a member of an ethnic group. And now that they are in the minority, many of them have begun to claim

---

Thurgood Marshall (1908–1993) The civil rights lawyer who successfully argued the *Brown v. Board of Education* case before the Supreme Court and who in 1967 was appointed by President Lyndon B. Johnson to be the first African-American member of that court.

that they are an ethnic group, too. A politician may be said to be practicing ethnic politics when he tells his Irish constituents of his support for a united Ireland, his Jewish constituents of his support for a strong state of Israel, and his Hispanic constituents of his strong support for bilingual education. Ethnic politics does not have to be substantive; sometimes it is nothing more than a "photo opportunity" of the politician eating ethnic food or attending an ethnic cultural festival or wedding.

A racist can be defined as any person or organization that either consciously or unconsciously practices racial **discrimination** against a person on the basis of race (or ethnicity) or supports the supremacy of one race over others. The most notorious of American racist groups has been the **Ku Klux Klan.** But anyone who is insensitive to the feelings of racial minorities and uses racially demeaning language or diction out of genuine ignorance may also be considered racist. Such people might deny they are racist; however, offended minority groups might still perceive them to be so. This is especially true with what is known as stealth racism—racist acts readily apparent to African-Americans but virtually invisible to whites. Well-to-do middle-class non-whites are routinely kept under greater surveillance at shopping places, find it difficult to get taxis, are automatically presumed to be dangerous, and are given unequal service in restaurants and airports. Such lack of respect, such affronts to honor, are difficult to deal with by legislation. The Civil Rights Act of 1964 mandated equal access to expensive hotels and restaurants. But it still hurts when an African-American guest dressed in a tuxedo is mistaken for a waiter or the valet parking attendant. That's stealth racism.

What distinguishes African-Americans from other ethnic Americans is not so much their color—many other groups are nonwhite—but their ancestors, who came to the United States not as the "huddled masses yearning to breathe free," as is engraved on the pedestal of the Statue of Liberty, but as slaves. And slavery has uniquely colored the African-American experience down to the present day.

The Bitter Heritage of Slavery

Slavery, which began in colonial times, was addressed, albeit obliquely, in various parts of the Constitution. Article I, Section 2, stated that slaves are to be counted for purposes of congressional appointments as "three-fifths" of a person. Article I,

---

discrimination Bigotry in practice; intolerance toward those who are of different races or have different religious beliefs.

Ku Klux Klan (KKK) The most infamous U.S. terrorist organization; a racist, white supremacist group established in the South following the Civil War. The KKK has a long history of intimidation, beatings, and murders of blacks, as well as other racial and religious minorities. Lynchings are a hallmark of the KKK, as is the burning of crosses, designed to instill fear into the hearts of onlookers. Klansmen traditionally cloak themselves in the anonymity of robes and hide their faces under hoods. Early in the twentieth century, the KKK had considerable political power; it dominated politics in a dozen states and counted dozens of congressmen as members. Today, the KKK has only the slightest influence in American politics. Thus it has traveled from the mainstream to the lunatic fringe, from millions of members to a few thousand. In recent years, successful lawsuits brought against the KKK by its victims have dealt the organization severe setbacks.

Section 9, stated that Congress could not pass any law banning the importation of slaves until 1808 (which it did). Article IV, Section 2, said that persons "held in service"—meaning runaway slaves—who escaped had to be returned. This was upheld by the ***Dred Scott v. Sandford*** decision of the Supreme Court.

Abraham Lincoln was, even before he became president, the most eloquent spokesman against slavery. He told the Illinois Republican State Convention on June 16, 1858, "'A house divided against itself cannot stand' [the Bible, Mark 3:25]. I believe this government cannot endure, permanently half slave and half free. I do not expect the Union to be dissolved—I do not expect the house to fall—but I do expect it will cease to be divided. It will become all one thing, or all the other." He was right.

In September 1862, President Abraham Lincoln, acting as commander in chief during a time of war, issued the **Emancipation Proclamation,** which became effective on January 1, 1863. The proclamation declared that all people held in slavery "are, and henceforth shall be, free; and the executive government of the United States, including the military and naval authorities thereof, will recognize and maintain the freedom." The Thirteenth Amendment was passed in 1865 to quell the controversy over the constitutionality of the Emancipation Proclamation and to settle the issue of slavery in the United States forever.

The history of slavery in the United States is still relevant today because it is the underlying basis for African-American claims for special treatment. Some argue that reparations are due and point to the Civil Liberties Act of 1988. This law authorized the payment of $20,000 to all living Japanese-Americans who were interned by the United States government during World War II. The act authorized a total of $1.25 billion in reparations payments. Of the 120,000 Japanese-Americans who were interned, about 70,000 were still alive when the act was passed. But these payments to Japanese-Americans went to the still-living victims. There are no direct victims of slavery still living. There is not much sympathy for reparation for slavery when most Americans are not descendants of slave owners but descendants of people who came

---

Dred Scott v. Sandford (1857) The second case in which the U.S. Supreme Court declared an act of the Congress (the Missouri Compromise) to be unconstitutional (the first was *Marbury v. Madison* in 1803). Dred Scott (1795–1858) was a slave who was taken to a free state in the North. The question before the Court was whether residence in a free state was sufficient basis for declaring Scott a free man. The Supreme Court in a 7 to 2 ruling said no. The chief justice, Roger Brook Taney, wrote in the Court's opinion, "The right of property in a slave is distinctly and expressly affirmed in the Constitution. . . . No word can be found in the Constitution which gives Congress a greater power over slave property or which entitles property of that kind to less protection than property of any other description." While it helped to further entrench the Court's right to judicial review, the Court's holdings—that blacks could not become citizens and that the United States could not prohibit slavery in unsettled territories—did much to make the Civil War inevitable, especially because the decision made a legislative solution to the slavery issue virtually impossible.

Emancipation Proclamation Lincoln showed his cabinet the draft of the proclamation about half a year earlier, on July 22, 1862, but felt that he had to keep it secret until the military situation improved for the North. While the battle of Antietam of September 17, 1862, was essentially a draw, Lincoln considered it enough of a victory to announce the proclamation.

to the United States after the Civil War—often with little more than the clothes on their backs. Still, the unfinished business of mitigating the heritage of slavery led to the second reconstruction.

From Reconstruction to Second Reconstruction

While the Thirteenth, **Fourteenth,** and **Fifteenth Amendments** attempted to settle the issues of slavery and civil rights, the issue of the former slaves remained. After **Reconstruction** many states enacted **Jim Crow** laws, which effectively made African-Americans **second-class citizens.**

This second-class status was supported by the Supreme Court in the separate but equal doctrine. In *Plessy v. Ferguson* (1896) the Court held that segregated railroad facilities for African-Americans, facilities that were considered equal in quality to those provided for whites, did not violate the equal protection clause of the Fourteenth Amendment. In a **dissenting opinion** Justice John Marshall Harlan wrote, "We boast of the freedom enjoyed by our people. . . . But it is difficult to reconcile that boast with a state of the law which, practically, puts the brand of servitude and degradation upon a large class of our fellow citizens, our equals before the law. The

---

Fourteenth Amendment The post–Civil War amendment to the U.S. Constitution that defines citizenship and mandates due process as well as equal protection of the laws for all citizens. Through the due process and equal protection clause of the Fourteenth Amendment, the U.S. Supreme Court has gradually applied (incorporated) most of the protections of the Bill of Rights to the states. The Fourteenth Amendment, which has produced more litigation and court interpretation than any other part of the Constitution, was enacted originally to protect the freed slaves from abrogations of their rights by the southern states.

Fifteenth Amendment The 1870 amendment to the U.S. Constitution that guarantees to all citizens the right to vote regardless of "race, color, or previous condition of servitude." This is the legal source of federal voting rights legislation.

Reconstruction The post–Civil War period when the South was divided into military districts and the states that were formerly part of the Confederacy were brought back into the Union. The official end of Reconstruction was 1876, when the last federal troops were withdrawn.

Jim Crow A name given to any law requiring the segregation of the races. All such statutes are now unconstitutional. But prior to the Civil Rights Act of 1964, many southern states had laws requiring separate drinking fountains, separate rest rooms, separate sections of theaters, and so on for blacks and whites. The name "Jim Crow" comes from a nineteenth-century vaudeville character who was called Jim (a common name) Crow (for a black-colored bird). Thus the name was applied to things having to do with blacks.

second-class citizen A person who does not have all of the civil rights of other citizens. Historically, African-Americans were called, and because of segregation and discrimination often considered themselves to be, second-class citizens. But since the civil rights movement and the new laws that flowed from it, there can be no second-class citizens in the United States. Nevertheless, the phrase is still used in various contexts: by minorities who wish to emphasize economic disparities, by women who feel that they have not achieved social equity with men, by prisoners who complain they cannot vote.

dissenting opinion The opinion of a judge who disagrees with the decision of a court. On the U.S. Supreme Court, these opinions have sometimes been extremely significant because they have so often established the intellectual framework for subsequent reversals of decisions. Chief Justice Charles Evans Hughes (1862–1948) observed that dissents are "appeals to the brooding spirit of the law, to the intelligence of another day."

thin disguise of 'equal' accommodations for passengers in the railroad coaches will not mislead anyone, or atone for the wrong this day done."

More than half a century later the Court overturned the *Plessy* decision and nullified this doctrine when it asserted that separate was "inherently unequal." In *Brown v. Board of Education of Topeka, Kansas (1954)*, the Court decided that the separation of children by race and according to law in public schools "generates a feeling of inferiority as to their [the minority group's] status in the community that may affect their hearts and minds in a way unlikely ever to be undone." Consequently, it held that "separate educational facilities are inherently unequal" and therefore violate the equal protection clause of the Fourteenth Amendment. According to Chief Justice Earl Warren, "We come then to the question presented: Does segregation of children in public schools solely on the basis of race, even though the physical facilities and other 'tangible' factors may be equal, deprive the children of the minority group of equal educational opportunities? We believe that it does."

This decision, one of the most significant in the century, helped create the environment that would lead to the second reconstruction: the civil rights movement and legislation of the 1960s. The first reconstruction, immediately after the Civil War, gave African-Americans their freedom from slavery. But the laws as enforced and customs as practiced did not allow for the full rights of citizens. That came in the 1960s, when public sentiment was aroused and legal action was taken to ensure equal rights for all Americans.

An Administrative Fix for Racism

The problem with the second reconstruction, with its outpouring of equal employment opportunity and civil rights legislation, was that the government formally got into the business of examining people's blood lines. Official race categories were established by the Equal Employment Opportunity Commission (EEOC), which had been created by the Civil Rights Act of 1964. The South once had miscegenation laws, declared unconstitutional in *Loving v. Virginia* (1967). Miscegenation laws meant that if one of your ancestors was African, you could not marry someone whose ancestors were all European. Now, in a reversal of fortune, if one of your ancestors is African, you are entitled, under affirmative action provisions of equal opportunity laws, to preferential treatment in employment.

To further this goal, the EEOC has established five racial-ethnic categories for reporting purposes:

1. *White, not of Hispanic origin:* Those having origins in any of the original peoples of Europe, North Africa, or the Middle East

2. *Black, not of Hispanic origin:* People having origins in any of the black racial groups of Africa

3. *Hispanic:* People of Mexican, Puerto Rican, Cuban, Central or South American, or other Spanish culture origin, regardless of race

A meeting between the two major leaders of the 1960s civil rights movement, Dr. Martin Luther King Jr. (left) and Malcolm X. They became the living symbols of the two extremes of the civil rights movement: King called for civil disobedience to gain voting rights for the disenfranchised, while Malcolm X offered white society a simple choice: "It's either a ballot or a bullet." Both would be dead from assassins' bullets by the end of the decade. •

4. *American Indian or Alaskan native:* Those having origins in any of the original peoples of North America and who maintain cultural identification through tribal affiliation or community recognition

5. *Asian or Pacific Islander:* Those having origins in any of the original peoples of the Far East, Southeast Asia, the Indian subcontinent, or the Pacific islands (These areas include China, Japan, Korea, the Philippine Islands, and Samoa)

These categories are used on the EEO-1 form, the annual report on the sex and minority status of various workforce categories, that is required of all employers with 100 or more employees. The report must be filed with the Joint Reporting Committee of the Equal Employment Opportunity Commission and the Office of Federal Contract Compliance within the Department of Labor.

The Supreme Court has also recognized additional race categories that are protected by the federal civil rights laws. In *Shaare Tefila Congregation v. Cobb* (1987), it held that Jews could bring charges of racial discrimination against defendants who were also considered Caucasian. And in *Saint Francis College v. Al-Khazraji* (1987), it held that someone of Arabian ancestry was protected from racial discrimination under the various civil rights statutes.

In addition to employment advantages, recognized minority group members have been granted set-asides—government purchasing and contracting provisions that set aside or allocate a certain percentage of business for minority-owned or female-owned companies. The use of set-asides was upheld by the Supreme Court in *Fullilove v. Klutznick* and *Metro Broadcasting v. FCC* but restricted in *City of Richmond v. J. A. Croson* and *Adarand Constructors v. Pena.*

Equal Employment Opportunity

Equal employment opportunity (EEO) is a concept fraught with political, cultural, and emotional overtones. Generally, it applies to a set of employment procedures and practices that effectively prevent any individual from being adversely excluded from employment opportunities on the basis of race, color, sex, religion, age, national origin, or other factors that cannot lawfully be considered in employing people. While the ideal of EEO is an employment system devoid of both intentional and unintentional discrimination, achieving this ideal may be a political impossibility because of the problem of definition. One person's equal opportunity may be another's institutional racism or institutional sexism. Because of this problem of definition, only the courts have been able to say if, when, and where EEO exists.

Nevertheless, it must always be remembered that EEO laws and programs were created to remedy very real problems of bigotry and sexism—problems that are still with us today. The word that summarizes workplace intolerance toward those who are different is *discrimination*. In employment, this is the failure to treat equals equally. Whether deliberate or unintentional, any action that has the effect of limiting employment and advancement opportunities because of an individual's sex, race, color, age, national origin, religion, physical handicap, or other irrelevant criteria, is discrimination—and illegal.

Origins of Affirmative Action

It was not until the Kennedy administration that EEO became a central aspect of public personnel administration. Between 1961 and 1965, the civil rights movement reached the pinnacle of its political importance and became a dominant national issue. Indeed, it was a sign of the times when Kennedy declared, "I have dedicated my administration to the cause of equal opportunity in employment by the government." His

---

Fullilove v. Klutznick (1980) The Supreme Court case holding that Congress has the authority to use quotas to remedy past discrimination in government public works programs, reasoning that the Fourteenth Amendment's requirement of equal protection means that groups historically denied this right may be given special treatment.

Metro Broadcasting v. FCC (1990) The Supreme Court case holding that the Federal Communications Commission could use "benign race-conscious measures" to increase minority ownership of broadcast licenses.

City of Richmond v. J. A. Croson (1989) The Supreme Court case holding that a minority set-aside program designed so that 30 percent of city construction contacts went to minority-owned firms was too rigid; it was not justified by past findings of discrimination.

Adarand Constructors v. Pena (1995) The Supreme Court case holding that set-asides could only be used when a minority group has suffered actual discrimination; thus they could only be used as a remedy for past discriminatory practices.

Executive Order 10925 of March 6, 1961, for the first time required that "affirmative action" be used to implement the policy of nondiscrimination in employment by the federal government and its contractors.

Affirmative action first meant the removal of "artificial barriers" to the employment of women and minority group members. Special efforts were made to bring more members of minority groups into the federal service. These included recruitment drives at high schools and colleges heavily attended by minorities. Agencies were encouraged to provide better training opportunities for minority group members.

The Kennedy program was carried forward and expanded by the Johnson administration. The Civil Rights Act of 1964 declared that "it shall be the policy of the United States to ensure equal employment opportunities for Federal employees." It also created the Equal Employment Opportunity Commission (EEOC) to combat discrimination in the private sphere. The coordination of all equal employment activities for federal employees was assigned to the Civil Service Commission.

The continuing rationale for government-sanctioned affirmative action programs was provided by President Lyndon Johnson in a June 4, 1965, speech at Howard University: "You do not take a person who, for years, has been hobbled by chains and liberate him, bring him up to the starting line of a race and then say, 'You are free to compete with the others' and still justly believe you have been completely fair."

The next major development in the evolution of the EEO program came in 1969, when President Nixon issued an executive order requiring agency heads to "establish and maintain an affirmative program of equal employment opportunity." It was also during the Nixon administration, when the federal courts associated affirmative action with specific **goals** and timetables for minority hiring, that the term was altered to include compensatory opportunities for hitherto disadvantaged groups.

The Equal Employment Opportunity Act of 1972 solidified the Civil Service Commission's authority in this area and placed the program on a solid statutory basis for the first time. It reaffirmed the traditional policy of nondiscrimination and empowered the commission to enforce its provisions "through appropriate remedies, including reinstatement or hiring of employees with or without back pay . . . and issuing such rules, regulations, orders, and instructions as it deems necessary and appropriate." It also made the commission responsible for the annual review and approval of agency **EEO plans** and for evaluating agency **EEO activities**.

---

executive order The principal mode of administrative action on the part of the president of the United States. The power of a president to issue executive orders emanates from the constitutional provision requiring him to "take care that the laws be faithfully executed," the commander-in-chief clause, and express powers vested in him by congressional statutes.

goals Realistic objectives that an organization endeavors to achieve through affirmative action. Quotas, in contrast, restrict employment or development opportunities to members of particular groups by establishing a required number or proportionate representation, which managers are obligated to attain, without regard to equal employment opportunity. To be meaningful, any program of goals or quotas must be associated with a specific timetable—a schedule of when the goals or quotas are to be achieved. Quotas tend to be mandated by courts to remedy patterns of past discrimination.

EEO plan An organization's written plan to remedy past discrimination against, or underutilization of, women and minorities. The plan itself usually consists of a statement of goals, timetables for achieving them, and specific program efforts.

TABLE 12.1   Average Income for Person with
a Bachelor's Degree in 2004

	Men	Women
All Races	$63,753	$38,766
White	$65,652	$49,318
Black	$47,648	$38,612
Hispanic	$53,814	$34,849
Asian	$57,236	$38,438

SOURCE: U.S. Bureau of the Census (2005).

The act also brought state and local governments under the federal EEO umbrella for the first time. The EEOC, hitherto primarily concerned with the private sector, was given equal authority over the nonfederal public sector. In 1979, as part of the overall federal civil service reforms then taking place (see Chapter 11), the enforcement aspects of the federal EEO program were transferred to the EEOC. So after starting out with enforcement authority over just the private sector in 1964, the EEOC by 1979 had been given responsibility for enforcing equal employment opportunity at all levels of government as well.

The Case for Affirmative Action

The case for affirmative action, for special efforts to recruit and advance minorities and women in employment, has always been based on statistics. According to the Bureau of the Census, white college graduate males earned about $65,000 in 2002. But black and Hispanic males with the same education earned 30 percent less. Even among high school graduates, black men earned 25 percent less than whites. These economic disparities in income carry over into rates of home ownership. In 2002 the national rate for home ownership was 68 percent, but for blacks it was 48 percent (up from 42 percent in 1990).

These disparities exist because of continuing patterns of discrimination that are easily traced back to the days of slavery. The only way to overcome and get beyond the **adverse impact** of **systemic discrimination** is to implement a vigorous affirmative action program. To repeal affirmative action and force minorities to compete

---

adverse impact When a selection process for a particular job or group of jobs results in the selection of members of any racial, ethnic, or gender group at a lower rate than members of other groups, that process is said to have adverse impact. Federal EEO enforcement agencies generally regard a selection rate for any group that is less than four-fifths, or 80 percent, of the rate for other groups as constituting evidence of adverse impact.

systemic discrimination Use of employment practices (recruiting methods, selection tests, promotion policies, etc.) that have the unintended effect of excluding or limiting the employment prospects of protected-class persons. Because of court interpretations of Title VII of the Civil Rights Act of 1964, all such systemic discrimination, despite its "innocence," must be eliminated where it cannot be shown that such action would place an unreasonable burden on the employer or that such practices cannot be replaced by other practices that would not have such an adverse effect.

on the proverbial "level playing field" would only perpetuate the existing patterns of discrimination.

Affirmative action offers advantages that go beyond its immediate beneficiaries. As civil rights activist Roger Wilkins wrote, "Racist and sexist whites who are not able to accept the full humanity of other people are themselves badly damaged—morally stunted—people." They, too, are victims of racism and sexism—even if it is their own. Affirmative action programs that bring them into contact with a more diverse group of associates will help liberate them from their own ignorance. They can go from being "morally stunted" to morally elevated.

And the same that can be said of people can be said of organizations. The less damaged they are by racism and sexism, the more productive they will be. This is the effect of diversity management—directing the work of a racially and culturally heterogeneous group of employees to bring a more varied set of perspectives to organizational problems. This variety can translate into greater productivity. Concerns for diversity that started as part of EEO programs are now less a matter of social equity than organizational survival. The simple demographic fact is that whites will be a continuously decreasing part of the national workforce. For large organizations, the future can be summed up in three words: "Diversify or die!"

diversity is just good business sense ✓

The Case Against Affirmative Action

The case against affirmative action can be stated very simply: It is unfair. It negates Dr. Martin Luther King's "dream that my four little children will one day live in a nation where they will not be judged by the color of their skin, but by the content of their character." Well-meaning opponents of affirmative action (as opposed to

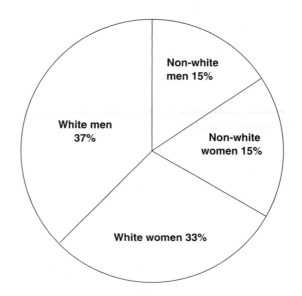

Figure 12.1   A Numerical Argument for Diversity: The U.S. Workforce in 2008 (Projected)
SOURCE: U.S. Bureau of Labor Statistics (2003).

> ## BOX 12.1   Why "Affirmative" Action?
>
> At the Texas State Society's inaugural ball [in 1961], Lyndon Johnson, the incoming vice president, was pressing flesh in the receiving line. When a young black lawyer from Detroit named Hobart Taylor Jr. . . . came through the line, Johnson pulled him aside and said he needed something. An executive order banning discriminatory hiring by federal contractors was being drafted for President Kennedy's signature; could Taylor help work on it?
>
> The next day, Taylor holed up in a room at the Willard Hotel with two future Supreme Court justices, Arthur Goldberg and Abe Fortas, to prepare a document with the not-very-catchy title of Executive Order 10925. "I put the word 'affirmative' in there at that time," Taylor later told an interviewer for the archives of the Lyndon Baines Johnson Library. "I was searching for something that would give a sense of positiveness to performance under that executive order, and I was torn between the words 'positive action' and the words 'affirmative action.' . . . And I took 'affirmative action' because it was alliterative."
>
> SOURCE: Nicholas Lehmann, "Taking Affirmative Action Apart," *New York Times Magazine* (June 11, 1995).

lunatic fringe racists) favor equal employment opportunity. They hold that race or sexual discrimination is wrong no matter who does it. Racial and sexual preferences in hiring women, blacks, or other ethnic minorities are not only inherently discriminatory, but they are also in violation of the Civil Rights Act of 1964, which prohibits discrimination against anybody—even whites.

Despite its best intentions, affirmative action programs have had the effect of stigmatizing minority workers as those who got their jobs not because of their intrinsic merit but because of pressure to fill a formal or informal quota. Thus such programs damage both the self-confidence and self-image of their beneficiaries while creating resentment among those denied such employment opportunities. Minorities who advocate affirmative action are essentially saying, critics charge, that they cannot compete on merit.

Finally, opponents of affirmative action argue that if compensatory benefits are to be provided, they should be based on class, not race. Why should a child from a black professional family making more than $100,000 a year be given special educational and employment opportunities when there is greater need for such opportunities in the case of a child from a poor white family with an income close to the national median? Besides, class-based preferences could gain the widespread political support that affirmative action now seems to lack.

Representative Bureaucracy

In 1944 J. Donald Kingsley, coauthor of the first full-scale text on public personnel administration, had published his historical analysis, *Representative Bureaucracy: An Interpretation of the British Civil Service*. In 1967 Samuel Krislov, a constitutional law scholar, expanded upon Kingsley's concept of a governing bureaucracy made up of representative elements from the population being ruled. In *The Negro in Federal Employment,* Krislov examined the advantages of "representation in the sense of personification" and thereby gave a name to the goal for the movement for the fullest expression of civil rights in government employment—representative bureaucracy.

In a subsequent work in 1974, also entitled *Representative Bureaucracy,* Krislov explored the issues of merit systems, personnel selection, and social equity. Krislov asked more directly, how could any bureaucracy have legitimacy and public credibility if it did not represent all sectors of its society? So, thanks in large part to Krislov, the term *representative bureaucracy* grew to mean that all social groups have a right to participation in their governing institutions. In recent years, the concept has developed a normative overlay—that all social groups should occupy bureaucratic positions in direct proportion to their numbers in the general population. Today, representative bureaucracy is commonly used as a shorthand phrase for the ultimate goal of equal employment opportunity and affirmative action programs.

Reverse Discrimination

Reverse discrimination is a practice generally understood to mean discrimination against white males in conjunction with preferential treatment for women and minorities. The practice had no legal standing in civil rights laws. Indeed, Section 703(j) of Title VII of the Civil Rights Act of 1964 holds that nothing in the title shall be interpreted to permit any employer to "grant preferential treatment to any individual or group on the basis of race, color, religion, sex, or national origin." Yet affirmative action programs necessarily put some white males at a disadvantage that they would not have otherwise had. Reverse discrimination is usually most keenly perceived when affirmative action policies conflict with older policies of granting preferments on the basis of seniority, test scores, and so on.

This has been one of the hottest issues before the Supreme Court over the last few decades. *DeFunis v. Odegaard* was the 1974 case concerning a white male denied admission to law school at the same time minority applicants with lesser academic credentials were accepted. DeFunis challenged the school's action on the grounds that it denied him equal protection of the laws in violation of the Fourteenth Amendment. He was successful in state court and was admitted to the school. On appeal, the school won a reversal. Nevertheless, DeFunis remained in school pending further action by the Supreme Court. As the nation awaited a definitive resolution of the issue of reverse discrimination, the Court sought to avoid the problem. Since DeFunis had completed all but his last quarter of law school and was not in danger of being denied his diploma, a majority of the justices seized upon this fact and declared that the case was moot—beyond the Court's power to render a decision on a hypothetical matter of only potential constitutional substance.

Then, in 1978, in *Regents of the University of California v. Allan Bakke,* the Court upheld a white applicant's claim that he had been denied equal protection of the law because he was refused admission to the University of California Medical School at Davis when 16 out of the school's 100 class spaces were set aside for minority applicants. The Court ruled that Bakke, whose objective qualifications according to the school's admission criteria were better than those of some of the minority candidates who were admitted, must be admitted to the Davis Medical School as soon as possible but that the university had the right to take race into account in its admissions criteria. The imprecise nature of taking race into account as one factor among many has created considerable confusion about voluntary affirmative action programs concerning employment. Nonetheless, Bakke was admitted, graduated, and today is a practicing physician. Ironically, it was these same regents of the University of California who would lead the nation in dismantling affirmative action in higher education. In 1995 it adopted a resolution that "effective January 1, 1997, the University of California shall not use race, religion, sex, color, ethnicity or national origin as a criterion for admission to the University or to any program of study."

Then in the 1979 case of *United Steelworkers of America v. Weber et al.*, the Court upheld an affirmative action program giving blacks preference in selection of employees for a training program. Justice William Brennan, in delivering the majority opinion of the Court, stated that "the only question before us is the narrow statutory issue of whether Title VII forbids private employers and unions from voluntarily agreeing upon bona fide affirmative action plans that accord racial preferences." The Court concluded that "Congress did not intend to limit traditional business freedom to such a degree as to prohibit all voluntary, race conscious affirmative action." Brennan went on to add that, because the steelworkers' preferential scheme was legal, it was unnecessary to "define in detail the line of demarcation between permissible and impermissible affirmative action plans."

The practice of reverse discrimination was finally given legal standing when the U.S. Supreme Court, in *Johnson v. Santa Clara County* (1987), upheld an affirmative action plan that promoted a woman ahead of an objectively more qualified man. Critics contended that this turned Title VII's requirement that there be no "preferential treatment" upside down because for the first time the Court sanctioned and gave legal standing to reverse discrimination. This was not illegal sex discrimination because Paul Johnson was not actually harmed. The Court reasoned that he "had no absolute entitlement to the road dispatcher position. Seven of the applicants were classified as qualified and eligible, and the Agency Director was authorized to promote any of the seven. Thus, the denial of the promotion unsettled no legitimate firmly rooted expectation on the part of [Johnson]." While Johnson was denied a promotion, he remained employed with the same salary and seniority, and he remained eligible for other promotions.

Race has always been a hot issue in American politics. But affirmative action policies were tolerated, if not actually supported, by most of the public until a sea change in public opinion began to occur in 1990. That was the year that Republican Senator Jesse Helms of North Carolina, running for reelection against Harvey Gantt, the black mayor of Charlotte, used a notorious television commercial in the last week of the campaign. Over a pair of white hands crumpling a job rejection letter, a voice announced, "You needed that job, and you were the best qualified, but it had to go to a minority because of a racial quota." Helms, who was well behind in the polls, then decisively won reelection.

Affirmative action is a wedge issue—it drives people apart. Since the 1980s, the Republicans have been quite astute in using the wedge. They branded the Democratic Party the champion of special privileges for minorities. This wedge deserves much of the credit for driving traditionally Democratic blue-collar voters into the political arms of the Republicans.

TABLE 12.2   Affirmative Action: A Chronology

1941	President Franklin D. Roosevelt issues Executive Order 8802, which (1) required that defense contractors not discriminate against any worker because of race, creed, or national origin, and (2) established a Committee on Fair Employment Practice to investigate and remedy violations.
1944	J. Donald Kingsley's *Representative Bureaucracy* develops the concept that all social groups have a right to participate in their governing institutions in proportion to their numbers in the population.
1948	President Harry S. Truman issues Executive Order 9981, which mandated the racial integration of the military and naval forces of the United States and called for an end to racial discrimination in all federal employment.
1961	President John F. Kennedy issues Executive Order 10925, which for the first time required that "affirmative action" be used to implement the policy of nondiscrimination in employment by the federal government and its contractors.
1964	The Civil Rights Act prohibits discrimination on the basis of race, color, religion, sex, or national origin in most private sector employment; creates the Equal Employment Opportunity Commission for enforcement.
1965	President Lyndon B. Johnson issues Executive Order 11246, which required federal government contractors to have affirmative action programs.
1969	President Richard M. Nixon's "Philadelphia Plan" imposes affirmative action quotas on federal building contractors in Philadelphia.
1971	The Supreme Court attacks restrictive credentialism when in *Griggs v. Duke Power Company* it rules that Title VII of the Civil Rights Act of 1964 "proscribes not only overt discrimination but also practices that are discriminatory in operation"; thus, if an employment practice operating to exclude minorities "cannot be shown to be related to job performance, the practice is prohibited."
1972	The Equal Employment Opportunity Act amends Title VII of the Civil Rights Act to include prohibitions on discrimination by public sector employers.
1978	The Supreme Court in *Regents of the University of California v. Bakke* rules that a white male applicant denied admission to medical school in favor of minorities with lesser objective credentials was discriminated against and had to be admitted; but at the same time the Court holds that race was a factor that could be taken into account in admissions decisions.
1979	The Supreme Court in *United Steelworkers of America v. Weber* upholds an affirmative action program giving blacks preference in selection of employees for a training program.
1980	The Supreme Court in *Fullilove v. Klutznick* (1980) holds that Congress has the authority to use quotas to remedy past discrimination in government public works programs.
1984	The Supreme Court in *Fire Fighters Local Union No. 1784 v. Stotts* rules that courts may not interfere with seniority systems to protect newly hired minority employees from layoff.
1987	The practice of reverse discrimination was finally given legal standing when the U.S. Supreme Court, in *Johnson v. Santa Clara County*, upholds an affirmative action plan that promoted a woman ahead of an objectively more qualified man.
1989	The Supreme Court in *Wards Cove Packing v. Antonio* puts the burden of proof upon the plaintiff in equal employment opportunity cases.
1991	The Civil Rights Act of 1991 overturns the *Wards Cove* decision.

TABLE 12.2   *(continued)*

1995	In reaffirming his administration's support for affirmative action, President Bill Clinton asserts that "affirmative action should not go on forever."
1996	The state of California repeals affirmative action by ballot initiative.
1998	The state of Washington repeals affirmative action by ballot initiative.
2003	The Supreme Court in two cases involving the University of Michigan reaffirms taking race into account in admissions decisions (*Grutter v. Bollinger* and *Gratz v. Bollinger*) but disallows automatic point systems in *Gratz*.

The raw political fact is that affirmative action has lost the support of whites. According to a 2003 *Newsweek* poll, 73 percent of whites oppose it. Even a clear majority (56 percent) of minorities oppose it. When the vast majority of citizens are opposed to reverse discrimination (which to many is just another term for affirmative action), it is absurd to brand them all as racists. True, opposition to affirmative action is a credo of racism. But most who oppose it are not racists; they simply believe that the present EEO program does not further equality, that it will ultimately be found to be unconstitutional, and that while it was once needed to jump-start black Americans into the economic mainstream, it now—on the whole—does more harm than good.

Justifying Diversity

The legal rationale for affirmative action—in effect, reverse discrimination—was to provide a remedy for past practices of discrimination. But how do you justify the continuation of such remedies when the practices they were designed to remedy were increasingly long in the past. This is the question that confronted the Supreme Court in 2003 in two cases concerning the University of Michigan.

In *Grutter v. Bollinger* the Court agreed that the University of Michigan Law School could continue to give advantages to minority applicants for admission. But the justification for such preferences was not to remedy past practices of discrimination but to further diversify for its own sake. The majority opinion written by Justice Sandra Day O'Connor, held that the Constitution "does not prohibit the law school's narrowly tailored use of race in admissions decisions to further a compelling interest in obtaining the educational benefits that flow from a diverse student body." In this 5 to 4 decision the Court asserted that "effective participation by members of all racial and ethnic groups in the civic life of our nation is essential if the dream of one nation, indivisible, is to be realized." Justice Lewis F. Powell had initially advocated the diversity rationale in the 1978 *Bakke* decision. In this 2003 case the Court endorsed Justice Powell's "view that student body diversity is a compelling state interest that can justify the use of race in university admissions."

But even in accepting that diversity is a "compelling state interest," the Court has asserted that this interest, no matter how "compelling," must be temporary because such compellance flies in the face of the Fourteenth Amendment's requirement for equal treatment. In an unusually blatant appeal to a future Supreme Court, Justice O'Connor stated, "Race-conscious admissions policies must be limited in time. This requirement reflects that racial classifications, however compelling their goals, are potentially so dangerous that they may be employed no more broadly than the interest demands. Enshrining a permanent justification for racial preferences would offend this fundamental equal protection principle." She concluded, "All governmental use of race must have a logical end point." Then she quite literally provided the end point: "We expect that 25 years from now, the use of racial preferences will no longer be necessary to further the interest approved today."

2028?

So the Court has ruled that racial preference for diversity's sake may extend another 25 years—but did not provide explicit criteria for their termination. In an unusually scathing dissenting opinion Justice Antonin Scalia asserted that the "mystical 'critical mass' justification" for racial preferences "challenges even the most gullible mind." The "critical mass" refers to the oft-asserted "fact" that significant numbers of minorities are needed in schools for everyone's betterment. The "gullible minds" seem to include the five justices that approved O'Connor's majority opinion. Scalia observed that the same academics who are among the strongest advocates of diversity tolerate "tribalism and racial segregation" on their own campuses, including "minority-only student organizations, separate minority housing opportunities, separate minority student centers, even separate minority-only graduation ceremonies."

In a parallel case involving the University of Michigan's undergraduate admissions process, *Gratz v. Bollinger,* the Court held that a point system that automatically gave black students an overwhelming advantage in admissions was unconstitutional. Race may still be taken into account but not in such a "non-individualized, mechanical" way. This means that affirmative action/reverse discrimination admissions (and hiring) programs may continue as before—so long as no hard numbers that look, smell, or sound like quotas are attached to them. Justice O'Connor expected a "highly individualized, holistic review of each applicant's file." Race is just one factor among many. To those who are annoyed that race is a factor at all (because they believe the Constitution should be color-blind), the Court has said, in effect, "just wait 25 years."

President George W. Bush had his administration formally ask the Court to reject both of Michigan's admissions programs as barely disguised quota systems. On first hearing of the Court's support for its version of diversity, the White House (on June 22, 2003) issued a presidential statement. It praised the Court "for recognizing the value of diversity on our nation's campuses." It then said, "Like the court, I look forward to the day when America will truly be a color-blind society." You could almost hear the president frustratingly shouting between the lines: "But why do we have to wait 25 years?"

The Ongoing Role of Race in Public Administration

If the role of racial discrimination in the United States had drifted from the everyday thoughts of most Americans by 2005, the aftermath of Hurricane Katrina reminded the nation that race continues to play a major role in government and society. As New Orleans was evacuated in the days and hours before Katrina struck, images of city residents left behind to ride out the storm in the Superdome demonstrated an obvious racial divide. Almost all of the individuals lining up outside of the mammoth sports stadium were African-Americans. While the city was attempting to protect its residents in a "shelter of last resort," one could not help but wonder why those unable to get out of the city were overwhelmingly black. The absence of white faces, even in a predominantly black city, made for striking television images. In the week following Katrina's landfall, the images grew even starker, with pictures of thousands of African-Americans suffering without food or water in the stifling Louisiana heat. These shocking photos reignited the national debate about the relationship between race and government policies. This debate is bound to have an impact on public administrators charged with providing equal protection under the law to 300 million Americans.

Nonracial Discrimination

Equal employment opportunity has been most controversial when race is at issue. However, it is equally illegal to discriminate against someone for reasons of sex, age, or disability.

Sex Discrimination

Sex discrimination is any disparate or unfavorable treatment of a person in an employment situation because of his or her gender. The Civil Rights Act of 1964 (as amended by the Equal Employment Opportunity Act of 1972) makes sex discrimination illegal in most employment, except where a **bona fide occupational qualification** is involved.

Sex discrimination in employment was by no means a significant concern of the civil rights advocates of the early 1960s. Its prohibition only became part of the Civil Rights Act of 1964 because of Congressman Howard "Judge" Smith (1883–1976) of Virginia. As chairman of the House Rules Committee in 1964, Smith was one of the most powerful men in Congress—and as unlikely a hero as the women's movement will ever have. As the leader of the South's fight against civil rights, he added one small word—sex—to prohibitions against discrimination based on race, color, religion, and national origin. He felt confident this amendment would make the proposed law ridiculous and cause its defeat. Smith was an "old style" bigot: To his mind, the one thing more ridiculous than equal rights for blacks was equal rights for women.

The "sex discrimination" amendment was opposed by most of the leading liberals in Congress. They saw it as nothing but a ploy to discourage passage of the new civil rights law. The major support for adopting the amendment came from the reactionary southern establishment of the day. There was no discussion of sex discrimination by the Senate. The momentum for a new civil rights law was so great that Smith's addition not only failed to scuttle the bill but went largely unnoticed. The legal foundation for the modern women's movement was passed with almost no debate or media attention. Once Smith and his supporters realized the true impact of

---

bona fide occupational qualification (BFOQ) A good-faith exception to EEO provisions; a job requirement that would be discriminatory and illegal were it not necessary for the performance of a particular job. For example, female sex would be a BFOQ for a wet nurse.

what they were doing, they sought to withdraw the amendment before the final vote but the few female members of Congress stopped this by insisting that it be done by a recorded, as opposed to a voice, vote. The male members did not want to be embarrassed by voting against women, so the amendment remained in the bill.

Although the sex discrimination prohibition was included in the new civil rights law almost in secret, word quickly got out. The new law brought into being the Equal Employment Opportunity Commission to enforce its various provisions. During the first year of the new commission's operation, over one-third of all of the complaints it received dealt with sex discrimination in employment. Typical complaints included inadequate consideration of female applicants for promotion, "help wanted" ads for separate male- and female-labeled jobs, and higher retirement benefits for male workers. All these practices and more were made illegal by Title VII. Over the next three decades, Judge Smith's unintended gift to the nation's women became the judicial reference for countless court cases and out-of-court settlements.

Women, far more than minorities, have been the greatest beneficiaries of affirmative action. Women are now almost a quarter of the medical and legal professions (and nearly half of all medical and law students), more than 30 percent of all natural scientists and 40 percent of all college professors, and about 60 percent of all public officials. While some complain of a **glass ceiling** that many women find difficult to break through, many others are happy to note that it is only a matter of time before it falls down by itself.

Sexual Harassment

When the Civil Rights Act of 1964 prohibited sex discrimination in employment, it would not have occurred to anyone to say or imply that the new law had anything to do with sexual harassment. The phrase "sexual harassment" was not even in the language. Yet today, for all legal purposes, sex discrimination includes sexual harassment—the action of an individual in a position to control or influence the job, career, or grade of another person and who uses such power to gain sexual favors or punish the refusal of such favors. Sexual harassment on the job varies from inappropriate sexual innuendo to coerced sexual relations.

The courts are only gradually giving us a general idea of what behavior should not be permitted on the job. Although there was universal agreement that sexual harassment was bad, there was no agreement as to where the normal give-and-take between the sexes ended and sexual harassment began. An old maxim of the common law in such situations was that "there is no harm in asking!" But the harm was always there. Countless women left jobs rather than submit to sexual requests. Countless others, out of sheer economic necessity, continued on in humiliation and fear.

Then a few courageous women enlarged the meaning of the law because they were mad enough about unwarranted sexual pressures to "go public" and test their

---

glass ceiling The unseen barrier through which an organization's highest-level positions can be seen but not reached. Women and minorities often perceive that a "glass ceiling" prevents their advancement to the top.

> ## BOX 12.2   The "Other" Affirmative Action
>
> A young white man . . . was not only troubled but choleric at the very notion that "unqualified minorities" would dare to demand preferential treatment. Why, he wanted to know, couldn't they compete like everyone else? Why should hardworking whites like himself be pushed aside for second-rate affirmative action hires? Why should he be discriminated against in order to accommodate them? His tirade went on for quite awhile. . . .
>
> When the young man paused to catch his breath, I took the occasion to observe that it seemed more than a bit hypocritical of him to rage on about preferential treatment. A person of modest intellect, he had gotten into Harvard largely on the basis of family connections. His first summer internship, with the White House, had been arranged by a family member. His second, with the World Bank, had been similarly arranged. Thanks to his nice internships and Harvard degree, he had been promised a coveted slot in a major company's executive training program. In short, he was already well on his way to a distinguished career—a career made possible by preferential treatment.
>
> My words seemed not to register, and that did not surprise me. Clearly, he had never thought of himself as a beneficiary of special treatment, and no doubt never will. Nor is it likely that either his colleagues or his superiors would be inclined to look down on him as an undeserving incompetent who got ahead on the basis of unfair advantage and was keeping better-qualified people out of work. Yet that assumption is routinely made about black beneficiaries of "affirmative action." *AMEN!*
>
> SOURCE: Ellis Cose, *The Rage of a Privileged Class* (New York: HarperCollins, 1993).

novel interpretation of sex discrimination in federal court. In 1974 Paulette Barnes started the first major case linking sexual harassment to violations of the federal civil rights law. She was an administrative aide in the Environmental Protection Agency when her supervisor began a "campaign to extract sexual favors." This included suggestions that sexual cooperation would advance her career and repeated requests for dates despite her consistent refusals.

After Barnes's supervisor finally gave up hope of seducing her, he initiated an "administrative consolidation" of his office which, as a by-product, eliminated the need for her job. A federal judge ruled that it was sex discrimination to abolish a woman's job because she refused her male supervisor's sexual advances. The Court of Appeals left no doubt that sexual harassment was sex discrimination when a woman's job "was conditional upon submission to sexual relations—an exaction which the superior would not have sought from any male." Consequently, in 1977 Paulette Barnes was awarded $18,000 in damages.

Over the next few years a variety of similar cases were successfully brought to court. They all involved women who had lost their jobs because of sexual harassment.

These women were not suing their actual harassers; they were going for the **deep pockets** and suing the organizations that had employed them.

In 1980, after the lower federal courts had decided that sexual harassment was sex discrimination in a variety of cases, the EEOC issued legally binding rules that defined and prohibited sexual harassment:

> Unwelcome sexual advances, requests for sexual favors, and other verbal or physical contact of a sexual nature constitute sexual harassment when:
>
> 1. submission to such conduct is made either explicitly or implicitly a term or condition of an individual's employment;
> 2. submission to or rejection of such conduct by an individual is used as the basis for employment decisions affecting such individual; or
> 3. such conduct has the purpose or effect of unreasonably interfering with an individual's work performance or creating an intimidating, hostile, or offensive working environment.

Finally, in 1986 the Supreme Court issued its first ruling on sexual harassment. In *Meritor Savings Bank v. Vinson,* it held that "a violation of Title VII [of the Civil Rights Act of 1964] may be predicated on either of two types of sexual harassment: harassment that involves the conditioning of concrete employment benefits on sexual favors, and harassment that, while not affecting economic benefits, creates a hostile or offensive working environment." The hostile environment standard was expanded upon in *Harris v. Forklift Systems,* discussed in the keynote.

In 1998, the Supreme Court offered further refinements in four sexual harassment cases. In *Oncale v. Sundowner Offshore Services*, the Court held that same-sex claims of harassment are permissible. In *Gebser v. Lago Vista Independent School District*, the Court held that school districts are not responsible if teachers harassed students when the school administrators did not know about it. In *Faragher v. Boca Raton, Florida,* the court held that an employer could be held financially liable for harassment by a supervisor. And in *Burlington Industries v. Ellerth*, the Court held that employers were liable for the threatening sexual advances of a supervisor even when the threats are not carried out and the harassed employee suffers no adverse effects.

Despite the clearly established illegality of it, sexual harassment remains a continuing problem. In 1995 the U.S. Merit Systems Protection Board released a survey, based on a questionnaire sent to 8,000 federal employees, that found that 44 percent of women and 19 percent of men said that they had been the victims of "uninvited, unwanted sexual attention." However, most of what was being complained about were the less severe forms of harassment—sexual teasing, jokes, and questionable remarks. A male referring to a female coworker as "honey" or "sweetie" or "doll" is not guilty of criminal sexual assault. But such verbal assaults, if perceived as inappropriate, do constitute sexual harassment, are inappropriate, and may be **actionable**.

---

deep pockets A person or organization with enough money to be the most worthwhile target in a lawsuit.
actionable Provides adequate reason for a grievance or lawsuit.

Pregnancy Discrimination

A 1978 amendment to Title VII of the Civil Rights Act of 1964 holds that discrimination on the basis of pregnancy, childbirth, or related medical conditions constitutes unlawful sex discrimination. The amendment was enacted in response to the Supreme Court's ruling in *General Electric Co. v. Gilbert* (1976) that an employer's exclusion of pregnancy-related disabilities from its comprehensive disability plan did not violate Title VII.

The amendment asserts that a written or unwritten employment policy or practice that excludes from employment opportunities applicants or employees because of pregnancy, childbirth, or related medical conditions is in **prima facie** violation of Title VII.

Disabilities caused or contributed to by pregnancy, childbirth, or related medical conditions, for all job-related purposes, shall be treated the same as disabilities caused or contributed to by other medical conditions, under any health or disability insurance or sick-leave plan available in connection with employment. Written or unwritten employment policies and practices involving matters such as the commencement and duration of leave, the availability of extensions, the accrual of seniority and other benefits and privileges, reinstatement, and payment under any health or disability insurance or sick-leave plan shall be applied to disability due to pregnancy, childbirth, or related medical conditions as they are applied to other disabilities.

While this amendment to Title VII did not require an employer to offer a specific number of weeks of maternity leave, the Family and Medical Leave Act of 1993 requires employers—in both the public and private sectors—with at least 50 workers to allow up to 12 weeks of unpaid leave (for childbirth, care of spouse or parent, new adoption of child, and so on) during a 12-month period for all employees (whether male or female) employed for at least a year.

Gender Discrimination and Education

For the millions of Americans who participated in sports during their high school or college years, the issue of gender discrimination has played a significant role. In 1972, Congress passed Title IX of the Education Amendments, requiring that "no person in the United States shall, on the basis of sex, be excluded from participation in, be denied the benefits of, or be subjected to discrimination under any education program or activity receiving federal financial assistance." Among the ramifications of this law was a major shift in the gender balance among sports teams in secondary and postsecondary settings.

Since Title IX was passed, the number of women in intercollegiate athletics has risen from fewer than 30,000 to around 150,000, while the number of female athletes in high school increased from 294,000 to 2.8 million in 2003. This increase was directly related to a tremendous increase in the number of sports teams offered by schools trying to comply with the requirements of Title IX.

---

prima facie Latin for "at first sight"; on the face of it; presumably. Said of a fact that will be considered to be true unless disproved by contrary evidence.

Yet, even as the door has opened for young women to participate in sports as part of their educational experience, it has closed for many men. With limited budgets for athletics, school administrators have chosen to pay for added women's sports teams by cutting men's sports programs. In particular, schools have dropped low-profile men's teams in wrestling and gymnastics as a way of complying with the gender equity requirements of Title IX.

Ironically, the equity provisions of Title IX were challenged in 2003 by the National Wrestling Coaches Association on the grounds that the act imposed quotas and illegally discriminated against men. While the Supreme Court refused to hear the *Wrestling Coaches Association* case, the Department of Education did relax the compliance standards for colleges in 2005 by allowing institutions to demonstrate lack of demand for women's sports teams through a survey of students. If women students tell their college administrators that they are not interested in water polo or lacrosse, schools can use that evidence to avoid adding women's sports teams and thus preserve the imperiled wrestling and gymnastic teams for men.

Age Discrimination

Ageism is discrimination against those who are considered "old." During the second presidential debate of the 1984 election, when there had been great speculation about Ronald Reagan's ability to continue to perform as president because of his age, Reagan literally turned the election around when he said, in answer to a question about his age, "I will not make age an issue in this campaign. I am not going to exploit, for political purposes, my opponent's youth and inexperience." Reagan went on to defeat the much younger Walter Mondale in a landslide.

Because not everybody has the Great Communicator's ability to turn the issue of age on its head, the Age Discrimination in Employment Act (ADEA) exists. First passed in 1967 and often amended, this law prohibits employment discrimination on the basis of age and (with certain exceptions) prohibits mandatory retirement. The law applies to all public employers, private employers of 20 or more employees, employment agencies serving covered employers, and labor unions of more than 25 members.

The ADEA prohibits help-wanted advertisements that indicate preference, limitation, specification, or discrimination based on age. For example, terms such as "girl" and "35–55" may not be used because they indicate the exclusion of qualified applicants based on age. Many states also have age discrimination laws or provisions in their fair employment practices laws. Some of these laws parallel the federal law and have no upper limit in protections against age discrimination in employment; others protect workers until they reach 60, 65, or 70 years of age. In 1983 the Supreme Court, in *Equal Employment Opportunity Commission v. Wyoming*, upheld the federal government's 1974 extension of the ADEA to cover state and local government workers.

Disabilities Discrimination

The federal government has a long history of legislative efforts to provide employment for the disabled. Disabled veterans were the first people formally given employment preference, toward the end of the Civil War. In 1919, just after World War I, employment preferences were extended to the wives of disabled veterans as well. However, it was not until the Vocational Rehabilitation Act of 1973 that federal contractors and subcontractors were required to take affirmative action to seek qualified handicapped individuals for employment. This Act also provided the now accepted definition of a handicapped or disabled individual:

1. A person who has a physical or mental impairment that substantially limits one or more of such person's major life activities
2. A person who has a record of such an impairment
3. A person who is regarded as having such an impairment

A qualified handicapped individual, according to the act and with respect to employment, is one who with **reasonable accommodation** can perform the essential functions of a job in question.

But it was not until the passage of the Americans with Disabilities Act (ADA) of 1990 that there was a comprehensive federal law to ban discrimination against physically and mentally handicapped individuals in employment, transportation, telecommunications, and public accommodations. All employers with more than 15 workers—not just federal contractors as before—are required to accommodate disabled employees. New buses and trains must be accessible to people in wheelchairs. Telephone companies have to provide hearing- or voice-impaired people with equipment to place and receive calls from ordinary telephones. Renovated or new hotels, stores, and restaurants must be wheelchair accessible. Existing barriers must be removed, if that is "readily achievable." Businesses that can demonstrate that these changes would be too costly or disruptive may be exempt from the law.

According to the ADA, "No covered entity shall discriminate against a qualified individual with a disability because of the disability of such individual in regard to job application procedures, the hiring, advancement, or discharge of employees, employee compensation, job training, and other terms, conditions, and privileges of employment." Among those protected by the act are individuals who are in or have successfully completed rehabilitation for drug abuse or alcoholism. However, the act states that "homosexuality and bisexuality are not impairments and as such are not disabilities under this Act." In seeking to limit the applicability of the ADA to those with traditional disabilities, the ADA also specifically excludes transvestism, pedophilia, compulsive gambling, kleptomania, and pyromania.

While the U.S. Supreme Court has not ruled that AIDS is a directly covered disability under the ADA, it has signaled the possibility that it might be. In its decision in *School Board of Nassau County v. Arline* (1987), the Court held that a public school teacher with the contagious disease of tuberculosis was "a handicapped individual" within the meaning of the Rehabilitation Act. Therefore, protection

---

reasonable accommodation Those steps needed to accommodate a handicapped employee's disability (e.g., adequate workspace for an employee confined to a wheelchair) required of an employer unless such steps would cause the employer undue hardship.

against employment discrimination was provided by the law. This case has been the basis for some lower court rulings that the Rehabilitation Act protects persons with AIDS from employment discrimination. In 1998 the Court offered its first substantial review of the ADA in *Bragdon v. Abbott*. Here it held that people with the HIV infection that leads to AIDS—people with no AIDS symptoms as yet—were protected by the ADA. While the scope of the case was limited, its tone strongly suggested that people with AIDS would also be protected.

The Equal Employment Opportunity Commission, which enforces the provisions of the ADA, requires that an employer may not ask about the existence, nature, or severity of a disability and may not conduct medical examinations until after it makes a conditional job offer to the applicant. This prohibition ensures that an applicant's disability that is not obviously apparent is not considered prior to the assessment of the applicant's nonmedically related qualifications. At this pre-offer stage, employers can ask about an applicant's ability to perform specific job-related functions. After a conditional offer is made, an employer may require medical examinations and may make disability-related inquiries if it does so for all entering employees in the job category. If an examination or inquiry screens out an individual because of disability, the exclusionary criterion must be job related—and the employer must be able to demonstrate that the essential functions of the job cannot be performed with reasonable accommodation.

Sexual Orientation Discrimination

The long history of discrimination against and hostility toward homosexuals—gays and lesbians—has been subsiding considerably in recent decades. While sexual orientation is not protected by the federal civil rights laws, many federal agencies have internal regulations prohibiting discrimination on the basis of sexual orientation. In addition, at least 15 states and more than 140 local jurisdictions have laws or executive orders that forbid sexual orientation discrimination in employment.

The core problem of dealing with the civil rights of gays and lesbians is that the activity that defined them (sexual relations with a member of the same sex) was a crime in many states. This, however, is no longer the case. In 2003 the Supreme Court in *Lawrence v. Texas* declared unconstitutional the Texas ban on "consensual sodomy" and in effect asserted a broad constitutional right to sexual privacy. Justice Anthony M. Kennedy in the majority opinion wrote that the case concerned "two adults who, with full and mutual consent from each other, engaged in sexual practices common to a homosexual lifestyle. The petitioners are entitled to respect for their private lives. The State cannot demean their existence or control their destiny by making their private sexual conduct a crime."

In an extremely strong dissenting opinion Justice Antonin Scalia said that the ruling "effectively decrees the end of all morals legislation," and could possibly pave the way for "judicial imposition of homosexual marriage, as has recently occurred in Canada." This case overruled a 1986 decision in which the court upheld Georgia's sodomy law *(Bowers v. Hardwick)*. The 2003 decision effectively nullified sodomy laws in the 13 other states besides Texas that still had such laws. The 2003 *Lawrence* decision on homosexual rights has its origins in the 1965 case of *Griswold v. Connecticut,* which first asserted that there was a constitutional right to bedroom privacy even when the word *privacy* does not appear in the Constitution.

✦ A CASE STUDY: SOCIAL EQUITY THROUGH SOCIAL INSURANCE

An anonymous Washington wit once observed that the federal government is basically just a large insurance company with a defense business on the side. While seemingly outrageous on the surface, this comment becomes more and more reasonable if its implications are closely examined. The reality is that most—far more than half—of the federal budget goes to insurance programs: Social Security, Medicare, Medicaid, welfare, and food stamps are the most obvious. But the federal government also runs insurance programs for banks (Federal Deposit Insurance Corporation), for pensions (Pension Benefit Guaranty Corporation), and for home mortgages (Department of Housing and Urban Development), among others. In terms of money, these programs represent more than 60 percent of the federal government. Defense—that business on the side—accounts for only 20 percent.

So how did the federal government evolve into the world's largest insurance business? The answer lies in the historical development of the American welfare state. The problem the welfare state was created to ameliorate was elegantly posed by Anatole France in his 1894 novel *The Red Lily:* "The law, in its majestic equality, forbids the rich as well as the poor to sleep under bridges, to beg in the streets, and to steal bread." Thus social equity in terms of political and civil rights is inadequate if not accompanied by minimal economic rights. This other side of the equity coin, often summed up in one word—*welfare*—has a long lineage.

Some biblical scholars contend that the commandment "Thou shalt not kill" contained the essence of a welfare program. After all, if a wandering desert tribe did not help those members in need (the ill, the old, the widowed and orphaned), they would surely die. Thus we can conclude that the social provision of welfare services has always been mandated from above—sometimes high above.

Economic security has often been an elusive goal. During the **Middle Ages** merchants and craft workers, any group with a common business intent, might form guilds

---

Middle Ages The historical time period that divides the classical world of Greece and Rome from the modern period; generally from the fall of Rome to the Italian Renaissance.

Griswold v. Connecticut (1965) The U.S. Supreme Court case that, in holding that the state regulation of birth control devices was an impermissible invasion of privacy, helped to establish privacy as a constitutionally protected right under the Ninth and Fourteenth Amendments. Justice William O. Douglas wrote, in the majority opinion, "The First Amendment has a penumbra where privacy is protected from governmental intrusion." He asked, "Would we allow the police to search the sacred precincts of marital bedrooms for telltale signs of the use of contraceptives? The very idea is repulsive to the notions of privacy surrounding the marriage relationship."

or mutual aid societies. While primarily created to regulate prices and employment standards, they also offered welfare benefits to members in times of poverty or illness. Beginning in the sixteenth century, friendly societies, the forerunners of fraternal organizations, emerged. They would grow rapidly during the **industrial revolution** and would often evolve into modern **craft unions**. They allowed members to provide for their own welfare by paying into funds for life insurance, burial expenses, and other forms of assistance in times of need. Many of these organizations still thrive in the United States and are well known: the Free Masons, the Odd Fellows, the Benevolent and Protective Order of Elks, and the Royal Order of Moose.

The rapid industrialization of the late nineteenth century transformed the concept of the worker. They were viewed less and less as human beings and more and more as **factors of production**. Like any other nonhuman resource, the laborer was increasingly a specialized "cog" in the manufacturing process. Workers also felt threatened by massive immigration from Europe, which assured a ready supply of "hands" to take their place. Finally, increasing urbanization made workers almost completely dependent on their wages—the proportion of factory workers who could "retreat" to a family farm continued to dwindle.

When the problem of what to do with displaced workers and their families grew too much for traditional charity to handle, the state stepped in. The English Poor Law of 1601 was the first systematic codification of English ideas about the responsibility of the state to provide for the welfare of its citizens. It provided public funds to pay for **relief**. It distinguished between the "deserving" and the "undeserving" poor. Relief was local and community controlled. Almshouses and poor farms were also established. This essential structure was the tradition the English settlers brought with them when they colonized North America.

The first colonial poor laws featured local taxation to support the destitute, distinguished between the "worthy" and the "unworthy" poor, and had relief as a local responsibility. This tradition continued until well after the American Civil War. It was up to local officials to decide who was worthy of support and how that support would be provided. Relief was made as unpleasant as possible in order to "discourage" dependency. Those receiving relief could lose their personal property as well as the right to vote.

Four important demographic changes happened in America beginning in the mid-1880s that rendered the traditional systems of economic security increasingly unworkable:

industrial revolution A very general term that refers to a society's change from an agrarian to an industrial economy. The industrial revolution of the Western world is considered to have begun in England in the eighteenth century.

craft unions Labor organizations that restrict membership to skilled workers (such as plumbers, carpenters, electricians, etc.) as opposed to industrial unions that seek to organize all workers in an industry.

factors of production The resources used to produce goods and services. There are three traditional factors: land, labor, and capital. Recently, management (or entrepreneurship) has come to be considered a factor as well.

relief Public assistance programs for the poor. Direct relief referred to straight welfare payments. Work relief referred to any of the numerous public works projects initiated specifically to provide jobs for the unemployed.

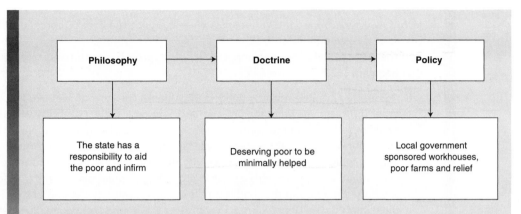

Figure 12.2   The Traditional Doctrine of Welfare

1. The Industrial Revolution transformed the majority of working people from self-employed agricultural workers into wage earners working for large, impersonal organizations. In an agricultural society, personal prosperity was linked to one's labor. Anyone willing to work hard enough could usually provide at least a bare subsistence for themselves and their family. But when one's income is primarily from wages, one's economic security can be threatened by factors outside one's control—such as recessions, layoffs, failed businesses, and so on.

2. Urbanization increased along with the shift from an agricultural to an industrial society. Americans moved from farms and small rural communities to large cities; that's where the industrial jobs were. In 1890, only 28 percent of the population lived in cities. By 1930 this percentage had exactly doubled, to 56 percent.

3. This trend toward urbanization contributed to the disappearance of the extended family and the concomitant rise of the nuclear family. Today we tend to assume that "the family" consists of parents and children—the so-called nuclear family. For most of human history, we lived in "extended families" that included children, parents, grandparents, and other relatives. The advantage of the extended family was that when a family member became too old or infirm to work, the other family members assumed responsibility for the individual's support. But when the able-bodied left the farms to seek employment in the cities (or other countries), the parents or grandparents usually stayed behind.

4. Finally, thanks primarily to better health care, modern sanitation, and effective public health programs, Americans began to live significantly longer. In the three decades from 1900 to 1930, average life spans increased by 10 years. The result was a rapid growth in the number of older citizens from 3 million in 1900 to 7.8 million by 1935.

The net result of this complex set of demographic and social changes was that America was older, more urban, more industrial, and had fewer of its people living on farms in extended families. The traditional strategies for the provision of economic security were becoming increasingly fragile—and with the Great Depression, they would be overwhelmed.

There were, generally speaking, three basic approaches to the Great Depression that began in 1929:

1. <u>Do nothing because nothing needed to be done</u>. The current problem was just another dip in the inevitable boom-and-bust economic cycle. Prosperity would eventually be just around the corner—just as it always had been. Nevertheless, the problem remained that prosperity was taking too long to turn the corner.

2. Rely on <u>"volunteerism" or private charity</u>. Traditional charitable good works were widespread in a nation with a large churchgoing population. But the problem was too huge for a nation that had lost half its total wealth by the end of the first three years of the Depression. Six years after the Depression began, President Franklin D. Roosevelt would say in his second inaugural address, "I see one-third of a nation ill-housed, ill-clad, ill-nourished." The nation was simply too ill for the "pill" of charity to make it better.

3. <u>Expand welfare programs</u>. Even before the Depression hit, the states had been forced to deal with the problems of economic security in a wage-based, industrial economy. **Workers' Compensation** programs had been established by most states. Once the Depression hit, all levels of government responded with expanded relief and public works programs. The main strategy for providing economic security to the elderly, in the face of the demographic changes just discussed, was to provide various forms of old-age "pensions." These were welfare programs, eligibility for which was based on financial need. By 1934, most states had such "pension" plans. However, these plans were so restrictive in eligibility and so minimal in payments that they were almost wholly inadequate to the task.

The essential problem with these three approaches was that the Depression just continued. While the New Deal of President Franklin D. Roosevelt fought the Depression traditionally with massive relief and public works programs, it also sought to change the debate on how to deal with economic insecurity. A long-term permanent program of social insurance, already widespread in Europe, would become the alternative to the current patchwork of ad hoc solutions.

Social insurance, as conceived by President Roosevelt, would address the permanent problem of economic security for the elderly by creating a work-related, contributory system in which workers would provide for their own future economic security through taxes paid while employed. Thus it was an alternative both to reliance on welfare and to radical changes in our capitalist system. In the context of its time, it can be seen as a conservative, yet activist, response to the challenges of the Depression. State-sponsored efforts to provide for economic security would come to be seen as the practical alternative to the siren calls of those who preached socialism.

Workers' Compensation Industrial accident insurance designed to provide cash benefits and medical care for a worker injured on the job and monetary payments to survivors for a worker killed on the job. This was the first form of social insurance to develop widely in the United States. Workers' compensation was first developed in Germany and Great Britain in the 1880s. By 1920 all but a handful of states had laws encouraging workers' compensation in private industry.

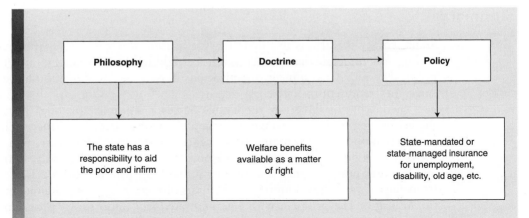

Figure 12.3   The Social Insurance Approach to Welfare

Social insurance has been the pragmatic answer to a variety of widespread problems—from disability and death to old age or unemployment. It is immediately obvious to think of death, disability, or unemployment as conditions that led to a loss of income and that can be ameliorated by a pooling of risk. It may be strange at first to think of old age or retirement in this same way. But social insurance looks at retirement much as it looks at death: A loss of income has occurred because of a cessation of work. Social insurance seeks to solve the eternal problem of economic security by pooling the assets (the insurance contributions) from a large social group and providing income to those members whose economic security is being immediately threatened.

As President Franklin D. Roosevelt signed into law the Social Security Act on August 14, 1935, he stated, "We can never insure one hundred percent of the population against one hundred percent of the hazards and vicissitudes of life, but we have tried to frame a law which will give some measure of protection to the average citizen and to his family against the loss of a job and against poverty-ridden old age."

Nevertheless, the Social Security Act did not quite achieve all the aspirations its supporters had hoped by way of providing a "comprehensive package of protection" against the "hazards and vicissitudes of life." Certain features of that package, notably disability coverage and medical benefits, would have to wait until 1954 and 1965, respectively. But it did provide a wide range of programs. In addition to the program we immediately think of as Social Security (old-age pensions), it included unemployment insurance and aid to dependent children. But this was just the beginning. The Act would be amended time and again to become the foundation of the American welfare state. (For details on the current welfare program, see the keynote in Chapter 4. For the current status of Social Security, see the case study in Chapter 13.)

For Discussion: *Why does social equity necessarily have two faces—civil rights and economic rights? Why has the American welfare state evolved as a pragmatic, not an ideological, solution to the pressing problem of social equity?*

Summary

Social equity is fairness in the delivery of public services; it is egalitarianism in action—the principle that each citizen has a right to be given equal treatment by the political system. Government organizations have a special obligation to be fair because they represent the citizenry.

The history of slavery in the United States is still relevant today because it is the underlying basis for African-American claims for special treatment. Equal employment opportunity, created to mitigate the heritage of slavery, is a concept fraught with political, cultural, and emotional overtones. Generally, it applies to employment practices that prevent any individual from being adversely excluded from employment opportunities on the basis of race, color, sex, religion, age, or national origin. The problem with equal employment opportunity programs is that they put the government into the business of examining people's bloodlines.

Well-meaning opponents of affirmative action (the means by which EEO is to be achieved) favor equality. They hold that racial and sexual hiring preferences are not only inherently discriminatory, but they are also in violation of the Civil Rights Act of 1964, which prohibits discrimination against anybody. Affirmative action has become a wedge issue—an issue that drives people apart. Since the 1980s, the Republicans have been quite astute in using this wedge to brand the Democratic Party the champion of special privileges for minorities.

When the Civil Rights Act of 1964 prohibited sex discrimination in employment, nobody would have said that the new law had anything to do with sexual harassment. Yet today, for all legal purposes, sex discrimination includes sexual harassment. A 1978 amendment to the act holds that discrimination on the basis of pregnancy, childbirth, or related medical conditions also constitutes unlawful sex discrimination.

The federal government has a long history of legislative efforts to provide employment for the disabled. But it was not until the passage of the Americans with Disabilities Act in 1990 that there was a comprehensive federal law to ban discrimination against physically and mentally handicapped individuals in employment, transportation, telecommunications, and public accommodations.

Review Questions

1. Why is social equity a critically important value for public organizations?
2. What is the difference between equal employment opportunity and affirmative action?
3. Why is a representative bureaucracy the inherent goal of all affirmative action programs?
4. Is reverse discrimination both legal and ethical?
5. How did the Civil Rights Act of 1964 eventually make sexual harassment illegal?

Key Concepts

affirmative action A term that first meant the removal of "artificial barriers" to the employment of women and minority group members; now it refers to compensatory opportunities for hitherto disadvantaged groups—specific efforts to recruit, hire, and promote qualified members of disadvantaged groups for the purpose of eliminating the present effects of past discrimination.

child labor   Originally, the employment of children in a manner detrimental to their health and social development. Now that the law contains strong child labor prohibitions, the term refers to the employment of children below the legal age limit.

discrimination   Bigotry in practice; intolerance toward those who have different beliefs or religions. In employment, the failure to treat equals equally. Any action that has the effect of limiting employment and advancement opportunities because of an individual's sex, race, color, age, national origin, religion, physical handicap, or other irrelevant criteria is discrimination.

equal employment opportunity   Employment practices that prevent any individual from being adversely excluded from employment opportunities on the basis of race, color, sex, religion, age, national origin, or other factors that cannot lawfully be considered in employing people.

new public administration   An academic advocacy movement for social equity in the performance and delivery of public services; it called for a proactive administrator with a burning desire for social equity to replace the traditional impersonal and neutral gun-for-hire bureaucrat.

racist   Any person or organization that either consciously or unconsciously practices discrimination against another person on the basis of race (or ethnicity) or supports the supremacy of one race over others.

representative bureaucracy   The ultimate goal of equal employment opportunity and affirmative action programs.

reverse discrimination   Discrimination against white males in conjunction with preferential treatment for women and minorities.

second reconstruction   The civil rights movement and legislation of the 1960s. The first reconstruction, immediately after the Civil War, gave blacks their freedom from slavery. But the laws as enforced and customs as practiced did not allow for the full rights of citizens. That came in the 1960s, when public sentiment was aroused and legal action was taken to ensure equal rights for all Americans.

sex discrimination   Any disparate or unfavorable treatment of a person in an employment situation because of his or her sex.

sexual harassment   The action of an individual (either a supervisor or coworker) in a position to control or influence another's job, career, or grade who uses such power to gain sexual favors or punish the refusal of such favors. Sexual harassment on the job varies from inappropriate sexual innuendo to coerced sexual relations.

Title VII   That part of the Civil Rights Act of 1964 that prohibits employment discrimination because of race, color, religion, sex, or national origin and created the Equal Employment Opportunity Commission as its enforcement vehicle.

Bibliography

Armas, Genard. (2003*a*). "Census Figures Show Economic Gains by Blacks," *Las Vegas Review-Journal* (April 26).

———. (2003*b*). "Earnings Potential Still Subject to Gender, Race Gaps," *Las Vegas Review-Journal* (March 21).

Bishop, Peter C., and Augustus J. Jones Jr. (1993). "Implementing the Americans with Disabilities Act of 1990," *Public Administration Review* 53 (March–April).

Boller, Harvey R., and Douglas Massengill. (1992). "Public Employers' Obligation to Reasonably Accommodate the Disabled Under the Rehabilitation and Americans with Disabilities Acts," *Public Personnel Management* 21 (Fall).

Cose, Ellis. (1993). *The Rage of a Privileged Class*. New York: HarperCollins.

Fineman, Howard, and Tamara Lipper. (2003). "Spinning Race," *Newsweek* (January 27).

Fletcher, Michael A. (2003). "Changes to Title IX Considered: Proposal Would Allow Scholarship Limits," *Washington Post* (January 24).

Frederickson, H. George. (1980). *New Public Administration*. University: University of Alabama Press.

Henry, William A., III. (1994). *In Defense of Elitism*. New York: Doubleday.

Jamieson, David, and Julie O'Mara. (1991). *Managing Workforce 2000: Gaining the Diversity Advantage*. San Francisco: Jossey-Bass.

Kingsley, J. Donald. (1944). *Representative Bureaucracy: An Interpretation of the British Civil Service*. Yellow Springs, OH: Antioch Press.

Klein, Joe. (1995). "The End of Affirmative Action," *Newsweek* (February 13).

Krislov, Samuel. (1967). *The Negro in Federal Employment*. Minneapolis: University of Minnesota Press.

———. (1974). *Representative Bureaucracy*. Englewood Cliffs, NJ: Prentice Hall.

Marini, Frank, ed. (1971). *Toward a New Public Administration*. San Francisco: Chandler.

Marshall, Thurgood. (1987). "An African-American's Perspective on the Constitution," *Vanderbilt Law Review* 40.

McAllister, Bill. (1995). "The Problem That Won't Go Away: A New Survey Finds Complaints of Sexual Harassment Are Still Widespread in Federal Offices," *The Washington Post National Weekly Edition* (November 20–26).

Pellicciotti, Joseph M. (1991). "Exemptions and Employer Defenses Under the ADEA," *Public Personnel Management* 20 (Summer).

Riccucci, Norma M. (2002). *Managing Diversity in Public Sector Workforces*. Boulder, CO: Westview.

Robinson, Robert K., et al. (1993). "Sexual Harassment in the Workplace: A Review of the Legal Rights and Responsibilities of All Parties," *Public Personnel Management* 19 (Spring).

Sowell, Thomas. (1984). *Civil Rights: Rhetoric or Reality*. New York: William Morrow.

Thomas, R. Roosevelt, Jr. (1990). "From Affirmative Action to Affirming Diversity," *Harvard Business Review* 68 (March–April).

Thompson, Victor A. (1961). *Modern Organization*. New York: Knopf.

———. (1975). *Without Sympathy or Enthusiasm*. University: University of Alabama Press.

Waldo, Dwight. (1968). "Public Administration in a Time of Revolution," *Public Administration Review* 28 (July–August).

Weisberg, Jacob. (1996). *In Defense of Government: The Rise and Fall of Public Trust*. New York: Scribner.

Wilkins, Roger. (1995). "The Case for Affirmative Action," *The Nation* (March 27).

Williams, John. (2001). "The Clint Eastwood Verdict Makes My Day," *Business Week Online* (October 6). www.businessweek.com.

Recommended Books

Arredondo, Patricia. (1996). *Successful Diversity Management Initiatives: A Blueprint for Planning and Implementation*. Thousand Oaks, CA: Sage. A how-to-do-it manual for workforce diversity program implementation; presents a prototype for measuring both qualitative and quantitative results.

Katznelson, Ira. (2005) *When Affirmative Action Was White: An Untold History of Racial Inequality in Twentieth-Century America*. New York, W.W. Norton and Company. An examination of racial inequity and its relationship to government policies that are believed to benefit blacks but that have actually benefited whites.

Olson, Walter K. (1997). *The Excuse Factory: How Employment Law Is Paralyzing the American Workplace*. New York: Free Press. A review of the unintended consequences of the Americans with Disabilities Act whereby it has become difficult to fire slacking employees because of the protections the Act offers for those with frivolous physical and mental "problems."

Reese, Laura A., and Karen E. Lindenberg. (1998). *Implementing Sexual Harassment Policy: Challanges for the Public Sector Workforce*. Thousand Oaks, CA: Sage. A review of the problems and opportunities of creating organizational policies for forestalling and dealing with sexual harassment.

Sowell, Thomas. (1990). *Preferential Policies: An International Perspective*. New York: William Morrow. An around-the-world tour of affirmative action policies and practices.

West, Cornel. (1993). *Race Matters*. Boston: Beacon Press. An explanation of how the intellectual frameworks about race used by both blacks and whites impede racial progress and understanding.

Related Web Sites

Affirmative Action and Diversity Project
  http://aad.english.ucsb.edu/
Affirmative Action Manual
  www.law.ucla.edu/Classes/Archive/CivAA/bible.htm
Americans with Disabilities Act Document Center
  http://jan.wvu.edu/links/adalinks.htm
  http://janweb.icdi.wvu.edu/kinder/
Avoiding sexual harassment claims
  http://www.gesmer.com/
  www.lgu.com/em49.htm
Black history and culture resource guide
  http://lcweb.loc.gov/exhibits/african/afam001.html
Civil Rights Division of the U.S. Department
  of Justice
  www.usdoj.gov/crt/cr-home.html
Commission on Civil Rights
  www.usccr.gov
Congressional Black Caucus
  http://www.congressionalblackcaucus.net/
  http://drum.ncat.edu/~drwww/CBC.html

Federal antidiscrimination laws
  http://www.policyalmanac.org/culture/archive/
  discrimination.shtml
  www.hronline.org/consult/hrtopic/anticisc.html
Martin Luther King Jr. Web site
  http://mlkmemorial.org/index.htm
  www.standford.edu/group/King/
National Committee on Pay Equity
  http://www.pay-equity.org/
  http://feminist.com/fairpay.htm
Sexual harassment prevention training
  www.sexual-harassment.com/
Title IX information
  http://www.titleix.info/index.jsp
U.S. Equal Employment Opportunity
  Commission
  www.eeoc.gov
U.S. Supreme Court decisions since 1990
  http://straylight.law.cornell.edu/supct/index.html
  http://supct.law.cornell.edu/supct/

CHAPTER 13

Public Financial Management

•KEYNOTE: TAKE ME OUT TO THE BALL GAME AND *YOU* BUY THE TICKET: PUBLIC STADIUM FINANCING

Large American cities of the late twentieth century have almost universally engaged the issue of the construction of sports facilities to house professional sports franchises. From the current debate in New York City regarding a proposal for two new baseball stadiums with a $1.6 billion price tag to a bitter debate in hurricane-ravaged New Orleans regarding the future of the Superdome, the nation's urban areas continue to wrestle with a topic of considerable controversy. While the issue of public involvement in funding can be viewed from a number of perspectives, it essentially remains a game in which primarily privately owned sports franchises attempt to maximize their bottom line by securing public funding from political officials who seek to keep franchises in their cities at the lowest cost to their constituents. In many cases these games are played out in the realm of public elections, where citizens decide the fate of deals developed through negotiations between the franchises and government.

The securing of public funds for the construction of professional sports facilities can be achieved through two broadly defined approaches: public approval or nonelectoral negotiations. In the most common approach, sports franchises can gain the support of government financial backing through nonelectoral avenues. In these approaches the sports organization and government institutions agree on a "deal" in which the sports franchise agrees to operate in the geographic confines of the city, county, or state in return for a set level of financing for the construction or renovation of the venue that houses the team. Of the 77 venue deals struck in the past two decades, 60 percent have been finalized through the negotiated mechanism without direct approval of the public.

In some cases final approval through negotiation came without the public ever getting a chance to vote on the use of public funds (e.g., Philadelphia baseball and football venues in 2000), while in other cases a negotiated settlement between organizations and government came after voters declined to support the use of public revenues for venue construction (e.g., Milwaukee's baseball stadium in 1995). A quote in the *Phoenix Gazette* by former Chandler, Arizona, Mayor Jay Tibshraeny in 1995 regarding renovations to a spring training facility in his city nicely demonstrates the dynamic associated with the process of getting deals done even without direct public support. Tibshraeny stated, "I believe the citizens should have a say in this issue. If the voters pass this, we'll move forward. If the voters don't pass this, we'll still move forward."

Avoiding public votes on the question of sports venue financing can be seen as an attractive option for sports franchises, but it can be a less positive option for policymakers. For the organizations, the opportunity to secure funds from the public without having to mount a campaign to sway public opinion may seem less risky and thus a first choice when seeking to raise revenue for a project. While less risky for sports franchises, the risks for elected officials concerned about the political liabilities associated with the transfer of public funds to private sports entities helps explain why many political figures seek public ratification before allocating funds. Thus in 40 percent of stadium construction projects involving public funds, the public has been asked to weigh in on the matter by voting at the polls.

While it may seem on the surface that the movement of a stadium finance decision from legislative chambers to the ballot box would place the organization's quest to secure public funding in peril, the track record demonstrates that the electoral approach usually bears fruit for a franchise. Of the 31 decisions that have been put forth to the voters, a vast majority (84 percent) were eventually approved. The remaining 5 (or 16 percent) that did not receive voter support were eventually approved with either a combination of public-private financing or completely private financing. A more detailed examination of the five cases sheds some insight into the resolution of these situations.

In the cases of stadium projects in Milwaukee, Seattle, and Pittsburgh, public referendums failed to gain public approval, with the projects in Milwaukee and Pittsburgh failing by nearly 2 to 1 margins and the proposal in Seattle failing by a narrow 51.1 to 49.9 gap. Nevertheless, substantial public funding was secured for the eventual construction of these venues through measures passed by the state legislatures in Wisconsin, Pennsylvania, and Washington. In the case of Columbus, Ohio's, attempt to build an arena to house a professional hockey franchise, voters rejected a proposal for stadium financing by a 56 to 44 percent margin in 1997. Following the failure of this plan at the polls, private financing by the Nationwide Insurance Company and other private investors allowed for the construction of an arena and the creation of the expansion Bluejackets franchise in the National Hockey League.

For elected officials the presence of a major league sports franchise in their city is a sign of prestige and economic vitality. Thus cities and states seek to both retain and attract sports franchises to their confines. While valuing the presence of sports teams, elected officials would rationally prefer to have their presence at the lowest possible costs to the public. In essence, the ultimate scenario for an elected official (like a mayor) would be a vibrant sports franchise in her city with the public paying none of the cost for the venue in which the team plays. This situation is optimal for elected officials because it would allow them to avoid entering the realm of revenue raising to finance a stadium or redistributing revenue from other areas while maintaining the benefits of the franchise's presence.

For the sports franchise the situation is even simpler. As profit-maximizing entities, an organization would like to receive as much public financing as possible for the construction and operation of the venue housing its team, thus allowing it to maintain a healthier bottom line and a more competitive position within the league it inhabits.

With such conflicting goals present, it helps to consider the negotiation between the franchise and government officials as a **zero-sum game**, with any movement toward greater public funding preferable to the franchise and any movement toward greater private funding preferable to government officials. With this scenario in mind, we can turn our attention to the relative bargaining positions of the negotiating parties and the impact of those positions on the setting of the referendum question.

---

zero-sum game Games where the amount of "winnable goods" is fixed. Whatever is gained by one player is therefore lost by the other player. Thus the sum of what's gained and what's lost is zero.

In terms of **bargaining strength**, the organization clearly has the upper hand because of its ability (at least perceived) to relocate to another city. As long as cities publicly court the relocation of franchises, elected officials are placed within the confines of a prisoner's dilemma. Former Washington, D.C., Mayor Sharon Pratt Kelly clearly describes this situation:

> The mayors of American cities are confronted with a prisoner's dilemma of sorts. If no mayor succumbs to the demands of the franchise shopping for a new home, then the teams will stay where they are. This, however, is unlikely to happen because if Mayor A is not willing to pay the price, Mayor B may think it advantageous to open up the city's wallet. Then to protect his or her interest, Mayor A often ends up paying the demanded price.

> While the presence of the threat of moving gives the franchise an enormous advantage in the negotiation, the strength of an elected official's desire to not use public funds is also mollified by the very presence of the ballot question. More specifically, given the cover of citizen ratification of the use of public funds, elected officials may not feel the urgency to strike a deal in which the franchise pays a larger share of the facility costs. Other than the opportunity costs for the revenue being directed to the sports venue, and the possibility of diminished reputation due to a failed referendum, an elected official can justify a large public contribution to the construction of a sports facility through voter ratification as a case of "the will of the people."

bargaining strength Relative power that each of the parties holds during the negotiating process. The final settlement often reflects the bargaining power of each side.

For Discussion: *Why do local and state governments direct public funds to the construction of stadiums and arenas when those venues are primarily used by privately owned sports teams? Do cities get back their investment in sports venues through added revenue from economic activity generated by the stadiums and arenas?*

The Importance of Public Financial Management

The flow and management of funds is the lifeblood of our system of public administration. No policy, however farsighted, no system of administrative performance, however well crafted, can function unless it is associated with the flow of funds that will make it possible. Like other parts of the story of public administration covered so far, the system of public financial management rests on designs and reforms adopted over many years. Administrators need to understand how that system has been designed, what it is intended to do, what it is capable of doing, and especially what it is *not* capable of doing. As with the machinery of government and the system of intergovernmental relations, many aspects of the design of the American system of public financial management go back to our deepest political traditions and compacts—to the ideas of the founders at the Constitutional Convention. Others, like the idea of the welfare state, go back only a few generations. Still others, such as the concept of "user pays," are at their height.

Public financial management is a dynamic, living, breathing system with which citizens interact every day. Think of this system as rather like a huge irrigation system: one that gathers rainfall behind large dams and distributes the flow of water through large and small pipes and channels to many disparate communities—to commercial users, schools and hospitals, parklands and charities, businesses and individuals, seaside areas and deserts. Such a system must be managed and regulated throughout its length, and its consumers must be billed according to some politically acceptable framework. If adequate rain falls, if the dams and pipes do not leak or burst, and if the supplies of water are not diverted or stolen before delivery, the system will become a precondition for life, growth, and even abundance. In one dimension at least, public administrators, as well as concerned citizens, are river wardens on this system. They are all sustained by its flow.

Six Principles

At the Boston Tea Party in 1773, America's pioneers began to lay down the design of this country's system of public financial management when they cast cargoes of tea into Boston Harbor rather than pay reasonable taxes on them to England. When they shouted their slogan, "No taxation without representation," they were also asserting a cardinal value—a design principle—for the future system of public financial management in America. Taxation and public spending must be voted for;

TABLE 13.1 The Federal Government's Fiscal Posture

Where the Federal Government Gets its Revenue

Source	Percent
Individual Income Taxes	40%
Borrowing	12%
Social Insurance Receipts	32%
Corporate Income Tax	10%
Excise Taxes	3%
Other Taxes (i.e., estate, gift)	3%

Where the Federal Government Spends its Funds

Area of Expenditure	Percent
National Defense	19%
Social Security	21%
Medicare	14%
Medicaid	7%
Other Discretionary Spending	30%
Interest on the Federal Debt	9%

SOURCE: Budget of the United States, fiscal year 2007 (estimated figures).

they must have, in effect, the stamp of democratic approval. This had not been the way most governments to that date had operated. States and potentates had levied and extracted taxes as a matter of the exercise of power. Then they kept or spent the money as they chose. America's founders made democratic consent to these things a fundamental design feature. This is why the Constitution requires that all tax legislation must originate in the House of Representatives, the legislative branch most responsive to the popular will.

At the heart of the design of the American system of public financial management are the following six principles:

1. *Democratic consent:* Taxation and spending should not be done without the explicit **consent of the governed**.
2. *Equity:* Governments should be equitable (treat people in similar circumstances similarly) in raising and spending taxes.
3. *Transparency:* What governments do in raising and spending funds should be open to public knowledge and scrutiny.
4. *Probity:* There must be scrupulous honesty in dealing with public funds, of which legislators and administrators are the stewards, not the owners.
5. *Prudence:* These stewards should not take undue risks with public funds.
6. *Accountability:* Those who deal in public funds can and should be regularly called to account for their stewardship through legislative review and audit processes.

These normative principles are "shoulds," but they are all too often breached in real life. Public financial management can be abused. Democratic consent is lacking when government is conducted in secret. Concerns for equity often yield to **pork barrel** favoritism toward areas, clients, or groups. Without transparency, probity, and prudence, the inherent caution so essential to the management of public funds is thrown to the winds. Governments then may incur substantial losses through risky investments or negligence.

Balanced Budgets

A balanced **budget** is a budget in which receipts are equal to or greater than outlays. A government that has one is financially healthy. The advantages of a balanced budget, not spending more than you take in, are obvious. But there are also advantages to "unbalanced" budgets, those that require public borrowing. The "extra"

---

consent of the governed The notion that the institutions of government must be based on the will of the people.

pork barrel Favoritism by a government in the allocation of benefits or resources; legislation that favors the district of a particular legislator by providing for the funding of public works or other projects (such as post offices or defense contracts) that will bring economic advantage to the district and political favor for the legislator.

budget A financial plan serving as a pattern for and control over future operations—hence, any estimate of future costs or any systematic plan for the utilization of the workforce, material, or other resources.

spending can stimulate the economy during economic downturns and provide needed public works and public support for the less fortunate. But these considerations must be weighed against the danger that large deficits over a significant period can devalue the currency, kindle inflation, and have such a **crowding out** effect on capital markets that an economic depression (or recession) occurs. Note that it is only the federal government that has the option of long-term deficit spending. The states all have constitutional or statutory provisions mandating balanced budgets (at least at the beginning of each year).

The Fiscal Year

Fiscal means having to do with taxation, public revenues, or public debt. The fiscal year is a 12-month accounting period without regard to a calendar year. The fiscal year for the federal government, through fiscal year 1976, began on July 1 and ended on June 30. But Congress, in part because of the invention of air conditioning, increasingly stayed in Washington through the summer. Since it usually waited until the last minute to pass the various appropriations bills, federal agencies increasingly had to depend on **continuing resolutions** for their funding. Finally, Congress realized how silly this was and simply moved the beginning of the new fiscal year to the end of the summer. Since fiscal year 1977, fiscal years for the federal government begin on October 1 and end on September 30. The fiscal year is designated by the calendar year in which it ends (e.g., fiscal year 2001 was the fiscal year ending September 30, 2001). Not all state and local governments follow the federal example. Most states begin their fiscal year on July 1, but a few use the first day of April, September, or October.

Fiscal is also used as an all-purpose adjective to refer to anything to do with government finances. Thus fiscal integrity is a characteristic of a government budget that spends no more than anticipated revenues. A balanced budget has fiscal integrity; a budget with a significant deficit does not. You will be deemed to have fiscal integrity when the person so deeming agrees with your fiscal policies. If that same person disagrees with your policies, you may be deemed so lacking in fiscal responsibility as to be considered fiscally irresponsible.

Budgeting Theory and Practice

Budgeting is the single most important decision-making process in public institutions. The budget itself is also a jurisdiction's most important reference document.

---

crowding out The displacement of private investment expenditures by increases in public expenditures financed by the sale of government securities. It is often suggested that, as the federal deficit increases, the money borrowed from the public to pay for it is therefore unavailable for private investment. Such crowding out could thus lead to a recession or worse.

continuing resolution Legislation that provides budget authority for specific ongoing activities when the regular fiscal-year appropriation for such activities has not been enacted by the beginning of the fiscal year. The continuing resolution usually specifies a maximum rate at which the agency may incur an obligation based on the rate of the prior year, the president's budget request, or an appropriation bill passed by either or both houses of the Congress.

In their increasingly voluminous formats, budgets simultaneously record policy decision outcomes, cite policy priorities as well as program objectives, and delineate a government's total service effort.

A public budget has four basic dimensions. First, it is a political instrument that allocates scarce public resources among the social and economic needs of the jurisdiction. Second, a budget is a managerial or administrative instrument: It specifies the **ways and means** of providing public programs and services; it establishes the costs of programs and the criteria by which these programs are evaluated for efficiency and effectiveness; it ensures that the programs will be reviewed or evaluated at least once during the budget year or **budget cycle**. Third, a budget is an economic instrument that can direct a jurisdiction's economic growth and development. Certainly at the national level—and to a lesser extent at the state and regional levels—government budgets are the primary instruments for redistributing income, stimulating economic growth, promoting full employment, combating inflation, and maintaining economic stability. Fourth, a budget is an accounting instrument that holds government officials responsible for the expenditure of the funds with which they have been entrusted. Budgets also hold governments accountable in the aggregate. The very concept of a budget implies that there is a ceiling, or a spending limitation, which literally (but theoretically) requires governments to live within their means.

The Taft Commission

Prior to 1900, the processes of public financial management in America lacked overall objectives. A particular need—to build a road, finance a war, or meet the costs of civil service and military pay—inspired an appropriate allocation by Congress. In the twentieth century the growing scale and complexity of government led to calls for budgetary reform. In 1912, the **Taft Commission** recommended a national budgeting system. Writing in 1918, William F. Willoughby (1867–1960), a member of the Taft Commission, outlined developments that were leading to the creation of modern budget systems in state governments. In *The Movement Towards Budgetary Reform in the States,* Willoughby argues that budget reform would involve three major threads: (1) how budgets would advance and provide for popular control, (2) how budgets would enhance legislative and executive cooperation, and (3) how budgets would ensure administrative and management efficiency. This is rather prophetic when you consider the topics of some of our everyday headlines: taxpayers' revolts, "Proposition 13" movements, and other forms of expenditure and revenue limitation laws (thread 1: popular control); continued infighting

---

ways and means The methods by which a state gains its funds, supplies, and other necessities. The English House of Commons has had a Committee on Ways and Means at least since 1644. The U.S. House of Representatives has had a Ways and Means Committee since 1795. All national tax legislation must originate in the House Ways and Means Committee.

budget cycle The timed steps of the budget process, which includes preparation, approval, execution, and audit.

Taft Commission The 1912 Commission on Economy and Efficiency, chaired by the president, which called for a national budgetary system. Its recommendations were incorporated into the Budget and Accounting Act of 1921.

between the executive and legislative branches over budgetary control, deficits, and balanced budgets (thread 2: executive-legislative cooperation); and the effectiveness, or lack of it, in overburdened budgeting systems in maintaining managerial practices (thread 3: management effectiveness). Finally, in 1921, the Budget and Accounting Act was passed, bringing into being the Bureau of the Budget and the General Accounting Office (GAO), responsible for budgeting and audit respectively. (See Chapter 14 for further details on the GAO.)

At first, budgetary and compliance procedures remained simple, with budgets constructed of "line items" allocating funds to particular expenditure categories in each department—so much for salaries, furniture, paper, and so on. The process of audit was correspondingly simple, emphasizing the examination of the extent to which expenditure had been in compliance with the purposes for which funds were allocated.

The 1930s saw the advent of increasingly larger government domestic programs and concomitant expenditures. Consequently, budgeting became of increasing importance. However, budgetary theory—that is, how to rationally allocate government resources—was woefully inadequate. The emphasis was on process and line-item budgeting, which stressed accountability and control. Performance

President William Howard Taft displaying his executive profile while thinking about executive budgeting. Taft was the only person to be both president of the United States (1909–1913) and chief justice of the Supreme Court (1921–1930). At 321 pounds, Taft also holds the record as the largest of all presidents. While he was the hand-picked successor of President Theodore Roosevelt, Taft quickly lost Roosevelt's support once in office. Roosevelt found him so unacceptably conservative that both men competed for the Republican nomination in 1912. When Roosevelt won the primaries but lost the nomination to Taft, he ran for president as a "Bull Moose" Progressive. This split the Republican vote and allowed Woodrow Wilson, the Democrat, to win.•

budgeting (allocating funds for sets of activities), which stressed work measurement, much as scientific management, was increasingly advanced and used as an appropriate management-oriented budgetary process. Nevertheless, there remained little integration of the budgetary process with rational policymaking and decision making. In 1940, **V. O. Key Jr.** wrote an article bemoaning the lack of a budgetary theory. Greatly concerned about the overemphasis on mechanics, he posed what was soon acknowledged as the central question of budgeting: "On what basis shall it be decided to allocate X dollars to activity A instead of activity B?" Key went on to elaborate on what he considered the major areas of inquiry that should be researched to develop a budgeting theory. This, along with continuing pressure for even greater increases in the size of government programs, would set the stage for the major advances to come—but they would not be coming until after World War II.

The Influence of Keynes

The British economist **John Maynard Keynes** showed how government spending could be critical in managing an economy, by stimulating demand when resources were underutilized and unemployment was high. His thinking created the notion of budgetary policy as an instrument—in some respects the primary instrument—by which a nation could execute **macroeconomic** policy. All U.S. presidents since Franklin D. Roosevelt have used Keynes's theories to, admittedly or unadmittedly, justify deficit spending to stimulate the economy. Even President Richard M. Nixon admitted, "We're all Keynesians now." Keynes observed in his *General Theory* that "practical men, who believe themselves to be quite exempt from any intellectual influences, are usually the slaves of some defunct economist." He even provided the definitive economic forecast when he asserted that "in the long run we are all dead."

   Aaron Wildavsky, in successive editions of *The Politics of the Budgetary Process,* highlighted the extent to which budgeting was a political and economic

---

V. O. Key Jr. (1908–1963) The political scientist who did pioneering work in developing empirical methods to explore political and administrative behavior.

John Maynard Keynes (1883–1946) The English economist who wrote the most influential book on economics of the past century, *The General Theory of Employment, Interest, and Money* (1936). Keynes founded a school of thought known as Keynesian economics, which called for using a government's fiscal and monetary policies to positively influence a capitalistic economy; he also developed the framework of modern macroeconomic theory.

macroeconomics The study of the relationships among broad economic trends such as national income, consumer savings and expenditures, capital investment, employment, money supply, prices, government expenditures, and balance of payments. Macroeconomics is especially concerned with government's role in affecting these trends.

Aaron Wildavsky (1930–1993) The author of *The Politics of the Budgetary Process* (1964; 4th ed., 1984), which reveals the tactics public managers use to get their budgets passed and explains why rational attempts to reform the budgetary process have always failed. For this classic work alone, Wildavsky would have earned his place in the pantheon of public administration. However, Wildavsky also made landmark contributions to the study of the U.S. presidency, policy analysis, and program implementation and evaluation. Because of the volume, quality, and diversity of his work, Wildavsky was one of the nation's most widely read and influential academic analysts of public affairs.

rather than a mechanical process. Later, James M. Buchanan and Gordon Tullock of the "public choice" school presented government budgeting as a battle among beneficiaries seeking to capture funds to their own ends. Instead of a lack of budgetary theory, as in 1940, we are now abundantly served with it.

The Objectives of Budgeting

The analysis of economists Richard and Peggy Musgrave in *Public Finance in Theory and Practice* provides a key to the understanding of the objectives of public financial management. They postulate that government revenue raising and spending serve one of the following four objectives:

1. *Allocation:* Ensuring that an appropriate level of funding flows into sectors of the economy where it is required

2. *Distribution:* Ensuring that the balance in public funding between regions, between classes of people in society, between public and private sectors, and between government and business reflects public policy

3. *Stabilization:* Using public spending to stabilize the macroeconomy (or in some cases parts of it) as prescribed by Keynes

4. *Growth:* Using the power of government spending to facilitate economic growth and wealth creation

When we look at the budget of the national government—or of a state or local government—we can use this perspective for analysis. Is this a budget aimed at supporting growth in the economy? If so, what are its strategies—perhaps a lower tax on business and less government regulation? Is this a budget aimed at distributional objectives? Perhaps it seeks to assist cities and the long-term unemployed? Or it may be designed to stabilize the economic cycle—to stimulate demand during a slump or to moderate it in a boom. There is often disagreement over just how to achieve stated goals. Those who espouse supply-side economics believe that lowering tax rates, especially on marginal income, encourages fresh capital to flow into the economy, which in turn generates jobs, growth, and new tax revenue. Because this concept was adopted by the Reagan administration, it has been popularly called Reaganomics, even though Reagan's actual economic policies were a melange of supply-side thinking, monetarism, old-fashioned conservatism, and even Keynesianism. While economist Arthur Laffer is generally credited with having "discovered" supply-side economics, the underlying premises of it were established almost 200 years ago by Alexander Hamilton in *The Federalist*, No. 21 (1787). Hamilton presented this argument:

> It is a signal advantage of taxes . . . that they . . . prescribe their own limit; which cannot be exceeded without defeating the end proposed—that is, an extension of the revenue. When applied to this object, the saying is as just as it is witty, that, "in political arithmetic, two and two do not always make four." If duties are too high, they lessen the consumption; the collection is eluded; and the product to the treasury is not so great as when they are confined within proper and moderate bounds.

Of course, one person's supply-side economics may be another's **voodoo economics**. Politicians are not always crystal clear in articulating what values and objectives underlie their budgetary strategies. Sometimes when these objectives have crass political motives—tax loopholes for campaign contributors—it is not polite or honorable to publicly admit them. Often, because budgets have grown so enormously complicated and detailed, those who are responsible for them literally do not fully understand the import of what they are doing—budgetarily speaking. Remember that it was David A. Stockman, Reagan's director of the Office of Management and Budget from 1981 to 1985, who, in 1981, confessed to readers of the *Atlantic Monthly* that "none of us really understands what's going on with all these numbers."

The Two Types of Budgets

There are two basic kinds of budgets. The most common, and what most people think of when the word *budget* comes to mind, is the operating budget. This is a short-term plan for managing the resources necessary to carry out a program. "Short term" can mean anything from a few weeks to a few years. Usually an operating budget is developed for each fiscal year, with changes made as necessary.

The second kind is the capital budget process that deals with planning for large expenditures for capital items. Capital expenditures should be for long-term investments (such as bridges and buildings), which yield returns for years after they are completed. Capital budgets typically cover five- to ten-year periods and are updated yearly. Items included in capital budgets may be financed through borrowing (including tax-exempt municipal bonds), savings, grants, revenue sharing, special assessments, and so on. A capital budget provides for separating the financing of capital, or investment, expenditures from current, or operating, expenditures. The federal government has never had a capital budget in the sense of financing capital programs separately from current expenditures.

Waves of Innovation in Budget Making

The structure and format of government budgets has been the subject of successive waves of innovation throughout the twentieth century. Why should this be so? It is simply because the ultimate statement of what a government stands for and spends is to be found in its budget. The budget is the key focal point of public administration. It places huge power in the hands of those who shape it. To the executive, the bureaucrat, and the "budgeteers," it is of incessant interest because of its timeless potency.

---

voodoo economics Presidential candidate George Bush's 1980 description of Republican primary opposition candidate Ronald Reagan's economic policy proposals. After joining Reagan as the vice presidential nominee on the 1980 (and the 1984) ticket, Bush thought he had better not say it anymore. And he didn't. But the press never let him forget it. When in 1982 he denied ever having said it—"I didn't say it. I challenge anyone to find it"—NBC News then showed a videotape of him using the phrase (*Newsweek*, May 23, 1988). Since then he hasn't denied saying it.

The Executive Budget

The first conceptual breakthrough in budgeting was really the conception that there could be a government budget at all—that is, a single document bringing together in one place the revenue, expenditure, and financing plans of government. Until the twentieth century, budgeting in **representative governments** was decidedly a legislative, not an executive, function. Congressional or state legislative **committees** would appropriate funds for an agency without regard for the other agencies of government. Without overall coordination there was considerable confusion and ample opportunity for both incompetence and corruption. The movement toward an executive (or comprehensive) budget in the United States began in the states and was adopted by the federal government with the Budget and Accounting Act of 1921. Today all state governments except South Carolina use some variation of the executive budget.

An executive budget is both a technical process and a physical thing. First it is the process by which agency requests for appropriations are prepared and submitted to a budget bureau under the chief executive for review, alteration, and consolidation into a single budget document that can be compared to expected revenues and executive priorities before submission to the legislature. Then it becomes a tangible document, the comprehensive budget document for an executive branch of government that a jurisdiction's chief executive submits to a legislature for review, modification, and enactment. The president's budget is the executive budget for a particular fiscal year transmitted to the Congress by the president in accordance with the Budget and Accounting Act of 1921, as amended. Some elements of the budget (such as the estimates for the legislative branch and the judiciary) are required to be included without review by the Office of Management and Budget or approval by the president. After all, the president has no say in the budgets of the other branches of government. It is just convenient to include the comparatively small budgets of other branches in the overall document. The president's budget is the president's "wish list"—his suggestions to Congress. Every president's budget is "dead on arrival" the moment it is formally sent to the **Hill**, since Congress always makes extensive changes. The same considerations apply to state governors. Thus a governor's budget is an executive budget prepared by a state governor.

Be aware that not all of the national budget is open to public scrutiny. The "black budget" is the classified (secret) portion of the federal budget that hides sensitive military and covert projects. According to Tim Weiner in *Blank Check*, "The

---

representative government A governing system in which a legislature freely chosen by the people exercises substantial power on their behalf.

committee A subdivision of a legislature that prepares legislation for action by the respective house or that makes investigations as directed by the respective house. Most standing (full) committees are divided into subcommittees, which study legislation, hold hearings, and report their recommendations to the full committee. Only the full committee can report legislation for action by the entire legislature.

Hill The U.S. Congress, because it is literally situated on a hill. It is 88 feet above sea level, while the White House is 55 feet above sea level. Now there can be no doubt about which is the "higher" branch of government.

Figure 13.1 The Executive Budget Process

black budget is a challenge to the open government promised by the Constitution. Today close to a quarter of every dollar in the Pentagon's budget for new weapons is cloaked in blackness. . . . Every dollar spent in secret defies the Framers' intent that the balance sheet of government should be a public document."

Line-Item Budgeting

The line-item budget was the original budget format—each item of expense had a literal line in a ledger book. It classified budgetary accounts according to narrow, detailed objects of expenditure (such as motor vehicles, clerical workers, or reams of paper) used within each particular agency of government, generally without reference to the ultimate purpose or objective served by the expenditure. It was useful as a record of expenditures and the criteria against which audits could measure compliance.

The line-item budget is still widely used. Most local governments use it either as their basic budget format or as a supplement to more sophisticated formats. Because it offers such comprehensive details on proposed expenditures, legislators interested in fine-tuning executive budget recommendations are particularly partial to it because it allows for greater control and oversight.

While the traditional line-item budget was a great step forward, it had a major weakness. It might allow the test to be made as to whether funds had been spent on the purposes for which they had been appropriated, and that truly was (and is) an important test. But it gave no inkling as to how well these appropriations had been spent, whether they had resulted in "value for money."

Performance Budgeting

The concept of performance budgeting, first tried in New York City in the early 1900s, was the first major step beyond the line-item budget. Performance budgeting required a performance measure to be stated alongside each line item so that elementary calculations of unit cost and efficiency could be made. Line items were grouped, or categorized, in functional terms. For example, a sanitation (trash collection) department's workload could be determined on the basis of the number of houses and businesses served, which made it relatively easy to calculate how much trash is generated each week, month, or year. Using this measure, the efficiency of collection could be compared to a base period and a base cost. At this elementary level, comparisons in relative efficiency could be made from year to year, and in concept, between governments (in practice, intergovernmental comparisons required standardized measurement, which usually did not exist).

Performance budgeting, which was in its prime after being officially sanctioned by the Hoover Commission of 1949 (see Chapter 3), stressed using the budget process as a tool for work measurement and efficiency analysis. The heyday of performance budgeting lasted from the 1950s through the 1960s, and even today in some local governments you can still find performance budgets. However, while line-item and performance budgets were helpful in addressing issues of control, compliance, and efficiency, they did not help in the planning dimension, in the identification of global resource allocation to purposes, or in the assessment of effectiveness (that is, the extent to which goals were attained).

Program Budgeting Versus Incrementalism

The next wave of budgetary reform followed hard on the heels of performance budgeting, and essentially met its deficiencies. In 1954, David Novick, an economist with the California-based **RAND Corporation**, proposed "program budgeting"—a form of budgeting that would permit global understanding of expenditure purposes, which consolidated spending into "programs," and that therefore laid foundations for a focus on effectiveness, since the total resources directed to any purpose should now be more readily apparent. Novick defined a program as "the sum of the steps or interdependent activities which enter into the attainment of a specified objective."

If a budget were to consist of large slabs of spending, called programs, directed toward particular objectives, the fragmentation problem common to line-item and performance budgeting would be overcome. Compliance could still be monitored, but the monitoring of efficiency and effectiveness would also be facilitated. And instead of being primarily an instrument of control and management information, the

---

RAND Corporation A think tank created by the U.S. Air Force in 1947 and located in Santa Monica, California. The name is an acronym for research and development, and came from Project Rand, in which Douglas Aircraft agreed to provide civilian advice to the Air Force about developing new bombers. Separated from Douglas in 1948, the RAND Corporation was located in Santa Monica partly on the grounds that it was better to have a think tank of this kind away from the political pressures of Washington. RAND was concerned with the application of scientific and social scientific methods to the problems of strategy and security in the nuclear age. It became the key institution in the development of civilian expertise on nuclear strategy and remains one of the most important think tanks on national and international security issues.

budget would become a planning document, and a document supporting the comparison of alternative expenditures at some meaningful level of aggregation. These were important conceptual breakthroughs.

The team that fashioned program budgeting at the RAND Corporation had an ambitious program, for they proposed not merely a rewrite of budget structure but a new framework for the analysis of policy and the review of accomplishment. They proposed not just program budgeting but planning-programming budgeting. This was a linked system with elements of forward planning, which they termed "the analytical comparison of alternatives," the allocation of resources in the framework of a multiyear cycle, and budgeting related to broad program groups rather than individual items. The "package" was named PPBS; it was intended "to create a new environment of choice." The document was now no longer about "Where are we?" but about "Where do we want to go?" It seemed that the theorists were at last making a contribution that had the potential to reshape government budgeting, planning, and resource allocation in a fundamental way.

Budgeting during the 1960s was dominated by PPBS—the planning, programming, budgeting system. First installed in the Defense Department during the Kennedy administration, it seemed to represent the height of rationality for the budget process. According to Schick, the stages of budget reform went from the development of budgetary theory, with its concerns for accountability and control, which were the hallmark of the line-item budget, to performance budgeting, with its emphasis on managerial efficiency, to PPBS, which stressed objectives, planning, and program effectiveness.

In 1965 Lyndon Johnson mandated the use of PPBS for all federal agencies. The application of PPBS, which required among other things that agencies detail program objectives and indicators for evaluation, make five-year expenditure forecasts, and generate numerous special cost-benefit analyses and zero-based reviews of program activities, marked perhaps the zenith of the management systems approach to public administration. Implemented hastily, with insufficient time for understanding, training, and development, the across-the-board implementation of PPBS failed quickly, leaving a platform for cynics and incrementalists to lambaste national initiatives and planning indiscriminately for many years.

PPBS was never without its critics. In 1964, Aaron M. Wildavsky published *The Politics of the Budgetary Process,* his immensely well-received critique of how budgeting was, in reality, an incremental process sharply influenced by political considerations. Incremental budgeting is a method of budget review that focuses on the increments of increase or decrease in the budget of existing programs. Incremental budgeting, which is often called traditional budgeting, is a counter-school of thought to more rational, systems-oriented approaches, such as PPBS or zero-based budgeting. But this old approach nicely takes into account the inherently political nature of the budget process and so will continue to be favored by legislative appropriations committees, if not by budget theorists. As Wildavsky wrote, "The largest determining factor of the size and content of this year's budget is last year's budget." And this is still overwhelmingly true, despite the reinventing government movement and the devolution revolution of the 1990s.

In 1969 Wildavsky wrote a devastating critique of PPBS. Aside from stating flatly that he thought PPBS was unworkable, Wildavsky demonstrated how the planning and analytical functions of PPBS were contradictory to the essential nature of budgeting.

What was once mandatory for all federal agencies and widely adopted by state and local jurisdictions, by the end of the decade was officially "un"-adopted by the federal government and was widely considered to be unusable in its original format. Nevertheless, the influence of PPBS as a major budgeting process remains. Where it is still in use, however, it tends to exist in a hybrid instead of a pure form.

Wildavsky, who would later form and be the first dean of the University of California at Berkeley's Graduate School of Public Policy, was greatly influenced by Charles Lindblom, under whom he studied while a doctoral student at Yale. Incremental approaches to budgeting, or what would later be called "traditional budgeting," was the counter-school of thought to the management systems emphasis. The principal contention of the incrementalists (such as Wildavsky and Lindblom) was that budgets are inherently political and that studying budgeting and budgets is useful because it explains how and what choices (political compromises) have been made. Wildavsky even rebutted V. O. Key's classic question, "On what basis shall it be decided to allocate *X* dollars to activity *A* instead of activity *B*?," as unanswerable and irrelevant. What mattered was that the process of budgeting should facilitate decision making and assist in obtaining consensus about policy goals and program objectives.

BOX 13.1   No One Can Do PPBS

In a better world, without the vulgar intrusion of political factors (such as the consent of the governed), PPBS would perform its wonders as advertised. Now it is clear that for the narrow purpose of predicting why program budgeting would not work there was no need to mention political problems at all. It would have been sufficient to say that the wholesale introduction of PPBS presented insuperable difficulties of calculation. All the obstacles previously mentioned, such as lack of talent, theory, and data, may be summed up in a single statement: No one knows how to do program budgeting. Another way of putting it would be to say that many know what program budgeting should be like in general, but no one knows what it should be in any particular case. Program budgeting cannot be stated in operational terms. There is no agreement on what the words mean, let alone an ability to show another person what should be done. The reason for the difficulty is that telling an agency to adopt program budgeting means telling it to find better policies and there is no formula for doing that.

SOURCE: Aaron Wildavsky, "Rescuing Policy Analysis from PPBS," *Public Administration Review* 29 (March–April 1969).

Zero-Based Budgeting

In 1952 **Verne B. Lewis** continued the quest for the development of a theory of budgeting that Key had sought a dozen years earlier. In his "Toward a Theory of Budgeting," Lewis presented a theory of alternative budgeting. His analysis marked an important link to the PPBS systems of the 1960s and, especially, to the zero-based budgeting systems of the 1970s.

Lewis advocated budget submissions prepared in a manner that would facilitate comparison and demonstrate a range of choices for service and funding levels and, at the same time, have the final choice provide realistic contracts—that is, specific, realistic expectations for the individual program managers. The implied rationale for this process almost seems a restating of Key's classic budgeting equation: For X level of funding, Y level of service can be provided; for $X + 1$ funding, $Y + Z$ services, and so on.

Alternative budgeting, Lewis's preferred solution, was a means to overcome traditional budgetary review techniques that focus on item-by-item control rather than on scaling levels of program services and goals to varying levels of funding. Lewis, a realist, saw clearly the influence of other factors such as "pride and prejudice, provincialism, and politics" in budgetary decisions. His hope was for the advent of budgeting systems that could overcome these noneconomic and nonrational factors.

The next stage of budget reform after PPBS, zero-based budgeting (ZBB), would fully incorporate Lewis's concept of alternative budgeting. Management consultant Peter A. Phyrr first developed it for Texas Instruments and then for the state of Georgia while Jimmy Carter was governor. In 1976, presidential candidate Carter made the installation of zero-based budgeting a campaign promise, and in 1977, as president, he ordered its adoption by the federal government. The initial reaction to ZBB paralleled the reaction to PPBS in the 1960s, only the downfall of ZBB was even more rapid.

Zero-based budgeting is a budgeting process that is, first and foremost, a rejection of the incremental decision-making model of budgeting. It demands a rejustification of the entire budget submission (from ground zero), whereas incremental budgeting essentially respects the outcomes of previous budgetary decisions (collectively referred to as the budget base) and focuses examination on the margin of change from year to year. So, under ZBB, an agency would have to rank each of its programs according to importance and face the possibility of the least important ones being discontinued.

In large part, ZBB failed because the conditions that had prevailed for most of the previous budgeting systems reforms had changed. In an era of acute resource scarcity, ZBB had little utility because there was little real chance that funding could be provided for any program growth. Critics assaulted ZBB as a fraud; some called it a nonsystem of budgeting. ZBB's fate in the federal government was tied to the Carter presidency. After the inauguration of a new president (Reagan) in 1981, it

---

Verne B. Lewis (1913–) A federal budget officer. After retiring from the U.S. Department of Agriculture, he taught public administration at the University of Washington.

was quietly rescinded. Still, numerous state and local governments use ZBB techniques or some adaptation of ZBB. Now that the hype has subsided, ZBB remains an important part of public budgeting.

Contemporary Budget Reform

It is useful to consider three important contemporary budget questions because they remain unanswered and are likely to be so far into the future. Should an integrated national budget and financial statement be created? Can multiyear budgetary cycles be effectively controlled through shorter-term political processes? And, finally, can a budget process with a greater policy focus be created?

Integrated Budgets

The concept of an integrated national budget and financial statement is an important one. No corporation would expect its shareholders to be content with less than an integrated **balance sheet** and operating statement. Yet the rule in government has too often been that the balance sheet is missing and the **operating statement** incomplete. The completion of the operating statement, after all, was the reason why the budget concept itself was originally created: to present a single document integrating at one view what was to be raised and spent. In 1967, the President's Commission on Budget Concepts reaffirmed the need for just such a unified budget, and one was adopted in 1969.

A unified budget is one in which receipts and outlays from federal funds and trust funds (such as Social Security) are consolidated. When these two fund groups are consolidated to display budget totals, transactions from one fund group to another (interfund transactions) are deducted to avoid double counting. The fiscal activities of **off-budget federal agencies** are not included in the unified budget. And this is precisely the problem. Because billions and billions of dollars of "off-budget" spending exists outside the unified budget, the budget is not all that "unified" after all. Some expenditures of this type were created to avoid political scrutiny of the costs of new programs, some represent the "black" expenditures of the intelligence community, and some are represented by the budgets of public enterprises whose financial affairs can be excluded from the unified budget if that will help the administration (as it usually does) to understate the total size of government spending. The goal of transparency in public financial administration is a strong argument for reform in this area, with the ultimate goal being an annual consolidated financial statement—both balance sheet and operating statements—which is unified, inclusive, and prepared on

---

balance sheet A summary of the financial worth of an individual or organization broken down by assets (what is owned) and liabilities (what is owed). It is called a balance sheet because total assets balance with, or are equal to, total liabilities plus net worth.

operating statement The detailed financial information that supplements a balance sheet.

off-budget federal agencies Agencies, federally owned in whole or in part, whose transactions have been excluded from the budget totals under provisions of law (e.g., the Federal Financing Bank). The fiscal activities of these agencies are presented in an appendix to the federal budget.

independently validated standards as to accounting, estimating, and valuation. Only then can we claim to have a mature budgetary document in line with community expectations and private sector norms.

In principle, the objective of a unified budget is important and should be observed: It is that all revenues and expenditures by government for the budgetary period should be brought into a single document and framework. Only in this manner can democratic control be exerted on a fully informed basis, whereby elected representatives can compare the costs and revenues that make up government activity and make judgments about alternatives. On the other hand, conflicting principles do apply. Details of secret intelligence operations overseas can hardly be debated during the budget session, lest the lives of operators be put at risk. The commercial latitude critical to public enterprise performance may be jeopardized if excessive detail of public enterprise budget issues is placed in the unified budget, rather than in the separate annual financial and performance reports of the enterprise.

We must be skeptical and suspicious whenever a government seeks to conceal an area of government activity from normal channels of democratic scrutiny; sometimes the reasons for seeking to place a particular category of spending "off-budget" may be at odds with the public's right to know. Just because an expenditure item is off-budget, it need not mean that all democratic scrutiny must be forgone. There are several courses that can be taken to provide alternative channels. Security-related issues could be vetted by a special congressional committee. Public enterprise or joint venture results could be covered by separate reports or covered in supporting appendixes to the main budget documents. All of these options are in use; the key requirements are that no significant area of public spending should evade democratic scrutiny altogether and that we should be able to rely on the unified budget to furnish the most comprehensive and feasible composite picture of public revenue getting and spending.

Multiyear Budgets

A second long-standing but essentially unresolved issue in budgeting concerns the need of some program areas for multiyear funding—for financing that extends over a number of years. Just as business demands certainty from government as to the rules of the game, so does effective public administration in many areas, from major infrastructure investment to strategic research. Effectively, the federal government uses a multiyear budget for a wide variety of programs, such as transfer payments to the states based on statutory formulas, **entitlement programs,**

---

entitlement program Any government program that pays benefits to individuals, organizations, or other governments that meet eligibility requirements set by law. Social Security is the largest federal entitlement program for individuals. Others include farm price supports, Medicare, Medicaid, unemployment insurance, and food stamps. Entitlement programs have great budgetary significance in that they lock in such a great percentage of the total federal budget each year that changes in the budget can be made only at the margin.

multiyear **appropriations** for construction projects, and, of course, long-term borrowing authority. Yet, our legislators might argue, if they do not have the opportunity annually to apportion public funds, how can they take an integrated view and place funds where today's priorities lie?

A strong case can be made for a biennial or triennial budget cycle. The advantages of such a horizon would include a better matching of known funding with the needs of longer-term projects and allocations; an ability for government and business alike to plan with certainty over several years; and the containment of the necessary political wrangling over budget making so that the crescendo of horse trading would occur less frequently. This would thus allow politicians, lobbyists, and bureaucrats more time to do other things—to consider longer-term policies, to engage in in-depth scrutiny of the implementation of programs, and perhaps to concentrate on cooperative rather than adversarial aspects of their responsibilities.

Until relatively recent times, biennial budgets were the norm in state government because so many state government legislatures regularly meet only every other year. Indeed, in 1940 only New Jersey, New York, Rhode Island, and South Carolina had annual sessions. Arkansas, Maine, Montana, Nevada, New Hampshire, North Dakota, and Vermont still retain biannual budget sessions. However, many states with annual sessions have adopted the biennial budget even when they have annual sessions.

Financing Public Expenditure

There are three basic elements to public financial management: (1) taxing, (2) spending, and (3) saving. Yes, unlike the federal government, many state and local jurisdictions do not spend all their funds each year. Contingency and "rainy day" accounts are common at the subnational levels. Still, taxing and spending are the essential elements of public finance. And it is a pointless chicken-egg argument as to which comes first. But they eventually have to be reconciled—sort of. Spending must always equal taxing plus borrowing. Because tax revenues tend to be **elastic**, one can only estimate yearly revenues. A booming economy will bring in a surfeit of taxes; a sluggish economy will bring in less revenue than before. This is why budget makers so often paint a rosy scenario—an all-too-optimistic estimate of economic growth and interest-rate levels made by budgeteers so that the estimated deficit will seem less than

---

appropriation An act of the U.S. Congress that permits federal agencies to incur obligations and to make payments out of the Treasury for specified purposes. An appropriation usually follows the enactment of authorizing legislation and is the most common form of budget authority, but in some cases the authorizing legislation also provides the budget authority. Appropriations are categorized in a variety of ways, such as by their period of availability (one-year, multiple-year, no-year), the time of congressional action (current, permanent), and the manner of determining the amount of the appropriation (definite, indefinite).

elastic The up-and-down nature of tax revenues; they will increase or decrease depending on overall economic conditions.

TABLE 13.2   Landmarks in Federal Budget Practices

1921	The Budget and Accounting Act establishes a Bureau of the Budget in the Department of the Treasury and the General Accounting Office as an audit agency of Congress.
1939	The Reorganization Act transfers the Bureau of the Budget from the Treasury to the White House.
1950	The Budgeting and Accounting Procedures Act mandates the performance budgeting concepts called for by the Hoover Commission.
1961	The Department of Defense installs a planning programming budgeting system (PPBS).
1965	A PPBS is made mandatory for all federal agencies by the Johnson administration.
1970	The Bureau of the Budget is given more responsibility for managerial oversight and renamed the Office of Management and Budget.
1971	PPBS is formally abandoned in the federal government by the Nixon administration.
1974	The Congressional Budget and Impoundment Control Act revises the congressional budget process and timetable and creates the Congressional Budget Office.
1977	Zero-based budgeting is required of all federal agencies by the Carter administration.
1981	Zero-based budgeting requirements are rescinded by the Reagan administration. David Stockman, director of the Office of Management and Budget, tells the *Atlantic Monthly* that "none of us really understands what's going on with all these numbers."
1985	The Gramm-Rudman-Hollings Act is signed into law; it seeks to balance the federal budget by mandating across-the-board cuts over a period of years.
1986	The Supreme Court in *Bowsher v. Synar* invalidates certain provisions of the Gramm-Rudman-Hollings Act.
1990	The Budget Enforcement Act amends the Gramm-Rudman-Hollings Act to require that new spending be balanced by new taxes or spending reductions.
	The Credit Reform Act (in response to the savings and loan scandal) tightens requirements on federal lending and loan guarantees.
	The Chief Financial Officers Act requires federal agencies to create a chief financial officer position to oversee agency finances.
1993	The Government Performance Results Act requires agencies to justify their budget requests on the basis of the results or outcomes to be achieved.
1997	Agencies are required to submit strategic plans, including mission statements and performance goals.
1998	A Government-Wide Performance Plan is first presented with the federal budget.
2000	Agencies must now advise Congress as to how well they met the performance objectives and goals set out in their strategic plans.
2004	The OMB no longer makes budget projections beyond five years, ending the practice of ten-year projections that had been in place since 1971.

realistic estimates would suggest. But beware the rosy scenario! If you are a budget maker, it will strain your credibility. If you are a consumer of budgets, it will set you up for a fall. Whether scenarios are rosy, neutral, or harsh, the fact remains that budget making involves the task of matching revenues and expenditures so that government can function in the coming year.

Governments have six principal means of financing their spending requirements. This is something of an advance from biblical times, when revenue from tax collectors and forced seizure of property were the main available strategies. Today, governments must choose from the following:

1. Imposing a **direct tax**
2. Imposing an **indirect tax**
3. Collecting revenue by imposing user charges for government customers
4. Obtaining grants from another level of government or an aid agency
5. Making profits from the activities of public enterprises
6. Borrowing from the public through bonds, or from private lenders through loans
7. Using innovative finance techniques, **public-private partnerships**, franchises, or the licensing of private sector providers
8. Using earnings from savings or investments, if any

Each of these methods of raising government revenue involves complex issues of policy, such as incidence (on what group the tax will fall); effectiveness (whether the tax will succeed in yielding the revenue it should); equity (whether it is fair); and administrative ease and cost. If these financing options are still insufficient, governments may turn to privatization, cost cutting, or the termination of programs to reduce the scope of what must be financed.

Taxation

General taxation (or a general property tax in the context of local government) is the most traditional means of financing public services. A tax is a compulsory contribution exacted by a government for public purposes. This does not include employee and employer assessments for retirement and social insurance purposes, which are classified as insurance trust revenue.

Taxes are generally perceived by a public to be legitimate if they are levied by that public's elected representatives. Indeed, one of the causes of, and principal rallying cries for, the American Revolution was that there should be "no taxation without representation" because "taxation without representation is tyranny." Consequently, practically all taxes at all levels of government are now enacted by popularly elected legislatures.

---

direct tax A tax (e.g., an income tax) paid to a government directly by a taxpayer. Article I, Section 9, of the U.S. Constitution holds that "no capitation, or other direct tax shall be laid, unless in proportion to the census or enumeration herein before directed to be taken." This inhibited the enactment of the federal income tax until the Sixteenth Amendment of 1913 changed the Constitution to allow for direct taxation.

indirect tax A tax (e.g., a sales tax) paid to a third party, who in turn pays it to a government.

public-private partnerships Joint efforts on the part of local governments and the business community to plan for, generate public support for, and pay for major social programs or construction projects that will be mutually beneficial.

People have been making poignant remarks about taxes since ancient times. For example, the first-century Roman historian Suetonius reported on a complaint presented to the Emperor Vespasian about taxes on the public toilets (in effect, user fees) in Rome. The emperor took a coin that came from this tax, stuck it in the complainer's nose and asked, "Does it smell?" Hardly even waiting for the answer of "no," he continued: "Yet it comes from urine." Since then, nothing has been in such bad odor that it could escape taxation. Sometimes tax reform is not as much reform as the addition of new kinds of taxes. New things to tax come about by the inventiveness of fiscal experts or by new technology. A vivid example is presented by James Kendall in his biography of Michael Faraday, one of the pioneers in the development of electricity. When Faraday was first explaining his invention to the British chancellor of the exchequer, he was interrupted with "the impatient inquiry: 'But, after all, what use is it?' Like a flash of lightning came the response: 'Why, sir, there is every probability that you will soon be able to tax it!'" Whether urine or electricity, it is all part of the cosmic, all-encompassing governmental revenue stream.

Taxes are one of the most volatile of political issues. Walter Mondale, in accepting the Democratic Party's presidential nomination in 1984, said, "Taxes will go up. And anyone who says they won't is not telling the truth." He lost by a landslide. George Bush in accepting the Republican Party's presidential nomination in 1988 said, "Read my lips. No new taxes!" He won by a landslide. So there is a lesson in this. Bush's lips, however, did not speak the truth. He raised taxes, and this was very much held against him when he futilely sought reelection in 1992.

There are major differences between the federal and state-local revenue systems. The federal system has experienced a trend toward less diversity; over two-thirds of its general revenue is provided by the federal income tax and the several insurance trust funds (such as Social Security). State and local revenue systems, in contrast, depend on a greater variety of revenue sources (such as property taxes, income taxes, sales taxes, user charges, lotteries, and federal grants). While local governments still rely primarily on the property tax, their states—with a few exceptions—rely largely on the state personal income tax. In addition, state sales and business taxes provide a significant source of income. This melange of taxing authorities creates great disparities in the state-local tax burden. A resident of New York may pay hundreds or thousands of dollars in state income taxes, while a resident of Texas—which has no state income tax—pays none. Virginians have to pay more than double the sales taxes paid by Vermonters. There are even greater variations in property taxes. A house in one jurisdiction may be assessed at three times the amount of an identical house in another.

The Ability-to-Pay Principle

Historically the art of taxation has been defined as "so plucking the goose as to obtain the largest amount of feathers with the least possible amount of hissing." While this definition is usually attributed to **Jean-Baptiste Colbert**, efforts to reduce the

---

Jean-Baptiste Colbert (1619–1683) King Louis XIV's controller general of finance.

"hiss" have continued unabated. Two of the classic means of doing this are using the "ability-to-pay" principle or "hiding" the taxes.

The ability-to-pay is the principle of taxation that holds that the tax burden should be distributed according to a person's wealth. It is based on the assumption that, as a person's income increases, the person (whether an individual or a corporation) can and should contribute a larger percentage of income to support government activities. The progressive income tax is based on the ability-to-pay principle.

The personal income tax is based on ability-to-pay, in that the tax rate is applied against income. But income is more than just money; it is any asset that increases one's net worth, and yet income taxes are not necessarily a straight tax on all of one's income in a given year. Remember all those millionaires that the press annually discovers who do not pay any tax on their income? They are able to do this because it is not their total incomes that are subject to taxation but their adjusted gross incomes. All taxpayers have the right to exclude certain kinds of incomes from their gross incomes for tax purposes. For example, interest from state and local bonds is exempt from federal taxation. Thus a millionaire whose sole income came from investments in such bonds would pay no federal income tax. (To ensure that such citizens pay at least something, there is now an "alternative minimum tax"—but emphasis is on the "minimum.") The taxpayer may also subtract deductions and exemptions from taxable income. Then the taxpayer can deduct a host of expenses, as long as they are allowed by the tax laws: medical care, state and local taxes (if a federal return), home mortgage interest, and charitable contributions. A taxpayer can itemize deductions or take a minimum standard deduction, which is a precalculated weighted average. Progressive tax rates are then applied to the taxable income to determine how much tax is due.

All states except Alaska, Florida, Nevada, South Dakota, Texas, Washington, and Wyoming have personal income taxes, as do many cities. Thus residents of Baltimore, Cleveland, Detroit, New York, and Philadelphia, for example, must pay personal income taxes to three different governments: federal, state, and local. With so many taxes at so many levels of government, it is no wonder that **tax avoidance** has become a national pastime rivaling even baseball. The very wealthy J. Pierpont Morgan (1836–1913) provided the intellectual foundation of tax avoidance when he said, "No citizen has a moral obligation to assist in maintaining the government. If Congress insists on making stupid mistakes and passing foolish tax laws, millionaires should not be condemned if they take advantage of them." The Tax Reform Act of 1986, designed to make tax avoidance more difficult by closing many **tax loopholes**, was with good reason informally, cynically, and accurately referred to as the "Tax Accountant's Full Employment Act."

---

tax avoidance Planning one's personal finances to take advantage of all legal tax breaks, such as deductions and tax shelters.

tax loophole An inconsistency in the tax laws, intentional or unintentional, that allows the avoidance of some taxes. An intentional tax loophole is a tax expenditure. A tax expenditure for one person is often viewed as a loophole by another. Tax loopholes are perfectly legal; but they have an unsavory reputation as the handiwork of special interest lobbyists.

The Flat Tax

An income tax that is flat has no brackets; it charges the same rate to each taxpayer. The concept has been put forward in a variety of proposals for reform of the federal income tax. This has long been advocated by prominent Republicans in the Congress such as Jack Kemp of New York in the 1980s and Richard Armey of Texas in the 1990s. It even became a major issue in the 1996 presidential race when millionaire publisher Steve Forbes based his campaign for the Republican presidential nomination on it.

The flat tax is attractive in large measure because it is so simple and seemingly fair. Everybody just pays the same percentage of their income. Tax returns could be completed on a postcard. Nevertheless, Democratic Party members tend to oppose it because it grossly violates the ability-to-pay principle. A flat tax is inherently regressive in that the poor pay proportionately more than the rich. When the idea became a

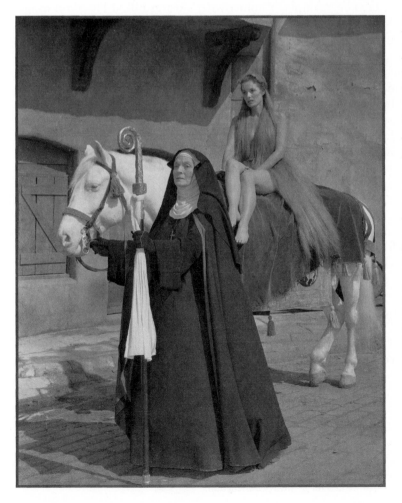

Maureen O'Hara, bare but for her hair, in the title role in the 1955 film *Lady Godiva*, acts out the most famous tax revolt in history. In 1057, so the legend goes, the vassals of Lord Leofric in Coventry, England, complained about their tax burden to his wife, Lady Godiva. Nice lady that she was, she then pleaded with her husband to lower the levy. Nasty fellow that he was, he agreed, but only if she would ride naked through the streets of the town. He didn't think she would do it. But she did. Then he kept his word, reduced the taxes, and thereby established public nudity as an effective tax reduction technique. Godiva chocolates, first made in Belgium in 1926, were introduced to the United States in 1966 with a massive advertising campaign featuring Lady Godiva's tax-revolting ride. Market research had determined that drawings of a naked woman on a horse combined with the subliminal advocacy of lower taxes would sell expensive chocolates to the Americans. After all, the only people who could afford them were already in a high tax bracket! •

major issue in the 1996 Republican primary elections, the accounting firm of Price Waterhouse did an analysis reported in *U.S. News & World Report*. They found that a couple with two children and an income of $60,000 would pay 2 percent more if there was a 21 percent flat tax instead of the current system. However, if that same family earned $300,000, they would have an effective tax cut of 31 percent.

Many forces in the economy are natural enemies of a true flat tax. Charitable and religious organizations do not want to lose the deductions that encourage contributions to them. The housing industry is concerned that the loss of the home mortgage interest deduction would depress housing prices. Corporations worry that the elimination of tax deductions for new equipment purchases would hurt profits. And public financial analysts express concern that a flat tax at the oft-mentioned rate of 17 percent could not raise enough revenue to run the government.

User Charges

User charges are specific fees that users or consumers of a government service pay to receive that service. For example, a homeowner's water bill, if based on usage, would be a user charge. Other examples include toll roads and bridges and charges to use public swimming pools. If a sports team plays on a publicly owned field that has been fenced in, gate takings should be the basic source of finance for that operation. Public transportation is a little different. There, some of the costs need to be recovered from riders. But since the existence of public transportation saves government the need to build new freeways, and since the limitation on the resulting number of commuter automobiles lessens air pollution, public transportation also offers obvious advantages. Accordingly, it is customary and proper for publicly owned transportation systems to be financed partly from user charges and partly from taxation. Freeways, because gasoline taxes are used to pay for them, are financed in this manner. Freeways provide some obvious public goods, such as mobility for the car-owning public and a capability for business to truck its products around. But on the other hand, particular freeways do benefit selectively the commuters that are able to access them. These commuters, some argue, should incur a user charge—that is, they should pay a toll—but this is not always politically possible.

While user charges are voluntary in theory, in practice they are often unavoidable. Few citizens consider municipal water and sewer connections among life's little options. Being essential, the charges are in actuality taxes that dare not use their name. Many user charges are more easily avoided. For example, if you do not attend a state university, you do not have to pay their fees—except for your portion of the overall subsidy such institutions receive through general taxation. If you do not hunt or fish, you need not buy a state license to do so. And if you do not build an extension to your house, you need not pay for a local building permit.

User charges are often treated as **earmarked tax** revenue in that the funds they produce may only be used for legislatively determined purposes. Thus charges for hunting and fishing licenses are often earmarked for wildlife conservation programs.

---

earmarked tax A tax whose revenues must, by law, be spent for specific purposes. For example, a state gasoline tax may be earmarked for highway construction.

Grants

Grants represent an important category of revenue for state and local governments in the United States, as well as in other federal systems such as Australia and Germany. As we have seen in Chapter 4, there are hundreds of federal grant programs, particularly reaching into the areas of health, welfare, and infrastructure (programs involving transportation, water, and sewerage). There are, as well, block grants designed to bolster the financial position of poorer states and regions. The block grants may be automatic, based on population. But when grants are a function of population size, counting people becomes a matter of counting money. Local jurisdictions, especially the big cities, often complain that they are shortchanged in grant money because of a census undercount—the contention that people are missed by the census because they move, are illiterate, or are fearful of filling out government forms, or for other reasons. Because the count is critical for congressional districting and for the funding level of many intergovernmental grant programs, jurisdictions are apt to make an issue of what they consider to be an undercount.

The Problem of Debt

Nowhere can the urgency of developing adequate standards of public financial management and reporting be seen more clearly than in the management of debt. The ability to incur debt is in many respects a hallmark of governments. They usually exist, in part, to undertake projects whose benefits will go on for many generations. This is why Alexander Hamilton wrote in an April 30, 1781, letter to Robert Morris that "a national debt, if it is not excessive, will be to us a national blessing." Of course, there have always been those who disagree with Hamilton's famous sentiment. Andrew Jackson, while a candidate for president, wrote to L. H. Colman on April 26, 1824, "I am one of those who do not believe that a national debt is a national blessing. . . . It is calculated to raise around the administration a moneyed aristocracy dangerous to the liberties of the country." This essential argument continues today among contemporary politicians.

Debt is a way of matching costs with those who benefit from the borrowing, of seeing that future generations pay their share of the costs of roads or buildings we put in place now, of ensuring "intergenerational equity." In the United States, tens of thousands of governments can issue bonds and incur debt. These range from the federal government to the tiniest local governments.

The national debt is the total outstanding debt of a central government. The national debt is often confused with the nation's budget deficit in a given year. The debt is, in effect, the total of all the yearly deficits (borrowing) that have not been repaid, plus accumulated interest. It is President Herbert Hoover who is usually credited with first saying: "Blessed are the young for they shall inherit the national debt."

Deficit financing is a situation in which a government's excess of outlays over receipts for a given period is financed primarily by borrowing from the public. Deficit financing, and especially the general acceptance of it by economic theorists, is largely a phenomenon of the last hundred years. Depending on the economist you listen to, a large deficit is either considered a major drag on the economy or a significant stimulus.

Abuse of Public Debt

Borrowing is a tool that has a clear purpose in public administration. It is a tool that in the right circumstances public administrators should use with confidence. It is also a tool notoriously open to abuse. There are six main categories of such abuse:

1. Borrowing to finance operating (or "recurrent") expenditure
2. Borrowing beyond the level of repayments the community can meet
3. Borrowing under poorly structured contracts that leave the borrower no protection against large interest-rate hikes by the lender
4. Borrowing to finance projects that give no return (like public monuments) or are highly speculative (like building facilities to host sporting events the tenure of which cannot be guaranteed)
5. Borrowing where government lacks the administrative capacity to manage or implement projects without major losses
6. Borrowing where there is widespread corruption and where a high proportion of the funds borrowed will be creamed off in payments to corrupt politicians and administrators, rather than applied to the purpose for which the funds were ostensibly borrowed

These risks are compounded by the fact that politicians often view borrowing as politically preferable to imposing higher taxes. Borrowing is virtually invisible to the electorate. If the projects produced by it are impressive, politicians see a painless way of "buying" votes—especially when the proverbial chickens do not come home to roost until a subsequent administration.

Overcoming these problems is not straightforward. There is not a high level of understanding and debate of these issues in the community. It is genuinely hard to assess the masses of confusing data that project boosters disseminate. Democratic oversight through legislative committees is of varying effectiveness. And audit scrutiny is often too late.

Municipal Bonds

A bond is a certificate of indebtedness issued by a borrower to a lender that constitutes a legal obligation to repay the principal of the loan plus accrued interest. Municipal bonds are the debt instruments of subnational governments. This causes some confusion because they appear to refer only to bonds issued by a local government. Yet bonds issued by states, territories, or possessions of the United States, or by any municipality, political subdivision (including cities, counties, school districts, and special districts for fire prevention, water, sewer, irrigation, and other purposes), or public agency or instrumentality (such as an authority or commission) are subsumed under the rubric "municipal bonds." While the interest on municipal bonds is exempt from federal taxes, state and local exemptions may vary. Tax-exempt bonds allow jurisdictions to borrow money at lower than commercial market interest rates. The buyers of the bonds find them attractive because their high marginal tax rates make a tax-free investment more advantageous than a taxable one paying even higher interest.

There are a wide variety of municipal bonds:

1. General obligation bonds, which are backed by the jurisdiction's **full faith and credit** with repayment, usually, from general revenues.

2. Callable bonds, which can be repaid totally or in part prior to the maturity date. For this reason, callable bonds ordinarily carry higher interest rates. Noncallable bonds, on the other hand, may not be repurchased until the date of maturation.

3. Revenue bonds, which are municipal bonds whose repayment and dividends are guaranteed by revenues derived from the facility constructed with the proceeds of the sale of the bonds (e.g., stadium bonds, toll road bonds). As revenue bonds are not pledged against the tax base of the issuing jurisdiction, they are usually not regulated by the same debt limitations imposed by most states on the sale of general obligation bonds. Additionally, revenue bond questions usually do not have to be submitted to the voters for approval, as they do not commit the full faith and credit of the jurisdiction.

4. Industrial development bonds, which are state or local government bonds issued to finance the building of a factory or installation that will be used by a private company. While such bonds are popular as a means of attracting new industry to a community, they are essentially fronts for private borrowing. Congress, sensing the loss of tax revenue from these fronts, has in recent years put a variety of constraints on their use.

5. Junk bonds, which are issued by a company or government with a poor credit rating; thus they pay higher than normal interest to compensate for the additional risk.

6. Moral obligation bonds, which are state or local government bonds that are backed only by the jurisdiction's promise to repay; they are specifically not backed by a jurisdiction's full faith and credit. Moral obligation bonds often carry a higher interest rate than other municipal bonds because full faith and credit bonds will always be paid first.

7. Serial bonds, which are sold in such a way that a certain number of them are retired (paid off) each year.

8. Term bonds, which all mature (must be paid off) on the same date.

The Rating Agencies

The problem of abuse of public debt is critically important for citizens, administrators, and honest politicians. But it is also very important to lending institutions. After all, borrowing is a two-sided activity: There can be no borrowing without some institution agreeing to lend. International financial markets are composed of many thousands of lenders. Their capability of assessing the merits of a project a government wishes to

---

full faith and credit The descriptive term for those debt obligations, such as certain bonds, that have first claim on the resources of the state.

fund by borrowing will vary greatly. Large lenders financing big governments might have an acute idea as to the merits of projects and the creditworthiness of borrowers, but the thousands of smaller governments and smaller lenders may well see each other "through a glass darkly"—that is, very imperfectly indeed.

The New York ratings agencies, Standard and Poor's and Moody's, exist to fill this gap, which they do by rating or assessing the creditworthiness of borrowers (public or private) and assigning them a credit rating—just like those that have long been assigned to individuals and businesses. However, at the scale of borrowing a government undertakes, the difference between a triple A rating and a rating of merely double A might amount to millions of dollars in loan repayments. Bond rating systems differ, but the highest or most **gilt edge** are triple A; the lowest rating of **investment grade** bonds is triple B. Bonds rated below double B are generally considered speculative or junk. The ratings agencies have independent teams of analysts permanently assigned the task of reassessing ratings, and governments are keen to persuade the agencies of the safety and security offered by their prudent financial management approaches.

The role these agencies have come to play in the financial management of governments is crucial. On the one hand, they are a clearinghouse for information and confidence. No doubt their activities facilitate lending that might not otherwise occur. On the other hand, they are not value free. By upgrading the ratings of the bonds of governments whose actions accord with their ideology, they impose a value scale on policy decisions throughout the world. It is a value scale that rewards balanced budgets and reductions in government expenditure. It gives a tilt to "the level playing field." And of course, these agencies work in secret and are not subject to any form of democratic accountability. When Standard and Poor's in 1995 rated Detroit triple B, Baltimore A, and Minneapolis triple A, it made judgments that will affect the overall quality of life in those cities for years to come. Minneapolis, because it has the best possible rating, will save millions. It will have more money to spend on police and parks than cities such as Detroit and Baltimore, which will have to spend those "extra" millions on interest.

Bonds, Debt, and Emergency Recovery

The terrorist attacks of September 11, 2001, and the major destruction from Hurricane Katrina in 2005 had a major impact on the area of municipal bonds and finances. Both 9/11 and Katrina left local and state governments with substantial financial difficulties that usually discourage investors from investing in municipal bonds for governments and authorities. After the disasters in New York and Louisiana, municipal governments needed massive amounts of money to rebuild destroyed infrastructure at the same time that tax revenues dried up because of crippled local economies. Not surprisingly, Standard and Poor's warned investors of possible downgrades of New York City and New Orleans municipal bonds in the wake of their catastrophes.

---

gilt edge A popular term for a stock, bond, or other security with the highest rating (for safety of investment) or for a negotiable instrument with similar safety.

investment grade Refers to securities that fall into the top four categories, AAA to BBB or Aaa to Baa, for Standard & Poor's and Moody's ratings, respectively. Some institutions are required by law to buy only investment-grade issues.

To help New York recover after 9/11, Congress, New York State, and local governments created a special financing mechanism that reassured private investors that it would be safe to invest in bonds from the city and Port Authority. In fact, a whole new category of municipal bonds, called **Liberty Bonds,** have been used to pay for the redevelopment of lower Manhattan after the destruction wrought by the terrorist strike. These bonds are part of a broader economic stimulus law signed by President Bush in March 2002 that let New York City real estate developers obtain lower borrowing rates by selling bonds in the municipal bond market. Despite some controversy over how the revenue is being used, the Liberty Bond provision has been essential to the rebirth of the area around "Ground Zero."

While this new bond helped New York City recover from 9/11, New Orleans's efforts to rebuild after Katrina may take much longer. The widespread nature of the destruction in New Orleans caused a significant loss in the city's tax base—most notably from property taxes. According to the Congressional Budget Office (CBO), New Orleans has about $800 million of outstanding bonds, with the water and sewer authority holding another $198 million and the convention center obligated to about $500 million more. It will be extremely difficult for New Orleans to meet these bond obligations without revenue coming in during the city's recovery period. For example, the Convention Center Authority pays its bond debt through taxes on hotels and restaurants. With the city's tourism trade in shambles, the Convention Center Authority is going to have a hard time meeting its obligations to bondholders. All major ratings firms issued warnings on debt issued by New Orleans and its special purpose districts but did not downgrade any bonds. The lack of downgrades is caused by the belief that both the state and federal government will step in and keep the city and its authorities from defaulting on their financial obligations.

Economic Policy

Isolationism, an option in foreign policy, is most decidedly not a possibility with a government's financial policies. Contemporary financial policies cannot stand alone. They are inherently part of the nation's overall economic policies.

Economic policy, the process by which a nation manages its trade, business, and finances, generally consists of three dimensions: (1) fiscal policy, (2) monetary policy, and (3) those other facets of public policy with economic implications, such as energy policy, farm policy, and labor union policy. The interaction of these dimensions of economic policy is crucial, since none operates in a vacuum. While monetary policy basically exercises control over the quantity and cost (interest rates) of money and credit in the economy, fiscal policy deals with the sizes of budgets, deficits, and taxes. Other policy areas, such as housing policy (also dependent on interest rates) and programs dependent on deficit spending, involve aspects of both monetary and fiscal policy, and vice versa. However, their interrelationship does not

---

Liberty Bond Refers to tax-exempt private activity bonds used to finance capital projects in New York City after the terrorist attacks of September 11, 2001.

exist with regard to implementation. Monetary policy, while receiving major inputs from the president and other executive agencies, is the responsibility of the Federal Reserve Board, an independent agency. Fiscal policy, while receiving similar inputs from the Federal Reserve Board, is primarily the responsibility of the president and Congress. The degree of equality and subsequent share of responsibility varies within a stable range. While a president may wish to spend this or that amount, only Congress has the constitutional ability to levy taxes (although tax laws, like any others, must be signed or vetoed by the president). Also limiting a president's discretion over economic policy is the fact that so much of it is controlled by prior decisions to fund, for example, welfare, entitlement, and pension programs, which are not easily changed.

Monetary Policy

Monetary policy consists of a government's formal efforts to manage the money in its economy in order to realize specific economic goals. Three basic kinds of monetary policy decisions can be made: (1) decisions about the amount of money in circulation; (2) decisions about the level of interest rates; (3) decisions about the functioning of credit markets and the banking system.

Controlling the amount of money is, of course, the key variable. In 1913, the United States passed into law the Federal Reserve Act, which created a strong central bank: the Federal Reserve. Like most central banks, the **Federal Reserve System** is empowered to control the amount of money in circulation by either creating or canceling dollars. The implementation of money control is achieved through the process of putting up for sale or buying government securities, usually termed **open-market operations**, which means that the Federal Reserve competes with other bidders in the purchasing or selling of securities. The difference is that, when the Federal Reserve buys securities, it pays in the form of new currency in circulation. If it sells some of its securities, it decreases money available, since in effect it absorbs currency held by

---

Federal Reserve System Colloquially known as the Fed, this is in effect the central bank of the United States, created by the Federal Reserve Act of 1913 and charged with administering and making policy for the nation's credit and monetary affairs. Run by a seven-member board of governors appointed by the president (who also appoints its chairman), the system includes 12 Federal Reserve banks, 24 branches, all national banks, and many state banking institutions. Three major monetary tools are available to the Federal Reserve System to control the economy's supply of money and credit: (1) open-market operations, which, through the purchase or sale of government bonds, increase or decrease the availability of dollars to member banks; (2) discount-rate adjustments, which increase or decrease the interest rate charged to member banks for the money they borrow; and (3) reserve requirements, which, through changes in levels of reserve, increase or decrease the number of dollars a bank may make available for loan. Two less significant tools, moral suasion and selective controls over stock purchase margin requirements, are also used to help manage the economy.

open-market operations The purchase and sale in the open market by the Federal Reserve System of various securities, chiefly marketable federal government securities, for the purpose of implementing Federal Reserve monetary policy. Open-market operations, one of the most flexible instruments of monetary policy, affect the reserves of member banks and thus the supply of money and the availability and cost of credit.

others. This does not mean, however, that the money stock fluctuates greatly. It steadily increases. It is in the margin of the increase that **money supply** has its impact. Through the use of the two other tools, the Federal Reserve can attempt to affect investments and loans. First, it can change its discount rate—the interest rate it charges other banks for loans of money that these banks can use to make loans. Second, it can change the reserve requirement—the amount of money a bank must have on hand in comparison with the amount of money it may have out on loan.

Fiscal Policy

Fiscal policy consists of the manipulation of government finances by raising or lowering taxes or levels of spending to promote economic stability and growth. Stability and growth must be combined, since stability without growth is stagnation. The use of fiscal policy for economic objectives is a decidedly recent phenomenon. For the greater part of the 200-plus-year history of the United States, fiscal policy was not a factor. The national budgetary policy was premised upon expenditures equaling revenues (a balanced budget). In fact, with the exception of war years, budgeting before the 1900s was primarily an exercise in deciding how to get rid of excess revenues, generated primarily by **tariffs**. This is not to say that modern fiscal policies would not have saved the nation considerable distress from assorted recessions and depressions, but the nineteenth century held that the economy followed a natural order. The first major tampering with the natural order of things came in 1913, with the advent of the federal income tax and the establishment of the Federal Reserve System. The Great Depression of the 1930s, along with the initiation of Social Security and unemployment compensation programs, provided the first recognition of the need for a national economic policy. However, legitimization of the goal of a national economic policy came with the passage of the Full Employment Act of 1946. The act not only created a **Council of Economic Advisers** for the president, but it prescribed objectives for economic prosperity and charged the president with ensuring their achievement.

Basically, fiscal policy offers discretionary and built-in courses of action. Discretionary fiscal policy, which involves changing policy, has two major facets: the level of receipts and the level of expenditures. The major fiscal policy actions of recent years are replete with tax cuts and temporary reductions. Given the time lags involved in legislating tax changes, it is easy to see why presidents have preferred to

---

money supply The amount of money in the economy.

tariff A tax imposed on imported products. A duty is distinguished from a tariff solely by the fact that the duty is the actual tax imposed or collected, while the tariff, technically speaking, is the schedule of duties. However, in practice the words are often used interchangeably.

Council of Economic Advisers (CEA) The U.S. president's primary source of economic advice. It assists the president in preparing various economic reports, including the annual *Economic Report of the President*. Established in the Executive Office of the President by the Employment Act of 1946, the CEA consists of three economists (one designated chair) appointed by the president, with the advice and consent of the Senate, who formulate proposals to "maintain employment, production, and purchasing power." While council members are now usually professional economists, Congress initially objected to them and preferred practical businessmen.

wage fiscal policy battles in terms of government spending. The second dimension involves built-in fiscal stabilizers—that is, preset or automatic policy. These are the **transfer payments**, the **progressive tax** rates, and the changing federal budget deficits and surpluses that move automatically to counter economic downturns or to control excessive periods of demand and business activity. For example, as people are laid off from work in a recessionary period, payments for unemployment compensation mount automatically. This increases the federal budget deficit, which in turn stimulates the economy and moves to offset the economic downswing. If the economy heats up, both regular and overtime wages increase, fueling demand for goods and services and creating inflation. As personal income increases, however, more and more people move into higher tax brackets. Thus the tax structure functions as an automatic stabilizer by absorbing more personal income and restraining demand for goods and services.

✦ A CASE STUDY: SOCIAL SECURITY REFORM

Social Security is the popular name for the Old Age, Survivors, and Disability Insurance (OASDI) system established by the Social Security Act of 1935. At first, Social Security covered only retired private sector employees. In 1939, the law was changed to cover survivors when the worker died and to cover certain dependents when the worker retired. In the 1950s, coverage was extended to include most self-employed persons, most state and local employees, household and farm employees, members of the armed forces, and members of the clergy. Today, almost all jobs are covered by Social Security.

Disability insurance was added in 1954 to give workers protection against loss of earnings due to total disability. The Social Security program was expanded again in 1965 with the enactment of **Medicare**, which assured hospital and medical insurance protection to people 65 years of age and over. Since 1973, Medicare coverage has been available to people under 65 who have been entitled to disability checks for two or more consecutive years and to people with permanent kidney failure who need dialysis

Medicare The national health insurance program for the elderly and the disabled authorized by a 1965 amendment to the Social Security Act. The two parts of Medicare—hospital insurance and medical insurance—help protect people 65 years of age and over from the high costs of health care. Also eligible for Medicare are disabled people under 65 who have been entitled to Social Security disability benefits for 24 or more consecutive months (including adults who are receiving benefits because they have been disabled since childhood). Insured workers and their dependents who need dialysis treatment or a kidney transplant because of permanent kidney failure also have Medicare protection.

transfer payments Payments by a government made to individuals who provide no goods or services in return. All of the social welfare programs at all levels of government that provide subsistence income support are transfer payment programs. They are often referred to as *entitlement programs* because one becomes entitled to transfer payments if one meets criteria established by the authorizing legislation.

progressive tax Any tax that has people of greater wealth paying a larger percentage in tax than people of lesser means. Income taxes are often progressive.

treatment or kidney transplants. Amendments enacted in 1972 provided an automatic **cost-of-living adjustment**.

The biggest problem with Social Security is demographics. In 1950 the ratio of taxpaying workers to pensioners was 120 to one. In the year 2030 it will be two to one. This is why Social Security payroll taxes have risen from 1 percent in 1940 to 7.65 percent in 2002. (Of the 7.65 percent, 6.2 percent is for traditional Social Security pensions; the remainder goes to fund Medicare.) And that percentage is for both employees and employers—so it is double if you are self-employed.

Brookings Institution analyst Paul C. Light contends that if you want to understand American politics, you must first study Social Security. "Those who care about budget deficits must know something about the single largest program on the domestic ledger; those who care about electoral politics must know something about the central concern of older voters; those who care about trust in government must know something about the lack of confidence in Social Security among young and old Americans alike." Nevertheless, even with all its problems and deficiencies Social Security remains "the most important program for helping elderly women and minorities."

The critical importance of Social Security as an antipoverty program can be summarized with a few statistics. According to the Social Security Administration, in 2001 more than 90 percent of all citizens over age 65 received benefits. For 20 percent of them Social Security was their only income. For 33 percent it represented 90 percent or more of their income. And for 65 percent of them it represented 50 percent or more of their income. And that Social Security income in December 2002 averaged $983 a month for men and $740 a month for women. More than 46 million citizens currently rely on monthly Social Security payments. And they tend to be experienced voters!

Social Security is not a static program. Discussions to expand and contract it have been going on since its inception. For its first four decades it kept expanding with additional classes of workers being covered and new benefits added. The high watermark of this expansion occurred in 1972 when benefits started being automatically adjusted for inflation. But by the 1980s it had become obvious that something had to be done if the system was to retain its long-term viability. So in 1981 President Ronald Reagan appointed the bipartisan National Commission on Social Security Reform (known as the Greenspan Commission for its chair, Alan Greenspan). The commission's recommendations, which were signed into law in 1983, sought to make the system fiscally solvent by raising Social Security taxes from 5.4 percent to its present rate of 6.2 percent, taxing the benefits themselves to recover a portion of benefits paid out to higher income recipients, and gradually raising the age at which one could receive full benefits from 65 to 67.

In 2001 President George W. Bush, motivated as much by ideological zeal as actuarial necessity, appointed the President's Commission to Strengthen Social Security—a bipartisan 16-member group "to study and report recommendations to preserve Social Security for seniors while building wealth for younger Americans." Then Governor Bush had campaigned for president in 2000, pledging to take Social Security to its "logical

---

cost-of-living adjustment (COLA) An increase in compensation in response to increasing inflation. Some labor union contracts and some entitlement programs (such as Social Security) provide for automatic COLAs if inflation reaches predetermined levels.

conclusion" by allowing Americans to use part of their Social Security contribution to create "Personal Retirement Accounts." These accounts—unlike the current Social Security program, which provides benefits only for recipients, their spouses, and dependent minor children—would facilitate wealth creation. Similar in concept to Individual Retirement Accounts and 401(k) accounts, the accumulated assets could be inherited as they would be personally owned and not subject to the vagaries of politics.

President Bush followed up on his campaign promise by formally introducing a proposal in 2005 that called for reform of Social Security that included elements of privatization. In this excerpt from his 2005 State of the Union speech, Bush makes his case for the creation of voluntary personal retirement accounts:

> As we fix Social Security, we also have the responsibility to make the system a better deal for younger workers. And the best way to reach that goal is through voluntary personal retirement accounts. Here is how the idea works. Right now, a set portion of the money you earn is taken out of your paycheck to pay for the Social Security benefits of today's retirees. If you're a younger worker, I believe you should be able to set aside part of that money in your own retirement account so you can build a nest egg for your own future.
>
> Here's why the personal accounts are a better deal. Your money will grow, over time, at a greater rate than anything the current system can deliver—and your account will provide money for retirement over and above the check you will receive from Social Security. In addition, you'll be able to pass along the money that accumulates in your personal account, if you wish, to your children and/or grandchildren. And best of all, the money in the account is yours, and the government can never take it away.
>
> The goal here is greater security in retirement, so we will set careful guidelines for personal accounts. We'll make sure the money can only go into a conservative mix of bonds and stock funds. We'll make sure that your earnings are not eaten up by hidden Wall Street fees. We'll make sure there are good options to protect your investments from sudden market swings on the eve of your retirement. We'll make sure a personal account cannot be emptied out all at once, but rather paid out over time, as an addition to traditional Social Security benefits. And we'll make sure this plan is fiscally responsible by starting personal retirement accounts gradually and raising the yearly limits on contributions over time, eventually permitting all workers to set aside four percentage points of their payroll taxes in their accounts.

While there was considerable national debate on the merits of such accounts and how they might be gradually implemented, the commission issued its report at a most unfortunate time: at the end of 2001 when the United States was deep in a recession and the stock market's decline was so severe that it was being compared to that of the Great Depression. This more than anything else took the wind out of the sails of this proposal. Consequently, the whole matter of reform and the creation of personal accounts to be invested in the stock market was quietly dropped from the national agenda.

Since being introduced, Bush's plan for Social Security reform has met with great resistance in Congress, and its future remains uncertain. The only certainty is that reform efforts will continue. The current system is simply not sustainable. Once the **baby boomers** start retiring in 2008, the system will suffer from a significant decline in the number of workers paying into the system, with a corresponding significant number of new retirees demanding benefits. In 2003 James Lockhart, the deputy Social Security commissioner, presented these stark facts in testimony before the Senate Special Committee on Aging: "If the system is not overhauled, workers eligible for Social Security income in 2042 would see a 27 percent cut in promised benefits. In 2077, a 35 percent reduction in promised benefits would be required."

Obviously something must be done. But it is hard to muster the political will to deal with a problem that is still decades away. Both Presidents Bill Clinton and George W. Bush sought to reform the system. But Clinton, who once thought that Social Security reform would be part of his legacy to the nation, instead spent his second term lying about his Oval Office sexual escapades and fighting impeachment. Then his successor's reform efforts were sidetracked by a recession and the war on terrorism.

Only two facts remain: (1) reform must come, and (2) the sooner it comes, the less painful it will be. One prevalent suggestion is to gradually raise the retirement age to 70 but exempt those baby boomers who are about to retire. If no one feels any immediate pain, this fix for the system becomes more politically palatable.

---

baby boomers That age cohort born in the two decades after World War II. This group of almost 74 million people makes up about 25 percent of the U.S. population. The boom came about because population growth was suppressed for more than a decade, first by the Great Depression of the 1930s and then by the prolonged absence of men for the World War II effort. With the return of prosperity and of the men in the postwar period, a baby boom commenced. As the babies in the boom continue to grow older, their sheer numbers will continue to have significant sociological, economic, and political implications. The apex of the baby boom, which began in 1946, was the year between April 1, 1959, and April 2, 1960. More living Americans were born in that year than in any other. Since then, there has been a steady decline in the birth rate.

For Discussion: *Why will it be politically so difficult to achieve a consensus on reforming the Social Security program? Why is it that the baby boom generation is in effect forcing political leaders to reform the system sooner rather than later? Why has President Bush's proposal to partially privatize Social Security failed to attract support?*

Summary

Budgeting is the single most important decision-making process in public institutions. The budget itself is also a jurisdiction's most important reference document. In their increasingly voluminous formats, budgets simultaneously record policy decision outcomes, cite policy priorities as well as program objectives, and delineate a government's total service effort.

There are two basic kinds of budgets. The most common is the operating budget: a short-term plan for managing the resources necessary to carry out a program. Usually an operating budget is developed for each fiscal year. The second kind is the capital budget; it deals with planning for large expenditures such as bridges and buildings. Capital budgets typically cover five- to ten-year periods.

An executive budget is both a technical process and a physical thing. First it is the process by which agency requests for appropriations are prepared and submitted to a central budget office for review, alteration, and consolidation. Then it becomes a tangible thing, the comprehensive budget document for an executive branch of government that a jurisdiction's chief executive submits to a legislature for review, modification, and enactment.

General taxation (or a general property tax in the context of local government) is the most traditional means of financing public services. There are major differences between the federal and state-local revenue systems. The federal system has experienced a trend toward less diversity; over two-thirds of its general revenue is provided by the federal income tax and the several insurance trust funds (such as Social Security). State and local revenue systems, in contrast, depend on a greater variety of revenue sources (such as property taxes, income taxes, sales taxes, user charges, lotteries, and federal grants). While local governments still rely primarily on the property tax, their states—with a few exceptions—rely largely on the state personal income tax.

Deficit financing is a situation in which a government's excess of outlays over receipts for a given period is financed primarily by borrowing from the public. Politicians often view borrowing as politically preferable to imposing higher taxes. Borrowing is virtually invisible to the electorate. If the projects produced by it are impressive, politicians see a painless way of "buying" votes—especially when the proverbial chickens do not come home to roost until a subsequent administration.

Economic policy, the process by which a nation manages its trade, business, and finances, generally consists of three dimensions: (1) fiscal policy, (2) monetary policy, and (3) those other facets of public policy with economic implications, such as energy policy, farm policy, and labor union policy. While monetary policy basically exercises control over the quantity and cost (interest rates) of money and credit in the economy, fiscal policy deals with the sizes of budgets, deficits, and taxes.

Review Questions

1. Why is government budgeting—meaning the allocation of public resources—an inherently political process?

2. What are the goals and tactics of a budget-maximizing bureaucrat?

3. What is the difference between an operating budget and a capital budget?

4. Why has the executive budgeting process evolved to be the most common means by which public budgets are developed and approved?

5. How is the ability to pay principal incorporated into all progressive taxing systems?

Key Concepts

budget   A financial plan serving as a pattern for and control over future operations—hence, any estimate of future costs or any systematic plan for the utilization of the workforce, material, or other resources.

budget cycle   The timed steps of the budget process, which includes preparation, approval, execution, and audit.

budget process   The total system a jurisdiction uses to make decisions on government spending needs and how to pay for them. The main difference between federal and state-local budget processes is that the state and local jurisdictions must have balanced budgets each year.

budget surplus   The amount by which a government's budget receipts exceed its budget outlays for any given period.

capital budgeting   A budget process that deals with planning for large expenditures for capital items such as bridges and buildings.

deficit financing   A situation in which a government's excess of outlays over receipts for a given period is financed primarily by borrowing from the public.

executive budget   The budget document for an executive branch of government that a jurisdiction's chief executive submits to a legislature for review, modification, and enactment.

incremental budgeting   A method of budget review that focuses on the increments of increase or decrease in the budget of existing programs. Incremental budgeting, which is often called traditional budgeting, is a counter-school of thought to more rational, systems-oriented approaches, such as zero-based budgeting.

line-item budget   The classification of budgetary accounts according to narrow, detailed objects of expenditure (such as motor vehicles, clerical workers, or reams of paper) used within each particular agency of government, generally without reference to the ultimate purpose or objective served by the expenditure.

national debt   The total outstanding debt of a central government.

progressive tax   Any tax that has people of greater wealth paying a larger percentage in tax than people of lesser means. Income taxes are often progressive.

regressive tax   Any tax that has people with lower incomes paying a higher overall percentage of their income in tax than people of greater income. Sales taxes are examples of regressive taxes.

tax   A compulsory contribution exacted by a government for public purposes.

unified budget   The present form of the budget of the federal government, in which receipts and outlays from federal funds and trust funds (such as Social Security) are consolidated.

zero-based budgeting   A budgeting process that is a rejection of the incremental decision-making model of budgeting. It demands a rejustification of the entire budget submission (from ground zero), whereas incremental budgeting essentially respects the outcomes of previous budgetary decisions (collectively referred to as the budget base) and focuses examination on the margin of change from year to year.

Bibliography

Anderson, Martin. (1988). *Revolution*. New York: Harcourt Brace Jovanovich.

Basler, Roy P., ed. (1953). *The Collected Works of Abraham Lincoln*, vol. 2. New Brunswick, NJ: Rutgers University Press.

Blais, Andre, and Stephane Dion, eds. (1991). *The Budget-Maximizing Bureaucrat*. Pittsburgh: University of Pittsburgh Press.

Boettke, Peter J. (1992). "Friedrich A. Hayek (1899–1992)," *The Freeman* (August).

Buchanan, James, and Gordon Tullock. (1962). *The Calculus of Consent*. Ann Arbor: University of Michigan Press.

Caiden, Naomi. (1983). "Guidelines to Federal Budget Reform," *Public Budgeting and Finance* 3 (Winter).

Cassidy, John. (2000). "The Price Prophet," *The New Yorker* (February 7).

Dror, Yehezkel. (1964). "Muddling Through—'Science' or Inertia," *Public Administration Review* 24, No. 3 (September).

Frederickson, H. George. (1995). "Misdiagnosing the Orange County Scandal," *Governing* (April).

Galbraith, John Kenneth. (1981). *A Life in Our Times*. Boston: Houghton Mifflin.

Gingrich, Newt. (1995). *To Renew America*. New York: HarperCollins.

Gore, Al. (1993). Report of the National Performance Review, *From Red Tape to Results: Creating a Government that Works Better and Costs Less*. Washington: U.S. Government Printing Office.

Grieder, William. (1981). "The Education of David Stockman," *The Atlantic Monthly* (December).

Hayek, Friedrich A. (1944). *The Road to Serfdom*. Chicago: University of Chicago Press.

———. (1960). *The Constitution of Liberty*. Chicago: University of Chicago Press.

Hyde, Albert C., ed. (1992). *Government Budgeting: Theory, Process, Politics*. Monterey, CA: Brooks-Cole.

Kendall, James. (1955). *Michael Faraday*. London: Farber and Farber.

Key, V. O., Jr. (1940). "The Lack of a Budgetary Theory," *American Political Science Review* (December).

Lewis, Verne. (1952). "Toward a Theory of Budgeting," *Public Administration Review* (Winter).

Light, Paul C. (1985). *Artful Work: The Politics of Social Security Reform*. New York: Random House.

———. (1994). *Still Artful Work: The Continuing Politics of Social Security Reform*, 2nd ed. New York: McGraw-Hill.

Lynch, Thomas D. (1995). *Public Budgeting in America*, 4th ed. Englewood Cliffs, NJ: Prentice Hall.

Lynn, Jonathan, and Antony Jay. (1984). *The Complete Yes Minister*. New York: Harper and Row.

Miranda, Rowan. (1994). "Privatization and the Budget Maximizing Bureaucrat," *Public Productivity and Management Review* (Summer).

Musgrave, Richard R., and Peggy B. Musgrave. (1984). *Public Finance in Theory and Practice*, 4th ed. New York: McGraw-Hill.

Mysak, Joe. (1995). "Winking at Debt," *New York Times* (June 23).

Novick, David. (1968). "The Origin and History of Programming Budgeting," *California Management Review* 11 (Fall).

Owen, Jeffery G. (2003). "The Stadium Game: Cities Versus Teams," *Journal of Sports Economics* (August).

Phyrr, Peter A. (1977). "The Zero-Base Approach to Government Budgeting," *Public Administration Review* 37 (January–February).

Quinn, K., P. Bursik, C. Borick, and L. Raethz. (2003). "Do New Digs Mean More Wins?: The Relationship between a New Venue and a Professional Sports Team's Competitive Success," *Journal of Sports Economics* (August).

Schick, Allen. (1966). "The Road to PPB: The Stages of Budget Reform," *Public Administration Review* 26 (December).

———. (1973). "A Death in the Bureaucracy: The Demise of Federal PPB," *Public Administration Review* 33 (March–April).

———. (1977). "Budget Gap," *Public Administration Review* (September–October).

———. (1978). "The Road from ZBB," *Public Administration Review* 38 (March–April).

———. (1983). "Incremental Budgeting in a Decremental Age," *Policy Sciences* (September).

Shenk, J. W. (1995). "Hidden Kingdom: Disney's Political Blueprint," *American Prospect* (Spring).

Strop, Leigh. (2003). "Report: Social Security Deficit to Boom," *Washington Times* (July 29).

Suetonius. (1931). *The Lives of the Twelve Caesars*. New York: Modern Library.

Weiner, Tim. (1990). *Blank Check: The Pentagon's Black Budget*. New York: Warner Books.

Wildavsky, Aaron. (1969). "Rescuing Policy Analysis from PPBS," *Public Administration Review* 29 (March–April).

———. (1984). *The Politics of the Budgetary Process*, 4th ed. Boston: Little, Brown.

Willoughby, William F. (1918). *The Movement Towards Budgetary Reform in the States*. New York: D. Appleton and Company for the Institute of Government Research.

Recommended Books

Blais, Andre, and Stephanie Dion, eds. (1991). *The Budget-Maximizing Bureaucrat: Appraisals and Evidence*. Pittsburgh: University of Pittsburgh Press. Everything you need to know about bureaucratic empire builders and how to help them or thwart them.

Bland, Robert L., and Irene S. Rubin. (1997). *Budgeting: A Guide for Local Governments*. Washington: International City/County Management Association. A succinct survey of the theory, obstacles, and practicalities of budgeting at the local level; offers many examples of how budgets are assembled and what municipal budget manuals need to contain.

Mikesell, John L. (1995). *Fiscal Administration: Analysis and Applications for the Public Sector*, 4th ed. Belmont, CA: Wadsworth. The standard text on managing governmental funds.

Wildavsky, Aaron. (1992). *The New Politics of the Budgetary Process*, 2nd ed. New York: HarperCollins. The last update of Wildavsky's *Politics of the Budgetary Process* (initially published in 1964); one of the most influential books in the history of public administration.

Related Web Sites

Congressional Budget Office
www.cbo.gov/
Federal Reserve System
www.federalreserve.gov
Federation of Tax Administrators
www.taxadmin.org/
Government Finance Officers Association
www.gfoa.org
National Association of State Budget Officers
www.nasbo.org

State and local government budgets
www.ipma-hr.org/index.cfm?navid=144&id=767&tcode=nws3
U.S. Bureau of Public Debt
www.publicdebt.treas.gov
U.S. Office of Management and Budget
www.whitehouse.gov/omb/
www.whitehouse.gov/WH/EOP/omb
U.S. Treasury financial manual
www.fms.treas.gov/tfm/index.html

CHAPTER 14

Program Audit and Evaluation

•KEYNOTE: CAPTAIN BLIGH'S PROGRAM EVALUATION OF THE MUTINY ON THE *BOUNTY*

For more than two centuries the ultimate South Seas adventure story has been the tale of the *Bounty* and its mutiny. But this is no tall tale; there really was a mutiny on the *Bounty* in 1789. William Bligh, the captain, and Fletcher Christian, the mutinous officer, were real people. A trio of Hollywood's greatest character actors (Charles Laughton in 1935, Trevor Howard in 1962, and Anthony Hopkins in 1983) have played Bligh—first as a sadist, then as an overbearing bureaucrat, and finally as a frustrated corporate climber. They were paired with Fletcher Christians who were among the greatest romantic leads of their day (Clark Gable, Marlon Brando, and Mel Gibson). The dramatic tension between these two estranged friends is the core of the film, of the mutiny, and of the legend.

Bligh was chosen to be the ship's captain because he was a young officer with Captain **James Cook** when Cook visited Tahiti in 1777. Cook, before he was killed by the local residents of Hawaii, wrote that the breadfruit plant would be excellent food for the slaves of the British-owned West Indian plantations. This is why the Jamaican slave owners lobbied the navy for the voyage. Bligh was one of the very few naval officers in England who had actually been to Tahiti and knew the people there. Besides, Bligh's wife had an uncle who was one of the plantation owners who successfully lobbied the government for the voyage. The uncle then continued his lobbying efforts on Bligh's behalf. While his political sponsor brought Bligh's name to the forefront of consideration, there is no doubt that Bligh was as fully qualified for the command as any officer in England. The *Bounty* command was considered such a choice assignment, one that could really make one's reputation, that Bligh, then a merchant ship captain, accepted the job for a vastly reduced salary (from 500 down to 50 pounds a year) and at the rank of lieutenant. So while Bligh was the captain of the *Bounty,* he was only a lieutenant in the Royal Navy. Bligh then chose Christian because he wanted his friend from two earlier voyages to the West Indies along for the ride. Good company can be scarce on the high seas unless you plan for it!

The *Bounty*'s mutiny was in reality a pathetic little affair as mutinies go. While passions ran high, the decks did not run red with blood. The crew totaled 44, but only 12 of them were actually mutineers. Aside from Bligh's bruised ego, nobody was really hurt. No blood was shed, and no shots were fired. After much shouting, the mutineers put Bligh and 18 other men in a 23-foot lifeboat, fully expecting all of them to perish. But Bligh, in one of history's most remarkable feats of seamanship, sailed that tiny, overloaded craft 3,618 miles to the Dutch colony of Timor, in present day Indonesia. There he found passage home to England. Had Bligh and his lifeboat colleagues died, there would have been no mutiny in that the world would never have known of it. The *Bounty* would have just been presumed lost at sea—a common enough occurrence in those days.

The mutiny became a cause célèbre because Bligh's account of it, his program evaluation, *The Mutiny on Board H.M.S. Bounty,* was published soon after he returned to England in 1790. It was an instant best-seller, what with its tales of the exotic South Seas with casual sex, betrayal, and a desperate voyage of survival. Adding to the sensationalism was the simple fact that this kind of thing had never happened before in the Royal Navy. Mutiny was a word used for insubordination, for resisting or complaining about orders. But to take over—to steal—one of His Majesty's ships was unthinkable for two reasons. First, under the **articles of war**, mutiny was punishable by death. Second, there was quite literally no place in the entire world where one could hide from the enormous Royal Navy. Thus Christian and company could only have committed such an act because they were deranged by the allures of Tahiti. Bligh's account, being first,

James Cook (1728–1779) The explorer who first sailed English ships to Australia, New Zealand, Antarctica, and many Pacific islands. While visiting Hawaii he was killed—literally hacked to pieces—by locals who wished to discourage tourism.

articles of war The traditional laws governing the behavior of military and naval personnel. The United States used articles of war from 1775 to 1950 when they were superseded by the Uniform Code of Military Justice.

supported the derangement theory and forever defined the terms of the mutiny. He wrote, "The mutineers had flattered themselves with the hopes of a more happy life among the Otaheiteans [Tahitians] than they could possibly enjoy in England." Bligh's analysis for the underlying causes have been quibbled with and expanded upon but never subsequently refuted:

> The women at Otaheite [Tahiti] are handsome, mild and cheerful in their manners and conversation, possessed of great sensibility, and have sufficient delicacy to make them admired and beloved. The chiefs were so much attached to our people, that they rather encouraged their stay among them. . . . Under these, and many other attendant circumstances, equally desirable, it is now perhaps not so much to be wondered at, though scarcely possible to have been foreseen, that a set of sailors, most of them void of connections, should be led away; especially when, in addition to such powerful inducements, they imagined it in their power to fix themselves in the midst of plenty, on one of the finest islands in the world, where they need not labour, and where the allurements of dissipation are beyond anything that can be conceived.

A contemporary portrait of William Bligh (1754–1817), captain of the *Bounty.* Because the *Bounty*'s saga has lent itself so well to novels and movies, readers (and viewers) often forget that this story is a case study in public policy and, particularly, program evaluation. True, the *Bounty* was a Royal Navy ship, but she was built as a merchant ship, was commanded by an officer (Bligh) with years of experience in merchant ships, and was on a merchant ship's mission. Today, private corporations have the National Aeronautics and Space Administration put satellites in space for them. In the eighteenth century it was the Royal Navy that was on the cutting edge of technological and navigational skills, so it was quite reasonable that they would undertake such a "scientific" mission. The Navy was only being responsive to the request of influential planters in Jamaica. These West Indian businessmen just wanted a cheap source of fuel for their slaves. Believing that Tahiti, an island in the South Pacific, had a nourishing plant—breadfruit—that could thrive in their climate, they used all their considerable influence to get the Navy to do the job for them. Just like today's corporate executives, they lobbied their government to take on their breadfruit research and development costs. Governments, then and now, are happy to accede to such requests in the hope that a relatively small investment would engender substantial economic development and concomitant taxes. The absolute immorality of doing something designed to make slavery a more economically viable institution never occurred to the English colonists, the Royal Navy, or the crew of the *Bounty.* While the *Bounty* was not a slave ship, it nevertheless was on a slaver's mission. This mission gave the *Bounty* its name. Originally a merchant ship named *Bethia,* it was rechristened to reflect the king's "bounty" to his West Indian subjects—and their subject slaves.

Bligh knew that there would be a clash of cultures when his normally sexually repressed and especially sex-starved crew met the sexually liberated Tahitians. But after a few weeks at most, they would all be back at sea. The problem was that the *Bounty* stayed in Tahiti for almost six months—mainly because Bligh wanted to make sure that the breadfruit shoots had rooted properly so that they would survive the anticipated seven-month voyage to Jamaica. This delay gave the men time to establish extremely strong relationships with the local women. In his analysis, the "allurements of dissipation" that Bligh only hints at are the prime causes of the mutiny. Bligh saw nothing else amiss. As he wrote, "Had their mutiny been occasioned by any grievances, either real or imaginary, I must have discovered symptoms of their discontent, which would have put me on my guard." Modern audiences of the films about the mutiny often think the crew revolted because of Bligh's harsh discipline and frequent whippings. But this is looking at eighteenth-century management practices with twentieth-century eyes. Lash for lash, Bligh was actually far less harsh than other captains of his era. Statistical analysis of the number and severity of floggings shows that Bligh used corporal punishment sparingly. According to historian Sven Wahlroos, "It was not his physical cruelty but, rather, his humiliating tongue—in an era when a man's honor was more important than his life— that contributed heavily to the most famous mutiny of all time." A very strong case can be made that Bligh, far from being too harsh, was too lenient. He allowed the crew almost total freedom to cavort among the Tahitians both on shore and on ship. This is what made it impossible to reassert traditional discipline on the return voyage. But the imagery of the floggings and the pleasure the actors playing Bligh gave to his countenance during the floggings has made his name a byword for a seagoing **martinet**.

Bligh was an astute organizational climber. He was not about to let those who would lead a life of dissipation ruin his naval career. Knowing that any officer who loses a ship by mutiny would be **court-martialed**, he craftily started making his case, writing his program evaluation while still in the lifeboat. Any court-martial is essentially an evaluation of whether an officer has conducted himself appropriately. Bligh had. But he also knew he had to defend himself before three courts:

1. The formal court-martial, which he had every reason to believe would be a formality that would (and did) exonerate him
2. The informal court of naval opinion, which would determine whether he would ever be given another command
3. The court of public opinion

He won all three at first. He was acquitted by the court-martial; the navy kept promoting him (eventually to admiral) and giving him progressively more responsible assignments; and the public initially considered him to be a great hero. But two years later, during the court-martial of the few mutineers who were captured, new information surfaced that branded him a villain.

---

martinet A strict disciplinarian. The word comes from an inspector general in the army of France's Louis XIV, Jean Martinet, who was so despised for his spit-and-polish discipline that he was "accidentally" killed by his own soldiers while leading an assault in 1672.
court-martial A military court that tries members of the armed forces for violations of military law.

Without ever using the phrase, Bligh was a practitioner of the "defensive program evaluation." His assessment of the mutiny prevailed at first because there were no contemporary contradictory evaluations. British Prime Minister Winston Churchill once bragged during World War II that history would look kindly upon his actions because he, as a professional writer, intended to write it. Bligh was no Churchill, to be sure, but they both knew the advantages of writing the history in which you participated—before the other guy does.

However, Bligh was not completely forthcoming in his analysis. He only told of one of the reasons for the mutiny. According to naval historian Richard Hough, there were two other major contributing factors: Fletcher Christian's tender sensibilities and the fact that Bligh was overwhelmingly detested by everyone on board. Bligh seems to have been unusually obnoxious and bad tempered. He was the worst kind of **Theory X** manager, giving so many orders that they often contradicted each other. When the resulting foul-ups occurred, he tended to blame anyone but himself—and his blame was expressed by language so constantly obscene and insulting that it shocked—yes, shocked—sailors who were, as sailors, thoroughly experienced with obscene and insulting language. By constantly impugning the honor and integrity of every sailor and officer on board, he created a situation such that, when push came to shove, not one officer would take his side. A mutiny must be led by officers for the simple reason that only they knew how to navigate. There would be no point in taking over a ship if you couldn't go anywhere with it. This is why the focus of the analysis of the mutineers' motivation has been on Christian. The lower-deck men encouraged and supported him because they knew he had grievances, and they wanted to return to Tahiti. Indeed, Christian, as a gentleman, would have felt obligated to challenge Bligh to a duel because of his verbal abuses had they been on land.

Bligh was absolutely correct about there being nothing amiss for him to discover. The mutiny was less a plot than a spontaneous outburst. Christian was in despair over his relationship with Bligh. He was effectively suicidal and preparing to jump ship in a makeshift raft when a fellow crew member, noticing his preparations, said the men were "ready for anything." Thus the mutiny began spontaneously because Bligh's treatment of Christian had pushed him over the proverbial edge.

What happened on the *Bounty* in 1789 was no different from what seems to happen a few times each year in the U.S. Postal Service—an overbearing supervisor psychologically pushes a mentally delicate clerk too far. So the clerk comes to work one day with a gun and kills the supervisor, a few bystanders, and maybe himself. True, the mutiny was aggravated by the allures of Tahiti, but its underlying cause was less a matter of sadistic perversion than bad management. The single most significant management blunder was the absence of the squad of marines almost always assigned to naval ships. Marines in all major navies originated not as soldiers to be landed on hostile shores, but as jailers for the sailors. Unfortunately the *Bounty* was a small ship, less than 90 feet long by 24 feet wide. With a crew of 44 there was simply no room. Many

---

Theory X The traditional managerial assumptions that people dislike work and therefore must be coerced or threatened to put forth adequate efforts.

other naval ships visited Tahiti and other friendly Polynesian islands before and after the *Bounty.* They did not suffer mutinies, but they had marines.

And there was one other contemporary element to the *Bounty* mutiny. One of the most respected accounts of the mutiny, Richard Hough's *Captain Bligh and Mr. Christian,* suggests that its underlying cause was sexual harassment. This suggestion is a mixture of fact and speculation. It was fact that the traditions of the Royal Navy included "rum, sodomy and the lash." We know that the *Bounty* made ample use of rum and the lash. Because sodomy was a capital offense, it was never lightly discussed. According to Greg Dening, shipmates on Bligh's two earlier voyages with Christian "remarked on Bligh's infatuation with the active, charming young man [Christian] who had begged—for the experience of it—to join his crew even at no pay, so long as Bligh permitted him 'to mess with the gentlemen.'" It was a fact that Bligh showed extreme favoritism toward Christian—a favoritism that stopped as the return voyage began. The speculation is that the 26-year-old Christian was not the macho romantic portrayed by Hollywood but that he had a homosexual relationship with Bligh before Tahiti, which he was reluctant to resume after his Tahitian interlude. And all accounts of the *Bounty*'s odyssey, including Bligh's, agree that Bligh was the only member of the ship's company who did not have a sexual liaison with any of the Tahitian women. Hough concludes that Bligh's pressure on Christian to resume their previous, not unprecedented, relationship led to the angst that forced Christian over the mental edge. If so, he would not have been the last worker driven crazy by a sexually harassing boss.

A court-martial declared that Lieutenant Bligh was personally blameless for the mutiny. He was then promoted to captain and given another ship—this time with marines. He returned to Tahiti for a second cargo of breadfruit plants, which were successfully delivered to Jamaica in 1793. The irony of all this was that even after a successful second voyage, it did not do any good. The West Indian slaves did not like breadfruit and would not eat it. The whole program was a total failure except for the blockbuster movies, the more than 2,500 books published on the adventure, and the still-thriving Tahitian tourist industry.

Popular imagery aside, Captain Bligh's adventures conveniently provide modern public managers with five valuable lessons about the politics of program evaluation:

1. **Be first.** Bligh arrived back in England just as promptly as he could. His account of the mutiny, mostly written on his voyage home, was practically ready for the printer. The first evaluation of a major program defines the parameters and sets the tone for the others that inevitably follow. Bligh's assertion that it was lust—and not lashes—that motivated the mutineers has never been completely refuted. Even though many subsequent analyses have shown Bligh's leadership style to be a major contributing factor, his **spin** on events is still spinning.

---

spin Efforts by an administration or an individual political actor to manipulate the media to contain, deflect, and minimize an unraveling scandal or other embarrassing or politically damaging revelation. The purpose is to keep the situation from spinning out of control.

2. **Have friendly evaluators.** Your best friend at evaluation time is your own pen—or computer. Imagine a continuum with yourself at one end and your worst enemy at the other—and everybody else aligned according to their affection for you. It is far better to have an evaluation written by someone leaning toward you on that continuum. Is arranging for an evaluation to be biased in your favor cheating or simply effective **public relations?** Hey, we're not talking objective social science here; we are talking management survival. The methodologies naturally differ.

3. **Disseminate your evaluation.** Just as the old adage says that there is no such thing as bad publicity, there is no such thing as too much dissemination of an evaluation. It creates notoriety and fame. In the entertainment business it means that whatever you did, good or bad, someone will hire you or offer you a book contract. There is no way of assaying how much good Bligh's widely disseminated account of the mutiny did him, but this much is for sure. Honor after honor and high office after high office came to him. So it probably did a great deal of good. Besides, it proved he could write. To the extent that real life—and especially public policy and its administration—is an essay contest, he won. Fletcher Christian lost. His name has become a synonym for a disloyal officer in large part because he never told his side of the story. Had he returned to England and challenged Bligh to a duel of evaluations, he might have been hanged for it—but Bligh's honor would have been at least sullied.

4. **Don't tell all.** Bligh knew more about events leading to the mutiny than he put in his report. He knew he stayed in Tahiti longer than necessary. He knew that he had allowed shipboard discipline to become so lax that the decks were filthy and some of the sails had been allowed to rot from neglect. He knew much more about Christian's motivations and mental state than he admitted. His report did not lie about these things. It was just self-servingly less comprehensive than it could have been. Bligh, no more paranoid than many a manager today, knew he did not have to say bad things about himself because so many of his enemies would be happy to do that for him. And they did. The mutineers and alleged mutineers who were captured in Tahiti and returned in chains for court-martial gave a devastating indictment of Bligh's management style. Only thereafter did Bligh become in the public mind what we still think of as "a Captain Bligh."

5. **Impeach the integrity or methodology of critics—or simply ignore them.** Bligh's court-martial was **pro forma.** However, while Bligh was off on his second two-year breadfruit-to-Jamaica expedition, the ten members of *Bounty*'s crew who were

---

public relations The management of the public's perception of a political figure or an agency. Cunning politicos throughout the ages have instinctively practiced effective public relations. Some techniques are timeless. When William Shakespeare's Richard III wanted to enhance his seeming worthiness to be king among the masses, he conspicuously went about carrying a Bible. President Bill Clinton did the same when the Monica Lewinsky scandal broke in 1998. The following Sunday he went hand in hand with his wife to church while conspicuously carrying his Bible. The Bible, in addition to its other uses, is a time-honored public relations prop.

pro forma A Latin phrase meaning as a matter of form or a mere formality. The phrase applies to requirements or agreements that are presumed to have no real effect on behavior.

arrested in Tahiti were court-martialed in England. (Christian and the other muti-neers fled with the *Bounty* to Pitcairn's Island, where they remained for the rest of their lives.) The crew's account of events on the *Bounty* fleshed out Bligh's earlier evaluation to such an extent that Bligh lost his stature as a national hero. Edward Christian (Fletcher's brother) wrote a stinging rebuttal to Bligh's assessment in *A Short Reply to Captain Bligh's Answer* (1795). Bligh then published a pamphlet attacking his accuser's methodology and facts. Edward Christian then published a rejoinder pamphlet attacking Bligh's attack on him. The attacks by supporters of either side continue to this day.

If you think that the mutiny and the debate it has fostered are ancient history, con-sider that its essence reoccurs every day in the United States. The nation is a ship in which we all sail. Indeed, the "ship of state" is a nautical metaphor that has been used since ancient times. All citizens are obligated on the voyage of their lives to obey the shipboard laws. Many people, especially young men the same ages as the *Bounty* crew, "mutiny" by violating the law of the land. They steal. They kill. They rape. The same people who would defend Christian and company offer a similar defense for these new-style mutineers—they lived in an oppressive environment and were treated too harshly by those who were "in charge." Those who would defend Bligh, who feel that there can be no excuse for mutiny, today assert that there can be no excuse for break-ing the law.

To the extent that we as a society refuse to excuse crime and demand longer prison sentences under increasingly harsh conditions, we are all "Captain Blighs." The debate over *the* mutiny is really a debate over the legitimacy of mutiny itself. Christian supporters will find ways to rationalize crime, will seek to understand the motivation of the criminals, and will demand more ameliorative programs, such as increased public housing. Bligh supporters see no excuse for crime of any kind anywhere. To those who demand such things as more public housing as a preventive measure, they say that the nation has been on a public housing building boom since the 1980s—only these "public houses" are called jails.

For Discussion: *Was Bligh's published account of the mutiny and the events that fol-lowed a good example of the assertion made in Chapter 1 that public administration is an essay contest? Are Bligh's five lessons about the politics of program evaluation still valid today?*

What Is an Audit?

Bligh knew that upon his return to England he would be subject to an audit, a word derived from the Latin word *auditus*, meaning "a hearing." *Auditorium* re-tains this original meaning. Bligh's audit, because he was a naval officer, took the form of a court-martial. But even if there had been no mutiny, Bligh's conduct would have been audited—reviewed by his administrative supervisors. Today *audit* is used to refer to any independent examination, any objective assessment of something. In public administration *audit* refers to either of two common activities:

1. The official examination of a financial report submitted by an individual or organization to determine whether it accurately represents expenditures, deductions, or other allowances determined by laws and regulations; or

2. The final phase of the government budgetary process, which reviews the operations of an agency, especially its financial transactions, to determine whether the agency has spent its money in accordance with the law, in the most efficient manner, and with desired results.

In all cases an audit connotes comparison with some standard. Bligh knew that his behavior would be measured against that of other naval officers. Administrators expect that their performance will be compared to that of other administrators with comparable responsibilities. And financial statements are audited to determine when they are in accord with generally accepted accounting standards. The essence of auditing is measuring something against a good example in order to make a critical, evaluative judgment.

Virtually all modern organizations, from a local tennis club to the U.S. government, have auditors whose basic task is to certify that the financial accounts of the organization are correct. Auditing has become a major branch of the accounting profession, with complex professional standards and procedures for admission, practice, and reporting. Large accounting firms such as Price Waterhouse are widely known throughout the developed world. In themselves they are multinational organizations of substantial size and complexity. The audit certifications of such firms are attached to the formal financial reports of all major corporations. This independent examination of the financial accounts of organizations is a process designed to establish that they comply both with the law and with national accounting standards. These pictures of an organization's financial position are essential requirements for confident decision making by senior managers, by boards of directors, and by stockholders.

Multiple Applications

Audit continues to evolve. Many new applications of the term now exist besides its traditional use for financial reports. Thus it is possible to have a management audit—an independent examination of an organization's management posture (policies, practices, and performance of management within an organization)—or a performance or efficiency audit. An audit undertaken within a single organization may seek to combine elements of the financial audit, the efficiency audit, and the management audit. To such global intentions the term *comprehensive audit* is often applied.

The concept of independent audit has not been limited to financial and managerial issues. Many other kinds of independent assessments are also called audits. For example, an environmental audit may seek to examine compliance with environmental laws and sound environmental practices. An energy audit may seek to independently assess how an organization uses or wastes energy. Water or telecommunications audits may do the same to help an individual or organization reduce its utility bills. And a social audit may assess social issues within an organizational context. Audit processes have in common a focus on the present and the immediate past. When the social or environmental effects of a future proposal such as a new airport or highway are examined, they are usually referred to as a social impact, or environmental impact, statement. Logically we cannot audit something that has not yet happened, although it is often possible to analyze or predict future impacts.

Independent examinations—audits—of an organization's finances or performance can be conducted internally or externally, by an organization's own staff, or by outsiders from a public (meaning private sector) accounting firm. In government the outsiders could be an independent audit arm of government such as a comptroller general's office. Large organizations are normally subject to both internal and external auditors. An internal audit group, independent of line management and with a reporting line sufficiently high in the organization, may seek to provide management with objective advice quickly so that problems can be identified and rectified before they grow worse. The external auditor not only comes from outside but often reports outside as well—to elected representatives, stockholders, or whomever it is that holds ultimate responsibility for an organization's destiny. Often, an efficient internal audit unit can simplify and prepare the ground to make the work of external auditors quicker and more focused. Nevertheless, neither internal nor external auditors alone are likely to be adequate for a large and complex organization—especially in the public sector where accountability is critically important.

History of Auditing

Government auditing goes back to ancient times. There are records of a Chinese audit function in the eleventh century B.C.E. and in Athens in the fourth century B.C.E. Modern audits in government, though, really developed in the nineteenth century when the growth of public sector activities became so complex that an independent and objective assessment of financial management became essential. With huge sums of money moving around global empires in the nineteenth century, the opportunities for corruption were effectively limitless. In this context it made financial sense to create strong government audit units with clear links to the top of government. Great Britain created its Office of Comptroller-General in 1857. It had independent links to a Parliamentary Committee of Public Accounts and strong legislative backing to enforce access to accounts and the disclosure of information. The U.S. General Accounting Office was established in 1921. Headed by the comptroller general of the United States, it is an agency of, and reports directly to, Congress. However, there were many other examples of government audit in the United States earlier than this. The progressive reform movement early in the twentieth century fought, often quite successfully, for state and local governments to have an appointed civil service commission to curtail patronage abuses, as well as an elected controller/comptroller whose job it was to inhibit financial abuses.

The establishment of prestigious and relatively independent national audit organizations like the Comptroller and Auditor-General in Great Britain and the General Accounting Office in the United States helps the audit function to stand above corruption and apart from the political administration of the day. Often the prestige and renown of the individual in charge of an audit office can be important in personifying the integrity and credibility of the office—particularly when (as is inevitable) some of its findings turn out to be unpalatable to the ruling administration.

The Government Accountability Office

Today, most people assume that it is the president who is responsible for the performance and accountability of the federal bureaucracy. That was certainly not the case in the nineteenth century, when it was assumed that Congress had the overwhelming responsibility for the national administration. But when Theodore Roosevelt became president in 1901, he led a two-decade-long cry that the president be given greater authority. Finally, after a variety of high-level commissions endorsed the notion that the president be given significant administrative responsibility, Congress passed the Budget and Accounting Act of 1921. The first half of the act (the "budget") gave in to the reform advocates by creating a Bureau of the Budget in the Department of the Treasury. This new bureau was authorized to prepare an executive budget and was given additional staff to conduct continuing studies of efficiency. So long before the Bureau of the Budget was renamed the Office of Management and Budget in 1970, it had a significant management role.

Congress, however, was institutionally suspicious of presidential power. So the second half of the act (the "accounting") created the General Accounting Office (GAO) as a congressional support agency to audit federal government expenditures and to assist Congress with its legislative oversight responsibilities. Because these two agencies have become so central to the administrative well-being of the federal government, Herbert Emmerich in *Federal Organization and Administrative Management* has called their creation "probably the greatest landmark of our administrative history except for the Constitution itself."

The GAO, which officially became the Government Accountability Office in 2004, is directed by the comptroller general of the United States, who is appointed by the president with the advice and consent of the Senate for a term of 15 years. While the GAO originally confined itself to auditing financial records to see that funds were properly spent, since the 1960s it has redefined its mission to include overall program evaluation. Its responsibilities include conducting financial as well as performance audits of all federal government agencies. Indeed, it was always intended that it be so. The 1921 act specifically authorizes the comptroller general to "make recommendations looking to greater economy or efficiency in public expenditures." And "all departments and establishments" are required by the Act to turn over "any books, documents, papers or records" that the comptroller general "or any of his assistants or employees" requests. Long before President Ronald Reagan popularized the phrase "trust but verify" in regard to nuclear weapons treaties with the Russians, Congress was taking this attitude with the president. Think of the GAO as the "Office of Verification" for Congress. In a typical year the GAO completes around 1,000 major reports for the members of Congress.

Often the information provided by the Government Accountability Office is delivered to Congress in written reports that include specific recommendations. According to the GAO's own estimates, the agency made 2,700 recommendations to improve government operations between 2000 and 2004, with 83 percent of those suggestions being implemented. However, there are numerous occasions every year where GAO staff provide testimony to congressional committees (217 times in 2004) or provide formal briefings to members of Congress. The issues covered may concern conventional financial management, but often the scope of reports

> ### BOX 14.1   What's in a Name?
>
> In 2004, the 83-year-old General Accounting Office officially changed its name to the Government Accountability Office. While still going by the acronym GAO, this organization's name change could be considered an act of "truth in labeling." While accounting has always been an important role for the GAO, this function is just one aspect of the office's broad mission. According to its Comptroller General David Walker, only 15 percent of the GAO's workload deals with the area of accounting. In reality, the GAO has been much more involved with the evaluation and analysis of government programs than with keeping the government's books. An examination of the agency's personnel helps to demonstrate the multifaceted nature of the contemporary GAO. While you will still find CPAs among the GAO's staff, you are more likely to find economists, policy analysts, and lawyers inhabiting the agency's offices. The GAO's staff does conduct audits to make sure tax dollars are being spent appropriately, but more often its employees are engaged in projects that attempt to measure the efficiency and effectiveness of programs. For example, the GAO has been highly engaged in the evaluation of the Social Security system and other federal entitlement programs. In addition, the agency has been deeply involved in examinations of the logistics and resource allocation of the United States military in Iraq. In this capacity it has evaluated the effectiveness of such endeavors from the security of its position within the legislative branch of government. Thus the GAO of today is much more than a group of grizzled bean counters with accounting ledgers. Instead, it is the government entity that is responsible for making sure the country gets the most bang for its tax buck.
>
> SOURCE: Adapted from the GAO Web site, www.gao.gov/about/rollcall07192004.pdf.

and briefings goes to matters of vital policy import of which Congress might otherwise not have been aware. For example, in fiscal year 2004 the GAO reported to Congress on Social Security reform, defense department procurement, the use of private contractors in Iraq, military peacekeeping operations, the No Child Left Behind Act, the Defense of Marriage Act, the renewable energy policy, tax policy, computer policy, flu vaccinations, managing human resources, the United Nations Oil for Food program, and lapses in security at federal agencies. The scope of these topics illustrates how far removed a modern national audit agency is from the kind of green eyeshade, quill pen audit that existed in the past. These are truly adventures in public policy where the auditor is not so much a "private" as "public" detective and the client not a rich widow but Uncle Sam himself.

Despite the wide scope of policy and performance investigations that the GAO undertakes, financial management remains a central concern. On the revenue side, the GAO identifies many cases where government agencies are not pulling in the money owed. The GAO found out, for example, in one of its studies that the Internal Revenue Service is less likely to catch high-income people who do not file tax returns than lower-income people and that Medicare contractors were not bothering to recover monies owed by other insurers. On the expenditure side, each year brings new examples of waste identified by GAO—for example, how Stanford University had overcharged the Office of Naval Research or how inadequate controls over Department of Defense subcontractors cost the federal government millions of dollars each year. Overall the, GAO measured its financial savings to the government at $35.4 billion in 2003, or a $78 return on each dollar in its budget.

The GAO, with its $464 million budget and a staff consisting of 3,200 accountants, lawyers, engineers, and other employees, is the largest government auditing agency in the United States. The GAO is vast both in size and reputation. Its national visibility and reputation for institutional integrity has made it a model for other levels of government. Every major subnational government has its auditors. They range from the elected auditor general of a state government to the local accounting firm retained by a small school board. Indeed, the state-level auditor is effectively part of a plural executive, the *de facto* arrangement of most state governments, because most governors share executive authority with other independently elected officers, such as a secretary of state, treasurer, attorney general—or an auditor.

Types of Audit

The GAO in its *Standards for Audit of Governmental Organizations, Programs, Activities, and Functions* maintains that a comprehensive audit program should include the following three types of audit:

1. **Financial and compliance:** Determines (a) whether the financial statements of an audited entity present fairly the financial position and the results of financial operations in accordance with generally accepted accounting principles and (b) whether the entity has complied with laws and regulations that may have a material effect upon the financial statements.

2. **Economy and efficiency:** Determines (a) whether the entity is managing and utilizing its resources (such as personnel, property, space) economically and efficiently, (b) the causes of inefficiencies or uneconomical practices, and (c) whether the entity has complied with laws and regulations concerning matters of economy and efficiency.

3. **Program results:** Determines (a) whether the desired results or benefits established by the legislature or other authorizing body are being achieved and (b) whether the agency has considered alternatives that might yield desired results at a lower cost.

Compliance Audit

The oldest and most traditional form of auditing activity is known as a *compliance audit*. Here the auditor is looking for the extent to which, in the financial management of an organization, financial inputs have been managed in compliance with the law and accepted standards and conventions for the treatment of accounting information. In the past, a traditional compliance audit was embodied by the annual visit of the auditor to remote parts of the organization, where the auditor would check each entry in financial journals and ledgers, making sure that arithmetic and balances were correct and that no mistakes had been made. At the end of this process, the auditor would certify that the financial records were correct.

The value of this traditional form of audit is clear. Officials dealing with funds could not simply dispose of them as they wished, keeping no records or records that could not be understood. The advent of traditional auditing meant that every public official had to (1) expect and prepare for a regular visit by the auditor, (2) keep accounts in a manner officially prescribed (often by regulations), and (3) make those records available for the auditor's scrutiny. In some jurisdictions the audit might be accompanied by an inventory of stores and equipment—hence, the at times derisive references to compliance audits as involving the counting of paper clips. In fact, the compliance audit was and remains a powerful primary tool for preventing many types of corruption.

But compliance audits often go beyond financial reviews. Voluntary compliance is the basis of a civil society. No government has the resources to force all of its citizens to comply with all of the criminal and civil laws. Consequently, all governments are more dependent on compliance than they would ever like to admit. The best single example of massive voluntary compliance is the U.S. federal income tax system, which is essentially administered by self-assessment and voluntary payment. The much-dreaded audit by the federal government's tax-collecting agency, the **Internal Revenue Service,** is an assessment not just of whether a citizen has paid taxes due, but also of whether the taxes were calculated in the appropriate manner. Compliance auditing is also undertaken by funding agencies to judge whether a grantee is acting (i.e., spending its grant funds) in accordance with the granter's policies or preset guidelines. For example, the aptly named Office of Federal Contract Compliance Programs within the Department of Labor works to ensure that (1) there is no employment discrimination by government contractors because of race, religion, color, sex, or national origin; and (2) there is affirmative action to employ Vietnam-era veterans and handicapped workers.

But compliance auditing is inherently limited. Conceptually it is part of a control system that focuses on the "inputs" or resources used in administration, not the "outputs" or results. An organization might well be able to comply with the letter of the laws concerning accounting for public monies and yet seem to achieve nothing. By the 1960s government auditors at all levels became increasingly discontented with performing such a confined role, of effectively "fiddling while Rome burned," by concentrating only on financial transactions rather than looking at the overall performance of the organization.

Internal Revenue Service (IRS) The federal agency, established in 1862 within the Treasury Department, responsible for administering and enforcing the internal revenue laws, except those relating to alcohol, tobacco, firearms, and explosives (which are the responsibility of the Bureau of Alcohol, Tobacco, Firearms and Explosives). The IRS mission is to encourage and to achieve the highest possible degree of voluntary compliance with the tax laws and regulations. The IRS is the largest controller of information about financial data on private citizens. The potential for abuse of this data and of the tax system is ever present. For example, major scandals about using the IRS for political purposes erupted in both the Truman and Nixon administrations.

> ## BOX 14.2   Auditing Katrina
>
> As the federal government began to pour billions of dollars into the Gulf Coast area in the wake of Hurricane Katrina, the inevitable specter of financial wrongdoings appeared on the scene. Within months of the storm's landfall, reports of misuse of financial resources started to surface in the media. For example, a number of media outlets reported that contractors were being paid $2,500 for two hours of work putting up tarps. Not surprisingly, both Congress and the Government Accountability Office quickly began hearings and investigations into the management of disaster relief and reconstruction outlays. In November 2005, a House special committee held hearings about the use of federal resources in the Gulf region, with testimony from lead officials from the Department of Homeland Security, the Federal Emergency Management Agency (FEMA), and the Army Corps of Engineers. The testimony demonstrated the lack of control that these agencies maintained over the $60 billion in federal appropriations that had been directed to the recovery efforts. Department of Homeland Security's Inspector General Richard L. Skinner's statement before the committee was quite illustrative of the confusion that enveloped the situation in Louisiana and Mississippi: "Obligations are being made at a rate of $275 million a day, in an unstable environment and in an expedited manner. When you mix it all together, it is a potentially perfect recipe for fraud, waste, and abuse." These concerns were echoed in preliminary reports from the GAO that found the awarding of reconstruction contracts appears to be fraught with problems. For example, the GAO uncovered a $39 million sole-source deal for portable classrooms given to an Alaskan Native corporation with headquarters in North Carolina, when a Mississippi firm was willing to perform the work for about half the amount awarded. Given the long-term recovery effort necessary, it may be these findings are the tip of an iceberg that will keep government auditors and watchdogs busy for quite some time.
>
> SOURCE: Adapted from the *Washington Post,* November 3, 2005.

Performance Audit

The possibility of auditors extending their scope from assessing compliance with law and regulations to the wider role of assessing efficiency and effectiveness began to be discussed late in the 1960s. By 1972, the General Accounting Office was formally advocating adopting such a wider role. The GAO's enabling legislation had from the beginning given it the legal basis for this expansion of its mission. Efficiency and effectiveness audits are the two steps in the performance audit chain, but in practice they may be telescoped into a single performance or comprehensive audit of the organization. An efficiency audit compares the activities of an organization with the objectives that have been assigned to it. In a sense, an efficiency audit still entails a compliance notion—though it is now the extent to which the organization has complied with and realized its objectives that is being examined. Such an extension of the auditor's role is compatible with an instrumental view of administration, since it is implementation of the objectives set by political leaders that is being reviewed. They and their constituents want to know how responsive the organization has been to their will and how effective they have been in playing the instruments of state.

When the scope of audit is extended beyond the efficiency of an organization to its effectiveness, attention now turns from the extent to which politically set objectives have been achieved to the broader question of whether the objectives themselves were right in the first place. This further extension of scope has been controversial, since it places the auditor firmly in the role of policy evaluator. Is this an appropriate role for an auditor? Does it invite political controversy of a kind that might reflect on the independence of the audit function? If auditors criticize political leaders or suggest that government policies are inappropriate, the audit entity itself could lose the capacity to review programs in a way that will be perceived as not only objective but above the normal political fray. Effectiveness or performance auditing in government is thus an inherently political activity that must be dressed in apolitical clothes. It must be free of methodological bias as a matter of science at the same time that it is perceived to be free of political bias as a matter of strategy.

Internal Audit

So far we have focused on the audit of governmental programs and activities by external auditors, such as the Government Accountability Office. However, line managers are often reluctant to wait until an external examination finds problems in their organizations. It is therefore common to find internal audit groups within larger governmental organizations. Such groups need to have a reporting line high in the organization (such as to the chief executive officer or to an audit committee at the highest level). They need adequate clear authority and support as well as resources and the right to enter all parts of an organization. Internal audit functions vary in the tasks they pursue and the way tasks are assigned to them. Sometimes (especially if the organization is a major cash handler), they may need to have a significant compliance audit role. In other circumstances they can virtually serve as independent troubleshooters, providing early warning to top management of emerging problems. While any such internal audit unit must have an **audit program** showing what it intends to focus on, CEOs sometimes give substantial latitude to internal auditors to roam freely around the organization and to add items to their audit program without top-management approval. In this sense they function as **inspectors general**.

---

audit program The detailed steps and procedures to be followed in conducting the audit and preparing the report. A written audit program should be prepared for each audit, and it should include such information as the purpose and scope, background information needed to understand the audit objectives and the entity's mission, definitions of unique terms, objectives, and reporting procedures.

inspector general The job title (of military origin) for the administrative head of an inspection or investigative unit of a larger agency.

Internal auditors are always in danger of losing their independence to line management. To ensure that the degree of independence needed for effectiveness is maintained, three key principles must be observed:

1. Location outside line management
2. A high reporting line for audit results
3. Reasonable latitude in selecting assignments

There is a significant role in the public sector for private accounting firms serving as auditors. Large public corporations, especially those operating under corporations law, normally employ accounting firms in some or all of their audit functions. The Government Accountability Office itself, quite appropriately, has been audited by a private accounting firm (Price Waterhouse). There can be many occasions when such firms with their wide networks and expertise can play an invaluable role in public audit.

However, those who imagine that the whole of government audit can or should be placed in the hands of private accounting firms are in the minority. While public administration remains a large complex and specialized field, with its own framework of accountability leading back to democratically elected representatives, there will remain a need for specialist internal and external audit capacities, such as the Government Accountability Office, within government.

Program Evaluation

A program evaluation is the systematic examination of any activity or group of activities undertaken by government to make a determination about their effects, both short and long range. Program evaluation is distinguished from management evaluation (also called organization evaluation) because the latter is limited to a program's internal administrative procedures. While program evaluations use management and organizational data, the main thrust is necessarily on overall program objectives and impact.

Policy Analysis Is Not Program Evaluation

The terms *policy analysis* and *program evaluation* are often used interchangeably, but they mean different things. A policy analysis is a set of techniques that seeks to answer the question of what the probable effects of a policy will be before they actually occur. A policy analysis undertaken on a program that is already underway is more properly called a program evaluation. Nevertheless, the term is used by many to refer to both before- and after-the-fact analyses of public policies. All policy analysis involves the application of systematic research techniques (drawn largely from the social sciences and based on measurements of program effectiveness, quality, cost, and impact) to the formulation, execution, and evaluation of public policy to create a more rational or optimal administrative system. A formal program evaluation effort normally implies that a relationship of "arm's length" independence has been established between the program and those evaluating it. In-house evaluations, however well conducted, are likely to be suspected of special pleading on behalf of the agency concerned.

Of course, program evaluations have always been done by executives, legislators, and their captains. (Remember Bligh!) But as old government programs expanded and new programs were initiated in the 1960s, program evaluations came out of the shadows. By the beginning of the 1970s, it was generally conceded that many of the Great Society programs initiated during the Johnson administration were not working nearly as well as had been originally hoped. As these and other social programs came under increasing criticism, the field of program evaluation gained increasing prominence.

Aaron Wildavsky, in his 1972 *Public Administration Review* article "The Self-Evaluating Organization," provided an insightful discussion about the difficulties of evaluating public programs in a dynamic political environment. Wildavsky wrote that the "ideal organization would be self-evaluating. It would continuously monitor its own activities so as to determine whether it was meeting its goals or even whether these goals should continue to prevail. When evaluation suggested that a change in goals or programs to achieve them was desirable, these proposals would be taken seriously by top decision makers. They would institute the necessary changes."

But the problem with evaluation, according to Wildavsky, was that no matter how compelling the case for change, change was precisely what evaluation emphasized most and organizations abhorred most. Most public managers, he argued, are hard-pressed to cope with day-to-day operational demands, so they strive for stability—not constant reorder and reformulation. The costs of change had to be borne, too, and evaluation seldom considered this. Finally, since the most politically feasible organizational strategies would be ones that minimized disruption, managers would tend to resist or ignore evaluation.

Wildavsky's arguments notwithstanding, evaluation would not be denied. In 1967, Edward Suchman of Columbia University published the first major work on evaluation theory, *Evaluative Research*. Suchman's work argued that evaluation was essentially a field of study; that evaluative research and practice can and must be studied in a general context outside of evaluation applications in the various fields of specialization; and that evaluation was generic. *Generic?* Yes. But in whatever context it surfaced, it was also intensely political. Evaluation researcher Carol H. Weiss discovered these four "less legitimate"—meaning wholly political in the worst sense of the word—reasons for evaluation:

1. **Postponement:** The decision makers may be looking for ways to delay a decision. Instead of resorting to the usual ploy of appointing a committee and waiting for its report, they can commission an evaluation study, which takes even longer.

2. **Ducking responsibility:** Sometimes one faction in the program organization is espousing one course of action and another faction is opposing it. The administrators look to evaluation to get them off the hook by producing dispassionate evidence that will make the decision for them. There are cases in which administrators know what the decision will be even before they call in the evaluators, but they want to cloak it in the legitimate trappings of research.

3. **Public relations:** Occasionally, evaluation is seen as a way of self-glorification. Administrators believe that they have a highly successful program and look for a way to make it visible. A good study will fill the bill. Copies of the report, favorable of course, can be sent to boards of trustees, members of legislative

committees, executives of philanthropic foundations who give large sums to successful programs, and other influential people. . . . The program administrators' motives are not, of course, necessarily crooked or selfish. Often, there is a need to justify the program to the people who pay the bills, and they are seeking support for a concept and a project in which they believe. Generating support for existing programs is a common motive for embarking on evaluation.

4. **Fulfilling grant requirements:** Increasingly, the decision to evaluate stems from sources outside the program. Many federal grants for demonstration projects and innovative programs are tagged with an evaluation requirement—for example, all projects for disadvantaged pupils funded under Title I of the Elementary and Secondary Education Act are required to be evaluated. . . . To the operators of a project, the demands of starting up and running the new program take priority. Plagued as they often are by immediate problems of staffing, budgets, logistics, community relations, and all the other trials of pioneers, they tend to neglect the evaluation. They see it mainly as a ritual designed to placate the funding bodies, without any real usefulness to them.

Legislative Program Evaluation

The General Accounting Office (now known as the Government Accountability Office), under the leadership of **Elmer Staats,** also helped elevate the general quality and value of program evaluation by setting evaluation standards and working actively to professionalize program evaluation as part of the **expanded scope of auditing.** Many state governments would initiate legislative evaluation commissions based on the GAO idea. Some state legislatures—most notably Hawaii, Wisconsin, and Michigan—have organized separate program evaluation staffs similar to the GAO. Another method used by state legislatures is that of the legislative commission. New York's Legislative Commission on Expenditure Review pioneered this concept, whereby a separate program evaluation staff, under an executive director, reports to the joint leadership of the legislature. New Jersey, Illinois, and Virginia now use variations of this theme. A third format exists whereby the evaluation function is located in a discrete committee that is linked to the several appropriations committees. Connecticut and North Carolina offer examples of this.

In 1976, Colorado, after a major lobbying effort by **Common Cause,** would become the first state to enact a sunset law—the requirement that government agencies and programs have termination dates. Many other jurisdictions subsequently enacted them as well. They require formal evaluations and subsequent affirmative legislation if the agency or program is to continue. Although the purpose of a finite life

---

Elmer Staats (1914–) The comptroller general of the United States from 1966 to 1981.

expanded scope of auditing Evaluating the results and effectiveness of a government activity in addition to delving into the traditional financial compliance concerns of auditing.

Common Cause A Washington, D.C.-based public interest lobby founded in 1970 and devoted to making public officials more accountable to citizens and to improving government performance.

span of, say, five years is to force evaluation and to toughen legislative oversight, the effect is to subject programs to automatic termination unless the clock is reset. Despite its widespread popularity, such time bomb evaluation is not without risks. There are limits to the abilities of any legislature's staff to do the kind of thorough evaluation required to make sunset meaningful. And, of course, the political reality is that the evaluation might become a tool of bipartisan infighting. Requiring organizations to submit evaluation data for review and to justify their programs may amount to little more than burying the legislature in an avalanche of insignificant paper—something at which agencies have a demonstrated prowess. Furthermore, some agencies, such as police, prisons, and mental health institutions, will be rightly skeptical of the chances of their programs being shut down. Nevertheless, by the mid-1970s evaluation was—and remains—a vital and integral part of public administration.

Types of Evaluation

There are many types of program evaluation and many perspectives from which it can be undertaken. For example, an *ex ante facto* evaluation, such as an environmental effects statement, might seek to assess the impacts and outcomes of a program before that program is implemented: Should the outcomes or impacts identified prove problematic, such a study may lead to a program being aborted, or at least significantly modified. A process evaluation may examine aspects of a program's operations while they are in place, and its results may be absorbed directly into the organization's management processes. An *ex post facto* evaluation, postmortem, or debriefing looks at a program or operation after it has been completed, and it has particular relevance when the nature of an activity is iterative, like dealing with a forest fire emergency, or a serious heat wave such as the one in Chicago in 1995 that claimed hundreds of lives. Such studies seek to establish the changes to policy, infrastructure, or operations that would allow a similar circumstance to have more positive results when it next occurred.

Perspectives in program evaluation also vary according to the discipline or paradigm from which they are conducted. Managers will usually think in terms of managerial paradigms and look at the nature and appropriateness of objectives, and the efficiency and effectiveness with which objectives were pursued. Lawyers may stress issues such as authority, compliance, equity, process, and culpability in examining an issue. A political analysis may look at issues of representation and accountability. Clearly, the purpose of undertaking the evaluation needs to determine the kind of evaluation to be adopted and the skills required in the evaluation team. Other decisions will include the type of supporting data and research to be used (and the provision of a budget to fund it); the extent to which there will be public hearings or consultations as part of the evaluative process; and whether there are hidden agendas to continue, terminate, or transform the program.

The zealous evaluator has one cardinal principle: Everything is evaluatable. There are no exceptions. However, many a public manager, while agreeing that most programs are evaluatable, will also argue that there are plenty of exceptions. In actuality, it is more a question of degree. Some programs have a high degree of "goal ambiguity"—a quality that can greatly inhibit evaluation. The public sector, because it tends to provide services rather than produce products, has always had more difficulty in defining its output—in measuring its goals. Further complicating matters is the fact that the different functions of government invariably involve different types of evaluation measurement. In evaluating highways we can focus on accidents, injuries, and fatality rates, which seemingly represent hard data; but the "data" quickly becomes soft once we move to such functions as parks, mental health, services for the elderly, education, and training programs for the unemployed.

Evaluation Standards

Generally speaking, evaluations refer to three standards against which a program can be evaluated: (1) compliance, (2) efficiency, and (3) effectiveness/relevance. These standards indicate the fundamental questions that must be asked of any program.

The first category of questions, compliance, essentially asks an auditing question: Are government business transactions being conducted in accordance with law? This can be broken down into more specific questions:

1. Were all financial transactions involving the acquisition and expenditure of resources consistent with legislative and administrative authorization/regulation?
2. Are financial records and statements rendered in accord with prescribed accounting standards?
3. Are they accurate and free from fraud?

Most evaluations for ensuring compliance on a regular basis are performed by various audit and control units.

BOX 14.3 The Bad News of Program Evaluation

The Book of Exodus in the Bible tells the story of Moses leading the tribes of Israel from bondage in Egypt to the shores of the Red Sea. Looking behind him, he saw the rapidly approaching army of the Egyptians and, naturally, became concerned. Looking then to the heavens, he called out for assistance. A voice from above promptly answered, "Moses, not to worry, for I have good news and bad news."

Moses replied, "Tell me quickly, for the army grows nearer."

The voice answered, "The good news is that when you raise your staff to the sky, the Red Sea will open, creating a path for your people to cross over in safety. Then the walls of the sea shall come crashing down and destroy the pursuing soldiers."

Moses, "Why, that's marvelous. But what's the bad news?"

The voice replied, "The bad news is that you will first have to prepare an environmental impact statement."

Questions of efficiency can be asked: Are government agencies getting optimum productivity out of the resources that they expend? More specific questions can be asked:

1. Is responsibility for specific tasks clearly delegated?
2. Are employees adequately qualified to perform their tasks?
3. Is the waste of resources being avoided?

Efficiency evaluation can also be readily used for comparative analysis: pitting various units, regions, or similar organizations against each other to ascertain who is more efficient and, conversely, who is less. But sometimes this kind of competition can prove counterproductive. For example, Jay Shafritz, Albert Hyde, and David Rosenbloom tell the story of a GAO audit of the U.S. Postal Service. After a new **postmaster general** sought to foster competition among post offices by generating a list of top offices in productivity, the Postal Service's productivity and mail volume appeared to increase nationwide. After starting at the bottom of the list, the Washington, D.C., post office reported consistently increasing mail volumes and productivity until it ranked at or near the top. The Postal Inspection Service estimated that the total amount of mail handled was inflated more than 60 percent. Sometimes the totals were overstated by as much as 110 percent. According to the GAO, these estimates were "supported by hours of videotape records showing individuals reweighing the same mail over and over to inflate volumes and by sworn statements from supervisors and employees admitting record falsification." The GAO concluded that "the most common reasons given by employees for participating in the fabrication were the pressure from higher management to achieve production levels that were unrealistic and a belief that their careers would suffer if these productivity levels were not met." Now "pressure for increased productivity" can be added to the list of all-purpose excuses such as "the devil made me do it" and "the dog ate my homework."

But it has been the third category of questions, those concerning effectiveness, that seem to now dominate the program evaluation environment. Questions of effectiveness ask, "Is the expenditure of government resources for a specific purpose contributing sufficiently to the achievement of that purpose?" This general question then can in turn be subdivided:

1. Are the various purposes involved in a program compatible?
2. How much of a reduction has there been in the problem?
3. Could the commitment of additional resources to the program have brought about significantly greater advances toward the objectives?
4. What would have happened if the program had not existed?

Despite the close relationship between the effectiveness and efficiency aspects of a program's operations, they can have an inverse relationship to one another. Thus it is possible to have a program that is relatively inefficient but nonetheless

---

postmaster general The chief executive officer of the U.S. Postal Service appointed by its nine-member board of governors.

effective (it squanders resources but nevertheless gets the job done) or one that is relatively efficient but ineffective (it may use its resources optimally but nevertheless has little impact on the problem it was designed to ameliorate).

Management Control: Evaluation in Microcosm

Control is that aspect of management concerned with the comparison of actual versus planned performance, as well as the development and implementation of procedures to correct substandard performance. Control, which is inherent to all levels of management, is a feedback process that ideally should report only unexpected situations. Some management control systems regularly report critical indicators of performance so that management will have advance notice of potential problems.

As we have seen, audits and evaluations provide important perspectives through which managers and elected officials may make evaluative judgments about the efficiency and performance of programs and organizations. However, it is not the only such perspective. On a day-to-day basis, within the organization, the manager must receive continual feedback, make judgments, and exercise corrective and directive control. Herbert Kaufman, in *Administrative Feedback: Monitoring Subordinates' Behavior,* notes that not all feedback is welcome. When organizations are rife with corruption, as is all too often the case with public administration, leaders "may resort to the strategy of discouraging feedback about administrative behavior because they privately approve of the behavior they know they should, according to law and morality, prevent." Such leaders want to be managers, but most specifically do not want to appear to be "in control" in case "a pattern of offenses by subordinates is disclosed." They want to be able to make "a credible claim that they, too, were victimized" by their organization's ne'er-do-wells. This is the tactic of the police chief (played by Claude Rains) in the 1941 movie *Casablanca* who was "shocked, shocked!" that gambling had been going on (as he pocketed his winnings) in Humphrey Bogart's nightclub.

Management control exists to ensure that managers are made aware on a day-to-day basis of developments within their program or organization so judgments and corrective actions can be taken. The process can be described as "evaluation in a microcosm." As with formal, external evaluation, the manager is likely to have strategic objectives in mind and to be forming progressive but increasingly formed judgments about the extent and rate at which objectives are being achieved. If they are not being achieved, or being achieved too slowly or in the wrong way, the manager will often "exert control" by stepping in and providing program managers with direction. The nature of this direction will reflect management style and the gravity of the position. It may range from a facilitative discussion of available options to a stormy injunction to "shape up or ship out."

Often the audit process focuses on assessing the adequacy of management control systems as a whole. Effective control seeks to ensure that all members of an organization are working together toward organizational objectives. It should provide an early warning system if strategic assumptions are wrong or if the environment has changed. An effective management control system will deploy many of the tools of longer-term evaluation; that is, it will involve references back to goals and objectives, the selective use of performance standards and performance measures to see whether and how well objectives are being achieved. It will also use informal networks and the **grapevine,** which helps to provide timely information and knowledgeable hunches as to what is happening "in the trenches." A framework of control that is well conceived, uses timely information, and is flexible can help the program or organization to avoid disaster. On the other hand, if the system of management control is heavy-handed, based on poor or incomplete information, and excessively rigid, it can frighten out innovation and fail to perform its key task of short-term evaluation and correction. This is what happened with the space shuttle *Challenger* disaster (see Chapter 2).

Evaluation and the Democratic Process

One of the distinguishing features of public administration in democratic societies is the extent to which government is conducted in a "fishbowl." The electorate and elected members of legislatures expect to be able to see clearly how governmental programs and organizations are functioning in "real time" so that policy adjustments and changes in direction can be made—and so that debate can occur about the practicalities of program implementation as well as about the theoretical niceties of policy.

Executive branch internal evaluations—essentially "self" evaluations—are normally incorporated into the management process. More and more budget offices are undertaking this role. Agencies need to be sure that they are accomplishing their objectives, that they are making progress. Of course, this "thirst" for evaluation may be induced from various motives. The noblest is the good management practice of assessing progress so that problem areas can be identified and remedial action taken. Equally necessary, though considerably less noble, are program evaluations undertaken for political considerations. A common gambit here is the "defensive program evaluation," whereby possibly controversial programs are evaluated to create, in effect, "good" report cards to show legislative committees or at least to provide some counterarguments against evaluations by others that might produce less-favorable results. This is what Captain Bligh instinctively knew he had to do. As a program evaluator, he was far ahead of his time!

The processes of audit and evaluation in government, and indeed many aspects of the exercise of day-to-day management control within public organizations, are no longer conducted in the expectation of secrecy. Rather, the expectation is that decisions and actions are likely to be publicly audited, evaluated, debated, and discussed. Sunshine laws exist to this end. Many state and local governments have such laws. The federal government's Sunshine Act of 1977 requires all independent regulatory commissions to give advance notice of the date, time, place, and agenda of their meetings. Closed meetings are allowed if circumstances warrant, but citizens have the right to take agencies to federal court if they feel that closed meetings were not justified. On the whole, this is a healthy development likely to weigh against corruption and incompetence, which fester best in dark places. Yet it must be acknowledged that the

---

grapevine The informal means by which organizational members give or receive messages. The word is derived from the practice of stringing early telegraph wires from tree to tree in a vinelike fashion.

weight and extent of accountability, evaluation, and scrutiny do impose costs on public administration. These encompass both the direct costs of documenting actions and making information available to inquiries through written or oral testimony, and also the more subtle constraint accountability may impose on spontaneous and flexible decision making. There will be times when administrators take the decision that can best be defended during audit and evaluation, rather than the judgment that is the wisest and best response to a problem.

Despite their imperfections, the systems of audit and evaluation within the public sector form part of the foundations of the public's trust in government. It is the ethical responsibility of public administrators to both improve and facilitate them. After all, as **Alice Rivlin** wrote in her now classic work *Systematic Thinking for Social Action*, "Put more simply, to do better, we must have a way of distinguishing better from worse."

✦ A CASE STUDY: JEREMY BENTHAM, THE PHILOSOPHER OF POLICY ANALYSIS AND PROGRAM EVALUATION

The ancient Greek philosophers and the political analysts that they inspired over the next two millennia were concerned with grand theories of the state and governance, of war and peace, and of power and politics. But with the rise of cities, with the advent of a merchant or middle class, and with the new problems and opportunities brought about by the industrial revolution, things had to change. Governments had to get increasingly involved with the minutiae of public policy and its administration. Someone had to start thinking about the relatively small issues, less about war and peace and more about how best to collect taxes, build sewers, and design prisons. This is where Jeremy Bentham (1748–1832) comes in. He was a one-man think tank for a great many of the petty details of governance. In consequence he is considered one of the founders of the practice—indeed, the science—of policy analysis.

Bentham was often referred to as a child prodigy because he was reading English by age 3, Latin by 4, and French by 6. At 12 he was sent off to Queen's College, Oxford, graduated in 1763, and immediately undertook the formal study of law. The family hoped he would join his father in the family legal business. But, upon hearing the lectures of the leading legal scholars of the day, he became disillusioned and disappointed with English law—but not discouraged. While called to the **bar** in 1769, instead

---

bar The once real but now imaginary partition across a court; lawyers stood at this bar to argue their cases. Thus to be "called to *the* bar" meant that you were thought to be enough of a lawyer to plead a case in court.

Alice Rivlin (1931–) The Brookings Institution economist and authority on fiscal policy and program evaluation who became the first director of the U.S. Congressional Budget Office in 1974. During her eight years as head of the CBO, she saw that agency earn a reputation for accurate fiscal and budgetary projections. She served as Director of the Office of Management and Budget from 1994 to 1996.

of practicing law, he decided to devote his life to reforming it. By "it" he meant both the established doctrines of the law as well as the laws themselves. While the life of a reformer seldom pays well, he worried not—especially after his father died and left him independently wealthy. Even today the life of the mind is ever so eased by a healthy inheritance.

Bentham is best known as the British philosopher who held that self-interest was the prime motivator and that a government should strive to do the greatest good for the greatest number. He wanted institutions to justify themselves on the practical grounds of the level of useful welfare achieved. He was thereby the prophet of the movement called Utilitarianism, which held that an action is right if and only if its performance will be more productive of pleasure than pain, more productive of happiness than unhappiness—than of available alternatives. In his best-known book *Introduction to the Principles of Morals and Legislation* (1780), Bentham wrote that "nature has placed mankind under the governance of two sovereign masters, pain and pleasure. It is for them alone to point out what we ought to do, as well as to determine what we shall do."

By using the principle of utility to explain all human motivation, Bentham felt he had found the key to a science of human welfare. The overall welfare of a society would be measured by how well off were each of its members. Thus governments, through their policies, should strive to achieve the "greatest happiness for the greatest number." This was not an attitude that endeared him to the British aristocracy who, as a class, were determined to keep themselves happy at the direct expense of the lower social classes. But the French were so pleased with Bentham's egalitarian musings that in 1792 he was made an honorary citizen of the fledgling French Republic. Those French revolutionaries regarded him as one of their own.

By holding that governments were created because of man's desire for happiness and not by divine intervention, Bentham antagonized both the monarch and the church—which denounced utilitarianism as "godless philosophy." His beliefs, writings, and actions made Bentham the major intellectual force behind social reform in nineteenth-century England. What actions? Bentham, a truly gentle man, was an intellectual agitator. He bought a house in Westminster near the British Houses of Parliament. He named his house "Hermitage" and there, unmarried, he devoted his life to writing and reform. On virtually every day of his life he wrote about 15 pages of proposals for and commentary on legislation. He was conveniently located to frequently entertain—rather educate—members of both Houses of Parliament. Not only was he a one-man think tank, he was a one-man lobbying organization. Ultimately, he succeeded in that his ideas, premised on their utility, contributed to all the major social and legal reforms in nineteenth-century Britain.

The difference between Bentham and other would-be reformers was that Bentham sought to develop techniques to deal with policy questions—techniques that others could use to apply to yet unknown problems. In effect, Bentham's patrimony is so great because he was the first methodologist in policy analysis. He showed the way to find a way.

Bentham admittedly did not originate the principle of utility, which can be traced back to the ancient Greeks. He first read of it in Joseph Priestley's 1768 *Essay on the First Principles of Government.* However, he was the first to rigorously and mathematically apply the principle to current and proposed public policies. Bentham was the first to empirically examine public policy problems, to use the investigation of social facts as a justification for reforming the law on a matter. A hundred years later this would be called a Brandeis brief, a legal argument that takes into account not only the law but the technical data from social or scientific research that have economic and sociological implications for the law as well as society. This kind of legal argument was pioneered by Louis D. Brandeis (1856–1941), who later served on the U.S. Supreme Court (1916–1939). It was a Brandeis brief, for example, that helped win the 1954 *Brown v. Board of Education* case, when, with testimony from psychologists about the effects of segregation on black children, the lawyers for Brown proved that separate education facilities were inherently unequal. "Bentham brief" would be the more intellectually honest phrase.

Bentham demanded that all laws and policies answer the question "Who benefits?" And if the proposal didn't meet his test of the "greatest happiness for the greatest number," then it was not deserving of enactment. Above all, Bentham urged practical, pragmatic solutions to the problems of crime, education, welfare, and public health, among others. He felt that he had a genius for legislation, for recommending new policies that should be enacted into law—which is exactly what he spent his life doing. And he demanded that legislators be guided not by their party but by his principle of utility. To do otherwise is to be dishonorably immoral. That is why his most influential work is called *An Introduction to the Principles of Morals and Legislation*. After all, the whole point of legislation is to do the moral, the ethical, thing. Isn't it?

For Discussion: *Is Bentham's criterion for a successful program as one offering the "greatest happiness for the greatest number" still valid as the underlying basis for a program evaluation? Is Bentham's principle of utility still visible in current social legislation and public administration practices?*

Summary

Organizations have auditors whose basic task is to certify that financial accounts are correct. New applications of auditing have evolved beyond this traditional meaning. Thus it is possible to have a management audit, a performance audit, or an efficiency audit. An audit undertaken within a single organization may seek to combine multiple auditing elements. Such efforts are called comprehensive audits.

A comprehensive audit program typically includes three types of audit: (1) financial and compliance, which determines whether the funds were properly spent and whether the law was complied with; (2) economy and efficiency, which determines whether resources have been used economically and efficiently; and (3) program results, which determine whether desired results have been achieved. The establishment of relatively independent audit organizations has helped the audit function to stand above corruption and apart from the political administration of the day.

Policy analysis and program evaluation are often confused and are often used interchangeably, but they are not the same. A policy analysis is a set of techniques that seeks to answer the question of what the probable effects of a policy will be before they actually occur. A policy analysis undertaken on a program that is already in effect is more properly called a program evaluation. Evaluations refer to the standards against which a program can be evaluated: compliance, efficiency, and effectiveness/relevance. These standards indicate the fundamental questions that must be asked of any program.

Review Questions

1. Why is an audit so often considered to be the final phase of a budgetary process?
2. What is the mission of the U.S. Government Accountability Office?
3. What is the difference between a formal compliance audit and a performance audit?
4. What organizations undertake governmental program evaluations, and why do they do it?
5. Are program evaluations more likely to be undertaken for political or for managerial reasons or for both?

Key Concepts

audit   An independent examination, an objective assessment of something; typically the financial reports of an individual or organization to determine whether they accurately represent expenditures and are in compliance with accounting standards and laws.

compliance audit   The traditional form of auditing where the auditor is looking for the extent to which an organization's funds have been managed in compliance with the law and that accepted standards and conventions for the treatment of accounting information have been used.

evaluation research   An attempt to assess specific policy options by conducting experiments, assessing their outcomes, and recommending whether the new concept should be broadly applied.

Government Accountability Office (GAO)   A support agency of the U.S. Congress created by the Budget and Accounting Act of 1921 to audit federal government expenditures and to assist Congress with its legislative oversight

responsibilities. Originally named the General Accounting Office.

internal audit   The function of audit groups within a larger organization. They vary in the tasks they are assigned. Sometimes they have a compliance audit role. In other instances they serve as independent troubleshooters, providing early warning to top management of emerging problems.

management control   That aspect of management concerned with the comparison of actual versus planned performance as well as the development and implementation of procedures to correct substandard performance.

performance audit   An audit that compares the activities of an organization with the objectives that have been assigned to it.

program evaluation   The systematic examination of any activity undertaken by government to make a determination about its effects, both short-term and long-range.

Bibliography

Bagby, Meredith. (1994). *The First Annual Report of the United States of America*. New York: HarperCollins.

Ball, Ian M. (1973). *Pitcairn: Children of Mutiny*. Boston: Little, Brown.

Bligh, William. (1961). *The Mutiny on Board H.M.S. Bounty*. New York: New American Library.

Bowring, John, ed. (1962). *The Works of Jeremy Bentham*, 11 vols. New York: Russell and Russell.

Brown, Judith R. (1984). "Legislative Program Evaluation: Defining a Legislative Service and a Profession," *Public Administration Review* (May–June).

Brown, Richard E., and Ralph Craft. (1980). "Auditing and Public Administration: The Unrealized Partnership," *Public Administration Review* (May–June).

Chelimsky, Eleanor, ed. (1984). *Program Evaluation: Patterns and Directions*. Washington: American Society for Public Administration.

Comptroller General of the United States. (1981). *Standards for Audit of Governmental Organizations, Programs, Activities and Functions*. Washington: General Accounting Office.

Dening, Greg. (1992). *Mr. Bligh's Bad Language: Passion, Power and Theatre on the Bounty*. Cambridge, England: Cambridge University Press.

Emmerich, Herbert. (1971). *Federal Organization and Administrative Management*. University of Alabama Press.

Hodge, G. (1993). *Minding Everybody's Business: Performance Management in Public Sector Agencies*. Melbourne, Australia: Montech Pty.

Hough, Richard. (1973). *Captain Bligh and Mr. Christian*. New York: E. P. Dutton.

Hyde, Albert C., and Jay M. Shafritz, eds. (1979). *Program Evaluation in the Public Sector*. New York: Praeger.

Kaufman, Herbert. (1973). *Administrative Feedback: Monitoring Subordinates' Behavior*. Washington: Brookings Institution.

Kearns, Kevin P. (1996). *Managing for Accountability*. San Francisco: Jossey-Bass.

Kelly, Paul Joseph. (1990). *Utilitarianism and Distributive Justice: Jeremy Bentham and the Civil Law*. New York: Oxford University Press.

Konigsberg, Eric. (1993). "Waste Watchers," *The New Republic* (April 5).

Morrison, Philip, and Emily Morrison, eds. (1961). *Charles Babbage and His Calculating Engines*. New York: Dover.

Normanton, E. L. (1966). *The Accountability and Audit of Governments*. Manchester, England: University of Manchester.

Postema, Gerald J. (1986). *Bentham and the Common Law Tradition*. New York: Oxford University Press.

Rivlin, Alice. (1971). *Systematic Thinking for Social Action*. Washington: Brookings Institution.

Shafritz, Jay M., Albert C. Hyde, and David H. Rosenbloom. (1986). *Personnel Management in Government*, 3rd ed. New York: Marcel Dekker.

Suchman, Edward. (1967). *Evaluative Research*. New York: Russell Sage Foundation.

Wahlroos, Sven. (1989). *Mutiny and Romance in the South Seas: A Companion to the Bounty Adventure*. Topsfield, MA: Salem House.

Webber, Carolyn, and Aaron Wildavsky. (1986). *A History of Taxation and Expenditure in the Western World*. New York: Simon and Schuster.

Weiss, Carol H. (1972). *Evaluation Research*. Englewood Cliffs, NJ: Prentice Hall.

Wildavsky, Aaron. (1972). "The Self-Evaluating Organization," *Public Administration Review* (32, No. 5, September–October).

Recommended Books

Normanton, E. Leslie. (1966). *The Accountability and Audit of Governments: A Comparative Study*. Manchester, England: University of Manchester Press. The classic study of how governments have conducted audits throughout history and throughout the world.

Sylvia, Ronald, Kathleen Sylvia, and Elizabeth Gunn. (1977). *Program Planning and Evaluation for the Public Manager*, 2nd ed. Prospect Heights, IL: Waveland Press. A systems approach to monitoring and reviewing internal processes as well as conceptualizing outcome evaluations.

Weiss, Carol H. (1997). *Evaluation: Methods for Studying Programs and Policies*. Englewood Cliffs, NJ: Prentice Hall. A primer on evaluation that deals with both the politics of why it is undertaken as well as the techniques of how to do it.

Wholey, Joseph S., Harry P. Hatry, and Kathryn E. Newcomer, eds. (1994). *Handbook of Practical Program Evaluation*. San Francisco: Jossey-Bass. A comprehensive reference offering all the how-to-do-it "nuts and bolts."

Related Web Sites

American Evaluation Association
www.eval.org/
Association of Government Accountants
www.agacgfm.org/homepage.aspx
Financial and auditing links
www.financenet.gov/financenet/start/topic/audit.htm

Mutiny on the *Bounty*
www.visi.com/~pjlareau/bounty1.html
U.S. Government Accountability Office
www.gao.gov/reports.htm

Glossary

accountability The extent to which one must answer to higher authority—legal or organizational—for one's actions in society at large or within one's particular organizational position.

administration The management and direction of the affairs of governments and institutions; a collective term for all policymaking officials of a government; the execution and implementation of public policy.

administrative doctrine The rules, procedures, and ways of doing things that reflect the basic values of an organization.

affirmative action A term that first meant the removal of "artificial barriers" to the employment of women and minority group members; now it refers to compensatory opportunities for hitherto disadvantaged groups—specific efforts to recruit, hire, and promote qualified members of disadvantaged groups for the purpose of eliminating the present effects of past discrimination.

agenda setting The process by which ideas or issues bubble up through the various political channels to wind up for consideration by a political institution such as a legislature or court.

assets All money, property, and money-related rights (such as money owed to one) owned by a person or an organization. Capital assets or fixed assets are those things that cannot be turned into cash easily (such as buildings); current assets or liquid assets are those things that can be turned into cash easily (such as cash or goods for sale); and frozen assets are those things that are tied up (for instance, because of a lawsuit).

audit An independent examination, an objective assessment of something; typically the financial reports of an individual or organization to determine whether they accurately represent expenditures and are in compliance with accounting standards and laws.

big lie An untruth so great or so audacious that it is bound to have an effect on public opinion.

block grant A grant distributed in accordance with a statutory formula for use in a variety of activities within a broad functional area, largely at the recipient's discretion.

bribery The giving or offering of anything of value with intent to unlawfully influence an official in the discharge of duties; a public official's receiving or asking for anything of value with the intent to be unlawfully influenced.

Brownlow Committee A committee appointed by President Franklin D. Roosevelt in 1936 for the purpose of diagnosing the staffing needs of the president and making appropriate recommendations for the reorganization of the executive branch.

budget A financial plan serving as a pattern for and control over future operations—hence, any estimate of future costs or any systematic plan for the utilization of the workforce, material, or other resources.

budget cycle The timed steps of the budget process, which includes preparation, approval, execution, and audit.

budget process The total system a jurisdiction uses to make decisions on government spending needs and how to pay for them. The main difference between federal and state and local budget processes is that the state and local jurisdictions must have balanced budgets each year.

budget surplus The amount by which a government's budget receipts exceed its budget outlays for any given period.

bureaucracy The totality of government officers; all of a government's employees; a general invective to refer to any inefficient organization encumbered by red tape or a specific set of structural arrangements.

bureaucrat bashing Either justified criticism or inappropriate condemnation of public employees.

bureaucratic dysfunctions The pathological elements of bureaucratic structures that often make them inefficient in operation; the pressures on workers to conform that cause them to adhere to rules as an end rather than a means.

bureaucratic impersonality The dehumanizing consequences of formal organizational structures eliminating personal and emotional consideration from organizational life so that the individual bureaucrat functions only as a cog in an ever-moving machine.

bureau movement The efforts of progressive reformers early in the twentieth century to apply scientific methods to municipal problems. Their efforts led to the creation of research bureaus, which in turn created the academic field of public administration.

cabinet The heads of the executive departments of a jurisdiction who report to and advise its chief executive; examples would include the president's cabinet, the governor's cabinet, and the mayor's cabinet.

cabinet government The British system, whereby the cabinet as a whole, rather than only the prime minister who heads it, is considered the executive, and the cabinet is collectively responsible to the Parliament for its performance. In addition, the cabinet ministers are typically drawn from among the majority party's members in Parliament, whereas in the United States the cabinet secretaries are only from the executive branch.

capital budgeting A budget process that deals with planning for large expenditures for capital items such as bridges and buildings.

casework The services performed by legislators and their staffs at the request of and on behalf of constituents.

categorical grant A grant that can be used only for specific, narrowly defined activities—for example, to construct an interstate highway.

charisma Leadership based on the compelling personality of the leader rather than on formal position. The word *charisma* is derived from the Greek word for divine grace. The concept was first developed by Max Weber, who distinguished charismatic authority from both the traditional authority of a monarch and the legal authority given to someone by law.

chief of staff The military title for the officer who supervises the work of the other officers on a commander's staff; civilian supervisor of an overall management team who reports directly to the chief executive officer.

child labor Originally, the employment of children in a manner detrimental to their health and social development. Now that the law contains strong child labor prohibitions, the term refers to the employment of children below the legal age limit.

civil service A collective term for all nonmilitary employees of a government. Paramilitary organizations, such as police and firefighters, are always included in civil service counts in the United States. Civil service employment is not the same as merit system employment, because all patronage positions (those not covered by merit systems) are included in civil service totals.

civil service reform Efforts to improve the status, integrity, and productivity of the civil service at all levels of government by supplanting the spoils system with the merit system; efforts to improve the management and efficiency of the public service; or the historical events, the movement, leading up to the enactment of the Pendleton Act of 1883.

classical theory The original theory about organizations that closely resemble military structures.

code of ethics A statement of professional standards of conduct to which the practitioners of a profession say they subscribe. Codes of ethics are usually not legally binding, so they may not be taken too seriously as constraints on behavior.

collective bargaining Bargaining on behalf of a group of employees, as opposed to individual bargaining, in which each worker represents only himself or herself.

common law The totality of judge-made laws that initially developed in England and continued to evolve in the United States. Whenever this kind of law—which is based on custom, culture, habit, and previous judicial decisions—proved inadequate, it was supplanted by statutory laws made by legislatures. But the common law tradition, based on precedent, is still the foundation of the American legal system, even though much of what was originally common law has been converted into statutes over the years.

compliance audit The traditional form of auditing, in which the auditor is looking for the extent to which, in the financial management of an organization, funds have been managed in compliance with the law, and to which accepted standards and conventions for the treatment of accounting information have been used.

congressional oversight The total means by which the U.S. Congress monitors the activities of executive branch agencies to determine if the laws are being faithfully executed.

constitutional architecture The administrative arrangements created by a government's constitution—from the separation of powers to the requirement that specific departments be created or services performed.

contingency theory An approach to leadership asserting that leadership styles will vary in their effects in different situations. The situation (not traits or styles themselves) determines whether a leadership style or a particular leader will be effective.

corruption The unauthorized use of public office for private gain. The most common forms of corruption are bribery, extortion, and the misuse of inside information.

council of government (COG) An organization of cooperating local governments seeking a regional approach to planning, development, transportation, environment, and other issues.

deficit financing A situation in which a government's excess of outlays over receipts for a given period is financed primarily by borrowing from the public.

devolution The transfer of power from a central to a local authority.

Dillon's rule The criteria developed by state courts to determine the nature and extent of powers granted to local governments.

dirty hands dilemma A graphic phrase for the tendency of public officials to commit an act generally considered to be a wrong to further the common good. This is a dilemma in the sense that doing bad seems to lead to something good.

discrimination Bigotry in practice; intolerance toward those who have different beliefs or religions. In employment, the failure to treat equals equally. Any action that has the effect of limiting employment and advancement opportunities because of an individual's sex, race, color, age, national origin, religion, physical handicap, or other irrelevant criteria, is discrimination.

e-commerce Selling and buying over the Internet, whether wholesale or retail.

e-government Conducting any aspect of government business operations over the Internet—from providing information by government to paying bills to government.

empowerment Giving a person or organization the formal authority to do something.

equal employment opportunity Employment practices that prevent any individual from being adversely excluded from employment opportunities on the basis of race, color, sex, religion, age, national origin, or other factors that cannot lawfully be considered in employing people.

evaluation research An attempt to assess specific policy options by conducting experiments, assessing their outcomes, and recommending whether the new concept should be broadly applied.

executive branch In a government with separation of powers, that part that is responsible for applying or administering the law. Thus a president, governor, or mayor and their respective supporting bureaucracies are the executive branches of their respective jurisdictions. But not all of the federal bureaucracy is part of the executive branch. Some agencies, such as the Government Accountability Office, are directly responsible to Congress. Others, such as the Federal Trade Commission (and other regulatory agencies), have been held by the Supreme Court not to be part of the executive branch.

executive budget The budget document for an executive branch of government that a jurisdiction's chief executive submits to a legislature for review, modification, and enactment.

Executive Office of the President (EOP) The umbrella office consisting of the top presidential staff agencies that provide the president help and advice in carrying out his major responsibilities. The EOP was created by President Franklin D. Roosevelt under the authority of the Reorganization Act of 1939. Since then, presidents have used executive orders, reorganization plans, and legislative initiatives to reorganize, expand, or contract the EOP.

federalism A system of governance in which a national, overarching government shares power with subnational or state governments.

federalism, cooperative The notion that the national, state, and local governments are cooperating, interacting agents, jointly working to solve common problems, rather than conflicting, sometimes hostile competitors, to pursue similar or possibly conflicting ends.

federalism, dual The nineteenth-century concept, now no longer operational, that the functions and responsibilities of the federal and state governments were theoretically distinguished and functionally separate from each other.

federalism, marble-cake The concept that the cooperative relations among the varying levels of government result in an intermingling of activities; in contrast to the more traditional view of layer-cake federalism, which holds that the three levels of government are totally or almost totally separate.

Federalism, New The Republican efforts begun during the Nixon administration to decentralize governmental functions by returning power and responsibility to the states. This trend was continued in the 1980s by the Reagan administration and culminated in the 1990s movement toward devolution.

federalism, picket-fence The concept that bureaucratic specialists at the various levels of government (along with clientele groups) exercise considerable power over the nature of intergovernmental programs.

financial report A written statement—also called an accountant's certificate, accountant's opinion, or audit report—prepared by an independent accountant or auditor after an audit.

fiscal federalism The financial relations between and among units of government in a federal system. The theory of fiscal federalism, or multi-unit government finance, is one part of the branch of applied economics known as public finance.

general staff A group of officers in a military's headquarters that assists their commanders in planning, coordinating, and supervising operations.

Government Accountability Office (GAO) A support agency of the U.S. Congress created by the Budget and Accounting Act of 1921 to audit federal government expenditures and to assist Congress with its legislative oversight responsibilities.

Grace Commission An attempt made by the Reagan administration to have business leaders study and reform the federal government; much was studied, little was reformed.

grant An intergovernmental transfer of funds (or other assets). Since the New Deal, state and local governments have become increasingly dependent on federal grants for an almost infinite variety of programs.

group cohesion The shared beliefs, values, and assumptions of a group that allows it to function as a team.

group dynamics The subfield of organization behavior concerned with the nature of groups, how they develop, and how they interrelate with individuals and other groups.

Hawthorne experiments The late 1920s and early 1930s management studies undertaken at the Hawthorne Works of the Western Electric Company near Chicago. Conducted by Elton Mayo and his associates from the Harvard Business School, the studies became the most famous management experiments ever reported.

higher law The notion that no matter what the laws of a state are, there remains a higher law, to which a person has an even greater obligation. A higher law is often appealed to by those who wish to attack an existing law or practice that courts or legislators are unlikely or unwilling to change.

honor The internalized moral compass by which individuals ascertain correct behavior in public and private life; the perception by others of one's reputation for integrity.

Hoover Commissions The post–World War II efforts to reorganize the federal government.

impasse resolution A condition that exists during labor–management negotiations when either party feels that no further progress can be made toward a settlement—unless the process of negotiating changes. The most common techniques used to break an impasse are mediation, fact finding, and arbitration.

implementation Putting a government program into effect; the total process of translating a legal mandate, whether an executive order or an enacted statute, into appropriate program directives and structures that provide services or create goods.

incremental budgeting A method of budget review that focuses on the increments of increase or decrease in the budget of existing programs. Incremental budgeting, which is often called traditional budgeting, is a counter school of thought to more rational, systems-oriented approaches, such as zero-based budgeting.

incremental decision-making model A view of the public policymaking process that assumes that small decisions made at the margins of problems are the usual reality of change.

integrity The core of honor. Those who have integrity live up to their stated principles, values, and, most important, their word. A person whose word is his or her bond gives the full faith and credit of his or her whole being to keeping commitments.

intergovernmental relations The complex network of interrelationships among governments; the political, fiscal, programmatic, and administrative processes by which higher units of government share revenues and other resources with lower units of government, generally accompanied by special conditions that the lower units must satisfy as prerequisites to receiving the assistance.

internal audit The function of audit groups within a larger organization. They vary in the tasks they are assigned. Sometimes they have a compliance audit role. In other instances they serve as independent troubleshooters, providing early warning to top management of emerging problems.

leadership The exercise of authority, whether formal or informal, in directing and coordinating the work of others.

learning organization Peter Senge's term for organizations in which new patterns of thinking are nurtured and where people are continually learning together to improve both the organization and their personal lives.

line-item budget The classification of budgetary accounts according to narrow, detailed objects of expenditure (such as motor vehicles, clerical workers, or reams of paper) used within each particular agency of government, generally without reference to the ultimate purpose or objective served by the expenditure.

management A word that refers both to the people responsible for running an organization and to the running process itself; the use of numerous resources (such as employees and machines) to accomplish an organizational goal.

management control That aspect of management concerned with the comparison of actual versus planned performance as well as the development and implementation of procedures to correct substandard performance.

management development Any conscious effort on the part of an organization, such as rotational assignments or formal educational experiences, to provide a manager with the skills needed for future duties.

managerial revolution James Burham's concept that as control of large businesses moved from the original owners to professional managers, society's new governing class would be not the traditional possessors of wealth—but those who have the professional expertise to manage, to lead, large organizations.

managerialism An entrepreneurial approach to public management that emphasizes management rights and a reinvigorated scientific management.

mandating One level of government requiring another to offer—and/or pay for—a program as a matter of law or as a prerequisite to partial or full funding for either the program in question or other programs.

merit system A public sector concept of staffing that implies that no test of party membership is involved in the selection, promotion, or retention of government employees and that a constant effort is made to select the best-qualified individuals available for appointment and advancement.

micromanagement A pejorative term for supervising too closely. Any manager may be guilty of micromanagement for refusing to allow subordinates to have any real authority or responsibility, thereby ensuring that subordinates can neither function as, nor grow into, effective managers. Also used to refer to interference by legislators with the minutiae of administration for the benefit of their constituents.

moral leadership Leading people in specific directions of action and thought based on morals and decency.

motivation An amalgam of all of the factors in one's working environment that foster or inhibit productive efforts.

national debt The total outstanding debt of a central government.

needs hierarchy Abraham H. Maslow's five sets of goals or basic needs arranged in a hierarchy of prepotency: physiological needs (food, water, shelter, etc.), safety needs, love or affiliation needs, esteem needs, and the final need for self-actualization.

neoclassical theory Theoretical perspectives that revise, expand, and/or are critical of classical organization theory.

new public administration An academic advocacy movement for social equity in the performance and delivery of public services; it called for a proactive administrator with a burning desire for social equity to replace the traditional impersonal and neutral gun-for-hire bureaucrat.

new public management A disparate group of structural reforms and informal management initiatives that reflects the doctrine of managerialism in the public sector.

nonprofit organization, An organization created and operated for public or societal purposes (such as alleviation of poverty) rather than private benefit purposes (such as return on shareholders' investments).

objective A short-term goal; something that must be achieved on the way to a larger overall achievement.

organization A group of people who jointly work to achieve at least one common goal.

organizational culture The culture that exists within an organization; a parallel but smaller version of a societal culture.

organization development An approach or strategy for increasing organizational effectiveness. As a process it has no value biases, but it is usually associated with the idea that effectiveness is found by integrating the individual's desire for growth with organizational goals.

organization theory A set of propositions that seeks to explain or predict how groups and individuals behave in differing organizational arrangements.

paradigm An intellectual model for a situation or condition.

patronage The power of elected and appointed officials to make partisan appointments to office or to confer contracts, honors, or other benefits on their political supporters. Patronage has always been one of the major tools by which political executives consolidate their power and attempt to control a bureaucracy.

performance appraisal The formal methods by which an organization documents the work performance of its employees. Performance appraisals are typically designed to change dysfunctional work behavior, communicate perceptions of work quality, assess the future potential of employees, and provide a documented record for disciplinary and separation actions.

performance audit An audit that compares the activities of an organization with the objectives that have been assigned to it.

performance management The systematic integration of an organization's efforts to achieve its objectives.

personnel A collective term for all of the employees of an organization. The word is of military origin—the two basic components of a traditional army being materiel and personnel. Personnel is also commonly used to refer to the personnel management function or the organizational unit responsible for administering personnel programs.

planning horizon The time frame during which the objectives of a strategic plan are to be achieved.

pluralism A theory of government that attempts to reaffirm the democratic character of society by asserting that open, multiple, competing, and responsive groups preserve traditional democratic values in a mass industrial state. Pluralism assumes that power will shift from group to group as elements in the mass public transfer their allegiance in response to their perceptions of their individual interests.

political culture That part of the overall societal culture that determines a community's attitudes toward the quality, style, and vigor of its political processes and government operations.

POSDCORB The mnemonic device invented by Luther Gulick in 1937 to call attention to the various functional elements of the work of a chief executive.

position classification The use of formal job descriptions to organize all jobs in a civil service merit system into classes on the basis of duties and responsibilities, for the purposes of delineating authority, establishing chains of command, and providing equitable salary scales.

postbureaucratic organization Constantly changing temporary organizational systems; task forces composed of groups of relative strangers with diverse skills created in response to a special problem, as opposed to continuing need.

postmodernism The belief that constant change is a new fact of life for large organizations that are living on the edge, on the boundary, between order and chaos.

principles of management Fundamental truths or working hypotheses that serve as guidelines to management thinking and action.

privatization The process of returning to the private sector property or functions previously owned or performed by government.

productivity A measured relationship between the quantity (and quality) of results produced and the quantity of resources required for production. Productivity is, in essence, a measure of the work efficiency of an individual, a work unit, or a whole organization.

professional A member of an occupation requiring specialized knowledge that can be gained only after intensive preparation. Professional occupations tend to possess three features: a body of academic and practical knowledge that is applied to the service of society, a standard of success theoretically measured by serving the needs of society rather than seeking purely personal gain, and a system of control over the professional practice.

program evaluation The systematic examination of any activity undertaken by government to make a determination about its effects, both short-term and long-range.

progressive tax Any tax that has people of greater wealth paying a larger percentage in tax than people of lesser means. Income taxes are often progressive.

public administration Whatever governments do, for good or ill. It is public administration's political context that makes it public—that distinguishes it from private or business administration.

public interest The universal label that political actors wrap around the policies and programs that they advocate.

public policy Decision making by government. Governments are constantly concerned about what they should or should not do. And whatever they do or do not do is public policy.

public program All those activities designed to implement a public policy; often this calls for the creation of organizations, public agencies, and bureaus.

racist Any person or organization that either consciously or unconsciously practices discrimination against another person on the basis of race (or ethnicity) or supports the supremacy of one race over others.

rational decision-making model A view of the public policymaking process that assumes complete information and a systematic, logical, and comprehensive approach to change.

red tape The ribbon that was once used to bind government documents; the term now stands as the symbol of excessive official formality and overattention to prescribed routines.

reengineering The fundamental rethinking and redesign of organizational processes to achieve significant improvements in critical measures of performance, such as costs or quality of services.

regressive tax Any tax that has people with lower incomes paying a higher overall percentage of their income in tax than people of greater income. Sales taxes are examples of regressive taxes.

regulation The totality of government controls on the social and economic activities of its citizens; the rule-making process of those administrative agencies charged with the official interpretation of laws.

regulatory commission An independent agency created by a government to regulate some aspect of economic life.

reinventing government The latest manifestation of the progressive tradition of continuously improving government—this time with an emphasis on privatization.

representative bureaucracy The ultimate goal of equal employment opportunity and affirmative action programs.

republic A form of government in which sovereignty resides in the people who elect agents to represent them in political decision making.

reverse discrimination Discrimination against white males in conjunction with preferential treatment for women and minorities.

rule of law A governing system in which the highest authority is a body of law that applies equally to all (as opposed to the traditional "rule of men," in which the personal whim of those in power can decide any issue).

scientific management A systematic approach to managing that seeks the "one best way" of accomplishing any given task by discovering the fastest, most efficient, and least fatiguing production methods.

second reconstruction The civil rights movement and legislation of the 1960s. The first reconstruction, immediately after the Civil War, gave blacks their freedom from slavery. But the laws as enforced and customs as practiced did not allow for the full rights of citizens. That came in the 1960s, when public sentiment was aroused and legal action was taken to ensure equal rights for all Americans.

self-directed work team A work group that will accept responsibility for their processes and products—as well as for the behavior of other group members.

separation of powers The allocation of powers among the three branches of government so that they are a check upon each other. This separation, in theory, makes a tyrannical concentration of power impossible.

sex discrimination Any disparate or unfavorable treatment of a person in an employment situation because of his or her sex.

sexual harassment The action of an individual in a position to control or influence another's job, career, or grade who uses such power to gain sexual favors or punish the refusal of such favors. Sexual harassment on the job varies from inappropriate sexual innuendo to coerced sexual relations.

spoils system The practice of awarding government jobs to one's political supporters, as opposed to awarding them on the basis of merit.

staff principle That a unit of a larger organization should have primary responsibility to think and plan, to ponder over innovations and plan for their implementation.

stakeholder Any individual or group that might be affected by the outcome of something. All decisions have their stakeholders. The responsible public decision maker seeks to obtain the maximum possible stakeholder satisfaction.

standards of conduct A compendium of ethical norms promulgated by an organization to guide the behavior of its members. Many government agencies have formal codes (or standards) of conduct for their employees.

strategic management A philosophy of management that links strategic planning with day-to-day decision making. Strategic management seeks a fit between an organization's external and internal environments.

strategic plan The formal document that presents the ways and means by which a strategic goal will be achieved.

strategic planning The set of processes used by an organization to assess the strategic situation and develop strategy for the future.

strategy The overall conduct of a major enterprise to achieve long-term goals; the pattern to be found in a series of organizational decisions.

strike A mutual agreement among workers (whether members of a union or not) to a temporary work stoppage to obtain—or resist—a change in their working conditions.

SWOT analysis A review of an organization's Strengths, Weaknesses, Opportunities, and Threats. This technique is widely used to examine the viability of strategic plans.

systems theory A view of an organization as a complex set of dynamically intertwined and interconnected elements, including its inputs, processes, outputs, feedback loops, and the environment in which it operates and with which it continuously interacts.

tactics The short-term immediate decisions that, in their totality, lead to the achievement of strategic goals.

tax A compulsory contribution exacted by a government for public purposes.

technocracy A contraction of "technical" and "bureaucracy," which refers to the high-tech organizational environments of the postmodern world.

Theory X The assumptions that the average human being has an inherent dislike of work; that most people must be threatened to get them to put forth adequate effort; and that people prefer to be directed and to avoid responsibility.

Theory Y The assumptions that work is as natural as play, that workers can exercise self-direction and self-control, and that imagination, ingenuity, and creativity are widespread.

think tank A colloquial term for an organization, or organizational segment, whose sole function is research, usually in the policy and behavioral sciences.

Title VII That part of the Civil Rights Act of 1964 that prohibits employment discrimination because of race, color, religion, sex, or national origin and that created the Equal Employment Opportunity Commission as its enforcement vehicle.

total quality management (TQM) A phrase for quality control in its most expanded sense of a total and continuing concern for quality in the production of goods and services.

trait theory An approach to leadership that assumes leaders possess traits that make them fundamentally different from followers. Advocates of trait theory believe that some people have unique leadership characteristics and qualities that enable them to assume responsibilities not everyone can execute. Therefore they are "born" leaders.

transformational leadership Leadership that strives to change organizational culture and directions. It reflects the ability of a leader to develop a values-based vision for the organization, to convert the vision into reality, and to maintain it over time.

unified budget The present form of the budget of the federal government, in which receipts and outlays from federal funds and trust funds (such as Social Security) are consolidated.

unions Groups of employees who create a formal organization (the union) to represent their interests before management.

vision A view of an organization's future. The purpose of strategic management is to make such a vision a reality.

vision statement The identification of objectives to be achieved in the future.

Watergate The scandal that led to the resignation of President Richard M. Nixon. Watergate itself is a hotel-office-apartment complex in Washington, D.C. When individuals associated with the Committee to Reelect the President were caught breaking into the Democratic National Committee Headquarters (then located in the Watergate complex) in 1972, the resulting cover-up and national trauma was condensed into one word: Watergate. The suffix "-gate" has grown to refer to any political crime or instance of bureaucratic corruption that undermines confidence in governing institutions.

whistle-blower An individual who believes the public interest overrides the interests of his or her organization and publicly blows the whistle on—meaning exposes—corrupt, illegal, fraudulent, or harmful activity.

zero-based budgeting A budgeting process that is a rejection of the incremental decision making model of budgeting. It demands a rejustification of the entire budget submission (from ground zero), whereas incremental budgeting essentially respects the outcomes of previous budgetary decisions (collectively referred to as the budget base) and focuses examination on the margin of change from year to year.

Appendix: Additional Sources

Chapter 1
"snow buttons" *U. S. News and World Report,* January 17, 1994

Chapter 2
"Just what is it . . ." Speech of January 29, 1916
"Remember, democracy . . ." Letter to John Taylor, April 15, 1814
". . . that my oath . . ." Letter to A. G. Hodges, April 4, 1864

Chapter 3
". . . are supervisors in California, judges in . . ." *Governing,* May 1989

Chapter 4
"What the judges say . . ." Hughes speech, May 3, 1907
"States are not colonies . . ." *The Economist,* November 26, 1984
"On bended knee . . ." Ibid.
"We do not want to be in the importing . . ." *Washington Post National Weekly,* September 18–24, 1995

Chapter 5
"The nation's honor . . ." Speech in Cleveland, January 29, 1916
". . . about a man who drives into Moscow . . ." *New York Times,* May 3, 1995
"Most of the material should not have been secret . . ." *Christian Science Monitor,* July 18, 1973
"When I order abandon ship . . ." *Time,* August 19, 1991
"Stand up, you man-eating . . ." *American Heritage,* October 1977
". . . have a duty to refrain . . ." *Times* (London), April 15, 1993
". . . that people shouldn't require . . . ." *U.S. News and World Report,* January 19, 1981
"McNamara went to the World Bank . . ." *New York Times,* April 15, 1995
"He kept his mouth shut . . ." *Newsweek,* April 24, 1995
"I think it's about 25 years . . ." *New York Times,* April 15, 1995

Chapter 6
"I found Rome . . ." Michael Grant, *The Founders of the Ancient World* (1991)

"No rule of war . . ." *Military Maxims* (1827)
"With 2,000 years . . ." Norman F. Dixon, *On the Psychology of Military Incompetence* (1976)
"There is nothing so practical . . ." Alfred J. Marrow, *The Practical Theorist: The Life and Work of Kurt Lewis* (1969)

Chapter 7
". . . the giant power wielded . . ." H. Balzac, *Bureaucracy* (1901)

Chapter 8
". . . if Congress . . . passed a law . . ." C. G. Dawes, *The First Year of the Budget of the United States* (1923)
". . . every revolution evaporates . . ." Kafka, quoted in *Newsweek,* October 14, 1968
". . . clocks look bureaucratic . . ." *Newsweek,* October 31, 1994
"All at once, five postal . . ." *New York Times,* June 6, 1993

Chapter 9
". . . the public be damned." Remark to reporter on October 8, 1882

Chapter 10
"Federal Centers for Disease Control . . ." *New York Times,* July 10, 1995
"The Presidency is not merely an . . ." *New York Times,* September 11, 1932
"This brand is cynically . . ." *Washington Post National Weekly,* February 5–11, 1990
". . . each year the military spends . . ." *U. S. News and World Report,* May 24, 1993

Chapter 12
"Effective January 1, 1997, the University . . ." *New York Times,* July 22, 1995
". . . the nation's first governor . . ." *Pittsburgh Post Gazette,* June 2, 1995

Chapter 13
"What the hell . . ." *New York Times,* December 18, 1994
"No citizen has a moral obligation . . ." *New York Times,* April 16, 1995

Index

Page numbers in italics indicate figures
Page numbers followed by t indicate a table

- Senator Joseph McCarthy (and in effect McCarthyism) censured by the U.S. Senate.
- Lakewood, California pioneers the service contract, whereby a small jurisdiction buys government services from a neighboring large jurisdiction.

1955
- The Second Hoover Commission recommends the curtailment and abolition of federal government activities that are competitive with private enterprise.
- Department of Health, Education and Welfare (HEW) created.
- AFL-CIO is formed by the merger of the American Federation of Labor and the Congress of Industrial Organization.

1957
- C. Northcote Parkinson discovers his law that "work expands so as to fill the time available for its completion."
- Chris Argyris asserts in *Personality and Organization* that there is an inherent conflict between the personality of a mature adult and the needs of modern organizations.
- Douglas M. McGregor's article, "The Human Side of Enterprise," distills the contending traditional (authoritarian) and humanistic managerial philosophies into Theory X and Theory Y.

1958
- NASA created.

1959
- New York City is the first major city to allow collective bargaining with its employees.
- Wisconsin is the first state to enact a comprehensive law governing public sector labor relations.
- The Advisory Commission on Intergovernmental Relations is established.
- Charles A. Lindblom's "The Science of 'Muddling Through'" rejects the rational model of decision-making in favor of incrementalism.
- Herzberg, Mausner, and Snyderman's *The Motivation to Work* puts forth the motivation-hygiene theory.

1960
- Richard Neustadt's *Presidential Power* asserts that the president's (or any executive's) essential power is that of persuasion.

1961
- President Dwight D. Eisenhower in his farewell address warns of "the military-industrial complex."
- President John F. Kennedy's Executive Order 10925 requires that "affirmative action" be used in employment.
- The Peace Corps is established.
- Alan B. Shepard becomes the first American astronaut to fly in space.
- The Rand Corporation helps the Department of Defense install PPBS.

1962
- President John F. Kennedy issues Executive Order 10988, which encourages the unionization of federal workers.

1963
- During the "March on Washington," Martin Luther King Jr. delivers his "I Have a Dream" speech.
- President John F. Kennedy is assassinated; Vice President Lyndon B. Johnson becomes president.

1964
- The Civil Rights Act prohibits discrimination in private sector employment and public accommodation.
- Aaron Wildavsky publishes *The Politics of the Budgetary Process,* which becomes the classic analysis of the tactics public managers use to get budgets passed.

- The Economic Opportunity Act becomes the anchor of President Lyndon B. Johnson's "war on poverty" and other Great Society programs.

1965
- PPBS made mandatory for all federal agencies.
- The Department of Housing and Urban Development established.
- Medicare is created through amendments to the Social Security Act.

1966
- The Freedom of Information Act allows greater access to federal agency files.
- Morton Grodzins in *The American System* asserts that the federal system is more like a marble cake than a layer cake.

1967
- Age Discrimination in Employment Act passed.
- The National Academy of Public Administration is organized; its first members will be all of the living past presidents of the American Society for Public Administration.
- Edward A. Suchman's *Evaluative Research* asserts that evaluation is a generic field of study.
- Terry Sanford in *Storm Over the States* develops the concept of "picket-fence federalism," which holds that bureaucratic specialists at the various governmental levels exercise considerable power over the nature of intergovernmental programs.

1968
- "Younger" public administration scholars meeting at Syracuse University's Minnowbrook Conference site call for a "new public administration" that would emphasize social equity.
- Martin Luther King Jr. is assassinated.
- Robert F. Kennedy is assassinated.
- Richard M. Nixon is elected president.

1969
- Laurence J. Peter promulgates his principle that "in a hierarchy every employee tends to rise to his level of incompetence."
- Theodore Lowi's *The End of Liberalism* attacks interest group pluralism for paralyzing the policy-making process.
- Neil Armstrong, an American astronaut, becomes the first man to walk on the moon.

1970
- The Bureau of the Budget is given more responsibility for managerial oversight and renamed the Office of Management and Budget.
- Postal Reorganization Act creates the U.S. Postal Service as a public corporation within the executive branch.
- Hawaii becomes the first state to allow state and local government employees the right to strike.
- Environmental Protection Agency established.

1971
- The Supreme Court attacks restrictive credentialism in *Griggs v. Duke Power Company.*
- PPBS formally abandoned in the federal government by the Nixon administration.

1972
- Equal Employment Opportunity Act amends Title VII of the Civil Rights Act to include prohibitions on discrimination by public sector employers.
- Watergate scandal erupts when men associated with the Committee to Reelect the President are caught breaking into the campaign headquarters of the Democratic opposition, located in the Watergate hotel-office-apartment complex.
- The Equal Rights Amendment is passed by Congress; it never becomes law because too few states will ratify it.
- Revenue sharing is introduced with the passage of the State and Local Fiscal Assistance Act (it will expire in 1986).